PHARAOH THUTMOSE III

With love and blessings,
Marisa & Kuthumi
xo.

1

Also by Marisa Calvi with Kuthumi Lal Singh
"You Don't Have Problems, You're Just Bored!"
available at www.newenergywriting.com

LET'S GO FOR A WALK

BOOK ONE

PHARAOH THUTMOSE III

A life adventure of
Ascended Master
Kuthumi Lal Singh
as told to
Marisa Calvi

BCC Publishing
GLENORIE, AUSTRALIA

First published in 2009 by
BCC Publishing
20 Pinus Avenue
Glenorie NSW 2157
AUSTRALIA

A CIP catalogue record for this book is available
from the National Library of Australia

ISBN 978-0-9803506-2-3

Cover artwork "J'Encore" by Jessica Simanowski
www.js-artist.com

Printed and bound by BA Printing
Brookvale, Australia

FOR
ISIS, KUAN YIN AND MARY

......THE DIVINE FEMININE,

OUR ETERNAL MOTHER......

PREFACE

I am not entirely sure where and when my journey with Kuthumi began. However I can offer you a most memorable occasion in July of 2006 when lying wide awake at 2 a.m. in a hotel room high up in the Rocky Mountains of Colorado I heard a voice, clear and distinct call out to me, "Oh good, you're awake!"

I knew it was Kuthumi instantly. He was on my mind as the very next day in the ballroom of the hotel I was to hear Geoffrey Hoppe channel him.

Kuthumi followed this greeting with a simple invitation, "Let's go for a walk."

That night accepting his invitation led to an etheric stroll through the hotel corridors and down to the ballroom. I sat upon a seat in the centre of the room and Kuthumi said, "Tomorrow when you are here, feel the energy that moves when everyone laughs."

The next day I slept in and ran down to the ballroom just as the day's events began. The only seat I could find was the very same place I had "sat" during my walk with Kuthumi. When the channel began the crowd laughed so hard at Kuthumi's jokes and I lost myself within the vibrations of their laughter.

When the laughter subsided then Kuthumi announced that he had written four books that were available for whoever should choose to "download" them and bring them into 3-D reality. My heart sang as he spoke of them. My passion for writing had been bubbling away since my childhood, pushed aside by some amazing distractions I created. Now in my mid-thirties it was ready to boil over and Kuthumi provided me with the platform to really begin.

I returned home to Sydney and six months later "You Don't Have Problems, You're Just Bored!" was almost complete. I was doing final editing, working on layout and writing my introduction when I realised that it would also be nice to write a page about Kuthumi and began to research what was known about him. I read about his past lives and all that he achieved and as I did so our connection deepened. Not least because he would watch over my shoulder commenting on what I was reading!

During this time I once again was lying awake in the early hours of the morning, breathing to calm my mind in the hope I would sleep, only to look at the clock and see yet another hour had passed. Then Kuthumi appeared by my bedside laughing. "Why do you think you need to sleep so much?" he asked this time.

I wasn't amused but I was grateful for the distraction he offered. "If you need to be here, could you at least be interesting. Why don't you tell me about your past lives," I answered.

I felt his delight at being asked and then what came next was beyond any experience I ever had meditating or breathing. Kuthumi didn't just tell me

1

about his past lives, he took me to them. For each life he offered me a different way to connect with his experience. For some he offered words, some an image and others a physical sensation.

I saw an image of ancient Egypt but I felt the grandeur, tradition and permanence. Pythagorus, he said, was of the "mind" and I felt the constant swirl of thoughts. I then rode upon a camel with him as the Magi known as Balthazar, feeling the camel sway underneath me while ahead in the sky I saw the star that guided them and I felt the knowing and excitement as they travelled to meet Jesus. I felt the harshness of being St. Francis yet the depth of his connection with St. Clare. Then I visited Shah Jahan and my heart swelled with warmth and I was wrapped in a red glow as he spoke of his beloved Mumtaz.

Then I fell asleep. Finally.

With my first book near completion I began to contemplate my next adventure in writing. I began yet another of the titles that Kuthumi spoke of during his channel at Colorado but it did not flow. I had an idea for a novel but that too seemed to falter as soon as I tried to type the words. Then one day while watching television a creative spark was ignited. It had nothing to do with what I was watching, more so that I had entered that zone where my mind was quietened. I suddenly had the idea that I should write the story of Kuthumi's lives. I heard a resounding "Yes!" It was Kuthumi and my heart agreeing in unison and in that very instant my new writing adventure was begun.

Adventures can be planned but the truly inspiring ones are those that take on a life of their own, offering up experiences that you didn't plan for. This is what my time with Kuthumi has been like. When I accepted his first invitation to go for a walk I never imagined what that could lead to. Kuthumi has become my teacher, my friend, my guide and my inspirer. My work with him has opened my creativity both artistically and with life in general.

The book you see before you now was supposedly going to be the first part of a single book covering five of Kuthumi's better-known lives. Yet when I began, Thutmose's story soon became its own entity, bursting to well over four hundred pages. To some people it will appear a simple collection of anecdotes and reflections. To those who will accept Kuthumi's invitation it will be much more.

KUTHUMI'S INTRODUCTION

Let me extend to you an invitation. It is not the most normal of invitations, as it doesn't require you to attend a party or function. It is an invitation to travel with me across time, across civilizations, across religions and across philosophies. I invite you to turn off your simple human limitations of time and place. I invite you to open your senses. With this opening I will share with you depths of sensation, perception and experience you haven't even imagined.

I am now sitting at a desk in my home in India. There is a bustle outside. There is always a bustle outside as that is part of Indian life. I sit here now at the end of my last human period of existence. I will leave this shell we call a body soon and I will do it without regret or fear for I know not only where I have been but where I am going. I have decided not to return to this human realm again. Well not within the way that we know as human existence and not within any time frame you can comprehend. I will experience it from the other side of the veil, from that place we all come from and yearn to return to, only to rush back to human life once again when we get there.

There will be those that follow in your time who will hear me from there. They will seek within their lives the knowledge that I have gained and I will share it in more ways than just with the written words that I will leave behind. They will choose to go beyond the limitations of the human mind. They will reach into my experience. They will choose to feel.

So now my friend I will invite you.

Will you choose to feel?

Wonderful.

Now, let's go for a walk…

 # CHAPTER ONE

We shall start our journey in ancient Egypt. I will indulge your limited concept of time by telling you we are now stepping back to the year you refer to as 1465 BC or thereabouts. Your researchers and archaeologists are so limited with their measurements. They have taken samples from my wrappings and scraped paint from my tomb. They put them into tubes with chemicals and shine different lights upon it so they can tell the age of things. This satisfies their scientific minds. They can put things into order and make sense of the things they find. However there are many things that still don't make sense despite all their knowledge and measurements. While I am telling you this story they still don't fully understand how the pyramids were built and I am not about to spoil my fun of watching them debate and theorize by telling you. Let's just say you can all let go of the alien theory.

Each culture of man is arrogant enough to believe that they are the pinnacle of development and knowledge. That those who follow will build upon what they have learnt and experienced but this is not always the case. Society and culture ebbs and flows through time. One culture can be flying a man to the moon while others still forage in jungles wearing handwoven cloths. A society can be so grand as to build monuments to last an eternity and yet end up having to ask of others to feed their children. It all goes in cycles and the highs and lows coexist on this planet as we speak.

So it was that I was born into one of the grandest, most spectacular and most arrogant cultures of them all. It was the time of the 18th Dynasty, part of the New Kingdom period of ancient Egypt's history. My heritage was immense. The pyramids were already a thousand years old when I was born and there would be over one other millennia of our culture as it was before it collapsed under Cleopatra's reign and the Romans invaded. Egypt's structures, codes and disciplines were well-established and it worked like a well-oiled machine with each cog knowing its place and how to work within it and with its immediate surrounds. The only changes to be made were in making the machine of the empire bigger.

Even my birth followed established rules and protocol. My mother was laid upon an immaculate birthing bed dressed with the finest linens embellished with gold. Not that she noticed nor cared, as the pains of her first labour were so overwhelming. As each contraction ripped through her uterus sending waves into her spine and down her legs she recalled yet another story or memory of hearing of women dying whilst giving birth. Unfortunately this fear shortened her breath, only intensifying the pain and making it more difficult for her to push me out and thus prolonging the birth and the pain.

Of course she was well attended to but those surrounding her were of little comfort. They too knew that women died while giving birth and having

4

seen or heard of it so many times had this thought weighing on their minds as they cared for her. She had two of her personal maids, both on the verge of tears as they watched their beloved mistress in her pain. They wiped her face and her arms to help keep her cool as well as any blood that appeared on her legs, quickly hiding the bloodied rags so as not to upset my mother anymore. It was their role to keep her in as pristine a condition and as comfortable as a royal mother should be.

There were two midwives to perform the actual delivery. They stayed at the foot of the bed and at regular intervals would peer between my mother's legs to examine the birth canal. They would then gently prod and feel for the expansion that they knew was needed before they could start coaching the final stages of my birth. One would feel and then silently murmur to the other and they would withdraw from the bed and allow the maids to continue on with their duties.

The midwives too had their fears. They had fears for the mother and child but above all for themselves. To be overseeing a royal birth and deliver a death instead would result in their reduction from royal midwives to anonymous women amongst the multitude of palace attendants. They would lose their fine clothes, their comfortable homes and their generous salary. Each stage of the birth had to be dealt with carefully and with utmost consideration. Getting the mother to push too soon would risk injury to the mother as she pushed through a birth canal not dilated enough. The resulting blood loss weakened many women and even caused them to bleed to death. However taking too long to start pushing would place the child at risk. The midwives knew that delaying the child's first breath would result in deficiencies to the child or have it stillborn. Being a royal heir and in direct line to the throne, either result would mean the same thing; for if I had been born incomplete or feeble I would have soon been allowed to perish and given some assistance to do so.

So the midwives had to carefully consider their timing and given the choice of favouring the mother or child, this time they would choose to favour the child. This decision was made even more easily given that they were delivering not only a royal child but a future pharaoh or queen. It was then this priority that kept them detached from my mother's pain. Her questions and pleas were met with simple, quiet and noncommittal answers that only fed her fear, causing her breath to shorten yet again and intensify her pain and discomfort.

In the corner, standing over a narrow table that acted as an altar, was a young priestess performing the rites for birth. She was burning incense and chanting over and over the same simple words that were prayed at all Egyptian births, "Make the heart of the deliverer strong, and keep alive the one that is coming."

With these words the great God Amun was supposedly summoned. He would relieve my mother's pain and deliver me safely. His arrival would be known when a breeze from the north would sweep through the room. Unfortunately Amun didn't seem to be favouring my birth as no breeze from any direction was travelling through the room. This made the young priestess nervous for several reasons. First of all she was concerned that she hadn't performed the rites properly and she might be responsible for an unsuccessful royal birth. However this could simply just be a birth that the Gods did not wish to favour and she would be the one having to report this to the Pharaoh and the other priests of the royal household. Neither scenario was one that she desired to be a part of. So she prayed harder, burnt even more incense and chanted more frequently with a stronger voice.

My mother was too consumed in her pain to be aware of any breeze or its absence. After twenty-four hours of pain and discomfort she was exhausted and could no longer hear the priestess chanting. In-between the contractions she would lay back drained of energy and in a state of half sleep only to be shocked back awake by the next pain. Her exhaustion worried the midwives, as they knew she would need her full focus and strength for the final stages.

Once again one of the midwives pressed her fingers between my mother's legs and this time looked up and smiled. "Your Highness! Your Highness! Your child's arrival is imminent!" she said directly to my mother, trying to summon some semblance of enthusiasm and anticipation. However it came out with such tension that it seemed to evoke more anxiety to the entire event. The midwife then addressed the maids, "It is time to move her to the chair."

The birthing chair was to the side of the bed and just as elaborate, for simple birthing bricks to squat upon would not do for royalty. The chair had a high back for my mother to rest upon between contractions and was painted with the entourage of Gods needed for a safe delivery. Amun who had failed us so far was there as was Bes, Tawaret and Hathor. The centre of the base of the seat was carved away in a "U" shape. The sides of the seat supported my mother's legs and the opening between allowed for my arrival. A bowl of boiling hot water was placed beneath and the steam rising played its desired role in soothing those delicate areas that would soon be tested so dearly. The clear water would gradually turn a shade of pink and then red as it also collected the blood that left my mother along with me.

Her maids gently helped ease my mother from the bed to the chair, talking so softly and lovingly to her as they made the short journey. They removed the skirt tied around her waist and, supporting her arms, lowered her with absolute grace upon the chair. They then stood one on each side stroking her hair, shoulders and arms. At the first sign of my mother wincing from a contraction they would firmly grip her arms as she leaned forward and rub her back until the pain subsided.

The elder of the midwives squatted between my mother's legs. A quick examination of the cervix made her look up with a smile. "Your Highness, your womb is ready for the child to leave," she beamed.

Her decision to move the birth to the chair wasn't entirely premature as now the cervix was fully dilated. Whether it was the small walk to the chair or the Gods finally favouring my birth somehow things were moving ahead quickly. The second midwife uncovered a small table of implements that would now be used in this final stage; scissors and string for the cord, small knives to cut an un-ruptured birth sac or my mother if needed and then dishes for the afterbirth.

Unfortunately there was still no breeze. Any breeze would have been welcome now as the clouds of incense smoke and its cloying fragrance hung still in the air. The priestess kept busy, partly for the birth and partly for herself. She hated the sight of blood and to even think about it brought on the light-headedness and nausea that was inevitable should she actually see it. This was an utter sign of weakness for a priest or priestess especially when they had to reside over sacrifices. She had thus far disguised it well and had many strategies to help her deal with the rare occasions that saw her duties involve the red fluid.

The priestess knew to focus on her breath and make sure she was breathing deeply to keep that awful dizzy feeling at a tolerable level. She would also avoid looking at the blood instead centering on the faces of those around her. Ironically the stiff poise and quiet concentration that this projected on such occasions gave her a reputation as a majestic and stoic priestess. Her subsequent high regard within the priesthood made her the ideal candidate for attending royal births so that the high priests were unanimous in choosing her to preside. This was an honour that could not be refused. So here she was ministering to my birth in all its gory glory. No one noticed that she would stop every so often and place her hand on her belly, close her eyes and take several deep breaths. Even if they had they would have assumed she was saying a quick silent prayer not realising that it was the only thing stopping her from fainting.

As my mother tensed her whole body with yet another contraction the elder midwife placed her hand upon her belly feeling for my position. She could feel me resting as low as possible and knew now it was up to my mother to coax me the rest of the way. It was during this contraction that my birth sac decided to break and a flood of fluid spilt from between my mother's legs. The elder midwife checked the colour quickly while the maids and other midwife scurried for the cloths to soak it up. It was clear apart from small traces of blood indicating that the child was still in good health. However it would now mean that I needed to get out of my mother and breathe.

Looking up at my mother the midwife spoke calmly yet firmly, "Your Highness, with the next pain you will bear down and help your child finds its way to its new life."

So with the next pain my mother indeed bore down with the hope that the pain would soon be over and I began my final passage to my own existence. Each pain saw her push harder and saw me closer to birth. The maids kept stroking and supporting my mother while the midwives kept a watchful eye and coached with gentle words. The priestess kept chanting, burning incense and deep breathing. My mother's pains came quicker so the pushing was more constant and soon my head started to make itself known to the midwife crouched before my mother.

"Ohhhh!" she gasped, "The child has hair!"

This was a good sign for it indicated a strong, well developed child was making its way. I had the thickest black hair you could imagine and the crown of my head made it known to all that a robust child was about to be delivered. Such progress spurred the women on, especially my mother who was happy to know a strong child was coming from her body. The priestess looked up excitedly as she finally had something positive to put into her report to the Pharaoh and other priests. She had to take the midwife's word for it. At this stage she wouldn't even dream of looking for herself and risk fainting during these final moments. The midwives were excited too as they knew the birth was now assured. My mother was staying strong and any bleeding was within a standard amount for a healthy delivery. By all accounts it would take some unexpected complication now for anything to go seriously wrong.

"Push, Your Highness, push," the midwife was shouting as the excitement of the end being close was engulfing us all.

I could hear the sounds so much more clearly. They were getting louder as the seconds passed. Each contraction not only pushing me further along my mother's cervix but also massaging and starting to squeeze out the fluids I had been living in. I felt some discomfort now in this tight, narrow passage after my slightly more spacious womb but I could sense the anticipation of those helping me out. My mother's moans were familiar as I had listened to her speak for months. Likewise were the voices of the handmaidens as they had talked with my mother each day.

Of course it was mainly muffled sounds but the essence of the words and who conveyed them was what I felt. I had felt my mother's anticipation and wonder at the pregnancy as well as when she was upset by goings-on in the palace. I was aware of the handmaiden's sense of duty as they spoke with her. There was one voice not amongst this group that I was searching for as I was being delivered--that of my father's. As a male he was not to be present in the birthing room. He instead would go about his royal court duties until word was sent to him. In the meantime servants would dart back and forth between the birthing room and the court with updates. The messages were simple: "No child yet." I longed for the sense of calm and reason that was always present with his voice.

Now the talking in the room became even clearer and suddenly I was aware of light as my head fully emerged. The midwife cradled my head tenderly, ecstatic to see my perfectly formed face.

"The child's face is here! Look Your Highness," she cried.

My mother slowly bent her head downwards to take in my features. She could hardly believe she was finally seeing my face but the immense pain of my body stretching her cervix delayed any sense of joy.

"One more push and the child is here," the midwife urged. "Now push…"

My mother bore down and as she strained each muscle and felt my body for the last time inside of her a great gust of wind burst into the room through the open window. Amun had finally arrived upon the scene and he did so with great effect. He swept into the room and greeted me as I slipped into this world. The midwife held me up and I opened my mouth wide and breathed him in as my first breath. Then I expelled that breath with the loudest of cries. I was here, I was breathing and everyone in the room had no doubts as to my state of health and that the Gods did indeed favour my arrival.

The priestess on hearing my cry took a very deep breath that was a combination of relief and anticipation for the next part of the proceedings. She would now have to determine my condition to report to my father and knew that I was covered in the blood and other fluids of the birth. Worst of all she would have to witness the cutting of the umbilical cord. So she walked towards me breathing deep and avoiding looking at me directly until the very moment she had to. My cries were now easing and my mother's relief at the end of the labour was clearly visible on her face as she smiled at me.

The priestess was now close by and it was time for my cord to be cut and for me to become a fully separate being. While the first midwife held me the second midwife tied a piece of string onto the cord close to my body and another piece a few inches away. She then looked up at the stiff face of the priestess. The priestess nodded and the second midwife swiftly cut through the cord.

The priestess quickly looked away and into my mother's eyes, "Well done Madam," she said curtly.

Looking back she did a quick scan of my body. There were no obvious deformities or conditions. My head was perfectly formed and my face although squashed from the birth was even and complete. There were two arms ending with hands that had the right amount of fingers, two legs ending with feet that had the right amount of toes. A solid chest that rose and deflated with strong lungs inside that had already made known their abilities. However the part of my anatomy that would receive the most attention lay between my legs.

"You have given birth to a complete and healthy son," the priestess announced with a smile, her first of the entire birth. "The Gods thank you for the next Pharaoh, as does all of Egypt. We shall now help you empty your womb of the afterbirth."

My mother could now relax and rejoice my birth. Her smile and joy spread to the maids who clucked and cooed their congratulations. As she rested back in the chair they declared me the most special child ever born and thanked her for the honour of allowing them to be present at my arrival.

The priestess walked to her altar and returned with the birth wand, a piece of ivory carved into a flattened curve much like a boomerang. Placing it upon my mother's belly and then looking away to the ceiling as though addressing the Gods directly she asked them to help clear my mother. The midwife massaged below the wand and my mother gently pushed out the remnants of the birth sac and the placenta.

These too would have to be examined as to complete the picture of my birth. If the placenta were too pink it would mean I had arrived early and my lungs may need herbs to help them. It would also indicate that I would have an impatient and ill-considered temperament. A more developed pregnancy saw the pink turn to red and a delayed birth saw the colour start to turn to dark red or brown. While the latter colour didn't affect my health it would mean I would be of a hesitant and too cautious nature. As it was my placenta was a decidedly strong red colour. I was neither too early nor too late. My arrival was completely appropriate. The midwife relayed this to the priestess who nodded and trusted her appraisal. Thankfully now she would not have to actually look at the redundant tissue that provided this information.

The midwife wiped my face and I was wrapped before being handed to my mother for her first embrace of me. No one will ever know the feeling of joy that she had as she took me in her arms. My eyes were wide open and she looked into them with awe trying to comprehend that this little person had grown inside her. She was overwhelmed with wanting to protect me and drew me close to her. I cooed and gurgled letting her know my happiness in my own way. All the formalities and expectations fell away for that brief instant. We were simply mother and child. There were no titles, no ritual and no other person needed. It was very short-lived though.

"Bathe the mother and child," the priestess ordered of the maids and midwives. "Prepare them for the Pharaoh's arrival to meet his son and heir."

I was promptly taken from my mother's arms and our precious moment was ended. The midwives carried me to a large tub filled with water and the maids led my mother to the next room where a huge sunken bath had been waiting. They knew not to hurry and that they could take their time. The Pharaoh would be at least an hour as the priestess had to go to him at the main court which was a long walk away. She would deliver the birth announcement as well as all the details and then return with my father and an entourage of officials to meet me.

The priestess went and opened the door leading out into the corridor. Two servants sitting outside jumped to their feet awaiting her order. "Get the others and prepare the room for the Pharaoh!" she instructed. They left immediately around a corner and she was finally alone. A wave of dizziness and anxiety flushed over her and she quickly sat down in one of the chairs vacated by the servants, closed her eyes and drew in a deep breath.

She had now been awake for more than twenty-four hours overseeing the labour from the first few pangs of pain, endured those awful final moments with the blood and now she needed to gather herself to present to the Pharaoh. The priestess rose, steadied herself and began the walk towards the court where she knew he was waiting. At the end of the corridor four young men stood guard and as she approached they stood to attention and snapped their posts straight.

"You--accompany me," she demanded as she pointed at one without even stopping. She didn't need him for security nor to help her find her way. He was insurance should she pass out within the maze of corridors along the way. To collapse in an area not frequented could have meant the announcement would be delayed for over an hour and the thought of this made her feel even more nauseous. He quickly stepped to walk ahead of her as any escort would, the priestess barking directions as they approached any turns or doors they would need to pass through.

It was a solid fifteen minute walk from the family rooms of the palace across to the other side where the court and other formal rooms were but despite her fatigue the priestess kept good time. As she walked she played over and over in her head the words she would use to announce to the Pharaoh that he had a son, embellished with the details of the mother's courage and the signs from the Gods. With the child and mother safe she was free to exaggerate and make it as grand as possible. Her simple walk to the court gathered a momentum of excitement through the palace for as she passed courtiers, priests and servants alike all knew her movement through the palace meant the birth was complete. She could never stop to share any details, as these were first and foremost for the Pharaoh's ears however she did satisfy their curiosity with a slight smile and a nod. Within these so small gestures they received the news that the royal birth had been a success.

As she passed more people her nausea and dizziness subsided as she too now joined them in the excitement. Those that were able to enter the court fell in behind her and the final moments of the walk saw a joyful procession heading along the corridor that approached the court. Twelve guards presided over that last stretch of hallway lining it with six on each side, and as they saw the priestess approach with the small crowd they all stood to attention as much with anticipation as duty. The two closest to the huge doors pulled them open, this was enough to let those inside know that the news they had been waiting for was about to be delivered.

As the priestess approached the guards she slowed her walk and stopped, letting her young guard approach the first of the court guards. "Priestess Arisina to be presented to the Pharaoh!" he delivered with the stiff decorum that was required of such a statement. He then stood aside and was replaced by this guard as well as the guard who stood opposite him. They stood side by side and led the priestess along the hall, past the other guards. The remaining guards stood at attention and looked straight ahead never making eye contact until the priestess had passed and they then scanned the crowd to make sure those following were actually allowed to enter the court. They grabbed a few who were trying their luck but the lightness of the whole event simply saw them scolded with a laugh as they were pushed back from the entrance.

The priestess looked ahead hardly believing that this moment had come. As she peered down this final part of the passage and through the doors she could see straight through to a small rise of stairs that led up to the platform on which the Pharaoh, my father, was waiting. This stage raised him above any others attending court as was befitting for a man viewed not only as a king but also as a living God.

He had paced here forward and back all day waiting for news while his attendants, army commanders and viziers had endeavoured to entertain him with stories and the latest of news. When the doors swung open a hush fell across the massive room and my father walked quickly to the front and centre of the stage, standing with his hands clasped behind his back trying desperately to appear regal but bursting with curious excitement. It felt like an eternity watching the guards walk the priestess in but finally they were at the base of the stairs. Following protocol the priestess didn't look up at him until they were finally in place and she was announced by the bellowing voice of the leading guard.

"Your Royal Highness Pharaoh Thutmose, Priestess Arisina requests an audience with you," he said looking straight ahead and never daring to look the Pharaoh in the eye.

"Priestess Arisina is most welcome," My father replied with the broadest smile, barely able to contain himself as he looked to the priestess.

The guards stepped away, each to one side of the floor of the main court where they would wait to escort the priestess and my father to meet me. Those that had followed also moved to the sides to take a place along the edges and amongst the columns that lined the grand hall, wherever they might be inconspicuous and yet still hear the news.

Arisina now looked up at the Pharaoh and was momentarily taken aback. There was my father not sitting upon his throne but standing and with a huge grin on his face, which despite the circumstance was certainly not within the disciplines of a pharaoh holding court. Even though my father was known as a gentle leader this was still somewhat discomforting for someone so entrenched in protocol and determined to execute her duties in the manner that was required of her.

"Speak Arisina. What news do you have for me?" he blurted out, leaning forward while he stood, almost as though it would help the words get to his ears quicker.

The priestess took a step forward, crossed her arms over her chest and bowed. She slowly raised herself back to standing straight and then after a deep breath to help quell her nerves and produce a strong voice she spoke the most amazing words my father had been praying to hear.

"Your Highness Pharaoh Thutmose, Queen Isis has given birth to a son," she announced with the solemnity and gravity she believed was required of such words. She barely had time to inhale in preparation for the rest of her announcement when my father suddenly shouted.

"Ahhhh!" he bellowed to the ceiling and clapped his hands, "Wonderful! Wonderful news! What a grand day that the Gods have given me," and with that he bounded down the stairs toward the priestess. There was momentary chaos as courtiers and guards rushed after him.

"Let's go and see him," he said to the priestess beaming almost wildly as he approached her rubbing his hands together.

"Ah--Your Highness…" she stammered in absolute confusion. My father had so seriously broken the procedure of a birth announcement as she had been trained to deliver it that the priestess was completely lost as how to react. Her exhaustion layered upon this didn't help and now she had courtiers and attendants all looking at her with the expectation that she would restore order.

As my father arrived by her side she once again found a steady voice, "Your Highness, your joy with this gracious gift from the Gods is truly inspiring, however there is much more for me to share with you," she said quickly.

"Oh, of course there is Arisina. Isis? Is she alright?" he asked, almost embarrassed that he hadn't immediately posed this question before the priestess had pointed out that there was much more to know.

"The royal wife is strong and healthy as is your son," the priestess recounted with the confidence that she was regaining order.

"Wonderful, tell me the rest along the way. I must see them," he was almost begging. He had truly forgotten his place, surrendering to his excitement and elation completely.

"Your Highness, your son and his mother need time to prepare for your visit. Let us talk here, it will give them the time they need," she said gently as she gestured to his throne and my father reluctantly but obediently walked back and began to climb upwards.

As he mounted the stairs to his throne he invited Arisina to join him and requested a chair for her. His mood was decidedly calmer when she sat before him but her dramatic re-telling of my birth, in particular the spectacular arrival of Amun at my emergence raised his spirits once more and he was soon leaning forward in his throne laughing and clapping as he heard the details. All the while a scribe sat cross-legged upon the floor nearby making notes upon a scroll that would be copied many times over and carried across the land to proclaim my birth. This of course would not include my father's interjections and whoops of laughter as my birth story was told.

The priestess drew to the end of the account and her weariness as well as her compassion towards my father made her grateful that she could now invite him to come and meet me. They both rose and made their way down the stairs, the priestess always remaining a step behind my father. The two guards came forward again to flank him and a small entourage of courtiers and officials gathered behind the priestess and together they set out to see me.

In the meantime the birthing room had been filled with servants who had stripped the bed of its soiled linen and replaced it with fresh bedding. The floors were washed and the birthing chair was scrubbed down with hot water. My afterbirth was removed in dishes for other priests to examine and perform ceremony over after which it would be buried along the banks of the Nile returning some of the nourishment that the river gave to our people over and over. The midwives' tools had been taken away to be meticulously cleaned and boiled before being stored away for the next birth. By the time of my father's arrival the birthing room would simply look like any other bedroom in the palace apart from the birthing chair, which was now pushed back into the corner.

My mother had been taken into an adjoining room to be bathed. It had an enormous sunken bath and the maids undressed what clothing remained on her and then walked her into its waters that had been kept ready for this moment since her labour began. Oils had been added to the water and they gave the air a syrupy fragrance and soothed her spirit while the warm waters refreshed her body and washed away the last traces of the birth from between her legs. She sat on a stair within the bath while the maids poured water over her, and washed her with soft cloths. She wanted so desperately to sleep and the warm water was making it so easy to close her eyes but knowing my father would be here soon helped to keep her awake.

After the bath the maids dried her and dressed her in beautiful fresh silks. By the time she was being led back to bed to lie down I too was being placed in my basket as I had also been bathed and dressed. My basket was woven of reeds and sat within a frame of gold decorated with the same Gods that had adorned the birth chair. Beside it was a small table upon which two statues of Bes and Hathor were placed. They would now protect me in these first days as I grew accustomed to my new life.

My mother came and looked over me before she climbed onto the bed and lay back. The midwives returned and checked her one last time. She was slightly torn from my birth and now that she was freshly bathed they could see this more clearly. They had prepared a poultice of crushed herbs and this was spread upon a leaf that would help hold the herbs against my mother's tender skin. The leaf was then bound between my mother's legs, protecting her more from infection than it would actually heal her.

With all the fussing finally over my mother lay back against the soft pillows. A young servant boy was gently fanning her and relieving her from the now stagnant evening air. She wanted so much to sleep but knew that my father would be there any moment and she was as eager to see him as he was to see us both. Looking over at me she could hardly believe that this was all over. Her joy at my safe arrival was equalled by her pride in giving my father a son. After all the favour that had been received by her in life thus far, she felt that she had somehow returned the good fortune that the Gods had given her. Within this pride there was also a sense of superiority. She could now walk with her head just a bit higher knowing that the palace and all its officials would have to respect her that much more.

In particular was one person who she knew would not take this news well at all. This person was also missing at my birth announcement in the court. It was Hatshepsut, my father's highest wife and my aunt. That is correct--she is my father's sister. Hatshepsut and my father were born of the same father but had different mothers. Hatshepsut's mother was a "full" royal having been born of a mother also of royal lineage. My father's mother was merely a "lesser" wife having been chosen by my grandfather from amongst his consorts within the palace. So my grandfather in order to strengthen the path of his sole male heir to the throne married his son to his daughter.

The fact that her life would always be lived below that of my father simply due to the circumstance of her gender never sat well with Hatshepsut, especially as she had been born first. By the time my father was old enough to be involved in court matters she was already well experienced and would take every opportunity to humiliate him and make fun of his lack of knowledge. Not surprisingly my father never exercised his marriage rights with Hatshepsut and despite their private chambers being next to each other he had never crossed her door. He didn't even know what the interior of her rooms looked like.

Some of your history books tell of them having a daughter together who would then become my wife. Hatshepsut did have two daughters though neither was of my father. A diplomat fathered one daughter as part of a marriage before that to my father. The other was by some anonymous courtier who she sought out to satisfy her one night. Hatshepsut had many male consorts who visited her chambers. They were ushered there with utmost discretion but it was common knowledge within the palace. There were few secrets any royal could truly keep beyond their private chambers.

Despite the urge to provide a male heir of her own body she now asked the physicians to provide her with the herbs needed for preventing pregnancy. She did not require the complications that an illegitimate male child would have brought upon her. All would know that the child had not been fathered by the Pharaoh. To have her daughters usurped by the son of a consort was bad enough, to have a son of her body usurped would be worse no matter how tenuous his claim to the throne. So on the several occasions that the herbs

15

didn't work Hatshepsut would remain in her chamber for several days while the priestesses and physicians arranged the necessary procedure. The court would simply be told she had a fever.

History would now repeat itself as I lay here the sole male heir born of a lesser wife. Isis, my mother, was one of my father's royal consorts, a group of women gathered amongst the daughters of senior palace officials and diplomats from surrounding regions. These women were here to please, pamper and indulge my father however he chose or required. While he did indulge his more carnal desires with many of them, he generally obtained them more for company and conversation as they were a wonderful relief from the heaviness of his official duties.

My mother would gradually become the woman that he sought more than the others. She loved discussion and was a born philosopher and this satisfied a part of my father that no other person, duty or worship could. He would call for her after a full day of court duties or training with the army and they would talk for hours eventually falling asleep, more often than not in each other's arms. The gentle love that overwhelmed them both helped my father forget his woes with Hatshepsut, even if it further inflamed her jealousy, as he grew happier by the day. It was upon the realisation that he wanted my mother and no other in his bed that he announced that she would become his wife and so began the union that would make my arrival possible.

Isis knew the extent of her luck at being chosen to be a royal wife and to be truly loved. Many consorts were merely toys or ornaments to their assigned patrons. Worse yet some were just a female to be laid upon and empty their seed into without any regard or affection. She understood and acknowledged the blessings that were granted to her and believed that her gratitude and thankfulness were now recognised by the Gods in the birth of a son.

My father, Arisina and the entourage were now nearly at the birthing chamber. As they got closer my father's excitement and exuberance escalated. His pace quickened which meant that of the guards and the exhausted priestess had to as well. The young guards stood tall as my father approached then two of them walked ahead and opened the doors. A wave of rose oil scent swept outwards greeting them all.

The opening of the doors saw the few servants inside run through side doors to adjacent rooms so that when my father finally entered the only people within the room would be the two midwives by the window, the maids in the opposite corner, the young boy beside the bed with his fan, my mother on the bed and me in my crib to her left and in direct line with the doorway. The guards stood back to flank the entrance just in time to avoid being pushed aside by my father as he made a beeline to my crib. The small entourage that had followed him waited in the hallway.

The smile he shone down on me as he first looked at me brought tears to my mother's eyes. It was the pure joy and love of a new father and he too felt tears. Once again his excitement overtook protocol and he swept me up in his arms, the sudden movement of his masculine hands jolting me from my first sleep and I bellowed.

"Ah, little one, your strong lungs were not exaggerated," he laughed as he spoke to me.

The midwives were standing in shock, as it was to be the priestess's duty to hand me to my father for his first inspection. Instead he had gathered me up for my first embrace without any assistance. He pulled me close to him, instinctively soothing me and I soon settled again as he carried me to the side of my mother's bed.

"Isis, what a wonderful gift you have given me," he said to her gently and bent to kiss her on the lips, "May the Gods eternally bless you."

The priestess now accustomed to the fact that this birth was not going to follow the procedure she had trained for smiled at the midwives who were still standing wide-eyed at my father's behaviour. She beckoned to them to come closer and they approached the foot of the bed. My father was too entranced by me to even notice them and so the priestess once again drew him back to some semblance of the required formalities.

"Your Highness, I present to you Maperre and Arahk-Ra, the midwives who helped bring your son," she announced gesturing with her hand towards them.

My father turned to the women and smiled. They would never understand just how much appreciation he held for having his wife and son safe and healthy. They bowed to him and then stood straight with their eyes cast down.

"Your skill and care will always be remembered," he continued to smile at them.

They nodded and bowed, both saying, "It was our honour Your Highness," softly as was expected and acceptable in return for this recognition. The priestess was about to deliver the dismissal signalling the end of their duties when my father once again spoke.

"Arisina, see to it that these women are rewarded for their wonderful work," he said.

"Oh--ah--Your Highness this is not necessary," she hesitated. Arisina was beyond exhausted now and knew every time my father broke from the set proceedings it just added to the time before she could sleep.

"Arisina, I insist!" he spoke stronger now. "Get one of the courtiers waiting outside to gather wine and meat for their families. He will also give them a gold piece each."

The midwives now gasped and looked up. The gifting of wine and meat was more than enough, but a gold piece was above anything that could be dreamt of. This would feed their families for months, provide new clothing and even buy a donkey. Arisina too looked at my father in shock. It took her a moment before she gathered herself and gestured to the midwives to follow her to the doorway. She took a deep breath, waved towards her a senior court official and repeated my father's orders. He and those around him looked at each other confused but were assured by the priestess that this was indeed the Pharaoh's command. The courtier then nodded and with the midwives smiling and giggling behind him they walked away down the corridor to gather their reward.

The priestess returned to the chamber where my father was now sitting on the edge of the bed next to my mother, alternating his smile from me to my mother. There was only one last duty for her to perform and that was to invite the officials milling outside the door to now meet me as well.

"Your Highness, shall I call in your courtiers?" she asked.

Without looking away from me my father nodded and with that the priestess waved to the guard by the door. The senior guard nodded to the group in the corridor and they silently walked into the room forming a single orderly row. One at a time they walked to my father, bowed, looked at me, gently relayed a congratulations or compliment to my parents and exited the room. It was the most simple of the requirements for the birth and the priestess wasn't going to even try and make my father place me back into my crib to receive the palace officials as was expected. She hid a yawn behind her hand as she watched them file quickly through the chamber and soon they were all done and gone.

"Your Highnesses, is there any other duty I can assist you with?" she asked, hoping there wouldn't be.

"Arisina, you have done more than enough, the maids and servants can now take care of us. You are free to go," he replied.

"It has been an honour," she said as she bowed low.

With a parting look at the lovely picture of the three of us Arisina left the room. There was one last duty she would have to do now and she dreaded this one most of all. She considered omitting it entirely but it would not be worth the complications that it in itself would then attract. She would now have to officially tell Hatshepsut about my birth. The priestess knew that she would in fact have already heard the news. Hatshepsut had many servants and maids who happily spied for her and one would have certainly carried this to her within the hour or so since my birth. Arisina had to pass the Queen's quarters on the way to the carriage that waited for her so she decided that she may as well get it over and done with, and then she could sleep in completion.

Arisina headed into the corridor that led to Hatshepsut's chambers and as she did another priestess entered from a side passage.

"There you are! Ready to break the news?" she smirked to Arisina. Ma-Keet was another of the senior palace priestesses. Her sole duty was in performing ritual and prayer for Hatshepsut. "She knows already and she is not happy," she said, gloating at the opportunity to spread her mistress's displeasure.

Arisina merely nodded. She was too tired to enter into small talk and she also knew that Ma-Keet had a tendency to take a conversation and twist it to serve her purposes. The less said around her the less ammunition she would have to use against her at a later time. Arisina kept walking towards the doors of Hatshepsut's chambers while Ma-Keet, following alongside her, yelled to the guards to open the door. The pair walked in to see Hatshepsut reclining on a lounge. Her two daughters were sitting nearby, one having her hair brushed by a maid, the other playing a game of Senet with another maid. They all appeared quiet and trying to behave as though things were fine.

Arisina had to act as though she was the first through the doors with the news of my birth and so she conducted herself as she did with my father. She took a few paces inside the door, crossed her arms over her chest and bowed. She then straightened up, keeping her eyes cast down until Hatshepsut acknowledged her.

"Speak! Is it true?" Hatshepsut commanded.

Arisina was accustomed to Hatshepsut's harshness and remaining composed she raised her eyes and calmly stated that a male had been born to the Pharaoh's lesser wife. Hatshepsut's face flushed and the muscles along her jaw sharpened as she clenched her teeth and lifted her chin while her daughters kept their eyes down.

The priestess was about to excuse herself when Hatshepsut stood and walked towards her, stopping next to a table. Hatshepsut absently started to stroke a statue that was on the table as she smirked, and then without looking up she asked the question, "Will the child live?"

"Yes," answered Arisina evenly. "He is most rigorous, one of the strongest babies I have ever seen."

Arisina needn't have added those other details and Hatshepsut certainly didn't want to hear them. The words had barely left the priestess's mouth when Hatshepsut reached down, grabbed the statue, and smashed it to the floor. There was no smirk on her face now as it turned the deepest red. She turned to look at her daughters, her hands clenched into fists by her side, shaking her head from side to side.

"This is not over yet," Hatshepsut muttered under her breath. Then she turned to Arisina and hissed, "Go! Your duties are over!"

The priestess barely bowed and quickly turned to leave the room. As she crossed the doorway she thought she heard whimpering tears from one of the daughters, however she was so overcome by exhaustion now she hardly cared. In a short time she would be in her chambers at the temple, on her bed and drifting off into a blissful sleep. Knowing this, Arisina's exhaustion seemed to accelerate and her feet grew heavy.

Arisina's two maids greeted her as she returned to her own room and they followed her as she crossed the floor and sat on the edge of the bed. They began to take off her jewellery and then her clothes. The priestess was starting to sleep even as they did this and they instinctively knew that she wouldn't be using the bath they had prepared, instead wiping her quickly with wet cloths to cool and refresh her. Then, not worrying about her makeup or even a nightdress, they helped her lie back onto the bed and covered her with a sheet. The maids silently collected her clothes, put away her jewellery and left for their chamber nearby. Arisina was in a deep sleep before they even closed her door and spent the night dreaming of breezes, statues smashing and my father's smile.

I was now stirring from my slumber as hunger pangs started to make themselves known in my stomach. As blissful as it was to be with my mother and father in our cosy configuration, my need to eat could not be delayed. My cries grew stronger and I began to thrash my arms and legs as best I could in my swaddling. Although my father was enjoying watching my display, relishing my physical strength, my nurses understood better.

I would have a team of three nurses who would care for me, alternating through the day and night to attend to my needs. There would also be two wet nurses to feed me. These were women from amongst the palace staff who had children recently and also enough milk to nourish a second child. It was a position allocated out of circumstance and meant their family would be moved to the more luxurious apartments of the palace to be near me while I needed milk. My mother would have loved to feed me. Her maternal instincts were also strong but she was not in the position to challenge protocol. So as one of the nurses stepped forward and collected me from my father explaining that I needed to be fed, my mother said nothing and watched me being carried away. Her heart ached and it would every time this happened. My mother and father both followed me intently with their eyes until I passed through the curtain that hid the doorway to the small room in which the wet nurse waited to feed me.

My father then turned to my mother. He was still beaming and leaned over her, cupping her face in his hands and gently kissing her hair and forehead. "Come to my room tonight," he whispered in her ear.

"Thutmose!" she giggled in response.

"I want you both with me tonight," he said, eyes wide, his voice full of love. "I want to wake and see you both there. I want to hear his cries during the night. Please come and stay with me."

"Am I allowed?" Unlike my father, my mother knew she had rules to follow. Amongst these were that she must stay within the birthing room for three weeks to recover and heal.

My father laughed, "I am Pharaoh. I think that I may decide where my wife and child will stay!" With that he gestured to the most senior of my mother's maids, "Arrange for my wife and child to stay tonight in my chambers."

The maid bowed and turned to the nurses and servants repeating this request. They began to hurry about preparing for the move. Thankfully it wasn't too far. However the maid had one concern; how to move my mother? She could never be expected to walk despite it not being too far but still it was too much to ask of a woman exhausted from her first birth. Also it was now up to the maid to ensure my mother healed, and even though there was minimal tearing my mother would still require utmost care. She walked to the door and a guard immediately came to her.

"We need to relocate the royal mother to the pharaoh's chambers. She cannot walk and must be carried. Can you arrange this?" she spoke with authority but it was more of a plea for help.

The guard merely nodded in response and then turned to some younger guards, "Go and collect the sedan, and don't waste time or I will have your heads!" He turned to the maid, "It is done. All will be ready shortly."

As the young guards ran down the hallway the maid returned to the room and continued to oversee the other servants. Cloths for me were being stacked in piles and my mother's clothes were being gathered. The senior nurse gave directions to the others and then left to oversee the set up of the nursery in my father's chambers. A short line of servants followed her, some with arms bundled with clothing, some carrying trays with bottles of oils and soaps.

My father remained sitting on the edge of my mother's bed stroking her hair as she told him about the birth. They were in their own world seemingly oblivious to all the movement around them until four guards walked in with the sedan, an elaborate chair with handles extending along the base from which it was carried. This now would be how my mother was transported. It arrived with good timing as I had just finished my first meal and was being brought back into the main room. The nurse was taking me over to place me into my crib, assuming that I would be moved to my father's room laying in it--but of course my father had other ideas.

"I will carry him!" he declared putting out his hands.

So it was that my journey to my new bedroom was taken in my father's arms. In fact if he could have, he would have carried my mother and me both. Instead, we now formed a procession starting with my father holding a very content child, flanked by guards, then behind us four guards carrying my mother in her portable throne, and lastly two more who brought my crib. Several female servants transported the remainder of my effects, including most importantly my statues of Bes and Hathor.

We walked along the corridors and on reaching my father's rooms they all once again dispersed into different duties. The sedan was carried straight to the bedchamber and once it was lowered her two maids helped my mother from it and guided her to the bed. The servants removed the sedan as my crib was put next to the bed and the servants who placed it also left. The women continued to fuss about placing my statues and organising my effects. All the while my father walked forward and back, cradling me and admiring every detail of my face. He would do this for another hour or so until the fuss and bother was settled and the senior nurse dismissed most of the servants.

My mother having known she was finally in the bed where she would sleep had drifted off soon after her arrival despite all the movement. My post-feed stupor had turned into deep sleep along the corridor and now my father too finally grew hungry and weary. He handed me back to my nurse who placed me in my crib and then after a quick meal allowed his butler and personal servants to prepare him for the night. My father slid into bed beside my mother, giving her one last kiss on the forehead, and then lying on his back he fell into a deep sleep where he dreamt of me growing into a warrior twenty feet tall crushing Egypt's enemies with the Gods Amun and Ra by my side.

CHAPTER TWO

My early days went by smoothly. I was bathed, fed, clothed and adored. A newborn child doesn't want or need for much more than that. My father continued to break protocol by keeping my mother and myself in his private chambers. His happiness at this arrangement flowed into the day to day running of the palace and therefore Egypt and this was indeed one of the empire's most peaceful times. He didn't seek to capture more land instead being content with what was and nurturing that. Of course none of this sat well with Hatshepsut who would have loved to have been expanding the empire and asserting herself over anyone that would allow it. However it was my father's happiness that agitated her more than any of his political decisions. She never came to visit me as a newborn. It was as if by not acknowledging me she could pretend I didn't exist. However I did exist and she eventually did have to see me no matter how painful it was for her.

A month after my birth I was taken to the Great Temple at Karnak. Here I was to be blessed, given my name and officially presented by my father as his heir. Any official within reasonable travelling distance had by now heard of my birth and had arrived in Thebes to attend the ceremony. Arisina stood at the altar with the Amun high priests of Karnak, the very highest of all the priests in Egypt. She was burning incense, the very same that was burnt during my birth and even at my young age I recognised it. It was a heavy smell and evoked emotions in many of us. My mother walking her required paces behind my father was immediately taken back to the pain and exhaustion. The tenderness between her legs almost felt as though it was freshly stretched despite a month of healing.

My father as always led the procession into the temple. Behind him four guards walked carrying me within a basket gilt with gold and lined with silks, followed by my mother and Hatshepsut side by side. My mother kept her eyes ahead the whole time, glad that she could keep her glance upon me. The truth was that she dared not look Hatshepsut in the eye, for to look that woman in the eye was as good as allowing her to drain you of your blood. Hatshepsut knew all too well how to intimidate and overpower with a mere glance and my mother had experienced this on many occasions. Today my mother would not allow Hatshepsut's bullying to spoil my first royal ceremony.

My basket with me inside sleeping and oblivious to all was placed upon the great altar as my parents and Hatshepsut settled into place kneeling before the stairs that rose up to it. Once all were settled the priests began their chanting, raising their arms into the air to call upon Amun to join us. The chanting stopped and my father stood and walked up the stairs to stand before the altar.

"Pharaoh, you have blessed us all with the arrival of a son. What name shall he be known by?" Arisina asked performing her part of the ceremony.

"My son and heir shall be named Thutmose, as am I and as was my father," he beamed back.

"And so it shall be," she stated, and all the priests bowed to acknowledge my title. "Hold your son for all to see, Pharaoh, so that all will know him and his name."

My father then carefully unwrapped the cloth I was cocooned in and with only my silk diaper tied upon me he turned to face all gathered in the temple and held me up for all to see. Being unwrapped and feeling the air against my skin ended my gentle slumber and I looked wide-eyed out to see a blur of people. He then placed me back within my basket upon the altar and Arisina anointed me with oils calling the Gods once again to protect and guide me. When she was finished I was re-wrapped and placed into the curve of my father's arms. He then walked down to the base of the stairs where my mother and Hatshepsut stood to either side of my father who then beaming the same smile he had carried since hearing of my arrival, called for those present to come and meet his son.

A slow procession of dignitaries and ambassadors from all over the empire and its neighbours, along with local nobility and the wealthy made their way to see me. Each carried gifts as a symbol of respect as well as to seek favour. They brought the finest offerings from their region or trade and soon beside us was a huge pile of gold, bags of gemstones, incense, scented oils, paintings, fabrics and leather. All would be used for me in some way. The gemstones and gold would be for adornments and eventually my funeral mask and sarcophagus, the incense and oils for rituals and bathing, paintings for my private rooms, fabrics for clothes and bedding. The leather though would become some of my most prized possessions; my saddle and battle clothes.

My first official duty was now over and I began to squirm with hunger.

My first few years of royal life flowed. I had a freedom that few children knew and was greatly indulged. I grew strong and had a vitality that surprised many, as this was not something my father or even his father possessed. Whispers amongst the palace and then out to the empire grew that I was indeed blessed by the Gods and was a great hope for Egypt and its people for another generation of abundance and prosperity.

I was able to walk by ten months of age, which was considered almost supernatural despite children often doing this, yet it somehow further reinforced my calling to the position of Pharaoh. To me it was simply a calling to assert some independence and I seized every opportunity to exploit my newfound skill. Anyone who cared for me soon developed a higher level of fitness or they would be moved on to other roles if they couldn't keep up with me. Of course like any child I soon found an amazing game within this and the act of slipping away from my nurses was as much fun as the ability to do so.

One nurse soon figured me out though. I could run and she wouldn't always follow. She would not get the anxiety or flurry that the others would succumb to. She wouldn't even sigh but remain calm and patient. She knew I couldn't get too far and that I was ultimately safe. So I soon knew that to run from her was no game and when I was with her I didn't try to escape her care. I would walk slowly and turn often to see she was still with me. I would look for her approval before touching anything and when I was with her all of my meal was eaten. I would wander through the palace as she calmly followed me, seemingly curious as to where I would lead her, enjoying watching me explore. Her care for me was not through fear of protecting a future king. It came from a gentle respect and wonder for the part I would one day play.

It was on one of the days that I was under her care that we were roaming through the palace corridors and I drifted into the area leading to the palace courtroom. As usual the corridor leading to the massive doors was flanked by a dozen guards, six on each side. They were dressed in their official uniforms, bare-chested but with a gold and blue woven kilt that stopped just above the knee. It was split along the side of each thigh to allow them movement. What this also allowed was for a tiny child to lift and see what was underneath and I decided to do this as I wandered even further into their space.

I stopped at the first guard who remained stoic, as was his job, looking straight ahead as though I was not there. They were never to address or acknowledge anyone unless they were addressed or acknowledged. So as I lifted his skirt to see what was beneath it he remained still and quiet. A few of his counterparts however found it somewhat difficult to maintain their poise and a slow wave of muffled laughs began to dissolve the stillness. I moved my way slowly down the line of guards, examining each the same way as the stifled laughs continued and more guards grew aware of what their future pharaoh was doing. A few were starting to shake with laughter despite making no noise and my nurse now had a very bemused look on her face. I was just lowering the skirt of the fourth guard I had inspected when the court doors opened. A high-ranking official, known as a vizier, stepped into the corridor. Within a split second all twelve guards had regained their composure; there was not the slightest sound or hint of a smile. My nurse dropped her head so as not to make eye contact, as was her place. The vizier looked at everyone with that knowing that he had interrupted something but not sure what. He just as quickly continued on his way bowing his head to me as he passed.

My nurse came to me offering me her hand, "Come along, young prince, it is time to return to your nursery."

I offered up both my arms, allowing her to collect me. As she carried me away I took one last look over her shoulder before we turned the corner and I saw the guards dissolve in quiet laughter.

When I was more of a toddler than a baby and was fully weaned, my father took every opportunity to have me by his side. My father did this as much to spend time with me as it was about helping me become accustomed to my duties and those serving me. He would sit me on his lap in court as he discussed business and policies with viziers and diplomats. I overheard diplomatic deals that would be in place for the next hundred years but this was all beyond my mind at this time. I would simply sit and enjoy being with my father as he bounced me on his knee whilst he talked. Sometimes I would get the odd piece of attention from those he was talking to but soon they would get lost in the serious aspects of their business and I would soon grow bored. It was then I would squirm and eventually my father would put me down to be collected immediately by one of my nurses who were always waiting nearby.

I would then return to the nursery to be entertained with my toys and hopefully any other children who were in the palace at the time. I had one loyal and trusted friend, Salas. He was born within a week of my birth to the cousin of my mother who was a palace attendant. Salas was an approved playmate, as I couldn't just play with anyone. His mother's close association to the palace and his blood ties allowed us to be friends and for this I would always be grateful as true friends in such a position are few and far between. Within the safety of the nursery rooms we could play for hours with our mothers close by and it was always wonderful.

However my most joyful times were when my father carried me; whether it be through the palace or into temple. The constant movement and changing scenery amused my child mind. Of all the places that he carried me to, my most favourite was the rooms of the army commanders. Even as a child I sensed the importance of these rooms but what truly captured my attention were the vast tables set out with maps. Upon these maps were models of armies complete with horses with chariots, weapons such as catapults and even ships within the waterways. They were a full detailed visual of exactly how things were throughout the empire as well as amazing tools for planning. However to a small child such as myself, they were a most delightful playground just waiting to be explored and played with.

It was within this room that I wasn't allowed the freedom of other places within the palace. As much as I would have loved to crawl and play upon the tables, rearranging the small soldiers and their equipment, it wasn't to be. My father would always hold me firm within his arms and if I squirmed too much then I would be handed to a nurse and sent back to the nursery. So by the age of three I understood perfectly that if I wished to spend time here I would need to remain quiet and still, with my hands by my side. While at first this was hard for a young child it opened up a new world for me. This was how I learnt to listen and within this listening space I was to grasp much of what would make me one of the greatest army commanders and pharaohs to ever rule.

By the age of six I had learnt all the terms and language used by the commanders. I knew of all the current placements of our army as well as those

of our neighbours. The more I learnt the hungrier I grew for the knowledge.
I could draw the map of our kingdom from memory and name all its parts as
well as the diplomats and rulers of the surrounding regions. My father would
quiz me to delight in how I was soaking up all the details that would one day be
needed when I ruled. He would often do this in front of visiting dignitaries and
court officials, seemingly to boast of my learning. I now know this was also to
make them aware of the formidable pharaoh that their country would one day
be dealing with.

Hatshepsut was often nearby when I was spilling out this information.
I often imagined this would inflame her hatred of me even more however
this was far from the truth as the more I learnt the less harsh she was towards
me. She was witnessing the growth of someone who would serve Egypt well
whether it was under her rule or as someone she could influence. She would
have been a fool to not nurture and support me.

If she did hold any anger towards my growing knowledge it was directed
at her daughters. Unlike myself, who savoured learning about royal duties;
her daughters were distracted by their female indulgences. They were happy
to avoid court proceedings in order to bathe and be preened. Hatshepsut could
only convince them to attend royal tours with the promise of shopping for new
silks and jewels. They could barely recite the names of our local court officials
let alone any neighbouring diplomats and as my reputation grew they became
more invisible. Even Hatshepsut soon tired of using any energy in encouraging
them to become informed on topics beyond appearances and manners.

As their mother lost interest in them and her interest in me grew this
soon gave rise to hostilities between them and I. As they approached and
entered their teenage years and understood more fully what was going on this
resentment mounted even more. I was subject to quips and teasing, always
perfectly choreographed outside of my father's and their mother's earshot. If
I retaliated they simply made fun of my attempts and their next attack would
be doubly vicious. So I decided to simply remain quiet. The one time I spoke
of it to my father I saw the pain on his face as he listened. He recalled his own
memories growing up and to know I now was also going through this hurt him
more than I could imagine.

"Be strong my son, these are just words. Words will never keep you
from your true destiny to be Pharaoh. The Gods declared it at your birth," he
said calmly to me.

I never talked of it to him again and each time a barb was delivered I
recalled his words and held onto the truth he spoke. The girls were reprimanded
but it didn't stop them, they just became cleverer in their timing and delivery.
They were the one blemish in what I knew was a blessed life and it ate away at
any other joy I had. Despite my young years I knew I would need to deal with
this by some means and the answer as to how to do this presented itself to me
quite simply one day in court.

I was aged eight and was well versed in court procedures as I have told you. I knew that on the sixth day of each month my father would preside over what you would call trials. He would be presented with cases in which someone was due punishment and he would decide upon the sentence. I made my way to court where I would sit beside my father to witness his rulings for that month. On this day a man who had been held in prison was hauled into the court. His hands and feet were bound so he was literally dragged along by guards and thrown at the base of the stairs below us. He had already been whipped and there were cuts weeping on his back where the cords of the whips had hit him. His binding and wounds already indicated a serious crime and my mind was racing as to whether it was murder.

It was just as bad as murder for this man was a tomb robber. Egyptian tombs were the most sacred sites of all in our religion. This was the final resting place of the physical form and the beginning point for the person to cross into the afterlife. These were sacred spaces, embellished with images celebrating the life that had been, as well as prayers to carry the 'ka' or spirit of the person to the afterlife. To interfere with this was to interfere with the rules of existence and the plans of the Gods. A tomb robber was the lowest of all criminals, as the effects of their desecration could never be rectified by men.

The magistrate presiding over the hearings for that day stated the details of the man's crime including witness reports and the site of his capture. My father sat still upon his throne as he listened to the magistrate's recounting and I saw his hands loosen and then tighten upon his crook and flail that were held crossed over his chest.

"He was only seen coming out of one tomb, Pharaoh," the magistrate continued, "however we have reason to believe there were more."

"Which tomb was he seen desecrating?" my father stated.

"That of Pharaoh Amenhotep, Your Highness," was the reply.

This was the Pharaoh who had preceded my grandfather. His daughter had been my grandmother and her marriage to my grandfather was what had sealed my family's destiny as royalty. However even if there had been no bloodline the rage that was now welling up in my father would have been just as potent. The nerve to desecrate a tomb was insulting enough to the deceased but to have done so to a Pharaoh and therefore a God was beyond any punishment that could be served.

I saw my father's hands once more open slightly and tighten. He squared his shoulders and I saw them rise slightly as he took a deep breath. He then delivered his decided punishment. It was one that I had yet to hear him deliver and I fell back into my seat.

"I have heard the crimes and there can only be one punishment to equal the desecration and disrespect that has been committed. This prisoner will be executed tomorrow!" my father declared boldly and decisively.

There was an element of surprise in the room as my father had so rarely been extreme in his rulings. This astonishment was matched by firm agreement though, as this would set a precedent and send warning to any other tomb robbers. The robber was dragged back out of the court far too weary and in too much pain to react. I doubt he even comprehended what had just occurred. I, on the other hand, completely comprehended this. At the age of eight I now realised the power that being Pharaoh entailed. I had been in the army rooms and knew of battles that a pharaoh could order but the concept of those orders deciding lives never really occurred to me. I understood my father's balance in how he usually delivered judgement but also recognised that someone different could utilise this power in a totally different way. This realisation now also gave me the final piece of clarity with which to deal with my stepsisters.

When the court proceedings for the day were over I marched with a strut to the girl's chambers. My side-lock, the single bundle of hair that emerged from my otherwise shaven head, swung and bounced as I walked. As expected, I found my stepsisters being preened and fussed over by their maids. They barely raised their eyes as I walked into the room.

"Oh look, the whore's little son has come to visit," the eldest Neferure said with a laugh. "Are you actually saving us time in finding you to insult you? Are you here to make it easier for us?"

I ignored her and cleared my throat. "Are you aware that one day I shall be Pharaoh?" I said with a clear strong voice.

"Oh yes," she snorted looking to her sister and they both laughed.

"On the day I become Pharaoh I shall have you both executed!" I declared.

I barely gave them time to react and turning on my eight year old heels I left with an even stronger strut in my walk, leaving the two princesses aghast.

It had the desired effect and they stopped their attacks--well verbally anyway. I would still get sly looks or the occasional snigger but the words stopped and that made life easier. However their hatred for me, embedded by their mother on the day of my birth, had well and truly taken a blow.

CHAPTER THREE

Unfortunately the day that I became Pharaoh came far too soon. Over the next two years my father's health started to fail and the once reasonably healthy man slowly turned into a thin and weak old man far too rapidly. In your modern times he would have been diagnosed within the first few months as having cancer but of course we did not have the tools and imaging machines you do now. In modern times he may also have sought assistance a lot quicker as well. My father being the man he was though suffered for some time before even telling his personal physicians of his ill health. By that time they had already noticed the changes.

What had began as deep pain within him seemed to start eating him away. He gradually lost weight and even seemed to become shorter. His energy was easily depleted and his time spent on duties each day grew less and less. The physicians were baffled and the priests grew scared as the illness confounded any form of treatment or any amount of prayer or ritual. His eyes grew darker and his voice became weak and there finally came the day that he could not leave his bed. People began to speak in hushed tones when around him and would leave his bedside with frowns or tears. Prayers and treatments continued but then talk began of death being near.

I was old enough to understand that things were not so well but the idea that my father may die did not even enter my thoughts--not yet anyway. My father had spoken to me many times of what would occur when he died, of me becoming Pharaoh and the duties and responsibility that would lie ahead. I hated to think of this time ever becoming a reality but I knew some day it would. I also imagined this day many years ahead with my father a very old man and myself fully grown and ready for my reign.

The last three months of my father's life consisted of bedside court sessions and an endless stream of physicians and priests. I would visit as often as I could between my lessons and army training and his smile when he saw me always made me feel that I was helping him get well. Eventually though he didn't smile when I stepped up to his side, he didn't respond to anyone or anything and this was when the reality of the situation set in. The frowns of people around him grew deeper and the tears flowed more. I would cry myself to sleep at night, often in my mother's arms. She would then leave me so that she could sit by my father so as to be near him should he slip away in the night. Her eyes grew dark from her lack of sleep and her heart grew heavy as she faced losing her love.

The fateful moment came in the early morning hours of a very hot summer day. The heat had barely backed off during the night and my father was surrounded by six servants fanning him with massive fans made from ostrich feathers. My mother sat in her chair by his bedside and my father slipped away so gently and quietly that no one noticed for some time. It was only when my mother got up from her chair at the first sign of daylight to gently touch his face that she realised he was gone. Her cries and sobbing alerted everyone else. Some joined her in the crying and wailing, others rushed out to let other palace officials and priests know.

I had just woken and was making my way to my father's chambers. Several people rushed past me, bowing to acknowledge me but not making eye contact, each one resistant to being the one who might let me know. The change in activity in the corridors alone let me know that something had happened and I felt it wasn't good. I walked into my father's bedchamber to see my mother laying alongside my father with her back to me. She was holding his hand as it lay on his chest and she sobbed uncontrollably. Two priests stood to the end of the bed with solemn faces but looked up at me wide-eyed as I walked in.

Walking to the bed I was somewhat confused. My father was still here, lying just as he had been last night when I left him but I didn't understand this new heaviness that was in the room. As I walked closer though I saw his face was changed in a way I could barely comprehend. His face was now a greyish white and looked waxy, his mouth gaped and the skin seemed to hang over the bones of his cheeks. It was no longer the face of my father. It was merely the face of the body lying before me. I felt no desire to touch the body or even be close to it, despite my mother doing so. This was no longer my father.

The quiet in the room was soon broken by the footsteps of Hatshepsut behind me. She stepped to my side and I felt her take a gasp as she saw my father's body. Despite having been summoned from her chambers for this reason she was still taken aback at the sight of his dead body. She placed her hand on my shoulder and gently squeezed it. This was closest she would ever allow herself to show me any sympathy and even at my young age I knew this. It was the start of my tears and they soon blurred the sight of my father's body.

"Has everyone else been informed?" Hatshepsut said quietly to the priests.

They nodded their reply and Hatshepsut walked towards the bed and placed a hand now on my mother's shoulder.

"Isis, he needs to be prepared for burial," she said gently but directly.

My mother lifted her head from the sheets leaving a black mark where her kohl-rimmed eyes had sobbed into them. Turning her head to Hatshepsut she nodded, her body still trembling from her outpouring. Even in the depths of her grief she understood the importance of the burial rites and the time frames they needed to done within. She stood up from the bed still holding his hand, keeping in contact for as long as she could, looking into his face for what she knew would be the last time as it would now be layered in cloths and finally his funeral mask. It was only when she realised I was beside her that she finally let go of him and turned away. My mother grabbed me and held me close against her, sobbing freshly against my head while behind us the priests moved in to begin their tasks.

So at ten years of age my reign as Pharaoh was begun. My first duties were to be the worst of my entire fifty-six-year rule. It would begin with two months of funeral rites for my father and the formalities for me to become Pharaoh.

Despite my father being physically gone I could still feel him around --especially at night. Sometimes I would think I heard his voice or I would see him disappear around a corner ahead of me. I didn't dare tell my mother or any of the priests, as they would be concerned that his spirit hadn't crossed to the afterlife properly. I was also scared they would think me bewitched as no one apart from priests ever talked of communicating with the dead so directly. The rest of us asked for signs or simply performed rites, always maintaining the mystique of the veil separating us from those who had passed. So I kept my visions and sounds to myself, fitting into my expected behaviour. The final week of the funeral rites was the time I saw and felt him most. It was almost like he was overseeing the preparations. Once when I was being consulted on a decision for his burial I saw him behind the priest shaking his head and so I said no, which seemed to delight him.

The lengthy period taken for these rites was necessary not only for the number of formalities that would need to be performed but also allowed for dignitaries from afar to travel and attend. And most importantly though, this amount of time was needed for the extensive procedures a body must go through to be entombed correctly. Only specific priests would attend and enact the preservation process. They began with dissecting the body and preserving the organs to be placed into magnificent canisters. The shell was then filled and covered with natron salts to pull out any last moisture. When it was dry the hollowed body would be stuffed with cloths that had been soaked in oils; then it would be wrapped in the same. Our methods were as amazing as we intended as it has allowed for your archaeologists to find our bodies thousands of years later. In fact if the tombs had remained untouched and intact you would have found us all in much the same state that we were interred, alas for the tomb raiders and fortune hunters who would decide otherwise.

When the wrapping was completed his burial mask would be placed and my father would be laid within a series of three coffins and placed upon the altar at Karnak for two days of prayers and sacrifices to honour his spirit. During this time last details at his tomb could be finalised and the possessions that he would need in paradise would be placed within it. The huge stone sarcophagus would be put in place within the burial chamber ready for the body within its nest of coffins.

There would be one last day of prayers at Karnak which would be his funeral day. The temple would fill with every dignitary from Egypt and the neighbouring empires. My father would then be carried out of the temple to make his way to the Nile edge. A majestic funeral boat would carry him across the river to the Valley of the Kings where his tomb was dug within the folds and crevasses of the cliffs. A procession of priests, the most senior ones carrying the Canopic jars and others carrying statuary would escort his sarcophagus the entire way to its tomb. I rode in the royal carriage that followed the pallbearers carrying the sarcophagus with Hatshepsut beside me, while my mother was carried in a lesser carriage with Hatshepsut's daughters.

When we reached the tomb the high priests escorted the body inside while we waited in the sun until they emerged letting us know my father was in place. Then we were free to enter and say our final goodbyes in the damp, coldness of the stone with the flicker of lamplights. Although I heard my mother's breath catch a few times as she held back sobs; it was a simple and dignified farewell and we were soon back out in the sunlight. The priests then went back in and placed the sarcophagus' lid and directed the placement of the blocks to seal my father's tomb. As I heard the last stone slide into place I felt a sense of accomplishment. We had done all that was required of us for my father's journey to the afterlife to begin and I sighed with relief that this was now complete. After this day I no longer heard or saw my father.

The end of the formalities for my father's death now signalled what was to officially be the beginning of my ruling years. I was now Pharaoh and although I had the knowledge of the state of affairs from being involved from a young age I did not have the maturity required to enact this knowledge. Lying in my bed the first night after the funeral my mind raced as to what my new life would be like. I was filled with a mix of warm pride to carry on my father's lineage whilst I also felt the quick stabs of fear. The priests would still support and advise me as they did my father, while the viziers and diplomats would still perform their duties as before. I would simply step into place and have the final say. This realisation made my heart sink. I wasn't ready. I wasn't sure enough. My father had been a man in his twenties when this was required of him whilst my voice had barely changed. I felt no one would take me seriously and I did not wish to be a pharaoh who was not fully respected.

I knew things were whispered of my father behind his back and my stepsisters were more than ready to continue this practice about me. A simple whisper in the corridors of the palace or temple could spread to the streets and then be amplified until it reached the outer regions of the empire. Those around Egypt constantly sought after the slightest sign of weakness in the kingdom. The mere fact that a ten year old was now Pharaoh would be reason enough for armies to be summoned and as I lay there I considered this. As I slipped into sleep I prayed to the Gods to help me.

I was not the only one evaluating these thoughts as at that exact moment down the corridor in her chambers Hatshepsut was pacing. She too was concerned at the prospect for Egypt of having a ten year old Pharaoh. She too had no doubts as to my knowledge but was fearful of my naivety. Other kingdoms would be waiting to pounce and despite them knowing she was by my side would that be enough to keep them at bay?

Aside from her political concerns Hatshepsut also had her personal concerns. She had increased her duties and influence in the months leading to my father's death and the two months of mourning had seen this continue as I was absorbed in grief and confusion. There was no way that she would now just step aside for a child.

She would need to make this clear to all that she was my main advisor and that the bloodline of the Pharaohs was totally in control of all. Her father's memory and work would not be negated now by the death of my father and the consequence of my age. The empire would not be compromised while she still had a breath. In that moment with the light of a full moon streaming in her window she looked up and out to the source of the light and was given the answer. She believed a God residing in the moon provided this solution and when she approached the priests to share this with them no one dared question it.

The next day was to be our first official session of court following the funeral. Despite having held court sessions during the two months since my father's death, today with the funeral over the palace was now out of mourning and normal life was resumed. This first session was to be the true showcase of my succession and there was an air of anticipation from everyone involved. It also required an even stronger sense of formality than usual.

Hatshepsut rose with the sun. Her maids came to dress her, and she requested her finest silks and her most decorative headdress and jewellery. She was full of energy and even smiled as she was being readied. This took her maids aback as they were rarely treated to such a sight, being more accustomed to her surliness. As always they acted indifferently simply taking orders or asking quick simple questions to ensure their mistress was being prepared as she wished. After an hour she was ready and she looked as magnificent as any queen should. She was laden with cloths, gold and jewels, her eyes pierced out from the deep borders of black kohl, her hair was thick and shone with henna. She carried herself with the assurance and poise that demanded respect and awe. Hatshepsut understood the role she had to play and performed it perfectly. Squaring her shoulders and tilting her chin upwards she began her walk to the court.

I now occupied my father's chambers and the butler and servants who had attended to my father now surrounded me. It was a natural progression for them and they fell back into their routine with ease despite the grief that many of them carried in their hearts. An elaborate box held within it my new clothes for court. A loincloth of finest silk was folded around me first, then a pleated skirt of gold silk, bordered in reds, blues and greens. My arms, chest and back were rubbed with creams embedded with gold dust so I shimmered. A heavy collar of gold links with jewels sitting within them was lowered onto my shoulders; it peaked down over my chest and curved over the top of my shoulders, covering my upper back. Its weight was immediate and I grimaced.

My butler saw my discomfort, "Your Highness, this collar declares your ruling status. Wear it with the pride your father intended you to."

I immediately cleared my face of any expression as I remembered the manner in which my father had worn his formal adornments. My preening continued and soon I was ready. My head was completely shaved smooth now with my side-lock of youth gone forever, covered with my headdress and a ceremonial beard tied into place over my ears. I crossed my arms behind my back and puffed my chest up as I looked into the mirror seeing a shorter version of my father and my heart tore at the thought he would never see me like this. I then wondered how his journey in the afterworld was progressing. My quiet contemplation was quickly disturbed as a high priest arrived and announced we needed to head to court for my first official session.

I exited my chamber door surrounded by priests, guards and servants. I was used to watching my father being surrounded but having them around me in this way was something else. They all towered over me and I felt consumed by them despite their intentions of servitude and protection. However as was expected in my role I remained poised and regal--that was until I caught a glimpse of my mother waiting for us along the corridor. It was her quick gasp that first made me aware that she was there. Seeing me in my official court robes for the first time brought her a rush of emotions. Her heart still ached at losing my father and seeing me dressed like this evoked so much.

"Mama," I cried, totally shattering any illusion of my readiness. It was all I could do to not run to her and throw my arms around her.

"Isis! You should be waiting at court!" a priest hissed.

My mother stood speechless. She had no answer for the priest--well none that he would accept or comprehend. With one hand on her heart she smiled at me with so much love that I beamed. In that moment my strength suddenly swelled.

"My mother will walk with us," I declared to the priest.

The priest bowed in recognition, but it was more like he cowered. I may have been a child but I was Pharaoh first and foremost. I put my hand out to my mother and she came to my side and taking my hand we all began to walk again. This however proved too much for the priest and he made his way to my mother's side, "You cannot hold his hand," he muttered through clenched teeth, "And you must walk behind him!"

My mother knew that we had pushed enough boundaries today and she was in no position to cause waves. She gently let go of my hand and giving me a nod she slipped a pace behind me. My entourage now continued in its new formation to the court.

Hatshepsut was already in place on her throne when I entered having arrived early to consult with the high priests who would attend court today. She remained seated while all else stood as I walked down the central aisle towards the raised area where my new throne waited for me beside hers. Those around me blurred as my focus was drawn to her. Despite her calm composure I could see a hint of her sly smile and my intuition cried, *"Beware!"* My breathing became shallower the closer I got to her. As I started up the steps of the altar my beloved Arisina came to my side to lead me to my throne and I felt a calm wash over me. Aside from my mother, this priestess was my rock within the palace having been there from my birth, overseeing my formal rites and to have her here now was a true comfort.

Hatshepsut now took it upon herself to begin the proceedings with the authority that she knew no one else at this time possessed. She coolly and calmly now delivered the solution that had been delivered to her the night before. This was a small assembly of the highest priests and most senior viziers of the palace. They stood in the main aisle of the court and were curious to see how this first session of the new reign would be held.

"As you all know my husband the Pharaoh left us all far too soon," she stated, her voice carrying evenly to all present. "Thankfully he left us with an heir, the blessed Thutmose, our son," she turned to me and gently smiled with a slight nod. "We are all aware of Thutmose's talents and passion for Egypt and his family. He is truly a magnificent Pharaoh and military leader in the making. This, my subjects, is the point that we need to consider."

I drew in my breath. All she said was true but to have my one weakness, that of my youth, spoken out before the entire gathering made my stomach tighten. I looked to my mother and could see her face had turned hard as she too waited to see what plot Hatshepsut would now deliver without my father to stop her.

With this Hatshepsut continued, "To appoint a ten year old to a full reign has never been done. The surrounding regions will pounce. We know of his talents and his knowledge, some of our neighbours do as well, thanks to his father's promotion, but it will not detract from the fact that a child sits upon the supreme throne and has the final say!" she ended with a flourish. "Last night I prayed to the Gods for a solution to this situation. I prayed on behalf of Egypt and I prayed for the bloodline of my ancestors that belongs upon the throne as the ruling family and I was answered. I consulted with Senemut and he deemed this to be truly a message sent to me from Amun."

Senemut was not only one of the highest of the Amun priests but also one of the priests who worked closest to Hatshepsut. He squared his shoulders as Hatshepsut acknowledged him and smiled at her, relishing this moment.

The priests surrounding Senemut all knew what was to be delivered, but my personal priests including Arisina did not. There were a few murmurs and heads turned but Hatshepsut put up her hand and instantly silence and stillness returned. My breathing began to quicken. I prayed to my father, to Amun, to any name I could conjure. I just wanted this over. Even if it meant she was going to order my death. I kept my eyes down, as I didn't want to see my mother's face when she announced her scheme.

"So it is that I have been told by the Gods that I shall be co-regent with young Thutmose! I have the experience and the bloodline necessary. This shall declare Egypt as a solid force. All can continue on smoothly and when Thutmose reaches maturity he shall become Pharaoh in his own right," she announced with all the coolness and authority she could muster and with that she was done.

It was a perfect plan and no one could dispute it. Not any priest or official, not even my mother. Sure it was obvious that Hatshepsut had finally secured her position of power, but it was delivered to her perfectly--almost as though it had in fact been delivered by the Gods. It would indeed strengthen Egypt's rule. There were many other benefits but I was unable to think of them at this time. My head was spinning with thoughts that there was more to come, that she hadn't yet delivered the true sting. Of course she hadn't because she had none; not yet anyway. For now though I needed to remain calm. This situation benefited me as well for now I had a reliable, if somewhat self-serving partner who would also serve as my teacher. My heart ached though for my father to still be here and for me not to have to deal with this at all. If only it had been even five more years later, then I would have been ready to rule in my own right, and this situation wouldn't even exist. This was my reality though, and I would have to accept it.

Looking up at those before us I saw Arisina who was standing off to the side. Her eyes locked on mine and within that contact I felt her support and understanding. She could sense my confusion. I was relieved yet suspicious, and on top of all this, I was disappointed in myself. Disappointed that I was not older, such a simple thing and yet it would have solved everything. I turned my head back and looked to the floor.

Hatshepsut asked if what she spoke was understood. One by one the priests and viziers all nodded and said, "Yes." I could hear their responses and knew that as each one replied my fate was being sealed as the proposal was accepted and acknowledged.

Hatshepsut turned to me, "Thutmose, do you understand?"

I was the only one to have not yet responded as I was so deep in my misery and confusion that I didn't even hear her address me specifically.

"Thutmose?" Hatshepsut repeated.

I looked to Arisina who gently nodded as though to say, *"Answer her Thutmose."*

I could hardly bear to face Hatshepsut but I turned my head to do so. I couldn't speak in that moment. I simply met her gaze and nodded once. I will never forget the look in her eyes. I expected them to be blazing with her new power but as they met mine they seemed to dim a bit. Instantly she recognised that I had tasted the pain of being held from what one knew was their destiny and right, and that scared her. She remembered what that had ignited inside of her and what that had made her become. In that moment she knew this would not be as easy as she had at first imagined.

The meeting continued on with the usual political discussions. Hatshepsut was correct--all fell into line smoothly as though this was the natural order of things. I fought all the aches of my soul and raised my head to meet the eyes of each priest or official who addressed us. I noted that they all addressed me first. Well by that, I mean that they made eye contact with me before turning to Hatshepsut. Although it was mostly Hatshepsut who replied they still acknowledged me as they finished their address and fell back into the crowd. This gave me some confidence and when questions arose regarding military affairs I readily gave my opinion and asked questions. Hatshepsut and I soon fell into a rhythm that was both comfortable and effective. This continued for three hours; it was a long court session but necessary after months of mourning and funeral rites. Everyone grew weary and Senemut declared we should all rest before continuing into the afternoon.

As we rose to leave the court Hatshepsut turned to me smiling. My back was up waiting for her next move and it was delivered with the precision that I was accustomed to. "Thutmose, won't you join me for lunch?" she said sweetly.

Ah yes, a delightful invitation to dine. To those around it was a solid gesture of hospitality and kindness, but to me it was being invited into the spider's web. However I could not refuse, for to do so would invite some form of open hostility, and it would express some weakness in the new "alliance" to those around us. Instead I accepted and then silently prayed to the Gods to protect me.

My entourage would follow but my mother knew this procession should not include her and she smiled to me before she left with the rest of the officials. Hatshepsut walked by my side to her chambers, not behind me, as all but my lead guards must. She was now my equal and would make sure she took every opportunity to display and experience this. We began our walk without speaking. I could think of no conversation as I had never indulged in small talk with this woman and had no desire to begin so now. Her occasional comments on such things as a wall hanging or the weather I met with a simple "yes," or just nodded in agreement. She soon gave up and we arrived at her private dining room in absolute silence.

I walked to my assumed position at head of the table, which didn't seem to please Hatshepsut at all. In public she would be happy to play the equal but within her chambers, on her private territory I would always be second. To have

38

me sit at the head of the table while she sat to the side was simply not to be accepted. Of course she could always have sat to the other end of the table and been opposite and equal to me there, but she needed to be close to talk to me.

She gestured to her maid and asked for a setting to be placed next to me. So at an entire table, which could have seated twenty, there sat the two of us side by side at one end. Thankfully the width of the table allowed this but the comfort did not detract from the pettiness of the situation. Hatshepsut dismissed our servants and guards, mine only leaving when I nodded my head in confirmation and soon it was just the two of us side by side heading an empty table with servants walking to and fro, serving and clearing as we ate.

I was grateful for the food not only to relieve the ache of hunger that was gnawing in my belly but also that it gave me something to focus on and lessen the discomfort of the situation. Finally Hatshepsut broke the silence by lifting her glass of wine. Sipping gently she turned in her chair to face me.

"How do you feel that this morning went?" she tilted her head and spoke as though genuinely wanting to know what I thought.

"I felt it went very smoothly. I appreciated your insights and opinions," I said directly and calmly.

"The officials accepted the new arrangement and worked well with it, don't you think?" she seemed to be probing me for a response I hadn't yet delivered.

I couldn't answer straight away and part of me knew this was to tease her, to not satisfy her that I did indeed realise that this was a fortuitous arrangement for us both. I acknowledged her with a simple nod as I took another mouthful of food.

"Thutmose, I know exactly what you are feeling!" she leaned in close whispering to me so that the few servants and guards nearby could not hear her clearly. "I know the pain of losing a father I loved dearly and to have that sorrow buried under duties. I also know what it is like to have your rightful place not recognised merely due to circumstance!"

"My rightful place is recognised!" I hissed back, "I am Pharaoh. It was told by the Gods at my birth."

"As it was at mine!" she beamed back, enjoying me finally biting. For indeed Hatshepsut too had been granted a grand birth story declaring her worthiness until that of my father's relegated her to second place. "Do you not think the Gods created this situation for us both?"

I dropped my head back down. I was horrified at how I had let that anger slip out. My pulse had quickened and I could feel a headache building. Taking a deep breath I calmed myself and turned to her once again.

"Thutmose," she said my name gently, "We have an amazing opportunity here. We need each other. Just think about that. You could declare tomorrow that this is not to be but where would that leave you? I can tell you exactly where; at the whims of the high priests and viziers who will exploit your youth for their own gains and interests! I know their foibles and games and they know they are no match for me. Keep me in place and the court stays stable. Dismiss me and there will be bedlam. Egypt will be attacked and raped within a month. Do you think this is what your father would have wished for the beginning of your reign?"

She paused just long enough for me to nod in acknowledgement and continued on, "I do not wish to see you pushed aside either. Everyone knows you have a natural aptitude for the military and at your age you understand more than I do. Is the military not your passion?"

"Yes it is. Our army could be even grander than it is now," my eyes lit up as I spoke of this.

"Then make it grander Thutmose!" exclaimed Hatshepsut. "Let me hold court while you immerse yourself in the army and its workings. Imagine an Egypt with two strong leaders! One who attends to the rulings and procedures while the other builds the mightiest military machine that any empire will know. Egypt will be indestructible, it will grow, and we will both be remembered forever as the ones who took it to its grandest and richest," her voice had grown louder. Hatshepsut finished this last sentence by flourishing her glass in the air.

I found myself nodding. We did indeed have an amazing alliance available to us both. Even though she had admitted her one weakness she had quite strongly made point of mine. However by combining our strengths we could indeed create a partnership that few would dare to test. I raised my glass and held it to hers and with a simple click we made the co-regency a reality.

We finished eating and I returned to my chambers to rest before the afternoon session of court. My servants removed the heavy collar and even though I felt immediate relief, I was amazed at how quickly I had adapted to it. I swiftly bathed and lay upon my bed to relax but sleep did not come. My mind raced with what lay ahead and I began to fantasise about my new role leading the army. I saw myself riding ahead of my men, strong and confident, annihilating all who came before us. I felt my energy surge as I stepped into these images sensing the power and control.

I arose from my nap no longer a boy thrown into such a heavy position but a young man with vision and direction. I summoned my servants to help me re-dress and made my way to court ahead of all others. As each person entered the court including Hatshepsut, I sat straight and tall upon my throne, looking at each and every person straight in the eye.

CHAPTER FOUR

Our formal coronation was held the following week at the Great Temple at Karnak. It would have been my ceremony alone but now Hatshepsut joined me as we were both officially recognised as my father's successors. The priests and priestesses performed what seemed like an endless array of rituals and prayers to bless and protect us. Two oxen were sacrificed; one for each of us and yes, poor Arisina had to help with the one allocated to me. As usual she displayed her stoic poise and no one noticed that her face grew pale as the blood flowed. Nor did they notice her slip away soon after to a small chamber behind the altar where she quietly sat and breathed deep until her vision cleared and the nausea subsided. Such was the crowd gathered to witness at Karnak, scattered amongst the columns and various temples, you could disappear and reappear and it was assumed you had merely been to another part of the celebration.

Of course Hatshepsut and I had to remain in our positions before the main altar as different priests came forward to perform yet another rite or regale us with another story relayed from the Gods confirming our appointments to our thrones. Scribes sat to the side scrawling the details to be recorded and reproduced. Visiting neighbours or local merchants would drop gifts at our feet begging for favour and harmony. They all became a blur as the heat of the day wore on us both and after four hours our empty stomachs made us light headed.

Finally it was over, the formalities were complete and we were now leaders. We were Pharaoh and Queen, rulers together but in our own right. However there was another layer to this. We were now also Gods. We were the physical manifestation of the God spirits sent to protect and lead Egypt. In truth it was a marvellous way to incite fear into the commoners, who were the only ones to take this seriously. Our palace officials and priests simply saw us as tickets to their own gain and increased stature. Leaders of other countries knew this game of superiority too well as they themselves played it in their own way.

To the pharaoh or queen it fed the ego wonderfully, but it also fuelled your fears. At your core some truth resonated that you were no different from the people around you, yet you could never voice that to anyone. Any crack in the façade would spoil the illusion and game that everyone played. So each ruler accepted their part and eventually the role became such second nature that many did believe they were Gods and acted accordingly. That is the power that built the pyramids. That is the power that after thousands of years enabled us to be remembered over the dozens of other cultures that rose and fell afterwards. Our buildings and records were never just meant to hold history; they were memorials to our power and egos. Thankfully they now create a wonderful tourist trade for modern Egypt so we weren't entirely selfish.

With the formalities of the day over we could now head into the social part of the day. This entailed a grand feast with lots of wine, gossip and the possibility of waking up in someone else's bedchamber. Of course at age ten this final option was not one that would be available to me, but Hatshepsut would certainly not end the evening alone. My night would end walking hand in hand with my mother, no longer a queen but now known simply as the "King's Mother". She would help bathe me and prepare me for bed, smoothing the covers over me as she kissed me on the forehead and then sitting by my bedside as I slipped into sleep. Only then did she let her tears fall. They were tears of joy for seeing her beloved son, her only child, now a Pharaoh. They were also the tears of a young widow wishing her husband and soulmate was still here to share in this love with her.

      The next day I rose slightly later than usual as did the entire palace. Court would not be held today due to the anticipated cloudy heads and queasy stomachs. Two parts of the palace would be operating as per usual though, the kitchens getting ready for the eventual onslaught of hungry late risers and the offices of the military. After getting ready as minimally as possible, I dismissed my servants and asked my guards to escort me to see the generals. As I walked along the corridors I couldn't help but smile as I headed off to perform my first duty purely of my own accord and preference. My entry was done with the ritual that would precede my arrival anywhere. A seemingly invisible servant would run ahead notifying any guards along the route so that they were presentable as I approached. The guards outside the army office doors would have already notified the commanders well before my arrival so their announcement as they opened the doors for me was no surprise to any within.

      In fact they were all standing in rank, with my highest commander near the door ready to greet me. There were no nerves or intimidation as I entered my favourite part of the palace. These rooms and these men were more familiar to me than my chambers or playmates. The respect I had for these men was more than reciprocated as we had grown to know each other since my early years when I accompanied my father here. My natural aptitude for the workings and energy of the military had now come to fruition as I walked in as their supreme commander. Ironically, my youth was not considered a weakness here; as far as anyone here was concerned I had ten years experience. I was met with smiles and despite the formalities of my arrival it was more like a friend being welcomed into another's home.

      Djehuty-Ken the most senior of commanders approached me and held his hand out in friendship, which I took. He bowed his head in respect and thanked me for visiting. This made me laugh. He had never been so formal with my father and I was bemused at his sudden change in behaviour.

      "Ken--you never did this with my father! Why now with me?" I gushed and half laughed as I said this.

This made him laugh too, "Your Highness, this is just what *your* father said when I greeted him the same way on his first visit to us as Pharaoh."

"I am not so different now I am Pharaoh. I just dress a bit different," I said joking.

At this all the commanders laughed. Ken turned to me smiling and replied, "He also said that to us!" He continued, "There is a difference, my King, for you now walk in as our leader."

I nodded at this, "Are you aware of the agreement of the co-regency?" I asked.

"We are aware that Hatshepsut will share leadership with you," he said gently and bowed his head. The commanders behind him seemed to all go still as this was discussed and was confirmed to them.

"There is a bit more to this that I need to make you aware of," I began. "Hatshepsut and I have agreed that she will deal with the majority of matters of the court," I said and slightly hesitated before adding, "and I shall deal with all matters military."

There was some movement amongst the men as they exchanged glances. Ken's eyes narrowed and furrowing his brow he asked, "So only you are our leader?"

"Yes," I answered, worried I had not spoken clearly.

"We shall answer to only you?" he restated.

"Yes--Ken--I will be working with you…" I stammered. I was now worried that this was displeasing them as there was more movement and murmurs behind him.

"We won't have to approach the Queen or get her approval, only yours?" My general seemed to need full confirmation on this.

"Yes--Ken…" I stammered again. If they did not accept this then all was fruitless and the stability of the co-regency and any power I had would be completely undermined.

Ken stood straight and a wide smile spread over his face. "Wonderful!" he declared with a clap of his hands. Behind him I saw all the men smiling and they too clapped their hands in celebration of my announcement.

The knot in my stomach was gone. The agreement was truly sealed and I could now fully step into my role with ease and grace. Ken smiled once again and nodded towards the map table where we would now go and continue our military plans.

My first year with the military as their commander would be spent on developing my skills. I had the advantage of ten years of listening to strategies and planning so now more time could be allotted to increasing my physical abilities. This would include everything from swords and arrows through to horse riding. I had been introduced to all these things from a young age, having shot my first arrow at age six with my father by my side. Now though was the time to make these skills as powerful as they could be, ready to lead my men into battle as strong as anyone who rode behind me. I had been on horses with my father as a toddler and so the day I rode upon my very own horse when I turned five was one of the most amazing days of my life and this would become one of my absolute passions.

I had my own saddle made from the leather gifted to me at my birth. It had been cured and toughened to perfection and the finest craftsmen worked it beautifully. It was decorated with the symbols of my name which I loved as these reflected those of my father and grandfather. Also upon it were the symbols of Ra and Amun. Whenever I rode I imagined all four of them on their own horses at my side, guiding and protecting me.

Horse riding had also given me my first taste of independence and freedom. Before my father had died and when I had truly gained confidence I would make my way to the stables by myself, order my favourite horse saddled up and, upon finding an opportune moment to escape my minders, would just ride away from the palace. I would dress as plainly as possible so I could make my way outside the walls with little notice. Once through the gates I would ride as fast as I could, leaving a huge cloud of dust behind me. I would go as far as my horse allowed and find a secluded place where I could sit and think. I cherished these moments to myself where I could be in silence and speak with the Gods. I wouldn't need long, barely an hour and I would feel refreshed and able to face everyone at the palace again.

This had all changed now. I was always accompanied by soldiers or guards when riding and although I could still pick up pace and not have to hear any sounds other than my horse's hooves pounding the sand and dirt I still craved those moments when I could be truly alone. I knew they were now lost. My alliance with Hatshepsut was all going smoothly but my duties and responsibilities were still overwhelming for me. To be able to escape for just an hour from everyone and everything would have been bliss. Even within the quiet of my private chambers I knew there was always a servant around a corner or behind a curtain waiting for a demand.

So I just had to find new ways of creating this space. As I grew older I soon learned to make this time for myself within the palace and touch this quiet wherever I was. I could do it while bathing or as I slipped towards sleep. With practice I could even do it within a room full of people talking. It was a simple way to restore my energy that did not endanger me or anyone that depended upon me.

The first two years of the co-regency were an interesting time of change for my family as we all settled into our roles and the new dynamics of the palace. Hatshepsut and I took our positions very seriously. We often met to update each other on what we were doing and any plans that were developing, however we always held back just a little information for ourselves. It was a little power play that fed our egos and nothing more. There became an understanding that there were "her" people and "his" people within the royal staff and a silent divide grew between them. It was never outwardly displayed or spoken but it was there. My army commanders would confide in each other and seek rites and advice from the priests and priestesses loyal to me, but never do the same with those close to Hatshepsut.

Even though it seemed to work for everyone it was feeding insecurities within Hatshepsut that grew each day. The indifference of her daughters to use their possible power was a constant disappointment, and even though I was a valuable and competent substitute, I was still not of her flesh. She longed for her true bloodline to carry on through the throne. One year into our co-regency this was dealt a huge blow when her youngest daughter died. Barely fifteen years old, she took ill and died within weeks. Death at a young age was not rare in our times, but the death of any child at any age is an anomaly in our human existence no parent can comprehend. For Hatshepsut though her grief was overtaken with the strike at losing a stake in the royal lineage.

Her remaining daughter, Neferure, then immediately had all focus put upon her. The quickest and simplest way to secure this child's position was to have her marry me. So at the age of eleven Hatshepsut had me marry her seventeen year old daughter. The marriage was never consummated and was merely a traditional political ploy to strengthen all of our positions and the family bloodline which was the only reason I agreed to take part. The bloodline would never continue via this new queen though. Our age long disdain for each other was the most powerful contraceptive. We could barely be in a room with each other let alone the same bed, but we played our parts well as had my father with Hatshepsut. I thanked the Gods each day that a pharaoh could take more than one wife or else my bloodline would never have been continued.

The fact I was a virgin and barely understood the mechanics of sex also spared my new wife of any expectations. I had begun to feel some stirrings during these years and was confused, as I had never been told of what changes were happening in my body. I knew I would grow bigger and stronger as I aged but the sensations and more intimate physical changes were a bewildering surprise. In our society's time you found out such things as was necessary. Women, for the most part found out as part of their wedding preparations and then on their wedding night, while men generally found out through drunken talks or the sheer luck of being with a woman who already had. My first scare was waking with an erection just before I turned twelve and thinking that my penis had been inhabited with illness. My panic soon helped it subside, but the fright was enough to carry with me all day. The next time it occurred was during being bathed. My servants acted as though they didn't see, but I knew that they did and this worried me as well.

My priestess Arisina was the only person I trusted to confide in. I decided not to say anything to my mother. I didn't want to alarm her with the possibility of a son with illness after the suffering of my father. So I made my way to Karnak under the premise of seeking a prayer session and while I was there requested a private audience with Arisina. She took me into a small room and reclined on a lounge in front of me. When she noticed that I remained seated upright and clenching my hands into fists upon my knees she too sat up matching my posture and enquired, "Your Highness, you seem incredibly troubled. What could this be?"

So I told her of the two incidences and several others that had occurred. As I spoke a smile spread across her face and she seemed to bite her lip. Looking away for a moment, she put her hand to mouth but behind it I could see her smile even more. If I knew better I would have almost said she was trying not to laugh. Finally she turned back to me composed, despite a slight flush across her cheeks. "My beloved Pharaoh, this is to be of no concern," she said through her smile, "in fact this is something to be celebrated as it signals your passage into manhood."

"Oh, then I am not ill?" I said shocked, "but why does it…"

"It is all quite natural and normal," she interrupted holding up a hand. "However it is a male priest's duty to explain all the details. I shall fetch someone appropriate for you. Wait here please."

With that she rose from her lounge, bowed her head and with her hand to her mouth once again, walked quite briskly out of the room. Within minutes she returned with an older male priest who looked quite embarrassed and directed him to sit opposite me. Arisina had collected him from nearby rooms where he was writing. He was unprepared and somewhat flustered, not because of what needed to be said, but that somehow due to his choice of rooms to write in that day he was now responsible for the sex education of the Pharaoh. Arisina excused herself saying she would be just outside. The door closed and the priest then began his discourse. It proved to be the most surreal half hour of my life. When Arisina re-entered the room, both the male priest and I were blushing, sweating and eager to get away from each other as fast as possible.

"Your Highness, do you have any questions?" she said smiling.

I shook my head slowly despite wanting to scream, *What were the Gods thinking when they decided children would be made this way!* I rose from my seat, making the priest jump up also. I mumbled thank you to them both and walked out of the room as though in a trance. As I rode back to the palace I could not come to terms with the fact that my parents had done this, that everyone does this and someday I would have to in order to have an heir. Thankfully Arisina took some initiative in clearing this deluge within my head.

That evening after my meal I returned to my salon in my chambers to practice my writing, yet another skill I was refining. There was some noise at my door and I heard the guards talking, followed by a knock at my door. I shouted out my acknowledgement from my desk and Arisina entered with the same priest who had spoken to me that day. He was still blushing madly and avoiding eye contact with anyone--especially with me. Then behind them was a woman who I recognised from around the palace. She was not a priestess; in fact I had no idea what her role was, having always assumed she was a maid of some sort. I also assumed that she was brought here to be introduced as a new member of my personal group of servants and maids, which I guess in some way she was to be.

Arisina instructed all the servants in the room to leave and ordered the guards to close the doors. This was a somewhat unusual way to introduce a new servant and I put down my quill and stood up from my desk.

"Your Highness, today has marked an important step in your progress into manhood," she started.

"Indeed!" I thought to myself. *"And I have never wished to return to my childhood more."*

I was speechless though as I stood before her wondering what the hell else they had to tell me now. Arisina stepped to one side and gestured to the woman to step forward. She was immaculately dressed and groomed and I could even smell the rich heavy scent of expensive perfume. She was incredibly beautiful and proportioned; a perfect example of an Egyptian woman in her twenties. My confusion continued to grow.

"I present to you El-Runa," Arisina smiled. "She is one of the palace's most esteemed consorts that we have hand chosen for you. El-Runa will aid your transition into manhood tonight."

My mind was now racing as I wondered what she had been hand chosen for and where was she going to take me. The priest kept his eyes away, while El-Runa smiled at me in a way I had never experienced before and which somehow gave me a stirring in my groin. This only added to my discomfort.

"She will be left here with you for some time so you can understand what you learnt of today," Arisina said. She now had the faint sign of a blush even though she spoke firmly.

I, on the other hand, was now completely blushing as I realised just what this woman was here for.

"Do you wish to speak with Minmose again before we leave you?" Arisina asked gesturing to the priest.

"No!" I reacted immediately and probably a little too loud. My head was racing with what I was expected to do to this woman and the last thing I felt like was another embarrassing talk with the man. Quite frankly, anything I might not know, I did not want to know.

"As you wish," Arisina said, "then we shall leave you. When it is over your servants shall return to bathe you and prepare you for sleep." She talked as though organising a temple ritual before finishing with, "You are in good hands Your Highness," and with this she bowed, then turned and left the room followed by the priest.

I was left standing in the room, all of twelve years old, facing a beautiful twenty-eight year old woman sent here for the sole purpose of relieving me of my virginity. I was never more scared of anyone or anything in any life as I was at that moment. I said nothing and she said nothing. We both stood still staring at each other for a very long and awkward moment. Finally realising that she would need to take the lead in order to achieve what she had been sent to do, she stepped forward and took my hand.

"It will be alright," she said so softly that she almost whispered and then she led me into the bedchamber.

She told the truth. It was alright. In fact it was quite amazing. It was also very quick. I believe it took longer for her to undress herself than the actual act did. The swirl in my head was replaced for a few minutes by a flood of sensations that she choreographed in a gentle and tender way. I am sure she was just as happy as I that it was over quickly and I lay in a bit of a stupor as she stood beside the bed and re-dressed. Once she was finished, she bent over and kissed me on the forehead. Running her hand down my cheek she smiled at me, then after covering me with the bed sheet, she left the room.

I now had the rare occurrence of being truly alone and my mind retraced what had just occurred. How could something that had sounded so horrible and wrong make you feel so good? How would you do this with someone you didn't like? Had I just made a child with the consort and what would I do if I had?

Of course I had not impregnated the consort. They knew how to take care of such things and would regularly take the required herbs to prevent such complications to palace life. They were mostly assigned to one man anyway, so if such a slip did occur the child would often be cared for as though a child of marriage, especially if the consort had provided a much needed male heir. There was also the scenario of that of my parents where a consort would actually be loved by her patron and be taken into a love marriage should the opportunity arise.

All these thoughts dissolved as I lay upon my bed with my groin tender and tiny shocks still being felt in the nerves down into my legs. I finally managed to smile and when my servants arrived to bathe me that was how they found me. This was lucky, as it was the task of my butler to report back to Arisina what state I was in. My stupor and foolish grin confirmed El-Runa's report that the mission had indeed been accomplished. I could now be officially regarded as a man and without realising it, I was now another step closer to taking full charge of the throne.

The news of my achievement spread through the priesthood and to those loyal to Hatshepsut, so that soon she also was aware of this. The reports did not please her at all for in my stepping closer to sole reign, she was closer to having to step aside yet again. Hatshepsut knew this situation was inevitable but a part of her had always hoped it might never occur. Her emotions swung from anger to fear, while her mind spun with the all the scenarios that she dreaded to face. The alliance that she had planned to serve her ambition would soon be over. The very qualities in the child that she had sought to strengthen her own position could now undo it and she needed to address this as soon as possible.

Each night she would sit by the same window as she did on the night of my father's funeral and pray to the Gods for the clarity they had bestowed to her then--but none was delivered. Slowly, what did come to her, was the realisation that I was indeed the one who should be leader and this only infuriated her more. She wanted to experience the full power, the enduring legends and myths her followers would create; she wanted the monuments and temples that would immortalise her here on earth and allow her to walk into the afterlife as grand as any male she had stepped aside for. The clarity for a God-given solution may not have been delivered with the moonlight, but within those hours Hatshepsut did indeed concoct the events that were as inspired as any story created about her.

We all continued on as normal with our duties and on the surface all protocols and procedures were executed and performed with no changes. Beneath the surface though, the bugs and mites were scurrying and rearranging their burrows. Those devoted to my father rejoiced at knowing I was now a fully functioning man ready to claim my rightful place and alone--no longer having my power diluted by another. Hatshepsut's camp in the meanwhile, had an undercurrent of anxiety surging through them all.

Hatshepsut herself started to lose weight and had dark circles under her eyes from sleepless nights. Her physical changes were soon matched by her demeanour. Her temper quickened and this initially saw her servants bearing the brunt of her general displeasure, having to deal with outlandish orders as well as verbal and physical abuse when her demands or expectations weren't met. Eventually this behaviour spilled into her court appearances as viziers and priests were questioned and criticised with such harshness they were left aghast. No matter the loyalty of those aligned to her, Hatshepsut's behaviour now began to eat at her supporters and gave those campaigning for me even more resolve.

Finally her frustrations sought out her remaining daughter and myself. My meetings with Hatshepsut now were no longer the relatively friendly and co-operative affairs that they were during our first two years ruling together. They were now tense and unpleasant, filled with jagged quips and barbs within her words, emphasised with searing eyes and scowls as I spoke to her. I imagined it was the continuous flow of duties, meetings and rituals that was wearing her spirit, never imagining that having begun my sexual life was at the core of all this.

Ironically, I had never been with another woman in the months that followed my night with the consort, mainly due to the fact I was too scared and embarrassed to ask for her return. In the meantime, I had instinctively sought my own private solution to reliving that escapade and it was serving me well. The whole sex thing was just another physical act to me. I treated it as another skill learned, much like any other I had acquired through my military duties. In no way did I imagine that it was as powerful.

Hatshepsut though was slowly becoming consumed with the fear that was growing within her. Her moods and violence had to be tolerated by all, including myself, but it raised concern in the priestess closest to her. Ma-Keet had been a confidante and mentor to Hatshepsut for many years. Whilst her loyalty served the priestess's own means, there was also a great sense of friendship and concern as she watched Hatshepsut slowly start her descent into anger and destruction. Ma-Keet could see how Hatshepsut was ruining the amazing work we had created together and how it ate away at the support and allegiance of the ones she needed to maintain her position.

Ma-Keet knew the fury that had been simmering within Hatshepsut since hearing the news of my developing manhood was now finding its way out. She watched over the months as the tension escalated; too scared to address her directly and hesitant to speak about it with other priests in case this was relayed back to Hatshepsut and she would be accused of being disloyal. However, one day this no longer was something to be just observed anymore.

After a somewhat arduously long day of court proceedings and planning, Hatshepsut returned to her chambers. Her servants lined up within the salon, their heads down, waiting for the inevitable barrage of demands and criticisms. Ma-Keet had accompanied her back to the chambers and stood in the background waiting to be dismissed. Hatshepsut had just finished giving orders to the servants when her sole-surviving daughter Neferure swept into the room followed by her two maids. The maids carried bundles of cloths tied with ribbon as well as other wrapped packages.

"Take these things into my bedchamber," she smiled and gestured to the parcels.

Hatshepsut stood silent watching this seemingly innocent entrance and waited for the servants to disperse before approaching her daughter.

"Daughter, where have you been?" Hatshepsut said with a calm air.

"I have been to the weavers for new cloths," she smiled, "and I visited the markets for other pieces to be added when they are sewn."

The last word had barely left Neferure's mouth when her mother's stiff hand hit the side of her face. The force combined with the surprise knocked Neferure backwards. Neferure held her face and tears started to stream from her eyes as her skin began to burn. She looked to Ma-Keet, but the priestess was just as stunned.

"Are you aware there was a court session today?" Hatshepsut now raised her voice and again stepped in close to her daughter.

"Yes," said Neferure, "but …"

Her words were cut short by yet another blow from her mother. Neferure stumbled back again, her tears now pouring down her face and she swayed as the pain was making her dizzy. Hatshepsut lunged forward again, her eyes now wild.

"You are a royal wife and daughter! You should have been there to support your husband and mother. You should be learning the ways of the court. Do you not realise that you would be the ruling queen if both he and I die?" Hatshepsut spat at her, "Instead you go gathering cloths and decorations. How will these serve you if you end up ruling?"

"If I end up ruling? And what are the chances of that?" Neferure yelled back, "I am barely a wife. You marry me to a boy I hate who will surely take other wives to create an heir while I will rot alone. Or should I sneak men into my chambers to console me as you do?"

Neferure's sudden burst of defiance was short lived and her mother saw to it that another would not occur. Her mother's hand struck her again, but now as a closed fist. It was followed by the other hand also clenched, and both hands now struck Neferure over and over. Neferure couldn't have hit back if she wanted as the first few blows blurred her vision with pain and shock. Her legs began to weaken and even as she fell the blows continued. It seemed to take forever yet to Ma-Keet standing nearby it all happened in a blur. She was horrified to see a mother hitting her child in this way and as Neferure began to fall she ran forward and pulled Hatshepsut away. Ma-Keet called out to some servants who ran into the room to find her pinning Hatshepsut within her arms and Neferure on the ground, with blood trickling from her nose, a split in her lip and her right eye starting to swell. Hatshepsut was breathing rapidly, her face was red and she stared down in disbelief at what she had done.

"Take Neferure and attend to her," the priestess commanded. "Call a physician!"

The servants gathered Neferure into their arms and carried her through to her bedchamber while Ma-Keet walked Hatshepsut to a lounge. They were both in shock and shaking but Hatshepsut was barely aware of where she was. Ma-Keet sat quietly with her arms around her until Hatshepsut's breath slowed and the muscles in her face softened. Then without warning Hatshepsut's head slowly sought out the priestess's shoulder and lowering her face she cried as Ma-Keet slowly rocked her.

Hatshepsut then confided to her friend and guide. She spoke of the rush of emotions within her, her confusion as to how to deal with them. Her sudden burst of anger and the violence it unleashed had scared Hatshepsut to her very core. It felt like something was growing within her and she didn't know what to do. Just as she was opening up more the physician burst into the room. Ma-Keet jumped up from her chair and rushed to him hoping to hide the state Hatshepsut was in and distracted him further by pushing him towards the door that led to the chamber Neferure was in waiting to be seen to.

"Our beloved Princess has had a bad fall," she said as calmly as she could, "Please make sure there is nothing broken and attend to her injuries," she ordered as she pushed him though the door.

Turning back to Hatshepsut she saw a very scared woman sitting before her. Ma-Keet hoped the quick interruption would not stop Hatshepsut's outpouring. Hatshepsut looked up at the priestess with red eyes that seemed to beg. She then began her final confession to her closest ally. Hatshepsut told of her fear of losing her power to me after finally being recognised by the palace in her own right. Now it seemed she was tampering with the plans of the Gods and that they were affecting her very spirit to pull her into line.

"But I know in my heart this position is my right! How can I fail my father by succumbing to a boy with such a weak bloodline!" she said passionately.

"His talents and skills are more valuable than any bloodline," thought Ma-Keet, but she could never say this. Instead she said strongly, "We all know your talents and blessings of the Gods make you just as worthy."

Hatshepsut straightened and smiled on hearing this and she nodded in agreement.

"Egypt is in a unique position. We have two strong and blessed leaders but our traditions have us play this out in a set way," Ma-Keet spoke as though every word was measured, "Your Highness you were clever enough to create the situation that we presently are blessed with. Surely you can create another?"

"Ma-Keet I have tried. Each night I pray to the Gods to support and show me the solution but nothing comes. It eats into my every moment! I allow myself some respite but then I see that boy or someone mentions him and the fire heats up within me again and wants to get out. Today it finally was released and see what it made me capable of."

With this the tears began again and Ma-Keet took her seat once more beside Hatshepsut to console her. As Hatshepsut cried Ma-Keet's mind frantically sought some insight to pacify or encourage her queen. Ma-Keet knew how power drove people; she had seen it within the priesthood over and over as men and women clawed their way to high positions. She had seen the ones who had risen through dedication and hard work, those that had been lucky reciprocates of circumstance and those who had made their way through less honourable means. There were many ways to climb and they all lead upwards; some just worked faster than others. Ma-Keet also knew the difference was about who you chose to help you.

"Your Highness," she whispered, "It is time for you to take rest. I will reschedule any court dealings so that you may have a day of refuge here in your chambers."

Hatshepsut nodded and squeezed Ma-Keet's hand in a gesture of gratitude for her support. The priestess then made her way to Neferure's chamber. As she entered the physician was just finishing. Any blood had been cleaned, however the swelling about her eyes was now worse and it was joined by more swelling to the side of her mouth. Neferure was awake but dazed and when she saw the priestess a tear fell through the puffiness of her eyes.

"She is a lucky girl," the physician sighed. "It looks worse than it is. There are no breaks and the contusions can be treated with poultices. I would suggest several days of bed rest, possibly longer until all is healed. I also suggest no social calls."

The priestess nodded. It was obvious these injuries were not from a simple fall but all those around Hatshepsut had learned discretion and double speak. The queen would indeed need bed rest, mostly for the shock, but also to hide the extent and nature of her injuries from those outside Hatshepsut's inner circle. Neferure had no intention of receiving people anyway but this additional recommendation of the physician was duly noted by all around her. The physician then gave his final directions to the princess's maids and he bid his farewell.

Ma-Keet approached the bedside of Neferure and gently stroked her hair. "Dear child," she cooed. "All will be well. Do not carry any ill for your mother. She is not well but will be."

The priestess then made her way to Karnak and the sanctuary of her own chamber. However she had someone she needed to see before she made way to her private room. Ma-Keet headed straight for the rooms of Senemut, now the most senior of priests. He was Hatshepsut's most revered advisor and much more, for he was also her most frequent late night visitor and Ma-Keet knew that he aimed to be Hatshepsut's only paramour. He was sitting at a desk pouring over scrolls that she could see were more to do with business than they were with temple rites. A cheetah skin was slung over one shoulder and bound at his waist and Ma-Keet almost wanted to laugh at the fact that despite the heat and with no one to see him he still felt compelled to don the fur to make his position known.

Senemut barely looked up the priestess, "Ah Ma-Keet, what news of the palace today. Has Our Majesty run out of kohl? Perhaps she needs new lotus plants for her garden pond?" He sniggered as he spoke.

"Thank you for reminding me of how trivial my position is compared to yours, my High Priest," she replied dryly and Senemut's head snapped up at her irreverence.

"You dare address me in that tone?" he challenged. "Perhaps you would like to serve in a temple on the Canaan border serving peasants and entertaining the savages who test our boundaries?"

"I am not here to play games Senemut," she retorted, her face stern and strong making Senemut turn in his chair to face her.

"Well then, I suggest you sit and enlighten me as to exactly why you are here," he gestured to a chair across the table. Ma-Keet sat forward in the chair, her chin squared and her eyes burning. This amused Senemut and he smiled.

He loved it when a lower priest came to him ready for a challenge only to be quashed within minutes. Ma-Keet had indeed come to play with him, she just didn't realise it. "Speak," he said and leaned to one side resting on the arm of his chair.

Then Ma-Keet began and Senemut's smile grew even more as he listened to her re-tell the afternoon's events. "You were right to come to me Ma-Keet," he said still reclining. "It seems our Queen has taught you much of loyalty and service." The priestess did not respond, still wary of her leader. Senemut sat forward, "It seems quite clear that our beloved queen is in need of help and together we shall provide it."

Ma-Keet now smiled back at Senemut. Everything she had sought the high priest out for was now in place and all that was left was how it would be enacted. Senemut, as resourceful as ever, had a plan designed in moments. He too had not been looking forward to Hatshepsut's demotion and the losses that would mean for him. Ma-Keet's visit this afternoon had not only delivered him a worthy accomplice but now the final impetus to put his ambitions into play. Timing was everything and now knowing that Hatshepsut was at her lowest only made this all the more easier.

Ma-Keet barely slept that night from the excitement as to what was about to occur. She could barely believe what she had sat there and heard Senemut plan, but what made her smile the most was that she was an integral part of its implementation. After their meeting she walked the temple complex grabbing those she knew were sympathetic to Hatshepsut and pulling them to a hidden corner or remote room to share with them Senemut's plan. They all listened intrigued and smiling, nodding their support. Ma-Keet knew exactly who to tell and who to simply walk past. Within hours a network had been created, so that when the message passed through the temple that all would assemble the next morning to hear Senemut speak, they knew exactly what was to be said.

They all gathered in the great hall the next morning after the dawn rites, including Arisina and others from my group of priests. Senemut sat at the front of the hall with Ma-Keet standing by his side. She was breathing heavy with nerves as she watched the others enter. Some walked in with knowing glances while others entered with brows furrowed, curious as to why such a meeting should be called. Soon they were all in their places and ready.

The air was thick with tension. Inadvertently those loyal to me gathered to one side while Hatshepsut's priests and priestesses gathered to the other side. Senemut stood from his chair at the front of the room and then invited Ma-Keet to speak. Arisina drew in a breath wondering what drama she would bestow upon us, but she could never have imagined what was about to be said. Ma-Keet spoke of the queen being ill due to growing concerns for the empire, the palace and our royal family. She declared that they must address the structure of the regency immediately in order to address the queen's condition and to restore stability to the palace and the kingdom.

My priests all looked between each other. *What instability? All was fine and progressing as planned.* Then they all slowly realised the truth of this meeting; to insure Hapshetsut's power until her death and their shackles rose.

"There is no concern for the regency," Arisina stated. "Our young King develops well and with great speed as he has since birth."

"He is becoming the great warrior that Egypt has prayed for!" another added.

"Yes, but he is still a boy and needs the Queen to support him for many years to come!" Senemut argued back.

"We need the Queen to maintain her role and continue the stability that is currently in place," Ma-Keet said backing up Senemut.

Many more added their comments and the meeting soon dissolved into a tangle of opinions and criticism being shouted from all corners of the hall.

Senemut soon pulled them all back to order. "We are achieving nothing with this rabble," he said coldly. "It is now time for the priesthood to show their support and plan the best possible outcome for all."

There was quiet in the room. With one simple sentence Senemut had called for the priesthood to act as one, and not just for the palace and kingdom but for the benefit of them all as a collective force.

"Hatshepsut must remain Thutmose's equal," he said bluntly.

"Senemut, the Gods decreed his position at his birth," Arisina stood forward and pleaded.

Senemut cut her short, "Oh you birth priestesses and your stories from the Gods!" he mocked. "And just how tired and hungry were you when you witnessed those signs? We all know the Gods decree them rulers by the very circumstance of the father they are born to, there is no need to justify anyone with those delightful embellishments."

Arisina had no answer for her leader and many dropped their heads at having a huge part of their mystical façade removed by Senemut. His brutish declaration now cleared the way for a down to earth discussion absent of myths and double talk. The reality of their roles and their privileged positions were now open to be examined.

"We have had two prosperous years with the co-regency as it has been deemed fit to operate. Our two leaders work well together and within their areas of strength. We, the priesthood, have had it easy being able to focus on one leader at a time and only the facets of the kingdom that lie in the jurisdiction of the leader we align with. Is this not true?" he asked of his group.

All of them nodded. They were all doing much better under the current situation than the priesthood had with any single ruler previously. They all were fond of and favoured their current alignments and any change would affect the very synchronicity of the priesthood. Surely they could adjust but to keep things constant served everyone equally. Arisina felt something tighten within her though; her instincts not liking where this was headed. They were acting as men and women, from their basic human fears and desires. It was against all their teachings to even speak like this about their roles. No good could come of it; if not immediately then the Gods would right this sometime soon and those responsible would pay.

Senemut continued with his campaign for Hatshepsut, "So my fellow priests and priestesses, I propose the following; that we support Hatshepsut in remaining co-regent with Thutmose, not only until he has reached manhood but until her death."

"That is outrageous!" Arisina shouted, any fear or subservience of her leader was gone. "It is unthinkable!"

"Then why was I able to think of it?" Senemut snarled back.

"It is offensive enough to ignore his birth story, but to ignore his birthright is an insult to the Gods and the kingdom," she continued shouting. "If this is executed then the souls of all responsible will pay in the afterlife."

Senemut laughed outright at this comment, "So would anyone else like to join Arisina in voting against me?"

"This is not something we can simply vote on!" her anger continued to boil. "Hatshepsut cannot be his equal once he has reached manhood. She is female! A queen can never equal a pharaoh. What do you intend to do? Conjure her some male genitals?"

"Not a bad idea, Arisina. I am so glad we have you here to provide us with these notions," Senemut smiled back at her, for she had just provided him with the perfect solution. "And you are also right about it not being something to vote on. I shall make the decision and you shall all follow. Ah, my dear priestess, you have indeed been helpful!"

He laughed outright now. Arisina in confronting and challenging him had in fact made his resolve greater and even though she had hit a nerve about Hatshepsut being female, she had also given Senemut an idea. Indeed a queen would never equal a pharaoh for a pharaoh had no equal. His only equals were those that preceded him in his role. But what if there were two pharaohs alive at the same time? Senemut looked up at his group knowing it was an outrageous scheme but also that without any precedence it would be hard to argue against. He simply announced that Hatshepsut would also be crowned a pharaoh and rule as my equal. They all stood quiet for as unthinkable as it were, no one could argue with Senemut.

The priests and priestesses all made their way out of the temple chamber to return to their ordinary daily duties. Arisina stood fuming, the anger and frustration within her was beyond words. She merely stood and glared, her eyes locked on Senemut as he once more sat and watched over everyone leaving. As the last few priests were walking out of the door and only Ma-Keet remained by the high priest's side, Arisina approached him.

Looking up he acknowledged her with a sly smile. "My sweet priestess, have you come to be thanked more personally for your help with this meeting," he laughed as he said it.

"I am here before you to ask as to how you intend to announce this to the Pharaoh and the Queen?" she spoke calmly despite wanting to say so much more.

"We shall have a private audience with the Queen," he answered, nodding his head toward Ma-Keet, implying her involvement.

"And what of the Pharaoh?" she pushed, her voice rising.

"Well, I imagine that should be your duty," he leant forward and crossed his arms, but just as quickly his face shifted and his arms dropped. Senemut's eyes narrowed as he took in Arisina's stance and the full extent of her anger registered.

"Perhaps," he continued, "this would be better executed with both of them present. Yes, that would be much better." His smile returned now, "Gather another priest Arisina and the four of us shall meet at the palace this evening to announce the decision to our beloved Pharaoh and Queen. We shall gather here at sunset and travel together."

Arisina was happier with this second scenario but her distrust of the old priest made her wary of why he suddenly changed his mind. She was relieved that at least I would be hearing it directly and with Arisina present as support. However it would not make the news any less devastating and this was still her concern. With the plan in place she bowed to her elder and turned to leave. Just as her back was turned Senemut said one last thing.

"Arisina, *please* remember your place tonight," Senemut drawled. "Save the dramatics for your birth stories and leave the talking to me. I will not tolerate any outbursts as I did today."

Arisina kept her back turned to Senemut. She fought against every desire to turn and deliver the tirade that that was at the tip of her tongue. A part of Senemut would have even enjoyed seeing her lose her composure one more time and Arisina knew that. Instead she simply drew a deep breath and walked away.

I spent that day oblivious to what had occurred the previous night and then that morning. News reached me of Neferure's illness and it was said to be quite serious, so I assumed that the cancelling of court was for Hatshepsut to be by her side. I spent the day on my duties with the military. As I walked about the palace though I noticed that I passed none of the more senior priests who always seemed to be wandering on their way to some consultation. This in itself changed the atmosphere but there was something else I felt stirring.

The palace seemed to take on a dreamlike state. Those around me knew nothing of what was decided at the temple that morning, but the decision itself seemed to be working its way through the building. No servant, guard or courtier would have admitted to it, indeed I doubt barely any of them would have been sensitive enough to feel it. The distractions of their tasks didn't allow them the time to tune into such greater things. This was within the sphere of the priesthood and the rulers. The energy around me began to feel increasingly suffocating; I wished to consult with Arisina, but something told me not to. Instead, I retreated to my chambers where I wrote and eventually laid upon my bed to rest.

I fell into a deep sleep despite the inevitable heat of the afternoon and was soon dreaming. Dreams confused me back then; they were supposedly sent by the Gods to warn us, but why would they scramble the message so much?

On this afternoon I dreamt I walked into court and there seated in the grandest throne at the centre of the podium was my beloved father. He was back! The emotions within me surged, the love was overwhelming and then there was the relief of simply being a prince again. I rushed towards the stairs that would lead up to him but as I ran I saw something was wrong. He stayed still and stiff, there was no expression of excitement or happiness to see me. I was confused. Why was my father not happy to see me? I kept running and as I finally arrived in front of him I understood the coldness. It was my father's body sitting upon the throne but as I looked closer the face was that of Hatshepsut, as though she had placed her own mask upon his body. I stepped back in shock and this horrible imposter of my father spoke a single sentence, "This is how it should have always been."

I woke feeling sick and distraught. I was sweating heavily from the heat and I yelled out for someone to fan me. Several servants came running and did so, while another started to wipe my face and arms.

My butler then entered and announced that the high priests had requested an audience with myself and Hatshepsut after dinner. Something inside me felt like I had been punched and within that moment I knew I was about to find out what that dream meant. I picked at my dinner, too distracted to eat as I thought about my dream and then the meeting. One thing I felt for sure though was that it wasn't to be pleasant.

I walked along the corridors towards the wing of the courtrooms. The meeting was held in a smaller, more private courtroom rather than the great hall and I was the last of the group to enter the room and felt everyone turn to watch me as I walked in. Hatshepsut was seated looking every bit the regal diva that she was, although I detected some nervousness there too. A seat was placed beside her and she motioned for me to sit in it. I sat and the four priests formed a line before us. Senemut stepped before them all reinforcing his leadership while Ma-Keet, Arisina and Hapuseneb, another of my priests stood still and quiet. Their faces were blank but serious and to see Arisina without any of the warmth she usually showed me only let me know this was a matter of utmost importance.

Leaning forward Hatshepsut now addressed our priests, "So my dear Senemut, what is this gathering all about?"

"My dear Pharaoh and Queen, we seek your audience this fine evening to relay some insights from the Gods," he replied with a smile crossing his face, although to me it looked more like a smirk.

The tightness in my stomach twisted even tighter and my mind raced. Was it a famine about to strike us? Perhaps an early flooding of the Nile? Or one of them had been sent a vision of an army sent to destroy us?

He continued, "The Gods have watched over your dual regency with much favour and pride. They have sent me to tell you that your alliance and actions arising from it please them greatly and to let you know that you ensure a stable and abundant future for Egypt." With this last word he bowed deeply in acknowledgment of our grand achievement.

Behind him Arisina took a deep breath and closed her eyes momentarily. *"Now who is conjuring great stories?"* she thought.

Hatshepsut and I sat still and quiet. This was a wonderful message to receive; in fact the most wonderful we could have hoped for. Hatshepsut turned to me and smiled as if to say, *"See I told you it was the right thing to do."*

I nodded to her as indeed this was the realisation of all that we spoke of that day two years ago when we began this. I couldn't help but feel there was more and then Senemut spoke again.

"It is with respect to this communication that I feel compelled to address your co-regency further. I feel there is more to this message sent to us than mere congratulations." His voice slowed to a drawl as he dragged out each word, enjoying the moment as much as he could. Senemut continued on smiling constantly and looking from Hatshepsut to me as he concluded, "We must advise that this alliance of leadership continue on."

Both Hatshepsut and myself were awestruck; but for very different reasons. She fell back into her chair and I heard her sigh. I however sat bolt upright and leaned forward. I wasn't even sure of what I heard but I knew it didn't feel right. The high priest now openly smirked at me as he was prepared for whatever I was about to say. That is one of the benefits of being the instigator of any confrontation--you get the option to plan, strategise and gather resources and allies whilst your victim has to think on his feet and often with no support.

"What exactly are you suggesting Priest?" I said sharply.

"We are advising that our beloved Queen remains your co-regent until her passing," he replied just as sharply confirming what had raised my shackles and what Hatshepsut had already understood. "Further to this we wish to tell you both that the priesthood has decided to fully support crowning our Queen as a Pharaoh that you may both rule as equals."

I turned to Hatshepsut, "This was not our agreement. It defies my rights and those of my forefathers, YOUR forefathers!"

Hatshepsut did not respond. Her eyes were glazed over as all that she had dreamed of had now landed right in her hand. She stared in the direction of Senemut and I turned back to face him again.

"I am rapidly entering my manhood; my training with the army and my experience in court will see me more than a competent Pharaoh in a matter of years. This is unnecessary!" I spat at him. "How dare you insult the kingship by declaring a woman to be Pharaoh? This is unnatural and an insult to every man who has been crowned."

"Oh yes, we are all aware of your skills and blossoming manhood," he conceded. "However, how can we argue with a message sent straight from the Gods?"

With that justification he delivered his trump card and it was one that I could not give an answer to. I looked to Arisina but she looked away. In that moment I knew it was all over. My allies had to succumb to this man and he hid behind the Gods. To go against a declaration of a high priest no matter how weak its assertions was a wary game to enter in my position. If I was sole ruler there would have been no problem as they would not have dared to challenge me but my power was diluted and now it would remain so. I too sank back in my chair. I barely heard whatever was said after that and suddenly the priests were gone.

I turned to Hatshepsut, "You planned this!" I hissed.

"Thutmose I swear I didn't. How could I?" she seemed genuine but something deep inside told me she had done something to instigate the whole event. I could never trust her fully now, whatever small amount of respect I had for her was gone. Yes, all would continue on, but the air of mistrust and suspicion would now thicken and envelope every meeting and activity within the palace.

Without so much as a goodbye I left the courtrooms and strode to my chambers. I thought I would feel better upon leaving her presence but as I walked the anger and frustration grew as my thoughts churned. By the time I reached my room my face was red and my pulse was racing. My mother was already waiting as she visited me each night, and when I walked in the look on my face scared her.

Jumping up from her seat she crossed the room, "What is it Thutmose?" she cried as she grabbed me and pulled me close to her. "What has happened?"

I pulled away and I paced the room as I explained what had just taken place. My arms flailed, my voice grew loud and my face grew even redder. It was the first time I had truly lost my temper before her. My mother listened patiently as she had done so many times listening to my father tell stories of court and his higher wife. My father however had never let himself get as angry as I was right now and this concerned my mother more than any of the politics that I was describing to her. She let me finish and then put her hand out to take mine and led me over to sit with her on a lounge. Pulling my head gently to rest on her shoulder she gently stroked my face and held me.

"My darling son," she spoke softly. "This woman has spent most of her life consumed by anger and jealousy. Look at what it has made her become. Your father lived life gently--please be more like him and not like this snake that remains with us. Tomorrow visit with Arisina. She will talk more when not in front of her high priest and others. Let her advise you on how to live this out as the true leader that you were born to be."

I wished I could have stayed in those safe arms all night but I was too old to be known as still needing my mother in such a way. Instead I retired to my bedchamber alone. I did not sleep so deeply that night but at least my mother had helped to quiet the noise within my head and the anger pounding in my chest. She reminded me that all was still well in its own strange way. The important things were the same. Now it was just how to live my life alongside a woman I truly despised.

The next morning I awoke and for a few seconds the world was alright. Then the events of the previous evening came flooding back and my mind fired up again. My body quickly responded with my stomach twisting and I felt my heart pounding again. I would arise and seek out Arisina. If there were to be anyone who was going to help me undo this, or make this alright, it would be her. My mother was correct to suggest Arisina, but to think now that she may have been part of this scheme tore at my heart; to lose the trust I had in her would mean I had no power left at all. I attempted to eat something for breakfast but anything I put into my stomach immediately felt like leaving it, so I gave up. I wanted to get my meeting with Arisina over and done with but was so scared that it would reveal her as yet another part of my undoing.

As I made my way to Karnak my mind created a myriad of ways in which this had happened. Hatshepsut had promised Senemut a position in line to the throne and next they would assassinate me and he would take my place. Senemut had taken bribes from traders who Hatshepsut was sympathetic to and thus ensured their businesses for decades to come. Of course, the rumours that Senemut and Hatshepsut were lovers also added a whole dimension to this too. The list of stories I was able to imagine was endless.

I was now close to the temple and as my horse arrived I quickly prayed to my father and grandfather that my beloved priestess had not chosen to betray me. I had sent ahead a messenger to let her know that I requested counsel with her so she was waiting and appeared nervous as I approached her. Arisina gestured me into the same room which only months ago I had sat and learnt about sex, the very occurrence that had inadvertently started the events that would lead to this meeting. We both sat down and my heart was beating against my chest bone as I started the discussion.

"I want to know how this happened!" I demanded. I tried to stay calm but we both knew I was far from that.

"My Pharaoh, I never imagined we would be having this discussion ever," Arisina's voice wavered and I saw tears start to form in her eyes.

This set me back completely. A priest or priestess never showed emotion--never--and especially not Arisina. Her chest lifted and fell several times as she sought to find more words but couldn't and she just shook her head instead.

"So you were not part of this?" I said.

She merely shook her head in response.

"It was all Senemut," I said as this was not a question but a simple realisation on my part. "There is nothing that we can do is there?"

Another simple shake of her head confirmed the reality of this. I recounted the conversation with my mother and how she sent me to see the priestess. This brought a smile to Arisina's face. "Your mother is a wise woman Thutmose. It is no wonder your father loved her so much, and that she gave birth to someone equally as wise. Come; let us take a walk together."

She rose from her chair and so did I. She then led the way until we were on a balcony overlooking our beautiful Nile River. "Tell me all you know about the Nile," she asked, turning and smiling at me.

I always loved to pour out facts and figures or history and even though I was confused by why she would choose to ask me this today, I launched into everything I knew about the river held within my head. I talked of how each year the Pharaoh would pray to the God Hapi and the Nile's waters would rise and bring nourishment to the land helping our farmers to feed our people and keep us strong. I talked of the wheat crops, the animals that it kept alive, the people and goods that it carried and the taxes it sent to the palace to support our beloved kingdom.

"This river has been here long before any of us Thutmose, and it shall remain long after we are all gone. It is part of the order of nature determined by the Gods, just as the sun and the moon will always rise and set. These are things that no man *or woman* can change," she said softly. "I stood and watched Senemut put all this in place, first with the priests and then before you and Hatshepsut. I wanted to cry and scream as much as you, for I know he has chosen to go against what the Gods truly want. This river though reminded me that with time the Gods restore order no matter the actions of man."

I now understood and nodded silently to her. Arisina leant towards me and gently laid her hand on my chest. "The one thing no man should ever be able to affect is the heart and spirit of another. So today my young Pharaoh I will ask you to keep this pure. Do not let Senemut's actions or that of your aunt affect this in any way." She spoke strongly and we looked deep into each other's eyes. "Stay strong and clear of their deceptions and delusions and the Gods will restore your rightful place. I was at your birth dear Thutmose and I know your destiny is to lead this country."

I felt the cloud of anger start to lift as Arisina gave me back my hope and in a way my power. My head started to nod as I felt the truth of her words. I would revisit this moment on many occasions through the years when times were trying. I could step back to the feeling in a single breath--that moment was my saviour.

# CHAPTER FIVE

The day of Hatshepsut's ceremony to become Pharaoh wasn't held until almost two years later. Apparently there was much to do in getting ready for the first woman to take on this role, despite the fact that the only thing about her position that would truly change was her title. Senemut and Hatshepsut seemed to revel in creating new rituals to prepare her for this and the entire palace as well as the city was encumbered in providing witness to them. They were full of theatrics and declarations from the Gods. All were recorded by scribes so that copies could be sent throughout the kingdom. They also apparently required Senemut frequently visiting her chambers until very late hours, which of course now established as true the rumours of a much closer relationship.

As each ritual was carried out I realised this was all an elaborate stage setting for her ascension to Pharaoh. Each performance was merely another piece of Senemut's public relations campaign, sending out the message loud and clear that this was ordained by the Gods and not to be challenged. So I sat through ritual upon ritual, bored stupid and often escaping into daydreams of battles with my army.

This transient year also saw Neferure seem to begin to take her duties more seriously. She was very changed after her "fall" and began to attend court on a regular basis. Senemut was personally tutoring her along with several others, preparing her to step into her role as queen when her mother became Pharaoh. As my wife she would now be recognised as the most senior of women in the palace. My mother, despite her marriage was now just the King's Mother, as her bloodline did not deem her worthy to carry a royal title outside of her now demised marriage.

So all the women then readjusted to their new duties and roles. Hatshepsut and my mother were fine as they were now right where they wanted to be. One was rising up higher than she ever imagined whilst the other was happy to return to a simpler role as a mother. Neferure however struggled. She was caught in a life she hated. Her only joys, those of adorning herself and collecting possessions, were now greatly limited due to her royal obligations and studies. She rose each day hating everyone and everything. She rarely made eye contact with anyone and her once loud voice filled with laughs and jibes was barely ever heard. Her sister, the only person who could have provided any allegiance, was long gone and she had no trust for any of the staff or priests who surrounded her as she knew the smallest things were reported to her mother.

She could not even hang onto the hope of finding a husband to confide in and be loved by as she had been forced to marry me, a boy she was taught to hate from my birth and who was six years younger. Of course there was the option of having a lover but she knew no man would be brave enough to risk that. As I had no heir yet, she continued to be such a focus for Senemut and her mother as she would be the one to assume the throne should both Hatshepsut and I head to the afterlife before I fathered a successor. However there was no affection within their attentions and of course Neferure had no passion or commitment for such things. They were simply preparing a shell to step into such a role if the need arose.

Neferure's body soon started to reflect the sadness and despair that was inside her. She grew paler and thinner as each day passed. There would be reports that she had fainted whilst walking through the palace. A day or two of bed rest would then follow these episodes while physicians and priests would attend her with herbs and prayers. Each period of illness seemed to restore some strength to her physical being but her eyes would look emptier and her head would hang just as heavy as before. Then came the day that she didn't arrive in court as expected; in fact Hatshepsut arrived late and looked flustered, announcing that a great illness beset her daughter through the night and Neferure would not be attending court for some time.

No one saw Neferure for well over a week that time and there began whispers that she may die. Hatshepsut cut back her duties to attend her bedside and things seemed to slow for a while in court. When I finally saw Neferure a few weeks later she came to court the thinnest she had ever been. She had a multitude of bangles upon both arms, which was not surprising as it was part of our women's style. However as she came and sat beside me on her throne I saw that each of her lower arms beneath her bangles was bandaged. I imagined she used one of her beloved hairpins sharpened to harm herself; but of course no one would ever tell me as anyone who had access to such knowledge was sworn to secrecy.

After this episode there was something different about Neferure. It was hard to define as she rarely spoke. There was something different in her face as darkness now pervaded her eyes. I don't just mean dark circles as they were always present, but that there was now a burn in her gaze. It was like the looks I would get as a child as she teased but even more intense. People were already avoiding the constantly ill woman but now they seemed to genuinely fear her and kept even more distance. Inside her, underneath the cloud of depression and frustration Neferure had finally found a way to escape all this. Her first effort was thwarted due to her own bad timing and the good timing of a maid, but next time she promised herself, she would be successful.

She didn't plan any better though. Her fatal, or should that be un-fateful flaw was to underestimate the lengths her mother had gone to in order to prevent her success should she try again. Neferure in her haze was unaware that she was constantly watched, even around corners. So within minutes of her next attempt she was once again attended to. The quicker care given to her cuts made this a less sinister recovery despite her more brutal injuries. This second effort revealed to her mother just how determined she was, a quality she knew all too well and that now Hatshepsut set about quashing.

Hatshepsut sought counsel with Senemut and they discussed at length how this would be dealt with. As usual Senemut had a simple yet effective plan and, of course, one sent by the Gods. Neferure upon being well enough to sit before her mother and the priest was told of the horrific consequences of taking one's own life. Those that saw to end their existence did not pass onto the afterlife with the recognition of their rightful place in paradise. They instead entered another world of darkness filled with pain and suffering hunted by all sorts of beasts and monsters. Neferure sat before them and for the first time in months actually made wide-eye contact with her mouth dropping open. It worked as they now had a woman whose fear of death now outweighed her hatred of life.

It didn't remove the secret thrill and liberation she had learnt from sliding sharp metal along her flesh. She would hide her tools within her mattress and when all thought she was asleep she would then slowly slice the skin on her legs. Legs were great to do as she could then hide the scars under her skirts and there were lots more places to reach and leave scars on. Her maids would often find her bed sheets full of blood but the more blood that was spilled during the night the less depressed Neferure awoke. She became quite talented at it, knowing just how deep to push to hurt and bleed yet avoid serious injury. She knew just how to reach a place which was far from living yet kept her from the dark world that ending this all would take her to--so too had Neferure found her own balance of power.

The day of Hatshepsut's coronation arrived and the dramatic ceremony and pomp outdid the years of preparation as everyone imagined it would. The deep smile on my aunt's face was matched by that on Senemut's as he led the prayers, sacrifices and declarations. It was like no other ceremony performed at Karnak in the temple's long history thus far. Certainly many pharaohs had been crowned here and walked out as living Gods but none had been women. Senemut made this point many times as the ritual proceeded so that by the end when he said it for possibly the hundredth time I was not alone in sighing and rolling my eyes. I did not care who saw my reaction and I am sure Senemut caught many of us doing this. It felt good to know that the priest was aware of how many of us recognized the ceremony for the sham that it was, and that our behaviour would have eaten at his confidence and pride.

When the ceremony was over Hatshepsut and I sat upon sedans to be taken back to the palace. Hatshepsut's sedan was beside mine and the bearers had been instructed and trained with such discipline that neither sedan was ever carried so much as an inch before the other. I stole a glance at Hatshepsut as we made our way back through the streets lined with our subjects who were all cheering. None would have been brave enough to do anything else. Hatshepsut still had the deep smile she had worn upon her face at the temple and now it grew even wider as she was carried as my equal for the entire city to see. I sighed and continued to wave to my people just as my father had always done while Hatshepsut's hands remained gripped upon the armrests of her chair.

At the palace a grand feast was held and I had to sit beside the newest Pharaoh and greet all her well-wishers as they came up to fawn and declare their obedience. A grand feast such as this would usually have continued on into the early hours of the morning but the sweets had barely been served and the dancers only just left the room when Hatshepsut rose from her chair. Everyone in the room also rose as was expected when the Pharaoh stood but I stayed slouched within my own chair and continued eating.

"This has been a most grand day and one that should be celebrated eternally," she shouted to the room. "However Egypt needs sound ruling and so I will retire and be ready to serve rested and fresh within our court tomorrow."

The room exploded with applause and cheers but I still looked down and chewed. Hatshepsut turned and looked at me feigning a smile. "Won't you also choose to retire now Thutmose," she said slyly and turned back to look upon the room, "that you might also be refreshed and ready to continue on with our work for the people?" She gestured her hand to the room adding a final flourish.

I looked up as I swallowed what was within my mouth and then lifted a glass of wine. "I do believe my youth will afford me several more hours of celebration dear Aunt," I said loudly, "but you go ahead and seek all the rest that your age needs." I finished and took a deep sip of my wine as my own final flourish.

I saw Hatshepsut's face grow red and knew she would have hated to be shown up like this on her grandest of days. Her eyes narrowed and she lowered her voice, "Fine then Nephew, but don't make issue if you oversleep and miss any important decisions."

She did not wait for a reply--not that I was going to offer her one, and left the room with her entourage and soon after the viziers and priests who were part of her alliance.

"Call back the dancers!" I demanded.

The next day I was awoken early by servants to begin the long and tedious routine that was needed to look the part of Pharaoh. As I was dressed and decorated I imagined Hatshepsut being also prepared in her finery. I was finally ready and I headed into the hallway where my mother and Neferure waited to join my procession to court.

We entered the corridor that led to the huge doors of the court and they were swung open for us to enter. My eyes were immediately drawn to the thrones that were in their usual place and for a second I stopped in my tracks.

There was a man sitting upon one just as in my dream. Just as it had within that dream my heart jumped at the thought that it was my father. It was no man. It was my co-regent and fellow pharaoh Hatshepsut sitting on her throne, and she had chosen to dress herself as a man. She had covered her breasts but in the style that I would have in the rare cool weather.

Her headdress was a copy of those my grandfather, father and myself wore in court and from the sides of this came two gold threads that held in place a ceremonial beard. This final detail was the element that took this from merely dressing up to a huge statement of her power. She not only now had a male title and clothes but somehow she had stepped into the physicality of the gender that had held her back. She had finally matched us in every way she could. The shock value worked wonderfully. Who would challenge any one brave enough to do such a thing?

As I walked closer the initial shock soon turned to amusement. Although I will admit I was a bit jealous as I loved wearing my ceremonial beard after watching my father wear his. It was also my declaration of manhood and to have this woman wearing one now seemed to mock all that. Still it was highly entertaining to see her dressed as a man, as though she seemed determined to grasp every part of her role no matter how ridiculous it seemed. A smile spread across my face as I stifled a laugh.

Arisina was waiting to the side of the podium to greet me and arrange my clothing once I was seated. She too was smiling as her eyes met mine and we intuitively shared our amusement at Hatshepsut's latest expression. As she leaned over me to smooth my clothes and then hand me my crook and flail she whispered, "What else do you think Senemut may have attached to her?" I now had to bite my lip to stop my laughter as Arisina stood back, her face returning to its usual composure as she bowed to me and then to Hatshepsut.

So there we all sat, Hatshepsut, to my left hoping that by impersonating a man she would be treated as one, myself in the centre biting back my laughter, and Neferure my self-mutilating sister-wife and now Queen of Egypt to my right. We were the perfectly normal and regal Royal Family of the most powerful empire in the known world.

CHAPTER SIX

L ife in the palace with Hatshepsut was actually quite easy for me. I was able to concentrate on the army, which was my passion, and the shorter hours in court also meant more time for horse riding and my new passion for writing. You have it so easy in English with your twenty-six letters and a handful of symbols. We had a myriad of symbols whose meanings could be changed simply by how they were placed. Salas, my cousin and childhood friend had now entered the priesthood and was chosen to become a scribe. This was wonderful for me as we could often use a writing practice session as an excuse to socialise. We soon learnt to avoid wine until after we were done writing, as the next day we would find that we had created new symbols or arranged real ones in a manner not befitting a king or priest.

The army flourished with me as their commander. My lifelong friendships with the established generals served us all well. I respected their experience and skills while they enjoyed having a fresh perspective and the energy that came with my youth. It was a perfect balance. My training leapt ahead and my physical attributes were soon an outward display of what I had learnt. I was growing taller by the week and my constant training was keeping me toned and muscular. I was growing into quite a male specimen and rather handsome to top it all off. I enjoyed my ride into manhood, relishing all the physical developments including a nice deep voice. Occasionally I would remember that these changes should have been my passage into sole leadership as well but I would remember Arisina's words or spend a stuffy day in court and I would let it go.

Another aspect of my physical being was also growing and now the hormones that fed this part of me were also in full swing. My body desires grew stronger and I finally was brave enough to request that consorts be sent to my rooms at night. I was fifteen when this started and they would send two or three each night. They were generally a bit older, which was expected but also nice as I enjoyed women with a bit more maturity. They would entertain me with music and singing, or join me in games such as Senet. Some knew how to massage and these were usually the ones that would end up in my bed. Once this pattern was established I soon found that they all knew how to massage.

Ending up in the Pharaoh's bed was not an assumption that any consort could hold, however it was a goal that they all aimed for. Being a consort to the Pharaoh gave you privileges and placed you above other palace consorts. To make it into his bed and be providing him with the most intimate of entertainment however took you above and beyond again. You would then be provided with the most luxurious of clothing and toiletries, given more time to bathe and preen, as well as not being expected to perform more menial tasks. It gave the chance of gifts that many intimate consorts would be given especially if they developed extra talents to make the sex even more thorough and exciting. An agile tongue could lead to a gold bangle encrusted in jewels! More valued though was the possibility that, as had my father, one of them may be chosen to become my wife and a queen.

So my penis became a prize that they all wanted. I only had about seven women that would come to my rooms and eventually I had sex with all of them so that level of competition was wiped out. So they replaced that with who was chosen the most often. This initially led to some very persuasive, even aggressive seduction techniques and our bed sessions became absolute adventures as they all consulted with more experienced palace consorts for techniques to set them above their colleagues.

Away from me there would be bickering and attempts to undermine each other began. They would arrive earlier to my chambers to be the first to gain my attention or they would sabotage each other by doing such things as spilling wine upon another as they dressed for the evening. Eventually a comment or two was made in front of me that would prove to be that woman's undoing. Having spent a childhood with squabbling stepsisters and an ice maiden as an aunt, I was hardly about to tolerate this from someone within my chambers who was barely above a servant--even if it wasn't directed at me.

After a day of battle training and strategies I hardly felt like continuing this on within my chambers. Initially I would simply not invite them back into my bed but it was eventually easier to just send them away. I settled on just three women after a year of this and chose just one to join me in bed when I so desired. She was far from the most adventurous in bed but she had the gentlest nature and it was this softness that I craved above all else to disappear into at night. I liked to have her nearby even without conversation and all soon noticed the way I favoured her. Without me knowing talk started that she was being considered by me as a wife. My favourite consort soon also started to believe this was her destiny and decided to act accordingly. She would order about the servants and the remaining two consorts, which at first didn't bother me until the day that I caught her stating her believed superiority over them.

Her tone and manner was such a reminder of Hatshepsut that I dismissed her immediately. My anger was quelled only by the look of embarrassment and the tears that fell from her face as she turned to leave my chambers. The competitiveness of the women and their desire to use their position to gain standing left me cold. I let the final two go for the night and sought my butler, Tati, to let him know that I would not be requiring consorts for some time. I lied and said I needed to reserve my energy for an intense period of army training. Not that he would have dared question me anyway, but it would provide an acceptable excuse for my actions. I would also not have to explain myself to Arisina and possibly get the consorts into any trouble or perhaps have them sent from the palace.

I didn't completely lie about the training as I was entering a rigorous regime and it was far simpler to climb into bed at night and relieve myself if I felt such a desire. Yes, I missed the touch of women but I didn't miss the complications of them. The cloths that I took into bed with me at night to collect my seed didn't go unnoticed by my servants. I could hardly hide them or clean them myself as Pharaoh and so after several months of this and still no request for the return of my consorts, Tati grew concerned and sought Arisina to notify her.

She arrived one day to my chambers just as I returned from a very enjoyable day of sword training. I was sitting in a large chair, sweaty, dusty and exhausted but elated from a wonderful day with my soldiers.

"Your Highness, you have had a successful day of training?" Arisina enquired.

"Yes, Arisina," I beamed back.

"You enjoy being amongst men don't you?" she continued in a soft hesitant voice.

I didn't hear the true nature of her question and replied with the enthusiasm that was afforded a proud army commander, "Yes, I do! It is always wonderful to be with my men," I answered and smiled.

Arisina looked to the side, took several breaths and then looked back to me with her solemn face. I knew I was about to get some serious advice and sat forward curious.

"Your Highness," she paused as she gathered her words and then continued, "I am aware that you have dismissed your consorts due to your training schedule."

"That is correct," I swallowed, and then knew I was having the conversation I so wished to avoid.

"It is apparent to your servants that you continue to--ahh--have desires and yet you do not ask the consorts to return," Arisina said. She maintained her composure as she spoke being as official as she could, although hardly believing that she needed to have this conversation. I hung my head and was just starting to find the words to explain myself when she spoke again, "Sire, would you prefer that we send you some male consorts?" she offered gently.

My head snapped up in shock and I stammered--umming and ahhing… until I regained my composure. "No! Male consorts will not be required," I answered emphatically.

Arisina bowed in acknowledgement and as she straightened back up I could see the relief on her face. It was not that preferring men would have made my chances of fathering a successor completely lost but she was thankful that there was simply one less obstacle to overcome. Now that I had reached the age of seventeen it was time to address this matter with me quite seriously.

"Thutmose," she knew using my name changed the mood, "You are of age now to be considering siring an heir. How goes things with your wife?"

I rolled my eyes, "I can't believe that you even ask. You know as well as

I what our relationship is like. It is as it always has been. Even if it were more cordial do you imagine her frailties would allow a child to bloom within her?"

Arisina nodded. I had summed up my marriage and possibilities of an heir with Neferure quite simply. "Then Sire, you must begin to seriously consider taking another wife and one that you feel will provide you with the heir that your family requires," she said almost begging.

I nodded in response and it was all that Arisina needed to know that I would take her words and truly consider what she had spoken of. The truth was I wanted marriage as my parents had. I didn't want a wife of convenience, or one to merely satisfy my ego's desire to keep my genes on the throne. I wanted a woman to love and to be loved by and to create children from that love. When the consorts first came to me I had hoped that one would warm my heart as my mother's had my father but it never happened. I believed this just added to my whole frustration with them all. I often scanned the court on the occasions when dignitaries brought their daughters to accompany them in the hope they would attract the attention of myself or someone from the palace as a spouse but none had done so yet.

If truth be told I was happy with life the way it was and felt that the more I avoided women the easier it was. With the exception of my mother and Arisina, the women in my life baffled me with their foibles and frailties. I was happy to keep my mind on my army and what was becoming a prosperous career as a general. The duty of providing an heir did weigh on me though. I cringed to think of repeating my father's fate, of siring an heir but then dying before they could rule with strength. I knew such things were destined by the Gods but I wanted to minimise the chances that my child's succession would be anything but smooth and unchallenged. The creation of an heir now would become my greatest priority.

Hatshepsut was likewise considering this very situation at the time. She sat in her chambers at night and considered it often. The most powerful woman in Egyptian history now had to face that her two heirs were a vacant shell of a daughter and a powerful army commander not from her body. She had been clever enough to have them married to each other but this was no guarantee that they would in turn produce the next generation. Hatshepsut desperately wanted the next pharaoh to be born of her daughter's flesh. She knew the dangers this presented considering the health of Neferure, but she was prepared to risk her own daughter's life should it provide a much-needed heir. I was strong and rigorous, unlike my father, and could raise and train the child on my own. The only real challenge would be in having us procreate.

Neferure's chambers were adjoined to my own as was befitting of my queen but we essentially lived separately. The doors that opened to allow passage between the rooms were never opened in our presence. We were happy to be neighbours but kept to ourselves. So you can imagine my surprise when one night as I was sitting in my room, quietly sipping on wine as I wrote, that these doors should open. I looked up in shock and my first instinct was to grab at the knife that I carried on my waist at all times for protection. It was just Hatshepsut minus her beard. In private she returned to her full feminine self and this was the version of the woman that now entered my rooms. The initial jolt was just settling when I noticed that Neferure followed in her wake, her head down as usual and shoulders slumped. She had already received her own special speech on her duties as Queen of Egypt and was being dragged in to bear witness to my impending lecture.

"Thutmose, how do you fare this evening?" Hatshepsut smiled at me.

"I am well and strong Aunt," I refused to call her Pharaoh as others were required. I had few ways to assert my equality and I used them as often as I could. I also refused to return the empty greeting, as I knew her presence here was far from friendly. "What brings you to my chambers this evening?"

"Thutmose, you may call me aunt as often as you like but you need to remember that as your father's first wife I am also your mother," she tilted her head and adopted a mock softness in her tone but the venom of her meaning came through loud and clear. "It is as your mother that I come here tonight to speak with both you and your wife. As mother to both of you it is time for me to address the issue of you producing an heir."

Neferure kept her head down as I looked towards her. We both knew what was required and neither of us wanted that. Hatshepsut let her words sink in and then pressed on. "Talk has started amongst the court that maybe our family's reign will end with you Thutmose. There is an endless line of priests, viziers and generals who will gladly step into our roles if we leave with no heirs. They would be planning their campaigns as we speak," Hatshepsut's tongue clipped out the words.

This was of course purely speculation and paranoia on her part. No one would even dare to speak such ambitions out loud. A mere whisper could lead to your demise and a confidante could soon turn traitor to gain favour within the palace.

"If either of you have a shred of family pride you will start to remedy this situation as soon as possible," Hatshepsut continued, "and if you think I will stand back and watch as you two let all that your grandfather built become nothing then you are very mistaken."

I furrowed my brows at this hollow threat and rubbed my chin while Hatshepsut stood silent. She knew she had nothing to really scare us with, essentially Neferure and I held the reins of this situation. Her silence spoke volumes though. Only the Gods knew what she could do with Senemut in her pocket.

"I expect for Neferure's servants to notify me of when she has spent the night in your bedchamber. I also expect that this will occur more often than not as this is what is required to plant your seed firmly within her," she said coldly. "Tomorrow morning you will have your butler bring the bloodied sheets to me."

With this she turned and left through the doors that returned to her daughters rooms and we heard her shout to the servants to close the doors. They snapped shut and I was alone with Neferure who still stood with her head down and shoulders slouched in exactly the same place that she had stopped behind her mother. It was as though a statue had been delivered to my rooms. I sighed and shook my head. All I could think was, *"what now?"*

"Neferure, come and sit down please," I gestured to the seat opposite me.

Barely lifting her head she shuffled to the table and took a seat, sitting sideways in the chair so as not to face me and she looked down once again. I could see her chest rise and fall quite rapidly; the only outward sign of her fear and anger.

"Would you like some wine?" I almost whispered, leaning forward lifting the carafe.

She shook her head in response. I poured myself some more wine and leant back in my chair as I slowly sipped. I glanced all about the room as I did anything to avoid looking at this poor figure sitting opposite me. I did seriously contemplate that I would need to take her to bed but the thought was not a pleasant one. I had never forced myself onto a woman and had no desire to take what had so far been a wonderful experience and make it into something that was unpleasant for either of us. My concerns were also for Neferure's lack of experience. I had taken the virginity of one of my consorts but she had been prepared and knew to not let the pain show in her actions. In fact I was only aware when I withdrew and saw blood upon the sheets. Hatshepsut's demand for such evidence added much to the pressure of this.

After what seemed an eternity I finally decided to talk. "Neferure, we do not have to do this tonight," I said but had barely finished the words when she turned to lock eyes with mine. Her eyes held the fire of anger that they did when she teased me as a child but they were now framed with dark circles, engulfed in despair. They bore into my own eyes and she didn't really need to speak to let me know her feelings.

"You will never touch me," she spat, "outside or inside!"

"As you wish," I quietly responded. "But tell me--do you not desire to have a child?"

"And bring it into this hideous place to be kept like a bird in a cage, taught to do tricks and not allowed to sing its song? I don't think so," she snapped again. "I curse the Gods who brought me to this life Thutmose. I curse them everyday and wish I could leave but then I would only curse myself."

I was horrified, for to openly curse the Gods was tantamount to inviting a punishment from them. Tomorrow I would have to get a team of priests together to cleanse my rooms and myself lest the words leave their energy on either. There was still the issue of presenting some evidence to her mother though.

"Neferure we need to send the sheets to your mother sometime soon so that she will know we have at least attempted to…" Once again I could hardly finish my sentence. Neferure interrupted me by rising from her chair and approached the door that led to my bedchamber. I jumped to my feet and followed in her steps wondering if she had changed her mind. As she entered my two servants who waited there each night to prepare me for sleep jumped to their feet not sure what to do.

"Turn the bed down and leave!" she ordered. "Close the doors behind you!"

They did so a bit quicker than usual and rushed out closing the doors with a bang in their haste. Neferure walked towards the bed and approached the wall to the side of it. She reached into her hair and pulled out a hairpin, a lock of hair fell to the side of her face but she didn't seem to notice or care as she then started to rub the end of the pin on the stone wall. I stood by silently, curious but too fearful to question her. This went on for only a minute or two, as she periodically stopped and held the pin close to her face inspecting the progress of her work.

When she was satisfied she crawled fully clothed into the centre of the bed and sat upon the mattress. She then began to lift her skirt to her knees. I approached the bed but she snapped her head up and I froze in place. The harshness of her glare was warning enough not to step closer but what truly shocked me was what she had revealed when she lifted her skirt. Upon her legs was a maze of scars that seemed tattooed. Some were faded, some dark and raised, while others still held the redness of new healing. Neferure looked down at her legs and began to run one hand along the skin while her other hand wielded her pin. She was doing this with the approach that an artist or craftsmen would when starting a new piece. It was almost like she went into another world completely oblivious of her surrounds or me.

I had no idea as she looked along her flesh she was assessing and contemplating. Each inch of flesh was measured for the possibility of a good blood source beneath the skin. Was it too close to another scar and just how much would it hurt? She finally found her target and without hesitation pushed the sharpened edge of the pin along her skin. I flinched as she did so but she barely reacted as if she was detached from the very flesh she was cutting. Neferure sliced along the back of her calf and as the blood started to seep from the delicate opening she had created, she lowered her leg against the bed sheet just at the appropriate place and allowed the sheet to be stained. Not quite satisfied with the amount that she had thus far produced, she gave her calf a squeeze to get another dose of blood out. Neferure wiped her leg against the sheet again spreading the stain and gathering the last drops as her skin began to pull together.

She looked up at me and there seemed to be an almost gleeful look in her eyes. "Do you think that is enough?" she asked.

I nodded. Even if it hadn't of been I couldn't bear to give her excuse or reason to repeat that act before me. I would see and inflict many injuries as a soldier but nothing would ever disturb me as much as seeing someone wilfully injure and scar themselves in this way.

"Ah, there would be other fluids," I stammered.

"Oh," she replied and leaning over the stain she spat into it, "I don't have much spit. You should add some too."

So I walked over and added a nice hefty mouthful to Neferure's contribution. In a way we sealed our pact to deceive Hatshepsut with that stain.

"I will stay here tonight to save any talk amongst the servants," she stated as she stood and smoothed her skirt back down over legs. Neferure still held her pin in her hand and she now looked me in the eye as she pointed it at me, "But let me warn you! If you so much as try to touch me and make a more authentic stain for our mother, I will injure you in such a way that you will never have an heir!"

To emphasise her point she finished by jabbing her pin in the direction of my crotch and I felt my testicles jump in horror. I had no doubt that she was more than capable of doing exactly what she threatened, and I seriously considered whether I should sleep wearing my leather battle cup lest I accidentally brush her in my sleep.

"Call my servants to dress me for sleep," she directed.

I was too shocked by everything I had just seen or heard to question her manner and so walked to open the bedchamber door. My servants were waiting just beyond the doors and jumped to their feet. "We are ready to sleep, please summon the queen's maids to prepare her and return to prepare me," I said.

I turned and walked back into the room and was greeted with the depressed, timid Neferure sitting on the edge of the bed, shoulders slumped and her head once again hanging low. The pin still grasped in her hand like a weapon didn't convince me that the feisty, cutting version of Neferure had left altogether though and I walked to the opposite side of the bed to get as far away as I could. The servants were quick to return and if they had any confusion over seeing evidence of sex and yet finding us both fully clothed they didn't show it.

They undressed us and redressed us in our bedclothes and I climbed into bed, laying straight and stiff upon my back as close as possible to the edge and stared upwards as Neferure finished dressing and assumed the same pose on the other side. The servants collected our clothes, closed the heavy drapes and walked out leaving us with just the light of one lamp flickering. We remained still neither daring to move lest the movement be misinterpreted in any way. I knew she still held her pin in her left hand ready for anything. The blood and spit upon the sheet between us was already starting to dry and I wondered just how closely would Hatshepsut and her priests examine it.

I had started to drift into sleep when a voice beside me broke the silence

"Thutmose, do you hate her as much as I do?" Neferure said barely above a whisper.

"Possibly even more Neferure," I answered, "but I choose to fill my life with things to enjoy and it helps me forget."

"That is the difference between you and me," she said even quieter, "I have nothing else to choose."

I was now suddenly wide-awake again and the words that Arisina spoke to me as we looked over the Nile came back. I eventually started to doze once more and as I did so I thanked the Gods for placing the priestess in my life to guide me and said a prayer for the soul of the woman beside me. A twist of fate could have easily placed me in her existence.

Neferure and I sat and discussed the details of our pact to deceive Hatshepsut over breakfast the next morning. Neferure would present to my chambers through our adjoining doors three nights a week. Her personal servants would be dismissed reducing any chances of them reporting anything untoward to Hatshepsut and mine certainly would never dare to betray me. She would be free to do as she chose on those evenings and I enjoyed seeing her face change on those nights as I allowed her some taste of freedom and fun. It was ironic enough that we had now plotted together against her mother but I never imagined that this would also open up a friendship within our reluctant marriage.

My evenings with Neferure became quite pleasant. She would practise her writing with me but would soon grow bored. We would play games or call in some palace musicians to entertain us. We drank wine and gossiped about people and events in the palace and eventually we even laughed together. I truly began to look forward to these nights of socialising and I believe so did Neferure. She began to gain some weight and the circles under her eyes lightened.

When I felt she was ready I began to invite some friends such as Salas to join us and soon these nights became even more fun as our group grew. It was with pure joy that on one of these nights as ten or more of us were gathered at the dining table that I looked down the table and saw Neferure deep in talk with one of my soldier colleagues, Samreen. She seemed enthralled with his conversation and beamed the most beautiful smile at him and my heart swelled to see her happy.

At other gatherings Samreen would also seek her out and they would soon disappear onto a balcony or into a corner to pay attention to each other. I'm sure that in these moments each made many declarations and kisses were quickly gifted. My close friends knew the truth of our marriage and in no way was my wife or my friend betraying me. However to take the relationship further was another matter.

One night when Neferure and I were alone she was very quiet and it was almost like the days of her darkest depressions, which scared me.

"Neferure, is something troubling you?" I asked.

She nodded and kept her head down.

"Please tell me," I begged. "Are we not friends now? I don't wish to see you like this again."

"Thutmose," she started, but her lip trembled and she began to cry.

"It is Samreen, isn't it?" I asked and she nodded again. "Has he done something to hurt you?" I was angry now and ready to avenge my sister but she shook her head.

"No, he has done nothing to hurt me," she said. "I have allowed myself to fall in love with him and it is beyond me to deal with these feelings."

"Has he indicated that he feels the same?" I asked.

"Yes, many times," Neferure looked at me and smiled. "He says he loves me and when he does then all the miseries of life disappear."

I slumped in my chair. How were we to deal with this now? Part of me was aching to feel this way for someone and have her love me too. I hated that our royal lives seemed to limit this happening and I decided to help Neferure experience this. I leant forward and took her hand. "Do you wish him to become your lover?" I asked, and once again she nodded her reply.

"So be it then," I gave my blessing and the tears flowed even more from her eyes. "You do understand that this will require all the discretion that we can muster. The room adjoining my bedchamber will become your private room. We will have a bed and furnishings placed within it to your choosing. No one can enter except through my chambers so you will be protected. Samreen will be allowed to stay with you on the nights that you would usually stay with me. If it becomes more often it will raise suspicion."

Neferure nodded continually as I spoke accepting all I said while inside her heart was bursting with excitement that this was happening.

"There is one thing I must ask of you," I continued.

"Yes, anything," she looked at me wide-eyed and grateful.

"You must somehow gain the herbs that will prevent you becoming pregnant," I demanded. "I can give my wife permission to lay with another man but I cannot accept a child of his seed to be my successor. Let us not complicate this any further. If I take another wife and she bears me a son than you will be free to have your own child."

Neferure understood completely. She asked to return to her own chambers for the night and stood. Before she turned to leave she approached me and bending down kissed me on the cheek. "I am very glad you forgot to execute me when you became Pharaoh," she giggled and floated out of the room.

I joined in her laughter and after she left I stared out at the moon that was full and round tonight. This situation only reminded me of the importance of finding another wife and I prayed that I too would find someone to ache for me the way Neferure did for Samreen. I had already had one woman forced to become my wife and although that had led to a somewhat agreeable situation I was reluctant to create a marriage that was anything but harmonious from the beginning.

Two nights later Samreen was announced at my chamber doors. He seemed nervous and there was even a blush to his cheeks as he entered. He approached me and was about to speak but I held up my hand to stop him. "She is waiting for you. Go to her," I said, and pointed the way through to their secret place. With a quick nod Samreen turned and almost ran through the doors to his lover.

CHAPTER SEVEN

The wonderful social gatherings that Neferure and I held grew and were now well-known. The cream of upper crust Egyptian teens and twenty-somethings attended them and to receive an invitation not only confirmed your place in Theban society but could offer you a chance to further yourself. Gorgeous and not so gorgeous young women, all properly chaperoned by a male family member, were brought to socialise and be paraded before me. Many found their way to sit beside me at dinner or on a lounge as we watched dancers and musicians perform. They would never be impertinent enough to start conversation with me but would steal glances at me from under their heavy fringes and thickened eyelashes.

I would engage with those I found attractive from time to time, but it seemed that the more attention they had paid to their appearance, the less capable they were of holding a conversation. They were all well prepared in their role as Pharaoh huntress and would gently guide the subject to praising me or asking about my army, as though they were interested or cared about such matters. Arisina would ask from time to time how my search for a wife was progressing and I would answer with a sigh and shrug my shoulders. She was at least thankful that I was mixing with women and considering my available options.

One day a young corporal, Ahmenmose, who was part of my Canaan border patrol, was back in Thebes for some de-briefing and training with the commanders and me. His family was also a powerful part of my army with his father having been a commander and court consultant for my father and grandfather. Ahmenmose was bright and loud, making him a perfect addition to our gatherings and an invitation was duly extended.

All our socials began with Neferure and myself seated side by side and as the guards approved each guest they would be then be escorted into the room by a servant. They would then approach us and greet us. Newer guests would always do the formal address of a bow and say, "Your Highnesses, what an honour to be your guest." Our regulars however would do the quickest of bows and then rush forward to grasp my hand and kiss Neferure, impart a quick compliment or snippet of gossip and then head off to mingle, drink and eat with the other guests. My visiting corporal entered the room in the more formal manner, unfamiliar with just what these gatherings entailed. Seeing me he smiled and began his approach while behind him I saw that a young woman followed. She matched his pace but not his poise, seeming quite timid and embarrassed to be here. Something about her intrigued me and I kept my eyes on her until the corporal began to speak.

"Your Highnesses," he bowed and swept up again, "what an honour to be a guest of the palace. I have brought my sister, Satiah to join the gathering also."

With this he stepped aside and the young woman stepped forward and bowed before Neferure and myself. When she straightened and our eyes met my life was changed. You humans talk about love at first sight and this was it. Every cell of my body felt like it wanted to explode as I looked at her. She didn't speak as she was too shy but smiled as her way of greeting and this melted my heart even more. Satiah was no more striking than many of the women who crossed my path but we all know that love transcends the mere physical and the illusions of what we think we see. She did not swamp her eyes with kohl or fake lashes and she did not layer herself with excessive cloths or jewellery. Whether this helped me see her more clearly I am not sure.

Our greeting soon ended and Ahmenmose with Satiah made their way to join the other guests and my eyes couldn't help but follow Satiah as she made her way across the room. My eyes kept finding her all night, drinking in her details, the way she smiled and tilted her head as people spoke to her--even the way her fingers curled around her wine glass. I was distracted by her all night and didn't hear much of the many conversations that I was a part of. When the farewells began around midnight, Ahmenmose with Satiah once again in tow came towards me to bid me farewell. Ahmenmose spoke his thanks while his sister, as timid as she was on entering the room, smiled but kept her eyes downcast. I finally though had my opportunity to talk to her and what I had to say would need to be said in front of her brother.

"Satiah, I hope you also enjoyed the evening?" I asked knowing I would have to get a response and eye contact.

She looked up and her smile spread even more, "Oh yes Your Highness, very much so," she answered and bowed her head to finish.

"Then you must join us again. I am sure that you have other brothers or men in your family to bring you once Ahmenmose returns to the border," I said not so much an invitation as a request. As I spoke the last part I looked at Ahmenmose and so did not see the blush that crept across Satiah's face.

Ahmenmose looked at me quite seriously. He knew immediately the agenda behind my request and nodded as though we had agreed on one of our battle plans. He held back his smile until he made his last farewell but as soon as Ahmenmose left the room his face lit up. It had been his father, Ahmose's idea to bring Satiah along and although he hated to parade his sister amongst Egypt's elite he knew it would help her secure a suitable husband as their father wished. Satiah was now turning fourteen and they wished her to attract a husband soon and although he and his father dreamt it would be me that would choose her, they never truly thought it would happen. As a palace carriage saw them home Ahmenmose spoke to his sister of my invitation and just what this implied.

"Satiah, if he chooses you then you would be Queen," he gushed. "Imagine the life you would have *and* you would be the mother of his heir--the mother of a Pharaoh, Satiah. You would have memorials built to you!"

Satiah had no desire for such a life though. Memorials and such grandeur did not appeal to anything within her for she had other plans for her life. She was in love with a shepherd who lived nearby and walked past her home each day. They had never spoken but his tender smiles as she looked out her window at him were enough for her to imagine him a kind and gentle man. She spent most of her time in daydreaming that he would one day come and ask her father for her hand. The reality though was that this would never happen. A simple shepherd could never ask the daughter of a palace official to be his wife but this didn't stop her fantasies.

Satiah had no desire for the luxuries, titles or power that a royal marriage would afford her. She hated the way the upper classes painted and decorated themselves and she was happy to spend her days walking in the sunshine and her nights staring out to the stars. Her only ambition was to marry so that she would become a mother and could teach her children the beauty and simplicity of the natural world.

However Satiah also loved and respected her family. If they were to ask of her to consider a royal marriage then she must. So once Ahmenmose returned to his posting on the border she returned to the parties with another brother or a cousin. Her family had much at stake and they could not refuse my invitations to ensure they continued to be a respected and vital part of the military. They also all knew, Satiah included, that her continual attendance at my gatherings was no guarantee of a marriage offer and it was this one key factor that Satiah held onto. Satiah knew that it wasn't so much what she would do that would save her from my attention--but what she didn't do. While other women would continually find their way to my side she simply would not. Her hope was that another would soon distract me from my interests in her.

They didn't though and their clamouring and eyelash batting bored me senseless. Satiah's disinterest in seducing me and not acting like the other women only made her more of a delight. She would float around at a gathering until she found an intelligent conversation and would lose herself within it while other women fluttered from one group to another, tiring quickly and soon settling into small groups of equally shallow decorations, happy to discuss their clothing and gossip. Initially I was happy to just have her in the room with me but this soon was nowhere near enough.

So I used my right as host and Pharaoh to simply request that she be seated near me at dinner tables or invited her to sit beside me as we all watched a performance. She would do as I desired as she had no choice but to accept this most grand of invitations. Satiah would sit quietly and turn her head to watch others. I would initiate conversation and she would reply quite simply and turn her head down. No matter how shy she wanted to appear it became quite apparent that my feelings were not being reciprocated and this made me ache. I would lie in bed at night and pray that she would change. I even asked Arisina to perform a ritual to help her emotions for me blossom.

"Thutmose, you are Pharaoh, she cannot refuse you," she stated matter-of-factly.

I made her perform the ritual anyway. Neferure and Samreen playing out their love affair before me made the turmoil of my feelings even more acute. One night I was looking at the stars and heard their gentle moans as they made love in the room nearby and I started to cry.

Salas and I were writing in my rooms one evening and the wine flowed freely. We were soon well intoxicated and my tongue began to flow too. I opened up to Salas about my feelings and my heartache but his drunken state didn't give me the support or advice I was hoping for.

Instead he began to tease, "Oh mighty Pharaoh!" He fought to speak through his laughter, "You can make the Nile flood every year and yet you cannot make a woman love you." With this he dissolved into such a fit that he fell off his chair and continued howling on the floor holding his stomach.

"Salas, tonight you are no friend of mine," I said flatly and pushed him with my foot.

However even in his inebriated state he had managed to succinctly sum up what was at the core of my frustration. I had the power of a God, I commanded the greatest army in the world and yet I could not sway the heart of another. My beloved priestess and now my best friend would not provide me with any answers, so I decided to approach this in the only way that was clear to me in my drunken state. I would draw up a battle plan. I pulled a fresh piece of papyrus before me and dipped my quill in the ink. Salas' laughter was easing and grabbing the side of the table he pulled himself to his knees to see what I was doing.

"Oh, are you writing a love letter?" he slurred. "Declare your love mighty one! Use bird glyphs. Girls like birds."

At this we both laughed and my mood lightened. Then Salas did indeed help me form my plan. "Can she read?" he asked genuinely.

Something inside me clicked and I finally understood the key to the whole scenario.

"I don't know," I answered.

I didn't know anything about her truly. I knew her family, her name and her age. In all the times I sat her beside me I never asked anything to truly know her. This needed to change and I finally had the key to making Satiah warm to me. I lay down the quill and decided that the night should come to a close. A quick shout to my servants and they entered the room to find me blurry-eyed in my chair while Salas had now returned to his slump on the floor. He was in no condition to make it back to his home at the Great Temple and I told the servants to make him comfortable in one of the many rooms in my chambers.

As I watched him be carried away between two male servants I felt the calm rush of sleep begin to fill me and walked with heavy feet to my bedchamber. My body may have felt much weight but my mind was now light as I began to prepare for the final stages of acquiring my wife.

The next day I summoned Arisina, her secondary priests and Neferure. I announced my intentions to now approach Satiah's family and begin my formal courtship of their daughter. Arisina beamed and promised the support of my priests, and spoke of plans for prayers and rituals to bless the union. Neferure nodded her agreement, happy that soon the pressures and questions from her mother to produce an heir could be directed at another. I also like to believe that on some level she was happy for me to have my own true love. The next step now was to have someone visit Satiah's home to speak with her father and Arisina would carry out this duty. She was well prepared for this moment and planned to do so that very afternoon.

When they all eventually left I was bubbling with anticipation like a child in your times would as Christmas approached. I left my chambers and made my way to my army offices but I was too distracted to truly focus and when it was clear there were no urgent matters I excused myself to return to my chambers. I summoned a palace goldsmith and commissioned a necklace, bangle and earrings for Satiah, then I had a palace seamstress come to me and show me cloths; but I was now way out of my depth. I had Neferure sent for and she helped me choose something suitable. In fact this is where she shone.

"Oh not that colour Thutmose, that is a consort colour," she would cry. "A future queen should wear this," and she would unwind a length holding it across her body to show me its beauty.

This went on for two hours as Neferure cooed and sighed with her maids over swathe after swathe of material. It ended with a pile of cloths deemed suitable for Satiah, one that was unsuitable and a third chosen for some new outfits for Neferure. Just when I thought it was over Neferure presented another challenge to me, "What shoes have you ordered?" she quizzed.

So the palace shoesmith was summoned and after another two hours of samples and sketches I placed an order for a dozen new pairs of shoes for Satiah. This of course was supplemented by an order for twenty pairs from Neferure.

"Oh that was fun!" she clapped as the shoesmith left.

I was exhausted and yet she was bursting with energy. I was thankful that my attire had no scope for choice. I had battle wear and Pharaoh wear. My Pharaoh wear consisted of a casual uniform and a formal one for court and temple events. The Gods granted us men a much simpler life.

During this time Arisina met with Senemut to let him know of my intentions and that her responsibilities would now also involve overseeing the impending marriage. Of course his first duty was to run to Hatshepsut and inform her and as expected she was not happy. It was now a year since her formal request for Neferure and myself to procreate and there was no sign of any child. Any husband was well within his right to seek another wife and create the children he needed to support and carry on the family. She could do nothing to stop me and must now face the inevitable fact that no direct descendant of hers would ever claim the throne.

There was one last way she could try to intervene and that was to not approve of my new wife but Satiah's family held immense respect within the military and their influence upon our border troops and trade routes only made the marriage more appealing than not. It would serve Hatshepsut as much as an heir would. In fact Satiah's father, Ahmose, had been one of the tutors called upon when Neferure was being groomed for her role as queen and possible leader. To interfere with this union would betray alliances that she needed and had spent years building. It was perfect and horrible at the same time. Her only response was to slump in her chair and grunt.

So while Hatshepsut sat and wrapped her mind around the new union, Arisina set about finding Satiah's father to begin the business of marriage. Now in your days you tag yourselves with technology and such a meeting could be organised and planned within minutes. Not so in ancient Egypt. Arisina began by sending six scouts to the various places that she believed she would find Ahmose. They scattered across the palace and the city searching everywhere from the military rooms to his home and in-between. The scouts would all run as fast as they could scouring the corridors and streets as they ran. Occasionally they would stop to ask of others if they had seen the man and might change their route depending on the information gathered. One scout through his interviews was directed to Ahmose in the markets where he was surveying and buying goods. The scout stopped and rested his breathing as best he could before approaching Ahmose.

"Sire," he said as he stepped towards the man and bowed waiting to be given permission to speak. Ahmose looked at the man and within seconds recognised him as a palace scout and messenger. His first instinct that he carried serious military news was quickly replaced with the hope that it was indeed the beginning of marriage talks.

"Speak young man," Ahmose said formally.

"High Priestess Arisina requests a meeting with you this afternoon," the scout declared, his arms stiff by his side, looking straight ahead but not making eye contact.

"Certainly," he answered nervously as his delight began to sweep through him upon realising it must be about Satiah.

"She has asked that you return with me to the temple in order for this meeting to occur," the scout continued.

"Of course," Ahmose answered, "let us go now."

Ahmose turned forgetting that he was in the middle of a transaction and followed the scout. Together they returned to Arisina albeit at a much slower pace. The whole market watched as Ahmose followed the scout and without so much as one word of marriage being mentioned between the scout and the man in their brief conversation, the gossip of my impending marriage was begun.

The meeting with Arisina was brief and to the point. She simply stated that Pharaoh Thutmose had indeed stated his interest in making Satiah his most royal of wives and a queen. Formal courtship meetings would begin the following day unless Ahmose objected to the union. He had no choice but to agree, for to refuse would almost be akin to political and social suicide for himself and his family--besides what man would deny his daughter such a life. This sealed his family's position and security. His own bloodline would now be merged with that of the throne. This was the grandest of blessings that the Gods had granted to him and his rightful return of allegiance that he had shown to three Pharaohs. He stated his utmost pleasure at this offer and outwardly thanked the Gods in front of Arisina. Once the meeting was over Ahmose rushed home to share the news with his family.

Satiah did not join the rest of us in the excitement of the official news. Her father burst into their home that afternoon beaming and talking loud as he called out to her to join him and her mother in their salon.

"Satiah, sit down. I have a grand announcement to make," he shouted as her mother sat by his side looking nervous.

Once seated, he told them both the news and then repeated it as each of her brothers joined them. As their mood heightened Satiah's sank. They spoke of moving into palace apartments as would be expected, the jewels they would soon own and the military positions her brothers would now be guaranteed. Satiah though ached as she thought of all she would now lose. There would be no more simple walks by herself along the river. She would be forced to adorn herself with all the trinkets that a queen was expected to wear and learn all the rigid ways of palace behaviour. Then she thought of her shepherd now lost to her forever and the man who would replace him. She didn't hate me nor did she even dislike me or find me unattractive but she was scared of my power and could not imagine how she would spend the rest of her life with me.

The following night Satiah's family joined my family for a dinner to begin our promise to each other. It was the first time in months that the three of us, Hatshepsut, Neferure and myself were at a table together. That in itself was uncomfortable enough. The greetings as the family arrived were stiff and awkward, each one of them so self-conscious and Hatshepsut's rigid demeanour only making them more so. We were finally seated along the table, Hatshepsut at one end, myself at the other. I took Satiah by the hand and invited her to sit by me. She nodded and let her hand rest in mine as we walked towards the table. Her parents delighted to see this affection and headed to sit near Hatshepsut, leaving us younger ones to the other end of the table. Ahmose and

Hatshepsut soon entered an animated conversation reminiscing of her father and my grandfather. Satiah's brothers quizzed me on military matters and their brother's posting along the border. Neferure stayed quiet sipping wine and picking at her food looking amongst us all with great bemusement. Satiah kept her head down and silently ate.

I answered the boys questions politely and normally would have been swept up in their enthusiasm as I loved to talk of the army. However my plan to get to know Satiah was being delayed and each minute I didn't speak to her was more time I lost in having her attention and gathering her affections. Waiting for a suitable break in their questions I turned to her.

"Satiah, how was your day," I cringed inside at the lameness of my attempt to begin conversation.

She almost jumped as if I startled her, having managed to drift off into another world to escape her unease. "It was--ahh—wonderful--ahh--Your Highness," she stammered and looked back down to her plate.

"What did you do?" I continued. I was genuinely fascinated and this was the only way I would find out about her.

"Oh…" She looked back up surprised at the question and unsure how to answer, "well--I always like to walk in the morning."

"Where do you walk?" I asked.

"I go to the riverside and look at the water," she said quietly and blushed.

From the corner of my eye I could see her mother watching us nervously hoping that her daughter was addressing me correctly. Her father was still too involved in conversation with Hatshepsut and her brothers were now also being entertained by their stories. Neferure though was watching me, sipping her wine with one eyebrow raised and smirking. She was thoroughly entertained with watching me court the young woman.

"What of your afternoons?" I kept on with my interrogation.

"Um--well this afternoon Mother and I went to temple to pray," she answered a bit more comfortably.

Her mother had prayed for the evening to be fruitful while Satiah prayed quietly for the strength to see her through this and not let her family down.

I continued on with a few more questions that she answered simply, never embellishing or asking any questions back. I now knew she walked along the river daily, her favorite God was Isis, and she couldn't read but was learning to. My plan was all coming along fine. With our eating done Hatshepsut led the way to a lounge area and we entered the formal procedures of the evening. Arisina and Senemut were called in and Satiah and her family were formally asked for their agreement to marriage with me. Her father's was the only answer we needed and once this was received and witnessed Arisina let the family know the events that would now occur.

The family would be moved into a royal apartment of the palace and begin their integration into palace life. This allowed Satiah to be close by to begin her training to become my wife. A wedding date was set for six months time. Satiah's father was thanked for his agreement to the union with a gift of money to begin his family tomb and to have his name recorded in the Karnak temple scrolls and a statue made. Tears began to fall down Ahmose's face as Arisina continued. Ahmenmose would remain in his elite position and upon the marriage receive a promotion in the army to become a senior general. The two younger brothers could begin their training to become officers as soon as the family moved into the palace. Satiah had indeed brought great fortune upon her family and hearing all this spoken so formally made her realise just what honour she brought to her family as well. Her father's tears were the most powerful reminder of all.

With the formalities agreed upon the family stood and farewells were made after plans for another dinner the following week had been decided. Satiah walked towards me and bowed, thanking me for the honour we would give her family but no mention of the honour that she would receive. I simply nodded and any words that I had planned to compliment her company at dinner were lost. Soon there was just Hatshepsut, Neferure, myself and the two priests remaining.

"My goodness," gasped Hatshepsut, "she is a bit timid for a queen don't you think Thutmose? I don't believe I saw her eyes once the whole night. They were glued to the floor!"

I didn't answer her as this was quite typical of her to throw her criticism over something that wasn't her doing. Instead I did something quite unprecedented in our relationship. I turned to Hatshepsut and addressed her with authority.

"There is one more matter that this marriage arrangement needs to address," I stated loudly and clearly. "Upon my marriage to Satiah I will release Neferure from her marriage with me."

Hatshepsut's jaw dropped not just for what I said but also for how I said it. I kept my eyes firmly upon hers and Neferure was delighting in watching me stand my ground. She adopted the same expression as me and locked her eyes upon her mother also. Hatshepsut looked from me to her daughter and in a split second she finally understood the alliance that we had made.

"Fine," she spat as she stood from her chair. "Live the lives you wish but if either of you act in anyway to injure this family's rule or the empire then I will enter into your lives with all the wrath of Osiris."

I returned to my chambers rejoicing my impending marriage and divorce, as well as an immense amount of pride at having stood up to Hatshepsut. I drifted to sleep with a smile on my face while across town my bride-to-be cried herself to sleep.

# CHAPTER EIGHT

The year of my marriage to Satiah was my eighth year as Pharaoh and I was eighteen years old. My beautiful bride was nearing fifteen, which may seem very young to you. However given that the ancient Egyptian life ended somewhere between fifty and sixty years of age even for those with good health it makes perfect sense for a woman to enter into marriage and begin having children as soon as she was capable. It allowed for the reasonable maturity of your children to care for you in your old age as well as for them to be of mature enough age to succeed you should you be Pharaoh. Neferure was now twenty-four, a somewhat serious age to be now single again, but she had her lover and now the freedom from her mother so she was beyond content.

Hatshepsut was now forty-two. She was well on the verge of middle age and beginning to ease into old age and she knew it. At times she would look at the four years she already had as Pharaoh and was grateful to have been allowed this time but then she would remember that she was not truly sole leader and that she could have had the throne years ago had it not been for my father being born. Then the hatred and anger would boil inside her. Her children were now grown and independent. In fact her plans to throw us together had allowed us to combine our strength and stand up to her. She had all the power she could ever wish for yet she had isolated herself. Hatshepsut's only true allies now were Senemut and Ma-Keet and the more she turned to them, the more power they gained. The three of them played together well and left me alone so I in turn left them alone.

I continued on with my beloved army. It was a peaceful time for Egypt thanks to the campaigns of my grandfather and father. Hatshepsut and I utilised this prosperity. She began some of the most amazing buildings the world will ever see while I trained and built up our army into an enormous machine.

I interacted with as many of my soldiers as I could sensing those with talents beyond wielding a sword and sent them to train directly with the generals. They would learn battle plans, tactics and most importantly the politics of the region. Some would return back to the soldiers as physical leaders with renewed vigour to inspire, others would stay as intellectual leaders and receive the knowledge of our aging generals. The old and new enjoyed interacting and at times creating animated debates. It was all in great fun and allowed the army to grow.

So my military and political life was fine and prosperous. My personal life was another matter. Within a month of our formal dinner with Satiah's family they were all moved into one of the royal apartments within the palace. There was much bustle in the days preceding their arrival with cleaning and furniture being arranged. I would arrive each day to make sure all was going well and my presence would incite even more activity as servants panicked upon my entrance. Some days Neferure would join me clucking and giving advice and other days Hatshepsut would call in too. No matter her personal feelings she would not let our family reputation nor that of the palace be tarnished by having any aspect of this marriage ill-handled.

The day Satiah moved into the rooms was amongst the proudest of my life. I stood by the doors beaming as her family all walked along the corridor towards their new rooms. Satiah walked behind her parents with her head down as always but as they approached her mother seeing me stepped to the side, grabbed her daughter's arm and pushed her to the front.

"Look Satiah," she whispered, "The Pharaoh has come to greet you."

Satiah looked up and she feigned a smile but it was short lived and her eyes looked down again. She was soon in front of me and I reached out to take her hand. Satiah gently placed her hand in mine as she bowed. I lifted her hand and gently kissed it. I still don't know how or why I did this except that I was totally carried away by finally having her at the palace with me. There was a moment of shock from those around me and I believe a few even gasped. Satiah, who had never had any form of physical affection from a man, took a quick breath and looked up at me. I know the minute our eyes met something inside her opened up to me so I have never regretted my action in the slightest.

Keeping Satiah's hand in mine I led her into what would be her home for the months before our marriage. I walked with her, talking loudly and quickly, pointing out all the different things in the apartment from the new curtains to the statues of Gods I had commissioned to protect her and her family. I talked so much and was so busy making sure I left out no detail of the tour that I didn't even realise that she was smiling and taking in every feature as I described it. The objects and decorations were not what made her smile though. In that short time as I walked, gushing over all the things I had organised just for her, I did more to win her love than I had in the months leading to this moment.

I finally led her to her bedchamber where her new clothes were all laid out upon the bed, while her new shoes were lined up on the floor. Satiah's hand slipped out of mine and I let her go imagining that she wished to examine her new wardrobe. She walked towards the bed but it was not the clothes that she went to see. Satiah made her way to a small table beside the bed and stopped. There upon the table was a statue of her beloved Isis that I had commissioned especially for her. It was exquisite, made of solid gold and I had even allowed some of my precious gems from my birth gifts to be used on it. She gently reached out and stroked Isis gold hair, mesmerised by it.

"Do you like it?" I asked, "I know you love Isis so I had her made especially for you."

"She is mine?" Satiah asked gently still looking at the statue, with her back to me.

"Yes, my first wedding gift to you," I answered smiling.

Satiah turned and gave me the first of many smiles I would have from her. Her eyes were glistening with tears. "She is truly beautiful Thutmose," she said softly. "I will treasure her always."

My heart almost exploded not just to see her smile but to know that I created something that touched her heart so much. Even more so was hearing her say my name for the first time, no longer addressing me as Pharaoh or Sire. All my praying and all my fussing to set up her home had all been worth it.

A short cough behind me made me turn. There stood Arisina with my two guards. I had been so caught in the excitement of sharing this new home with my beloved that I had forgotten that my entourage and in fact the rest of her family would have been trailing behind us the entire time.

"Sire, it is inappropriate for any man to be in the bedchamber of a virgin regardless of his intentions to marry her or his standing as Pharaoh," she said bluntly and with this she turned in the doorway, gesturing for me to exit.

"Satiah, my beloved I shall leave you now," I said. "Enjoy your new home and I shall see you at dinner."

I turned to leave but stopped. I walked back to Satiah and taking her hand once again raised it to my lips. We shared once last smile as I looked into her eyes and as I walked out a blush swept across Satiah's cheeks.

The next few months of what you would call our engagement were very different for us both. Satiah had to learn and grow accustomed to palace life and her new role. I had been lucky in that I had grown up in the palace and all was second nature to me. Also being Pharaoh meant that if I didn't always follow protocol then people just had to accept the fact and fall inline with my behaviour. Not that this happened so often with me; pushing boundaries and testing people was more Hatshepsut's way.

Satiah though had to learn the new manners and quickly. Arisina oversaw her training and tutelage. This consisted of daily prayers to guide the new queen-to-be. Ladies-in-waiting or high servants would then teach her how to dress and present herself. Even though she would have maids to dress her she still needed to know what was expected to ensure they were doing their duties correctly. Satiah started to attend court sessions with myself, Neferure and of course Hatshepsut. These bored her rigid, as they did everyone but Hatshepsut, and the sooner she learnt to adjust to the boredom the better.

Neferure enjoyed having a new playmate not least because Satiah's arrival had been another key to her freedom. She rewarded Satiah by having her join her on shopping expeditions and advising her on behaviour, especially in how to deal with Hatshepsut. In fact one night we both did just that although it did end up being more just Neferure and myself re-telling stories and gossip about Hatshepsut while we laughed. Satiah sat and listened to us, mostly shocked at our disrespect but often joining in on the mirth.

Hatshepsut seemed pleased with Satiah's progress. Not that she would ever admit to it; we would just need to assume this through her lack of criticism or interference. The truth was that as long as we didn't get in the way with her rulings or cause her embarrassment she wasn't that fussed with anything we did.

The day of my marriage arrived amid blistering heat and we all piled on our regalia and finery to celebrate. All the royal entourages of myself, Hatshepsut, Neferure and now Satiah met at the grand entrance courtyard of the palace. Satiah and I sat upon sedans and were raised by the bearers to be carried side by side to lead the procession. Hatshepsut and Neferure followed us in sedans also, and then my mother and Satiah's family on foot behind us. Guards flanked us all as we made our spectacular way through the streets to the greater temple at Karnak.

The procession continued into the enormous main hall of the largest temple where before the grand altar sat two thrones waiting for my bride and I. Guests including relatives of both families, visiting dignitaries and wealthy traders were scattered throughout the temple and they all bowed as we made our way past them. Arisina and Senemut stood at the altar with a legion of other priests behind and to their side ready to assist. As soon as everyone was settled they began to chant loudly and fan the already lit incense. The chanting seemed to go on forever but we all knew it was necessary to summon the Gods so that they would protect and bless our marriage.

The heat was suffocating, or maybe it was the crowds of people surrounding us as the clouds of incense smoke filled the temple. I heard Satiah sigh next to me as she drew a deep breath and I reached across to hold her hand as it rested upon the arm of her chair. I quickly dared to glance sideways to check on her and saw she kept her eyes closed. I imagined she was silently saying her own prayers and gently squeezed her hand. A very gentle squeeze in return was the only acknowledgement she would show me. She had indeed taken her training seriously.

Three hours later the rituals were complete including those to recognise and pray for the new Queen. Once more we were lifted in our sedans and the procession made its way back to the palace; this time with the addition of all the guests as well. We were taken to the great dining hall where everyone feasted for the afternoon and well into the night. Dancers, musicians and magicians entertained us. Deals were struck in quiet corners while new romances or affairs were created in other places. The noise and movement was relentless, yet Satiah and I remained in place observing it all.

Finally the time came when my wife and I should leave the party and begin our married life. I was indeed tired as was Satiah and all who had been part of the entire day. Arisina and Senemut approached us at the table and simply nodded their heads, signalling that it was time for us to head to our private chambers. Servants helped us from our chairs and as we rose from the table so did all within the room. There was finally quiet in the room as we walked out led by the two priests and followed by our mothers. Each guest bowed their head as we passed by them. We walked through the doors and they were closed quickly behind us. As we continued on the corridor the sound of music and chatter once again filled the dining hall. Our small party though remained silent as we walked to my chambers.

On entering my chambers Arisina took Satiah and her mother in to the bedchamber while I remained in the salon with Senemut and my mother. Servants were waiting in the bedchamber making sure the bed was ready and they assisted Arisina in undressing Satiah and bathing her. When Satiah was clean of all the gold dust, kohl and sweat from the day they lay her in the wedding bed naked. Arisina took a bottle of rose oil and gently drizzled it over Satiah's pubic area and upper thighs. She then gently smoothed it over her skin and through the wisps of hair that Satiah had protecting her womanhood.

"Your Highness, you need to part your legs," Arisina said gently.

Satiah did so and clenched her teeth. Part of her training had been to prepare her for this night so she knew what was about to occur and she was petrified. Arisina poured some more oil into her left hand and now rubbed this along the folds between Satiah's legs and into the crevasses. When she felt there was enough she returned the bottle to a table beside the bed, in case I should need more during the proceedings. Then with her left hand again she touched Satiah's forehead, then mouth, throat, upper chest, solar plexus, belly and pubis. As she touched each spot she recited a different God's name, asking for their blessing upon her deflowering and to make her womb fruitful.

When she was done Arisina drew a sheet over Satiah and bowed. Satiah's mother stood nearby crying as she watched the priestess and now she stepped forward and kissed her daughter gently on the forehead before leaving. Arisina and the servants followed swiftly behind her leaving Satiah lying stiffly in the bed with only the soft flicker of a lamp in the room with her. It seemed an eternity until I joined her yet not long enough.

In the meantime I too was being undressed and bathed. A simple kilt was wrapped around my waist so that I could walk and enter the bedchamber with some dignity. As the women walked back through my salon Arisina nodded to Senemut before they continued out into the corridor. I saw the nod and knew that my bride was ready.

I was expecting Senemut to dismiss himself and let me make my way to my bed but instead he stepped before me. In his hand he held his own bottle of rose oil. He poured some into his hand and handed the bottle to a servant. As he rubbed the oil into both his palms he gestured to another servant.

"Lift the front of his skirt," he ordered.

The servant did so exposing me and just as quickly Senemut reached down and slathered my genitals in the oil. Let's just say if you want to kill any romance in a situation get some guy you hate to rub your genitals with oil. Thankfully this was over quickly and as he pulled his hands away he looked me in the eye and delivered some advice.

"Enter her slowly to cause the least pain," he said frankly, "but don't be too slow else you will prolong her inevitable discomfort."

Ah, such wonderful cold advice. It made me wonder of his skills in Hatshepsut's bed. He walked me to the bedchamber doors and opened them. Standing to the side Senemut bowed and I walked past him to see Satiah lying in the bed. Her nervousness was obvious even at a distance and in lamplight.

The doors closed behind me and we were alone. I made my way to the opposite side of the bed and slipped under the sheet beside her. My first glimpse of her skin soon wiped any memory of Senemut's handling of me and my body responded. Satiah kept her eyes straight ahead at the ceiling as I fumbled to pull my skirt off and throw it out of the bed. I slid beside her and she jumped as I placed my hand upon her belly. I gently kissed her cheek and whispered sweet assurances to her. I repeated my love to her and promised I would never hurt her.

My body now was aching with all the impatience of my young hormones and I slowly lifted myself over her. Diligently she opened her legs so that I was now lying between them but she jumped as she felt my hardness push against her. I kept whispering as I slowly entered her but all the affection and oil in the world was not going to make this any less painful for her. I may have well sliced her with a knife. Her face tightened with the pain but I persisted knowing that it should subside as she opened up. It didn't though and when I saw a tear fall down the side of her face I pulled out and drew her into my arms apologising. I too had tears as I was horrified to have hurt her and we fell asleep with my arms wrapped around her.

The next day the bloodied sheets were taken to show the priests and Satiah was now fully accepted as Queen. Our relationship would need a bit more work though. I was upset that our first night had not been as pleasurable as it should have been. I didn't even empty any seed into her so despite the bloodied sheets it hadn't truly been successful. I had even had my consorts return to my bedchamber in the months of our engagement to practice. However women who had been trained for pleasure were very different to a woman who had been trained for breeding. Satiah had been taught that sex was a duty to be performed for me with the goal of creating a child. Despite her yearnings to become a mother she believed there was no element of pleasure in the act.

My interactions with the consorts and the stolen moments overhearing Neferure and Samreen make love had me craving this more sensual interaction with Satiah. Over the initial weeks of our marriage we continued and Satiah suffered less pain. I was finally able to place my seed within her but the act remained mechanical. I interspersed nights with Satiah with nights with the consorts hoping this would help me understand more but it didn't change anything. I finally decided to consult someone who should not only be knowledgeable but owed me a favour--Neferure.

Neferure's chambers were no longer adjacent to mine as these rooms were reserved for my queen. As happy as we both were to have moved on from our marriage we both did miss each other's company as we used to share it. I sent a special invitation for her to join me after dinner one night and she was glad to see it was just myself when she arrived.

"Oh a private audience--I do feel special. I just hope you aren't planning to beg me back to your marriage bed!" she teased, somewhat ironically given why I wanted to talk to her.

She sat herself on a lounge and I began speaking. Neferure listened intently as I opened up but as I confided more and more I saw her eyebrows rise higher and higher. I was just about to say something further when she started shaking her head and raised her hand to stop me.

"Stop, stop, stop!" she cried and looked at me incredulously. "Please tell me that you don't just dive upon her?"

I stopped and couldn't answer. *"What else was I supposed to do?"* I thought to myself. My hesitancy was answer enough for Neferure.

"Oh dear, Thutmose!" she now raised her voice, "Have your consorts taught you nothing?"

Now I was confused. Just what were the consorts meant to teach me? The Gods themselves knew I had continued on with them seeking some means of revelation but to no avail.

"Well what do you mean by that?" I replied just as loudly.

She continued on a bit gentler, leaning forward, "Thutmose, your consorts, they do more in bed than just--umm--*receive* you? Yes?"

"Well, yes of course," I said.

"Maybe then you could consider treating your wife in the manner that the consorts treat you," she said this with a smile on her face.

I sat and looked down at the floor still not quite grasping what Neferure was trying to convey to me and she could tell.

"Thutmose, your consorts are trained to pleasure you and in doing so many of them learn to receive pleasure for themselves in the act," she continued with a chuckle. "I dare say your little virgin has never been told of or shown the more enjoyable aspects of sex."

"Does Samreen do such things for you?" I asked, my curiosity now peaking.

Neferure burst into laughter. "Indeed he does," she beamed. "Why else would I have him return to my bed!" She continued laughing but I was now very serious about finding out what I needed to do.

"Tell me what he does," I said almost demanding it.

Neferure sat back in her chair and cleared her throat. She sighed and looked away as though she was slipping into a daydream. After another sigh she closed her eyes and began reciting a description of all the things Samreen would do to and with her. I sat riveted by her descriptions, sometimes wishing for more detail, and my loins began to stir at the prospect of trying some of them out. Neferure was soon finished and let out another sigh.

"Ahh…" she sighed and then giggled. "Now I wish I had summoned him tonight."

I had been leaning forward the whole time soaking up the information and now I sat back in my chair as my mind raced. Neferure rose and said her goodbyes satisfied that she had helped me sufficiently. I muttered a "thank you" and barely noticed her leaving.

I immediately called upon my most talented consort to join me in my bedchamber for a practice session. I tried most of Neferure's suggestions and soon my consort was moaning. Afterwards we both lay breathing heavily and I was almost tempted to head straight to Satiah's private bedchamber to begin with her. However I knew she would not be ready for my visit and that wonderful post-coital sleep began to wash over me. Well sleep did try to work its way on me--but the tempting hand of my consort making its way down my belly soon had me wide awake and another practice session was soon underway!

The following night I requested Satiah to join me in bed and all began as we normally did. Her maids prepared her for bed and breeding while my servants did so for me. I walked into the bedchamber as usual to find her lying stiffly and staring at the ceiling. The bottle of rose oil still sat upon the bedside table, as much a part of the ritual as the bed beneath us.

I climbed into bed with the rush that lifting the sheet always gave me but tonight it was even stronger. I slid across to Satiah and she opened her legs ready to for me mount her as she expected. Instead I remained by her side and started my new repertoire. My hand began and was soon followed by my mouth as I explored her body. I didn't quite get the moans of my consort but I was grateful for the few gasps and sighs that I heard. My nights with Satiah would never be quite like those with a consort but thankfully they stopped being the mechanical ritual of our first month of marriage.

Our nights together would soon be no more because as expected Satiah became pregnant. In a royal marriage every month that passes without the announcement of an impending birth raises questions as to the fertility of those concerned, the success of the marriage itself and the fate of the throne. We both felt this pressure and Satiah's tears would flow each month as her menstruation began and the priests and I were made aware that no pregnancy had been achieved. Prayers and rituals continued along with sex of course. When it reached the sixth month of our marriage and another menstruation began all these elements had their frequency increased and success was finally reached.

When Satiah had reached her fiftieth day without bleeding the physicians and priests declared her pregnant. A great ritual was held at the main temple to celebrate and bless the new child. We prayed for its protection and that it should be a boy to become Pharaoh and rule. I watched over all this with my mother by my side and imagined what her ceremony had been like when she was declared pregnant with me. I wondered how my father had felt and for the first time in years his memory brought tears to my eyes.

The months of Satiah's pregnancy seemed to go on forever, as does the time of every first pregnancy for the parents. Satiah would remain in her chambers at night, as a pregnant royal woman was considered sacred and untouchable. I would visit her each day and again before I retired. My army duties still required my attention and short times away from the palace were rewarded with an even more noticeable growth in the child. I delighted in her rising stomach, picturing our child within it.

Satiah's days were filled with bathing, praying and preparing for the birth. Her personal excitement at finally becoming a mother made her glow more each day. All who saw her believed the child to be strong and prosperous by the very nature of the pregnancy. She attended prayer rituals diligently and listened to advice from the midwives fervently. I do believe no other royal wife would ever have been as prepared as Satiah was for birth and motherhood.

Much of this preparation was kept from me as was expected. I did not need to know of placentas, contractions or umbilical cords. A Pharaoh just needed to know that the qualified people would attend the birth and he would arrive to the birthing room and have a clean, healthy child handed to him. I am glad though that I was able to share with Satiah her preparations for the nursery and commission the myriad of God statues that were needed.

One day close to the end of the pregnancy I sat and watched her fussing about the nursery placing the final statues that had just arrived. She seemed quieter than usual when doing this and I asked if she was feeling alright. Satiah dropped her head and started to wring her hands.

"If this child is not male what shall become of it?" she said and her lip began to tremble.

"She will be a grand princess," I stated honestly. "She will be no less loved than a male."

Tears fell from Satiah's eyes as she looked up at me and nodded.

"Satiah, we will have other children. One is certain to be male and take the throne," I continued, as though this was already fact. "They will all be loved as much as the other."

"Yes, Thutmose," she smiled. "We will have many wonderful children."

I replayed that conversation as I drifted to sleep that night. I felt that a son was about to arrive but no one could be certain until he was delivered. Even if a son was born that was no reason for me to relax and assume my lineage was secured. Infant mortality, disease, even a possible assassination could quickly rob me of my child and successor. Satiah's desire for children could soon make sure that there were others but a woman had physical limits on producing children. The risks of childbirth also meant I could lose my beloved with each attempt. No matter how much I loved Satiah I required a second wife. Indeed you could call her a back up and this all seems so cold, but you must understand that from my birth I was trained to ensure my family retained power. It was as second nature to me as it is to any of you reading this to protect and nurture your own families.

It actually would have been considered somewhat unusual if I did not take another wife. A pharaoh was expected to have several for the very reason that I intended. Of course now I would have to once again consider a woman for this role. I had no intention of falling in love with another the way that I had with Satiah in that moment when I first met her. In fact, I could never feel for another woman they way I felt about Satiah. This new union would be a simple one, made with clear intentions and purely for the purpose of insuring my bloodline. I would not begin anything though until after the birth of my first child. I would enjoy the build up to their arrival with no distractions other than my ordinary duties.

Satiah went into labour a bit sooner than was expected. In fact she was two weeks short of full term. This in itself set about some worry for the child as showing their nature as impulsive. My beloved Arisina would oversee the birth as she had mine. She was summoned from the daily sunrise ritual at the great lake at Karnak by a palace messenger and told that labour had begun. Concerned by the pains coming so soon she called for a carriage, not willing to risk the time it would take to walk and almost ran through the palace corridors to the birthing room. Her anxiety at the early birth helped to distract her from thinking about the blood she was about to see and she entered the room as confident as she could.

She walked through the doors of the birthing room just as a contraction subsided and Satiah fell back against the pillows. Arisina had not overseen a royal birth since mine and the memories of that day flooded back to her. It all felt so familiar as though she had almost stepped back into that very day. Arisina stepped towards the bed and bowed.

"Madam, I am at your service. We all have an immense duty to fulfil and I shall summon the Gods to guide and protect us," she said strongly.

Satiah nodded, comforted to see the priestess had arrived, and now all the people who were required were within the birthing room. Satiah's faith in the Gods was much greater than that of the midwives despite their skills being far more important than the burning of incense. Satiah's mother Ipu was wiping her daughter's brow and felt her relax. Not that my wife was particularly scared or anxious. She had been warned of the pain and knew it was necessary. Satiah also wished it was all over and she was holding her child.

Arisina retreated to her corner, began the chanting and lit the incense.

She recalled how my birth had begun in less than favourable circumstances and then the wonderful success with which I arrived. She smiled and thanked Amun for showing her this memory as a sign for the day ahead. Arisina also had the grace to turn and share this sign with my beloved. As a huge grin swept across Satiah's face another contraction began and somehow it didn't seem to hurt so much.

In my chambers my morning also began with the news that Satiah had begun labour. I fought every instinct to run to the birthing room and force my way in but instead I did as I was expected and walked to court. I sat as my father had on the day I was born and waited. Hatshepsut and Neferure were there too, waiting as anxiously as I. We discussed court matters but I could not concentrate on anything. Every so often a messenger would arrive to tell us all was well but that no child was born yet. Hatshepsut babbled constantly and I wanted to yell at her to shut up and then run to Satiah but I couldn't. So I remained still, spoke when I was addressed and prayed for good news to arrive.

The birth continued on at a fast pace. Satiah rapidly moved into the final stages, remaining calm and strong, which impressed everyone present. A timid lover and wife she may have been, but approaching motherhood had brought out the lioness within. She listened intently to the midwives, joined Arisina in her chanting and let out screams as she felt she needed to. The midday heat was now hitting the room hard but each scream from Satiah's lips seemed to summon a breeze through the windows. Arisina smiled as she recognized the raw power of a woman giving birth to call upon the Gods over that of some incense smoke. Amun had been called with a most powerful voice by the one who needed him most in this moment. The speed and passion in which Satiah was pushing the birth along gave my beloved priestess no time to think of blood as she mentally pieced together a magnificent birth story for my child.

Within the next hour Satiah was upon the birthing chair with everyone, including Arisina, gathered close by. Satiah knew now that she was so close to birth and a fire lit in her eyes. Instinctively she grabbed the arms of the birthing chair making her knuckles white and breathed deep as she anticipated the next band of tightness to strike her womb. The midwives cried to her to push but she began before she even heard them. A rapid succession of contractions followed, like none that the midwives or Arisina had ever witnessed. Within minutes of that first push our gorgeous, beautiful, wonderful son was born and Satiah's last screams of labour were replaced by the cries of our first-born.

Her happiness and excitement at seeing a healthy noisy baby made her cry with relief. In fact it wasn't until Arisina brought it to her attention that she realised that she had in fact delivered a son.

"A son!" she wept. "My Thutmose has a son!"

"Yes Madam," Arisina smiled. "You have given our Pharaoh an heir."

Satiah was so lost in the stupor of such an achievement that Arisina and the midwives continued on with the last details of the birth in a blur around her.

Satiah did not hear the comments from the midwife to Arisina that the placenta was "pink". She may not even have realised what this may have meant--but for Arisina it took a shine off the celebration. The priestess looked at Satiah holding what was a perfectly healthy baby. The colour of the placenta as some omen seemed to mean nothing as she watched their joy and she knew I would be crushed to hear of it. Many a priestess had added details to birth stories to comfort a Pharaoh before. She didn't see how leaving such a detail out was to be any different.

So nineteen years after she had walked the corridors to announce to my father that I was born, now Arisina walked to tell me of my son's birth. She thanked the Gods that at her age now she had been spared a tortuous or long birth as she fatigued somewhat quicker these days. She breathed away some giddiness from seeing some blood in the final stages and smiled as she imagined my face when she made the announcement. In fact she felt tears begin at the honour of announcing yet another birth of a Pharaoh and to someone she loved so much. As before she was greeted along the way and returned the inevitable questions with a nod and a smile. She arrived at the court doors and they were swept open as she approached and two guards walked her in announcing her obvious arrival. At the sight of Arisina walking through the doors I leapt forward in my throne.

"Stay seated! Remember your position!" Hatshepsut turned to me and spat through clenched teeth.

I remained forward in my chair. I could feel my heart racing and my breath quickened as Arisina approached us. She seemed to take forever and there were murmurs and movement through the court as people gathered to also hear the news. The priestess continued towards us and made her way up the few stairs to stand directly before us. She bowed to each of us in turn and I thought I would explode with anticipation. Then she turned to me and uttered the words that I was aching to hear.

"Pharaoh Thutmose, Queen Satiah has given birth to a son," she said clearly and loudly and bowed once again. She didn't need to bow again but she needed to hide the smile she couldn't hold back at catching a glimpse of the envy clearly visible on Hatshepsut's face.

With those words I began to cry from every fibre in me. My body shook as I leaned forward and sobbed. Everything was now made right. All that my father had raised me to be would now be honoured. The lineage had been corrected and no matter how much longer Hatshepsut kept me from being sole leader she could never stop my son from his rightful place. The next generation had been created and my son was its leader. The tears continued and I didn't care who saw them or what gossip arose. My beloved Satiah had helped me make things right and I thanked the Gods for sending her to me.

Hatshepsut remained still and silent beside me. I imagined she was horrified at my crying but as always her mind raced at calculating how this affected her. There was now the solid reality that no direct heir of hers would ever take the throne. She took small consolation in the fact that it was still her father's bloodline but she would never have the joy of passing on her title to another. She became aware of my weeping and was suitably appalled but not surprised and she sniggered, recalling my father's emotive character.

Neferure rose from her chair as she saw my tears subside and walked over to me. Planting an ever-so-gentle kiss on my cheek and squeezing my hand she murmured her congratulations into my ear. This calmed me even more and as she straightened to walk away I looked past her to Hatshepsut. Our eyes locked and I felt the silent fury of our competition that was once again burning inside her. My red eyes refused to look away. She would now have to also congratulate me in front of everyone present. This I knew would be one of the hardest things she ever had to do and that only added to the sweetness of hearing her utter the words. We continued our stand off for several seconds and when it became apparent that I would not turn away she opened her mouth.

"Thutmose, dear son, our family is honoured that you have given Egypt an heir," she said barely above a whisper, with her chin pointing to me.

Only those upon the podium area would have heard the words but all saw that she had said something. So it was noted by those present that Pharaoh Hatshepsut had indeed given her well wishes to her son on the birth of his first child.

Arisina was given a stool to sit before me and as she had done for my father so now she sat and recounted the story of my son's birth. My tears flowed again as each sign and stage was told to me and my heart ached to finally see my wife and child. Soon enough Arisina rose and announced it was time to meet my son. Hatshepsut had every right to attend with me but I wished that she wouldn't.

It was almost as though she read my mind for as I stood her heavy voice began, "I shall meet the child soon enough. There is still business to be done today and the empire cannot stop for the arrival of a child," she declared as she smoothed her skirt.

I did not answer her but exited the courtrooms grateful for her absence. Once we were well away my mood lightened. I gestured for Arisina to walk beside me and began to ask questions. I wanted to know whether she thought my son beautiful, did he remind her of me when I was born and had Satiah asked for me. She answered them all patiently and with positive, glowing terms. It may have appeared that she was playing the diplomat but she sincerely wanted this day to be as special for me as my birth was for my father.

We arrived at the freshly cleaned room and a waft of scented oils rose up as the doors opened. Satiah was sitting up in bed glowing and smiling despite what she had been through. She was only tender now having torn minimally and a soothing bath had refreshed her. Her excitement at my arrival was not at all hidden and she sat even straighter as I entered and ran to her. I grabbed her as she sat in bed, almost lifting her out of the sheets and indeed did start to cry yet once again. Just as quickly I let her go and turned to the crib beside the bed where Arisina stood.

"Your Highness, here lies your son." she gestured and bowed as I walked towards him.

No parent forgets their first glimpse of any of their children. This moment was like that but magnified for this was not just my child but also a future king. He was the saviour of my family lineage and he was the product of my love for Satiah and her love for me. As I leant over him and saw his face for the first time everything I had felt at the announcement in the court, the pride, the love and the protectiveness that came so instinctively was now sealed. There were no more tears to be shed as I looked upon him. Now I was simply in awe of this precious little being that I had created.

Arisina stepped close to the crib and gently lifted him from his bed. He was bound tightly with just his face showing but I could see the movement within his bindings and I smiled at his vigour. He was gently placed in my arms and despite never having held a child before I instinctively cradled him and pulled him close to me. My son opened his eyes and he appeared to measure me for a brief moment. I smiled down at him as he gently closed his eyes and returned to sleep. I wanted this moment over and over, with a hundred more children. As each of my children arrived, that first embrace was always what I treasured most.

Finally I turned back to Satiah smiling, "He is the grandest child that was ever born," I declared and we both laughed.

# CHAPTER NINE

My first-born was named Amenemhat in a grand ceremony held the following month at Karnak. He bellowed and kicked the entire time impatient for the warm breast of his wet nurse and her sweet milk. The priests and officials all moved a bit faster to bring the ceremony towards its close as soon as they could. No matter how small a child is, their cries of hunger can dominate a room of people ten times their size. The officials, diplomats and visitors all came to see him in my arms and give their gifts but there were no lingering glances as they backed away as fast as possible. I often wished I could manifest the power of a child's cry at battle. We would drive back the enemy's forces in no time at all.

Satiah recovered quickly from the birth with a vitality that surprised all. The newfound strength that had emerged during her labour did not wane and she walked taller and spoke stronger. After all she was now the mother of a future Pharaoh. She also revelled in the joy of having a child and the love he had brought into her life. So much so that she returned of her own volition to my bed eager to create more children. A year later our first daughter, Beketamun was also born and a princess balanced our prince.

All in the palace celebrated Satiah's fertility as my lineage was now well-established. The rapidity in which Beketamun followed Amenemhat also showed we had a healthy and strong marriage. However no matter how fertile or successful our relationship was I would still have to consider another wife. I met with Arisina to discuss with her my intentions.

"Do you wish to take one of your consorts as royal wife?" she asked.

My answer to this was no. None of them felt suitable in either their character or background. I had three consorts that had been chosen for me and tended to me for the past six years. They were all daughters of Syrian diplomats sent as peace offerings and to generate good will with a somewhat tempestuous neighbour. They served their positions well but I wanted a woman of Egyptian blood who was born respecting our ways and not transplanted into the palace as a political move. This would require some searching and screening by those around me. The parties that Neferure and I held as teenagers were now a thing of the past as we both matured. I was more interested in spending time with my family and the army rather than socialising. The very fact that this new wife would be found through those around me would also establish the marriage as one merely of duty and hopefully draw someone who would understand this.

So after Arisina and the priests were told I also gathered the palace butlers. My butlers were the uppermost of my servants. In fact they were not servants at all. They were of high breeding, their families having served and held positions of great importance for generations. My butlers oversaw my needs, directing servants and ensuring that all my daily requests were executed smoothly. They were like extensions of me, anticipating my every desire before I even needed to ask. If anyone should know the sort of woman who would be suitable--these men would know.

As it was my chief butler, Tati, knew of a young woman who would indeed be fitting. On the outskirts of Thebes there was a temple presided over by a specialty priestess, an adoratrix, called Huy who performed rituals for the people who lived in that area. She was not as high a priestess as those at Karnak but well regarded nonetheless. She had a daughter Matreya who had reached womanhood and was well versed in religious practice. To be well versed in religious practice meant that she was well versed in the Egyptian ways. Her natural beauty and apparent solid health rounded out her appeal. Tati approached Arisina with his suggestion and the next day Huy was visited by Arisina to begin discussion and to assess Matreya closer.

Huy was not surprised when she received the news that Arisina would be visiting her. In fact she had been waiting for such a day. Huy had dedicated her life to prayer and ritual for others but she had never forgotten to hold prayer for herself and her family. She had prayed to be recognised as a great priestess but the invitation to attend the palace was never extended to her. Her days serving commoners had sufficed, giving her the recognition and respect she craved. Yet she still harboured the hope that one day she would be elevated to a higher rank. As her age progressed she knew that her chances were growing smaller so she turned her attention to grooming her daughter. Matreya was developing into a more than able priestess under her tutelage and she was quick to let everyone and anyone know about it. Hopefully those words would one day reach the right ears and her daughter could become all that Huy had aimed for.

She smiled as Arisina arrived and walked into their home. Huy lead the priestess into her finest room and called out to servants to bring beer and sweets. The two women made some small talk about their work, asking polite questions and complimenting each other though all the while Huy wished that Arisina would state her real reason for being there. The drink and food finally arrived and once the servants were dismissed Arisina could now begin her true business. What Huy was about to hear was beyond anything that she had imagined or prayed for. Huy nodded her agreement before Arisina was even finished.

"This is an immense honour," was Huy's simple reply. And it was for this not only meant her daughter would be something far greater than a priestess, but that Huy herself too would finally make it to the palace. Huy was to be the mother of a queen and the grandmother of future princes and princesses.

"May I see your daughter?" Arisina made it seem like a question but it was in fact a command.

Huy took a deep breath and nodded. She called for a servant to summon Matreya and the two women sat in silence until she arrived. Huy's heart raced as Matreya's behaviour would now secure or refuse her this opportunity. If only she had time to speak to her first but this was exactly what Arisina wished to avoid. Any woman could be primed to act and speak appropriately when given time to prepare. If this young woman were all she had been described as then there should be no problem. Huy also knew this to be true. She had raised the girl well and her hard work thus far had led to this moment. Huy just prayed that the girl's youth and naiveté didn't let anything untoward leave her lips.

Her maids had already told Matreya that a high priestess of the palace had indeed entered their home. While her mother and Arisina had chatted lightly over their refreshments Matreya sent one of them to listen in on the conversation. The moment the discussion of marriage began the maid ran back to Matreya.

"Madam, the priestess is here to consider you for marriage--to the PHARAOH!" she repeated breathlessly.

"What! Are you sure? I will have your head if you are wrong," Matreya stressed with her eyes wide.

"I am certain Madam," the maid said nodding her head.

"Then quickly, make sure my hair is alright should she ask to see me!" Matreya snapped.

Matreya had openly spoken with her mother and prayed with her to become a palace priestess so that Arisina's arrival now made this appear to be becoming a reality. She had sat in her room picturing Arisina announcing her invitation to attend the palace and her reply. Now though this was going to be something even grander and she looked into the mirror as the maids fussed, scanning every detail of herself to make sure she looked perfect. When she felt sufficiently groomed she sent her maids away and sat quietly. So when another maid finally tapped on the door and said that her mother wished for her to join them in the parlour she stood and walked as though she was already a queen. Huy really had nothing to worry about.

Matreya walked into the room before Arisina with her shoulders squared, her chin up and looking straight into the priestess's eyes. Her poise was enough of a sign for Arisina that Tati's suggestion was insightful, even if there was something that did jar inside the priestess as their eyes met. Arisina let this go though as she felt it was just Matreya's vast contrast to Satiah's nature. When she heard Matreya speak it was a done deal. Her confidence and clear voice were additional assets and yet they also alerted something in Arisina but once again she dismissed this. Arisina was soon satisfied that she had sufficiently scanned the girl to report back to me and bid Huy and her daughter farewell.

"I shall meet with Pharaoh Thutmose and if he is also satisfied with my assessment than we shall begin marriage arrangements," she stated, "Until then

I suggest you keep this meeting secret. Idle gossip reaches far and quickly in the city and Pharaoh detests it. Should it reach the palace Pharaoh will certainly not pursue the arrangement."

The warning was duly noted by Huy and Matreya and Arisina returned to the palace. Huy wasted no time in returning to her temple with Matreya by her side and they fervently began prayers to Isis and Ra to bless and make this union possible. Despite how serious they were supposed to be in temple neither woman could hide the smiles on their faces that would not subside.

Arisina found me as soon as she could and briskly stated Matreya's suitability. As she listed each of her attributes I nodded as I checked against the list I carried in my head. It all matched up with what Arisina described and my infinite trust in her knew that if she was happy with this woman then so would I.

"Let us begin the marriage arrangements then," I said as she finished.

"Do you not wish to meet with her first or consider other women?" Arisina asked, most surprised at the speed of my decision.

"That will not be necessary," I answered. "I trust your observations and don't wish to give this matter any more time."

With this she nodded and we discussed the details of what should ensue. Once again my new wife-to-be would be moved into a palace apartment with her family and begin her training to become a queen. Although she had younger brothers they would not be offered military roles, as they were not considered suitable. There would be opportunities to become scribes or court assistants as they reached a fitting age.

"What of Huy?" Arisina asked. "Do you wish to offer her priesthood within the palace?"

"Is she suitable to join you?" I asked as such an invitation never crossed my mind.

"We could offer her a role as one of her daughter's counsellors and then for any children she will bear," she answered.

Huy was a more than capable priestess but there was something in her that Arisina had never really warmed to. Besides she had grown and trained outside the palace hierarchy and to step into it at her age would be disruptive and unfair to the established palace priests. A somewhat glamorous, if minor role, would be more than sufficient recognition for raising a queen for the empire.

That was the extent of my involvement with the marriage preparations. I did not fuss with ordering the clothes and jewellery that I did for Satiah. I would leave all this to my butlers. There would be no formal dinner with her family and in fact I would not set eyes upon Matreya until she arrived at the palace to begin her marriage preparations. The excitement and warmth of my first marriage simply was not to be had. I also felt that by treating this as the business arrangement that it was then lessened any betrayal I felt for Satiah. In fact in the time leading up to this marriage I spent more time than before with Satiah and the children. I showered them with gifts and by the time of the marriage ceremony Satiah was certain that she was neither being replaced nor was the second marriage any sign of her incompetence as queen or wife.

My engagement to Matreya was much shorter than with Satiah. From that first day that Arisina met with Huy to the day of the ceremony was only two months. I met Matreya as she arrived to move into her palace apartment and was struck by her beauty and poise. Her confidence didn't even falter in my presence. At the age of fourteen she had accepted the grand role offered her with a total sense of her worthiness to be queen. To be honest this scared me a little, not just as a man but also as a King. For all the dominance of husbands over their wives in those times, a clever woman could still exert some influence. I knew too well what a woman with a lust for power and an inflated ego could achieve. I made a silent pact with myself to be wary of my new bride.

Everyone noted Matreya's confidence and people around her began to act accordingly. Her maids and servants performed their duties diligently and never attempted to nurture the tenderness or friendship that Satiah had enjoyed with her attendants. Her character was not openly spoken about amongst the priests but the more ambitious amongst them soon knew that if they wished to play games with her they would need all the cunning they could muster.

Hatshepsut sensed this also within seconds of meeting her. As Hatshepsut looked upon Matreya and heard her speak for the first time she saw much that she admired and feared. Hatshepsut saw herself as a young woman once again, and as much as she loved to see another woman with such qualities, she also knew this girl could prove her undoing. As the old saying goes, "keep your friends close and your enemies even closer" and Hatshepsut knew that to make an ally of someone with such fire was her best course of action. This may seem all pointless as Hatshepsut's power was well and truly established while her life and reign was drawing to a close. I, nor anyone else, had ever challenged her position and certainly was not planning to. Such though is the fragility of a life that is based upon ego and control. Even if Hatshepsut had been upon her deathbed she would still have been scheming and manipulating those around her.

With only two weeks before my wedding to Matreya, Hatshepsut just "happened" to find herself wandering past the rooms where Matreya lived. Of course no Pharaoh just wanders--especially given the entourage that we must have with us. As Pharaoh she could go into any room of the palace as she pleased and so she entered Matreya's rooms unannounced. The servants there went into a spin but Matreya remained as cool as ever, delighted that Hatshepsut had sought her out. Matreya revelled in having the elder woman's attention. She knew that to have Hatshepsut's favour would be her key to being more than just a Pharaoh's wife and would set her apart from Satiah or any other wives who may be yet to come. She was also thankful that Hatshepsut's visit coincided with her mother's absence, as Matreya was tiring of her mother's premarital coaching and was looking forward to its end. Of course Hatshepsut's timing was not mere coincidence.

The older and the younger sat down together and made idle conversation over palace goings-on, clothes and the like. The air seemed jovial and friendly but each knew this was far more than a social call and Hatshepsut soon made her purpose very clear.

"Matreya, it is apparent to all how appropriate a choice Thutmose and his counsel made in selecting you as Queen," she drawled, tilting her head and smiling.

It seemed a smile but it was really a smirk as Hatshepsut spun out her threads to entrap the young woman. Matreya was already well entangled when she looked up and smiled her recognition. Hatshepsut instantly saw the fatal flaw of Matreya believing the Pharaoh was enamoured by her charms and took the opportunity to deliver a barb and a lesson in one hit.

"However don't think that your beauty and poise are enough to carry you through this," she sneered. "Beauty fades and poise can falter."

Matreya's smile disappeared as she was now lost as to what Hatshepsut's intentions were. She also reeled at the words, as her looks and demeanour were her only strategy in conquering the palace. What more could Hatshepsut be inferring?

"I would like to think that there is an active mind behind those seductive eyes," Hatshepsut goaded. "This is what will set you apart from Satiah. This is what will place you ahead as a royal wife. So tell me, Matreya, what sort of queen do you wish to be?"

Matreya sought the words but she hesitated; too frightened to share her ambitions with this woman so soon and before she was even married. Hatshepsut began to laugh quietly as she watched the girl struggle. She knew very well what Matreya aimed for however here sat the girl too weak and timid to even speak it. Yet another of Hatshepsut's threads tightened around the girl. Matreya's head suddenly snapped up and she looked intently at Hatshepsut. The laughter had wounded her as intended, but Matreya was nobody's fool--not even to the most powerful woman upon the planet. Hatshepsut's amusement came to an end as she was taken aback at the girl's disrespectful stance. Then Matreya began to speak with a voice well beyond her years.

"I desire to be a queen as you *were*!" she boldly stated.

Hatshepsut sat straighter in her chair and a smirk once again crossed her lips. She opened her mouth to deliver another barb but Matreya was not finished and openly spoke right over the Pharaoh.

"I desire the respect and adoration that you command. I desire to be feared as you still are. I desire that my child shall be the successor to the throne," she spat out with force and her eyes darkening.

Hatshepsut sat silenced--her mouth still open. She had not anticipated this little speech and display and it scared her as much as it impressed her. Hatshepsut had underestimated the fire in Matreya and she would now have to reassess her approach. She could not resist one last swipe of her paw to see how this might rouse the little vixen.

"So what makes you believe that you are worthy of such things?" Hatshepsut purred.

"Because, I above all other women is the one sitting here before you!" Matreya replied without hesitation or humility.

The girl's arrogance struck Hatshepsut hard. All she could do was nod at her astute observation. Matreya had not even attempted to sugar-coat the fact with signs from the Gods. She knew the game as instinctively as did Hatshepsut. They had both been groomed and trained for this from birth. Hatshepsut stared at the girl before her only wishing that it were Neferure instead who sat there. She had never understood just how she had failed in having her own child crave these same desires that Matreya did. Her chances with Neferure were long lost and now Hatshepsut had a fresh candidate before her to mold. Yes, Matreya would serve the empire well and she would bestow the blessing upon her that would decree it to everyone.

"Don't ever forget that very fact Matreya, but also don't ever forget the fact that I am Pharaoh and can easily undo you. While I live I am before you and above you," she lectured.

"But of course Your Highness," Matreya replied and bowed her head.

Hatshepsut enjoyed this display of humbleness from Matreya. She was reassured that the girl still acknowledged the respect she must show to her. Her next step could go ahead as she intended.

"Matreya, as a future queen of my family I wish to show you and all our people my acceptance of your position. You are free to take on the name Hatshepsut when you become Queen," she offered with a flourish of her hand.

"Oh Your Highness," Matreya's eyes lit up. She would be recorded with this name in scripts and tombs. It would make her be seen as Hatshepsut's daughter by all but birth. Matreya would be a grand queen to follow in her steps and with Hatshepsut's recognition.

"You shall still be known first and foremost by your given name Matreya. My name shall follow that. Do you understand?" she asked.

Matreya nodded. She was in no position to question any conditions of how she would use the name.

"In exchange, my sweet child," Hatshepsut continued with her smirk renewed, "I expect that you will return the respect to me that I have shown you. The thrones of this land have coexisted in peace before your arrival and so shall upon your marriage. You shall support your Pharaoh and husband in continuing this harmony and prosperity. You shall provide more heirs to continue our family lineage. That is all that is required of you until I pass to the afterlife.

Then you are free to act as you wish. Do you understand this also Matreya-Hatshepsut?"

Matreya nodded gently and smiled for she understood perfectly. She knew that wives were expendable no matter what their status within society. The rules were clear and defined. She would follow them knowing that if she didn't her new name might be revoked and also that she might just disappear from the palace. Now that she was here there was no way she would hinder her opportunities.

When the news of Hatshepsut's "blessing" reached me I merely rolled my eyes as I saw straight through it. The woman had no limits to how she would protect herself. I do admit that I enjoyed the fact that my new wife obviously scared her so much that she needed to do such a thing. I myself chose not to be intimidated by Matreya. I interacted with her but did so with a detachment that didn't allow for any games to be played. Any ambitions that she wished to express through me would never be realised and she knew this. She revelled in her new name, as it was the most powerful thing she would ever be granted. Ironically the one woman who could have manipulated me, Satiah, never chose to.

My wedding to Matreya was held with all the pomp and circumstance that it deserved but essentially as the business agreement that it was. We feasted all afternoon as before, though this time I sat with a wife on either side of me. Once again the time came for me to leave the celebration with my new wife. I turned to Satiah and squeezed her hand before I rose but she didn't respond and kept her eyes downcast. She knew that it was inevitable that I should lay with Matreya as much as she knew that I lay with my consorts, but this didn't stop the jealousy and hurt. She excused herself shortly after Matreya and I left to sit quietly in her rooms knowing that exactly as she had been prepared for me on her wedding night so too was Matreya being washed and oiled nearby. Satiah hoped that it would hurt as much as her first time and then hated herself for thinking such thoughts.

I do believe that it did hurt as much, not that Matreya would let it show. As stoic and professional as ever she received me without so much as flinching. I didn't warm her nor treat her to any of the affections that I did with Satiah. She would be deflowered with the duty required of me and with the duty required of her as my wife. Matreya knew no differently as was appropriate of a virgin on her wedding night. She understood though that the sheets would be taken tomorrow for the priests to pray over and bless. So as I slipped into sleep she gathered the sheet between her legs wiping as much of the blood and fluids upon it as she could. She lay back and smiled, enjoying the pain deep inside her where she had been torn and prayed for my seed to thrive within her.

As my newest wife it was considered Matreya's right to bear my next child and so Satiah was not to be summoned to my bedchamber until this had been achieved. This was also a way to establish my new wife's fertility and cement the marriage. She would have six months to prove herself and being the only woman to share my bed was considered more than ample opportunity in which to do this. I missed the tenderness of my Satiah and would see her as much as I could which also allowed me time with Amenemhat and Beketamun who were both growing rapidly. Some nights I would allow myself to be more tender with Matreya to relieve the coldness of being with her but it would never be the same. Thankfully Matreya's fertility was all it was predicted to be and in the second month of our marriage her bleeding did not commence and the priests' day count slowly reached the necessary fiftieth day. On the fifty-first day she returned to her private rooms and Satiah returned to mine.

Matreya's pregnancy developed well and Satiah carrying her third child joined her in pregnancy three months later. Each woman bloomed and blossomed in her own way. Matreya became more demanding of her attendants while for Satiah her routine of pregnancy was once again the joyful process that it always was. Matreya could well have sought Satiah for advice but never would. She was determined to move through this with the independence she always showed and would certainly not allow Satiah the opportunity to openly display her seniority. For Matreya it was bad enough that Satiah had given me my first son.

As always with Matreya things went according to plan. Her labour began on exactly the day calculated by the priests for the birth and once again Arisina was summoned to oversee another birth for the palace. As she approached the room she heard shouts but they were not the screams of a woman responding to the pains of labour so she quickened her steps. Entering the room Arisina found a maid bright red in the face having just bore the brunt of the last tirade from Matreya's mouth. The midwives had retreated to their corner pretending to check their implements while Huy was by her daughter's side whispering something in an attempt to calm her daughter; especially now that the high priestess was present. Arisina had seen women change in many ways during labour out of fear, pain and eagerness but this outright anger was something totally new.

"Finally you arrive!" Matreya shouted at seeing the priestess, lifting herself up on her arms.

Arisina bowed to the young queen somewhat bemused as she was here well within an hour of being summoned. She was also concerned as there could be very many more hours to come and if Matreya could not cope with these first pains then how would she be after a day. Arisina turned to her corner to begin her work and saw some incense had already been lit. This was to be no ordinary birth she decided.

Huy was quickly by her side apologising, "Please Arisina, I did not mean to interfere," she whispered, "Matreya was just so agitated that I had to do something."

Arisina took a deep breath and nodded to Huy. She was about to speak when Matreya began again.

"What are you whispering about? How dare you create secrets on such a day! I will tell Thutmose all about this--*and* Hatshepsut! How dare you! How dare you!" she screamed getting louder with each word.

Huy burst into tears totally lost as what to do for her daughter. Arisina though knew exactly what to do and walked to the bed with her chin up and her shoulders squared. Matreya knew by her walk that she meant business and sank back into the pillows ready to receive the lecture that she knew was about to be delivered.

"Your Highness! I have attended two queens and assisted many other noble wives in successful births. None have ever felt the need to behave in such a way. Such dramatics do nothing to protect yourself or your child. In fact you are placing your child at risk. The Gods will surely not arrive for any woman who feels the need to treat those assisting her birth in such a way. I suggest you remember your role and act accordingly." Arisina finished and turned her back to return to her corner to begin the chanting.

The screaming stopped but the attitude didn't. Matreya's attendants instead received scowls as they continued on with their duties. As the hours continued she fatigued somewhat and even gave up on the scowls. There was still some fire in her though. After five hours of labour when the midwife examined Matreya and announced that she was still not ready for the birthing chair she received a kick to her side. The midwife holding herself retreated from the bed while Matreya lay back and closed her eyes to avoid the stern look she knew she would be receiving from Arisina. It would be another five hours before my second son Amenhotep was born. A huge sigh of relief swept the room on his arrival. The women surrounding Matreya were all glad their ordeal was over while Matreya herself was happy to be holding a son.

"I have given birth to a Pharaoh," she declared.

There was silence from all in the room for indeed she hadn't. Amenemhat was to be the next Pharaoh while Amenhotep was simply a prince. To speak anything other than this was heresy. The women surrounding Matreya all looked to Arisina not knowing how to respond. Arisina herself was for once lost for words. The ill omen at Amenemhat's birth had never been discussed and to hear such words spoken added to the silent curse he was already carrying. She dare not add to this by acknowledging Matreya's words.

"Your Highness, you are tired from your first birth," she said. "Bathe and prepare for Pharaoh to visit his new prince."

With one simple sentence Arisina corrected Matreya's faux pas and all carried on as though it was never said. This of course included Arisina making her way to announce the birth. She would have no trouble in making my new son sound majestic and blessed, as everything physically about the birth was perfect, including the placenta. However she could not make a prince's birth sound more successful than that of a future king. She decided that the breeze had not been so strong today.

# CHAPTER TEN

Satiah delivered my third son Siamun three months later. My family grew rapidly and fourteen years after the arrival of Amenemhat, my tenth child Isis completed my children. Menkheperre followed a year after Amenhotep and Siamun and my pride at having four robust sons was evident to all. Amenemhat learnt from an early age that he was to be the next king and revelled in this as I had done when I finally understood my destiny. All of my sons took to their roles with the drive and passion that was expected of them. As had my father I took them from an early age to the army quarters and they soaked up the details and energies of the army as quickly as they could. Each boy took on an aspect of me and it was as though there were extensions of me walking the palace and journeying out through the lands. My greatest joy was to walk or ride with all four following behind me. Never was there a greater declaration of my power.

Amenemhat was as able a horseman as I ever was and loved the planning and strategies of the military. Amenhotep soon decided that he would be his brother's right-hand man as he idolised his elder brother. He sought to learn anything that he did and would follow him wherever he went. Their friendship and allegiance was impenetrable and never once suffered the jealousy that you would imagine. They sat together in court and listened intently often seeking me out to ask questions and support me as best they could.

Siamun became a man of the mind. He was fascinated in the trade routes and business and became an invaluable support to the courts and myself during my reign. His business mind though was always balanced by the gentle nature that he inherited from his mother. You would think this would leave him open to manipulation by traders and viziers but it didn't. In fact he was so well respected that no one dared ever betray him. I often felt that my father's spirit resided within him.

Menkheperre carried the ambitious fire of Matreya within him. Thankfully he directed this into becoming a most able and ferocious soldier. Many an unwitting partner in sword training returned to their quarters with cuts, scrapes and bruises while my prince remained unscathed. Egypt was also equally blessed that he had the leadership skills to compliment this and he was an able general as much as a warrior. He also loved talking about himself. His sisters would often be treated to animated accounts of his adventures and they would encourage him with squeals, gasps and clapping. Like the rock star that he was, he lapped up the attention and when he realised that his stories impressed women--he would practice them on his sisters before using them to seduce women throughout the palace and the empire. After a while his reputation preceded him and the women would be waiting within his chambers or army tent with no stories or performance necessary from him.

Now please don't think that I loved or valued my daughters any less. Each of my children was as precious as the other and was just as important a part of my life. I cherished every one of them and after having no siblings, apart from Neferure, I loved seeing them play together and watching their friendships and loyalties grow. There was never any division based upon who was born of which mother. I never held back on my affections to any of them and it was returned a thousandfold. I would leave for expeditions and they would hug me and cry as I rode away. Then when I returned I would be greeted with more hugs and crying. They all filled my life with more love and joy than I could ever imagine.

Egypt was still Egypt though and women had their roles, as did the men. Having grown watching a woman corrupt the true path of her country to satisfy her craving for power and glory I could not let my children repeat such an aberration. Yes, I know that Hatshepsut oversaw one of the most peaceful and prosperous times of the empire but this was as much due to her father, brother and myself as it was her own ruling. It was to be my family's responsibility to correct the family lineage and four sons were more than sufficient to do this. My daughters learnt from a young age that their brothers held such a duty. They also learnt what was expected of them. The gossip and murmurs about Hatshepsut reached their ears too as they grew older. They all soon understood that a woman taking power did not always gather the love and respect that would be expected.

My eldest daughter Beketamun loved to be around her brothers. She attended court and learnt the minutiae of Egyptian business and processes as soon as she could. She worked closely with Siamun in running the day-to-day business of the palace but as was expected of her being a woman she always remained in the background. Beketamun was not fussed with the trappings of femininity but was always immaculately groomed and carried herself with all the grace of a princess.

Deep down though she craved the experiences her brothers were all having. While she wanted to do such things as speak before court what she really desired was all the physical activities that they were allowed and expected to have. She longed to sit straight upon a horse and gallop across the sands with wind through her hair. Beketamun would listen to Menkheperre's stories full of brandished swords and flying arrows, smiling with joy as she took in all his details. She would then lie in bed and dream that she had done all these things herself, imagining the dust and sweat on her skin and the sun burning down on her. If she had the freedom allowed women in your times I believe she would have proven herself an amazing athlete. Of course dreaming would be the closest that she would ever experience such things and the next day when she arose she would resume her duties in respect for her family and the palace.

Nefertiry my second daughter with Satiah was named for one of the greatest women in our family, the first of the great queens of our dynasty. She however quickly became her own person and was like no other. She took to reading and writing with great aplomb, studying diligently and practising whenever she could. Writing in our time though was essentially for business, which was a male territory, or it was for record keeping and adornment, which was the territory of the specialised priests or scribes. Nefertiry found a way around all this though and took to drawing. Through drawing she could do her own form of writing through images. Glyphs would be worked into becoming part of the story that she was creating. She would paint portraits of all of us as well as landscapes that surrounded the palace. These then progressed into her painting scenes from our life. Nefertiry delighted Menkheperre by painting scenes of him triumphant in battle. She created a family album like no other and if only her paintings had survived you would know so truly our family life, free of the propaganda and formalities that overlay the records you study to learn of this time.

I had four daughters with Matreya and they were a bundle of hyperactivity as young girls and Matreya did little to control this--allowing them all the indulgences of young princesses. They were more like an entity than four separate girls until they reached their teenage years. The corridors surrounding their rooms always echoed with screams and giggles. Not surprisingly, I did not encourage them to attend court too often. They were doted on by their older sisters and adored by their brothers. The richness of affection that they were showered with was returned to the palace with smiles and laughter. After the heaviness of Hatshepsut and the depressing childhood she created for her daughters, their energy cleansed the palace.

The two eldest are both recorded as Meritamen, named for their mother and the God Amun. The second was actually named Hatshepsut at birth, in honour of her great aunt and at the insistence of Matreya, despite my less than perfect relationship with her. Royal daughters were always given family names to bless them, and with the elder Hatshepsut reaching her last years and with her health failing at the time of my daughter's birth, it was also a wonderful way to smooth the final days of the co-regency and allow her to depart to the afterlife knowing that some formal legacy was left amongst my children and her family. However, what would seem a minor incident soon changed my intentions for how my daughter's name would be struck in my tomb and upon records.

It was some years after the elder Hatshepsut's death and my eldest children had attended a full formal day of court with me receiving news from traders and the chief stewards who oversaw the farmers. We were all dressed in our full finery making it a most auspicious day for the family. Amenemhat was also home from his outpost on the Nile delta, so it was a wonderful day having all my sons in court to be followed by dinner with all ten of my children seated at my table. I dismissed the older children from court early in order that they should gather the younger ones and be ready to dine with me. I was exhausted from such a full day of business but the laughter and talking I heard from the dining hall as I approached lifted my spirits. This was short lived and any smile I carried was gone the second I entered the room and saw the scene before me.

Young Hatshepsut, barely nine years of age, was parading around the huge dining table wearing Menkheperre's headdress and collar. This was bad enough to see, but to make it complete, she was also holding to her chin a piece of bread to act as a ceremonial beard. She was marching around the table dressed as such while her siblings laughed and giggled hysterically.

"I am Pharaoh Hatshepsut!" she shouted. "You! Go and build me a temple--and you--go and fill my bath!"

She pointed to each of her brothers and sisters one at a time shouting a demand and they all laughed louder at each one. For me though this was not a joke at all.

"ENOUGH!" I roared.

They all jumped and turned to look at me shocked at my outrage. Young Hatshepsut froze in place fully aware that she was the cause of my anger. I am sure her little heart was pounding and while I hated to see my children so scared of me I had to continue.

"Hatshepsut, take off your brother's adornments at once," I yelled.

Beketamun silently slid from her chair and helped her little sister take off Menkheperre's adornments while the rest dropped their eyes. As Beketamun placed them on a side table Hatshepsut quickly took her place at the table and assumed the same downward eyes as the rest of her siblings. I strode towards the table and stood over Menkheperre. I could see him shaking as he anticipated my lecture.

"Menkheperre, do you think so little of the honour of being born a prince that you allow your adornments to be mocked?" I shouted.

He shook his head but knew that this would not be enough of a response. "No Your Highness," he said as strongly as he could, still looking down.

"Then I trust this will never occur again," I said.

"It will never happen again Father. You have my word," he said and looked up at me, his eyes wide seeking approval.

I nodded to him satisfied he understood the lesson I had wished to show them all and made my way to my seat at the head of the table. Satiah and Matreya walked into the room as I was seated and sensed the atmosphere immediately. It was not hard to notice as there was no chit-chat amongst the children as was usual. They all had their heads still down and the younger girls had red faces. Satiah looked to me with an expression that I knew asked of me to explain.

"Look up all of you," I said, and obediently all of the children did.

I could see young Hatshepsut eyes were red and watery as she held back tears. She feared that she would be reprimanded in front of everyone again, and worse still with her mother present.

"It is all very well to joke of things past as though they no longer exist. The truth is that people and events of the past can still exert influence over our present moments. This can be either good or bad. Tonight you *all* chose to recreate something that was a dark stain on your family history. I appreciate that you did this in jest but humour still allows such thoughts and ideas to evolve. Each one of you has it in your fate as handed to you by the Gods to correct our family lineage and history. Do not disappoint the Gods or your family by acting or thinking in any way that does not serve this end. Do I have your understanding? "

I finished the lecture with a simple question and looked at the children one at a time as they either nodded their agreement or spoke a simple "yes Father". I finished by turning to their mothers one at a time, receiving their acknowledgement also, and having their children witness their solidarity with me. Satisfied that all was complete with this issue I clapped my hands to signal our meal be served. The dinner was not as joyful as I would have liked but it was productive none the less. Some gentle talk began soon enough as I asked questions of Amenemhat's recent expedition and his brothers and sisters joined in. Young Hatshepsut remained silent though and I noticed she did not eat so much.

The manner in which I had dealt with the children had been necessary. There was no other way in which I could have done this. Yet the sight of little Hatshepsut with her red eyes picking at her food weighed upon me. When they had all been sent to their bedchambers I quietly entered hers and her eyes flew open as she saw me approach her bed so fearful of yet another reprimand. Instead I simply kissed her gently upon her forehead and whispered, "Dear sweet one, I love you as much as ever," as I stroked her hair. This was all that was needed to be said. I left her room and the incident was never spoken of again.

Now you may wonder what this has to do with me changing her name, especially as I seem to have dealt with the incident quite decisively. I decided though that it was more than coincidence that the young Hatshepsut should choose to imitate her namesake. What if I had cursed my daughter's blood with my aunt's spirit in naming her so? There was a simple remedy to this so upon young Hatshepsut reaching womanhood she was referred to as Meryt but recorded as Meritamen also.

The younger girls had a very simple life within the palace. They watched their brothers and eldest sisters take on serious duties but were never motivated to do so themselves. This did not please Matreya so much as she wished her girls were more ambitious but my crusade to have my children act according to their gender suited these princesses well. They would spend their days playing and preening themselves much like Neferure did. They were happy to come to court or temple when needed and enjoyed the excitement of dressing in their full princess attire as well as the adoration they received. Each would follow the lead of their older sisters in how to behave, walking in their footsteps and mimicking their behaviour. They were indulged one fit of giggles during a ceremony but the swift reprimand of their mother's dagger eyes made sure there was no repeat of such behaviour.

The two youngest, Nebetiunet and Isis were thankfully a bit more subdued than the two Meritamens. Regretfully I have to admit Nebetiunet is the child I knew the least. In any family of this size some will simply fade into the background. She was the quietest of all the children and quite happy to step aside as her more boisterous brothers and sisters took the limelight. Nebetiunet was also the only child of mine who sought a life away from the palace, choosing to become a priestess and eventually living at Huy's temple to serve.

Such too was the role of Isis within the family. Even though she was quieter, her sparkling eyes and warm smile made her a favourite with everyone. Her older siblings doted on her endlessly and she showered affection on anyone close to her. If I entered the room I would have Isis jump on my lap and remain there until I left. I will admit that giving her my mother's name made her that little bit more special to me.

CHAPTER ELEVEN

So now you have the full picture of my family life. Having two wives and children arriving made my manhood complete. Hatshepsut watched my family grow knowing that I could take over the throne with minimal notice or disruption to the empire. I never once sought to usurp her role despite my maturity or my ever-growing military prowess. Yet she remained as wary of me as ever. Her tenuous claim to her position required this despite our harmonious partnership and the wealth of the kingdom. A life built on shaky ground is never truly stable or happy and Hatshepsut lived such a life everyday. A Pharaoh though could never show such fears or doubts.

Hatshepsut had something huge on her side though. Our heritage had landed us both in an amazingly prosperous time. We had no immediate threats from any enemies. Our trade routes were secure and our lands producing well. Regardless of the different groups aligned to Hatshepsut or myself within the palace all was running smoothly. I will happily take credit for the peace within the palace, as I consider my lack of antagonism was what created a most solid understanding that our co-regency was amicable. Well, at least it was on the surface. The ace up my sleeve of course was that I controlled the army and Hatshepsut knew that this power could be her undoing. So we danced a most polite dance, each needing each other, and each believing that they themselves were leading.

I wish I could look back and say that I stayed completely true to Arisina's advice that day overlooking the Nile but ego can be a powerful thing. As each child was born, a part of me rejoiced that my family grew and overshadowed hers, no matter how much I loved Neferure. I paraded my sons in front of Hatshepsut whenever I could and spoke loudly of their attributes. When her health slowly started to fade before us all I silently celebrated that her days were finally numbered and looked forward to preparing her funeral. Of course I kept all this to myself not even sharing such thoughts with Satiah, my mother or especially Arisina who would have been horrified with me. Then in a quiet moment I would reflect on the priestess's words all those years ago and the sad life Hatshepsut had lived consumed by such ill thoughts and motivations. I would soon let such thoughts of my own float away.

A fragile ego needs to create a façade though to protect itself. Hatshepsut did this with such amazing skill that you still have the results of this. An abundant time in any culture is celebrated through its arts and architecture and never was this done more spectacularly than with her mortuary temple. This was just one part of her campaign for eternal remembrance. Hatshepsut also added to the Great Temple at Karnak and even the palace, though never as grandly as I did. Smaller temples were revamped throughout the land and you could not ride or travel anywhere without some reminder that this woman was

Pharaoh and that she was as strong and majestic as the land she ruled.

The high priests and viziers all revelled in this too with Senemut at the lead. He was now known as the "architect" overseeing her building works and business with as much attention as he could. Their other relationship was still kept hidden from public eyes but the way they interacted left no question as to how close they were. Senemut would grow angry on her behalf, Hatshepsut would gaze adoringly as he spoke. There are only so many aspects of a relationship you can hide and despite them both thinking it was not known it was actually considered common knowledge throughout the country. Senemut was even so blind to his actions revealing this that he was stupid enough to create glyphs within both his tomb and Hatshepsut's temple basically confirming it.

I had heard so much about this amazing temple and tomb being built that I decided I should go and look for myself. I used the excuse that I was checking on the progress of my own tomb to venture to the Valley of the Kings. So I set out one day for the burial valley with the usual entourage trailing behind me as well as Salas for company. I sat astride my horse and acknowledged the bows of the commoners we passed as we made our way to the boat that would carry us across the Nile to the Valley. On reaching the other side of the river my heart sank as we approached the pier to disembark as this was all too familiar to my father's funeral day. I kept my head high though, as any Pharaoh would when he was out on an official trip.

The Valley was not somewhere that people went to without reason. You went to the Valley to work upon tombs or to be buried. It was as simple as that. It was sacred land not just due to the fact that it was a burial site but it was our human representation of the world of the afterlife. It was not just the physical gateway for the pharaohs to meet Osiris for it was also his land to rule over. We lived our lives to the East of the Nile where the sun rose each day. We then watched it cross the river and begin its descent and then it would set to end the day in this very valley. The jags and crevasses of the Valley were all portals to leave and so they were perfect places to dig for tombs. The endless folds of the land were also ideal to hide tomb entrances and hopefully escape the attentions of tomb robbers.

The burrow of tunnels and tombs is endless beneath those rocks and for each tomb your archaeologists have found there is still another untouched but for subterranean waters and shifts in the land. I bless my descendant Tutankhamun for being the pop star of Egyptian burials. He wonderfully distracted you all from looking in places that will hopefully remain unfound. So too I would aim to find a place that would protect my body and allow me an eternity in the afterlife. However any thoughts of this were soon well and truly gone as I now rode into the opening of the Valley.

It was the noise that greeted my entourage first--the sound of chisels on rock, the calls of a team leader directing the movement of a stone block, the occasional crack of a whip upon a donkey or worse yet a slave not moving fast enough. Then as we passed between the hills that formed the entrance to the Valley we saw the entire scene. It was beyond any construction that I had witnessed in my life. There were hundreds of men but it looked like thousands and they were scattered like ants across their mound, working in teams but working as one huge machine. I stopped in my tracks dumbfounded and my entourage halted too. Our jaws dropped as we took in the sheer scale of what we were observing. The temple seemed to be growing out of the very ground it was being built on. It did not have the height that the pyramids used to overwhelm you but the scale of this temple was awesome. Huge ramps that were as long as the temple was high rose before it making the journey to reach it as majestic as the temple itself.

It was spectacular and sickening at the same time. Our family had never done anything like this. Each forefather created monuments to Gods and had grand yet reasonable tombs hidden from sight. Yet here was the hugest statement of all, crying out to Ra above and declaring her grandeur in the most outward display she could. I rode as close as possible to the construction and as the workers were so invested in their duties they were oblivious to me. The few that did realise who I was bowed and then turned so their backs were away from me, often signalling to others my presence as they did so. I dismounted and with Salas by my side we walked along the ramps and terraces that were complete and made our way to the main temple building.

The workers parted and cleared the way for us but I barely noticed. As I got closer and closer to the main part of the building with its rows of columns it seemed to grow in size. The main structure was all but complete. The work that was taking place was the embellishments with most of the blocks being placed now ready for carving into statuary or being marked to have reliefs carved upon them. Salas followed close behind watching me and waiting for me to comment but I couldn't. I knew that close by also watching and listening were any number of people who would report back to Hatshepsut any reaction I showed. Finally we were inside and knowing I was safe I instructed my guards and servants to wait on the terrace and with just Salas by my side I wandered into the cool interior.

There were no builders inside as it was complete in here but there were dozens of scribes, each with a wall to themselves marking out the glyphs and pictures that would be carved and painted into later. On the floor beside them, lay papyrus scrolls and sheets with the plans for what they would mark with charcoal and chalk. A servant boy would hold a torch or lamp to the wall lighting what they were working on. There was minimal talking as they were so focussed on what they were doing and many of them also did not notice me pass them. The walls were being filled with stories and scenes about Hatshepsut. Some were true, some highly exaggerated and some pure fiction. I turned a corner and found two scribes working on a huge wall. The space here was clearly lit from the sun and they moved quickly, consulting back to their papyrus plans and to each other. One had just taken a step back to check his markings when he saw me in the corner of his eye and turned. He recognised who I was in a split second, dropped his charcoal stick and quickly bowed, followed by his comrade who just as quickly realised who their visitor was. The priest overseeing the scribes seemed to appear out of nowhere, despite the fact that I am sure he had been trailing us since we stepped onto the terrace.

"Your Highness," he bowed low and dramatically. "What an honour to have your presence. Might I show the work that we have completed so far?"

He gestured as though to direct Salas and I outside the temple but I felt the ruse immediately and held up my hand to stop him.

"That will be most unnecessary. I believe I have seen it all as I entered," I said firmly. "Continue on with your work."

The two scribes hesitated to return to their work as it meant turning their backs to me but I nodded and they did so. Of course having a Pharaoh watching while you work incites certain self-consciousness but I was not watching them work. My eyes scanned over what was already marked above their heads. Salas did also and on discerning what was being depicted he turned to me to gauge my reaction. I looked at him but said nothing with the priest still nearby.

Upon the wall was being recorded an epic journey that had been taken to Punt. It recorded the produce that was brought back or discovered from this different land by the water. There were drawings of the fish, the trees that had been carried back and piles of precious incense. It showed Hatshepsut meeting the Queen of this area, of course depicted not nearly as beautiful as herself.

It was an artistic and thorough recording of a historic event during her rule now about to be preserved for evermore. There was just one slight problem with it all in that Hatshepsut had never taken this journey. Certainly it had occurred under her rule but Hatshepsut had never dared to stray too far from the palace. Her natural tendency towards self-preservation most certainly would never have allowed travelling somewhere so precarious either.

I wish I could say that it had been my journey but I had been too young to journey when it did occur. However it was my army and my men that had done so. I guess I should be thankful that it was at least recorded and in such a spectacular way but to see Hatshepsut claim it as her exploit and sole success burned me inside. I took a deep breath and turned to Salas to suggest we leave. He nodded to me and we turned to exit. The priest bowed to us and watched us walk away. I imagine he ran off to watch us from another vantage point and to also get a messenger to notify Senemut of my appearance. Salas and I walked back through the various rooms and corridors on our way out. As we passed though one corridor it was peculiarly empty, though a papyrus scroll and some charcoal lay on the floor. Possibly the scribe had taken his meal or a toilet break.

Salas stopped and picked up the charcoal, "Sire, would you like me to add something of our own to the beloved Pharaoh's records?" he said with a smile.

"Salas, my friend, whatever could we add?" I said and smiled back.

"Surely Her Highness would like a picture of herself and her beloved architect planning this temple in her bedchamber?" he said teasingly.

I now laughed outright at Salas' humour. As tempting as it was to say yes, even knowing that it could be corrected before the permanent markings were painted, I shook my head no.

"Drop the charcoal, my scribe. I have much better glyphs to occupy your time," I said still chuckling.

Hatshepsut was finally placed into her tomb after twenty-two years of sharing the throne with me. That sounds like such a long time for someone still occupying human time frames does it not? For a young Pharaoh eager to rule on his own it certainly could have been. However twenty-two years filled with army training, marriage and parenthood can move quite quickly. I am glad I chose the latter over the former. There were times that I imagined she had struck a deal with Osiris and was going to remain on the earth forever, or that I would be slain in battle or be struck by disease and never outlive her. Then there were times I would be so focussed on an army campaign or expedition that months would pass and then I would be sitting next to her in court and realise just how much she had aged as she wheezed or groaned beside me.

Her death was far from sudden and I believe it began around the time that Amenemhat was born. Her usual robust nature suddenly began to fade and each year she seemed to attract a new pain or condition. It was a strange reminder of my father's last years, as she seemed to suffer in the same ways that he did. The difference though was that Hatshepsut had an underlying vigour that saw her survive far longer than my father's frail shell could. She was not going to let something as pathetic as a disease rob her of her place on the throne. No indeed, she would hold onto it with every last breath of her very being. In those years that she slowly faded, not only did she see the births of all my children except Nebetiunet and Isis, but she also witnessed the passing of all she was connected to, except for me.

None of these deaths would effect her more than losing her beloved nurse, Sitre. A wet nurse was not so much chosen for royal babies as they were appointed out of sheer luck. A pharaoh or queen could not plan who would breastfeed their child. Miscarriages and death in childbirth could soon see any such expectations quashed. A wet nurse was simply someone who was available and producing milk at the right time. Often they were a servant of the palace who had just given birth or a consort who was nursing her own child. Sitre was neither. Sitre was a commoner, a relative of a royal butler, whose pregnancy just happened to time with that of my grandmother, Nefertiry. Her own daughter was born the day before Hatshepsut and had died within hours, her lungs too frail to sustain her. So in that first day as Sitre sat wishing she too were dead and with her breasts aching with the first rush of milk she was summoned to the palace. No one else was available or trusted and Sitre could not refuse. So she sat in the small room next to the royal birthing room, listening to the cries of the queen in labour just as she had cried in pain the day before. The chief midwife walked in and asked to see her breasts and she uncovered obediently, sitting quietly as the midwife squeezed them to ensure that some flow was there. She then handed Sitre a cloth to wipe her nipples dry and allowed her to recover herself. Sitre contemplated running away but the fatigue of her own labour wouldn't allow it so she sat and listened to the activity beyond the curtains.

Sitre had just started to doze off when she was awakened by the loudest shrieks of the birth so far. These were then followed by the cries of the newborn Hatshepsut, so similar to the sounds of her daughter barely a day ago. The tears flowed freely now down Sitre's face as she knew the moment she dreaded was soon to occur. The bustle in the room next door continued as the birth was completed and she heard the servants begin to prepare the room for the Pharaoh to visit. Then suddenly the curtain was opened and there stood a maid with the baby princess in her arms. Sitre's heart jumped and began pounding as the child was placed in her arms. The maid turned and left, she didn't need to instruct the woman as it was quite clear what was needed.

Sitre looked down at the newborn Hatshepsut. She looked so much like her own child that Sitre actually felt her own child had somehow been returned to her. Any hesitation at having another woman's child at her breast was now gone and Sitre quickly pulled at her clothes and let Hatshepsut latch onto her as though she was truly her own. It was a moment that never really ended and their bond grew everyday. So much so that Sitre soon became Hatshepsut's only wet nurse, luckily making ample milk for the princess who rejected other women's breasts anyway.

When Hatshepsut was weaned Sitre also became one of her nurses as few could comfort the crying princess as she could. Sitre would always be the one that the princess sought for solace. There became an uneasy relationship between Nefertiry and the nurse as the Queen observed what was becoming far from the usual relationship between a nurse and her charge. Nefertiry could not do much about it though as she was kept busy with her royal duties.

Like my mother, Sitre was happy to remain in the background and to be there for the one they loved when they were sought. She acted more as a mother to Hatshepsut than Nefertiry ever would and when Sitre finally slipped away Hatshepsut cried more than when either her father or mother died. It was the only time that Hatshepsut showed any softness that I can recall but the minute the funeral was over all tears stopped and her stone-like demeanour returned. Her grieving though continued within her and Sitre's death signalled the change in Hatshepsut's health and the beginning of her decline. She arranged for the woman to be interred within her own incomplete tomb so that she could rejoin her one day. Ironically after all the movement of mummies over the centuries the two women's remains would be found side by side in the massive cache of mummies which also contained my own remains.

It is surprising that given this relationship with Sitre that Hatshepsut never sought to nurture a similar relationship with her own daughter. Perhaps she had been too well trained by her actual parents in treating their offspring as a political commodity. Perhaps Hatshepsut was only capable of receiving and did not understand how to even share affection. I believe she did, but life was a lot simpler for her when people were kept at a distance with very clear boundaries and expectations. This indeed does keep life simple as you avoid heartbreak and deception; however you also avoid affection and deep love. Hatshepsut missed this in many ways but never more so than from Neferure.

My beloved cousin delighted in seeing me become a father. She still had not a maternal bone within her and despite her ongoing affair with Samreen had no intention of providing him with children or of approaching her mother to allow them to marry. Neferure continued to enjoy her clandestine affair. The very idea that she was defying what was expected of her only made it more delicious. While Samreen would have loved family he enjoyed her attentions and the treats and rewards it gave him. He could leave with the army for a mission and return with no pressures to provide for anyone. Neferure made sure he was always satisfied physically in return for his unspoken fidelity.

The life of a soldier though is always precarious and despite living in a peaceful time there were always risks. Even a fall from a horse in these times could be fateful. Samreen was in much greater danger when a border skirmish suddenly erupted. Word travelled back to the palace quickly of the small but vicious battle with the notice that several men were dead. Their bodies were being carried back just an hour or two behind the messenger. My gut sank at the news. Such reports were inevitable to a leader but you still did not want to hear of fatalities at any time. My stomach though felt something much worse than losing some of my valued soldiers. I knew that this area was where Samreen had just travelled to and without even knowing the names of the fallen I felt him among them.

I did not want to frighten Neferure until I knew for certain but the news reached her anyway. I was walking along a corridor, making my way to the army quarters where the bodies would first be taken to be identified, when she appeared before me.

"Let me come with you," she begged.

I couldn't though. Aside from the fact that no women were allowed in the army quarters I could not bear for her to see what state a battle-slain body could be in.

"Neferure, go back to your rooms. There is no reason for you to come and I can't allow it," I said, half trying to convince her and myself that my instincts weren't correct.

"It's him Thutmose. I know it. I heard him cry out to me during the night," she said, and her tears began to flow.

"Go back Neferure, I cannot let you come," I repeated, now holding back my own tears. *"How could two of us feel the same thing? It surely must be true,"* I thought.

"Then promise me that you will let me know as soon as you know. Please!" she begged. "Just yes or no is all I need to hear."

With that she turned and walked back to her rooms to begin the wait. I continued on my way to the army rooms where I would begin my own wait for the cart carrying the bodies to arrive. I was barely at the army quarters for half an hour when it did finally reach the palace. The drivers looked grim and were wearing their own injuries. The bodies of the six men were arranged with all the respect that any dead body was expected to have. A heavy canvas covered them to protect them from the sun as they were carried and one of my generals climbed up on the cart to pull it back. I also climbed up in a hurry to witness for myself what was to be Neferure's answer. As the canvas pulled back I looked at the faces and my heart lifted. I could not see Samreen but then as the last of the cover was flung back there he was. The last to be uncovered, he lay with a massive wound across his shoulder to the base of his throat. He would have bled to death in seconds from such a cut and I thanked the Gods for not having him suffer any longer than he needed to.

"Do you know all their names for the records and telling the families?" I asked my general beside me.

"All but two, Sire. I shall call some others to identify those," he answered. "Sire, do you recognise who this is?"

He pointed to Samreen and I nodded. Samreen and Neferure's affair was about as well hidden as that of Hatshepsut and Senemut.

"How shall we let the princess know?" he asked.

"I shall," I said softly. "I don't know how but I shall."

I remained a few minutes more to hear the drivers' recount of the attack on the border patrol. I instructed more troops to the area immediately but left my generals to organise the details as well as the burial of the men. I could not bear to have Neferure wait any longer yet wished I would never reach her rooms to give the worst news possible.

I entered her room and found her slumped upon a lounge. She had been crying the whole time she waited and she looked up at me with red eyes

I stood silently for a moment wondering how I would tell her.

"Yes or no," she said softly.

I could not even say the word so I just nodded.

"Are you sure? Did you see him?" she asked hoping that I was wrong.

I merely nodded again. Neferure sat in shock for a few seconds but as the truth registered she began to cry again with such sobs that her entire body shook.

She cried, "No, no..." over and over as she refused to believe that her lover was gone. I did not know what to do and her maids stood by also in shock. Her sobs continued to grow.

"I want to die too," she screamed over her sobs. "I cannot go on without him."

I went to her side now and sitting down I took her in my arms and held her as she cried. The cries soon softened and the woman who once threatened to stab me if I touched her went soft in my arms as she grew exhausted. I ordered her maids to prepare her bed and carried her there limp in my arms. As she fell back into the bed she looked up at me and locked eyes with mine. There deep inside her I saw the old Neferure came back to life. The Neferure who hated life looked up at me and a chill ran up my spine. I turned to her chief maid and ordered her to call a physician.

It would not matter what potions or tonics she was given--the happy, cheerful Neferure would never return. She had lost the one person she felt truly loved her without conditions or rules. Samreen had been her escape from royal life and without him and their love affair to distract her and occupy her thoughts she was flung back to her reality with a crash. Neferure appeared less and less at court and I heard via my servants that most of her days were spent dozing or sleeping. Her frame once again dissolved and her lack of eating just added to the lethargy. Hatshepsut seeing Neferure return to her depressive stupor simply gave up on her. Hatshepsut didn't reprimand her daughter for letting her royal duties slide and in fact removed most responsibilities from her. This made it all the more easy for Neferure to be consumed by her depression.

We imagine that a tumour or infection as something that eats at our bodies, robbing it of vigour and stealing our life force. Our minds can just as insidiously invite us to our deaths. Those voices within us that tell us we are not worthy of happiness, that life is cruel and harsh, that tell us that we need to suffer and lets us focus on tragedies as punishments or penances. This part of us that sees only the darkness robs us of the joys and magic that we have all around us. I imagine if I had said all this to Neferure she would have sneered at me and asked what joy and magic was there in the death of her lover. In truth that is a quite impossible question for a human to answer.

Once again Neferure looked to death with a longing. It would now not only be an escape from a life she once again hated but she would reunite with Samreen. The pull was strong but so too was the reminder that if she left by her own hand she would not join Samreen but be sent to the "other" afterworld of demons and beasts. Human desire though is amazingly powerful and the more she thought about leaving the closer she pulled death towards her. So Neferure slowly allowed her life to end by simply fading away. Suicide does not always have to be quick and sudden and Neferure chose a slower method. The less she ate, the weaker she grew, the more she slept, then the less she had to deal with life. In some ways she was gone long before her last breath.

The body will follow what the mind is directing and so it slowly started to shut down for Neferure. She eventually couldn't walk and became bedridden. Herbs would be forced down her throat by well-meaning physicians only to be vomited within minutes. Neferure's mind, body and spirit had made their pact and nothing was going to interfere with their mission. She eventually slipped into a coma and her final days were begun. Satiah, Matreya and I visited her daily to sit with her in an attempt to be some kind of comfort even though we believed she could no longer hear us. Hatshepsut would come each day but she would not sit with her daughter. In fact she barely looked at her as she asked the physicians as to her state. She would receive her update and leave with no emotion showing.

My blood would boil when I heard of this. Not even in Neferure's final days could she receive any affection from her mother. What I did not know and what Hatshepsut would never admit was that she was in extreme pain. Her hours sitting in court were more than she could bear. To come and sit by her dying child though was even more unbearable. Hatshepsut carried herself through this also with her unrelenting stiffness. She would slip to her chambers where her physicians would be waiting to give her their latest potion and balms. Hatshepsut would say she was still in pain and each day saw the pain growing greater. She asked for larger doses but they didn't stop her symptoms from progressing. Now she was watching her daughter die before her. This was a cruel irony as she should be the one leaving.

Neferure slipped away quietly and gently during the night with only a maid and a priest in her room. They did not even notice she was gone for almost an hour as they tended to their duties, oblivious to her cooling body and the greyness that washed over her face. I was called from my bed as was Hatshepsut and we each made our way to witness her body before it was carried to the mortuary for its final attentions. I arrived first and seeing Neferure's lifeless body was not the sorrowful experience I had thought it would be. I expected to be overcome with grief but I could not cry. Instead I was happy for her. I was happy that she was no longer suffering a life that she hated. Her body did not look as horrifying as that of my father's. Perhaps this was due to my age now but more so because I did not see it as a shell robbed of its life force. I saw a spirit that had been set free.

There was a rustle behind me and I turned to see Hatshepsut, hastily dressed and without her usual kohl lined eyes. I almost didn't recognise the pale, crumpled figure limping through the doorway. She nodded to me as she passed by, making her way to the bed. Hatshepsut also didn't cry as she stood looking at her daughter's body with her face soft and her mouth seeming to be slipping downwards.

"She should not have gone first," she said barely above a whisper.

I jumped slightly, thinking she meant I should have died first, but this was not what she meant at all. We stood silent for a few minutes more.

"Such a wasted life," Hatshepsut still whispered. "To have so much at your fingertips and yet not want any of it." Hatshepsut shook her head and turned to me, "She did not even choose a tomb," she said.

This was not a criticism of her daughter, even though it would seem so. I nodded. "Neferure will have mine. I will find another," I said.

"Thank you Thutmose. You are a most generous brother to your sister," she replied.

This was the closest I ever came to receiving a warm comment from my aunt. Hatshepsut left the room and I nodded to the priests, signalling that they could now take the body to the mortuary.

So my beloved sister-cousin took my original tomb as her resting place. We would not paint stories of her depression or her love affair with Samreen upon its walls. She was depicted as a grand princess destined for amazing things and all were happy for her to be remembered as such. After her mummy was placed in her tomb I would lie in bed at night and picture her walking through the golden gates of the afterworld. In my visions she would reach the last and as she stepped through Samreen would be waiting to greet her and they would walk together in their new amazing life.

CHAPTER TWELVE

Death is not uncommon in anyone's experience of life, but the deaths of those close to us can affect and define us in many ways. Hatshepsut losing Sitre took away any warmth in her life. Neferure's death was a harsh reminder of her shortcomings, not so much as a mother but as a Pharaoh in failing to create a bloodline successor. Even though I was much more able and willing I was a poor substitute for her. Neferure's death was also a reminder of her own mortality. Her body was growing weaker by the day and she knew her final years were now in place. So she grasped onto the last person who she trusted and who served her better than anyone else--Senemut.

Senemut was almost running the country as it was. He made all her decisions for her and would often initiate processes without even consulting her. Everyone from the high priests to the viziers and butlers knew that if Senemut spoke to them it was as good as if Hatshepsut spoke herself. You could imagine that this might have irritated a woman who loved her power so much and who needed to control everything but instead it provided her relief. It meant less time sitting in court, which was now so painful. It also meant that she did not need to travel anymore which was both agonizing and exhausting. She trusted him implicitly, knowing that he understood her and her intentions for the land. That he was also wary of me was a bonus.

Senemut though was running on pure adrenalin. His days were long and frenetic. The more he did to "support" Hatshepsut the more she seemed to hand to him so he that was on the move constantly. When he was not at court then he was riding out to oversee a building project or make his presence known to the traders and commoners. Senemut though was aging also. He was the same in years as Hatshepsut and, while not cursed with the genetic afflictions that she was destined for, his body was simply not as rigorous anymore.

The two very buildings that let Senemut be known to you today caused his ultimate downfall. He was so passionate about creating that most incredible temple for Hatshepsut that he spent as much time as possible at the site. From the first strike of chisel to the last stroke of paint, Senemut was there breathing in every detail, making sure that it was all going according to plan and as magnificent as he intended for her. In ancient times though there were no such things as dust masks so not only was Senemut breathing in his building's details he was also literally breathing in dust and stone particles. He followed this construction soon after with the building of his own temple nearby, adding to the sediments already settling in his lungs. His lungs coped for a while with the irritation but they eventually inflamed and began to fill with fluids. His breaths began to shorten and though he continued on with his duties as busy as ever he would have to sit often or stop to catch his breath.

Eventually he had to slow right down and like Hatshepsut was soon only to be found around the palace and court. Their deteriorating health gave them the perfect excuse to spend their final years in each others company virtually twenty-four hours a day. They would sit side by side, she grimacing from pain and he wheezing with each breath. Of course Senemut would be the first to give up and we once again had a death occurring within the palace. Senemut did not return to Karnak to die in the temple as was the custom for any ordinary high priest. Hatshepsut insisted he stay within the palace and had the same vigil that any of our royal family would have been afforded. She wouldn't let the physicians try to delay his death with herbs or tinctures. Hatshepsut finally had reached the conclusion that sometimes things just needed to run their course. Watching the slow prolonged deaths of parents, her brother, her nurse and daughter had taken their toll and she gave Senemut the death that she hoped the Gods would allow her soon also. Senemut was kept comfortable of course but Hatshepsut did not see why he should be delayed his passage to the afterlife where he would breathe freely and walk tall once again.

Senemut passed within a few days of taking to bed for the final time. They were not his most pleasant days but they were soon over and he was placed into his tomb below that of Hatshepsut's, the only person to be placed so close to her aside from Sitre. Hatshepsut once again mourned silently, five years after losing her daughter and eight years after losing Sitre. Her lover, her confidant and only true friend were now gone. All that Hatshepsut had now was I, a strong and capable man, ready to succeed her in a blink. Not surprisingly her health failed rapidly after the death of Senemut.

Knowing her final days were now approaching Hatshepsut sought to make sure that despite my outward signs of capability I was indeed ready to take over the throne. She called meetings almost daily and would perform an almost comedic mixture of quizzes and hypothetical situations to test what I had learnt. I would answer as diligently and knowledgably as ever, when I was unsure of what to answer I would make up an answer which I knew would placate her and we would both leave the meeting happy. As her pain grew she would eventually need to be carried to court but then even that was too much and Hatshepsut ended up addressing or receiving people from her private rooms, some days even in her bed.

Our last meeting was held in her bedchamber late in the afternoon. The heavy drapes were still drawn from the night before in an attempt to keep the heat out and despite the servants continually fanning Hatshepsut the room was stale and musky. The incense and herbs being brought to her made the room smell the same as any death room. She was sitting up in bed breathing so shallow that it recalled my father and Neferure's last hours when they too breathed this way. Hatshepsut's face though was swollen and not sunken like those that were about to pass. It was also not pale but red and she was sweating profusely. I approached the bed and bowed with the respect I always tokenly gave her, and sat in the chair that was made ready for me.

As usual Hatshepsut spoke first. "Young Pharaoh, it is good to see you," she spoke in a barely a whisper and her breath rasped as it entered her. I could tell that every word was painful. "I will not question you today, I know you are ready," she said.

Hatshepsut stopped and closed her eyes and I saw her chest rise as she tried to take in a deep breath. She slowly raised her right hand to her face cupping her jaw.

"My final days are here Thutmose, I know you have been waiting for them," she managed to say before another awkward breath made its way into her. "How you were so patient bewilders me." Another breath and she grimaced, cupping the side of her face again. "You have been true to our family from birth--stay true until your death--as have I."

I could do nothing but sit in silence and nod.

"I will be gone soon, do not let them prolong anything," she begged. "I am ready to join our fathers."

I nodded again. "As you wish," I answered.

"Go now," she said softly.

"Yes Pharaoh," I said addressing her for the very first time as such, knowing also that it would be the last time I would have the opportunity.

I stood to leave and bowed but as I rose I saw Hatshepsut in an entirely different way. This powerful woman who had ruled and shaped my entire life was now lying before me frail, vulnerable and soon to be gone. All my hatred evaporated in a second and I was overcome with sympathy for her. I walked to the bed and leant over and kissed her forehead. Hatshepsut's eyes grew wide as I had never attempted such affection before. I'm sure for a moment she also suspected that I was about to finish her there and then. Of course that never crossed my mind and as I pulled away I smiled.

"Farewell. May your journey with the Gods be grand," I whispered.

Hatshepsut smiled back ever so slightly and closed her eyes. I left her as she headed towards sleep and walked back to my rooms.

As I walked into the corridor I suddenly became aware of what had just happened. I had said my final goodbye to my co-regent. In effect I was now sole ruler. I was finally the only Pharaoh. The realisation made me stop dead in my tracks. The elation of finally reaching this moment though was washed over by an equally strong rush of fear. Now I was standing as Pharaoh just as I did twenty-two years ago when my father died and was scared once more. There was no other Hatshepsut to step in and guide me or to be my backup. I could never reveal my fear to anyone. It would be the same as going into battle without my shield and sword. So I squared my shoulders and walked as I knew the ruler of Egypt should. I recalled my work so far, my amazing army, my sons in line to succeed me and the fear soon fell away.

Hatshepsut's last days were intense for her and those who attended. I did not intervene as she requested. Even though Senemut was gone she was still surrounded by devout and loyal priests, courtiers and butlers determined to save her. While she still had a pulse and breath she was Pharaoh and it was their duty to preserve her. If I had spoken and asserted her unwitnessed last request it would have been akin to assassination. Their transition to my rule would be hard enough for them without adding such a tension to these days. So I watched and spoke when asked anything but did not interfere with their fussing and attentions. Besides I had matters of court to now watch over and an army to lead on my own. The news of Hatshepsut's imminent death would be spreading fast and setting up possible opportunities for uprisings or attacks by neighbours seeing this as a time of weakness.

Hatshepsut's death was as dramatic as her life. Despite her claims to be ready to leave she did not slip away with grace but went out almost with an explosion. A massive abscess on her right jaw now matched the crippling back and hip pain that had dominated her last few years. As the arthritis and now bone cancer ate away at her lower body her jaw was on fire with infection. The abscess sat like a suicide pill within her mouth waiting for when it would unleash its poison. The physicians would normally have pulled all the teeth around it but when they looked they knew this was far worse than anything they had ever seen. Too scared to touch it and deciding to rely on potions the abscess merely festered.

Finally in the night that followed my last meeting with Hatshepsut it released its poison into her bloodstream, making its way through her body and inflaming every cell it passed and touched. Her body was on fire inside and maids would end up wiping her continually to soak up the sweat and attempt to cool her while inside Hatshepsut's body fell apart. Blood vessels swelled and burst, shutting down her kidneys and smaller organs. Then within her brain, strained and squeezed by the fluids accumulating around it, one final artery split open and it was over.

The final moment was quick and her final gurgle was her last attempt to address those around her. Those watching her at the time all heard something different. Some heard goodbye, some heard one last demand, and for others it was a cry for help. I know though it was none of these. It was that split second all humans have as their body lets the spirit slip away. Hatshepsut saw her reality clearly and with her last breath sighed with her realisation. If those in the room could have heard beyond words they would have been privy to a great secret but they would know in their own time, as we all do.

The news of Hatshepsut's death reached me in my private rooms where I was sitting with Satiah, Matreya and my mother. With one simple sentence delivered by a priest our lives were changed. We sat quietly for several minutes and took in the news. Satiah walked to me and placed her hand on my shoulder.

She did not need to say anything and I looked up at her and nodded. I looked at the three women with me who were now all the family I had along with my children. There was no one to challenge me anymore.

I stood and turned to my mother. "Shall you join me to say our last goodbye to Hatshepsut?" I asked her.

My mother nodded and I put out my hand so that we could walk hand in hand on my first walk through the palace as the rightful Pharaoh I was born to be. As I walked through the door to begin the walk I turned to Satiah and Matreya who were also making their way to follow us.

"Wake our sons," I said. "They will join us also."

The women did not question me and made their way to the nursery rooms to gather each of the four boys. I had seen my first dead body at age ten and it was my father's. The shock of seeing the first body is huge I know but I would rather that they see it of someone who they had no immense affection for, and one that had passed from illness rather than battle wounds. This was the perfect opportunity to teach them and make them stronger, without causing the hurt of it being someone they cared for.

My mother and I continued our way to Hatshepsut's room. Despite the wafts of incense we could smell her death as we reached the door. The heat not only of the air but also within her body was helping the decay begin almost immediately. Her body did not have that sunken look as it was still swollen from fluid but the grey had finally taken hold. We both stood hardly believing that this woman was finally gone and listened to the physician describe her final hours, almost begging to be believed that they had done all they could to spare her. Finally his discourse was ended and we were able to stand in silence, still holding each other's hands.

Satiah and Matreya soon arrived each leading a son in each hand. Satiah had whispered to Amenemhat and Siamun along the way as to what my request would involve. Amenemhat was scared but intrigued and asked no questions and Siamun followed his example. Behind them Matreya walked in silence, scowling at Satiah's attempt to prepare her sons. She said nothing to Amenhotep or Menkheperre knowing they would find out soon enough and would not baby them as she thought Satiah chose to do with her sons.

However Menkheperre at seven years old was inquisitive and hyperactive, bouncing beside his mother, barraging her with questions. "What is mother Satiah saying? Where are we going? Why did father not call the girls?" he asked quickly and loudly.

"Hush!" Matreya hissed back. "Be quiet and stop jumping. We are almost there."

They rounded the last corner and Satiah stopped talking knowing they were in earshot of the room. The boys could smell the room and while Amenemhat and Siamun were prepared, Amenhotep was hit with an instinctive fear and stopped walking, pulling on his mother's arm and shaking his head.

"Keep walking!" she said, and dragged him forward.

My sons entered the room, some ready and understanding what they would see, one with his heart racing knowing only that it was not something good and the youngest bursting with curiosity. I turned to greet them with a stiff face and put my hand out. "Come here," I directed and beckoned them towards me.

By this time they had seen Hatshepsut's body lying upon her bed. Amenemhat walked towards me, looking at the body the whole time. Amenhotep ran and buried his face in my belly to avoid seeing her and began crying. I grabbed his shoulders though and turned him around to face the bed. I kept one hand on his right shoulder to keep him in place and pulled the other boys towards me, turning them also to face Hatshepsut's body. Amenhotep stopped his sobbing but tears still fell.

"Your aunt, the Pharaoh, has crossed to the afterlife," I stated.

Amenemhat looked up at me confused. "Father, but she is still here," he said.

"These are but her remains," I answered. "Her *ka* has left to journey with Osiris and begin her new life."

Amenemhat and Siamun nodded their understanding. Amenhotep finally stopped weeping, somewhat comforted by my words--but he still wasn't happy to be there.

"It is good for you to see her my sons, for this is the order of life and as royal princes you need to be aware that while you will live forever in the afterlife, your time here is short," I said. "Live with this knowledge and make your lives as grand as they can be."

I wanted to say more but tears began to well in my eyes and my voice faltered. Here I stood behind my sons, the eldest were as old as I was when my father passed and I became Pharaoh. I could stand here now knowing that no one would stand in Amenemhat's way if I died soon. Thankfully this was not to be the case. I only hoped that I would be enough of an inspiration to my son to create his own successor and carry on our lineage with the pride that I now would.

Once again the palace sent a body to the mortuary for its funeral rites and preparations. A Pharaoh takes somewhat longer to prepare for internment as they must be prepared in the most detailed of manners. Not only is the mummification process done most seriously but it was our duty to also gather her adornments and commission her funeral mask. Needless to say the sporadic funerals of royalty were quite an industry for Egypt and no less than five hundred people went to work from the announcement of her death to prepare not only her body, but her tomb, burial jewellery, the procession and rites that would be performed until her burial. The amount of people involved ensured that all went smoothly and you would assume expertly also.

Hatshepsut's mummification was done with all our grand society traditions and of course her own special twist that would ensure that three and a half thousand years later all would know just who these remains were of. The mortician priests assigned to her remains were of course the most experienced and knowledgeable of any in the land. There were two of them overseeing the technical side whilst two high priests, including Hatshepsut's beloved Ma-Keet would oversee and chant during certain procedures. They began with the draining of blood and removal of the organs as always. The air was tense as the morticians were nervous due to the serious nature of this particular embalming. Hatshepsut's personal high priests were also notorious for embodying their mistress's demanding and aggressive nature, and their sharp eyes were constantly upon them measuring their every move. The body was finally emptied and the process of cleaning was begun when a simple accident ensured Hatshepsut's remains did indeed achieve their eternal notoriety.

The younger mortician began to swab inside Hatshepsut's mouth, paying attention to the pus-ridden remains of the jawbone where her fatal abscess had begun. He was gentle and would swear this to his dying day but Hatshepsut's teeth had long ago began to rot so that his final prod with the cloth wrapped around his finger was enough to break away one of her molars. His horror as he felt it give way registered so plainly on his face that the second mortician did not even have to ask what had happened and he gasped while the high priests rushed forward.

"What have you done?" screamed Ma-Keet.

"One of her teeth--it has dislodged," stammered the mortician.

"Show me!" she screamed.

The mortician gently reached in and removed the tooth, petrified that he might break another tooth in the process. Fortunately he didn't and standing up he raised his hand displaying the bloodied yellow tooth between his trembling fingertips. Ma-Keet and the other priest looked to each other, their faces red with anger and frustration. You may think it peculiar that such a small accident would be taken so seriously especially at this stage of the Pharaoh's existence. However the preservation of the body is a serious matter and the manner in which it is entombed is the manner in which it will enjoy the afterlife. The person required their organs preserved and the shell intact, including their remaining teeth. Any damage no matter how small at this stage was sacrilege, especially to a Pharaoh.

Ma-Keet knew it would be up to her to decide how this would be dealt with. She rubbed her forehead and looked at the Canopic jars ready to be filled with their respective organs. Then she looked to their side and saw a small wooden chest with Hatshepsut's cartouche upon it. This was to house Hatshepsut's liver and bowels upon the completion of their own preservation but was sitting empty at this moment.

"Place it in there," she said pointing at the chest. "When the liver and bowel are placed make sure it is well secured between them. No one is to ever speak of this."

Ma-Keet sighed and prayed that this was the last royal death she would have to oversee, never knowing that her simple decision that day would thousands of years later lead to Hatshepsut's mummy being identified by your modern scientists.

# CHAPTER THIRTEEN

While Hatshepsut's death set those of us within Egypt into a flurry of activity, the news also spread quickly to our neighbours and they began their own preparations. The female Pharaoh was gone and the boy King was finally ruler. Despite my age I was still seen as some sort of junior and my prowess as army commander and soldier were yet to be fully displayed or tested. Hatshepsut's reign had been peaceful and our borders so well protected that any attempts to challenge them were quashed quickly and easily. There had been no need for battles and we had not sought to push ourselves any further.

A change in any government though is seen as a vulnerable time as officials and stewards realign to their new leader. A time of change is a wonderful opportunity to expose weaknesses and there is little time for strategizing. The difference with my stepping into sole rule was that I was indeed not fresh at my duties. I had twenty-two years as Hatshepsut's co-ruler and as army commander. I doubt anyone could deny that is more than a reasonable training period. In fact my training had ended long ago. I was able and ready, as Egypt needed me to be.

The lands to our northeast were always tempestuous. Indeed they still are. It's as though those souls who wish to experience tension and drama at its highest levels are drawn there. The kings of the regions here had sat back and accepted Egypt's dominance but after twenty years of being subjugated by a woman they began to talk to each other. They knew Hatshepsut would soon be gone and that if they were ready her death would be a perfect time to reclaim their lands from Egyptian rule and possibly claim Egypt itself. These small countries and tribes also knew that it would require their unity and they swore an allegiance between them.

The lands of Canaan, your modern day Israel and Lebanon were precious to so many of us. They were the area that lined the sea and crossed inland to Assyria and Mesopotamia. They swept down from the lands ruled by the emerging Greco-Romans to my lands of Egypt. They were not vast but they were the focal part of several key trade routes. Harmony here was essential to all--but especially to Egypt. Controlling the movement of goods through here drove our prosperity and stability. The dominance of these lands through tributes and taxes funded our buildings and luxuries, relieving our own farmers and craftsmen of taxes that would compromise their lifestyles. Past uprisings had also allowed us to enslave vast numbers of men, depleting their armies and tradesmen. It had all worked quite well until now and it was no wonder their kings were itching to reclaim their independence and rightful wealth.

At the first news of Hatshepsut's death the four major kings gathered and held conference at Megiddo. They underestimated my planning and leadership though. Hatshepsut's death was far from sudden and as I told you I was well prepared for this time. I had slowly taken over the policies and trade whilst maintaining my army. I now had the full picture of what lay at my fingertips. I was thankful to Hatshepsut for leaving me to focus on the army for all those years and now the duties of trade were a simple addition, aided by the loyal and talented viziers and stewards we had surrounding us. The well-oiled machinations of the palace and its people helped me beyond words and I thank them eternally for giving me the foundation upon which my skills as king and commander flourished.

I can tell you now that every great general did not win his battles through sheer skill and force. Just ask any of the Spartans who stood battle at their pass. There are many elements that come into play. Strategy and tactics are just the skeleton. Determination, loyalty and courage are the flesh that ultimately moves the victory. What I can also tell you is that there is an aspect that no general can define with words; but I will try to share this with you anyway. Napoleon stood overlooking hills and sensed the best way to ride, Alexander the Great would wake in the morning and know what he needed to do that day, Ramtha would feel the wind and smell which way he needed his men to march. It is the inner knowing that we all possess and tune into sporadically. You think of someone and the phone rings and it is that person. It is within experiences of déjà vu and also as the chills that course down your spine when someone shares an epiphany.

Yes, men have utilised this knowingness for battles and that seems like some sort of incongruence for a sense that is so pure and universal. A sense that we imagine should only be used for achieving peace and harmony. This is the trap of good versus evil that humans have learnt to live their life by. Any battle begins with the agendas of each of its combatants and each will tell you that they are the one who is right and worthy of victory. They begin with the hope that they will succeed and defeat their enemy. They picture the spoils of the win and their egos swell in anticipation. At the core of all the human machinations is one desire that drives all the surface elements of power and glory and that is the fundamental desire to survive. You grasp onto this sheer animalistic reflex to keep breathing and existing. It is this drive that fuels all your actions. This basic desire and need to survive connects us to this sense--as long as we are willing to listen. Those that do listen allow a flow that is unpredictable and undefinable but enables the greatness that will be spoken of for years to come.

I know now that I began to open that sense from an early age, but then I imagined it was just my calling to be leader and the subsequent skills showered upon me by the Gods. The true awakening though was standing on the balcony with my beloved Arisina. When she placed her hand on my chest and invited me to remember the truth I carried inside, it awoke something that I would never forget across all my lives. In that moment I connected to that inner strength and knowing that is within us all and that connection allowed me to be the greatest pharaoh of the 18th Dynasty if not of all ancient Egypt.

It was that knowing that sensed the dissonance brewing to the north and east of Egypt and I did not stress or display any anxiety as the border skirmishes began. My army was ready and my court prepared. In fact a good stoush with our neighbours would be a wonderful exercise for us all to show just how strong, powerful and organised I was--not only to our neighbours but also to Egypt. When our scouts returned from reconnaissance missions across the ridge into Canaan and reported that the great armies of Mitanni, Kadesh and the Canaan plains had gathered and joined at Megiddo, we all became excited. Finally there was no more speculation and no more arranging for possibilities. Our call to action had been made and we were itching to get started. The war rooms buzzed with plans as my generals consulted and sent orders. Troops from southern Egypt were ordered back to Thebes to prepare for the journey north and the city swelled with thousands of soldiers overflowing from the barracks and mixing with the civilians. Their very presence notifying all that a huge battle was imminent.

I hardly slept at all during these months of preparation and yes, it was months. How I managed to impregnate Matreya with our final child Isis during this time is beyond me. She must have persuaded me after a quieter day. My children soon learnt that I was no longer able to spend the time with them that I used to. The boys were excited to know that this was because of my impending adventure, the likes of which they one day would also take part in. The older girls, Beketamun and Nefertiry though felt Satiah's apprehension and avoided all talk of battles. Satiah had good reason to fear. She feared not only losing her husband but would look upon Amenemhat knowing that at just thirteen years old, all of Egypt would look to him if I did not return alive. Thankfully she chose not to speak to him about this and I also chose not to, so firmly did I believe that I would return. Besides, I had able priests, priestesses and courtiers who would guide and support him in the highly unlikely event that it should occur. In the meantime he and the three younger boys would follow me to the courts and army rooms as I had with my father. While none seemed to show the same accelerated rate of learning that I had, they were all taking in the rapid amount of plans and ideas quite ably. I would leave knowing that they were quite aware of what was unfolding.

The final week before we left was a blur to anyone involved in the army or the palace. The soldiers were all busy with last minute fittings for armour and having their weapons checked and refined. Tens of thousands of arrows were bundled and ready to carry, swords and daggers were sharpened and shined, while the horses were checked and rechecked by the grooms. Every shoesmith in the land had spent the last two months hurriedly making new sandals for every soldier who would fight with me. We had a long march and campaign ahead and I would not let my men begin with fatigued and splitting footwear. We needed to start with all the glory and splendour that we would ride home to celebrate with our people. I decided footwear would not be enough and commissioned new silk flags to brandish as we rode towards our enemy, showing them the riches and prosperity that was about to conquer them. A little bit of showmanship can go a long way in battle.

The night before we left Thebes every soldier of my army, along with our attendants, the grooms, sword smiths, arrow smiths, physicians and priests gathered at the Great Temple at Karnak for final prayers and blessings. There were eight thousand men that night gathered throughout the main temple and spilling out around the grand lake and smaller temples. Many others, their wives and children, palace officials and curious city dwellers came also to strengthen the prayers. There were tears shed but that night strengthened us beyond words. To finally be gathered in one place, and realise the might that we were, cemented our resolve for victory. To be surrounded by those who we would fight for and have them praying for us, reminded us of what we had to lose.

The ritual was over early enough so that the men could have some final goodbyes, a solid night's sleep and be ready to march at first light. I made my way back to the palace with my usual entourage of bodyguards and priests including Arisina. Satiah, Matreya and the children were also with me and we all made our way in the carriages in silence. My mind was heavy with thoughts of what lay ahead and I could barely focus on enjoying my last night with them all. The younger ones were asleep when we arrived back at the palace and had to be carried to their rooms by servants. I went to each child's bed and kissed them goodnight. They would be awoken the next morning to bid me and my men farewell, but it seemed right to pay special attention to this bedtime. Satiah and Matreya waited in the corridors and when I stepped out to make my way back to my room they both bowed and wished me goodnight. I imagine they assumed I would like my last night alone to rest and I had been quite sporadic in requesting either of them to join me in my bed these last few months. They were about to walk away to their rooms when I stopped Satiah.

"Satiah, I wish you to stay in my bedchamber tonight," I stated as I would have any other night.

However this was no ordinary night. It was possibly my last night in the palace and I had chosen Satiah over Matreya to be the one who would share it with me. Satiah nodded and if I didn't know her better I imagine I saw a faint smile cross her face. Matreya though stiffened and shot me daggers with her eyes. She could not hate me for my choice; after all she was pregnant with Isis and an unsuitable choice to be my bed partner no matter the circumstances. Matreya knew that her continuing pregnancies were the one thing she had over Satiah who had never conceived again after Nefertiry. Now that one thing would mean that Satiah would be the woman to lie with me on my last night before battle and everyone in the palace would know it. Without a word Matreya turned her back on us and made way to her own room.

To be honest I had no desire for sex that night. I just truly wished to have the woman I loved by my side and feel her warmth and softness as I slept. Of course once I was in bed and that warmth and softness was pressed against me it was an entirely different matter and we made love so gently I would almost cry when I thought about it later. I awoke the next morning with my arms still around her and my body encircling hers. I did not want to let her go but I had to. So when my butler summoned me an hour before sunrise to get dressed I sent him from my rooms with the order to wait until I opened the doors. I then made my own private and intimate farewell to Satiah, promising her my return and protection for eternity.

Satiah rose and walked to a table nearby the bed on which her personal things were placed as she prepared for bed the night before. With tears in her eyes she picked up a cloth, one that all women carried that was embroidered with royal symbols and her name. Laying it out in her hand, she picked up one of her earrings and placed it upon the cloth. Opening a drawer now she found some small scissors and walked towards me, the cloth in her left hand with the earring laid upon it and the scissors in her right hand. When she got to me she put the scissors down upon the bed and lifted my right hand and gently laid the cloth and earring upon my it. She then picked up the scissors and reaching up took a lock of hair in her hand and cut a short length. I sat silently as she placed this beside the earring, and then gently folded the cloth over them both.

"Carry these with you and I will always be with you," she whispered.

She gently kissed me on the lips to seal her pledge.

"I will carry it next to my heart in every moment," I promised her.

I did carry it as I promised against the centre of my chest, tucked within my armour. I would pull it out from time to time and touch the earring or lock of hair and my heart would swell. It would help me forget the dustiness of the plains, the searing heat of the sun and the loneliness that would engulf me at times during the night despite being surrounded by thousands of men. I cherished that quiet moment with Satiah, thankful that we had created a night and now this moment of intimacy. However duties beckoned and it would not seem right for the King and chief commander to keep his men waiting. I called to my butler and my first day of campaign was officially begun.

My family gathered to bid me a final goodbye. My mother and Satiah with tears coursing down their faces brought me to the verge of tears also. I needed to remain strong and firm, so even though their embraces made me want to melt I kept my words short and straightforward. This was not the time for flowery diatribes or emotional outpourings. It was a farewell not a goodbye. The children cried also through eyes still sleepy and I cherished their hugs and kisses sending them back to their rooms as soon as I could leaving only the adults around me. Matreya stood back from Satiah and my mother with her chin held high and her eyes still glaring from the sting of my rejection the night before. I approached her to receive a final embrace but her hands remained by her side and I knew not to even attempt contact. She merely bowed her head and wished me luck and protection with the decorum that I would expect of a loyal servant. Matreya made her point as she always did.

I began my walk to the entrance of the palace where my chariot was ready and waiting. Behind it were my generals all on horseback and behind them as far as the eye could see was my army, all lined up and arranged perfectly. They were silent but for the occasional snort or stamp of a horse and a cough from a soldier here or there. I looked upon them with the fiercest pride and thanked my father and Hatshepsut for all they did in placing me in this position. I was so overwhelmed with respect for my men that I stepped forward and crossed my arms before my chest and snapped them back against me; the highest salute that you can give and one usually only given to a king. The generals' momentary shock was replaced with huge smiles at my solidarity and it only took one general to return the salute and bow to me and then all the others followed, creating a wave of salutes and bows throughout the entire army. We had made our pact to each other and I nodded to my generals.

"Let us ride!" I shouted and climbed aboard my chariot.

I snapped the reigns and rode off leading my men out of the city. I did not look back to the women at the palace doors, I was partly too involved in the moment but also knew it would have broken my heart. Instead I led my army out of the city to the cheers and applause of my people as they came out into the streets or leaned out of windows to bid us farewell. The sun was just lifting its lowest edge over the horizon when the very last of the army left the city outskirts and full light was now upon us as we made our way through the smaller towns and headed north.

As the hours passed our formation became less formal and the lines the men began in disappeared as some men fell behind and others quickened their pace. No one totally faltered though and we were all happy to be finally on our way. There was no sense to rush and to do so in the heat of the sun would only wear my men down and they needed to conserve all their strength for the battles that lay ahead. I would order them to rest every few hours, when we found somewhere suitable to stop such as a small town with a spring or well where the men could refill their canteens. All the villages were expecting us, word travelled fast through Egypt, and we were greeted with the respect and reverence we deserved. Many were waiting with banquet tables laid out for me and my generals while barbeque pits roasted meats for the men. Of course few villages could provide an elaborate feast for eight thousand men but the soldiers were always grateful for a fresh cooked meal no matter how small, and the generosity was always well noted by me as their form of tribute and allegiance to Egypt.

It took us eight days to march north towards the Mediterranean Sea and then begin to turn east towards our border town of Tharu. As we headed toward the border region those who had been patrolling the district joined us. We would see them approaching across the sands with their flags held high and as they drew closer with shouts of joy to see the huge army they would now become part of. Over the next three days our numbers would swell to ten thousand men, the most formidable army that Egypt would ever have. The rebels knew this too. Just as we sent spies to them to collect information so too did they. As we rode closer and closer to Canaan, the message was received without any doubt that I was about to wage a battle of unprecedented might and magnitude. I relished every message returned that our enemy knew our power without seeing us and would smile as I was told of the panic and turmoil that was being incited amongst the tribes.

The psychology of war came naturally to me and I knew that being able to manipulate your enemy before you so much as stood on the same ground could be as powerful as any strategy. That is why I spent the time and money on such things as my men's sandals and silk flags. I knew that not only would the size of my force be something to be reckoned with but that an army displaying its wealth and prosperity would also demoralize and intimidate the enemy on another level. Indeed the word did get back to the rebels that not only was Pharaoh Thutmose proceeding with an epic armed force but that it was one filled with elaborately dressed men, armed with endless resources. This scared the rebels more than anything and as each day passed they would re-meet and re-plan, going over their options and ideas, arguing fervently to have their strategy chosen over that of another tribal leader. This lack of total unity within their alliance was like a cancer that was not yet detected. It was a weakness that would soon express itself as time wore on.

The rebels agreed on one thing though and that was that Megiddo would be the site of their confrontation. Megiddo was a fortified city and the largest after Kadesh, which was further north. Megiddo was like a gateway for the region; the layout of the land meant that it was the city which oversaw any trade movement from Mesopotamia to the sea and back again. Its position just north of the Mount Carmel ridge made it a guardian of all that lay north of these mountains. The rebel alliance was quite clever to make this their battlefront. It was the most southern of the major cities. To use a smaller and unprotected town situated before it would have been suicide. Instead they had a massive fort to act as a protective backdrop and from which to draw upon resources. They also assumed we would be fatigued from the long journey from Thebes to make our way there. All of these things had an element of truth to them but they would not ensure their success, instead it merely ended up drawing out the battle for months instead of days.

Ten days after leaving Thebes and upon the twenty-third anniversary of my coronation, we entered the city of Gaza, the southernmost city of Canaan, and claimed it for Egypt. The city was not stupid enough to pit their small force against our army and we arrived to find their leaders prostrating themselves upon the ground and begging for mercy--which of course we gave. A bloodless victory is always the easiest, especially when no blood of your own men is spilled. So Gaza, instead of being our first taste of a fight, was merely our first conquest. I did not deplete the town of its men to swell my ranks any more as this was not needed. Instead I made them pay tribute to me and depleted them of their gold, jewels and excess food. Bringing a town to its knees is just as effective as wiping them out. Reduce them to their basics and they are reverted to survival mode. They have no time or money to plan an uprising or confrontation when their day-to-day needs of food and shelter are not being met. This became our strategy as we moved through each small town or village on our way north. Word spread ahead of us and we arrived at each place without any struggle and with their tributes ready.

We left Gaza after only one day, rested, fed and encouraged at having conquered the southern port city. We all rose before dawn to pray before we recommenced our march north. My priests gathered in the pharaonic tent in which I slept at night and planned our campaign each day. They chanted and burnt incense to protect me and my men for the day. They asked for me to be blessed with the wisdom to make successful decisions and for plagues and misfortune to visit our enemy. I would take this time to sit quietly and see the day ahead, listening for the guidance that the Gods would send me for victory. We would then head out of the tent to greet the rising sun, the symbol of Ra, and give thanks for our fortune and progress so far.

During this ceremony each day the priests would look for signs to provide some message or for acknowledgment of what was achieved so far. The curl of the smoke off the incense would be Horus sending his blessing, a sharp wind making the embers glow would be Amun's embrace. On this morning though, we received the most amazing sign ever.

As we left the tent and turned to greet the sun we all gasped. There just above where the sun was about to rise was a star glowing like no other we had ever seen. A trail of stardust extended beyond it and faded into infinity. It was an amazing meteor, unexpected and never before seen by any of the priests, generals or myself. Certainly we knew such things could happen, but even our amazing grasp of astronomy did not know when to predict such occurrences. We all stood in silence, overwhelmed at first by its beauty, and then by the timing that had to be far from any coincidence. The priests fell to the ground and my generals followed suit. I however remained standing to acknowledge this sign with all the majesty and authority I possessed. I did not need the priests to interpret or conjure a story. I understood completely. The Gods were congratulating me and telling me to continue onwards. I too would sweep across the land leaving a trail behind me, shining brighter than all others. Any doubts that anyone or I had as to the destiny of our campaign were now totally relinquished and we marched that day knowing that we had the full blessing and command of the Gods to continue onwards.

It took us another eleven days to arrive at Yehem, our final town at which we would take rest before we would cross the mountain ridge and move upon the truly major cities of Canaan. It took us this long for the short distance as the land was now rougher and we of course would stop at least a day within each town to collect tribute and be assured of their succumbing to our dominance. So we arrived at Yehem and the soldiers were ordered to rest, the tradesmen to attend to any repairs and the grooms to ensure the horses were at their best. My tent was struck as always and I gathered my generals within to unroll their maps and finally plan our attack. We had barely begun when a small cloud of dust in the distance announced someone arriving. One of our scouts was returning at breakneck speed to share his news. He rushed up to the tent bringing his dust cloud with him, dripping with sweat and his horse on the verge of collapse.

"Sire!" he shouted without even bothering to dismount. "Megiddo is being prepared for battle!"

"Get down from there," snapped a general. "How dare you address the Pharaoh like this."

Jumping down from his horse, he bowed low to me, as he should have in the first place, breathing quickly with excitement and the strain of his horse ride.

"I am sorry Sire," he carried on, "but there is much to tell and it is occurring quickly."

I nodded at him, appreciative of his passion and exuberance in returning this news. My heart jumped. If they were still in the throes of decision-making then they would be easy to defeat, however we also were yet to solidify our plans and that too could be our weakness. I knew that a steady head was what was needed right now.

"Come inside and sit in the shade," I ordered. "Fetch this man some water and food."

My scout needed to calm down and be refreshed; then I was sure to receive his news clearer. It also gave my generals and myself some time to settle after his dramatic arrival. We were all seated again inside, gathered around the map table. The scout's maps were retrieved from his horse pack and unrolled before us.

"Here Sire, just past the ridge of Carmel, at Megiddo. All the kings are gathered. *ALL*! From Kadesh, Mitanni and the Canaan coast, they are all here with their armies and banded together with the smaller tribes. They know of your army and they know they will only defeat you as one," he spilled out as he pointed to places marked upon his maps. "Megiddo is being fortified as we speak, filled with provisions for them all. It is a massive city Sire--it is surrounded by huge walls and would prove a formidable refuge for them all."

My generals looked to me; all seemed to be somewhat thrown by this news. We had expected the kings to unite, but the addition of the tribes was another matter. The southern tribes had been left to fend for themselves and had been easy acquisitions but this northern area was to be another matter. I however was not worried at all. I was ever confident of my army and knew that we could deal with whatever we would meet.

"How many men?" I asked.

"They would match us but not exceed our numbers." He then went on to describe the composition of the army--how many archers, the swordsmen and the amount of chariots. They were not yet officially positioned and were in the midst of forming their placements before the city when the scout decided he should ride back to report to us.

I sat for a moment and looked to my map. The mountain ridge was our last bastion. Once we crossed this we would be finally confronting the enemy with all their might and we needed to be prepared.

"How shall we approach them?" I asked the scout.

He jumped up and pointed along the map. "There are two ways Sire. We can round the ridge north via Zafti, a small town with no armed forces present--or we can go south through Taanach, which is already deserted as they are expecting you to pass this way."

"Surely there is a more direct way?" I asked. "Is there not passage through the mountains?"

"Sire, even if there was it would be treacherous and time consuming," he said, shaking his head to emphasise his feelings about this.

As I looked at the map I could not see us passing north or south; I only saw us passing through the mountains directly into Megiddo. The Gods would clear a way for us I just knew it. I looked up at my men and smiled.

"Send scouts to the ridge. I wish to know any of the ways that we can pass through," I demanded and my generals all jumped in their chairs.

"Your Highness, can we afford this time, when we know we can pass safely by two other means?" one asked.

"Can we afford the time to ensure a victory?" I asked in return.

This silenced any murmurs or mutterings that began but they were far from happy and I am sure several of them questioned my sanity in that moment. The scouts were dispatched in three teams of three, one towards Zafti in the north, the other towards Taanach in the south and the third team straight ahead towards Aruna and the centre of the ridge. They rode at night under only the light of a waxing moon that shone brightly for them. The scouts sent to the north and south returned by mid morning confirming both routes as easy and unobstructed. Their sighting of the enemies' scouts in the distance as they cleared the mountains confirmed that we were indeed expected either of these ways and their sighting of my men proved to be fortuitous in the enemy making their plans as such.

It was midday and the Aruna scouts had not returned. My generals began to grumble that this was indeed already an indicator of the unsuitability of this route but I was not going to make such a conclusion yet. As the afternoon wore on there was discussion that perhaps the men had been captured or the pass so dangerous that they had fallen to injury. I felt none of this to be true and kept my vigil in my tent awaiting their return. The first signs of dusk were beginning when a telltale dust cloud could be seen on the trail leading to Aruna. The men were back, albeit weary, dusty and sporting some scratches and scrapes.

The news they carried was double-edged. Yes, there was a pass through the mountains and they had succeeded to ride completely through to the northern side to ensure we would not march into a dead end. It led to an opening and small plain area directly opposite Megiddo at which no enemy forces were waiting. Indeed the men had been able to ride into the open without any fear of being noticed. My eyes lit up and I smiled to my generals. Then came the "however" and it was a pretty huge however. The trail through the ridge had parts that were steep, their horses had only just been able to climb them, in other parts it was so narrow that they had to pass one rider at a time and no doubt the chariots would scrape as they did pass through. It took the three men two hand fells of the sun to pass through, which you know as two hours. This was the final straw for the generals and they began their blustering.

"Why would such a pass be chosen when there are two far more fitting?"

"We will be trapped like cobras in a basket if the rebels realise…"

"What if there is a rock fall--or the scouts do not recall the way and we are led into a closure…"

"Ten men could simply slay us as we emerge…"

I remained quiet and continued to stare at the map before me. We now had three lines drawn on the map and it would be my decision as to which line would become our route to Megiddo. The more I looked the more my eyes were drawn to that central line. The more I closed out the voices around me arguing and debating the clearer I heard the "yes" each time I looked at this central route. I took a deep breath and announced my decision to the generals.

As expected this only increased the debate and their gesturing grew stronger and their faces grew redder. I remained calm and they soon remembered their places and settled but they were far from happy and I knew I had more work to convince them.

"My men please listen," I asked of them. "The Gods are telling me that Aruna is the path we must take. Did you not all witness the miracle in the sky they sent to bless us? Surely we would not have been sent this sign if we were to be defeated? My calling is now to go through this pass. The scouts have told us that they are not waiting as they expect us to take the easy paths. The easy path is not the way for us though. We will burst out of the mountains and surprise them. All their planning and preparations will be undone but we will be ready. We will be victorious and Egypt will remember us forevermore. So I now tell you as your Pharaoh and commander that tomorrow morning I will ride to Aruna and begin the journey through the ridge. Those of you who choose to join me shall follow. You may choose to lead your divisions along the other ways but you will tell the enemy that we fight divided and fear my decisions."

A silence fell through the tent as the men took in my words. My speech had not been a mere political spin and they knew it. The image of the comet was burned into their memories and connected with them stronger than any logical strategy I could have laid out on a map for them. The first general stood and bowed to me.

"Your Highness--as the Gods have decreed you our leader by breathing life into you, I cannot do anything but follow you and claim victory for Egypt," he said. The rest of the men began to pound the table with their fists showing their agreement and solidarity, cheering and shouting as they did so.

I looked upon them smiling, "So go and tell our men that we ride once again at dawn to take the town of Aruna and begin the final ride to Megiddo to make Egypt the grandest it has ever been."

CHAPTER FOURTEEN

Aruna fell easily. It did not matter that they knew the size of our force heading towards them--to see us finally approaching their town with my men fanned out behind the bank of chariots was enough for them to fly their surrender flags. They resisted the tribute we demanded but that only meant we resorted to plunder. I could now say I possessed all of southern Canaan.

I allowed only one night of rest and we continued on again the next morning at dawn. Seeing the mountain ridge ahead of us and knowing that we were so close to displaying our might had our adrenalin pumping and I am sure many men joined me in a very light sleep as we imagined what the following day would bring. I had the scouts who had found the way through the pass ride close behind me where they could shout out directions, but it would be I who led my men through. The scouts did not exaggerate at all as to the perils of the journey here. I had to step off my horse many times to make an easier climb or to lead him through a narrow corridor, as did all the men following. Chariots were indeed scraped, men fell, or twisted ankles but we all made it.

Two and a half hours later, just as the sun reached its peak in the sky, I finally emerged through the rocks on the other side and onto the plain. As promised there were no enemy waiting here and I looked across the empty ground to see Megiddo sitting atop her rise. It looked like no city of Egypt with its high walls forming an almost perfect circle around her, wrapped like a present, protecting its prize within. I smiled at the thought I would soon be her ruler. I now turned back to the valley opening and stood within my chariot for the next couple of hours watching each and every man of my army arrive through the valley, giving my thanks and accepting their bows. There were natural rock escarpments which protected them as they came out and it was not until over half my forces were spilled onto the plain that the rebels realised what had happened and reports of their movement filtered back to me.

My first strategy worked to perfection. Their forces went into panic and began to rearrange in a state of alarm and confusion. Not least because they had split their forces into two, each half to meet us at either the north or south route that we were expected at. Instead we had arrived in-between both their divisions, and at the rear of both. All the logistics of battle aside this scared the kings and tribal leaders beyond anything I could imagine. I was described with words such as "lunatic" and "madman" for attempting such a journey with a force my size, but alongside these names I was also called "formidable" and discussions of me having supernatural powers abounded. If I was prepared to risk my men in such a way and succeed, then what else was I willing to risk, and what else was I possible of achieving? The fear it struck in the men was beyond anything they could admit. They knew of our Egyptian Gods and had laughed, but today they now met with the possibility that these very Gods they ridiculed were about to send this single king to defeat them all.

I further confused them by not attacking immediately upon our arrival. Yes, this allowed them to reconfigure and plan, but it allowed us rest and an opportunity to plan as well. It also afforded us time for prayers and the rebels knew this also.

"Call all the men together before the walls of the town," ordered the King of Kadesh.

"Surely we should attempt to attack tonight?" retorted the King of Megiddo.

"That is what they want!" the King of Kadesh declared. "A panicked, unplanned attack. No, my friend, we shall use their tactic and attack when we are truly prepared. Besides let us give them the time to pray to their animal headed Gods. They will need all the help they can get."

"Have you seen the size of their force and their resources? I truly doubt they need much more help," said another king.

"We match them with everything and we have the city for protection. What do they have but a mountain range and a suicidal tunnel for retreat behind them!" was the reply from the Kadesh leader.

They could use all the bravado that their words could elicit, they could pretend to be as unified as they liked, but they had already lost and they knew it. Being the proud leaders that they were though, they would put up a fight and not accept this until they were captured. The King of Megiddo spent the afternoon listing his regrets whilst the others kept plotting and planning for battle the next day. They all met in their tent just outside the walls and bickered and moaned as to the undoing of their initial plans. They had no back up--and why would they have had one--as the Aruna pass was never considered an option.

I sat with my generals and we watched the movement of their men as the afternoon passed on. They gathered from north and south and fell into the usual formation. Then an hour later, after I assumed a meeting of the kings had been held, we watched them rearrange, and then again two hours later. Our bemusement at this indecision was a victory all in itself. When we watched them rearrange for the third time my generals and myself actually broke out in raucous laughter.

"If only we had music, this would be a wonderful dance," one of my generals bellowed and we all laughed even harder.

In the meantime, my men rested within their standard formation and I was grateful that I did not react to all the movement of the enemy. My men remained quiet and calm while I imagined and hoped that the panic and confusion I was watching would tire the men outside Megiddo. As darkness fell there was no movement within the enemy lines and I knew that they had finally decided on their final formation. I called my generals and we had our final meeting and within ten minutes had our simple plan in hand and ready to be shared with our men. No one would sleep that night on either side but we would rest and this is enough for any soldier. Each army would have their guards watching intently ready to alert all and sundry.

Our priests walked through our men praying continually through the night and my tent was thick with incense to protect and guide me. I never prayed as hard as I did that night. I prayed for victory, I prayed for the might of Egypt to grow stronger, I prayed for my men to return home, I prayed for my own return home. I thought of Satiah, my mother, even Matreya and most of all my children. I did not want to let them down, especially my sons. I lay in my armour that night as we all did, ready for battle in an instant. I reached inside my chest plate and pulled out the cloth Satiah gave me the night before I left. It had been twenty-four days and nights now. The cloth was dirty and dusty and smelled more of my sweat now than the rose oil that she always wore, but if I pressed it to my nose I imagined I could still smell her. I opened the cloth and gently touched her earring and lock of hair, and I ached to touch her skin as she lay beside me. I folded it all back up and returned it to its place behind my armour upon my chest. I would be with her soon. I knew it.

The men were silently roused while it was still dark so as to be ready to strike before daylight. Yet another tactic we knew the enemy would not expect, despite being awake and as ready as we were. Our simple plan was ready to be unleashed. We had watched the rebels organise themselves with their majority centred like an arrowhead ready to pierce our forces. So we arranged ourselves the same way. However this was a ruse and the next day our true intentions would unfold as we began our assault. How did we know that our enemy was not also creating a tactical ruse? Because their astonishing display of indecision the day before was a solid indicator to me that these men could not think on their feet. The slightest change to anything that lay within their expectations undid them. They were men that needed a plan, as did all leaders, but flexibility and spontaneity are what makes a great army commander and they did not possess either of these qualities.

I stood in my chariot with my archers within theirs flanking me. They would provide the first assault, initially with their arrows and then with their wheels as they crushed whomever they rode into. The chariots would be followed by those on foot; first the swordsmen and then the truly brutal footmen wielding clubs and maces. I breathed deep and listened to the chants of my priests. Twenty-three years I had prepared for this moment. In fact it was longer. I should count from the first day my father carried me into the war rooms and I looked upon the maps and listened to the generals. From my birth I was destined to do this for Egypt and every moment of my life had been in preparation. I looked up to the stars that were starting to dim, as the sun was about to be reborn and I knew that today was going to be my rebirth also. Today

I would make my name known to all as a great Pharaoh and warrior, just as my father had dreamed. No longer in the shadows of anyone else I raised my hands to the skies, my sword pointing to the stars, and joined the chanting.

Across the way the kings sitting to the front of their men heard the hum of the chanting. The King of Megiddo felt a chill run down his spine as the sound reached his ears. He was the most fearful of all, as he had the most to lose by hosting the battle alongside his home. He almost wished it was over, but he sat straight and stoic, matching the King of Kadesh who believed he would ride north to his home triumphant within days. Their men behind them like mine had never attended a battle on such a scale and were wary of the strange men they had heard so much about who were protected by hundreds of Gods.

The battle prayer was finished and I leaned forward on my horse. The sky was gaining light but far from seeing the first curve of the sun. I turned to my generals. "We have walked and ridden for twenty-four days and nights to be here. Let us not wait any longer to claim victory," I said.

The generals all nodded and turned to their next in charge, telling them to alert the men that we were about to begin. My heart quickened as my adrenaline began to pump with anticipation for what was about to happen. It was all up to me to begin it. I knew the acceptable way; I would raise my sword and point it forward signalling to my men to begin, which they would by releasing the first wave of arrows and then charging within their groups with all the precision of a highly choreographed dance. I lifted my sword and not an ounce of fear was within me as I pushed it high in the air. Then I did what no one expected and released the most guttural of cries. I still do not know how my men decided to join me in that scream, whether they heard my heart cry out within it to the Gods for victory, or that it simply appealed to the barbaric event that we had been building up to, but the sound of ten thousand men roaring across the plain to the enemy was more powerful than any sword or arrow.

The sound swept across to them and hit the walls of the city to bounce back upon them and surround them. The kings and commanders jumped with shock as did all their men and within those few seconds as they gathered themselves we won the battle. The roar and its echoes masked the thunder of our horses as we began our approach, and the still dark sky hid the first wave of arrows until they were falling just above their heads. They were hit hard by those arrows and panic washed through the ranks of troops and especially the kings.

They too began their advance but we were upon them before they could build up their speed and momentum. We crashed and collapsed their front lines easily, ploughing through to their lesser forces. As we had planned our arrowhead of men fanned out as we neared, engulfing the cluster of chariots that they had focussed to the centre and within half an hour we had them surrounded on the front and sides. The rebels fell into panic, they had no plan that could match our sheer brute force and the kings and commanders soon retreated to the city walls. The King of Megiddo had instructed that the fort not be opened unless the Egyptians suffered defeat and he yelled this again to his guards through the gates. He knew that to open the gates now would be total annihilation; we were making our advance so steadily that we would make our way in if they were open. Instead he yelled for ropes to lift them over the wall. Within minutes hundreds of ropes and cords, even twisted and knotted sheets were flung over the ledge to the men waiting. The wall behind the battle was soon a scene in itself, with men climbing up the curtain of ropes. They even tried to lift one of the king's gold chariots within all this, while before them on the plain their men were being slaughtered.

The utter bedlam that was unleashed abated within an hour. My men high on their quick and savage victory began to ransack the dead bodies of the rebels surrounding them. This unfortunately was the one flaw of our day, for within this distraction few men continued on to the city walls and the escape of the enemy leaders into the city was little hindered. I will admit that I too was distracted by how suddenly we had overcome them and riding through my men I was part of ordering them to capture the surviving men and to collect as much as they could. I never imagined that the men that were scaling the walls were the leaders we needed to slay or subdue in order to claim total victory and to have this confrontation finalised. I could never have imagined leaving my men to be slain while I ran and hid. What sort of leader would do this? So it was not until the battlefield had been completely rifled that I knew no royal bodies had been found--they were instead now safe behind the city walls. I ordered my men to surround Megiddo.

Our plunder though was immense and the joy the men had in gathering weapons, armour and any gold upon the soldiers was their celebration. I sent for the ox carts to be brought from Aruna. They were unable to make the pass through the ridge and could now be brought through one of the easier routes to collect not only our spoils of victory but also our dead to return home and given the honour of a proper burial. One cart was reserved for something more gruesome; the left hand of each of the slain enemy soldiers. All two thousand of them piled upon a cart to be carried back to the temple at Karnak; not only to be offered to the Gods in thanks, but a wonderful sight for my people to see carried back to Egypt to show the might of their Pharaoh and his army. I took great delight in cutting some myself, hoping I would see the face of one of the kings as I did, but instead I saw face after face of anonymous soldiers staring blankly at me.

Our piles of hands grew higher, and each dead hand was matched with the capture of a live enemy soldier. Our plunder grew to include the enemies' carts full of food and water and two gold covered chariots abandoned to climb the walls. There were dozens of horses, scratched but worthy to be taken back to our stables. In fact our stables would never be able to house all the animals we captured and additional ones were built. I was watching all our goods being packed upon a convoy of carts to carry home when I noticed the king's tent was still standing and I made my way to it.

Within its silken walls were rugs and furniture, set up as though it was a room in a palace. It was unscathed so far; no one daring to enter it to pilfer, as all knew this would be my right. I walked through taking in all the details, the closest glimpse I would have to how my rebel kings lived their lives. There were the gold trimmings that I was used to but also an abundance of colour. Rich red cloths covered every inch, embroidered with gold, orange and yellow. It was dazzling and ostentatious and to see so much crammed within a small space was overwhelming after living a life in such huge spaces. There was not one idol or image of a God anywhere, just layer upon layer of opulence and comfort. These were men who served themselves with nothing higher to guide or bless them. I smirked at their humanness and what it had cost them today. Two of my generals were behind me and stood open-mouthed as well.

"Where is their map table?" one questioned, his brow furrowed.

"This is not a tent of an army commander," the other said. "It is one of a spoiled princess."

We all laughed as we compared it to my pharaonic tent, which did have its own comforts befitting a king but was centred on our map table and arranged for the ease of our planning.

"Let us gather all we can. My wives and daughters will be most pleased to have new trinkets and rugs," I laughed. "We shall leave this tent standing but change the flags to our own. It will be a wonderful warning of what is to become of their city also."

I turned to leave the tent and once again assess what was occurring outside when I heard a cry from behind me. I drew my dagger and spun around imagining that one of the kings had indeed emerged, ready to slay me here. Instead I saw one of my commanders standing by the corner of the tent, in his hand a blanket he had just lifted ready to collect, and there lying below him a whimpering scared boy.

This was no ordinary boy though as he wore the clothes of royalty. Without any doubt this was a prince, brought here to the battle to witness his father's works, but instead left behind as the king cowered in his retreat. As we all stared at him he began to cry and call out in his native tongue. I imagine he begged for his life but that was irrelevant. I stood over him with my dagger still in hand and imagined if my father would ever have taken me to battle so young and so ill prepared. I knew one thing for sure though; my father would never have abandoned me nor allowed me to be placed in such danger. How could anyone be so stupid as to risk their successor like this? I thanked Amun for giving me the sense to leave my sons safe in their palace.

I replaced my dagger in its scabbard. I could not kill a child this way, besides to have a royal hostage would be a powerful tool to manipulate the kings hiding within the city.

"Take him to someone who understands his words. Find out exactly who he is," I ordered. "He must not be harmed in any way. He shall be our new weapon to get within the city walls."

My men understood completely. We all had grown in a culture that revered its male leaders. To have captured a prince was worth as much as any gold that we collected that day.

I left the tent to the ongoing scene of dead bodies being stripped and hacked at. The smell of blood was mixed with waste as the dying bodies emptied themselves in their death throes. I saw my cavalry had encircled the walls of Megiddo. All was going well but we would need to make more decisive moves soon. The sun was high in the sky as I called for a horse and made my way to the walls of the fort. I rode around eyeing it all, taking in its details. I could see the amazing way it had been built and as I realised that there would be no way for us to penetrate it with our weapons or means, several of my troop leaders having circled the city entirely rode to me to confirm this.

There was no assault upon us from within the walls. All the arrow men had idiotically been sent to battle on the plain and we had made short work of them. Instead the kings and leaders were now all hiding as far within the palace at the centre of the city that they could. There was an eerie silence from within the walls and whilst I knew there must be someone watching us clear the battlefield and reporting to the kings, we could hear no movement. There was no clatter or thumping as new troops came into place and we now knew that they had not kept any reasonable force within the city as backup. We just needed to play a waiting game and the length of the game would depend upon the resources such as food that they had within the walls.

My generals and commanders sat nearby on their horses waiting for my direction. I turned to them and asked their thoughts.

"Sire we simply surround them--they have no choice but to surrender," offered one and they all nodded in agreement.

This had been my intention all along and I smiled as I knew my general had not merely said this anticipating my own words, but because my men were aligned with me not just in loyalty but in my thinking.

"Excellent. Maintain the guard around the city perimeter. Let no one leave unless it is to surrender," I ordered. "Collect the bodies of their dead and pile them outside the main gate. We shall set fire to them tonight so that when the sun sets their town will be lit by their dead burning, reminding them of their folly in rebelling."

The men dispersed to ride off and instruct their divisions and I once again rode through the battlefield to see the reality of my victory. I then rode back to the place at which we started the day and looked back upon the scene. I saw my flags flying everywhere, high and proud and now through the lines of cavalry encircling the city. Foot soldiers continued to move through the carnage collecting spoils and now beginning to move the dead. There was movement everywhere, even behind me as grooms and servants collected our equipment to relocate closer to our men who would now camp around the city. There was still no movement within the city though and I pictured them all in shock at how we had crushed them.

I kicked my horse's flank and headed as fast as I could towards the fort city. As I approached my men I slowed, and screamed out as loud as I could: "Eternal Egypt, blessed of Ma'at and Ra, today we claim this town for Amun and all the Gods. Let those godless cowards hiding within these walls know of their foolishness!"

An almighty roar once again rose up from my men and heartened by their resurgence of energy, I once again set my horse off at a gallop to ride the entire circle of city wall, roaring and waving my sword in the air as I rode. As I passed each group of men setting up their places around Megiddo they too joined me and our celebratory growls and roars circled the city. If the men within had thought we were insanely driven before they now knew it for certain.

The night and the following day passed without incident. We remained encircling the city, alternating those who guarded with those who rested and those who attended to the horses and repairs. Our dead, the spoils and the hands of the enemy left at dawn to make their way to Egypt and give confirmation of the news that I had sent ahead with a messenger. When the second and then the third day went by yet again without incident we all became restless, partly from the frustration of not ending the battle completely, as well as being sick of wondering just what the men within the walls had planned. At least our march here had some activity, not least the capturing of cities along the way. I wished to return to my home and family, as did all of my men.

I called upon my general Tjanuny and asked of him to write a letter demanding the city's surrender. We demanded that their surrender be signalled by the opening of the gates. Until that time our men would remain. It was quite simple. We also included that we held the Prince of Kadesh hostage and would be taking him back to Egypt as a prisoner. His life could not be guaranteed without the King of Kadesh bowing before the Supreme Lord Pharaoh. The letter was made and thrown over the wall on the morning of our fourth day. That afternoon we received our reply and their letter was simple also. There would be no surrender. The Egyptians could wait all they wanted but they would never bow to me. They demanded their sovereignty.

I was incensed, not only at their arrogance in wishing to challenge me further but also at their stupidity. They were completely circled, they had nowhere to go, were already depleted of resources and had already lost a prince. It had now just become a battle of patience and there was no way that I was going to give up. I had waited twenty-two years to lead my army as sole Pharaoh, and I could wait weeks for this surrender. We would just wait until they all grew hungry enough to give up.

For the smaller tribes this was soon so one week after the battle a letter dropped from the sky announcing the apologies of thirty smaller tribes and begging for mercy. They had sat within the walls for the week brewing their anger at the kings for convincing them to take part. They sat day after day and talked amongst themselves, amplifying their anger and discontent as they shared their thoughts.

Things had not been so bad had they? Now what did it cost them--their men annihilated and they now sat here like animals, unable to return to protect their own homes that the Egyptians would target next. It was madness to stay here and let those kings tell them what to do and when. So, to the absolute ire of the kings, the tribes announced they would be leaving.

I gathered extra men around the main gate through which they would leave, prepared in case this was a decoy to launch an attack, no matter how futile one would be at this stage. The men walked through the gates carrying their flags to identify the tribes they were head off. They walked through a corridor of my men who all had their swords drawn and arrows at the ready. The gates soon closed and we had our first group of defectors. I stood back from the exit and they were dragged to me and pushed to the ground to prostrate themselves as they begged for mercy, promising support to defeat the kings. I nodded and let the men stand up.

I saw that it was not just the tribal leaders but women and children had also followed them out of the city. They had all brought their families, including their successors, to stay safe within the city walls in case we had chosen to attack directly the less protected towns in the surrounding plains. This would have been a wise move if the coalition had won--but they hadn't--and it would now inspire me to enact one of the most effective plans to ensure my long-term control over this region. This was a plan that would see the force of my victory being felt well into the next generation.

Some of the princes were mere children but others were bursting into manhood, some standing as tall as their fathers. As I looked at each one I saw the potential of each tribe and town they represented. I saw the pain and fear in their eyes as they looked at me and I knew that they would return home with hate and anger for Egypt. This could not be easily cleared. I would expect my sons to be wary of our northern neighbours even once I was gone so I could not stand here looking at these sons and expect them to view me with any respect.

Then I heard my father speak to me so clearly in that moment. The sound of his voice overwhelmed me and I gasped. Those generals close by saw the same expression I wore as I decided to take the pass through the mountains. They knew I was deep in conversation with the Gods once again and stood quietly beside me waiting to hear their wisdom through me.

My father spoke, "My son, Hatshepsut was your enemy but she still gave you support and allowed you to flourish in your own way. You would not be standing here, the commander that you are, without her presence in your past. What nourishment shall you offer these boys to make them your allies?"

Then his voice was gone, and I once again heard the noises around me and knew that my generals were standing by for further instruction. I turned to the gathering of defeated tribes, "Today you stand as fallen men. You flourished under the rule of Hatshepsut and so too would you have under my rule. Instead you bit the hand of your keeper like ungrateful animals and now you kneel like servants before me instead of the leaders you born to be," I spoke calmly and clearly. The words flowed as though I had rehearsed them a hundred times. "You risked leaving your sons nothing. The Gods lead me to fear that this mighty battle will not be enough to quell your desire to rebel. So I shall take it upon myself and Egypt to ensure your sons will inherit the legacy they deserve. Your sons shall return to Egypt to be raised by me. If you have no sons then I will take your closest brother. Rebel again and they lose their lives. Live in harmony and they will return ready to lead, trained by the greatest army and educated as well as any noble."

After the tearful goodbyes to their sons and brothers the tribal leaders were allowed to return to their homes. I knew they had no means to stage any further attacks and the sight of the young heirs sitting upon an ox cart ready to be shipped back to Thebes killed any last vestiges of fight left in them. When the leaders returned to their homes they were to send back to us their tribute, to make further amends and reparations for their rebellion. They all kept their word and within a week the carts began to arrive full of more gold, jewels, incense and fabrics to send home; but more importantly food and wine for my men. A soldier can endure the worst of weather and the most boring of posts as long as they have a full and satisfied stomach. A hungry soldier has no vigour, nor can he maintain the loyalty and respect that is needed of him.

As I looked upon yet another cart full of apologies, a small sack caught my eye. I lifted it and when I opened it I saw it was full of small rolls of silk. I unrolled one and there within it was a magnificent necklace of fine gold woven into a cord, hanging from it were teardrops of lapis lazuli, bordered with more gold, and in-between each teardrop was an oval ruby also encircled with gold. The feature though was a massive ruby beautifully polished that would hang against a woman's chest. Its colour was so deep and red that it looked like blood. It sang in my hand and almost seemed to pulse like a heart. Yes, it was like holding a heart, and to see it against the chest of a woman would be like seeing her very heart. I knew this must be for Satiah.

I opened the other rolls and saw jewellery also beautiful, but none as grand as this ruby. I would make sure that Satiah would receive this but did not wish to inflame Matreya's jealousy anymore. So I laid out all the jewellery upon their fabric rolls and called over one of the scribes who were recording the spoils. I pointed out another necklace for Matreya and another for my mother, along with a special piece for each of my daughters. He was instructed to send a note with each piece and that they were to be carried on the body of the lead escort back to Thebes. With full faith that this would indeed happen I walked away, but then stopped, and returned to look one last time at that ruby for Satiah.

I had no lock of hair that I could cut and send to her as my head was shaved. There was no jewellery to shed either. There I stood in my Pharaoh battle regalia and could not think what of my person to send back. I took out my dagger and lifted one of the leather strips that formed my skirt, each piece hung to protect me like armour and at the tip of each strip was a gold stud. My dagger did not cut through so easily, but it did eventually. Along with the necklace going home to my beloved I sent her a smelly piece of leather that had been against me the entire time. Satiah would treasure it more than the necklace.

All the food and wine in the world though could not break the frustration at having the kings continue their standoff. After two weeks I held a counsel with all my commanders to make a plan. We contemplated a barrage of arrows, but this would not guarantee us any damage to the enemy, and we would only end up supplying them with arrows to aim back at us. We could use our might to bring down the walls, but Megiddo was valuable to oversee trade routes and it would cost dearly to rebuild a city that we needed. So this ruled out also the option of sending hails of fire catapulted over the city walls. The quick destructive options were all soon won over by our original plan. We would simply hold out until they gave up.

Word had reached the generals that there were some weak spots within our encirclement. Whether by negligence or by bribe some passage had been made though the city walls via smaller gates or hidden doors that were in different places. No part of me wanted to believe that my men would betray me in such a way, and so I pictured these couriers making their way in the dead of night using darkness to shield them. Whatever the circumstance, this had to be halted. The key to our plan was their eventual depletion combined with the knowledge that they were cut off from the world and that the only way out was through their surrender to me. We did this through the only means we knew and that was to now surround the entire city with a moat.

Our men dug for an entire week creating a trough over ten feet deep. No cart or wagon could pass, and no man could climb out without a ladder or being hauled by rope. Certainly this would not stop all men from crossing but they most certainly would not be able to move the supplies needed to support the city. Just to make it interesting, at the places that were near these smaller gates we embedded sharpened stakes at the base. Anyone who dared to jump into the moat in the dark would impale themselves upon them or suffer an injury that would see them bleed to death at the bottom of the ditch. Each morning these areas were surveyed and we often found men lying there dead or close to it, like rats in traps, for us to dispose of. We could tell from the way that they lay which direction they had entered by and would write this onto a note. Just something simple such as: *"The man on his way from your city failed."* The note would then be tied to the severed head of the man that we found and this would then be thrown over the city wall to let them know their courier or spy had failed. Whether they learnt of the places without the spikes or soon gave up, there were fewer bodies as time wore on. I was very proud of that little tactic.

Time continued to wear on and we were soon in the sixth week of siege. We had now been out of Egypt for ten weeks, which also meant that I had been away from my palace duties for ten weeks. Despite my faith in my viziers, courtiers and butlers I needed to get home. I remained with my men another two weeks though without any further developments or happenings apart from the odd severed head message being sent across the walls. News trickled back and forth between the palace and my siege site, but then came the day that I received the news that would make me truly want to return home.

Matreya had given birth to my sixth daughter and tenth child. My beautiful little Isis was born without me to greet her and my heart broke just a little. A priest read the story of her birth to me as I sat in my tent, dusty and sweaty. I closed my eyes as he read and I pictured it all. The sunrise that morning had been the most beautiful pink meaning that the calling of the Goddess Isis was with her from the first pains that Matreya felt. The breezes had been so gentle as she left her mother's body and my new little daughter sang rather than cried as she was bathed for the first time. Tears fell down my face at how beautiful it sounded and when I finally did see her she was just as I had pictured her as I sat so far away.

The birth of Isis added to the need for me to return to Thebes. I had one final meeting with the generals and commanders I would leave behind to oversee the siege. The effectiveness of the moat now meant that we could organise for regiments to return to other regions to create a presence throughout our newly acquired land and collect the continual tributes and taxes required of the villages and tribes now under our rule. I climbed onto my horse to begin my return and as we made our way to the southern edge of the Mount Carmel ridge, I turned one last time to look at the city still resisting us, quiet and solid like the mountains we were about to pass. I had no question that we would win, but prayed to the Gods that this should end soon.

My passage back to Thebes was a lot quicker than our journey to Megiddo. We had no need to neither stop or challenge anyone, nor halt for hours to consult or plan as to what we would do next. I made my way into Egypt with all the glory that a victorious Pharaoh should. When I rode upon my chariot into Thebes the streets were lined with my people shouting and cheering, the temples overflowed with people attending to give their thanks for the success of Egypt. Music was everywhere and as I passed by in my chariot, people threw flowers and coins to honour and thank me. When I finally made it to the palace doors my feet were buried beneath my gifts, with most of it having spilled after me to be collected by children brave enough to run amongst the procession to grab them. My palace attendants were all there to greet me and I quickly made my way through them all anxious to get to my family.

My family would be waiting in my private rooms, all lined up awaiting my walk through the corridors to get to them. Satiah was already crying, having been told I was here and making my way to them. I was tired and hungry but my pace did not slow at all as I made my way through the maze of corridors that crossed the palace. Finally I was walking the final few steps and the doors behind which my family stood were opened for me. I was expecting to see them all in line, quiet and regal, with wives followed by boys then girls, waiting for me to greet them one by one. Instead the second the doors began to open there was an almighty shriek followed by a blur as my Meritamen and Meryt burst forward to run to me and hug me, crying and shouting their love over and over. I could not move as they clung to either side of me and I did not want to. The rest of my children not wishing to be left out were upon me also within seconds, all talking at once, all crying and all clawing to try and hug me. I was almost dragged to the ground and loved every second of it.

I finally was able to pry them off me and hug each one in turn, surprised at how they had grown in the few short months I had been away. I lifted Nebetiunet into my arms and with Beketamun holding my free hand I walked to lead them into the chambers where I would see Satiah and Matreya. However when I walked in only Satiah was there to greet me and I was glad. She looked so beautiful having spent all day preparing to greet me and there upon her chest sat the ruby necklace, as amazing as I had imagined it would be upon her. With a blur of noisy children still jumping and grabbing at me I made my way to her, or maybe it was she to me, I don't really remember or care, but she was soon standing in front of me. I placed Nebetiunet upon the floor and took my beautiful Satiah into my arms.

Matreya was nearby in the birthing room still in her official recovery period. When Arisina went to her to announce that I was merely hours away and perhaps Matreya would like to reconsider her recovery status and prepare to greet her husband in his rooms with the rest of the family, her response was very clear.

"I have just produced my sixth child for him. He shall come and greet me," she snapped, and turned her head dismissing the priestess and ending the conversation.

This would have been a wonderful opportunity to caution or even punish my headstrong wife--but in fact I was grateful. I could enjoy my children and Satiah without her harsh glances and aloof air in the room. I took my time in going to her though. Matreya may well have gotten away with her petulance and disrespect but I would not run to her bedside like a servant being directed and ordered. I waited until late the following day, which made her blood boil as she pictured me spending this time with Satiah and in rooms so close to where she lay. I did not wait to see my new daughter though, and sent the order that Isis be brought to my rooms straight after her next feed so that I would get to hold her finally.

It was very different holding Isis for the first time. She wasn't the first I hadn't held within hours of her birth but as I held her something felt different. At the time I imagined it was my fatigue from the battle and travelling. Then I realised that she was the first baby that I held as sole Pharaoh and decided it was just that. However it was there as I watched her grow up too. This child was tenth in line to the throne and I knew that apart from some horrendous tragedy that would wipe out her nine older siblings it was near impossible that either she or any of her descendants would ever take the throne. She was born with no expectations or pressures upon her and somehow she tuned into this from her birth. Isis walked the palace with joy and each day was an adventure filled with people she loved and all the comforts she needed. As I grew older there were days when I wished that we could swap lives.

CHAPTER FIFTEEN

My days back at the palace fell into a new routine. I would sit in court in the morning and hear the usual reports on crops, trade and temple goings-on. Then the afternoons would be spent with the generals who remained at Thebes. A messenger would arrive daily with any updates but they were always the same. Things had not progressed any further than the day I left and we continued our waiting game, with patience as our best and only weapon. Megiddo was much better resourced than we could ever have predicted. Its king had also used his extra sense in preparing his city for just such an outcome. However he too did not expect his enemy to be so well resourced and he also spent his days hoping and praying that we would give up and leave. Most importantly, he prayed that this would occur before his city began to wilt.

Wilt it did. The months passed and the food became scarcer. His people began to suffer and as news of infant and elder mortality reached him, he merely accepted this as yet another wave of war casualties. Such casualties are necessary for the greater cause he decided. When the trials of hunger and disease though reached into the palace walls and claimed a daughter his view changed. Even the kings surrounding him and supporting the standoff took note. Was this also what was happening to their families and people back at their homes?

So it was that our patience finally won. It was six months after our arrival at Megiddo. My generals and men had not lost an ounce of their vigour or determination and were alert as ever when for the first time in six months they heard movement behind the main gates of the city. Looking up early one morning they saw the flags of the King of Megiddo being lowered and smiles spread across their faces as they recognised the first signs of surrender. However being the well trained commanders that they were they did not accept this as given and alerted all men to possible attack. When the gates opened though there was just what they had spent six months expecting and hoping for.

An emaciated soldier walked through, his hands outreached, palms showing forward displaying his lack of weapon. In the waistband of his skirt was stuck a scroll. My chief general walked up to him, horrified at the physical state of the man and grabbed it from his body. Before he read the note he waved to some men to bring the soldier food and water. As the general unfurled the scroll and began reading the messenger ate and drank, taking in the sustenance as quickly as the general took in the words of the scroll.

"We offer our absolute surrender. Our lives are at risk from hunger and disease and we ask your clemency in granting us our lives and those of our peoples. In return we offer full allegiance to the grand land of Egypt. We ask your Gods to forgive our folly."

Not only was it surrender but the most humbling as well. To bring men to such a state of begging made the general proud of our stamina in maintaining the siege, but it also sickened his heart to know leaders would crumble in such a way. He turned to the soldier still gorging himself; water and food spilling down his front from his bestial eating. Behind he could see our own men, healthy and rugged, ready to battle anyone or anything.

"Today the might of Amun has shown his favour on our Pharaoh and his people. We will send a message back with this poor wretch that we accept and will prepare to enter the city," he said to his surrounding generals and waved for the scribe to come forward.

My general dictated a grand acceptance letter and within the lines accepting the pitiful surrender he outlined exactly how the city and its captured kings would behave as it was entered. Clemency and honour would be shown to all who displayed the intended subservience of the surrender but those that showed the slightest sign of resistance would soon be added to the pile of charred bones outside the city gates.

A relay of messengers was begun immediately passing on the letter through each of our bastions throughout the kingdom. Each messenger rode with their adrenalin pumping at the sheer joy of passing on this glorious news. The last of the chain arrived just as I walked into the army rooms. He could hardly breathe as he spoke the simple words, "Megiddo has surrendered!"

I cannot describe the feeling that washed through the room as those words were spoken. There was several seconds of silence as our minds processed what we heard and we looked at each other, almost asking silently, *"Is it true?"* For that moment I thought I was in a dream. So many times did I wish to hear those words and in fact had dreamt this moment that it was hard to believe that it was now true. Then like a quick snap, reality kicked in and the room filled with cheers and hugs.

My generals based at Megiddo needed no guidance or direction. So by the time the news reached me down at Thebes they were well into the procedure of securing the city, only this time from the inside. Before they even sent one man through the gates they sought the final insurance that the city had indeed succumbed. They ordered the kings and remaining tribal leaders to exit and make their final confessions and surrender in person to my chief general

They did so in a steady stream for two hours, accompanied by their families and the few army leaders that had survived. After their audience with my generals they were herded like livestock and surrounded by a line of soldiers whilst another division made their way into the city walls.

The initial fears of a surprise final attack were dissolved within the first few moments. The stench that had made its way beyond the walls was almost suffocating now they were inside. Dead bodies lay in the streets waiting to be collected but those who should have gathered them were also dead or sick from the diseases that the bodies carried. The people that were alive were frail and their bones poked through their skin. As the soldiers passed on the streets the people put out their hands pleading for some food or wine.

"Disgraceful," muttered my general, "that a king would allow his people to come to this--all because of his vanity and pride." He turned to a small group of our soldiers nearby. "Go and fetch all the food and wine we have and bring it to the survivors. Make sure no one misses out."

The generals around him nodded knowing that for our men to go one night without food was a small sacrifice in order to show these people the generosity of their new ruler. The kings and their families also went without, sitting like dumbstruck pigs within their makeshift prison while the innocents of Megiddo ate and tasted the mercy of Egypt. More food was sent from amongst the local tribes as they had also done during the long siege so that our army and the town were fed well again the next day. The scraps were thrown to the kings and their families.

The next day the clean up of the city also began beginning with the dead bodies that were scattered throughout it. The soldiers, assisted by those Megiddians who could help, carried them out on carts. As the bodies were piled upon the coals and bones of the original pyre, the King of Megiddo broke down and wept as he saw the reality of what the siege had cost him and his people. The men who carried the bodies were washed thoroughly with heavy soaps and flushed themselves internally with strong wine to cleanse themselves of any diseases they may have picked up from the bodies--lest they too should meet the fate of the very bodies they carried.

That night as the pyre burnt and the smell of the burning flesh met the noses of all, the general looked at the downcast royals wishing they too could be thrown upon the flames. In that way they could make amends for the loss of innocent lives now burning before them. This however was not an option and to take a life, even if it was that of an enemy, outside of a battle was not only cowardly but also against the laws of the Gods.

On the fourth day of our success over Megiddo my orders arrived to be exacted by my general. The city was near to being entirely secured. Each sector had been searched and cleared and the funeral pyre outside the gates was finally diminishing rather than being replenished by dead bodies. The royals and their commanders grew weary in the sun without their comforts. The women and children were moved to tents or under canvas shades but we left the men to suffer as much as they could.

With the city now secure the general could focus on how to deal with the rebels. My instructions were quite simple. Each king or tribal leader would go back to their home accompanied by a sector of my army to ensure that upon their return they announced immediately their fall to Egypt and began the necessary changes to align with our government. A small group of soldiers would stay in each town to monitor their behaviour and the rest would return to Egypt with tribute from each city and town. The kings were all informed of this and their heads hung low.

Their dreams of independence were not just shattered but washed away without any hope as they also learnt of the last and final instruction. It was the same fate that the tribal leaders faced when they surrendered eight months earlier but was unknown to those still within the walls. As each king rode away accompanied by my soldiers they were required to leave possibly their most treasured and important asset behind; their heirs and successors. There was no leniency in this and while the kings rode away, holding their heads straight with what scraps of dignity they held, they were surrounded by the cries and screams of mothers and sons being separated.

I spoke before of the power of a child's cry so I could well imagine how my general felt as he stood at the door of the tent holding the princes. Toddlers were screaming, children were crying out for their mothers and nurses while young teens curled up and wept into their hands. I imagine a part of his heart did break and he suddenly realised that he should have indeed ordered their nurses to remain, but they were long gone and he could not now send for them. Instead he sent the appeal to within the walls of the city and women came forward to comfort and quiet the boys. The gentle warmth of the women did much to calm them. It also helped that they did not have swords and daggers strapped to their sides stained with the blood of their relatives and kinsmen.

The boys were carried back to Thebes in a small convoy of carts. The young women of Megiddo who had stepped forward to be their nurses accompanied them and they would now officially be nurses of the palace when they arrived in Thebes. Some of these women had been orphaned by the siege and some were simply sent with the blessings of their families to make a new life in Egypt. None of them had ever been further south than Megiddo and as the boys and their nurses travelled down to Egypt they saw the landscape change and the different faces of the south Canaanites. Their fear and longing for home now mixed with curiosity and some even began to point and call out to the younger ones when they saw something new and different. They still cried from time to time for their family and homes but the further we travelled, the more resigned they were that they would never see them again.

Just as they entered the lands of Egypt proper they saw the first of our temples and the older ones looked intently but did not point out like before. The older ones knew of our different ways and now here they were looking at the reality of it. The general escorting the convoy ordered it stop before the temple. As with any journey away from our homeland, they would stop and give thanks to the Gods for their safe return. The children were lifted off the carts and waved towards the temple. The smaller ones were carried or walked by the hand of their nurses while the older boys made their own way to the stone building. A priest stood waiting before the line of massive columns at the entrance. He had seen them make their way across the sand and by the time they were walking upon the stairs, the other priests inside had finished preparing a welcoming ceremony.

As the Priest watched the group of young boys with their nurses scattered amongst them, he smiled. The Goddess Satet who guided the Nile to rise had helped send even more nourishment to the land this year. The general walked towards him, nodded and bowed. The priest nodded back then raised his arms to the sky and cried, "Oh beloved Satet, Goddess of our lifeline, mother of the seasons, we thank you for guiding our men home safe and with new blood to invigorate our empire."

The children and nurses all watched enraptured. They did not understand a word but were very entertained by the theatrics of this greeting. They watched the priest intently with his shaved head and strange robes twisted around him. They then turned their attention to the soldiers all with their heads bowed. They seemed as scared of this bald man as they had been of the soldiers on the first day. Then suddenly the priest turned and walked into the temple with the general following. The other soldiers snapped out of their reverie and started to wave their hands once again directing the children to follow also. They didn't need to be told to be quiet now as they were all still dumbstruck by the display upon the steps. Their curiosity was now at a bursting point to see just what would happen inside.

The cool and shade inside the temple was a welcome relief after the sun and helped provide some comfort in this unknown space. As they walked in with the Priest and general way ahead of them, the boys and nurses all craned their heads upwards. None had ever been in a place like this with a roof so high you could barely see the outlines of the stones that made it. The hieroglyphs and pictures, some carved and some painted were fascinating, especially when they glimpsed an animal. The Gods with animal heads set off some giggles, quickly hushed by the nurses.

The soldiers left the children in the centre aisle and walked to the front of the altar where the main priest was now joined by four of his fellow priests. The soldiers prostrated themselves, first kneeling and then bowing low on the floor as the priests began their chanting. The children too sat on the floor and watched intently for a while, until the decorations and desire to explore the shadows between the columns flanking the aisle became too much.

The cool of the temple refreshed the children and their energy levels were soon evident to all. Suddenly there were the sounds of feet running, more giggles at the hieroglyphs and the muted pleas of the nurses to stop and be quiet. It did not abate, in fact the noise and movement grew by the second, echoing off the stone walls and columns making them seem even louder. The priest knew that these coarse children, born into godless lives would need much educating to understand the sanctity of a temple. As he looked down at the general and saw his jaw clenching tighter at each scream or outburst, he stopped the prayers.

"I suggest you continue to make your way to Thebes," the priest said calmly. "We can continue the prayers for you as you travel."

The general looked up and nodded a silent thank you to the priest and quickly made his exit. The children all followed, although some were quite reluctant to leave their new playground. In fact it took several nurses and soldiers to chase them through the columns and make sure none were left behind. They were all finally back upon the carts, still bouncing and beaming from their playtime. Now when they passed a temple there was no fear, instead they all pointed, screamed excitedly and begged in their own tongue for the soldiers to stop. This of course did not happen. The general was far from ready to repeat that last incident under his supervision and now his focus was on getting these children to the palace and ending his responsibility for them as soon as possible.

The general was thinking how wonderful it would be to see his wife and his own civilised children when their convoy approached a small village. On the roadside two priests were walking and the soldiers bowed their heads as they passed. The children though on seeing the men and recognising the bald heads and priest's robes all began to scream and jump about in their carts, pointing and shrieking with excitement. Both priests were so startled at this reaction that one almost fell over, being saved only by the strong arm of his fellow priest. They stood still; their jaws open at this brazen lack of respect not knowing who the children were. The general had no intention of wasting time by stopping and explaining either. So the carts moved on with the children still waving, pointing, giggling and calling out to the two priests who stood frozen in place by shock as the dust of the carts settled around them.

As they moved away from the priests and the villagers, the general could hear behind him muffled laughs slowly making their way through all the soldiers. He surrendered his demeanour and joined them.

They were soon upon the outskirts of yet another village. The general looked ahead and saw a quick straight path through the town. He also saw ahead the temple in the town centre and a gathering of priests in their red robes upon the temple stairs. Trying not to laugh he turned to his men and grinned widely, "Perhaps it is best to emulate our Pharaoh and take the longer more difficult route for this passing," he smiled.

The men looked ahead at first puzzled but they soon also saw the temple and its gathering. The soldiers all laughed and turned the horses and carts to make their way around the village on a rocky bypass.

The small convoy finally made its way into Thebes and though the boys were excited to see the huge buildings of the capital and then the palace, they were all too weary from travelling to show any of their previous excitement. Some were even asleep as the cart finally stopped by the army barracks where they would stay for now. Having so many of our men now posted through

Canaan to ensure the rebellion was quashed meant that there were many beds here empty and ready to be used until special quarters for our hostages were prepared.

I now had fifty princes under my care and direction. Those taken earlier, including the Prince of Kadesh, who was possibly the most valuable, were housed in converted servants' quarters. They were already well-established in their routines of training and schooling. In fact many had lost their mother tongue and could only speak our language. This in itself was a major triumph. So the next day when the new arrivals were taken to the courtyard to mix with their neighbours and begin their indoctrination they saw before them their fate. They saw the clothes they would be wearing, the way their hair would be cut or even shaved and the way these boys did not laugh or point when they saw a picture of a man with the head of a jackal painted on a wall or standing as a statue.

Children can be much like pets. They can be given to a new owner and while they will pine and whimper for their past owner, if they are fed and cared for they will soon come to revere their new master just as much. So it was that after months of being fed well and possibly more soundly, with opulent surrounds that befitted their birth, they grew happy and content with their new life in Thebes. Certainly they did not have their freedom but no child is truly free. They rely on parents for care and sustenance. To reject that would almost be suicide.

Several of the older boys did attempt to escape their new life and make their way to their homelands but would return within days scorched by the sun and dehydrated. Their lands were very different to the deserts of Egypt and they soon learnt the safety and nurturing energy of the Nile and why we all stayed so close to her.

My sons were made to mix with these foreign princes. Firstly, they were their peers. Yes, my sons were their rulers and actually their superiors, but these boys were born to rule as mine were, and I wanted my princes to associate with others of strong destinies. Secondly, these foreigners should know their rulers and my sons should be able to walk amongst them receiving the respect that was due to them. However children add many layers to such power plays. Birthrights are only one element of superiority to a child. Size, age and punching skills are others. Menkheperre soon found out that having a father as ruler of the empire did not ensure his safety when mixing with other children.

I was sitting in the war rooms with my generals when Nira, one of my sons' nurses, appeared at the door and looking down I saw her hand held that of Menkheperre who was crying with his left eye red and swollen. He broke free of the nurse and ran to me, jumping into my lap and burying his head upon my chest sobbed inconsolably. I let him weep for a moment as his nurse begged

171

apology for seeking me out here.

"Sire, he insisted we find you immediately," she tried to explain calmly fearing she would be reprimanded for entering the war rooms.

I nodded my approval. She had been right to listen to the demands of a young prince and now I was curious as to the cause. I gripped Menkheperre's small shoulders and lifted him away from me so I could see his face. He still sobbed but he was settling, which was more than I could say about his left eye. Made worse by his crying; he was sure to have a phenomenal black eye develop during the night.

"So my youngest prince, how did this occur? Playing rough with Amenemhat again?" I asked gently.

Menkheperre shook his head, "No," he started to sob again, each breath making his chest heave but he continued on in-between his sobs. "It was that pig, Suresh, the prince from Megiddo. Why did you bring him here? I hate him!"

"My son, you know why those boys are here," I replied.

"I don't care. Send them home! It was nice here when it was just *us*! Send them back, they are pigs and don't deserve to live here!" he cried, tears rolling down his face.

My generals looked on somewhat bemused but proud of his fire. I would never have spoken to my father in such a way and yet part of me was quite warmed by his spirit.

"These boys are here to learn the might of Egypt and its men. You, my son, are one of those men and even though you may be smaller and younger than such ones as Suresh, you are no less worthy of their respect," I stated. "The Gods are giving you a lesson my young one. Just as I was given one when my father passed and had to wait for my time to rule. Fear not for Suresh will be punished for striking his ruler's son. However you must also choose to find your own way in this situation."

Menkheperre looked at me intently. The tears had stopped and his brow furrowed as he took in my words. I knew this expression well as this was his demeanour when truly listening.

"Now I suggest you make your way back to the family chambers and bathe. Then visit the temple to pray for your guidance," I finished my lecture by placing Menkheperre on the ground and looked up at Nira. "Send for the physician to make some salve for his eye and make sure he uses it."

Nira nodded. In fact she had already sent word to the physicians. Taking Menkheperre's hand she began to walk him out of the room. As they reached the door though he pulled on her hand to stop and turned to me one last time, "Father, what would you do?" he asked.

"My son, I have never been in quite that situation. I look forward to what you will teach me," I smiled.

It was true. The only young male I grew up with was Salas who had been nothing but a loyal and true friend. My dealings with Neferure and her sister were nothing like this at all. I was intently curious as to how my eight year old son would deal with this.

As I had directed Menkheperre bathed, rested and redressed to make his way to the temple. All the while his mind raced with possible ways to deal with Suresh. He rode to the temple in a carriage with Nira by his side but did not speak nor point out to things as he usually did. Nira thought it was because of the pain that he was in as his eyelid was now swelling even more and closing his eye. Menkheperre indeed was in pain and the salve was proving nothing more than a slight comfort to the ache that now worked its way behind his eye and into his neck. His vision was altered as his eye could not open fully and each wave of pain or blurred image only made his mind churn more and solidified his determination to deal with Suresh.

He arrived at temple and Arisina was waiting to greet him. She knew of the situation as I had sent word that Menkheperre would be coming and why. The sight of my son now swollen and scowling made her sigh and shake her head. Arisina may well have been just our family's priestess but to see one of my children in pain made her heart ache as if her blood was within them. She bent down and gently kissed him upon the forehead.

"Come young one, we shall go and begin your true healing," she said softly.

Arisina did not move so quickly these days but she walked my young son through the corridors of the temple with all the gentility and love that she had ever shown me when I came to her as a young boy. In fact at one point she looked down at my son, so much like me in face at that age and felt that the years and events between had never occurred. The priestess smiled and looked ahead. So much water had coursed down the Nile and yet it all looked the same. In a hundred years another priestess would walk these corridors leading a young prince by the hand. *"What would they look like?"* she thought.

They reached the small altar especially made for my family to pray privately and Menkheperre knelt down, as he knew to, while Arisina began to speak the prayers. They prayed to Amun and Ra to protect Menkheperre and share their wisdom. Incense was burned and Arisina gently stroked rose and myrrh oil around his eye as she chanted to the Gods to help him heal. The cool of the temple, the gentle chants and now the soothing scents so close to his nose made Menkheperre drowsy. Closing his eyes he slipped into a half asleep state as Arisina moved back to the altar to continue. He was still aware of the sounds around him and now he felt some movement nearby and without looking he knew that someone else had joined him, kneeling to my son's left. This person leant in close so as to speak to him without disturbing the priestess's chants and although Menkheperre would never be able to repeat the words spoken he understood everything that was said to him.

Arisina looked down at my young prince and smiled. She saw no one by his side but felt the presence and looking upon his face knew he was deep in communication with the energy that had honoured him by attending their little session. Arisina returned to her prayers and gently blew upon the piles of incense to keep the embers smouldering and sending out their scented smoke. Then she gently lowered herself upon a pillow to the right of Menkheperre and waited.

Menkheperre lifted his head and slowly opened his eyes. He seemed a little confused as he opened his eyes and realised that Arisina was no longer chanting. The pain behind his eye and in his neck was now gone and despite the haze of the incense smoke his sight was clear also. He turned to speak to Arisina and she saw that the swelling around his eye had subsided and his eye was now open almost as fully as the untouched one. Of course none of this surprised a woman who had spent her life dedicated to the magic of prayers and faith. Arisina knew that Menkheperre's own spirit had played a large part in this also.

Menkheperre looked to his left suddenly remembering his visitor and saw just an empty space. "Did you see who was here?" he said.

"No I did not," she answered softly and smiling, "but I felt them."

"Arisina, I heard them!" he exclaimed, and leant forward towards her bursting with excitement as he realised he had been visited by one of the spirits he had heard so much about.

"Tell me little one, what did they say?" she asked, partly from curiosity, partly from wanting him to exercise his memory and pull his message into this realm.

"He said so much," he began, and started to shake his hands and look around trying frantically to remember.

"Shhhh," she hushed him gently. "Sit still and breathe Menkheperre."

Menkheperre dropped his hands and sat still once again. He slowly drew in a big breath but she could tell he was still forcing his mind to recall.

"Close your eyes," she told him. "Now breathe gently and step back to the moment they were speaking."

She watched his breathing slow down and work its way further into his body each time he inhaled. He closed his eyes and Arisina knew he was re-listening to what he had heard. When Menkheperre opened his eyes he was calm and in this much quieter state he re-told the conversation. He could not repeat the words exactly as he had heard them but he knew the message in his own words. Arisina listened and nodded. True to her training she would never repeat what was said--and so nor will I and keep that sharing as sacred as it was in that moment.

As she walked him back through the temple, she looked down once again and his face was changed and not just from the healing of his eye. He once again had some light shining from him. Arisina did not need to wonder what different princes would walk these corridors, she could watch those under her care transform within an hour and this filled her heart and spirit more than enough.

They stepped together into the sunlight where the carriage and Nira waited patiently. Menkheperre turned and grabbed Arisina, wrapping his arms about her waist and gave her the tightest hug he could. She bent down and kissed him on the crown of his head, squeezing him gently in return as she did so. Menkheperre jumped back into the carriage and turned once more to Arisina, "One day I hope I shall have a daughter and that she will be a wise priestess as you are," he beamed.

With that he was gone and the priestess turned to walk into the temple with a tear falling down her cheek. Back in the carriage Menkheperre continued to smile and Nira smiled also, happy to see her young charge content once again.

"Your prayers were most powerful young Sire," she said.

"Oh Nira, they were amazing," he gushed. "Amun himself spoke to me."

Nira had no response to this and sat with her jaw open as Menkheperre looked out of the carriage and smiled. His smile did not stop and was still across his face when I entered the children's chambers to visit with them before dinner. Menkheperre sat back as my daughters crowded me, and spoke hurriedly of any news to share. They clambered over me each vying for my attention first, eventually retreating when they were satisfied they had received their due time with me.

As Menkheperre finally made his way to me I almost thought that his afternoon visit with me had not occurred. I expected to see him swollen, black and still sullen. Instead a smiling boy walked towards me with just a slight shadow of a bruise under his eye. I took his chin in my hand and turned his head in a mock examination of his injury.

"Well Menkheperre," I said seriously, keeping up the guise of a formal procedure, "what or who did you sacrifice to the Gods to manifest this amazing recovery?"

Menkheperre laughed and then put on a serious face to continue the game. "Sire, before you are shown the powers that were conjured by the prayers of your grand priestess," he replied.

Now we both laughed.

"Yes, an hour with Arisina is truly being in the presence of Gods," I said as I continued to laugh.

"Father, it was even more incredible than that…" he gushed, and then leaning in close he talked softly so only I should hear, "I spoke with Amun himself."

I couldn't help it but my body went stiff--not from disbelief, but that one of my children should be gifted with the skill of hearing across the silken veils that separate us from the God realms.

"You don't believe me but it is true! Ask Arisina. She believed me!" he cried.

"Oh my son, I believe you," I emphasised. "I am so surprised that you have done this so young. I am very proud. I hope you continue to do so."

I lied though. I did not believe that it was Amun who spoke with Menkheperre. I believed it was my father. He had spoken to me at Megiddo and now he came to speak with my son. He was safely through the gates of the afterlife and now in my sole ruling he sent his spirit voice to guide and counsel my family. I thanked Menkheperre for his sharing. He had indeed taught me also through his prayers.

The next day Menkheperre rose and knew what he must do with Suresh to ensure that their discord would not escalate and Suresh would give him the respect that was expected. When he woke his eye was no worse than when he took to his bed as the salve and the Gods worked upon him during his sleep to continue his healing. We were all most grateful that Menkheperre could return amongst the hostage princes with barely a shadow under his eye, not giving his attacker the glory of seeing his victim wear the fruits of his blow.

Indeed when Menkheperre walked into the courtyard many of the boys expected to see his eye swollen shut and the blackness of a bruise spreading well into his cheek. Many had suffered or witnessed a blow from Suresh so were well aware of his force and the subsequent injuries. So when Menkheperre walked in a day after receiving one of his brutal punches there were surprised faces all round. Not least upon the face of Suresh, who having being reprimanded by the priests educating the boys, knew his only delight now would be in seeing my son carry his attack for the next week--a warning to all others as to his power.

Menkheperre strode amongst the boys with his head high and smiling. He knew where Suresh was after having glanced him in the corner of his eye. He ignored the foreigner and went to seek out those whose company he enjoyed. In fact, he did such a wonderful job of avoiding Suresh and acting as though he had never been struck, that even Suresh himself forgot about the altercation. This was when Menkheperre enacted his coup d'état.

It was mid afternoon and the boys were resting, bathing or playing together within the courtyard of their school. Suresh was in one corner talking big to a few boys. Menkheperre approached so silently that not even the boys facing his direction saw him until he was only a few paces away from them. The distracted expressions on their faces alerted Suresh and he turned to see what they were looking at. When he did turn Menkheperre was right in front of him and within that second that it took to for Suresh to register who it was Menkheperre's fist slammed into his stomach, sending him gasping to the ground.

Now you may call it dumb luck, but I call it perfect alignment. Alignment of my son to be born to a father who ruled all, a family priestess who could help a young boy open his insight, a call from spirit to step into his grandeur and genetics that provided him with the lightning reflexes that could deliver a punch sharp enough to fell a boy twice his size. It was also alignment that allowed Menkheperre's punch to hit Suresh perfectly on the solar plexus, temporarily paralysing his diaphragm so that not only was he curled in pain but left struggling for breath as though he was drowning.

All the boys in the courtyard gathered around in shock. They had never seen anyone suffer such an injury and many of them were delighted that it was Suresh who was on the ground writhing. Several ran to call a priest though, believing that Menkheperre had delivered a deathly blow and that Suresh was actually dying. No one though was as scared as Suresh, a simple boy who so far had only landed blows to faces and arms and now had been truly undone by this single punch. He too thought he was dying.

Those left in the courtyard though saw my son stay calm as he stepped in close to the boy who now had tears streaming down his face as he gasped for breath and tried to call for help. Menkheperre did not falter at all. He stepped so close that his feet were touching Suresh as he bent down, his finger pointed and almost touching Suresh's face, his other hand in a fist.

He now spoke as though he had been Pharaoh a hundred years. "You shall never strike me nor any others here ever again!" he bellowed, and then stood straight. He stayed standing over Suresh watching his gasps grow longer and smoother. He knew the boy would be alright as all was going according to plan.

This was the way that the priests who ran to the courtyard found them all. Menkheperre, calm and still, stood over the gasping Suresh while the other boys surrounded them. The priests ran forward demanding to know what had occurred and waving the boys aside to help get air to Suresh. As one priest knelt down to check on Suresh, Menkheperre turned to the other and with the same authoritative voice in which he had addressed the foreign prince he spoke once more. "This barbarian has been corrected of his ill behaviour. He is now aware of his rightful place and no others shall fear him again," he announced. "Now I shall take audience with my father the Pharaoh to inform him of this."

With that he bowed to the priest who could not argue or stop him; the priest merely stepped aside and let him leave to seek me just as he had stated. When Menkheperre came once again to see me at the war rooms he was smiling as he had the night before when he returned from his temple visit--but this time it was different. It was the smile of a worthy victor. The generals that saw him that afternoon would comment it was the same smile I wore when I heard Megiddo had fallen.

Menkheperre spent a delightful hour re-telling the day's events. It was one of the most wonderful afternoons of my life. The generals who were present laughed and cheered as he re-told the story, delighted to see yet another able warrior growing and developing for Egypt. They christened him "Little Cobra" that afternoon and the name would hold for his entire army career, with only the

"Little" being dropped as he reached manhood.

The foreign princes developed well and Menkheperre's small battle with Suresh taught me much about how to now maintain my victory over Canaan and its regions. Having their sons hostage did not prove to always be a deterrent for rebellions or uprisings. I never again had to mount a battle as at Megiddo but over the next eighteen years of my reign I would trek seventeen times within this region with my army behind me. Murmurs would grow and action would begin to evolve, but they were foolish to even whisper of it as the Egyptians planted throughout this region to oversee trade and collect tribute would soon hear them. We would not give warning but make our way and deliver our sting, leaving them on their knees and in no doubt as to who ruled their land.

Our conquering of the northernmost reaches of Canaan was the most tenuous as that wretch, the King of Kadesh, was the proudest of all the hundreds of leaders in this land. He was burnt badly by the loss at Megiddo and his ego ached for retribution in order to restore his lost dignity. Unfortunately I proved a formidable conqueror and every attempt he made was quashed decisively; crushing his reputation even further. He declared me an infection upon his very soul and that of his people, but in truth his people were happy under Egyptian rule. They were all doing fine. The crops were abundant since the defeat of Megiddo and as long as food was plentiful in our time all else flowed. They resented their king continually increasing his taxes to raise money for the army and they hated even more the constant recruitment of their men to become soldiers. Women were sick of seeing their men called away for another futile rebellion which saw them return home bewildered, injured or, even worse, to not have them come home at all.

So families began to lie about what they were harvesting and they joined together in their deceit of their king. They found caves or dug storage and camouflaged their stores. Newborn sons were not registered and boys already alive and nearing manhood were declared dead or having had runaway to the lands of the north when the men sent to enforce conscriptions arrived. Some even went so far as to create fake tombs to make the deception as authentic as possible. They even had men close to the palace paid to forewarn the commoners so that they were ready when the king's men arrived.

Finally after ten years of continual defeats, with his resources drained and undermined by his very own people, Kadesh truly submitted. The king consumed with remorse and anger never enjoyed the time of peace and would eventually die still hating himself for his failure to free his land of the disease he saw as Egypt.

CHAPTER SIXTEEN

In the meantime Egypt flourished like never before. It was now the largest empire it would ever know and I had well and truly established myself a worthy leader. Building work continued at a rate to match that of Hatshepsut, including a new pylon at Karnak and now my own inscriptions upon the temple to immortalise our victory at Megiddo and our might over Canaan. New temples were built across the land and some of the ancient ones were rebuilt or embellished.

My children grew and blossomed into young adults so fast that I felt I would return from a few weeks of campaign and find them aged a year. My sons embraced the grandeur of our new power. Amenemhat and Amenhotep found new enthusiasm for the army and they more than ably took in the knowledge of the generals and myself. Amenemhat was now well into battle training with Amenhotep just a year into his. Their eyes would light up whenever they spoke of what they were learning with Menkheperre sharing their excitement despite his own training being a few more years away.

Siamun though was never comfortable in the war rooms. I would find him looking out a window or yawning. He would never ask questions and when talk of his battle training was mentioned it was met with no enthusiasm. However when we sat in audience at the court, listening to endless reports from viziers or witnessing a judgement being passed down, it was Siamun who sat forward, eager to drink in every detail. Meanwhile the other boys would sit back, yawning, swinging their feet or looking around at anything they could find to distract them. Siamun would run to be beside me when we left court, repeating what he heard and asking questions fervently.

It was after one incredibly long day in court that I realised that I would need to rethink my dream of four warrior sons, one in each direction charging from the palace defending the empire. Amenhotep had even managed to fall asleep that day much to my embarrassment, but not unexpected after listening to a continual drone of numbers in reports. I too had grown weary within a couple of hours, but as was my position, I remained straight and attentive even though I joined my sons in the dreams of escaping to the less stuffy war rooms or outside on my horse.

Siamun though was far from bored and as he listened his eleven year old mind was constantly measuring and weighing up all that he heard. That day he was quiet when we left court and walked the corridors back to our family chambers. I did not particularly notice his head looking down and his forehead furrowed, deep in thought, as being tired myself all I could think of was being bathed and relaxing in my private garden with some wine.

It was here a few hours later that Siamun approached me, carrying a scroll. His face was quite serious and I knew this was not some frivolous issue to garner my attention, as so often my children would do. Instead he walked to me and when he was near, stood straight, took a deep breath and spoke. "Father, might I have your time to share some ideas I have about our wheat supplies?" he said, with such maturity I could not help but smile. He spoke as though he was a vizier in court.

"Well of course," I replied. "I am most interested to hear of your thoughts always Siamun."

Siamun smiled as he stepped close to the small garden table at which I sat. He moved aside my carafe of wine carefully and unrolled his scroll that was actually two pieces of papyrus, smoothing them flat carefully and then separating them so that the two pieces lay side by side. On one I saw a map of Egypt hand drawn by Siamun with place names and trade routes marked out. Small numbers were drawn at several places. I smiled even more now, remembering my father's pride at my ability to draw such maps with only my memory to guide me. Siamun's maps were just as accurate. On the second paper was another copy of the map but with some different lines and numbers drawn upon it. I leant forward curious now as I did not recognise these lines as Siamun launched into his presentation.

"Father, I listened to the reports today and I think there is a better way to move around our goods," he began. Siamun spoke for almost twenty minutes giving me a thorough overview of his vision for an upgraded trade route network that would not only save time but overlap deliveries, so that many perishables didn't have to travel as far.

I was flabbergasted. It was so simple and obvious that I was embarrassed to not have thought of it myself. We had all grown so accustomed to a system that had been passed down for almost five generations of Pharaohs that none had even questioned it. Those that probably had thought of it would never have had the courage to challenge what was.

Of course the particulars would need to be looked at more closely by the viziers. As you know, I was far from comfortable with the fine details of our trades, entrusting it to my viziers while I focussed on our military. So the next day I approached them warily hoping it was not my lack of knowledge that let me see this as an amazing opportunity. My apprehension was unwarranted and they too were impressed at the simplicity and efficiency this new approach would offer us. They were further impressed that it was my young son who had the mind to create such a plan and were comforted to know that the next generation of royals held some skill with the business side of the empire. They had never said anything, but many of the older viziers and stewards who had worked with Hatshepsut knew that I did not have the inherent interest or natural tenacity for this side of my duties. Yes, they respected my military prowess, and appreciated that without these skills we would possibly not even have the land of Egypt to oversee.

While many of them enjoyed the trust I held in them to perform their duties with little interference, many of them worried about what would lie ahead. Everyone knew my true passion was the military and word was now spreading as to how my sons were also highly skilled soldiers. The viziers had begun in earnest to pass on their knowledge and experience to their sons or nephews in the hope that their traditions and sensibilities could live on to support the empire. Today though gave them all the hope they needed. This new map drawn by Siamun was like a breath of fresh air to the business workings of the empire in more than one way. It was with genuine respect and concern that my most senior vizier, Rekhmire, now turned to me and spoke what I had already felt.

"Sire, I must speak and please know I do so for the good of the empire," he began nervously. "To have a son with such an aptitude for business at such an age is a blessing to us all. I thank you for siring him."

He bowed and I nodded acknowledging his compliment.

Rekhmire then continued. "I beg you Sire, let him develop this skill with us," he now spoke quicker, "and not let this talent be diluted within military training."

I nodded once more. Rekhmire had been brave to address me in such a way but I could not ignore such advice from someone who had worked so hard to keep our economy and resources strong. I also knew that there was much more that Rekhmire did not say that I felt in his address. So that afternoon it was I who went to Siamun and asked if he might give me his time. We sat and I offered Siamun a new path that he might choose to travel upon.

He smiled intently as I described the delight of the viziers. "They could see it too?" he asked eagerly.

"Of course!" I answered. "And they are most grateful that such a mind had been born into one of their princes."

"I have more ideas Father," he spurted. "Do you think perhaps you and the viziers might like to hear them also?"

I stopped and smiled as I realised Siamun would always be one step ahead--yet another sign of his calling. "Yes we all would Siamun," I answered proudly. "In fact, we have decided that if you would like, you may study with the viziers and stewards. Would you like to do that rather than train with the army?" I asked.

Siamun's eyes grew wide and he could not speak, but he nodded his head slowly. I had just handed him his passion on a plate and he would devour it, making it bigger than ever. Of course Siamun would still learn some sword play as all men are taught how to protect themselves, but from that day on his mind was allowed to enquire and analyse. He could solve any problem placed before him and Siamun become one of the grandest economists and negotiators that the palace ever saw.

This left my remaining sons to carry the mantle of the military. Of course Amenemhat had also been learning some business, as he would need knowledge of this element of his rule when he took to the throne. He too was relieved to know that Siamun's study and training would now focus upon business, as he would have a ready ally within the court when he was crowned Pharaoh. Amenemhat threw himself into his training with full determination and with the ambition to be the best he could to continue the heritage that his forefathers and I had created for him.

Amenemhat trained hard and fast, all with Amenhotep by his side. They created a wonderful dynamic as they trained together. Having grown up as close friends and playmates they now drove each other on in friendly competition. If Amenemhat could throw a spear fifteen lengths, then Amenhotep would train until he could throw it sixteen lengths--spurring Amenemhat to now out throw him. Chariot races became perilous, but exhilarating to watch, and I am thankful their mothers never knew of their competitions or they would never have slept well at night.

Their competition and dedication to continually better themselves flowed onto the other young men they trained amongst which was wonderful for morale. However their trainers soon lectured them all when the escalating competitions soon resulted in an escalation in numbers of injuries.

"Have you no desire to make it to a battle that you must try and injure or deplete yourselves in training?" one finally implored. Amenemhat and Amenhotep listened intently to this lecture knowing their part in this. They soon restricted their competition so as to garner less attention but still created great benchmarks for the rest to aspire to.

As my two eldest boys reached fifteen and thirteen I began to take them on smaller expeditions where they might witness the carriage of justice. Of course I would never risk my heirs by taking them close to a battle. I also would not risk giving the rebels a chance to take my sons in any way. They would be placed nearby on a rise surrounded by bodyguards to watch our men enact the will of Amun. It was wonderful training not only to see an army in action but to experience life upon a campaign, from the long horse rides, setting up camp for the night and consulting with my generals before a battle.

It also allowed my sons to see more of the land that they would oversee. Even more importantly it allowed the people to see my sons. They were now robust young men, well toned from activity and with skins gleaming from their time in the sun. It also helped that they had inherited their father's good looks. This not only made them pleasant to look upon but also displayed my paternity with significant power. There could be no question as to their lineage.

On one occasion we made the journey north upon the royal touring boat to approach the delta and the lush farmlands surrounding it. This area was always buzzing, as it was our access to the sea. Caravans made their way here to meet the ships that would transport their wares across the waters to Minoa and beyond. Our own boats made their way up the Nile carrying goods traded with Nubia while grand sea ships greeted the land here to bring us their delights. The boys were fascinated at the mosaic of different skins and languages that filled the city that would be eventually known as Alexandria. It was after this visit that they truly understood our place within the world, not least when they saw the foreign traders bow to me as we passed them.

We travelled back down the Nile again after letting as many people see us as possible. The boat heaved with gifts and tributes showered upon us by the foreigners visiting our ports, honoured that the winds should have them arrive upon our land at the time that I should also be there. We carried richly scented liquors that would be shared at special gatherings, baskets of their spices for my chefs to experiment with, cured meats that would be given to my soldiers for long journeys, perfumed oils for bathing and bags of jewels.

The jewels fascinated Amenhotep and as we drifted down the river he sat cross-legged upon the deck of the boat with one of the small silk bags resting on his legs. One by one he pulled the coloured stones from the sack and held them to the sun, fascinated to see them glisten and sending a thousand rays of colour bouncing around the deck as the sunlight reflected off them. I sat nearby entertained by his play and joining his admiration for the beauty of nature.

"Father, I feel the power of Ma'at in each and every one of these," he said, never taking his eye off the emerald that he turned in his hand.

Amenhotep now joined us upon the deck having finished his rest below in our cabin space. He stood beside his brother and bent down to take the emerald half the size of his palm from Amenemhat's hand. He turned it over and over, looking at all the cuts in it, seeing how it was polished.

"Isn't it amazing?" Amenhotep asked, now holding a ruby up to the sun, sending shards of red light over us all.

"Yes," Amenemhat replied, "I would quite like to keep this for my funeral mask."

It was a simple comment but its implications were far from simple for me. I lunged forward from my seat and in one step had reached Amenemhat and snatched the stone from his hand. The two boys looked up at me stunned.

"It is not your place to plan such things!" I shouted. "This stone cannot be used for anything else now that you have placed such intent upon it."

With that I hurled the stone into the river. It landed with a small splash far from the boat and to this day lies within the mud of the river floor. I returned to my seat, my chest heaving, overwhelmed at my rush of emotions at the thought of one of my children lying beneath a funeral mask--least of all my successor. Amenemhat looked out to where the stone fell, now getting further and further away. Amenhotep placed the ruby he held back within the sack and drew tight its cord. We continued on in silence.

Late that afternoon we docked at Giza, the ancient capital of our land before my forefathers moved to Thebes. As we disembarked and made our way to our rooms for the night we saw the peaks of the pyramids in the distance, shining brightly in the sun. Their limestone skins were still in place and the sunlight reflecting off them was dazzling. The boys said nothing as the carriage rolled along taking us to our home during our stay but looked intently, now too afraid to make any comments referring to death lest it inflame me again. I saw them looking at the monument and could see the curiosity in their eyes.

"Tomorrow we shall visit the grand pyramids and pay honour to our ancestors," I said simply.

So the next morning after breakfast we climbed upon horses kept in Giza for royal visits, and rode away from the city to the pyramids. I still loved to ride so much and to have my two sons with me made it even more special, especially now as they were such able riders in their own right. When we were clear of the city with its crowds of people and I could see we were on the road that would carry us straight to the pyramids I turned to our entourage of guards, priests and local viziers.

"Gentlemen, I am in the mood for a race," I grinned despite being met by confused looks from everyone including my children. I now turned directly to my boys. "Sons, let's see who of the three of us the Gods have given the fastest horse to today!" I teased leaning forward on my horse.

Amenemhat and Amenhotep looked at each other smiling. Any competition was a delight for them, and to have their father join in with such playfulness made it all the more exciting. So we lined up our horses equally and chose a bodyguard to signal the start. We all hunched forward on our horses, our legs tensed ready to kick their sides and make them run. The bodyguard lifted his hand.

"Enjoy the taste of my dust in your lungs!" cried out Amenemhat.

The bodyguard dropped his arm down and our three horses burst forward. Amenemhat did indeed streak ahead filling our faces with dust and the occasional rock, but I was far from riding my horse hard. Amenhotep kept his place tight by my side, which surprised but impressed me. We were now fast approaching the site and as the Sphinx grew larger I dug my heels into my horse and burst ahead of my two sons. Yes, I could have let my son win, but it would be far from right to hand him a victory. Also I was still Pharaoh and commander of all the warriors in this land.

Not that my sudden gain of the lead was a guaranteed win as the boys also pushed their horses to the limit and were close behind me, but it was I who pulled up beside the Sphinx first. My sons came and gave the traditional congratulations to the victor as our entourage arrived with much needed water.

Rested and rehydrated we walked towards the pyramids and now stood dwarfed by their size. Amenhotep ran to the first one, wanting to touch its surface but stopped. "Is it alright to touch them?" he asked, wary that there may be some protocol that needed observing.

I nodded to him and he continued to run along its edge with his hand sliding along the stones that formed the base level while Amenemhat stood by my side looking up in awe. "How did they manage such a height, Father?" he asked.

Yes, I did explain to him how it was done. That knowledge had been passed on through the generations as each new Pharaoh looked on at them in wonder. The process had been recorded officially but as no others sought to replicate these structures, those records were soon considered unimportant and were lost over time. There used to a library beside the Sphinx to store such things but it was pulled apart so that its precious stones could be used for a less wealthy Pharaoh to build his own tomb. The scrolls within were sent to some anonymous storage place where they would disintegrate before I was born.

"Why do we not build such tombs anymore if we have the knowledge?" he continued to ask.

So I went through the list of reasons, beginning with the depletion of resources upon a Pharaoh's reign through to the beacon these were for tomb raiders. Standing before them now a thousand years after they were built it was well-known that they had been plundered mercilessly. This was most possibly by other Pharaohs desperate to fill their own tombs with a taste of Khufu's grandeur or simply out of jealousy, believing that his monument was glory enough to make his way in the afterlife.

"Are you not proud that your great-grandfather found the grand valley in which our family lies?" I asked wanting to hear his feelings. "We were blessed that he should choose to begin our tradition of lying within tombs that Ma'at herself created."

"I am very proud of all that my family has done. I am just curious that such men who were even grander than Khufu chose more modest ways to be remembered," he said earnestly.

"Ah," I nodded, "so you believe that a man's tomb is about remembrance?"

"Well yes," he answered and waved his hand at the pyramid. "Why else spend so much time and money to build something? It worked for Khufu. Here we stand a thousand years later talking about him."

I laughed outright. He was absolutely correct. Khufu had indeed made his mark upon history and our land. "Well this is one way to be remembered through grand buildings," I kept laughing, "but tell me son, how would you wish that you and I were remembered--for grand buildings or grand actions?"

Amenemhat turned to me puzzled. "Well isn't a grand building in itself a grand action?" he said.

This made me laugh even more. Once again he was right so I offered another perspective hoping he would see the intent of my words. "Tell me what else we remember Khufu for?" I said plainly.

Amenemhat stopped and stared blankly for a minute or so. "I can think of nothing Father," he answered.

"Now tell me what I will be remembered for?" I asked.

"The grand battle of Megiddo and for making Egypt the greatest it has ever been!" he answered proudly.

"So what would you rather be; a Pharaoh remembered for spending his money and time building monuments, or one that trained and led his army into battle victorious every time?" I posed to him.

Amenemhat did not need to answer for this truly was not a question at all. Amenhotep appeared from around the corner of the pyramid having run its entire perimeter and stopped at the place where he had started, panting, sweaty and dusty, but delighted that he had done this. A minute later his bodyguard followed behind panting even heavier.

"Catch your breath Amenhotep!" I cried out to him, "I wish to defeat you and your brother in yet another race back to the city!"

Over the next year Amenemhat, now almost sixteen and having mastered his core army training, would make his own way north to visit the delta and oversee the goings-on of the region and most importantly the ports. It helped him make his name amongst the traders both foreign and native. He was always sad to leave his home and his family, despite his joy at finally having some independence. All of his siblings missed him dearly when he was gone but they too rejoiced in his passage into manhood and taking on more of his princely responsibilities. When he returned home he would always seem so much older despite having been gone only a month or so. He would bound back into the palace and we would all celebrate his return. While his sisters would coo and sigh at the gifts handed to them, his brothers would beg for stories of his adventures.

That year I did not see Amenemhat so much. We would often alternate our journeys so that while one of us was away the other would be resident at the palace. He revelled in his duties and that all those around him acknowledged his manhood so. Amenemhat, Amenhotep and Siamun were now lying with the consorts as was expected having reached an age where this was needed for their body as well as their spirit. It would only be a matter of time before they would father a child and possibly elevate the mother to a wife. In Amenemhat's case this was quite serious as that child would be the successor to the throne and create the next generation of our family and royalty. So his consorts were selected with a bit more care should their herbs preventing pregnancy fail or should Amenemhat fall in love with one of these women, as did his grandfather.

Satiah raised the issue of marriage with him as he turned sixteen, this being the age where I began to consider such things also. However when his mother spoke of this to him he dropped his eyes and shrugged. "Are such things so important?" he answered. "I am serving Egypt and there are many others who can provide an heir."

Satiah gasped, thankful that I was not present to hear such words. She was horrified that he would avoid his duty so and broke into a truly uncharacteristic barrage of pleas to our son. It was quite simple, Amenemhat had inherited my passion to rule and lead an uncomplicated life, which at this point did not entail what he saw to be the worries of marriage. What he failed to inherit from me was the drive to keep his genes upon the throne. He was right in a way as if he failed, he had three brothers who could ensure the bloodline for between them all there was surely to be one son. Amenemhat did not have the burden of solving this problem solely upon his shoulders, nor did he have the shadow of a stepmother and her team hovering over him. He could enjoy his youth and his travelling and be concerned about such things later.

Satiah would never share with me Amenemhat's exact words that day and I am glad I did not know them. She did however mention that he appeared to have no interest in taking a wife and I laughed remembering my own hesitancy to enter this purely from duty.

"Leave him be, Satiah," I responded. "He will soon find the desire to do so as did I. He just needs for his own Satiah to arrive and open his eyes.

I was on tour to Southern Egypt--which I rarely made it to as Canaan required such maintenance. I was standing overlooking a wheat field as the vizier for that region recited its expected harvest when in the distance I saw a palace messenger on horseback approaching us at great speed. My heart sank as I watched him approach knowing deep inside it was bad news. I no longer heard the words of the vizier as the rider stopped nearby and spoke earnestly to the priest who had accompanied me. The priest's face confirmed for me that this was indeed something terrible as he now walked towards me, his brow lined with worry. I raised my hand to the vizier, signalling him to stop talking and walked to meet the priest.

"Speak!" I bellowed impatiently.

"Your Highness, there has been an accident. The Royal Prince Amenemhat has been injured," the priest relayed as fast as possible, "and his life force is weak Sire. Her Royal Highness Queen Satiah asks that you return to the palace."

Of all the bad news I never imagined it was this. I imagined an uprising at Gaza or that the King of Kadesh was once again travelling south. Anything would have been better than to know one of my children was on the precipice of the afterworld. A haze washed over me and for a second I felt as though my legs may not be able to move me, then another wave of energy came crashing through and I had to get to my son as fast as possible. I brushed past the priest and towards my chariot.

"Unharness the horse!" I shouted to my guards.

I turned to the priest and the rest of my entourage. "I shall ride on horseback, those of you that can keep up my pace shall escort me," I continued firmly.

One of my guards began to change the horse with lightning speed and I helped him to make it even quicker. All had heard the report and knew the urgency so that when I mounted my horse less than ten minutes later I looked behind me to see three other horses unharnessed and mounted by my guards ready for the hard journey ahead. If we went as fast as possible we could be there in four hours. I kicked my horse and we were off.

I arrived at the palace as the sun was beginning to set. They had no warning of my exact arrival time as no one could have paced themselves ahead me. A butler ran to greet me, stumbling over his words, but words were not necessary as there was a heavy pall over the palace that you could almost see. My heart sank even further as it knew the truth already.

I ran through the corridors to our family chambers, cursing every turn, shoving doors open as I made my way. I reached the final corridor that led to Amenemhat's rooms and stopped. That smell, that cursed mix of sandalwood and myrrh that I had despised since my father's death met my nostrils and I knew. I knew. The door was open and I saw darkness with flickers of lamplight. The curtains had been drawn as they always were for someone's final hours.

My eyes did not need to see what was in the room but my feet carried me onwards. Perhaps Amenemhat just needed shade for his recovery and my mind so tired from the ride played tricks with the scents. As I drew closer though I heard some crying and my heart once again sank.

I walked through the door of the bedchamber and for a moment I was that ten year old boy standing in the dark watching my mother cry over the dead body of my father. Only this time she was joined by Satiah who was also crying and the body was not my father's but that of my precious first-born son. Arisina stood beside the bed silently mouthing the chants for the dead and I saw tears streamed down her face also as she looked up and saw me. My mother and Satiah too looked up, but seeing me only brought on a fresh flood of tears.

I slowly walked towards the bed and gazed down upon the shell of my son, his skin now that horrible waxy grey. As I rode home I had hoped that my return would bring with me some surge of protection to hold his spirit with us, but his call to leave was beyond anything I could offer. The only thing I could do now was to fall to my knees beside the bed and join the women in their tears.

# CHAPTER SEVENTEEN

I t was a simple injury that took Amenemhat from us. He had fallen from his horse during some basic training but the angle at which he hit the ground snapped his neck and he was instantly paralysed. He lay upon the ground gasping, trying to understand what was happening to his body when all went dark. He slipped into a coma before the others were at his side and he would never open his eyes again. He was put upon a stretcher and with this act the soldiers who did so helped to end his life even quicker. Unwittingly their handling created the last elements of bruising and twisting to his spine that would interfere with the nerves that fed his lungs.

Amenemhat was rushed back upon the stretcher to the palace, the jolts shaking the shards of the fracture even more. When the physicians and priests were finally by his side they knew just by looking that his spirit had already moved on. It was just a matter of when his body would finally also succumb. Satiah rushed to the room and she too knew that this was so as the body that lay before her had no life force despite the shallow breaths that persisted. It was then that Satiah sent the messenger to me, also hoping that my return may in some way call Amenemhat's spirit back.

The palace now fell into mourning. We had done this many times within my life, for my father, Neferure and Hatshepsut. We even had official mourning for Senemut. This time was different though. A shining star had been extinguished; the light that had shown all the way beyond Hatshepsut's shadow was no more.

I sat once more upon my throne recalling the day that he was born. The anticipation and then the soaring joy when Arisina came in to announce I had a son. To me he had been the right to correct all the wrongs made to our family by my awful aunt and for a moment my bile rose as I imagined her reaching out from the afterworld to hurt me still. All the anger that I held for her, that I had pushed down from my childhood until now rose up in one mighty wave so that I thought if I screamed the very walls around me would crumble. I choked it back though, calling upon calm to wash over me, only this time it would not come and I forced myself to steady my façade before the court.

I watched over my children as their hearts grew heavy with the loss of their beloved eldest and it made my anger at Hatshepsut grow. Every tear that fell from a daughter's eye, every dark look of despair within a son's eye, they all added to my hatred of this woman's spirit. I watched my beloved Satiah grow frail as her grief overwhelmed her. Beketamun and Nefertiry would spend their days comforting her and my anger would churn that at such a young age they would need to.

Evil could have come and just taken me. I could have fallen to the illness that took my father or be struck by an arrow in battle. Instead it was sent to my son, an innocent who threatened no one. Evil though does not act so simply or with such consideration. In choosing my son it tore at my love for my son and my pride as a Pharaoh, it ripped into the heart of his mother and pulled at the weave that held together my children. Evil is cruel beyond all reason and with no sense of consequence--other than to satisfy its own end. It exists to feed off our very misery and, in taking my son, it reached out with a thousand hands to touch as many as possible.

Amenhotep joined me in this anger albeit in his own way. He too watched his brothers and sisters grief-stricken at their loss. The girls in particular made his heart ache, as their rooms no longer rang with the sounds of their laughter and talking. He also felt for Satiah. Despite not being of her womb he held a love and respect for her that equalled that of his own mother, as did all of my children with Matreya. To see Satiah in pain made his own pain even deeper.

He began to question the Gods and their workings. Why would they let such a thing beset the son born to rule? Why had it not taken himself or Siamun or Menkheperre? Part of him started to think that it had always been his destiny to now rule after me and as soon as he thought this he hated himself for allowing such thoughts to enter his mind. Amenhotep had never dreamt of ruling. He had never been jealous of his older brother for even a second. No matter of his love for me, or his will to continue the family honour, there would always be a part of him that felt he was not the rightful Pharaoh to succeed me.

Despite this conflict within him he rose to his new role and responsibility with maturity that outstripped his years. During the sixty days that the palace waited for Amenemhat's body to be prepared for entombment it was Amenhotep who held the family together. Yes, it should have been my place to do so, but the anger consuming me had given me a cold veneer that all took for grief. I would sit and stare ahead of me for up to an hour at a time lost in my thoughts. My children could enter the room and I would not even notice their presence and this made them even sadder. Amenhotep saw this distance I had created with all around me and knew that this was a time for him to begin acting as the eldest son. So only a few days after Amenemhat's passing, he approached me during one of my statue-like sittings and stood before me so that I would have to acknowledge him.

"Father," he spoke softly holding back tears. "If it pleases you I would like to oversee Amenemhat's funeral preparations."

I looked him in the eye, the only one of my children that I had dared to in a few days. It was a request made with such love and honour, not only for his lost brother but also for Satiah and me, knowing that the removal of that burden would make these days easier. I nodded and as I did so closed my eyes and began to cry. I held out my hand and took Amenhotep's in mine.

"You were a wonderful brother and friend in life," I said. "I thank you for continuing to do so for him in death as well."

Of course Amenhotep would consult with Satiah and myself as to the details we wished for our son, and then with the priests for more essential matters. It would be Amenhotep who would oversee the mummification, visiting each day to ask as to how the mortuary priests were progressing. Amenhotep watched as his brother's body was covered in the natron to dry it and on his sixteenth birthday stood and watched the layers of bandages wrap around Amenemhat's body and was proud that he was able to see his brother's face until the last moment possible. He would ride out to the Valley and see that the tomb was being prepared to my satisfaction and all would respect him as though it were I standing before them giving orders.

Amenhotep though had an agenda in asking for this role. It was not one done with deceit or any selfish motivations. Another task involved in a burial is the commission of the adornments. These are the jewellery and decorations that accompany the body, signifying the grandeur in which the person lived. It was within this part of his duties that he wished to make his own special tribute to his brother.

Amenhotep made his way to the treasury to collect the jewels gifted to Amenemhat at his birth. The treasury was one wing of the palace with a large foyer at its entrance. The two pillars within it were gilded with gold. Understandably it was the most heavily guarded part of the whole palace due to the riches within it. Here was stored any gold, silver and jewels received in tribute or trade. During my family's reign it was expanded to hold all the worth we collected but there would be many reigns in which these rooms would sit empty.

Amenhotep was led to the room that contained the gifts given to each of us at birth. Lined up on a shelf were the silken bags containing jewels that were given to each of my family, each bag bearing a tag that bore the name of the person to whom the contents had been gifted. The largest of course was tagged with my name, and then one equalling mine was tagged with Amenemhat's name. As was custom for a son birthed as successor we were both showered somewhat more abundantly than others. Smaller bags, each with the names of my remaining children nestled next to them as they all waited to be collected to be made into the myriad of jewellery, statuary and eventually funeral adornments each one would require. Amenhotep reached out and picked up Amenemhat's with a sigh.

"It is truly tragic that his should be needed so soon for such things," muttered the treasurer behind him.

Amenhotep turned and nodded then asked, "Now where are the jewels from Minoa stored?"

The treasurer looked confused. There were more than enough jewels within the sack Amenhotep held to make the adornments for a prince. In fact there were enough for a Pharaoh as they were intended. It was not his place to question though and he gestured with his hand for Amenhotep to follow him

They were soon within another small dark room. Narrow shelves lined one wall filled with similar silken sacks while chests were piled upon the floor. Amenhotep saw what he wanted immediately and crossed the room picking up the blue bag that he had sat with upon the boat as we had floated down the Nile. It had only been a year or so yet it felt like so much longer. He opened it up praying that he would find the stone he sought and within a minute his hands found it in the lamplight. He held the ruby that he had been holding that day as I snatched the emerald from Amenemhat's hand. He slipped it within Amenemhat's sack and drew it tight.

As he placed the Minoan bag back upon the shelf, another sack caught his eye. It lay flat upon the shelf, its drawstring loose and its mouth gaping. He probably would not have even noticed but for the flicker of light coming from it as his lamp moved near to it. Placing the lamp next to the sack he reached in and pulled out the first jewel he touched. When his hand pulled it closer to the light he gasped. In his hand he held an emerald so much like the one his brother admired on the boat that day that he truly believed it was one and the same. He turned it in his hand letting the lamp light play upon it and he began to smile. There may have been little pleasure in overseeing his brother's funeral but at least now he could enact one of his brother's wishes.

From the treasury Amenhotep travelled straight to the royal goldsmiths who would make the adornments. Together they sorted through the jewels and Amenhotep directed them as to what should be used where. Armbands with lapis lazuli and diamonds were designed, followed by a pectoral of rubies, clear quartz and amethysts. Then the crowning glory was decided upon, his funerary mask that would capture his magnificence for eternity. Amenhotep followed the priests' advice and held to the traditional standards of our family period. He asked for one small adjustment to the design.

He handed the emerald to the goldsmith and instructed him to place it so that when the mask was lowered the stone would rest upon Amenemhat's chest. They did so and when the mask was complete it was so magnificent that all who saw it were reduced to tears at its grandeur. Many proclaimed that Ma'at and Amun had worked the gold and stones that made that mask in order for it to affect our emotions so. I know now that it was the love with which Amenhotep commissioned its creation and the magic that was held within that emerald that sought to move them.

There was one stone that Amenhotep did not leave with the goldsmiths that day. He walked away with the ruby in his hand with much greater plans for it. On the day that he stood and watched his brother's body brushed free of the natron salts he did something no one else had ever thought to do. He did not flinch as he saw Amenemhat's dried shell with the huge cavity that once held his organs. Instead he smiled as he watched the priests carry back to the body the separately preserved heart and lay it back within the body, and then he stepped forward and held out his hand with the ruby upon his palm.

"Place this with his heart," he said without any air of an order, just as a simple instruction.

The priest did not respond for a moment unsure what to say to this. They had such strict protocol as to how things were done that the eldest of the funerary priests could not help but step forward.

"Sire this is not the way for such things," he explained. "Let us bind it against his chest within the bandages as an amulet."

Amenhotep could not accept this alternative for he knew that grave robbers existed and he wished to guarantee that his gift would remain with his brother always.

"No," he answered calmly. "It shall be placed with his heart."

This was now a command and the Priest had to oblige. His knowledge of embalming knew that the gem would not compromise the mummification. If it should somehow interfere with the passage of Amenemhat's spirit then it would be Amenhotep who would face the consequences. So the priest laid the stone beside Amenemhat's heart and they continued to refill the body with wads of linen and began to bind it with the bandages. Amenhotep never spoke of the gift he gave his brother to anyone and the priests kept this little ceremony to themselves also.

When Amenemhat's body was ready he received a grand ceremony within the Great Temple at Karnak and anyone who could attend swelled the temple full. Those that could not fit inside lined the streets and wept for my lost son as his coffin passed, making its way to the pier on the Nile where it would cross to enter the Valley. Twenty men skilfully lifted the huge coffin upon the ceremonial boat and it made its way across the water while my family followed behind on the royal boat. As we entered the Valley, now upon carriages, Satiah and the girls began to cry as we were now sharing our last moments with Amenemhat.

I did not join them in their tears. As I entered the Valley my eyes saw the temple that Hatshepsut built and my anger raged again. I imagined taking my son to her tomb just below it, throwing her body out into the sun, stripping it of its adornments while he rested within its grandeur instead. Of course I would do no such thing and continued on in the cortège to where he would lie. I had my son placed within the tomb of my father that they should join together in the afterworld having never known each other in life. He was placed within a small annexe tidied of my father's treasures to make room for his sarcophagus.

I waited with my family in the entrance chamber while priests and servants carried the coffin through the narrow corridors to place him within the sarcophagus. The return of the pallbearers signalled that we could now enter and make our final goodbyes. I led the way and was strangely comforted to see his coffin nested within the granite box that would now protect it. Satiah though saw no comfort in this and broke down in sobs that soon were shared with my daughters. The children took turns to place gifts upon his coffin or beside the sarcophagus. Menkheperre placed a bow and quiver of arrows, Nefertiry a scroll of pictures, some flowers from Isis and Beketamun, different oils and incense from Meritamen, Meryt and Nebetiunet, and a shield from Siamun. I did not notice that Amenhotep did not place anything.

We all eventually made our way back out into the sun. It was very hard for Satiah to truly leave her son and I am still stricken by the courage she showed in doing so. While her grief for her son was enormous it was matched by her respect for his spirit and she knew now it must be left without the pull of her heart to hold it from its journey.

As we rode back through the Valley and we passed Hatshepsut's monument I once again scowled. I was now certain that it was her jealousy that beset this evil to come to us. All the warmth and respect I had shown for her was decimated in the loss of my son. I silently vowed to seek revenge. If she could affect me from the afterworld then I could affect her there from this life.

The strains of grief and the thoughts it lets your mind create can consume you. Whether you lose yourself within this to spin and churn, or move on with the life that actually exists around you, can be a hard path for many-- especially when the loss is too soon and so tragic. For a parent to lose a child is beyond any law of nature and spirit. We create children to replace us and continue our likeness. They are meant to see us into old age and give us the grandchildren that will continue on like an echo of ourselves. A parent buries a child and they not only grieve for what they have lost but also for the future that is lost in that death.

The palace soon filled with the sound of my daughters' chatter once again. The tears dried and the eyes of my sons once again shone brightly. It was hard now not to watch Amenhotep carry on the duties of Amenemhat and imagine how Amenemhat himself would have done those things. To also wonder what children Amenemhat would have fathered, what buildings he would have commissioned, and what victories he would have led our empire in. These thoughts grew less as I returned to my Pharaoh duties.

The thoughts that I held about Hatshepsut though did not fade or grow less frequent. Every time I walked through the Great Temple at Karnak I saw the images she had commissioned, I sat in court with men who had been her allies, and as I ventured into the Valley to oversee my own tomb construction I saw that pretentious temple. I had reminders of her everywhere and they all reactivated the hate and paranoia within me in seconds. This soon affected my sleep and once I was not well rested then of course such unbalanced thoughts grew more easily. I felt my own emotions start to eat me away from the inside and the more I fought them, the stronger they seemed to get. Then I was able to hate her for letting my mind grow so malignant and so the spiral continued.

I did not notice that Amenhotep himself had begun to harbour his own churn of thoughts in his mind since his brother's passing. Like myself, he did not wish to burden others with his own grief but the conflict he felt at replacing his brother as successor continued to weigh heavy. The funeral preparations had given him some distraction but now as he took up his extra duties they returned and the burden of them made some days a true struggle.

The first court session after the funeral seemed to make everything so real. The line of chairs that my sons sat upon to the left of me now only numbered three. We had left Amenemhat's throne in place until the funeral, partly out of respect for him but also as we did not consider him truly gone until his body was within the tomb. It had sat empty when he was on his excursions to the delta and it gave us some comfort to see it and know he would return to it. However Amenemhat was now gone forever and his throne joined him within his tomb, so that he would sit upon it in the afterlife with all the glory that was his as a prince. As my sons walked into court that day and took their places I felt their discomfort to sit within their new positions, all one space closer to the Pharaoh. Amenhotep wore it on his face plain for all to see.

I looked around and noticed that no one within the court would look at my sons as they normally would to acknowledge their entrance and kept their eyes upon me or to the floor. Unexpected change never sat well within the palace and least of all within court. My wives sat to my right and Satiah too had her head down as the boys now sat upon their thrones. It was hard enough to walk in and see Amenemhat's throne missing but now to see his brothers without him was too real. Next to her though sat Matreya looking ahead with her usual aplomb, across her lips a slight smile. No matter how slight--it offended me to the core. I held back with all the strength that I had my desire to stand and strike her with my flail. Instead I turned back to the people waiting before me to begin session and started the day's work.

While the rest of us were lost within the cloud of grief, Matreya had spent the days since Amenemhat's death revelling in a new self-made glory. Having never shared any love for Satiah's children, despite Satiah showering all my children with love and affection equally, Matreya had no emotions of loss or sadness in Amenemhat's death. Instead she spent her days boasting to her personal servants that finally she would be recognised for the grand queen she was born to be.

For you see as Matreya had so quickly stated when she saw Amenhotep finally leave her body, she had in fact given birth to a Pharaoh. For her Amenemhat's death was no loss but her final step into immortality. Now she would be recorded as my first wife, as mother of my surviving eldest son. She would be called "King's Mother" some day and delight in the respect and power that would bring. On the day of Amenemhat's funeral as we passed by Hatshepsut's temple, while I scowled Matreya smiled at the thought that now she could commission a grand temple for herself and she could not be denied it.

Her cunning and ego at least found some balance with the shreds of tact within her. She kept her plans and bragging to herself during the mourning period. Matreya would sit quietly and pray along with us when needed and even took to wearing the attire and lack of jewellery seen as appropriate during this time. She would retire to her private chambers as quickly and as often as she could though. Once there she was quick to strip the mourning clothes off and return to her usual overdone style. The servants would listen to her gripes of how boring the palace was at this time, how she craved for a party and some music and how horrid the mourning clothes were.

Once the funeral was over though she felt free to campaign her cause with all the energy she could muster. Her first assault was upon me. That first day in court she had expected that she would now sit within the seat closest to my right. As she was now mother of the heir this was her rightful place and Satiah should now be the one to sit away from the Pharaoh. As was Matreya's usual routine she was the last to arrive at court, taking her time with her grooming and making her own entrance.

Satiah would always be ready before all else and would walk with me to court, partly to give me company and also because she loved to be with me whenever she could. Since Isis' birth Matreya no longer shared my bed. She had provided more than enough children and her behaviour upon my return from Megiddo had given me more than enough reason to not request her company again. Satiah now shared my bed with me as since Amenemhat's death we had needed the nights to comfort each other. While our closeness annoyed Matreya she was relieved not to be required for any more children. It also gave her the space she needed to indulge her vanities, including sneaking in young soldiers or courtiers into her chambers to entertain her.

Satiah knew that despite our closeness and love, Matreya now outranked her so on that first day when we walked to the rise upon which our thrones were placed she automatically and respectfully went to sit to the queen's chair furthest from me. I was seated first as was protocol and as I realised what she was doing I sat forward.

"Satiah, your place is here beside me," I hissed, hoping no one would hear my words.

She looked at me shocked and said nothing. She had never been comfortable to speak in court even when addressed.

"Your seat remains beside me," I repeated emphatically.

Satiah nodded and took her place beside me. A few of the courtiers noticed and were desperate to speak between themselves but of course they couldn't. Then Matreya made her entrance and they all watched to see how this scene would transpire.

Of course Matreya saw Satiah within what she now considered her own position the instant she entered the court. She quickened her pace and by the time she was at the top step her face was blood red. Matreya walked to stand in front of Satiah. "I believe this seat is now mine!" she snapped.

Satiah kept her eyes ahead and did not make eye contact. This was awkward enough and she did not know what to say to Matreya. Also she knew it was up to me to let Matreya know of my decision.

"Satiah shall remain in her throne and you shall remain in yours," I said bluntly.

Matreya snapped her head towards me so quickly that her heavy earrings swung. She sneered as though about to speak but knew matters were bad enough. To have such an outward display of disrespect shown towards her in front of all the court was embarrassing enough as it was and she should not make it worse by acting with a lack of poise. She bit her tongue and sat within her usual place but all saw the colour of her face and her chest heave. It was a simple act but within it I had declared to all who I still favoured of my wives. So when Matreya looked across and saw that her son was in his rightful place she could not help but smile. I could do such things to her but it would never change the fact that a child of her body would one day rule.

Matreya did not shake the throne incident so easily though. She knew how to behave before the court but that afternoon as I sought to rest in my rooms she burst in. I was expecting her to do so and did not even flinch as she began her tirade.

"How dare you!" she began yelling. "To show me such little respect and in front of the entire court."

"I do not answer to you Matreya," I responded. "That court is under my rule and you shall accept however I choose to run it."

"But I am the mother of your successor!" she yelled even louder.

I did not answer her for I had no need to. I did what I did and it was of no consequence whether this satisfied her or not. So I sat in silence hoping she would tire of my silence and leave but she didn't and instead continued.

"I demand that you recognise me as the mother of your successor, Thutmose," she persisted. "You may not love me as you do Satiah but you cannot change the fact that it was I who gave you your heir."

Now I could not help myself. She had cut me to the core with those words; to speak so soon as though Amenemhat had never existed. I jumped to my feet and stepped towards her so quickly that she cowered. I stopped myself in time from hitting her but I desperately wanted to hurt her in some way. I wanted to make her share the pain that I was feeling inside, the pain that we were all feeling yet she somehow remained immune to. The roar of my voice inside also held back and I grabbed her by the arm pulling her close and spoke low so that not even the servants just beyond the doors heard my words.

"Satiah gave birth to my heir and evil took him away. I was blessed that he has brothers to continue our family legacy," I spat at her.

Her eyes grew wide in defiance. Even with my grip upon her she did not show any humility. "You sought me for marriage to provide you with children and I did! Six times over and with two sons that may even surpass your military skills," she snarled. "To not respect me will make all wonder why you choose to abandon the woman who birthed the next Pharaoh. They will question his lineage, and when they do I shall not speak to either confirm or deny it."

I looked deep in her eyes and the fury there along with her fervour made it clear to me that she would indeed be happy to begin such idle gossip. No matter how false or how incredulous the rumours would be someone would believe it. I released my grip upon her arm roughly sending her a step backwards. Her glare was still burning in her eyes. Such talk would prove to be a political cancer to Amenhotep's reign and I found it hard to believe that Matreya would take an action that would harm our son and ultimately her position.

What I could not underestimate though was Matreya's ambition. She had stabbed at the weakest place she could. Given time though she would think of some way to hurt me that would not affect Amenhotep and once again Hatshepsut and her unending grasp came into my mind. I gathered myself and sat down once again, leaning casually in my chair. I sat silent for a moment and rubbed my chin with my hand. Matreya watched me, waiting now for me to speak.

"You have always been considered a great wife, Matreya," I began. "All know you were brought to the palace for marriage and you were never a common consort raised above your station through luck or pregnancy. You have given the family six children who all bear my likeness or that of my mother. There is no question of your virtue as a queen, despite the rumours that have been shared with me that you receive male visitors in your chambers."

Matreya recoiled slightly as I delivered my own sting to her. She was completely unprepared for that revelation believing that she had been discreet. Her mind now raced wondering who had betrayed her.

"So my beloved queen and great wife," I leant forward in my chair, resting my arms upon my legs. "You understand that your role is important in having your son recognised and this is correct. So you shall be observed as such where and when it matters."

Matreya straightened up and smiled at her first triumph despite being wary of what else I might say now.

"So I shall sit beside you in court and at temple?" she said.

"No you shall not," I answered calmly and as she opened her mouth to begin another tirade I cut her short. "There is no need to pretend before those of the palace or court. All of those close to us, even the tribes of Canaan, know of my love for Satiah. She will remain by my side while we both live."

"This is disgraceful," Matreya hissed.

"Is it Matreya? Would you care to be cast aside but for the wicked hand of fate taking your first-born?" I asked.

"It is the will of the Gods," she answered coldly.

"Well it was also the will of the Gods which sent Satiah to me before you," I shot back half laughing. "You should feel blessed that Satiah has a more warm respect for protocol than you do. She will thankfully understand when I have you recorded as the first wife, but do not take it as personal flattery. I will merely do this to make sure Amenhotep's succession is as smooth as possible."

I then continued to outline a kind of package deal to satisfy Matreya's ego. She would be written in all records as my first wife including within my tomb. I also threw in some extras such as my promise to cast a blind eye to her male visitors. I gave her every means to be recognised except that seat beside me that she craved so much. Matreya though knew she had pushed as far as she could. If she could not have the respect or honour within this life then she would be satisfied to know that she would at least have it from generations to come. She accepted what I outlined but did so quite begrudgingly so as not to make me feel totally victorious over her.

Finally she turned to leave but chose to take one last parting shot at me. "Someday you shall see the folly of your love for that woman," she drawled. "She has blurred your sense of duty."

She turned her back to me now to walk out of the room thinking she had the last word but I was far from letting her.

"Whichever of us passes first shall be waiting to greet the other in the afterlife. Who shall be waiting for you Matreya?" I shot back.

She stopped her exit for one second but seemed to move even quicker when she once again continued. My final remark rang in her ears as she walked down the corridor but she would soon shrug this barb off. She had never come to the palace with any romantic ideals of a relationship with me so my words were not that sharp. It was just that once again she had to be subject to another's will. First she had to submit to Hatshepsut, biding her time until the old witch's death. Then by the time Hatshepsut had died Satiah had won the hearts of all in the palace while Amenemhat was well on his way to being Pharaoh, supported and idolised by her very own first-born.

Amenemhat's death should have changed all that. Instead she would remain a seat away from the Pharaoh, as voiceless as ever with token drawings and scrolls recording her—and those were all the records from *my* life as Pharaoh. However she did have one other person who could still grant her the power and glory that she sought. So instead of continuing on to her chambers, Matreya turned and made her way to Amenhotep's rooms.

When Matreya entered his rooms Amenhotep was with his personal butler organising for his first official trip away to Memphis. There were a dozen or so chests within the room, some already full, some still being filled by servants as directed by the butler while Amenhotep watched. He looked up as his mother walked in and as was customary he bowed to her leading the servants to do also.

"Oh, look at my son making his way out on his own finally!" she gushed.

You would never have imagined that she had just had the confrontation with me. The redness on her arm from my grip was gone and so was the scowl. Her face was soft and smiling. Amenhotep not being used to any affection or attention from his mother was puzzled by her appearance in his rooms and her attempt at some emotional connection with him immediately raised his suspicion.

"Yes Mother, I prepare for my first journey to oversee trade in Memphis," he answered simply.

"Amenhotep, you prepare for your first journey as heir to the throne," she said as though correcting him.

He turned his head away. It burned him to be referred to as this so soon despite its truth. Amenhotep tried to make small talk about his luggage but Matreya interrupted. "My son, let us share a private moment while your servants finish your packing," she drawled, and made her way to the small garden next to his rooms.

Amenhotep followed behind her reluctantly and truly uncomfortable at the prospect of being alone with his mother. They walked into the garden and Matreya sat upon a bench then gestured beside her, hoping Amenhotep would sit close by her. This invitation though was well beyond Amenhotep's comfort level with his mother and he shook his head.

"I shall stand Mother, I must return soon to oversee the preparations for my journey," he said awkwardly.

This far from pleased Matreya but she maintained her smiling face and they looked at each other in awkward silence for a moment. Finally Matreya was the one to speak, "I must say I am so proud to see you taking to your new duties so efficiently," she said. "All the palace speaks of your competence and maturity."

"I had a wonderful example to follow," he said, his eyes cast down. "How could I not know how to act as such."

"You know how to act as it is in your blood. Don't be fooled that this is purely from teaching," she said strongly, her eyes growing dark. "This is your destiny Amenhotep."

Every word she said made his muscles tense tighter and he felt his stomach twist. She had dared to say the thoughts that had made their way to him since his brother's death. He had pushed them aside and now here sat his mother saying the words out loud.

"It was Amenemhat's destiny, robbed by a simple accident. My only destiny is to continue his work to honour and respect my brother and Father," he said softly, hoping his words would correct the ill spirit of his mother's heresy.

Matreya looked at her son with his eyes still downcast and part of her was disgusted at his lack of strength to confront her, as she knew he truly wanted to in this moment. She stood and walked towards him, grabbed his chin and turned his face up so their eyes could meet.

"On the day you left my body they held you so that I could see your face. I knew that I was looking at a Pharaoh," she hissed. "Finally the day has come that everyone else must know this also and you stand here looking at the ground denying your own glory."

Amenhotep clenched his jaw and his eyes flared. He fought every impulse to push his mother away or strike her but she felt the anger boiling in him and this satisfied her. She at least knew he had some bite within him. Matreya dropped her hand away and Amenhotep kept his eyes locked on hers, his face growing red as he sought the words to match hers.

"Son, you do not wish to say anything harmful right now, after all I am your mother," she stated. "What greater ally or mentor could you wish for than the one who knew your grandeur from the moment of your birth?"

Matreya looked into his eyes and within her gaze Amenhotep saw everything. He saw her ego and its calculations, its desperate grasp for power. Within that split second he saw his mother's true self and knew her completely. Matreya in one sentence had revealed so much that her true motivation in visiting her son had been said and undone within that one sentence.

Amenhotep had been warned that he would have to deal with those wishing to share in his power for their own good. I had warned him, the priests and even his butler-- all that were used to the power plays of the palace had done so also. Amenhotep though had never imagined that it would be his mother who would be the first to manipulate his new position. The betrayal and disappointment was beyond words and he hated that he was now in this position more than ever. He closed his eyes, thought of Amenemhat and renewed his commitment to carry on for him.

Opening his eyes he turned to Matreya, "I have all of Egypt as my ally and the Gods to mentor me," he said calmly. "For any man or woman to think they can outdo either shows the folly of their spirit. Good day, Mother."

Amenhotep walked into his rooms fighting back tears. As he looked at the chests being filled for his journey the longing to not leave his family and home were now replaced with the desire to get as far away from this place as possible.

CHAPTER EIGHTEEN

y children were now young adults or rapidly approaching adulthood.
As they approached twelve, the age at which the Gods came to call
them to vocation, they would sit with me to discuss their role for the
family and of course for Egypt. For my sons this was simple. Amenhotep had
already chosen to oversee trade and our military station at Memphis but this
all changed when he became successor. Siamun and Menkheperre made their
callings known well before the age of twelve and were well-established in their
vocations by that age.

My daughters though weren't so straightforward. Not that any of them
proved difficult. It was just that royal daughters who weren't immediately in
line to the throne were offered much more choices as to how their life could be
spent. They could study the ways of the priestesses and support the Pharaoh in
this way. A princess could practise as an artisan, choosing to embroider, create
paintings or play music. Of course her arts would be solely for the enjoyment
of the palace. Lastly a princess could be simply a princess and spend her days
frivolously exploring her vanities at leisure, indulging in endless grooming and
bathing. All of these options would also involve the inevitable choice; that of
marriage.

Beketamun, being the eldest, was the first to choose her way. Satiah and
I secretly hoped that she would be an example for all her younger sisters. We
needn't have worried as Beketamun would step into womanhood with all the
grace that she had lived her childhood. She still managed to surprise me though.
Having been a quiet child who doted upon her younger sisters and always the
first by Satiah's side when a trip to temple was announced, I always saw her
as a priestess. My preoccupation observing my sons in court had meant I did
not see the way Beketamun leaned forward in her chair to listen the same way
that Siamun did. As it happened it was in the same year that Siamun began his
studies with the viziers that I called Beketamun to my chambers to speak of her
plans.

I believe she knew that her mother and I had a desire for her to study
with the priestesses so she was nervous when she entered. Her hesitancy in
speaking her truth though was unwarranted, as I would never force any of my
children along a path they did not wish. I had seen so clearly with Neferure
what happened to one's spirit when they were forced to act against it. I will
even admit that if Amenhotep had rejected his duties as successor I would
have happily groomed any willing brother to replace him. A reluctant Pharaoh
replacing me would have been worse and far more damaging than to die with
no successor at all. It was the fire of my great-grandfather Ahmose who had
placed our family upon the throne and if I did not create heirs with this passion
then the Gods would assist a family that did.

Beketamun came into the room blushing. She bowed and then stepped forward to let me kiss her cheek and hug her, turning to Satiah to do the same and then taking a seat before us.

"So my eldest daughter, share with me your path as you see it," I spoke, leaning forward in my chair.

Beketamun looked to me, then her mother and back to me again. She twisted her hands in her lap as she took a deep breath and prepared to speak. She had rehearsed this over and over as she lay in bed last night. Knowing that her request could be denied she planned on delivering it as soundly and passionately as she could.

"Father, Mother, I wish to study the trades of the court," She said quickly and then pushed on as Satiah and I looked at each other surprised. "I know this is not what you imagine for me but I know I will serve it well--and also--would it not support my brothers… Amenemhat will have yet another he can trust--and I can work with Siamun--and then Amenhotep and Menkheperre can spend more time with the army!"

She stopped and looked at Satiah and I waiting for our reply. We were too surprised to speak immediately however I was most impressed with the conviction of her address. Indeed her reasoning to support her choice was not only virtuous but also a wonderful understanding of our family needs. Something though did not feel quite right with her decision so I decided to push and see what else she would reveal.

"This is very noble and ambitious Beketamun, but tell me, why is it that you do not choose the priesthood as we imagined you might?" I asked gently.

Beketamun winced at my question. She had been expecting the choice of priesthood to be raised and she also knew that she could not lie. However within her truth she would reveal parts of herself that she knew would disappoint both her mother and me. Beketamun was mature enough to know how to filter the truth without lying or deceiving. She now cast her eyes down so as not to look into our eyes when she answered, "I feel no connection to the priesthood," she stated. "There is no calling for me there."

It was a simple enough answer and we would never truly know of just how uncomfortable Beketamun was at temple, especially around the priestesses. She had been sent to temple many times to spend days studying their ways and even Arisina seemed like a foreigner to her within the temple walls. As human embodiments of the Goddess energies, our priestesses lived and breathed their sacred femininity. They were aware of their sleek bodies and their soft curves and walked with all the sensuality that such awareness awakened. Do not confuse this with the seductive quality of a whore though. It was far from this energy. When a man looked at a priestess he saw all the nurturing power of the true Goddess. Some did indeed slip, using it to seduce, sometimes to gather more power or sometimes just to indulge a carnal need but the truly gifted priestess knew the fine balance of this energy.

Beketamun was thrust among these women as she was just becoming aware of her own sexuality. This was not only confusing but actually scared her. Having grown up with a conservative mother and two refined grandmothers, the priestesses were like elaborate witches dragging her into a world she did not understand. Each of her days of study with the women had her return home with a headache or nauseous--not that she would ever have admitted this to anyone.

In contrast she was happy to sit in court, dressed in more concealing clothing that did not hug her hips and behind, nor reveal the curve of her developing breasts or let her nipples show through the fine cloth. She could sit amongst the men with their strong energy and discuss matters that truly existed. They did not need to sing words or burn incense to know when shipments would arrive or what taxes would be collected. The court spoke of and with actual people, not some half-human creatures in the ethers.

If Beketamun had been able to request a placement in the army she would have. For all the praying and grandeur of the temples she truly believed it was simply my might as a commander that won Megiddo. If the Gods protected us so, then I would not need to wage war or continue my campaigns, she thought. It was by the virtue of a man's or woman's mind that they achieved anything. So my eldest daughter became a secret atheist, never revealing her true philosophy lest she break her mother's devout heart nor risk derision from the priests or confrontation with me.

I granted Beketamun her wish and she joined Siamun in his studies, which delighted him to no end. Now he had someone he loved by his side as he worked and their sibling bond grew even stronger. Beketamun had indeed chosen well and her presence in the court, though not as prominent as her brother's, was always well regarded. I was especially grateful after Amenemhat's death that she was well-established within this role as she was integral to maintaining the flow of the court at that time.

The example had been set so that my daughters as they reached twelve stepped forward and spoke with honesty knowing that I would support and guide them no matter what they chose. Nefertiry chose to become an artisan, which was no surprise to anyone. Her drawings and paintings adorned many a room of the palace. Whenever Nefertiry visited the temple she would make her way to visit the scribe rooms and see what they were doing. The scribes all grew fond of her visits and she would often make the carriage ride home carrying a new colour or a small scroll with new glyphs to learn.

Meritamen and Meryt had the smallest of ambitions and chose to simply be princesses, eventually. Meritamen made a token choice of being a priestess to pacify Matreya and her grandmother Huy, who ached to have a female follow in her ways. Huy had elevated her daughter to a queen and now to have a royal granddaughter choose the ways of the priesthood would round off her accomplishments.

Meritamen however proved my philosophy perfectly. One cannot follow a path that does not begin within their heart. Such an ill-founded path is one that the traveller will grow weary of and soon wander off. Meritamen never even remotely stepped on hers. She was moved to live at Karnak temple within the rooms of the other young priestesses beginning their studies and was instantly appalled at the simple surrounds. Still she was excited to be somewhere new and with other young women.

This was soon replaced with a desperate longing to see her sisters and the gentle maids that cared for her at the palace. Several times she would venture back to the palace wandering through the streets of Thebes unrecognisable as a princess in her novice temple gown. Her sisters would hide her as best they could but Meritamen would soon forget herself and someone would hear her voice and summon Matreya. A suitable lecture would ensue, she would be dragged before me to apologise if I was home and then she would be returned to temple. All this was considered a small price to pay for the joy of seeing her sisters and besides Meritamen enjoyed this simple act of defiance. I however knew that this could not go on.

The following year Meryt joined Meritamen at the temple. Meryt chose to become a priestess citing that, "It is in my blood." This translated to mean, "because my mother and grandmother suggested it and I can finally be with my sister." So the two sisters were reunited and in no way did this inspire them to commit to their studies. Instead Meritamen now had an ally to play with again.

While the other girls would follow the rules strictly, grateful for the opportunity to study at the Great Temple, my daughters decided this was merely a place to misbehave without the ever-watchful eye of their mother and the maids who reported to her. They would stifle giggles in prayer sessions, extinguish lamps when no one was looking and sneak into rooms that were off limits to the students with the goal of rearranging or hiding the high priests' scrolls and oils. Worse still they would mislead their classmates with false myths of the Gods. One would recount the story with a straight face while the other nodded and backed up the story declaring that their grandmother, the most noble adoratrix priestess, had told them such as children.

The high priests knew of their lack of interest and their ill behaviour but all hoped that both girls would soon open to their teachings and settle down. It was nothing new to have a young girl explore her independence upon entering temple life however these two, especially Meritamen, were going beyond the bounds that any girl had shown. The other dilemma facing the priests was that none of them had a princess studying with them before. Those that had taught Neferure were long gone and now there was no precedent as to how to deal with my daughters. No one wanted to risk the questions from me that raising the issue of their behaviour would lead to. So they all played along with the girls, giving light counsel at their misgivings. These talks only amused the girls. They would return to their rooms and fall into fits of laughter as they impersonated the priest who had scolded them and celebrated yet another successful prank.

This all played out well until Meritamen went too far. Each month, for five days, the rituals of the full moon enveloped the Karnak temple. The usual routine of an early night to meet the dawn was suspended as the priests stayed awake long into the night celebrating the light and majesty of the moon in all its glory. A group of statues of different Gods from various places within the temple were carried out into the moonlight where they would sit for the five nights as the moon reached its full circle and then began to wane. There were twelve statues, all about four feet high, carved of wood and painted in bright colours that looked amazing in the moonlight. The priests would sit them in a courtyard forming a circle to view the moon so that in turn the moon should view them also. When the five days were passed the statues would be returned to their place within the temple.

On the night of the full moon, elders and students alike gathered in the moonlight to pray and give thanks. They stood outside of the sacred circle of statues praying, chanting and playing music until the moon reached it highest point in the sky. Thankfully my daughters chose to behave during this ceremony but it turns out their being quiet was due to Meritamen scheming as to what they would do later.

It was about two in the morning when Meryt was shaken from her sleep. She opened her eyes to see Meritamen beside her bed, with a lamp in her hand.

"Quick," she whispered. "Let's go have our own moon ceremony!"

Meryt gathered a blanket around her as had Meritamen and they silently made their way to the courtyard. The moonlight was so bright that the statues were casting shadows. Meritamen placed her lamp upon a ledge and dropped her blanket to the ground. She began to giggle with the anticipation of what she would now do. "Let us commence," she said, throwing her hands into the air impersonating the high priests and walked towards the circle. Meryt giggled as she too dropped her blanket and followed her sister.

The circle of statues was carefully arranged. There were stone markers that permanently held their place in the courtyard and no one was even to step onto them in the days the statues were not performing their moon duties. They were aligned so that each statue was perfectly spaced thus allowing each God to stand opposite their counterpart. This allowed perfect balance in the circle and strengthened the energies that each God held. Each male God stood opposite his female counterpart, reflecting their power and creating a union that we believed would be consummated or strengthened in the moonlight. When they were returned to the temple they would carry the energy of their union to all who prayed before them.

Meritamen had some other ideas for this full moon. She walked up to the statue of Horus first and grabbed his head. Wrapping her arms around it she was delighted to see that she could move him with ease and burst out laughing.

"Oh this will be wonderful!" she exclaimed to her sister.

Within ten minutes they had successfully rearranged the statues and walked within the sacred circle to admire their work. Males stood opposite males, Gods of war stood opposite Gods of farmers. The girls stood leaning against each other, trying their hardest to not laugh too loud as they admired their work.

"What will they think?" Meryt whispered.

"They will think that Amun came and set them as he desired!" Meritamen answered and they both collapsed into laughter again.

The priests though would know the truth. My daughters did not realise that as part of this monthly ceremony a scribe would remain awake in a nearby room writing the accounts of that month's ceremony including any signs that may be shown to them. As he wrote he did not hear the scrapes and bumps as the statues were moved but the hum of the girls' conversation caught his attention and he stopped writing. A short shriek of laughter made him leave his chair and he entered the courtyard to see my two daughters not only within the circle but playing.

Meryt saw him first and stopped laughing so abruptly that Meritamen followed her gaze and they both looked upon the priest. His mouth and eyes were so wide with shock that they almost began to laugh again but they at least had the sense not to and make matters worse. Instead they too froze in place and all three of them momentarily were like statues themselves. The priest soon gathered himself and began to walk towards them.

"What--how--Get out of there NOW!" he stammered then shouted, still not believing that the girls were in there. "Why are you out of bed?" he continued, "When Akhenamun hears of this--OH NO!"

He finally saw exactly what the girls had done and stopped once again speechless. The girls quickly left the circle and stood behind the priest as he looked upon the sacrilege they had performed. He actually began to hyperventilate as he surveyed the new arrangement of the statues. This had to be corrected and quickly. Hopefully they had not done too much damage. Of all nights to choose to do this too; the night of the full moon when the energies were summoned the strongest.

He turned to the girls, his fear outweighing his anger. "Get back to your rooms immediately!" he bellowed. "In the morning Akhenamun shall deal with you!"

As the girls gathered their blankets and lamp and walked back along the corridor the echoes of the statues returning to their rightful places followed them.

The following morning Meryt dressed and ran to Meritamen's room. At least that way when Akhenamun confronted them they would be together. They were both sitting upon the bed silently when Arisina herself entered the room. Akhenamun unsure as how to deal with my princesses had summoned her from her duties to come to the temple school. It was hoped she would act as liaison with the palace due to her closeness with me. Her appearance made the girls realise they were in serious trouble this time and the look of disappointment on her face would cut them even more than my own.

"When I attended your births I never imagined one day we would gather like this," Arisina said, and the girls hung their heads low.

She led the girls to Akhenamun's rooms for their official dressing down. When they entered they saw that he had gathered all the high priests of the temple and the girls' heart grew heavy at how serious this had now become. While they all stood one priestess sat upon a lounge and wept. It was their grandmother Huy, devastated and embarrassed, summoned to the temple from her own to bear witness for our family. The girls ran to her side, buried their heads upon each of her shoulders and cried. Through their sobs they begged her forgiveness. Huy quickly quietened them, drying her own tears in the hope it would also stop theirs and made them sit still and straight to hear their judgement.

Akhenamun looked at them sternly and began, "Royal Daughter Meritamen and Royal Daughter Meryt, the sacrilege you performed last night is beyond any desecration that I--nor any of my priests have witnessed. It went against the very order of the Gods and you denied your family honour also in the process." He spoke as officially as I did within court. "Meritamen, we have continually indulged your humour and adventures for well over a year now. Meryt, when you joined us we hoped you would be an anchor for your sister and together you would settle into the ways of the temple. Together though you have only made greater your lack of respect for our teachings."

Akhenamun was tired of my children beyond anything he could say. He had even begun to hate them. While many girls ached for an opportunity to join the temple, these two had chosen to be here and mocked it at every opportunity. Akhenamun had longed for a solution to aid him in removing them from his school. He had always imagined that it would be a marriage arranged by the palace but last night the girls handed him all he needed. This was no frivolous prank that I could ignore or reason with. There was also no way that they could remain here unpunished, as that would show no example to any of the others. Such sacrilege could not be tolerated in any case.

Akhenamun now turned to the priestesses. "Arisina and Huy, I called upon you today as the priestesses most involved with the upbringing of these girls. We have joined you as their guides in this lifetime and your decision as to how this is dealt with must be considered. Together we must also share that Meritamen and Meryt are a reflection of your teachings."

At this last statement Huy's tears began again as Akhenamun spoke what she feared all would say about her teachings not only as a priestess but also as their grandmother. She had no suggestions on how to deal with this and she dropped her head. It was Arisina who spoke up.

"Akhenamun, I feel the girls have had ample time and opportunity to display their affinity for the priesthood. Perhaps it would be best that they return to the palace and seek the lives of royal wives," she said calmly.

"What reparations do you suggest that they make?" he answered.

"I believe their attendance at this meeting and the meeting that their father shall request will be ample," she stated.

This did not satisfy Akhenamun at all. The scribe had described in detail how they had maliciously placed the statues. Ironically they had used their knowledge to set them in order with as much disrespect as possible, including coupling a father with a son. Now they would as much as be rewarded by being returned to their palace with all its luxuries.

Arisina knew though that this stunt had taught them about consequences more than Akhenamun could ever understand. For all the silliness and misbehaving that Meritamen and Meryt loved to indulge in they would never dream of hurting their family. To have Arisina have to rescue them while their grandmother cried was worse than anything they could ever imagine. Meritamen sat and wished that she had stayed in her bed last night.

Akhenamun did not challenge Arisina. As I said before he had no precedent to go by and what could he order two princesses to do anyway. He also knew that he could not challenge a priestess with such high ties to the palace and over a matter that involved royal children, as that would be political suicide. So he sat and nodded his agreement. The fact that these two troublemakers were being removed from his school would have to be enough and for that he was truly grateful.

So with the utmost discretion Meritamen and Meryt left the temple school. They would never be spoken of as having been "expelled", but merely that their studies were complete. Only the high priests and their fellow students would know the truth and they would never gossip idly to damage my family's reputation. A carriage was summoned from the palace and the girls began their journey home in tears as they anticipated both their mother's harsh words and my final judgement.

I was not even remotely aware of what had happened until my butler announced to me that a carriage had arrived with Meritamen and Meryt within it, escorted by Arisina and Huy. My immediate response was that my daughters were ill and sent home to recuperate. However when I made my way to their rooms to see what had occurred I entered to see both girls in tears as Matreya stood bellowing over them.

"Such a disgrace that this family has never seen, and to wound your grandmother so!" Matreya shouted as I walked in. When she saw me she stopped and addressed me. "Our daughters have behaved unthinkably!" she yelled.

So now I imagined the worse. I conjured scenes of them banished for lying with men and my bile rose as I prepared to have those men killed. It was somewhat of a relief to know that they had in fact just ruined one of the most solemn of ceremonies by rearranging some statues. While this was still a most serious matter it could be rectified.

I sighed deeply and pulled a chair to sit in front of the girls. I did my customary rubbing of my chin as I looked at them and considered how I would deal with this. The girls were too scared to look into my eyes and understandably so. I waited until their sobs settled and spoke.

"This is most unsuitable behaviour for those learning the ways of temple--let alone a royal daughter," I began. "I can't imagine what you thought you would achieve or that you would not be held accountable."

"Father, we are so sorry," said Meritamen begging for forgiveness. "It was my idea--please do not give any blame to Meryt."

"That is very noble Meritamen," I acknowledged. "I see this has taught you a new sense of honesty and honour. However I believe Meryt took part of her own accord. Is this not right?"

Meryt looked up and nodded.

"So Meryt, you are accountable for your actions just as much as if you instigated them," I reasoned and leaned back in my chair and rubbed my chin again. "I have no idea how you shall be punished," I said.

"I do!" burst in Matreya, "They should be forced to serve in their grandmother's temple and eat with the servants."

I nodded in agreement. This would be a most suitable punishment but I knew that to throw them back into the very surrounds that they respected so little would only make matters worse. They had already lost a year in their development and in fact Meritamen had lost almost two. They could not afford any more time wasted and would now be made to focus on their palace life.

"We gave you the indulgence and luxury of choosing a path for yourselves. Not only did you disrespect your mother and I in allowing you to do so, but you also then chose to disrespect your very choice. You shall remain in the palace and study the crafts of your gender," I said. "You shall begin tomorrow after you travel with me to the temple to make an offering to the high priests as your apology."

So Meritamen and Meryt learnt the ways of embroidery and painting to while away their days until their husbands were found. Their story would soon waft through the palace and all would be horrified that the princesses had acted so. There were even whispers that the spirit of Neferure, their rebellious aunt, was within them. One person though was not horrified. When Beketamun heard what her younger sisters had done she had to bite her lip to not laugh out loud and envied that she had not been brave enough to act so during her time at temple.

Almost three years later when Nebetiunet announced that she would like to become a priestess, her choice was not received so lightly. In fact we were all hesitant lest she repeat her sisters' disgrace despite her having a totally different character to her more naughty sisters. So instead of being sent straight to Karnak, Nebetiunet began her studies at her grandmother Huy's temple. This way Huy could keep a close eye upon her and measure her commitment and competence. If she were satisfied, then after a year Nebetiunet would move onto the Great Temple at Karnak to complete her studies and serve.

"How can you bear to leave us?" asked Isis on the day she left.

"I am sad to go Isis, but it is not like how Amenemhat left," she answered. "I will just be a carriage ride away. You will come to pray and I will visit here with you all. It's just that I will not be in the bed besides yours anymore."

Nebetiunet's ride to her new home was a tearful one. Her first night alone in her new bedroom did not give her much sleep as she heard new noises in the night and she missed the murmurs of Isis's sleep talking from across the room. Within a few months though she was comfortable and began to open up new parts of her that she didn't even know existed. No longer within the shadows of her ambitious brothers and more charismatic sisters, she found her voice and her confidence. She embraced walking equally with the other priests and priestesses she served with. They did not bow to her or ask her needs and she enjoyed that.

Her favourite days were when the local people would come to ask counsel and join the temple prayer ceremonies. She could sit for hours and listen to their woes and trials, happy to listen as Huy gave guidance and then assisted the prayers they needed. She was fascinated in their lives and her understanding of people opened up. No longer protected by the palace walls she was seeing the reality of the lives of the commoners that I ruled over. Nebetiunet saw just how the decisions I made affected the Egyptian people.

Nebetiunet saw women attend who mourned their husbands and sons lost in battles I had led. She also saw those who came forward to give thanks for the abundance and safety that our land was blessed to have due to these battles.

She now saw all the facets of life and how they worked together, from my highest command through to the simple act of driving a plough through a wheat field. Nebetiunet saw the dance of every person, animal and object around her. She felt the magic that was held within the connection of all that was. Every day she could serve to honour this magic was a blessing.

Nebetiunet had indeed chosen the most perfect path for herself and Huy delighted in recounting this to myself and Matreya, as well as the high priests of Karnak. Huy also delighted in having one of her granddaughters so close to her. Having sent her only daughter to marry me had made life a bit lonely and there was a comfort in having someone of her blood within her temple once again. Although she would show no special favour to Nebetiunet they developed a new closeness. So much so that as Nebetiunet's first year began to reach its end,

Huy was almost sorry that she had done so well and would soon move on. Still it was far better than sending her back to the palace as a failure.

Huy's regret was matched by that of Nebetiunet. Her year spent with her grandmother had been the most wonderful of her life. She too had enjoyed studying under Huy and had developed a new sense of respect and deep love for the woman. Nebetiunet had also grown fond of those that worshipped at the temple. She knew that at Karnak she would be serving prayers of the highest order but this did not interest her. Karnak was the temple that served the palace. Apart from myself and the rest of the family, this is where the court officials, viziers and generals all went to pray and Nebetiunet had no interest in their concerns. She would rather attend to prayers for a baby who was teething than a general seeking to improve his battle skills.

So in the final month of her trial year Nebetiunet with her new-found confidence requested an audience with me to ask that she might stay within Huy's temple to serve her priesthood. When she walked through the door I almost didn't recognise her. Apart from the obvious physical changes and her new dress, she walked with such poise that I could have mistaken her for one of her older sisters. There was no doubt that my quietest daughter was now a very powerful priestess so I was rather disappointed when she made her request to remain within Huy's temple. I could not deny her passion to serve the traders, farmers and families of our common people though and granted her request.

Nebetiunet's service continued on and her skills grew more with each year. She would even become a birth priestess, travelling to homes to pray as women delivered their babies and would delight in the sight of every new birth she witnessed. Huy continued to savour every day with her granddaughter and as she grew older Nebetiunet was able to care for her. Eventually Huy would pass away and Nebetiunet became the high priestess of the temple. She then returned her grandmother's love and teachings to a new generation of priests and priestesses. Some of these included her own children as well as several of my other grandchildren. In fact those of my descendants who did choose the priesthood would always aspire to train with Nebetiunet--such was the warmth and wisdom of her temple.

Isis was the last to choose her path and with five sisters before her to act as examples she was well aware of what her choice could lead to. Isis had no business aspirations as did Beketamun, nor did she feel the pull of temple life as did Nebetiunet. As she was always, Isis was content with her palace life and could not imagine any other way. Her days were spent socialising with Meritamen and Meryt as they pursued their feminine hobbies and even though they were married when Isis turned twelve they still spent most of their time with her.

She was used to being surrounded by her family and the staff that she considered her friends. As her nieces and nephews began to arrive her company grew even more and the space created when Nebetiunet left for the priesthood was filled. For Isis life was just fine the way it was and had always been. She understood that old adage that if something was working you didn't interfere with it. What she didn't understand was her brothers' desire to travel to strange places or how Nebetiunet could want to leave such happiness. So my little Isis chose to remain in the palace and continue her days pretty much as they already were.

CHAPTER NINETEEN

The flow of vocational choices intermingled with marriages. As the younger children entered adulthood the older ones found partners and began families. Amenemhat had begun to have relations with several consorts before his death but none had been recognised as wives and thankfully none had fallen pregnant. Amenhotep soon had three consorts he favoured but refused to elevate any to a great wife, even when they eventually bore him children. I did nothing to convince him otherwise as I saw beyond his conduct and knew that he acted with the cunning and power that I had lacked and yet had helped him make this decision.

Amenhotep's meeting with Matreya that day in the garden had opened his eyes in many ways. Matreya's ambition had hissed at him like a cobra about to strike and he could easily have taken on her poison. He was also well aware of how Hatshepsut had kept me from my rightful place as ruler for all those years. The thought that a woman had manipulated the priests made him sick and a part of him also hated me for not having stood up to her. The night that I had caught Meryt imitating the old woman had let him know that there was some anger there, but he still could not understand why I had not acted this way when the woman was alive.

So Amenhotep decided to consider what would happen if one of his consorts also had delusions of power that she would develop further if given the position of great wife and eventually queen. If she didn't try to undermine his rule would she then be like Matreya and try to work through their child when it succeeded him. He considered himself lucky that he had been old enough to recognise Matreya's game. Had he been young, as I had been when my father passed, then she could easily have manipulated him. Amenhotep knew that his grandfather had been ill and neither he nor I shared this weak physical condition but then a simple accident could take him. His heir could be left vulnerable and he decided that only those he trusted would be in positions to raise the child and protect his rights. So Amenhotep did not marry any of his consorts. They would merely be his companions and provide him with heirs. He would allow them the care and luxuries that this role was worthy of but they would never sit beside him in court.

Beketamun tried her best to avoid marriage believing it would rob her of the independence she had gained from being involved in the court. While she had enjoyed fussing over her younger siblings Beketamun had no grand desire for her own children so not even that aspect of marriage appealed to her. Unfortunately the eldest daughter of a family carried her own responsibility towards her family and none of her younger sisters could marry until she did. If she had chosen the priesthood Beketamun may have bypassed this by joining one of the sects that advocated celibacy. Her work in court though didn't exempt her from this duty.

Ironically she was surrounded by more men than any of her sisters ever would be. Apart from the palace officials, priests and staff there were always traders visiting from the more remote regions of Egypt as well as diplomats and leaders from throughout Canaan and Punt. Many of them were quite enamoured with Beketamun who carried the understated beauty of her mother. She would lean forward in her chair or be attentive as they spoke of their trades and gave their latest reports. This led many of the men to mistake her interest in their words as actually being an interest in them. Beketamun would soon correct this though. When they sought her out to speak privately she would soon find ways to escape when the talk was obviously not business. The slightest attempt at any amorous talk was met with a furrowed brow and Beketamun would turn away as fast as she could, leaving a very puzzled man behind her.

For all her attempts at avoiding any men though it was something that needed to be addressed. When Beketamun reached the suitable age of fourteen the priests began to approach with offers from men that they may be considered for marriage to Beketamun. Unlike my sons who would be reasonably free to choose when and whom they married, my daughters had to enter a marriage that was wholly approved by myself. In the past many princesses were forced into marriage. Sometimes too, a princess would be married to a brother to provide him with a royal wife, or even to her father to provide him a queen and make her succession easier if there was no male heir. This practice had placed Hatshepsut in her position of power that she was so reluctant to relinquish and it robbed Neferure of her chance to marry from a young age to someone she could have loved. I would never make my daughters do either and so it was that my daughters would always be noted as the ones who broke from that tradition.

Any man from beyond the Egyptian borders would never be approved of as a husband and the priests would not even waste my time to approach me with these offers. Quite a few of the princes that had been raised in Thebes and were now of age to return to their homeland felt they might be considered due to their Egyptian tutelage but they would not. No Egyptian royal woman would ever be allowed to bear the child of a foreigner. This was in order to protect our bloodline. Now you may feel this hypocritical as our men could bed foreign women and the offspring of this union could rise to the throne. In our time we believed the man was the true creator of the child while the woman provided the fertile soil for his seed to grow within. We had no knowledge that a woman provided an egg and so to us they were exclusively the haven for a child to grow.

In accordance with this my daughters must have suitable Egyptian men seek marriage with them. Beketamun had army commanders, high priests and viziers ask for her. Each time I approved of a proposal she would be brought before Satiah and I. She would sit patiently but we both saw her flinch when the man's name was put to her and she would shake her head. In truth I was happy some days that she did say no, but I felt compelled to present her with any suitable proposal lest she had honest or secret affections for the man. As she approached fifteen though allowing her to continually supply refusal after refusal was becoming a worry.

Amenemhat's death allowed her some relief from the proposals as the official mourning period suspended any activities not deemed urgent. Indeed even when the funeral was complete I hardly was focussed on such matters and Beketamun despite her sadness at losing her brother was relieved to have some respite from the attentions upon her. However Nefertiry and now Meritamen were menstruating and must also seek marriage. Men were becoming hesitant to approach the priests with offers of marriage for Beketamun as they knew of the high calibre of the men who had been refused.

Rumours began that I was saving my daughters for sham marriages to my sons to protect the throne. My history with Hatshepsut only helped these stories. I called Beketamun to my rooms one day for a talk about the situation. The night before though I lay in bed with Satiah and I spoke of my concerns as I wondered aloud what could be done with this situation. Satiah understood her daughter all too well. Yes, Satiah was happy and loved me but she remembered the heartache of being forced into a marriage and she secretly was glad her own daughter could be so strong as to shape her own future. Satiah also recalled her shepherd and what could have been a much simpler life that was forever lost to her.

"Thutmose, do you suppose she has a secret love that she is scared to reveal?" she whispered in the dark.

That thought had indeed crossed my mind. I had lived in a palace rife with love affairs, including Neferure's that I had helped to orchestrate. The thought of an inappropriate man touching my daughter made my blood boil though and I sat up in bed and turned to Satiah.

"You know who it is don't you? I know our daughters confide in you! Have you been assisting this affair?" I demanded.

Satiah lay still beside me and sighed. "Thutmose, you know I would never deceive you," she answered calmly. "Now rest."

I lay back down roughly. I had to be satisfied with Satiah's answer, as I don't think she even knew how to lie to me. However I was not happy with my still foggy view of the situation. Satiah could feel my agitation and knew I was a long way from sleep.

"My Pharaoh, your daughter's heart is one land you cannot rule over," she said softly. "Women guard their hearts and none more so than from their very fathers whether they are Pharaoh or not. Tread lightly tomorrow lest you close your daughter off completely from you."

She said nothing more and was soon asleep. As I lay listening to her gentle breath of sleep I reflected on my own marriages. One was of warmth and love, the other cold and of duty. I had always believed my relationships with

Satiah and Matreya were due to their inherent personalities but now I wondered if it was the intent in which I had summoned them to palace life. I soon drifted off to sleep also, but my dreams were filled with wives clamouring for my attention and priests lined up with marriage proposals.

The next day Beketamun came to my rooms knowing exactly what was about to be addressed. She was not looking forward to it any more than either Satiah or myself. Once again we sat in the familiar formation. I sat in my imposing chair with Satiah beside me and Beketamun took her place before us silently praying as she sat that this would be over quickly.

"Beketamun, I am sure you are aware of why you are here," I began.

She nodded and attempted a smile.

"So my daughter, today we do not present you with any proposals passed on by the priests," I continued. "Instead your mother and I would like to hear if you have any suggestions as to who you desire as a husband?"

I had sat and thought of my words carefully that morning. I did not want to demand that Beketamun declare a secret lover and scare her from doing so. Instead I would simply ask her who she desired. Also I did not wish to assume my daughter had anyone in mind. This would be like considering a man guilty of a crime before he even had the chance to present his defence. So I devised different sentences and practised them in my mind until I was happy with the one I now used.

The look upon Beketamun's face alone answered my question as she looked at me and her brow furrowed to confirm her confusion. She attempted to answer but her words came out stammered so Satiah stepped in.

"Beketamun, we are just concerned that you have affections for someone who does not approach with an offer of marriage," she said gently.

"There is no one," Beketamun answered firmly, although now she wished there was someone and this whole situation could end.

"You do understand that you cannot refuse marriage offers much longer," Satiah continued.

Beketamun nodded to this also.

"So my daughter you understand that if you do not accept an offer soon we may simply choose for you?" I asked.

Beketamun nodded and once more her eyes were downcast.

"I do not wish to make you a marriage that you are not happy to enter," I continued, "so I shall also offer you the opportunity to enter the priesthood where it will be acceptable for you not to marry."

This was the last thing Beketamun wanted and I had now placed her between a rock and a hard place. However when she had to weigh up the options she would certainly choose marriage over temple life. Either life would be one that she would be just acting within, but at least if she was married she may still continue with her court work. She would rather deal with one man than a herd of priestesses and their legion of silly Gods. She took a deep breath and looked up at Satiah and myself. "Father, Mother. I will honour your wishes and choose a suitable husband soon," she said.

I missed the slight tremor in her voice as I was so ecstatic to hear her words. I nodded and Satiah smiled. It was done and clear. Beketamun would soon choose and the situation would be resolved.

"Thank you Beketamun, you may now leave," I said.

Beketamun rose from the stool and her mind was racing so much that she did not even offer her mother or I a farewell kiss, and even turned her back just a little too quick for protocol. I was too happy at the outcome to care for such gestures and continued to smile as she left the room. Once outside the doors though as she made her way back to the rooms that she worked within, Beketamun's eyes filled with tears. She held back from letting them flow too much as she did not wish for guards or servants to see her so upset after her meeting with me. She gently dabbed the few tears that were there, careful so as not to smear the kohl around her eyes and entered the record rooms of the court hoping that some work would help her forget the huge task of selecting a spouse.

When she entered the rooms she expected to be alone and looked forward to the solitude with just the chests and shelves full of scrolls to keep her company. No sooner had she unrolled one to begin her work when the door opened and Kamankh, one of the viziers entered.

"Ah Beketamun, how glad I am to see you. I have some great news from our farmers in the south lands," he declared in his usual loud manner. When Beketamun looked up with her eyes still red from tears his voice softened. "Oh--oh my dear. What is it? Are you okay?" he asked tenderly.

This was all Beketamun needed to let her tears truly flow and she now sobbed openly. Kamankh quickly closed the door to the room and rushed to her side, pulling a chair so as to sit close by her and hold her hand as she cried. Beketamun knew she could not hold back her tears forever and it was just timing that allowed this display before Kamankh. What she would never know is what made her open up and reveal her entire situation to Kamankh of all people.

Kamankh and Beketamun had known each other since she had begun in court. They were not close friends but had worked together often and in harmony. They had never spoken of their personal lives but Beketamun knew Kamankh was a widower, his wife having died in childbirth three years earlier. At the age of twenty-eight he was almost twice her age and they looked upon each other more as a teacher and student as Kamankh had been a key part in Beketamun's training. He knew all too well that her impending marriage was being spoken of frequently and he also knew many of the men who had been refused.

The thought had crossed his mind to also approach the priests as he did hold some affection for my daughter but his list of excuses was immense, starting with what would be considered their huge age difference. Kamankh had seen younger and more strapping men be rejected and to have a princess settle for him with his rounded belly was unimaginable. So he stepped back and heard the mutterings of yet another man who had been unsuccessful. Now here he sat and his affections swelled even more as he held her hand and shared this moment.

"Beketamun, I am sure the Gods will make this all clear for you soon," he said, and his voice soothed her as did his hand stroking her hair.

Beketamun looked up at Kamankh and suddenly he looked different. However her naivety did not understand the affections behind his actions or words. She thanked him for his listening and excused herself so that she may go to her rooms to bathe and clean her face after crying. As she was about to walk out the door she turned back to him. "Kamankh, I am so sorry. You came here to do business and instead you gave me counsel," she said, her face still swollen. "Perhaps we could meet tomorrow to enact our duties."

"Yes Beketamun. I would be most happy to meet tomorrow with you," he answered and smiled.

The next day when they did meet again Kamankh did the unthinkable. After completing the business that was needed of the court he proposed marriage directly to Beketamun. Beketamun was so taken aback that she could not answer at first so Kamankh continued on until she nodded. As he sat across the table from her he poured out his intentions in just the direct and no nonsense manner that Beketamun admired. He would be happy to be the husband that would solve her situation and in return she would simply be his wife in name only. They soon had an agreement and understanding that satisfied both.

"Why did you come to me instead of the priests?" she asked.

"Because I wanted to know from you directly," he answered. "I did not fear your refusal Beketamun. I just wished my intentions to be clear between us so that no matter your decision we could still work together as friends. Now that I am certain I shall see the priests."

Beketamun smiled at Kamankh. He had saved her from another possible meeting that would otherwise have ended in her disappointing me again. In truth she may well have turned down Kamankh if had gone directly to the priests--such would have been her surprise at his proposal. Kamankh left the room to continue his bid for a royal marriage and within minutes of his leaving Beketamun suddenly wished he would return.

Beketamun soon exited also and made her way to the main court where I was residing for the afternoon. She slipped into the large room and took her seat that was near my throne. As she walked all that she passed bowed and I was momentarily distracted not so much by the movement but the huge smile upon her face. She sat quietly and waited for a break in the proceedings and then approached me.

"Father, I wish to meet with you before dinner," she said simply.

"Certainly Daughter, I shall have you sent for when I have finished with court for the day," I answered.

My curiosity was killing me over the next few hours until the session was complete and I could leave the court. I had Beketamun summoned as well as Satiah as I suspected it was to do with our talk only the day before. So once again we all met in my private chambers in exactly the same formation as previously.

"Well--it is not often the Pharaoh himself is summoned," I began. "I hope this is to share good news?"

"Yes, Father it is," she beamed. "I have selected my husband!"

"Which man is it that you choose Beketamun?" I asked formally.

"Kamankh, of the upper Egypt viziers," she said, looking me directly in the eyes and ready for anything that I might have to say.

Satiah sitting beside me turned her head quickly to gauge my response which she was sure would be one of shock as that was what she too felt. We had imagined she would have reconsidered one of the men who had already proposed. Instead Beketamun had chosen a man who had not stated any interest in marriage at all.

"Are you not happy?" she asked and her brow now carried this question also.

I looked to Satiah who was grasping for words and holding her hand to her heart. I too was lost for words and still couldn't speak.

"You asked me to consider the situation and I did," Beketamun stated, her unending logic perplexed that we did not seem to accept her words.

I cleared my throat and grabbed Satiah's hand, as much to comfort me as it would her. This was not so bad. She had chosen a fine Egyptian male, well respected and a loyal servant of the palace and Egypt. I started to nod my head as I weighed up his attributes. Satiah watched me, holding her breath until she saw me nodding. Satiah turned to Beketamun but my daughter's eyes were fixed on me weighing every second of my reaction.

"You would not rather someone closer to your age?" I asked pulling forward the one factor that might be an issue.

I knew before Beketamun said no that this was nothing to be concerned of. Many marriages throughout the land had this age difference and it was nothing for a royal daughter to have been married to men up to thirty years older. Beketamun continued to keep her eyes locked on mine and I knew this issue could now be resolved and I sighed. Then the thought struck me, "*How exactly do we deal with this proposal in reverse?*"

As Beketamun met with me, Kamankh was meeting with the priests stating his cause. If Beketamun had done nothing all would have proceeded as normal and you may wonder why Beketamun chose to override all this with her actions. This was because Beketamun knew that the priests could refuse Kamankh and his proposal may never reach my ears. Her impetuousness had indeed paid off in guaranteeing that no matter the actions of the priests, Kamankh would be successful. A shrewd businessperson leaves nothing to chance, and just as she would have made sure a trade agreement was performed as agreed upon, so too did my daughter set out to honour her agreement with her future husband.

The priests sat in their palace room after Kamankh left and discussed his case and how it should be presented to me. They had no concerns in presenting Kamankh to me but their hesitancy came from their fatigue at presenting suitors to me for Beketamun. It had been a very long time since a royal daughter had been married and they were sure no previous princesses had been indulged with making their own choice. The last princess to be married had been Neferure and that had been to me. Neither of us had any say in that matter and all knew my feelings about that union despite my eventual friendship with her.

The priests had just finalised what they would say to me when my butler was announced at their door and all their concerns were allayed. My butler carried with him the message of Beketamun's choice, my approval of this choice and the direction to summon Kamankh to court to discuss this. Of course there would not be a discussion as such. Any man would be insane or contemptuous to decline a royal offer of any kind. As with Satiah's family being summoned to the palace for my marriage so too would Kamankh come to court to do nothing other than formally accept to become my daughter's husband.

The curiosity that now faced the priests was the fact that Kamankh had been to see them of his own accord and at the same time Beketamun had been to see me. Of course this raised theories that my daughter and the courtier were already romantically involved. Not that this mattered at all as my butler's message covered my approval. The relief that a marriage was imminent soon outweighed the curiosity and ended the need for speculation.

"Let us offer prayers to Amun that the five remaining princesses shall not possess the active mind of the eldest in arranging their marriages," said one of the priests and the other two nodded.

Their prayers were answered. Six months after the festivities of Beketamun's wedding I received an offer of marriage for Nefertiry. One of the scribes of the temple who she often went to ask questions of was presented as a suitor. It was the first and only marriage proposal Nefertiry would receive as she accepted it wholeheartedly. The scribe Serkhet was the one who shared his skills and knowledge with her the most. It also turned out that he was the one who was gifting her colours and tools to work with when she visited the scribes.

Meritamen and Meryt would marry soldiers on the rise in my army. The mens' swarthiness and the drama of seeing them off on campaigns satisfied the girls' need for excitement. Choosing husbands that travelled also gave them ample time alone to indulge their vanities and minimised the chances of pregnancy that brought with it physical discomforts and social limits. Nebetiunet found marriage within the walls of her temple cementing her position there and delighting Huy with the knowledge that the temple would pass onto not just her granddaughter but now also to a family of her blood. This just left Isis.

My beloved little Isis watched her sisters grow into womanhood with some sadness. As each one took up a vocation or study she lost another companion--and even when her sisters did spend time with her now they were not interested in playing games. They just wanted to talk and preen themselves. They spoke of boys in a different way and she did not understand many of the things they spoke of, but she sat quietly and listened. So Isis began to spend time alone. Some days it was just easier that way. She would wander the palace watching the goings-on within it. A quick walk through the kitchens to taste some fruit, and then along to the courtroom to listen to me speak to my nobles, followed by a walk outside in the gardens could amuse her for an hour or two. Then she would crave some company and seek her sisters only to be bored within minutes with anything they spoke of.

One day she crossed paths with Menkheperre and Amenhotep on their way to the stables for a morning of riding.

"Take me with you," she begged. "I want to ride too!"

"Little Sister, go back to your hair brushes and perfumes," Amenhotep said, and the boys both laughed at her as they kept walking.

Isis was used to being treated as the little pet of the family and had enjoyed the attention. However to have her two brothers mock her like this did not feel so good and as she watched them walk away she clenched her fists. *"Stupid boys!"* she thought to herself, *"I could ride as well as any of them."*

Too angry to be around anyone, Isis made her way to the gardens hoping to find some solace there in which to nurse her loneliness and hurt. Isis knew I was at court and no one would be in my private courtyard. She snuck through my rooms and made her way into my oasis. My courtyard was an interesting place, filled with exotic plants carried from the very edges of our empire. It was filled with fruit trees and other specimens unknown to most Egyptians. This garden was like my own private reminder of the vastness and diversity of the empire I ruled over. It was filled with sweet scents and colours not seen anywhere else in Thebes and Isis delighted to hide here and take in the richness of the surrounds. For Isis, like myself, stepping into this garden was like stepping into an amazing painting and you could almost imagine you had left the palace to visit a new land.

Isis was sitting beneath my prized persimmon tree, her back resting upon its trunk, counting the fruit that was budding above her head when she heard a sound. Looking across the garden she saw a door open within the boundary wall and through it stepped one of my gardeners. He bumped through the doorway, balancing two buckets hanging from each end of a pole across his shoulders. The buckets were full and he splashed some water as he manoeuvred his way into the garden and eventually set them down. He sighed as he stood up and stretched his arms above his head, noticeably relieved to have the load off them.

Isis sat still and did nothing to make herself known. She now had something to amuse her and was fascinated as to what the gardener would do next. Strapped to his waist was a pouch and he removed this now to take out his tools. The first was a ladle and he used this to scoop water out of the buckets onto some small delicate plants. As he did so he examined them, stopping to caress a leaf or two. Sometimes he would put the ladle down and reach for his snips to trim a browned leaf or tame an unruly branch. He even began to sing as he worked--just soft and low as if to the plants themselves.

Isis continued to sit still and watch. She was intrigued at how he lost himself in his work, like the plants were enough company for him. He had been working for over ten minutes and was still unaware that she was there on the other side of the garden. Isis was quite bemused that he had not noticed her and just as she was deliberating as to whether she should make her presence known the gardener turned and saw her. He was startled for a moment, almost dropping the snips in his hand. He immediately knew this was one of my daughters, her presence here alone was enough to indicate this, but her dress and jewellery confirmed it. He quickly put his right hand to chest, still clutching his tool and bowed to her. He straightened back up but kept his eyes down, as he knew he should.

Isis got up from her place under the tree and walked towards him. "Hello, I didn't mean to scare you," she said as she walked towards him.

The gardener kept his eyes down and seemed to be frozen in place. In truth he was petrified to be in the presence of royalty. He was the same age as Amenhotep and somewhat new to his palace duties. His role at the palace meant he rarely had to even be in the same room as any of the royal family, let alone speak to them; and even though he tended my garden, he was sent to do so when I was at court. A butler and guard would ensure the garden was empty of any workers when I chose to go there. All he knew to do now was stand silent lest he say something that would get him in trouble.

"You are doing a wonderful job in my father's garden," Isis continued on.

The gardener remained silent and still.

"Is there something wrong with you? Why do you not speak?" Isis was puzzled. Despite having grown up with servants, in her eleven years none had ever behaved like this. Now that he had been addressed though--the young man needed to reply.

"Forgive me, it is not my place to speak to a princess," he said.

"Not your place to speak? How silly!" Isis replied.

"Your Highness, I should not have disturbed you. I shall gather my things and return later. I beg your forgiveness," he said, and bowed again.

"There is nothing to forgive. If anything I disturbed you," she laughed. "Anyway if you leave then you will be in trouble for not doing your work and then it will be known I was here without permission and I will be in trouble. So you should indeed continue your work and I shall continue counting fruit."

This was as good as an order and despite Isis's youth she was the most superior present and he would need to obey.

"Yes, Your Highness," he replied, and turned to continue on with his work.

"What is your name?" Isis asked.

The gardener turned back to her. "My name is Menket, Your Highness," he answered, bowing and once again returning to his work.

Isis walked back to her spot under the tree smiling, happy that she could remain and watch the gardener until he was finished over an hour later.

The next day Isis made her way to my garden again at the same time in the hope of watching Menket at work once again. When she stepped through the doorway that led from my rooms he was already there, trimming an orange tree. Her movement caught his eye and once again he bowed and wished her good day.

"You don't need to bow to me Menket, we are not in court," she said. "Besides I am not so important."

Menket did not answer and continued to trim the tree. He felt self-conscious now, knowing her eyes were following his every move. It wasn't that he lacked confidence in his work for in fact he was highly skilled. No gardener would be assigned such a duty if he weren't. He was just wary that anything Isis saw could be spoken of later. He was also very uncomfortable to be alone with a royal daughter. If anyone found out the gossip would be horrendous for them both.

Isis would continue to sneak into my garden regularly and the discomfort Menket felt in her presence soon eased, especially as no one seemed to be aware that she was doing this. They eventually grew quite comfortable in each other's company. Isis began to ask questions of Menket's work and the plants while Menket enjoyed sharing his knowledge and her questions even amused him.

"How do you know which leaves and branches to cut?" she asked one day.

Menket stopped and thought. It had been so long since he had been taught how to trim and prune that it was now second nature. He shrugged his shoulders. "I don't truly know how to tell you, Your Highness," he answered. "The plants tell me. I look at their shape. It shows me the leaves and branches it doesn't need. See here," Menket pointed to a small shrub. For the most part it was rounded and compact but one branch was extending beyond all others. "It is like the plant is throwing it away." With that he trimmed the extension back and the shrub was now a perfect shape.

"But plants that grow in the countryside do not have gardeners to tend to them," Isis queried. "So why should these be cut so?"

"Well this is not the countryside. This is the Pharaoh's garden. Do you think it would honour the Pharaoh that he could not walk amongst his own garden without unruly branches scratching his legs or face?" Menket said, and Isis shook her head. "It also allows the plants their space. To be walked against and brushed would damage them," he continued.

Isis didn't quite understand but she nodded anyway. To her all that really mattered was that I had a nice space to relax within. This of course I did and it was one morning that I was sitting here that Isis appeared in the doorway. She stopped short seeming surprised to see me, for indeed she was expecting to see the gardener instead.

"Hello Daughter," I greeted her. "Have you come to give me some company?"

"Ah, yes Father," she answered, and as she walked towards me her eyes scanned the garden looking to see if Menket was there.

Of course I knew nothing of their friendship and the time that they had been spending together. I innocently made small talk about the palace and an upcoming banquet--all of which Isis responded to with her usual joyful manner. I then turned and looked upon my garden.

"Is this not a beautiful space, Isis?" I said, "I am so lucky to have this."

"Yes, it is Father," she answered, "it is well tended to."

I turned and looked at Isis. This last comment astounded. I expected an eleven year old girl to comment on the flowers and their colours, not to have any regard for the work involved in maintaining this space. I smiled, and looked back upon the plants. "The persimmon tree is almost finished its fruits. I will miss them as they have been most delicious," I said.

"Oh no Father, you shall not miss them so soon. There are much more to come!" she exclaimed, and then stopped as quickly.

Now I turned to her and my curiosity was well and truly piqued.

"Daughter, how do you know of this?" I asked, wanting to know the basis of her comment.

"Ah--well--just look--you can see many more beginnings of fruit from here," she stammered.

"Isis if you can see such things from this distance then I shall make you a scout of the army!" I said, and rose from my chair to walk towards the tree. There were indeed the beginnings of many more persimmons. They were not only small but hidden behind the other fruit and leaves. One needed to be right by the tree to see them. I looked back at Isis who was looking anywhere but at the tree or me. I walked back to my seat and sat down. "Isis you will not be in trouble for having come here without me, but I would appreciate your honesty in sharing this with me," I said firmly.

"Yes Father, I have been coming here," she said quietly. "It is just so boring now. My sisters are all busy with things that do not interest me. I like to come and sit here."

I understood completely. Just as I used to have my horse to ride upon and find places of quiet away from the palace goings-on, so too did my daughter need to find her place of solitude.

"I usually come most mornings, just for an hour or two. No one even misses me. They are all so busy," she continued.

I nodded my head. "That is fine Isis. You visit as often as you like. Let us just keep this agreement between us though. I do not wish for all to come and use this space. It is delicate and easily disturbed. You seem to know how to respect that," I said, and our pact was made.

I had now given my permission for her to spend whatever time she liked here. This pleased Isis to no end as not only had I given her permission to visit here but now she felt she had permission to visit with Menket also. The next day she made her way to the garden after checking that I was in court or at the war rooms. Menket was there and was picking the persimmons that had just that morning reached the stage for eating. Isis stopped and watched him for a moment, smiling at the way he treated each one as if it were the only fruit the tree had ever made.

She walked towards him and called out as she did so. "Good morning Menket," she said loudly.

Menket stopped what he was doing and looked to her. "Your Highness, should you speak so loud? Someone might hear you," he said softly.

"Menket, it is alright. My father has given me permission to visit his gardens. There is no need for secrecy anymore," she laughed.

However, Menket was not so sure that his presence at the same time was something that would please me--and he was right. I was still unaware of this friendship and if I had been, I would never have allowed Isis such freedom to enter my private garden unescorted.

The two young friends though continued on for several weeks more. Isis began to ask questions of Menket's family and where he lived.

"I would like to see your home one day," she said.

Menket did not answer, as he knew this would never be possible. It was far from his position to explain this to a young princess though. He quickly changed the subject back to the plants before them.

Not long after this Isis once again joined me in the garden. It was an evening after court and I sat relaxing and sipping on some wine, admiring my garden in the dusk light.

"I do believe these persimmons will be the last for some time," I said, nodding over towards the tree, "unless you wish to challenge my observation Isis?"

"No, Father--you are right. Menket says that also," she answered smiling.

"Who is Menket?" I asked softly. This name was unfamiliar to me and I made a point to be aware of the names of those around me.

"Menket is your wonderful gardener who keeps your garden so," she answered smiling even brighter now. "He is so clever Father. Don't you think he does a wonderful job?"

"Yes, he does," I answered, and looked at my daughter who glowed as she spoke.

I felt a sharp stab inside my chest. It was a familiar feeling. I had felt it the day Amenemhat spoke of his funeral mask, I also felt it every time I watched one of my daughters leave her wedding feast to lay with her husband for the first time. Now here sat my youngest daughter and I saw in her face the rush of affection for this servant that could never be. My heart ached, as I could not allow this to be, yet I would never want to hurt my baby daughter no matter her age. I had two ways to deal with this: I could be heavy handed and simply refuse her access to the garden and therefore to this boy, or I could simply let it run its course and Isis would learn in her own time and way.

As with most matters concerning my children I would take the middle ground. I did not stop Isis visiting the garden or her friend. I did though inform my butler Tati, who was suitably horrified that such things had occurred within his jurisdiction.

"Sire, forgive me! Had I known the Royal Daughter had been alone with this boy I would certainly have let you know," he gushed.

"It is alright. I believe no harm has been done *so far*," I said. "Perhaps it may be wise though if someone should just keep an eye on them."

"Of course Sire, I shall make sure of it," he answered.

So from now on when Isis visited the garden she was watched from around corners and through windows. My butler did this himself to make sure his promise to me was held. As discreet as he thought he was Menket would see him briefly and know what Tati was doing. Isis though remained oblivious and her affections grew. She would visit my garden most days and when she couldn't she would be miserable. Her time away was always spent thinking of Menket, of something he said, the way he walked or even how he had trimmed a plant as she watched.

All of her sisters, except Nebetiunet were now married or promised in marriage and Isis knew her time was not so far away either. In her naivety Isis imagined that she had in fact done a wonderful thing for her family in having found someone so soon. She knew that Menket was not the noble, priest, courtier or soldier that would be approved by them--but she was Isis the tenth child. What did it matter who she married? She did not affect the throne nor would she ever. She herself would barely be recorded in my history let alone her husband or children. So Isis's daydreams persisted and her emotions swelled. Then one day, just weeks shy of her twelfth birthday, she decided to act on her feelings with the hope of progressing the situation.

The night before Isis snuck a headdress into bed with her. It was her favourite and the one she wore to temple for special ceremonies. In the centre was a ruby, it was not as grand as any others I have spoken of--but it was beautiful enough. After she was left by the maids to sleep, she went to the window and there with just the moonlight she twisted and bent the headdress, picking at the stone with a hair pin until the ruby was free of its setting. She snuck back into her bed, clasping the jewel and smiling. When she woke the next morning the ruby was still in her hand and she once again smiled, remembering her plan for the day.

That day she would head to my garden knowing that Menket would be there. It was the day when the small plants must be watered and trimmed. She rushed through dressing and could barely eat her breakfast, prompting her nurse to ask if she was not feeling well. Isis felt fine apart from her heart pounding so strongly with excitement that it hurt. She walked quickly along the corridors to my chambers and past the few servants who were sweeping and polishing my rooms. They had almost no time to acknowledge her, she moved so fast. As she made her way into the garden the servants all looked to each other and one volunteered to let my butler know. The butler would be too slow that day to witness what would happen and maybe this was a blessing so that Isis's moment remained private.

When Isis entered the garden Menket was yet to arrive. She thought of sitting beneath the persimmon tree as she had been that day when they first met, but decided not to. Today she would wait for him as a lady. Isis sat upon one of the stone chairs that faced across the garden to the door he would enter through. She smoothed her clothes and hair as she had seen Meritamen do before her suitor would arrive to visit, and then she waited.

It seemed an eternity before Menket arrived, but he did finally bumping through the door with his water buckets as he had done on their first meeting.

"You are here!" Isis cried, and jumped up from her chair rushing across the garden to him.

"Yes, Your Highness," he replied plainly.

Isis began her usual blabbering and Menket smiled as he listened, trying hard to keep as much focus upon his work as he could. Today though, he noticed that she seemed agitated but as was his place he would not make comment on this and continued on. Then finally the source of her agitation was revealed.

"Menket, come and sit with me for a while," she said.

"Your Highness, you know that I cannot. I must keep with my work,"

Menket pleaded.

He was kneeling by a small plant and he turned back to it, turning the soil. This did not deter Isis at all. She simply walked over to him and knelt beside him. Menket stopped for a moment, he shouldn't have been as shocked for she had done this many times, but today it felt different. Isis leaned in close to him and whispered. He could feel her breath upon his ear and the folds of her dress brushed against him. He prayed the butler was not watching.

"I have a gift for you," she whispered.

With that she took Menket's hand and placed within it the ruby. He looked down and froze. Here in his soil dusted hand was a stone worth more than he would earn in a year. It could build his family a new home, or buy them enough livestock to begin their own trade. It had been handed to him so simply that he wondered if Isis even knew its worth. He quickly looked around to see if they were being watched knowing this was more than likely. Menket's mind raced as to what to do. If anyone was watching this he could be killed--quite literally. He could be accused of seducing a young princess or stealing royal treasure. Either charge would be his death should he be brought to me. He turned to Isis and though he whispered his tone was far from soft.

"Your Highness, I cannot receive this! You place us both in great danger!" he spoke strongly. "Have you no idea the worth of what you hand me?"

"Yes, I do Menket," she replied, her eyes wide. "Would this not allow you to improve your position? Then you would be able to ask my father for marriage to me."

Menket's jaw dropped as he sat back upon his feet. This he had not seen coming, and he was truly shocked. He knew Isis enjoyed his company and attention but that she should have such affections for him had completely evaded him. A simple gardener would never imagine capturing the heart of a princess. His head continued to spin and he actually felt nauseous as he searched for a way to deal with this. He looked to Isis, her eyes wide and a blush across her cheeks. He had no desire to crush her heart, but he could not humour her advances either. Menket took a deep breath and finally spoke a simple lie that abruptly ended the scene.

"Your Highness, I am already promised to another," he said as delicately as he could.

Isis sat still trying hard to not believe she had just heard his words. She felt a rush of humiliation, hurt and betrayal all at once. It was as though someone had punched her in the chest. She did not cry immediately as she was too shocked at his answer. In all her daydreams it had never occurred to her that it might go like this. Menket was supposed to have declared her wonderful for this plan, then gathered her in his arms for a gentle kiss. Instead they both sat here on their haunches staring at each other shocked and embarrassed.

Isis had no words in reply to Menket's announcement. She just rose to her feet and walked away.

"Your Highness, your jewel!" Menket cried out to her as she walked through the door back into my chambers.

Isis did not hear him though and continued on in a daze until she reached her rooms. Then as any young woman suffering her first heartbreak; she threw herself upon her bed and sobbed unashamedly. Her cries were so loud that her nurse came running and tried to extract the source of Isis's torment. My daughter though would never repeat to anyone the cause of her sadness. Her romantic adventure had been her secret and it would remain so. As her sobs subsided and she lay with her eyes red she vowed one thing--that she would never return to my garden.

Isis needn't have decided this in order to avoid Menket. After she left he looked down at the jewel. He knew it was highly likely someone had seen it handed to him. As he pondered upon the possibilities it offered him he knew there was only one action that he would pursue. That day when his work was complete he stepped to the door of my chambers and asked to see my butler. When Tati came to the doorway he simply handed the jewel to him.

"The Princess Isis left this behind in the garden today. I collected it lest a less honest servant should find it," Menket said stiffly. "I also think it best that I no longer attend the Pharaoh's private garden."

The butler nodded, understanding completely. He thanked the gardener for his honesty and told him to report to the kitchen gardens in two days time. Later that evening the butler came to me as I sat at my desk writing and he placed the ruby before me.

"Sire, Princess Isis left this in your garden today. It was returned to me by the gardener Menket," he said drolly.

I looked upon the ruby and knew immediately what had happened.

"I think it best our young gardener is now given alternate duties," I said as I looked at the stone.

"It is already done Sire. He requested this himself," my butler replied.

I simply nodded my reply. The boy had honoured and respected not only me but also his position. I asked that the butler ensure he was placed within a position that recognised his skill and worth.

As I looked back upon the ruby I now understood why people prayed for their offspring to be male. It was not just about carrying on family traditions, nor providing labour or protection. Males just did not bring the complexities of emotion that women carried. In all my years my four sons would never cause me a tenth of the heartache or headaches that my six daughters did. I thanked the Gods for my masculinity and the seemingly more simple life that it had granted me.

As for my Isis, time healed her heartache and a year later a young soldier caught her sight. He was the younger brother of Meryt's husband and a good friend of Menkheperre. His attentions and affection helped ease the pain of the gardener but I truly believe that she always held a place in her heart for Menket until she died.

CHAPTER TWENTY

As Isis farewelled her youth with heartache, my eldest children became parents and the next generation was begun. When the first of Amenhotep's consorts fell pregnant it was as though the entire palace took in its breath and held it for the duration of the pregnancy. I anticipated this child as much as I did the arrival of Amenemhat but there was a whole other layer of joy with this child. My pride swelled with the possibility that I would see my son's successor and know the fate of my lands but on top of this, my family would experience the joy of having three generations within the palace. This had not occurred for some time and certainly not during the dynasty in which my family had ruled.

Throughout the land it was spoken that the riches of my family life were the reward for my success in expanding my empire. It made perfect sense that a man that could oversee many lands and scores of people would be a man who heads a family of many. I was celebrated as a true born leader and when it was announced that my successor had fathered yet another generation I was further exalted for ensuring the future of the empire.

The day my first grandchild was born was wonderful. I was making my way to court when I noticed some scurrying of servants in the corridors ahead of me. The sight of a priestess making her way to the palace birthing room soon satisfied my curiosity. She was wringing her hands in front of her and while this small slip in composure should have concerned me it didn't. If anything it made me more satisfied at the temple's choice in choosing her for this royal birth. I would much rather someone who understood the levity of this birth than someone who sauntered in as though it was a standard ritual.

It would have surprised me to no end if I had only known that this was exactly the way Arisina herself had made her way to the birthing room for my delivery. That too had been her first royal birth and Isis had been her last. Arisina was now too old to attend a birth and focussed on the adult requirements of my children whom she adored. It also seemed quite fitting that a new priestess should now be assigned this duty as a new generation was begun. Like Arisina, Bet-Ankh would now have a special link to my grandchildren and their lives.

I continued on to court to find Amenhotep waiting in his chair that was placed beside me today in anticipation for what would hopefully be the big announcement. Being the consorts' first birth no one knew whether she would be a slow or quick birther. So once again I settled into my throne to discuss business until news of the birth arrived. Amenhotep sat beside me and tried his best to stay focussed on the court. Every time the doors opened for a courtier or vizier to enter he would jump in his chair, only to slump back down when he saw it wasn't the priestess. It was somewhat weird to look upon him sitting there, almost the same age as I was when I waited for the news of my first-born. I too had been that nervous and excited, but then Hatshepsut was still alive and by my side reminding me to bury my emotions.

Court was adjourned for lunch and as it was announced Amenhotep turned to me flustered. "Father, it has been since before dawn that Tiaa was taken to the birthing room. Something must be wrong," he concluded.

I tried my hardest not to laugh but couldn't help myself. "Son, I took over a day to leave my mother. You took from dawn until well and truly into the sun's decent to arrive. All is quite well and you just need to trust your child will arrive when it is ready."

"How did you do this ten times Father? I feel like my heart is going to explode," he said, screwing his nose up and clutching his chest.

I looked away and sighed. "Well the first time was the hardest," I said honestly. "It is especially so for us Amenhotep as our first child holds much in its arrival. Each time after is still hard as you pray for the mother and child to be safe, but you then know the joy of seeing that tiny face for the first time."

These words did nothing to ease Amenhotep's stress and he continued to rub his chest and furrow his forehead.

"Let us go and relax. Eating and bathing will help us both release some of the torment of waiting," I said.

So while we sought comfort from what we saw as our terribly hard part in this whole procedure, the birth was progressing at an unforeseen rate. My new grandchild was most anxious to make their way into the world and the attendants were picking up their pace to match. While we were walking to the dining room to eat, Tiaa was being walked to the birthing chair. Her child crowned as she walked after having spilt her birth waters upon the bed.

"You have a very ambitious child Your Highness!" Bet-Ankh declared.

Arisina had shared so many stories of long births such as mine and several of my children that Bet-Ankh was beyond relieved that her first royal birth was heading to the final stages while the sun was still high. Tiaa herself was relieved also despite the pain of her child's head stretching her. The young mother felt strong through the pains and looked forward to it being over. The months of preparation and prayers would soon be over too and the arrival of her child would change her life forever. Tiaa would no longer be an average consort amongst the women of the palace harem but just how far she was elevated would depend as always upon the sex of the child. If she delivered a son and therefore a future Pharaoh she could become a royal wife, but if she delivered a girl then she would still merely be King's consort but now a royal mother. This too was a rise in her placing in the palace but nowhere near that of being declared a wife.

Amenhotep returned with me to court several hours later not realising that as we walked to take our places upon our thrones Bet-Ankh was actually waiting for us.

"This is absurd," she muttered to another priest from the palace. "Pharaoh and Prince should have been summoned the moment I left the birthing room."

Indeed she was correct and this is exactly what should have happened, especially given the importance of this birth. The court priest just exhaled deeply and turned his head away, unwilling to be reprimanded by a birth priestess. The court priests had their own protocol to abide by and were too scared to detract from them for any reason. They would never summon me to court for anything other than a military emergency. All other matters could wait--or so they thought.

I was most displeased to enter court and find the priestess waiting for me when I should have been the one waiting for her, as should have my son. I rarely lost my temper before any of my officials, even when on military campaigns so when I spoke before even reaching my throne all present in court knew of my at this. "How long have you been here priestess?" I bellowed as I made my way towards my throne.

"Not long Sire," she said, bowing and scuttling behind me, struggling to keep her composure. "Your courtiers knew of your imminent return Your Majesty, and suggested we allow you to arrive in your own time."

This appeased my temper and I calmed down. Bet-Ankh had been chosen well; not just for her ritual skills, but also for her diplomacy. Her simple white lie settled me and saved the courtiers. It didn't however settle my son who now knew he was a father and was desperate to know of his child. Amenhotep almost ran to his throne hoping the quicker he was seated, the quicker he would receive his news. I too walked briskly and didn't care that Amenhotep had seated himself before me. Such days were for breaking from protocol as my father had known so well. I settled into my chair and brushed aside the priest whose job it was to smooth my clothes. I saw Amenhotep lean forward in his chair just as I had when Arisina came to tell me of Amenemhat.

"Speak Priestess," I said loudly.

Bet-Ankh gathered herself before us both, any sign of fluster in her now fell away as she took a deep breath, squared her shoulders and bowed. This little gesture seemed to take forever and she finally raised her head and spoke. "Pharaoh Thutmose and Prince Amenhotep, the consort Tiaa has given birth to a son," she said gracefully.

Amenhotep and I looked to each other. I had a deep smile on my face while he sat with his mouth gaping trying to comprehend what was held within those simple words. He had an heir and a successor. A future Pharaoh was born and of his seed. My reluctant successor had once again risen to his duties with the seeming natural synchronicity that made him once again appear to be the one the Gods had chosen from the beginning. I spoke my congratulations and thanked him for honouring our family so. Amenhotep was too shocked to even acknowledge me, so I reached out and grabbed his hand as it rested upon the arm of his throne. My touch soon pulled him back to the moment.

"I thank you Son," I repeated gently. "You once again honour our family."

I saw a tear form in his eye and all he could do was nod. Turning back to the priestess I asked her to tell us about the birth and this new prince of Egypt. As she delighted us with the birth story of this child eager to make his way to his family and empire Amenhotep's tears fell freely and so too did mine. Our tears both fell with love and pride, however Amenhotep's also fell with some pain. Once again he was part of an event that should have been Amenemhat's joy and celebration. The tarnish that had followed him since Amenemhat's death now was upon him in the strongest guise ever. Not only did he sit and mourn for the loss of his brother once again but he now also had a son who would benefit from his brother's misfortune.

The priestess finished her story and I suggested to my stunned son beside me that we make our way to meet his child. He nodded slowly and spoke his first words since the announcement. "Yes Father." There had not been one question to Bet-Ankh during her story and I believed it to be as he was so overcome with emotion, which he was. It just wasn't the emotion that I imagined.

We made our way to the birthing room and in retrospect I was chattering like a girl as we walked; so eager to see my grandson and reminiscing along the way about the same walk to see my own children. Amenhotep kept his eyes ahead the whole time just muttering a "Yes Father" or nodding to acknowledge my onslaught of stories.

My blabbering made the walk to the birthing room seem a lot quicker than it ever had for my own children although to Amenhotep it still seemed long. A few paces from the door I stopped walking, bringing the entire procession of courtiers, guards and priestess to a halt and I turned to Amenhotep.

"My son, you should be the first to greet your own child as my father did for me and I did for you," I said with a smile. "I shall wait here until you are ready to present him to me."

Amenhotep looked at me, nodded once again and walked through the door of the birthing room. I stood in the corridor smiling, knowing the magic that my son would now experience, while all around me my courtiers shifted uncomfortably in their places. I looked amongst them and realised this is exactly what they had done all those times they followed me here for my children. I considered making a joke to alleviate the increase in discomfort they now shared by adding my presence to this part of the procedure, but decided against it, and looked to the door waiting for my signal to enter.

The doors soon opened again and Bet-Ankh, the only other person to enter with Amenhotep invited me to meet my grandson. As I walked through the door I saw Amenhotep holding his son gently in his arms. Across my son's face was the gentlest of smiles. The first smile he had shown all day. Tears were once again in his eyes as he looked up at me.

I cannot begin to describe how it felt to see my son holding his own son. As I walked into the room to that scene it was as though time suddenly slowed. I was grateful for this as I wished to savour every detail of this moment from the sunlight streaming in the window through to the way Amenhotep's arm curved around his son. Within that soft energy I suddenly realised I was being given a magic opportunity to witness the many moments I had held my own children for the first time. It was as though I was revisiting those times and in a new way. Here I stood as an observer to an intimate moment, yet I was connected to them both in my own intricate way.

Amenhotep tried to speak to me but couldn't find any words. I just nodded and turned to Tiaa who was freshly bathed and lying upon the newly cleaned birthing bed waiting to receive us. As I turned and looked at her she dropped her eyes and blushed. She had so rarely been in my presence that she was still nervous whenever she was near me.

"Thank you Tiaa. You have honoured our family and your own with this child," I said as officially as I could, and then turned back to my grandson not even waiting for her response. "When you are ready Amenhotep I might like to embrace my first grandchild," I laughed as I asked this.

"Of course, Father," he answered and stepped towards me.

Amenhotep handed me his son with all the awkwardness of a new father and the baby's wrapping began to loosen as I took him into my hands. I did not pull him close to me. Instead I held him up in front of me, one hand forming a seat beneath his behind and the other supporting his head and neck. I admired his perfect little face that twitched with new sensations. His features recalled every likeness of my family, especially the rounded face that Menkheperre and I carried. It was of no doubt that this child carried the blood of my family. Then this future Pharaoh made his claim to the throne in a way that would erase any trace of doubt I could have. As the wrappings loosened even more with his squirming he pulled his arms free then stretched them above his head. Bringing them back down to rest upon his chest his forearms crossed over each other as though ready for a crook and flail.

"Father, if it pleases you I was hoping he might be named Thutmose, as you are and our forefathers were," Amenhotep said.

"He most certainly may," I answered never taking my eyes from the tiny Pharaoh-in-waiting.

My delight at having a third generation in the palace and having it begun by my son's successor was celebrated with a week of feasting at the palace and elaborate ceremonies within the Karnak temple. Word was sent throughout the empire that a male was born to my successor and that the might of the Pharaoh was confirmed by the Gods with a lineage that would continue for many years to come. Temples throughout Egypt held celebrations and money was sent that these temples would also hold feasts for my subjects. It was our land's greatest celebration since Megiddo fell.

While the empire celebrated young Thutmose's birth as a sign of prosperity our family was overwhelmed by our sudden unexpected affection for this baby. His nurses would have the easiest job of any women assigned to a prince as he was barely ever without one of his young aunts visiting for a cuddle and to coo over him. His uncles were also fascinated with him but didn't line up for embraces, as did my daughters. They would instead watch from a safe manly distance and ask masculine questions.

"What age will he start riding?" asked Menkheperre.

"Where shall his throne be placed in court and temple?" asked Siamun.

Matreya even showed a softer side at becoming a grandmother, showering the baby with attention. Despite my cynicism that this was to gain favour with Amenhotep she did have genuine feelings for the baby. Of course she still understood the importance of a relationship with an heir apparent and while she rocked her young grandson she vowed not to make the same mistake that she had with Amenhotep. However within her plan to gain the affection of her grandson for her own future purposes she fell to his charms. Eventually when she entered a room he would run to her crying "Grandmamma" wishing for an embrace and his attachment would be greeted genuinely. Matreya surprised herself with the warmth she invited into her life through this boy.

My beautiful Satiah shared my joy at becoming a grandfather but I am also sure that a part of her heart ached, as did mine, that we would never know Amenemhat's children. Satiah and I now watched upon Beketamun waiting for news of her first child but despite being married for over a year there was no sign of her belly rounding and the announcement that would accompany this. This caused us concern in a few ways. If Beketamun remained without providing a child to her husband he could simply dissolve the marriage. As a man this was his right no matter the standing of his wife and I could not punish him for exercising this right. Well, not directly or officially anyway.

This raised the concern that Beketamun could be barren but her hesitance to enter marriage made me think otherwise. Suddenly the events in which Beketamun entered into her marriage with Kamankh started to look suspicious and I imagined the very things that were murmured amongst the palace. I knew Beketamun was an intelligent and resourceful young woman and the possibility that she had arranged her own marriage as nothing more than a business agreement with her husband now appeared more than likely. Of course to Beketamun this had been the case. No matter the friendship that was between my daughter and the courtier or his hidden affections for her, their marriage was one of convenience. The fact that Kamankh had secured himself as part of my court only made this situation more obvious.

I began to watch them when they were together, hoping for some signs in their behaviour that would confirm my suspicions. At family gatherings, within court or wherever they would appear together before me I would scan every gesture looking for the slightest sign of coldness or distance between them. No gesture presented itself though. They would arrive together arm in arm, Kamankh would hold a chair for his wife to be seated, and they smiled as they spoke to one another. If anything they appeared more affectionate than any other couple in my presence. My cynicism wanted wholeheartedly to believe this was an elaborate performance but all I truly could see was a doting couple. They even reminded me of Satiah and I in the early years of our marriage.

The behaviour between them certainly was no act. Kamankh used the premise of "saving" Beketamun to enter into marriage and his genuine affection for my daughter blossomed as the days passed and he knew her even more. Though he would lie beside her at night and his body would ache to make love to her he remained on his side of the bed and respected the agreement with which he began the marriage. Instead he would find satisfaction in the attention he could shower upon her in other ways.

Meanwhile Beketamun had fallen in love with Kamankh even though she did not know it. Her feelings for Kamankh were buried in relief that she would no longer have to consider marriage proposals or my lectures about this. As Isis enjoyed the secrecy of her romance with the gardener, Beketamun too relished her secret agreement with Kamankh. In a life filled with servants and attendants a princess rarely had true secrets or privacy but the truth of her marriage was both of these for Beketamun. She allowed for her marriage preparations and played along with the priestesses and her mother as they performed prayers for her union. She also kept her composure as they informed her of the duties of a wife within the marriage bed. The biting of her lip and the blushing as a priestess explained the mechanics of sex were quite customary for a young bride-to-be. What they did not notice was the colour drain from Beketamun's face as she was also told the marriage rights of a husband in bed and the wife's role to provide him this.

Suddenly Beketamun was faced with the reality of her agreement with Kamankh. No matter their understanding he could exercise his physical right over her. To refuse could be the end of the marriage, the agreement and the approval she had won from her mother and I. So upon her wedding night she lay in her new marriage bed, oiled and ready for her husband with her heart pounding the same as any new wife. Kamankh though was a man of his word and when he slid into bed next to her he merely squeezed her hand and bid her a goodnight before turning to sleep upon his side with his back facing his new bride. Beketamun went to sleep with tears of relief in her eyes. Each night they would repeat this same scene. Beketamun would head to bed wondering if tonight would be the night that Kamankh would exercise his right only to have him turn his back to her once again after bidding her goodnight.

Their days though evolved as Beketamun found she enjoyed her husband's company beyond the space of business within the court. When they dined alone in their rooms she loved that they could exchange stories of their day's duties often giving each other advice or sharing a snippet of gossip that would not entertain anyone else. Beketamun also grew to love Kamankh's small physical gestures. She loved his arm underneath hers as they walked the palace or a gentle brush to her shoulder or stroke of her hair as he walked past her. There were even the occasional times in bed that his arm would brush her body when he turned in his sleep.

As that first year of their marriage progressed, these small gestures multiplied and Beketamun found she sought them more often. She would find new ways to be in his company and even asked that she would accompany him on his trips to the south for business. In bed she would sleep closer to the centre of the bed and some nights would end in Kamankh's arms. However, he would soon turn away; not from any desire to end the embrace, but to hide his arousal. Beketamun though not realising his noble intention believed that he had no desire for her sexually despite his affections when they were out of their bed.

Now their first anniversary had passed and Nefertiry married for only a few months had just announced her first pregnancy. Beketamun wept when she heard the news, as she knew that comments were being made of her fertility and now this would only make the gossip worse. Most of all she wept for the final act of intimacy that she wished her husband would seek with her. To make her woes worse Satiah, under my direction, would now approach her to discuss this.

"Has she approached the physicians for the necessary herbs? What about prayers? Has she been to temple enough?" I asked of Satiah.

Satiah just sighed and within this sigh we both felt that much more needed to be addressed. Beketamun had in fact been taking the herbs to help pregnancy following a very gentle and caring suggestion from one of her maids. All the herbs in the world though would not help if she remained a virgin. Whilst neither of us could imagine that Kamankh had not exercised his marital rights it now faced us as a serious possibility. More seriously though, was the possibility that Beketamun refused her husband this right and that her position as princess made him feel useless to challenge her.

"Wasn't Beketamun advised on her wifely duties?" I continued.

"Well of course Thutmose," Satiah answered, "I would never allow my daughters to marry without knowing of this part of married life."

"Then you must discuss this situation with her," I ordered.

So Satiah made her way to her daughter's chamber one afternoon when she knew Kamankh would not be there. As was Satiah's nature she ensured Beketamun's privacy and began the discussion as gently as she could. Beketamun responded with a flood of tears and the most honest outpouring that only a mother could receive from a daughter. Satiah listened to the truth of the marriage arrangement and despite her shock at her daughter's deceit of her mother and I, she remained quiet and calm. When Beketamun then spoke of the confused emotions that she now felt for her husband, Satiah reached forward and stroked her daughter's hair.

"My dear daughter, you have blessed yourself by choosing a man of honour," Satiah said softly. "It is now your duty to let him know he can truly be your husband."

Beketamun nodded her agreement. Her recent visits to temple as part of her charade to invoke her fertility had given my atheist daughter some quiet time to reflect upon her situation. Whilst the priestesses chanted to Bes and Hathor for her womb to ripen she had even ventured her own silent prayers for guidance from whatever God might listen to her. Satiah's guidance to her had been the answer she had already heard many times over as she prayed. To now hear it from her mother's mouth confirmed that this was indeed the solution she sought. Only now she would need to find a way to actually let Kamankh know that their marriage could progress.

It took Beketamun almost three weeks to find not only a suitable time but also the courage to speak the words. She would open her mouth to say something whilst they ate dinner but would stop, as a wave of fear would sweep over her. They would be walking in the gardens and once again she would think the moment had arrived only for a servant or one of her sisters to appear. Kamankh did sense something but when he did query his wife she would dismiss his observation.

"You do know that you can speak to me of anything, Beketamun," he told her after one of her false starts.

This did help lessen her fear of telling him. In the meantime they would enact the same routine each night in bed. One night though her desire was too strong to wait any longer. Kamankh climbed into bed and after wishing her goodnight began to turn away as he always did. Beketamun reached out and grabbed his arm, stopping his movement and Kamankh turned to her, "What is it Beketamun?" he asked, thinking she had one last thing to say before they slept.

"Please don't turn away tonight," she whispered, nervous and scared that he may refuse her.

Kamankh's heart raced and he put his arm over his wife. "Are you sure?" he asked gently.

Beketamun smiled and nodded. This was all Kamankh needed to turn to her fully and pull her close to him. My third grandchild was conceived that very night and Beketamun delivered a healthy daughter nine months later--just four months after Nefertiry gave birth to my first granddaughter.

If any of my other children had marital woes they kept them to themselves. In public all was smooth and proper and any indiscretions were kept behind closed doors. The only murmurs I ever caught wind of alluded to Menkheperre's philandering amongst the palace women and while I hope this ended when he finally sought marriage I am sure it didn't. The heavens only know just how many children Menkheperre fathered yet were raised by my courtiers, believing them to be their own offspring.

The one visible indicator of any trouble was when Meritamen's husband came to dinner one night with a large graze and bruising on his forehead. Having just returned from a military expedition with Menkheperre I assumed it to have happened whilst they were travelling.

"That is quite a mark there," I noted. "Menkheperre reported an uneventful patrol so I am surprised to see you carrying such a scrape."

"It was a peaceful journey, Sire," he answered. "I slipped whilst climbing the loose surface of a valley."

Menkheperre snorted and laughed out loud. "Were you not trying to pick some wildflowers for your wife?" he teased as my daughter's husband scowled at him.

I did not continue with any questions. It was obvious that there was some private joke between the men. What I did not know was that the injury was quite fresh, not having occurred upon the journey at all. The only slip my son-in-law had made was in not bringing home his wife a gift from his travels. She had expressed her distaste at this with a well-aimed statue. Suffice to say he never made that mistake again.

# CHAPTER TWENTY-ONE

Thirty-eight other grandchildren followed young Thutmose and the two girls as all of my children became parents. The palace size and population grew even more and only Ramses would ever top this due to the age he lived to and the amount of wives he kept. Each child was born strong and healthy and brought their own flavour of joy to our family and the palace. The nursery was the most active part of the palace for many years with mothers, fathers and even grandparents coming and going from dawn to dusk. This place was the centre of the children's early lives as it had been for my own children. Here they played with each other and began their lifelong friendships and allegiances with each other. They would all follow in their family traditions becoming pharaohs, soldiers, viziers, priests, artisans and glamorous princesses.

Each day of their births was a grand celebration, although none would be matched by the birth of young Thutmose. Only my sons would wait in court for grand announcements of the arrival of their children. My daughters' children were granted the more humble arrival of one who will never see themselves upon the throne despite their blood ties to the Pharaoh. Whilst my daughters' children would be reported to me there was no need for an elaborate announcement or a birth story. I would simply be told their sex and be invited to meet my new grandchild at my convenience. I would always make my way as soon as I could though as the delight of holding a new grandchild no matter whether of a son or daughter was always joyful.

The announcement of my daughter's children also brought relief that I would not feel when one of my son's wives was in labour. To hear of the safe arrival of my daughters' children would also mean I would hear of the health of my daughter. No matter my desire to continue my family lineage I would never wish to lose one of my daughters in doing so. I was fully aware that I had been blessed that my own wives had survived all of their labours and this was also noted as another of my acknowledgements from the Gods. The day Nefertiry delivered her first child I prayed silently all day that the God's blessings would continue on to my daughters. When I was finally told that she and her child were okay I took my first deep breath since her labour began. This is how it would be for each of my daughters' labours.

Visiting the birthing room after Nefertiry had given birth was a very new experience. Walking into the room to see my daughter lying within the bed, respectfully covered and ready to greet me was uncomfortable for both of us. The moment each of my daughters married and shared their bed with their husbands I had to respect them in the way that I would any woman married to another man. I no longer visited them for a goodnight kiss as they began to doze in their beds, nor did I invite them to sit on my knee. Such intimacies were now reserved for their husbands. So while part of me loved to be so close to Nefertiry once again I was glad for the distraction of my new little granddaughter to dispel the uneasiness the scene also brought.

This was a scenario I would soon get used to with six fertile daughters, not to mention my sons' abilities to father children as well. Each year saw at least one pregnancy at the palace and one year we even had five new children arrive within months of each other. Each time a daughter went into labour I would pray for my daughter's safety as much if not more than the child's. I would spend the day suffering with more nerves than their husbands did. Each time one of the girls gave birth her mother would be by her side to comfort, coach and reassure them. Satiah would rub muscles between contractions for Beketamun and Nefertiry while she recounted stories from their births or their brothers. Matreya would pace the room for her daughters ensuring all was being enacted as was proper for a princess giving birth, barking orders at servants. If any of her daughters should begin to whine at the pain or fatigue she would remind them that she had endured this six times! She never mentioned how atrociously she had acted during Amenhotep's birth though.

Their mother's presence was a comfort not only to my daughters but also to me. I was most grateful that I had someone present who could monitor everything. Not that I didn't trust the staff assigned to this duty but it was nice to have someone there to care for my daughters as much as I would if it were my place to be present. My wives would also recount a more casual report after that of the birth priestess. I would hear details of my grandchildren's first moments that only a grandmother would notice or care to recount.

The day that Nefertiry delivered her third child I was more grateful than ever that Satiah should choose to be with her. Nefertiry went into labour in the very early hours of the morning. It was still dark when a maid slipped into my bedchamber to summon Satiah who was sleeping in my bed that night. I roused from my sleep just enough to realise what was happening and then returned to sleep, hoping that upon awakening I would hear news of the child's arrival. However when I woke the next morning I was greeted with only news that the labour was still continuing. Nefertiry had not proven to be a quick birther before so I did not become any more anxious than I would normally. However, when it was once again dark I did begin to worry.

I was just finishing my dinner when Bet-Ankh was announced at my private rooms. I quickly moved to a more suitable chair to receive her news. When the priestess entered the room she did not walk with the usual poise that she did regardless of the length of the labour or her own fatigue. Her face too was pale and I saw her wring her hands as she had that day she arrived to attend to young Thutmose. My heart sank, as I knew that my new grandchild had not arrived safe and healthy.

My instincts were wrong, as my new grandson had arrived safe and vigorous. It was my beloved Nefertiry that was no more. Her torn birth passage spilled her blood so quickly that nothing of our times would save her. The midwives and priestess did all they could. As the midwives tried to staunch the flow Bet-Ankh conjured the Gods with all her heart. Satiah grabbed Nefertiry's hand and begged her to live as our daughter gasped her last breaths. My only consolation was that she was gone quickly and did not suffer any longer than she needed to. I can say that gives me consolation now but as I sat there and heard the priestess tell me that my daughter was gone nothing could stop the explosion that I felt inside me.

I did not go to the birthing room to visit my daughter one last time before she was taken to the mortuary. I could not bear to see her beauty washed grey with death. So I remained within my chambers, still and silent as servants moved around me in awkward silence. The priestess left and with her gone I could almost believe that our conversation had not happened. Soon though the news moved through the palace and I heard the wails and cries of my remaining daughters as they too heard the news of their sister's passing. I closed my eyes and clenched my fists and for a moment closed out everything.

I was soon shocked back to reality as the doors to my rooms burst open and I looked up to see Isis standing in the doorway. Tears streamed down her face and she ran to me. "Father," she cried, and threw her arms around my neck. "It is not fair, she should not have died."

"I know, Isis, I know," was all I could answer.

Satiah had to be carried back to her room by a guard and physicians were called upon to treat her. Satiah had watched a son slip from life before her and now she had watched a daughter take her last breath also. The heaviness of grief weighed upon her like never before. It had been almost seven years since Amenemhat had passed and while Satiah mourned him every day she had never let her grief engulf her. Now though with the loss of her second child every hurt of losing Amenemhat resurfaced and multiplied. She would not leave her bed for almost two weeks after Nefertiry's death and when she did finally walk the palace corridors again she was not the same woman.

Nefertiry's husband shared this debilitating grief. Any delight at having a son after two daughters was not to be experienced for him. In fact he could barely look at the child whose birth had robbed him of his wife. Despite the ample support he had to raise his three children he was overwhelmed to do so without Nefertiry by his side. He would occupy the first two months after losing his wife by spending his days and most nights painting her tomb himself. He took her paintings and copied them upon the walls. In-between them he would write the story of their marriage and he even brought himself to paint the story of her passing. He painted his son as being held by Hathor to protect him while Osiris stood over Nefertiry taking her to the afterworld.

He was so consumed by his work that often he would simply sleep there and begin again upon waking. A fellow scribe had to persuade him to finally leave and prepare for Nefertiry's funeral. He had spent so long in just lamplight that when he emerged into the bright Egyptian sunlight he could not see for several minutes and had to ride upon a cart back to the palace with a cloth over his head. He had grown frail not only physically but in his spirit as well. His eldest daughter walked to him and he didn't recognise her. When asked if he might like to see how his son was flourishing he even answered, "What son?" He was allowed his grief, and we accommodated his behaviour as best we could in hope that the passing of the funeral might help to heal him.

As for myself, my grief far from paralysed me. All the anger that followed Amenemhat's death that I had allowed to weaken with the passage of time came back with all the might that it could. I did not sit in a stupor beyond the day of Nefertiry's death as I had when my son died. This time I paced the palace and courts barking orders for her funeral, demanding the physicians create new concoctions for Satiah's malaise and calling for every ritual of the temple to be performed. My remaining children, Matreya and my mother came with me to Karnak each day to perform the rites for Nefertiry. Then I would ask that we pray to Isis to protect my remaining daughters. We would continue on with prayers for Satiah, prayers for Nefertiry's children and then prayers for our family in general.

The priests at Karnak spent their nights revisiting their scrolls for rituals and prayers that had not been performed in years and even generations. They did this to find any possible rite that they could that might satisfy what seemed to be my insatiable quest to cover every possibility of protecting my family. We did this for six weeks after Nefertiry's death and I was so consumed that I did not see the toll it was taking upon my family. One day as we rode back to the palace I heard a shriek from Meryt in the carriage following my chariot. I stopped and in the middle of Thebes with commoners flowing by I raced to my daughters' carriage to see Meritamen collapsed. In the first flush of her first pregnancy she had fainted from exhaustion after six hours of prayers amid the clouds of incense. We hurried back to the palace and after some rest and a tonic she thankfully was fine.

I lessened my family's involvement in my eagerness to protect us all but my priests continued on with their duties as directed by me. This eased the atmosphere at the palace but that at the Great Temple remained heavy. Talk began amongst the priests as to my state of mind as they grew weary of the continual chore of pacifying my suddenly heightened fears for my family. Arisina, now frailer than ever, felt the heaviness of this time more than most. She found it harder each day to attend to prayer sessions but she continued to do so through her love for me. As she attended me though during these sessions, she sensed something within me that all others missed. She waited hoping that I would come to her to seek counsel but I did not. I hardly could form the words to share what was in my mind.

It was only days before Nefertiry's funeral that Arisina decided she would approach me. Old age had provided her with a sudden lack of fear in approaching me. Not that she should ever have had any fear to speak with me; such was the closeness of our relationship. However there was always the measured respect that a Pharaoh must be approached with and this respect had increased as I grew older. Addressing the Pharaoh as a man was very different to addressing the Pharaoh as a child. Arisina no longer had any fear of losing my favour or her position. She knew her time in the living world was fast coming to an end and was happy to live these last days in whatever way presented. So one day as the prayers drew to a close and I lifted my head acknowledging that my prayers were complete, Arisina ordered that all other priests should leave as she had a private message from Amun for me. My guards looked to me and I nodded my consent. Within moments I was alone with my beloved priestess.

"What is this message that you received?" I asked now curious.

"Thutmose I have no message from Amun," she began, "I know it is the only way to truly speak to you alone."

I felt a slight betrayal at her deceit but I knew that she would never use such a ploy in any way unless it was to help me. I asked her to continue.

"My beloved King, I doubt there is anyone apart from your mother or wives who knows you better than I do," she said. "For almost two months now I have received you at temple but the face you arrive with here is not that of the man I have helped nurture and guide. Instead of wisdom and courage I see fear and hatred. Within the depths of your grief I have looked for the strength you have shown since you were a child and I cannot sense it. I fear if we do not call it back soon it will be lost forever."

I looked at my priestess and began to shake my head. She knew me better than my mother or my wives. She had described every aspect of emotion within me. I had become prey to my anger and hatred just as she had advised me upon my father's death not to. However now after losing two children my spirit was lost to these parts of me. Each day I prayed more, hoping for them to lift yet I only buried myself within them more as I sought some passage from their darkness. I finally spoke what I believed to the priestess.

"She did this," I spat through a clenched jaw.

"Who Thutmose?" she asked concerned.

"Hatshepsut!" I yelled, my face red and tears beginning to fall down my face.

Arisina leant forward. "Your dead aunt?" she asked.

"Yes! Who else could unleash such evil upon me in this way?" I continued to raise my voice. "She was not satisfied to take my heir--now she sends her demons to rob me of a daughter. How clever she was to make sure that both were from my most beloved wife. My daughters now fear to have children. My enemies can delight in my loss. No matter the riches I possess, the lands I rule or how wise I am I cannot stop death so she chooses this way to hurt us all."

Arisina nodded gently as she heard my words. She had experienced Hatshepsut's wrath and tactics firsthand. She too knew it was possible as much as she did not want to think this. The priestess had waited since the beginning of my regency for the day that I might forget my balance and seek revenge but she had always imagined it would have happened whilst Hatshepsut was alive.

"Thutmose, do you ever wonder why the Gods have favoured your rule?" she now asked.

"You will now say that it is because of my patience and dedication to my people," I answered almost sarcastically.

"I know that you wonder what things would be like if you had overthrown Hatshepsut while she was alive," she continued calmly, "but I also know that your heart recognises the reward of your actions as they actually did occur. I do not wish to make light of the loss of your children, Thutmose. Only you can know the pain that is within you. Can I ask the man before me to once again look to his inner wisdom as I did to the child so many years ago?"

"That naïve child is long gone Arisina," I answered.

"Oh yes, I know," she said without flinching. "I now sit before a noble warrior who has conquered more lands than any other, who has built taller temples than any other and who fills the palace with more family than any other. When you look into your mirror, who do you see Thutmose? Is it that warrior or a man broken by loss?"

Arisina delivered these words sharply to me. She locked her eyes upon me as though she demanded a reply. As she did so I felt an inner turmoil. The voices of my conflict rose up within me fighting for attention. I heard them calling out and overlapping each other. The confusion was almost overwhelming. I buried my head within my hands as though that might help stop them.

Arisina remained still and calm but when I lowered my head she stepped towards me and gathered my chin in her hand. She lifted my head so that once again my eyes were locked to hers as she stood over me.

"Thutmose, I won't be here much longer to guide you like this. So I will ask you one last time. Do you choose to live a life consumed in anger and hate or will you remember your courage and wisdom?" she asked me again and more forcibly than ever before.

I gave her the answer she wanted to hear. I chose my courage and wisdom however it was not so easy a choice this time. Arisina nodded gratefully.

"Thutmose, the most efficient fuel for evil is simply more evil. Be careful how you choose to act upon any anger now or in the future," she said.

I made my way back to the palace where I went directly to my chambers and slept for fourteen hours straight--something I had never done in my entire life. My servants did not panic as they knew of the exhaustion of grief. They also knew too that I had received private counsel with the high priestess delivering a message from Amun. It was no wonder that I would need such rest with this combination of events. I awoke groggy from so much sleep but my mind was lighter. The darkness that had weighed upon me had lifted but I will be honest and say there was a corner in my thoughts where it still sat, watching how I was reacting.

It was now the day of Nefertiry's funeral and my swirl of thoughts would now be pushed aside to deal with the ceremonies of the day and one of the hardest performances of my life. Satiah was by my side, with her eyes cast down and tears flowing freely from them. My daughters and even Matreya joined her in crying while my sons followed my stoic example. The exhausted priests and priestesses performed majestically at the altar of Karnak but all the grace in the world could not alleviate the pain of seeing Nefertiry's body bound and sitting within her gold coffin before us. With the prayers over eight priests stepped forward carrying the lid of the outermost gold casket, chanting as they lifted it into place and sealed her mummy within. Nefertiry was another step away from us and I know that each of us in our way sighed, took a sharp breath or sobbed again as we heard the sound of the lid resting against its base.

With the temple rites over we now made our way to the convoy of carriages and carts to begin Nefertiry's final journey. My loyal commoners lined the street as we made our way, wiping their own tears and shouting out prayers for her and for me. Some followed us to the edge of the Nile to watch as Nefertiry was lifted upon the funeral boat and it began to slide across the water.

As we entered the burial valley and Hatshepsut's temple greeted us as it did anyone entering the Valley, the anger I felt the day of Amenemhat's funeral did not have its embers fanned as I imagined it would. Instead a steady calm washed over me. I did not see a monument built by a woman consumed by power and control. I saw her pathetic attempt to make herself something that she would never truly be. Her grief in life may never match mine but her triumphs most certainly never would. It was all I could do to not smile as I continued on in my daughter's funeral procession.

My moment of gloating was soon ended as we arrived at Nefertiry's tomb and began her final rites and our final goodbyes. Glorious treasures including enough blank papyrus and colours for her to paint for decades surrounded her sarcophagus and her sisters scattered flowers throughout her tomb as their final gift. Their scent would follow us through the corridors as we made our way back out to the sunlight. Each of us would smell them again in the following weeks. We would be sitting quietly and alone and the scent would waft near us while not a flower was in sight. We knew it was Nefertiry saying a gentle hello but we were also grateful when after a few weeks we no longer felt this, as we knew she had made her way through to paradise.

The slight relief that is felt at the end of the funeral period though was short lived. The very next morning Nefertiry's husband was found hanging from the frame surrounding his bed. He had twisted one of the curtains that surrounded the bed into a rope and artfully applied it around his neck snapping his vertebrae when he slumped into unconsciousness as the blood flow to his brain slowed. There was no question of foul play, as all knew his intense grief. The distraction of preparing Nefertiry's tomb now over, he had returned to the palace after the funeral completely bereft. Lying within his marriage bed without her by his side was the final test that he simply could not endure. In the small hours of morning, when all was quiet and still, he sought his escape from the pain.

A servant was the first to find him and despite her horror at finding a dead body she also immediately saw the cause and acted with utmost discretion just as I would have directed her. For you see suicide in our time was seen as an evil equivalent to murder--for it was indeed murder of the self. It was an affront to the laws of nature and therefore an immense disrespect to the Gods. The perpetrator was doomed to the darkness of the afterworld as they left with a heart heavier than any truth the Gods could offer for salvation. They also brought disgrace to their past existence and any family remaining. This last point was the first thought that entered the servant's mind and her loyalty to my family would override any horror of dealing with a dead body.

She quickly summoned another servant and together they unwound the curtain and dragged the body back upon the bed so no one else could see the state in which it was found. Then she made her way to my chambers and summoned my butler and discreetly shared the truth of the cause of death. My butler nodded and sent her back to the bedchamber to watch over the body while he made his way to summon the priests that he knew he could trust to deal with such a matter. One hour later Tati and two priests entered the bedchamber to witness the body and begin the preparations. All in all only five people within the palace would see his body with the head sitting awkwardly upon its broken neck, a collar of purple and red bruising where the fabric had crushed his life away. The priests rushed the body away to the mortuary before anyone could become aware and when the cart left the palace anyone seeing it assumed that it was an anonymous servant who had met their demise.

I was sitting in my beloved garden that morning when my butler and the priests appeared at the doorway that led from my chambers looking even more serious than usual. They rushed into the garden, bowing and apologising for their disturbance.

"Sire," the first priest began, "I have some disturbing news. If only it was not so soon after your recent loss!'

I sat upright, not even capable of imagining what could possibly have occurred as the priests relayed my son-in-law's death.

"Such a sudden and unexpected death Sire--and so soon after that of his wife, the Princess. We can only imagine that his intense grief allowed something quite powerful to enter his body in such way," he offered. "We hope that it pleases you that we rushed the body from the palace lest this illness enter any other members of your family while they too are deep in grief."

He finished with a bow, as did the other priest, as they sought my approval.

"You did as I would have myself commanded. I thank you for your concern and adeptness in dealing with this," I replied.

The priests once again bowed in gratitude and letting them believe that I accepted their explanation for his death I dismissed them to continue on with their duties. Tati remained by my side and once the priests were gone I turned to him. "How did he do it?" I said simply.

"Hanged by a curtain on his bed, Sire," he answered dryly and not at all surprised that I had seen through the priests' story.

I shook my head. "How many people know?" I asked.

"Myself, just the two priests and the two servants who found him. All have pledged their discretion Sire," he answered again.

"Ensure that it remains so," I said.

While we went back into mourning it was not the grand or involved affair that had been enacted for either of my children's passing. He was not of my blood and his own son was far from a successor so he did not command such treatment. It all passed as simply as possible and while I understood his grief I could not understand his lack of respect for his own life and his family that would allow him to have done such a deed. I was actually grateful that someone so weak was now removed from my family and could no longer influence the grandchildren of mine that he had fathered. Their aunts and uncles would raise them now and much better than he obviously could have.

What pained me the most though was thinking of Nefertiry. I had no doubt she would make her way through the afterworld, and now would never be joined by her beloved. She was now destined to paint alone. For this I vowed never to forgive him. He was doomed already by his choice of passage and yet I wished it would be as difficult as possible. His body was placed by Nefertiry's side within her tomb so that in some way they would always be together. It also helped hide the circumstances of his demise, which many had guessed despite the official story. Their tomb remains one of the many that are undiscovered and untouched, so in a way they are still together.

There was one thing that I would thank him for. Within displaying his weakness in the face of grief he had shown me my strength. Despite my anger and heartbreak I could never act so. I could now look back into my mirror and truly see the warrior and leader that Arisina described. The scribe's weakness called back my strength more powerfully than ever.

CHAPTER TWENTY-TWO

I was now in my forties and had been a Pharaoh for just over thirty years -- more than three-quarters of my life. The sands of time flowed. Things slowly shifted, with changes so small that I hardly noticed and then suddenly it was all different. The people who had surrounded me in court and temple when I became Pharaoh with Hatshepsut were all but gone, replaced with a new generation of courtiers and priests, all chosen by me and loyal to me. The last of Hatshepsut's people, the priestess Ma-Keet, died soon after Nefertiry and her passing turned a corner for my time as Pharaoh. The last living shadow of my aunt was gone and the timing of her passing so close to that of Nefertiry helped me to believe that Hatshepsut had hopefully lost her last human grip upon my family.

It was with some irony that Ma-Keet and Arisina should be the only surviving members of the priesthood or palace who were in place during Hatshepsut's time. These two women had been our greatest confidants and guides, outliving men who had been more powerful and influential, while they had remained quietly serving us with grace and discretion. Of course Ma-Keet did not work close with me, not even after Hatshepsut's death, yet she had remained at Karnak and continued in general service to the palace. While she never was fully aware of just how she had shaped our history she was aware of how she had affected the lives of those around her and this grew as her final years came to be.

Arisina and Ma-Keet were now into the sixth decades of their lives which was a very long life for anyone in our times to have lived to. They were the oldest priests now at Karnak, highly respected not only for their longevity but also for the services to the palace that they had conducted during their lives. Between them they had overseen births of Pharaohs, conducted naming ceremonies, royal marriages and funeral rites. No other priests had experienced as much as these women and they were treasured as much as any statue or scroll that was within Karnak.

As they grew older young scribes sat with them for hours as they spoke of their experiences and what they had learnt, recording their invaluable words. Ma-Keet revelled in her sharing, embellishing her stories and making her time at the palace as grand as any novice in the priesthood would imagine it to be. Arisina though would keep her stories simple and as short as possible. A scribe who had been working with both women was quite amused at how differently they were approaching this honour.

"High Priestess, you seem to have some reluctance in sharing your life story," he observed with a smile one day.

"My reluctance, young scribe, is in knowing that simple marks upon a scroll will never truly share what I have experienced," she replied.

"But cannot the words at least open the opportunity in some way for the reader to imagine beyond the words?" he pushed.

Arisina laughed outright. "And that my dear is my whole point. Why waste time reading another's story when you have the imagination and skills to create your own."

"Yes, but did you not learn from your elders' experience in order to create your own story?" he continued.

Arisina nodded contemplatively as she recalled her very own teachers. It had truly not occurred to her that her story could in any way teach others as she herself had been taught. It was all so long ago that she had recited prayers as she went to sleep in order to remember the words, or watched every hand movement of an old priestess as she lit and fanned incense, trying to memorize every aspect, so that she too would serve and honour the Gods with as much skill as possible. Every last detail of her work now was so second nature and immediate that she actually had forgotten that she too was once a student. Now a young scribe sat before her wide-eyed, wanting to soak up her knowledge just as she had from her elders all those years before and she was bemused at his dedication and interest in her. The priestess just wanted to sigh as suddenly she was overcome with just how full her years had been and how quickly they had passed.

"One day you will sit here and be sharing your story, young scribe," she said, sitting straighter in her chair. "What would you wish to share with the priesthood?"

The scribe stopped and looked away for a moment. He turned back and smiled. "That I should have served as best I could, that my records are complete and correct, that each scroll has been attended to with care to help those who will come and honour those that have been."

Arisina nodded. "There is not much more that a scribe could ask for."

"Was your life as a priestess how you imagined it to be?" he continued.

Arisina laughed again and this time she shook her head. "My young scribe, lives sometimes have a way of creating themselves beyond the boundaries of what we imagine for them. My time as priestess has been a grand example of that. Now put down your quill and move away from your writing desk and I will share with you a story that can never be contained within a scroll."

With that Arisina shared the story of her life with me and how it had shaped my time as Pharaoh and the history of Egypt. This was not a narrative to be struck upon a scroll or found within history books. This Arisina knew well, for this account of her and I was beyond politics, religion and official record keeping. It was not a story that should be lost either, so with an enraptured scribe before her she re-told my story from my birth to becoming ruler and warrior, from child to husband and father. She told of the guidance she had given and how I had received it.

The scribe nodded as she spoke, taking in so much more than words. He too knew this was far too valuable to be lost and the scribe would share it again and again as he grew older, passing on Arisina's wisdom more powerfully than if it had been read upon a scroll. The listeners in turn would repeat the story, and it continued being told well into the times of my great-grandchildren. The story would soon be considered mere legend as it travelled the words and the details would change but the truth and love it carried with it would never be altered.

Ma-Keet's story was told and recorded also upon scrolls as was the tradition. Each roll of papyrus contained the "correct" re-telling of history to confirm that already told by Senemut and others who worked with Hatshepsut. There were the flourishes to make it all the more dramatic and the scribe could not help but smile as he compared Arisina's modesty to Ma-Keet's embellishments. He sat cross-legged before his low table fanning the very last scroll he had recorded with Ma-Keet, trying to aid the ink in drying so that he might roll it up and finally end these boring sessions with her. He looked upon the marks he had made, quickly checking for any errors to correct as it dried, when he recalled the story that Arisina had shared with him.

"High Priestess, while the ink dries perhaps you would entertain me with a story of your time in the palace," he asked curiously. Perhaps she too had something less formal to share and hopefully more entertaining than anything he had recorded.

"Scribe, I have shared with you all that you need of my time in service," she answered dryly.

"I was hoping that maybe you could offer a more personal story of your time with Hatshepsut. Perhaps something amusing that could prove a tender anecdote to provoke her memory," he continued.

Ma-Keet's scowl was answer enough. He may as well have searched for some water in the desert sands.

"Do you seek gossip, Scribe?" she snapped.

"No, Priestess!" he fumbled. "It's just that I was hoping that perhaps you had a fond memory of your time so close to the Queen. Something that is a bit less formal."

"I have no such *stories* to tell you about my mistress *the Pharaoh*," she corrected. "All that is needed to be shared with the priesthood has been relayed to you as required. I bid you farewell scribe," she finished bluntly.

Ma-Keet stood as quickly as her now frail legs would permit her and left the room with a flourish of her robes to give her exit the dramatic touch that her aging frame would not allow. She stomped her way back to her private rooms, her brow furrowed as she reflected on the audacity of the scribe to forget his place and attempt to trivialise her records with some irrelevant anecdote. She reached her room and brushed her maid away as the young girl approached to see what she needed. Ma-Keet went to her bed and lay down, her chest heaving as much from her anger as the strain of the short walk back to her room.

Her hip burned with pain as her breath slowed and her mind began to search back through the years to the time she spent with Hatshepsut. She recalled the pride and fear of being appointed by the temple to attend to her as queen. Despite being only a few years younger, Hatshepsut had always seemed so much older so that Ma-Keet had never been the teacher or guide that Arisina was to me. Hatshepsut instead had a personal assistant: someone to conjure prayers as she desired, to carry messages to her favoured courtiers or to help a lover make his way through the palace corridors unnoticed. None of these were stories or duties that Ma-Keet wished to reveal to anyone.

There was of course all that had occurred when Ma-Keet had unwittingly helped put in place the events that would lead Hatshepsut to being crowned a Pharaoh. As Ma-Keet recalled that day when she stood and watched Hatshepsut beat Neferure and then held the queen as she cried afterwards, a tear fell from the corner of her eye and curved around her cheek. It had been so long since she had thought of that moment. She had worked so hard to forget it all this time and now just when she least expected it was back, calling for one last round of her attention.

"Damn that scribe to the crocodiles!" she thought. If he hadn't pried, if he had kept to his duty, this could have stayed deep in the dark recesses of her forgotten memories. However, now it was back and she wondered why it haunted her more than ever to once again picture this incident. Her heart even began to race and her stomach twisted just as it did that day as she relived the anguish she shared with mother and daughter. Ma-Keet knew why this moment cut her as sharp as it did the day it happened. She knew this was why she had pushed this memory aside as soon as she could. For this remembrance was the key to so much. It was the moment she truly fell prey to the darkness of Hatshepsut's heart.

Ma-Keet recalled the day at fourteen years of age that she had left home to begin her training at Karnak. It was the noblest day of her simple family's life for a daughter had been chosen to serve at the Great Temple. One day she may even guide and serve a pharaoh or queen and this she did. She thought of her mother's tears as the carriage arrived to take her to Karnak. Ma-Keet was about to climb aboard to leave and she turned to kiss her parents and sisters one last time.

Her father grabbed her face between his hands and kissed her forehead roughly. "My daughter, never forget the grandeur of being chosen to serve as you have been. Don't ever forsake this honour for your family--but most of all for yourself," he said strongly, squeezing her face as though to emphasise his words.

Ma-Keet nodded through tears making her vow to her father and then climbed aboard the carriage to begin her new life. It would be four more years until she was chosen to attend Hatshepsut and she spent those as virtuous and servile as she promised her father and herself. Life in the palace with Hatshepsut though would change all that. Ma-Keet's position as a priestess was indeed nothing as she had imagined it would be, and as she thought about how it began, another tear curved around her cheek to fall upon the sheet as she lay there. She could not leave this existence with this heaviness in her heart, as she would fail the tests of the afterlife and never reach paradise. There was only one person who could help her cleanse her soul in readiness to leave the earthly realm.

The next morning when Ma-Keet woke she bathed, dressed and ate as she always did. Then she sent her maid to find out where Arisina was. Arisina was walking back from the dawn rites at the grand lake when the maid found her and asked that she might find time to visit with Ma-Keet. Of course this piqued Arisina's curiosity. They may be the two eldest serving priestesses but this was all they held in common these days. The silent divide set in place during the co-regency lingered on, and though the division was no longer needed amongst the priesthood, the old energy of those days was somewhat hard to shake for either woman. There was no bitterness though, and Arisina nodded and told the maid she would visit after her morning meal.

Arisina was just finishing her last piece of fruit when her own maid appeared and announced that Ma-Keet was in fact at her door. Ma-Keet shuffled in, adding the occasional grunt as her left hip ached as she walked.

"Sister, I did say I would come to you," Arisina said. "Did your maid not tell you? You could have saved yourself some pain."

"Pah! You are in just as much pain as I am!" she snapped in response. "You just hide it better."

Arisina gestured to some lounges and soon the two women were settled into their places facing each other.

"Arisina, it is much more appropriate that I should come to you, for today I seek your help and guidance," Ma-Keet began. Arisina's eyebrows lifted and Ma-Keet continued, "Oh yes, I see you now are wondering what it is you can help me with, and now that I am here sitting in front of you I can barely find the words to begin."

Ma-Keet stopped and looked down. Her aged hands rested in her lap and she lifted them up, looking at them and turning them before her. "Arisina, do you sometimes see parts of yourself and wonder how they suddenly changed so much?" she asked.

"Most days Sister, and when I don't see how my body has changed then it sends me pain to remind me," Arisina said, and wanted to laugh but she knew not to.

"See this mark here," Ma-Keet pointed to a dark line across the base of her left thumb, "I burnt myself with hot oil from a lamp during the very first ceremony I conducted at Karnak. It ached and ached as I finished the prayers and it seemed forever until I could get to my room and put cool water upon it. One of the elder priests saw me burn myself and later he found me to check upon it. As he held my hand he said to me that I would scar and this would be a good thing. It would be with me forever to remind me of my error and to help me be more vigilant. The burn ached for over a week and eventually the pain stopped. The priest was right, it did scar and I would look at the mark often and think of his words." Ma-Keet stopped for a moment and gently touched the mark on her hand. "It has faded with time but it holds on." Ma-Keet now looked up at Arisina. "My sister, I fear there are scars within me that will not fade and if I carry their mark with me to the afterlife then I am doomed."

Tears fell down Ma-Keet's face and Arisina leaned forward waiting for her to continue.

"You are the only one alive who will understand my pain, and Sister, you are the only one who can help me cleanse my soul. I just ask that you listen to my words without interruption and then I will receive any judgements and guidance that you will see fit to bestow upon me." That being said, Ma-Keet truly began.

Ma-Keet spoke of the deceptions and games she had helped Hatshepsut play. Then, after a very deep breath, she spoke of the day in Hatshepsut's chambers where the most serious of collusions began. Arisina sat, not entirely surprised by the general confessions Ma-Keet made. She had been present in the palace and there was enough talk amongst servants for much of Ma-Keet's divulgence to have become common knowledge. However as Ma-Keet told of how she helped begin Hatshepsut's coronation as Pharaoh, Arisina's eyes grew wide in shock. As she had promised though, she remained silent.

Ma-Keet was soon finished and sat waiting for Arisina to speak. It was Arisina who now could not find the words to begin and she opened her mouth several times only to close it again. Ma-Keet was ready for anything that she may receive now: abuse or anger, maybe even being hit. This was not Arisina's way though. The anger that she had shown that day at the temple meeting when Senemut announced that Hatshepsut would become Pharaoh was long gone. She nodded her head and her face softened as she turned to Ma-Keet.

"It is nor I nor any prayer that will heal your heart, Ma-Keet," Arisina said. "There is only one way that this can be done. You must speak these words to Pharaoh."

Ma-Keet nodded, accepting her guidance as she had promised she would. She too knew that in order to clear her conscience she would need to make amends with the person she had affected the most. An instinctive fear though crept in beneath this, as she knew now that to face a Pharaoh with such a confession would surely mean her execution. Even worse yet, I could order her banishment from the temple onto the streets of Thebes where she would perish homeless and destitute, ending her life as a beggar. Ma-Keet knew that whatever trial she would endure following her admission would be one less trial that she would face as she journeyed the afterlife, and despite her fears she could accept whatever lay ahead.

The very next day I received the two women in my private courtroom as Arisina requested, without the usual viziers and scribes floating around as in the public court. I smiled as they entered; imagining Arisina was here to check on me after my daughter's death to ensure I was holding true to my agreement from that day in temple. The addition of Ma-Keet I imagined was merely to make this a formal event. As they walked in though I knew this meeting was something very different. For a start, Arisina was not smiling as she always was when she greeted me. Ma-Keet, who had always been the epitome of priestly poise and confidence walked with her eyes down and her shoulders slumped. My smile dropped off my face as they stopped, bowed and sat down in the chairs before me.

"Good day to you both," I said warmly. "What honour to have our two grandest priestesses before me."

Both women nodded their head in acknowledgement.

"It is our honour Pharaoh," replied Ma-Keet.

I nodded and smiled once more. Never had any of Hatshepsut's priests spoken with such reverence to me, not even since her death. Such a comment from me would normally have been met with a blank stare. I sat back in my chair, relaxed and asked that I might now know what brought them both to me in private audience.

Ma-Keet looked to Arisina and then dropped her head down again. Once again she was paralysed at having to begin her story. Arisina knew this and she chose to begin, "Pharaoh, it is Ma-Keet who wishes to address you today. She comes to you to speak of some pain in the hope you may help her find some healing and forgiveness. I trust that you can listen with the wisdom and compassion that I know you possess," she said softly.

I nodded and agreed as I always did when Arisina asked something of me. Then Ma-Keet, though she fumbled over some words, slowly revealed to me the truth of how I was held from my sole rule for so long. Each detail of the story should have shocked me but it didn't. It all made perfect sense to me as I sat here at this age and thought back to the series of events. How clever my aunt had been in creating all that she wanted. She had surrounded herself with loyal but weak people, also consumed with their own ambitions, who were more than ready to be her pawns. Before me sat the last one, the one who had helped this all begin. Part of me wanted to step forward and strike her but I could not do this. The woman before me was frail and weak, literally begging for her forgiveness and here I sat in my grandeur, the only one who could grant it.

Questions swirled in my mind. *"If I forgive her do I truly allow her passage through the afterlife? If I forgive her do I release the last of Hatshepsut's presence in my life or do I make it stronger?"* I did not hear any answers. All I could do was look back at the feeble woman in front of me and I remembered Hatshepsut on her deathbed.

"My dear women, so many times through the years I have wondered how my life would have been had I ruled without my aunt. As my dear Arisina reminds me, my life has been grand regardless--or possibly even because of this," I began, "Ma-Keet, I cannot sit here and now pass any judgement upon you for your part in what happened nor can I offer you forgiveness. That is for the Gods to do and decide. What I do know is that the strength and bravery that you acted with in coming here to seek resolution makes your words heard through the heavens where they are needed."

Arisina nodded and smiled as I spoke. She had taught me well as I spoke the very words that she hoped I would. I returned her smile and leant forward in my chair, resting my elbows on my knees, "Ma-Keet, I have no doubt that your heart will not outweigh the feather when you stand before Ma'at. You are the only person to have sought me out to speak of such things and for that I thank you. Your heart can now be healed, and my mind can now rest, as the truth has been spoken. Your courage has blessed us both today."

My words were met with tears and Ma-Keet stepped from her chair and fell to her knees before me, thanking me for my mercy and wisdom. I hated such displays and made her get up, which unfortunately took some time as well as assistance from some servants. She was soon back seated upon her chair and I knew the meeting should end.

"Go and rest now Ma-Keet, then perhaps you and Arisina might offer some prayers for the completion of this," I said.

"Yes, Sire," Ma-Keet responded, and then both women sat still not making any gesture to leave.

"You may both go now," I said, thinking they waited for a more formal dismissal.

"Is this all you require of me, Sire?" Ma-Keet asked.

"Why yes," I answered and turned to Arisina. "Should I ask for anything else?"

Arisina looked to me and bit her lip, then looked at Ma-Keet. Suddenly I realised what they were waiting for and I couldn't help but throw my head back and laugh.

"No, my dear Ma-Keet, I have no other orders for you. I do believe that serving so close to my aunt was surely more than enough punishment or suffering for anyone in one lifetime. Go, live your final years free of that woman. That is my only other order for you today."

Both of them smiled at me, bowed and then left the room. I almost believe that Ma-Keet walked a bit lighter and quicker as she left. I called for a servant to bring me a glass of wine and laughed to myself a little more as I thought of how poor Ma-Keet might have envisioned me punishing her. What would I have done? Had her executed and robbed her of three, possibly five more years of her pain riddled old age? Had her thrown out of the priesthood despite all the wonderful service and teaching she had done? I was thankful for the momentary distraction from the truth of what had just been uncovered but as my wine arrived and I took my first sip I once again turned my thoughts to Hatshepsut and how her presence continued to make itself known in my life.

The meeting with Ma-Keet had done so much more than I imagined. Her heart now lightened and her fear of the afterlife finally quelled, she rapidly moved closer to leaving. The speed at which it happened even startled her as she suddenly lost the last vestiges of her strength and was soon bedridden. Not that she was in much pain, nor did she seem to contract any illness--she simply just could not summon any physical strength. She was well attended to of course and Arisina sat with her each day for company. Arisina was not surprised at Ma-Keet's decline as she had attended births in which the child seemed to delay their arrival, as though not ready to experience life. In much the same way she had seen people endure life, not ready to experience death. As Ma-Keet lay before her she had no doubt as to how ready she was to leave.

There would be no deathbed confessions as Ma-Keet had said all she needed or should have before her final days. She would not need potions or have incense burnt while a team of priests stood over her as she struggled for her last breath. She sat up each day and spoke clearly to whoever attended her or visited. Her final words were, "I'd like some water." By the time the maid poured the water and turned back to the priestess, Ma-Keet was gone and the maid stood dumbstruck with the cup in her hand. The last of Hatshepsut's people had left with all the simplicity and selflessness that my aunt had never possessed.

Ma-Keet left six months after Nefertiry and her husband--yet it seemed to happen within days. The Great Temple at Karnak fell into the mourning that was only offered for a long serving high priest or priestess. No bright colours were worn through the different sects as all wore simple white for the months while Ma-Keet's body was prepared. The priestesses covered themselves more discreetly and the men walked a bit slower as they made their way through the temple. Whispers were made as to what her final meeting with me had been about but none were correct. Most imagined she had requested a burial in the

Valley, an honour only afforded to royalty or those chosen by the Pharaoh. When her simple tomb was made within the mausoleum of the temple where all priests were placed this rumour was quashed. No one dared ask Arisina the truth of the matter and she would never offer anyone an explanation, staying true to her discrete conduct as always.

With each death of a priest or priestess within a temple there is a certain knowledge that things will change. This was ever so slight of course as this was still Egypt. It was more a sense of movement as the temple rearranged itself to a new formation. When Ma-Keet died though, there was not this same feeling in the temple. No one felt this more than Arisina did and it puzzled her. It was about a week after Ma-Keet's death, and Arisina made her way to her favourite place at the temple; the balcony overlooking the Nile. In the exact place that she stood and placed her hand on my heart she now stood still and looked out to the massive river. She closed her eyes, pulled her breath in deeply and called to Isis for insight.

All she heard from the Goddess was, *"Open your eyes"* and so she did.

Arisina looked out to the Nile and for a moment she was sure the waters had stopped but then the small waves and ripples made themselves known again and the boats flowed as they always did.

Then she heard Isis again, *"Look up."*

Arisina looked to the palm trees and grasses that lined the Nile. They stood still, not a frond swayed nor did a blade of grass move. Then suddenly they began to shiver and sway as a breeze made their way through them once again.

"Look higher," Isis called to the priestess.

Arisina now looked to the skies and saw a blue sky--empty and clear. To look upwards without the horizon edging it or clouds to break the blue it seemed eternal and limitless. Once again this stillness ended as clouds began to drift across this beautiful blue. They were at first white wisps, twirling as they made their way, pushing into each other and becoming bigger, then just as suddenly evaporating into the blue background. Then more clouds came in this time large, thick clumps that held their shape and cast shadows below them. They were purest white at first but then grey washed through them, they blocked more of the sun and their shadows grew heavier. On the river fisherman looked up and began to collect their lines and nets.

"There is a storm coming," thought Arisina.

"Indeed there is," replied Isis and with that she was gone.

Arisina stood a moment more, looking out to the river flowing and the trees swaying harder as the clouds carried even more of a breeze with them. The first drops of rain began to fall breaking the river surface with its dots and a rumble of thunder echoed through the sky. A drop landed on Arisina's face so strongly that she jumped as it pulled her out of her reverie. She smiled and put her hand out before her, watching the drops miss her hand to land on the ground below. Finally two drops landed in her palm within a second of each other. She closed her hand and made her way inside the temple where she sat and watched the rain from inside. It was just a short storm, enough to break the afternoon heat for a while, replenish the soil for the plants and wash the dust from the stones. The priestess watched it calmly and heard Isis one more time as the rain stopped. Arisina smiled as she felt the Goddess with her again.

"Even when there is stillness, there is much happening. A calm is merely the energies gathering to be felt more strongly afterwards."

These were the Goddess's final words for the day. Arisina thanked her heavenly mother and teacher for her words and then also thanked the river for its part in her lesson. She closed her eyes once again. All would be well as all was well.

# CHAPTER TWENTY-THREE

In my own life this calmness was felt as my duties, procedures, ceremony and consulting all continued on with routine precision. Routine is the only calm that political life and responsibility knows. Even the trials of dealing with Canaan were now mundane and predictable. We were so assured of quashing any uprising that the mere news that my army were on their way could settle any disturbance. Family life was subdued, with each family member acting as pleasant and co-operative as they could, almost as though Nefertiry's death had caused enough pain and they couldn't bear to be the one that would add to it. Even Meritamen and Meryt suddenly matured and walked the palace with the dignity young royal wives should.

It was the peace and stability I had always craved. This is how I had dreamt ruling life would be. Don't think I did not enjoy the battles and policy making, but I always endured them hoping that one day my prowess and dedication would lead to this stage of my life. Now here I was and most days I relished it, while on other days I would almost have wished for an excuse to climb on my chariot and lead my men to a bloody battle. It was two years of this calm and then the storm arrived to wash away the dust.

I was awoken one morning by my butler with the simple words "Sire, It is your mother…" He needn't have finished the sentence as I knew the rest. The look on his face told me before he started. My beautiful mother had left during the night, quickly and quietly. It was probably a stroke but no matter how her heart chose to stop beating it had been quick and without suffering. I made my way to her room to see her one last time before she began her journey to the mortuary. I entered the room expecting to be overcome by the grey and waxiness of her dead skin but this time it was different. She looked as beautiful as she did walking the palace. It was difficult to believe that beneath the slack skin her heart did not swell and squeeze, nor did her lungs. She lay gracefully upon her back, her legs straight and her hands crossed upon her chest. Her mouth did not gape and it looked to have a slight smile.

I actually waited for her to open her eyes and say, "Thutmose, what are you doing here?"

I turned to her chief maid, "Thank you for setting her body this way." I knew they would have done so for my sake as I made my way despite the fact that the priests should be the first ones to do so.

"Sire, we have not touched her. This is how we found her this morning," she replied quietly.

I turned and looked upon my mother once again and I smiled. Ever thoughtful, she had even begun her own preparations. As I looked upon her mouth with its slight smile I could hear her voice and with it my father's. They did not speak to me but with each other, laughing as they talked. They were together again I knew it. My mother had made her passage through the night and joined him in paradise. No one was more worthy to have made the journey so quickly. For the first time with the loss of someone I loved I felt peace. For the first time with the loss of someone I loved I reached down and touched her hand, then bent and kissed her cheek.

"Farewell Mother," I whispered. "Enjoy your time in paradise. You will be missed but I will join you one day."

I did not cry so many tears at losing my mother. Every time I ached with missing her, the pain was soon replaced with the joy of knowing my father had his lover once more by his side. She had lived a full and virtuous life in choosing to stay and be with me. It was only fair that I should now celebrate their reunion.

She received a grand funeral as was befitting the mother of a Pharaoh and the grandmother and great-grandmother of a successor. I had her placed within my father's tomb, making way for her by moving Amenemhat to his own personal tomb, something I did not have the strength to commission or enact when he had died. These days the certainty of death was something I was much better prepared for, although the thought of another child leaving before me was still unbearable.

I watched the priests move my son's sarcophagus as I sat upon my horse in the burning sun but I did not feel its heat today. Amenhotep, Siamun and Menkheperre sat upon their horses behind me watching also. For a short time it was just my sons and myself, all five of us together once more, then Amenemhat's body was gone again within its new cave tomb. Watching his body disappear despite there being twelve years between twisted my heart and I swallowed hard. I turned and looked at my remaining sons, robust and vital men, and I tried to imagine him among them as strong as any of them. I turned my horse and gestured for our return to the palace. Siamun and Menkheperre turned with me but Amenhotep sat in place just a bit longer, riding at the very back so no one could see how red his eyes were.

We rode back through the Valley in silence. There was not much else to say and it would be hard enough to repeat the event to the women made to wait back at the palace. As usual our last scene to ride past before we left the Valley was Hatshepsut's temple. Following her death her devotees had kept it maintained, visiting to care for the trees sitting in pots along her terraces, or to burn incense and say prayers for her hoping that she would send them help. Her followers were scarce nowadays though and many of the plants were shrivelled or their pots were cracked from the roots pushing past their limits. Dust lay thick upon its surfaces and the sand was slowly creeping up the stones claiming the foundations.

I saw no need to spend time or money on its care. It symbolised all that I hated of the woman; her immense ego, self-serving and self-satisfying and I had to pass it every time I buried someone I loved or truly honoured. I would always look away as we rode past but I still knew it was there. I also hoped my apparent lack of recognition would reduce its importance in the eyes of my children.

This day as I rode past I looked away as usual, acting as though we were just passing yet another expanse of hillside or cliff face. Our silence was suddenly broken by the sound of a horse running hard in the dirt. Immediately our guards surrounded us and pulled their swords or daggers ready to protect us from any danger. My sons and I had also pulled our knives as quickly as the guards and we now all scanned around us for the source of the noise. It was no one approaching us. Instead we all just as quickly saw it was someone riding away.

Amenhotep had broken off from the back of the cortege and was riding furiously towards Hatshepsut's temple. He pulled up sharply at the base of the temple, pulled his head back and then flung it forward spitting upon the stone. Just as quickly he was riding again. He was high out of his saddle as he rode around us and ahead to the barge waiting for us at the river edge. We all sat in place stunned as he whipped past.

When we arrived his horse was upon the barge and Amenhotep was sitting down on the bench that ran around the edge of the deck. His arms rested upon his knees and his face was hidden as he looked down at the floor. He didn't look up as we all rode aboard the barge and dismounted. Siamun and Menkheperre stood silently and stared at him, as did I, not knowing what to say or do. As the boat pulled away Menkheperre stepped forward and simply placed his hand upon Amenhotep's shoulder. Without looking up Amenhotep placed his hand over his brother's in a silent thank you. Then just as suddenly Amenhotep's shoulders heaved and as they dropped back down he began to cry. His tears continued until we were almost across the river and the yelling of the boatmen preparing to land signalled the end of the boat ride. Amenhotep said nothing and still did not look at any of us as he once again mounted his horse and prepared to ride back to the palace.

I should not have been so surprised that my successor should feel such hatred towards Hatshepsut. Despite my steady nature I had never exactly spoken of my aunt in glowing or fond terms. I had always hoped that my actions would teach far beyond anything I spoke. The incident when Meryt had donned her brother's crown to play Pharaoh had been long forgotten by me, buried within all the other events that had occurred after. However Amenhotep had not forgotten that day and the seeds of hate and confusion that were planted then were now bearing fruit.

Amenhotep had sat that day and laughed as hard as any of the children as they enjoyed their sister's humour and playfulness. He looked around at his siblings still all living that day, and his heart was full. Then I entered the room and unleashed my anger and rant. When the lecture was over and we all began to eat Amenhotep looked around once more at our family. He looked at his mother and Satiah, then at each of his brothers and sisters in turn. As he looked at them all he wondered what ambitions each one held. The blood of their aunt Hatshepsut was their blood also and any one of them could carry her drive and ability to undermine and usurp Amenemhat. He looked to Amenemhat and tried to imagine himself being the one that would do this. Instantly he shook away the thought. It would be impossible--he simply loved his brother too much and would never think of robbing him of his birthright. *"No,"* he said to himself, *"This would never happen in my family."*

Thirteen years later though things were much different. It was now Amenhotep himself in the position that could be challenged and when he looked at his brothers and elder sister he was not so sure that they held the same love for him that he had held for Amenemhat. They were all adults now, established in their vocations and noted for their skills in each. Beketamun was older than him, just as Hatshepsut had been to my father. Amenhotep knew this had been the main claim that Hatshepsut had over my father, until my grandfather chose my father to succeed him. Beketamun was well respected in the court and throughout the palace and that very respect could soon be turned into favours amongst the priests and viziers. Siamun was only three months younger than him and like Beketamun he was also well-established in court and well respected. Siamun also had the close association with his full blood sister. It would be easy for the two to stage a coup, to claim the throne, to even say they were doing it for their lost full blood brother so that they may live out his true destiny for him.

Then there was Menkheperre, his own full blood brother, now a senior commander of the army, leading campaigns and noted for his physical skills. Amenhotep also knew of his dalliances with women through the palace including several young priestesses. Menkheperre had possible allies everywhere. He could arrange an "accident" during Amenhotep's next journey or training, then use the army to establish his own power.

This was how Amenhotep's mind now played with him. He had been put into a powerful position after a slight that may never have occurred. Now he wondered if such a slight, whether accidental or not, might remove him from his place. Despite his initial reluctance in replacing Amenemhat, Amenhotep had now settled into his role as successor. He had accepted that as the next eldest male it was his duty to take the throne and lead the country. He had already even produced his own successor. However he was also aware of how fragile his place was and this was the source and refuge of all his fears and anxieties.

As Amenhotep watched his brother's body moved to its new resting place he was reminded of how differently his life had turned out due to Amenemhat's death; the deeper responsibilities, the people who clung to him to share the power and the paranoia he now held for those he should have nothing but love for. All these feelings were made raw as he sat upon his horse and watched the sarcophagus come back into the sunlight. Amenhotep pictured the ruby he had placed within his brother's chest and suddenly he felt a pain within his own chest. He wanted to scream as though somehow that would release it but he stayed silent not daring to disturb Amenemhat's rites.

If only Amenhotep possessed the hearing that I, Menkheperre and Nebetiunet could often open up to, for that day Amenemhat spoke to his brother. Amenemhat felt his pain and confusion and he called out for his brother to release these things. Amenhotep did feel something but he pushed it aside with the rush of thoughts in his mind. So Amenemhat sent him one last message and touched his heart, hoping this would reach him. All Amenhotep felt though was pain.

As Amenhotep rode towards Hatshepsut's temple it no longer looked to him as just a temple. It was a monument to his fear and paranoia, symbolising all that he was going through. Here before him in eternal stone was the result of deceit, greed and power. The pain in his chest swelled again. Amenhotep kicked his horse and was heading towards the temple before he could even think about what he was doing. It took all his strength to stop himself from being thrown from the horse as he pulled hard to stop before the stone stairs but the adrenaline that was coursing through him made it feel like nothing. He wished he could trample the building with his horse or conjure the cliffs above to collapse upon it. If he could make this temple disappear then maybe everything it stood for would also disappear. This was not to happen though, so Amenhotep did the only thing he could in that moment. He spat upon the temple and he imagined he sent a message to the demons that he would no longer play this game of fear with them, that they would waste their time in seeking anyone to undermine his position and that they should not poison his siblings in the way they had Hatshepsut.

Just as quickly Amenhotep turned and rode past us all while we watched with knives and swords drawn, in complete shock. The adrenaline got him to the boat and then he collapsed upon the bench. He lowered his head as much from exhaustion as to avoid our looks when we arrived. Amenhotep was surprised that when I boarded the barge I did not say anything but he was not surprised when his brothers followed my lead. He kept his head down and felt his body start to shake as the adrenaline slowed and his chest eased as his heart began to calm. It was at this point that Menkheperre walked to him and placed his hand upon his shoulder and Amenhotep saw this as a sign from the Gods. The sibling that he truly feared the most had shown him that the Gods had listened. Within that simple gesture Menkheperre had shown Amenhotep more love than he ever could have imagined. It was no wonder he cried as much as he did.

All this however was not so clear to me. I had seen an act of absolute desecration as Amenhotep may as well have spat upon her body and to do so before our priests was a gesture of arrogance and aggression. Not that either of these are considered entirely bad things for a man who is set to rule. However to have them shown in such an impetuous and emotional way was a sign of weakness. There were priests and viziers just waiting to find a Pharaoh's foibles to allow their manipulations to gain passage to power. Today my son had exposed a part of himself that no one should have seen. We would need to talk soon to make sure this never happened again.

       I sent for Amenhotep the next day. A palace messenger notified him that the Pharaoh sought audience with him as soon as possible. He was just dismounting from a ride with Menkheperre when the messenger found them. Amenhotep had never been summoned in such a formal way before nor had he been summoned to my private courtroom before. He knew this was a serious matter and he also knew it was to do with his behaviour in the Valley the day before. He looked at Menkheperre, who also knew that Amenhotep was to receive a lecture. Menkheperre merely raised his eyebrows and then as he turned to throw his reins to the waiting stable hand said quite seriously, "Good luck, Brother."

       The room in which I waited was like a sauna. It soaked up the morning heat and then seemed to hold onto it until the sun was long gone. I rarely took audience in here for this reason but it was the room furthest from straying feet or wide ears so I would forsake my comfort for this meeting. I asked for the drapes to be pulled but that shut out the miniscule breeze that was the room's only saving grace, so I had them pulled open again, letting the room flood with light. I considered calling for the boy servants with the ostrich fans but I wanted as few people near us as possible and their incessant movement would only annoy me today. So I sat and had a lovely coat of sweat upon me by the time Amenhotep sat before me.

       Amenhotep tried his best to act as regal and mature as he could but beneath he was as scared as the day he was dragged to see Hatshepsut upon her deathbed. He sat before me only years short of the age that I was when I gained sole rule and for the first time I had to question if he would be ready to rule alone if I should pass soon. This probably was not a fair comparison, as my son had never been thrown into the responsibilities that I had from a young age. Yes, he conducted his own expeditions and had his own appointments but decisions and direction always came back to me, as they should. Perhaps now was the time to push my heir just a little bit more.

       As he took his place before me and sat back, arms upon the rests of the chair, his back straight and his eyes meeting mine, I leant forward and began.

       "My son, yesterday you enacted a desecration and you did so before the high priests, your brothers and our most intimate of guards," I started. "I would like to hear what possessed you to act so."

"I find it hard to imagine that you need to ask," he said, so softly I barely heard him. "You have been quite clear in your feelings towards this woman and all she did to manipulate our family history. Yesterday I chose to express my own distaste at what the demons allowed to happen."

I sat back in my chair and sighed, "Amenhotep, despite my words, have you ever seen me carry out an act of desecration or behave so impulsively?"

He shook his head.

"We are in official audience Amenhotep--answer properly!" I snapped.

"No, Sire," he said flatly.

"Do you understand that all those present merely saw an impetuous man performing an act of utter disrespect?" I asked strongly.

He could not answer and looked down.

"Look up while I address you Son!" I snapped again.

Amenhotep looked up again but still did not answer, so I continued on.

"Do you want to take to the throne known by the priests as being a man of such actions? Or do you wish to be known as someone as just, wise and brave as your grandfathers and myself?" I asked loudly.

"Of course I wish to be known as my forefathers. I would never wish to disgrace our family in any such way!" he answered just as loudly and strongly. "I was just so overwhelmed with emotion yesterday. Father, seeing Amenemhat's coffin again and then seeing that woman's monument--it was suffocating." I nodded my understanding, and he continued on, "I couldn't help but imagine that such forces could continue on in our family. I hate to think this of my brothers, and even my sister, but the thoughts come anyway. Yesterday I prayed to stop these thoughts, but even more so, to warn the demons they were no longer welcome to play with us. My actions yesterday were my warning."

He finished and I could see his eyes were moist with the emotion that he had just expressed. One part of what he said alarmed me.

"You fear your sister? Which one?" I asked anxiously.

"Beketamun, Father," he answered matter-of-factly.

"No!" I cried back, as surprised as I was anything else. "You would never need to fear Beketamun. She is as loyal and trustworthy as I am to you. Why would you say this? Has she indicated otherwise?"

"No, Father, but her circumstances, if you just consider them," he leaned forward in his chair thrusting his hands before him. "She is older than I, just as Hatshepsut was to your father, and she is so knowledgeable of the court, I dare say as much if not more so than myself. Her marriage only bears this more weight."

The first part of his reasoning did not surprise me, but the second part hit a nerve. Hatshepsut's knowledge of the court had been her greatest strength and provided the leverage to work her way amongst the priesthood as well. My dear Beketamun may seem loyal and respectful now, but what if this changed when I was no longer around.

"Father, I hate to have these thoughts and I fight them whenever they raise themselves up, but they return," he pressed on. "My siblings show no sign of challenging me but is that guaranteed to continue…"

I leant to one side of my chair and raised my hand to my chin with my mind racing. Everything he had just said to me was so true and like my son I hated to think such thoughts. I believed I had raised children who were respectful and honourable. However I believe that my grandfather had thought the same of his daughter. It was time to make solid my son's path to the throne. I dismissed Amenhotep and it was only after he had left the room that I realised we did not even resolve the real reason I had summoned him. His behaviour now though was understood and I was sure that once we had cleared the path to his succession fully that would no longer be a problem. The problem that remained now was in how I would do that.

As I made my way back to my chambers for my afternoon rest my mind once again went to Beketamun, such a strong and intelligent woman sent by the Gods to be my daughter. I could never imagine her even beginning to plot or bargain to usurp her brother. I shook my head, as the woman in my imagination could not even begin to look remotely like my daughter. However I also knew people could change. Even worse I knew that beyond my family were waves of priests, viziers and merchants all wanting more power or to ensure their positions. Many would be willing pawns of someone stronger than they were. I recalled listening to Ma-Keet confess her part in Hatshepsut becoming Pharaoh, hardly believing that someone I imagined was a mere assistant to my aunt could have set into place the actions and events necessary.

On the way to my chambers I passed Satiah's private rooms and as I did I saw her sitting looking out to the gardens. I stopped and just watched her for a moment. She looked so peaceful but so small these days, as though she was fading away before me. Her grief at losing Nefertiry had been so much deeper than that for Amenemhat, or perhaps it was both losses combined. No matter how deep the pain though she resumed her duties, even if it did take longer for her to recover from our daughter's death. The malaise though never fully lifted and all knew that. She spoke quieter and even less than before and people mirrored this by seeking her less often and spoke softer when they did. Beketamun and Siamun though saw as much if not more of her than before hoping as much to comfort her as to fill the void. They truly were her saving grace as were our grandchildren.

Satiah had only ever wished her children to love and be loved. When she was brought to the palace to become a queen, she knew her duties involved providing me with heirs but as she held each baby she never thought ahead to their roles. She just saw a tender pink child that needed her. Her pride in delivering me my first son never went beyond that. For Satiah, giving me an heir had never been about her own ambition; it was about making me happy. When we lost our son, it was never about losing rank or recognition; it was just the raw pain of losing a child. Satiah never nurtured ambition in any of her children, but she did nurture their aspirations. When Beketamun or Siamun spoke of something new they had learnt about trading she would share with them their delight. She never though once asked how they were asserting themselves in court or whether anyone had been disrespectful to them.

Both children knew such high ambitions like dominating court were not something their mother would be proud of. They also knew that to do so would upset the balance of power I was establishing for Amenhotep. In truth neither actually had any ambitions for the throne. Although they did sometimes feel the pain of knowing that their full blood brother would not rule as he was born to do, they were quite happy that Amenhotep had been the one to replace him. Beketamun would have been more than able to rule and with a worthy husband by her side, but she liked her life the way it was. She could support and help her family rather than being a decoration as her younger sisters chose to be but yet she did not have the weight of the empire upon her.

Siamun often thanked the Gods that Amenhotep was fathered three months before him. He saw this timing, however slight it seemed to so many others, as a blessing. He had avoided having to deal with the army any more than he had to. It also meant no long trips away from home and his family that grew each year with thanks to a fertile wife. It also meant that he could enjoy his food and not feel wary of his rounding belly. Siamun was a man of simple pleasures and ambitions. His situation suited him immensely.

Menkheperre likewise had simple ambitions; that he be able to have sex as often as possible with whatever woman he pleased, and that the army should provide him the excuse to leave Thebes when he was sick of any of them. If he was successor he could take more wives and have endless consorts but it would be harder to seek affairs with married women. It would also tie him to the palace more and then he would miss the taste of foreign women as he travelled. His role in the army served him well. I was thankful that he never had any desire for the throne, as the list of claims to being *his* heir could have been a national crisis.

Satiah had not moved the whole time I was watching her. I knew it was only fair that I let her know what was about to happen in the family. I took a deep breath and walked into the room. She stayed quiet as I sat beside her, taking in my words and nodded from time to time. Satiah did not look up at me though, she just reached out and touched my hand and said quietly, "Do what you must Thutmose." Inside though all she could think was "*If Amenemhat had not died the others would not need to go through this.*" A fresh wave of grief washed over her that afternoon.

I made my way to Matreya's rooms next. I did not sit and neither did she. Instead we stood across the room from each other; I with my hands on my hips while she stood arms crossed. We both raised our chins as though a duel was about to begin. I spoke my words and her response was terse but delivered with a smile, "As you should have done years ago!" A fresh wave of arrogance washed over Matreya that afternoon.

# CHAPTER TWENTY-FOUR

It was a full week later that I called the family to meet. I did so once again in the small court but with the forethought of arranging the time in the evening to avoid the heat, as well as not to disrupt anyone's duties or commitments. The room had been arranged just as I asked. My chair sat before the single row of chairs that waited for my children and their spouses. Beside my chair were the usual two chairs to my right for my wives. To the left though I added a chair for Amenhotep and I made sure that he arrived before all others so that as the rest of my children walked in they saw him in place, sitting beside me and facing them.

Whether for a formal occasion or a family meal altogether my wives and children knew how they were to sit. Satiah was always the closest to my left with Matreya next to her. Then my sons in age would be to my right, followed by my daughters also by age, so when they all arrived within the meeting room and saw Amenhotep next to me they automatically arranged themselves. Siamun as the next son took the first chair with his wife beside him, then Menkheperre with his wife, followed by Beketamun and Kamankh, then the other girls with their husbands. I sat and watched as they took their places along the line of chairs, all kept in a single row on purpose, and only just able to do so in this room, with barely space remaining at either end to pass.

As usual Matreya was the last to arrive and as she did the quiet conversations that were happening ended and a priest walked over and handed me my crook and flail. As I took these symbols into my hands all knew it signified the most serious of duties was about to take place. They all knew what they stood for; my crook to lead and guide and the flail to call to order and the right to punish. They knew that when I held them in my hands I was about to do either or both.

"Today you will not sit in rank," I said. "Arrange yourselves by birth."

This was simple enough. It just required Beketamun and her husband to stand and move to the first seats on the left, whilst Siamun and Menkheperre moved two seats to their right with their wives. My younger daughters sat still with their husbands and watched. I am sure Isis noted yet again how unaffected her life was by such formalities. The three eldest were quite uncomfortable now though. This simple act had them even more worried. They were not so surprised by Amenhotep sitting before them for his position as heir made that perfectly acceptable, but to do this now and play with protocol in such a way confused them.

Beketamun felt it the most, sitting ahead of all now, including her brothers. Since Amenemhat's death all focus had been upon Amenhotep despite her being a year older than him. She had understood from an early age that this was the way of things within royalty. Never once did she ever imagine that she could lay claim to the throne based upon her age. They all understood that it was their gender that decided such things. Beketamun shifted in her seat, and Kamankh took her hand, reminding her that he was by her side. She looked at him and her worry as to what this all meant was clear in her eyes even though she could not say anything. I looked at them all now sitting in order of their ages and began.

"It seems only yesterday that you were but babes before me and yet here you all sit as adults and with your spouses. You serve your family and country well and I could not be prouder of each and every one of you." I started softly and felt them all ease a little within their chairs. "Your brother sits before you as the next Pharaoh, as he is the eldest son and this is the way of succession in Egypt, as you have all been taught from childhood. You all understand this?"

I waited until they all nodded or murmured "Yes Father" and then continued on.

"You are also aware of the history of my reign and how my aunt saw fit to lay claim to the throne due to her perceived seniority. It is now time to make sure that this will not be repeated within our family." I paused as I saw Beketamun's eyes grow wide. Menkheperre even glanced towards her understanding what I was inferring and then just as quickly looked back. "Beketamun, as the eldest living child of mine you would have the strongest claim above all others. You are now in the same position that your aunt Hatshepsut was. Like her, you are also a powerful courtier." Beketamun's face grew red with alarm and embarrassment. She looked to her mother but Satiah's head was down. "How say you for your brother's succession?"

"I support my brother as I always have," Beketamun said, but her voice trembled. She sat forward as though to speak more but I raised my flail, the signal for silence, and she complied sitting back in her seat.

Siamun and Menkheperre twisted in their chairs sharing in Beketamun's mortification. Their minds though were racing; had Beketamun in fact made some claim or attempt to challenge Amenhotep? Was this the true reason for this meeting?

"Siamun and Menkheperre," I began again and the men sat straight and looked square at me. "You may also have some taste for succession and both of you have means in which to attain it. How say you both for your brother's succession?"

Siamun answered as respectfully as ever he would. "Of course you have my support and honour, brother Amenhotep." He finished by bowing his head. Inside though his stomach churned wondering what had led his father to even contemplate such thoughts. Siamun was beyond embarrassment. He knew such things were necessary but the hurt of being questioned or considered a threat to his brother sat heavy within him.

Menkheperre though was simply furious and as Siamun finished his pledge he knew it was his opportunity to express it. "Of course I pledge my alliance to my brother!" Menkheperre shouted. "Now I demand to know who has given you such ideas that I or my siblings would ever act any other way."

"Menkheperre, remember your place!" I shouted. "You are not the one to make demands here."

"Father, we have done nothing but remember our places!" he snapped back. "Now in return we are addressed as though our actions are not enough."

"Stop," I roared and held the flail up. "This is not a meeting to accuse or incite any of you! Do you not understand I do this for you all?"

"If you did this for us all Father, then you would not address us as though we are threats," Menkheperre continued. "You point out the very qualities that you value us for as though they are now liabilities."

This was not going well at all and I took a deep breath. I had imagined the words to use over and over again but today as I spoke them they did not achieve any of what I desired. Beketamun sat with her head down but I could see her chest heaving from anxiety. Siamun looked ahead and sat straight, as noble as ever. His face though was cold and stern. Menkheperre was still forward in his chair, his face red, eager to continue on with his affront. Meritamen looked down awkwardly as did Meryt who was reminded of the reason she no longer carried her birth name. Nebetiunet sat gracefully in her chair. Her eyes were closed and I knew she was praying for us all and I imagine also wishing she was back at her peaceful temple. Isis had begun to cry. In-between them all their spouses sat still and quiet--Kamankh as always with Beketamun's hand in his.

Menkheperre now addressed Amenhotep. "Are these your thoughts?" he said strongly. "Do you believe that your own blood would challenge or threaten you so?"

Amenhotep looked to me, unaccustomed to such confrontations within our family and stammered to answer. I decided to rescue him lest this situation should become any worse.

"This meeting was my initiative Menkheperre," I answered.

"That does not answer my question Father," he snapped again. "I wish to hear your successor's answer."

Menkheperre's assertions were not going to be easily quelled tonight. I knew Amenhotep would need to speak and claim his part in this. I looked to Amenhotep sitting beside me and nodded, indicating he should reply. He sat for a moment looking down.

"Lift your head!" hissed Matreya, saying the very words I was thinking.

Amenhotep looked up and across the faces of his seven siblings before him and saw anger, bitterness, confusion and sadness. Beketamun with her chest heaving and gripping her husband's hand as though she may fall out of her chair and then at the other end, Isis trying to hold back tears with no success as her husband stroked her arm. Each woman sat like a bookend to the myriad of emotions between and he knew he was responsible for them all.

"I have held back my fears so long, hating myself that I could think such things of the people I love the most," he began. "I look at each of you and I see so much love and honour. These parts of you are so strong but I also know that we all have parts within us that are not so good."

Amenhotep spoke with much honesty yet this did not appease Menkheperre in any way.

"So this is how you choose to establish our loyalty, by dragging us to court as though we are common viziers or merchants that you need to strike a deal with? Do you fear these unspoken parts of us so much that you cannot even talk to your brother? These parts of us that may not ever come to be and yet you act as though they are all but guaranteed. Is this how you will rule?" Menkheperre continued on ruthlessly.

"I said that the meeting was my idea," I shouted again.

"I understand that Father," Menkheperre yelled back. "But do not insult my intelligence, nor that of my brother and sisters in denying the fact that there must have been some discussion to lead to this." Menkheperre fell back in his chair, his point finally made but he was far from finished. "Is this throne so important that you can forget the love we have? Could you have not come to me and shared these fears in private? I would readily have shared with you my joy at the fact that I am *not* the one to bear your duties!" he said to Amenhotep.

Amenhotep could not answer him, instead I did. "Can you understand that we needed these things made clear and agreed upon together as family with all present?" I asked him.

"Yes Father, I can understand beyond anything you can imagine of me," Menkheperre answered. "I am just disappointed at the way you and my brother have chosen to do so."

Menkheperre slumped in his chair, satisfied that he had spoken his mind but far from relieved. I knew we would not get anywhere with further talk as it had all broken down into disarray. The meeting needed to finish lest things get any worse and hopefully in concluding it I could somehow dissolve the tension. I sighed and looked towards Beketamun, her head still down and her hand gripping Kamankh's.

"Let us remember the simple reason you have been called here tonight. I wish for you all within the presence of each other to declare your support for Amenhotep." I called out to my daughter, "Beketamun, as the eldest I wish you to start and restate your support."

Beketamun looked up at me with dark eyes and then turned her gaze to her brother. "Amenhotep, you have my support and allegiance, just as you always have had and always will." Her words came out clipped and harsh and then she dropped her eyes again. To a stranger they would have imagined that she spoke this way to make her words strong, but I could see her jaw muscles tense and I knew that she wanted to add so much more.

Siamun was next and he too repeated the same words as Beketamun.

Not only did he choose the same words, but he also spoke them with the same tense jaw and dryness that his sister had. Menkheperre was next and once again the same words came from his lips. He knew exactly what Beketamun intended and he delivered them loud and strong with just a hint of distain to make sure everyone knew he was still far from pleased.

My remaining daughters had the precedent well and truly set for how they should now respond and so each in turn once again repeated the same words, albeit in much softer tones and with Isis still in tears. When my children were done then their spouses began. Kamankh started and once again chose the very same words so each spouse that followed spoke them also. Fourteen times Amenhotep had to hear those words and each time he did, no matter the tone and no matter the person, he felt a barb hit his chest. Each echo was a reminder of the weakness of distrust he had fallen prey too.

I felt it differently though. I now had their clear promise to Amenhotep, our country and myself. This was something that could now be recorded and referred back to. My children had declared their unity and their support for a clear succession. Part of me was relieved and sighed, but another felt heavy. I did not bear it much significance, as I was just thankful to end the meeting. Another feeling was now upon me also--that of hunger.

"Our duties here are done my family," I said. "Let us adjourn to the dining room and eat."

I stood first as always and began to lead us all to the dining room. We made our way for quite some time in silence. As we passed near the private rooms that we all lived within it was Satiah who broke the silence. "Thutmose, I will not dine tonight," she said simply. "I ask that you excuse me so that I may retire to my rooms."

"Of course my dear," I answered, and leant forward reaching out to take her hand and kiss her cheek when for the first time in over thirty years of marriage Satiah drew her hand back and turned away so that I could do neither. I was too shocked to say or do anything and watched her walk away. Matreya though was smiling from ear to ear and was beside me in Satiah's place in an instant. We continued on to the dining room.

Finally all seated my family was served a meal as sumptuous as any celebration feast which was what I imagined this meal would have been. There was no sense of celebration in this room though. Most plates were carried back piled with food. Our servants, allowed to eat the remains, were the only ones to truly enjoy the food tonight. Talk was scattered and quiet; not even I felt compelled to make any small talk to break the silence that dominated most of the gathering.

I looked amongst the children and saw not one smile amongst them. Beketamun was still dark and I saw Kamankh tenderly offer her a piece of fig, her favourite fruit, in the hope that she might eat something but she just shook her head. Nearby Isis would speak quietly with Nebetiunet who would answer politely but not encourage any further talk. Amenhotep would look at no one, studying his food intently, seemingly to avoid eye contact with anyone. The heaviness I had felt at the end of the meeting was thicker than before. When the final course was served and I ended the meal we all shared the relief of retreating to our private rooms.

When I entered my salon my butler and chamber servants greeted me as always but I looked past them all hoping for some sign of Satiah being here.

"I trust your evening went well Sire," Tati spoke politely as he removed my collar and headscarf.

"Yes it did," I lied just as politely in response. "Has Satiah already retired?" I wanted to see her so badly. Satiah would know where I had gone wrong tonight and she would help me correct this.

"Your Queen has chosen to spend the night in her private chambers, Sire. Do you wish us to summon her to your rooms?" My butler hesitated a little before he spoke. It was a given that Satiah spent most nights in my chambers-- needing my company as much as I needed and wanted hers. This simple act of Satiah seeking her own rooms after such a meeting was a strong message to my servants that things had not gone so well

"No, the Queen was very tired and feeling poorly. Leave her to her own rooms to recuperate," I carried on my performance with another lie.

Tati nodded and left the room to put away my adornments. I called for some wine and sat near one of windows that looked out over my garden. I didn't feel like drinking though and set the glass down before me, choosing instead to merely stare out at the night sky. Not a star was visible that night and the moon though full, was hiding elsewhere in the sky away from my window. Suddenly I was aware that my servants had withdrawn into other rooms and I had the rare occasion of being truly alone. I sighed and continued to look out to the almost blank sky when I heard some noise outside my door. Beketamun's voice suddenly echoed inside my chambers.

"I know the hour, butler. I wish to speak to my father," she said firmly.

Some more murmuring followed this, presumably from my butler then Beketamun's voice broke through again.

"Open this door or I shall do so myself!" she now shouted.

I stood knowing that the doors would now open for my daughter to be presented to me. The doors opened and Beketamun walked though them before they were completely open or before she could be announced. As she saw me she stopped and breathed in sharply, suddenly losing the bravado that I had heard her display before she entered. She stood looking at me with her eyes wide, knowing that I should be the first to speak.

"Come Daughter, sit with me," I gestured to the table by the window.

"I will not sit, Sire," she answered, and she crossed her arms before her grasping each elbow as though to hold herself. She lifted her chin and I could feel her gathering her confidence to speak with me.

"As you wish, Daughter. Now to what do I owe this visit from you?" I continued on, trying to be as casual as I could.

"This is no social visit, Sire," she snapped and I saw her eyes were red. "I simply wish you to know my feelings following the events of this evening."

"Please stop calling me Sire and call me Father," I said softly. "We are not in court."

"I cannot use that word tonight," she said shaking her head. "I now feel that each moment of my life in the palace is one of being in court."

"Beketamun! No! This is nonsense," I cried. "I cannot believe you all took such offence and affront at something that needed to be done for you all."

"Sire, this evening you called me to court and in front of my brothers and sisters, my mother, Matreya, the court priests and my husband, you compared me to that woman," she spat the words and tears fell down her cheeks. "All my life I have heard of her desecration of the family lineage, I saw your looks of hate directed at her when I was a child, I see your abandonment of her memorials and now tonight you looked me in the eye and in front of everyone you compared me to her."

"No, Beketamun, no!" I shouted. "I would never..."

"I have been a most loyal and faithful daughter and princess," she continued speaking over me, determined to be heard. "I have helped guide my younger sisters, I have served the courts as well as any priest or vizier could do or have done, I married even though I had no desire to. Never have I challenged your teachings or orders and yet tonight you repay my dedication and allegiance with this defamation and insult to all that I truly am."

"Beketamun, no!" I repeated and now too I had tears in my eyes. "I would never dream to insult you so. You cannot imagine how proud I am to have a daughter such as you. You embrace all that is magnificent and admirable from your grandmothers and mother. Then you have a mind that your grandfathers would have wished for. My daughter, you are the most amazing woman I know. My sweet, I could not admire you more."

"Yet it is these very qualities that make you question me also," she answered dryly, her arms still tight around her.

I sighed and rubbed my face, lost at what to say. "Beketamun, I could see no other way to do this," I cried, waving my hand at nothing. "There truly is no more to say of this matter."

Beketamun's chest heaved and her arms dropped by her side. She did not believe that I could not have found another way and now I was dismissing any further discussion. Her anger now was joined by an absolute distaste of me and as she looked at me her eyes narrowed and she began to shake her head.

"Sire, you may well have achieved much tonight as a Pharaoh, but you failed as a father!" she said strong and loud, then without a farewell or waiting to be dismissed she turned her back to me and left the room.

No blade or arrow tip could have wounded more than her words. They stung even more so as I had the deep knowing that she was in fact correct. I walked back to my chair by the window, collapsed into it and cried. As I did so I saw the moon outside my window. During my time with Beketamun it had made its way in the sky to now be seen from where I sat. As I looked at it my tears stopped and I felt its essence call down to me. I somehow became calm as I looked at it, shining so bright but I could see that it was not complete. It had already started to wane, having reached its fullness the night before. To one side I saw the slight collapse of its edge where the earth's shadow had begun to claim its hold over the moon's light once again. Each night it would slice away at its glow, wearing it down to a sliver of white. Then the moon would make its own power known again, growing each night and returning to its magnificence.

"All things can be healed. Nothing is permanent in this earthly realm" the moon seemed to whisper to me and I kept looking at it as though in a trance. A cloud wafted across its white surface and as it passed to the right, a star appeared from behind it. Then another and another made itself known. They glistened and sometimes seemed that they might fade, instead they hung tightly in place. I lost myself in their simple beauty, forgetting for one sweet moment all that had happened tonight. My eyelids began to drop and I knew I should get some sleep soon but as much as I wished to end the day I wanted this moment to last also. I opened my eyes wide again and just as I did a brilliant shooting star shot across the sky leaving a trail shimmering behind it. It was gone as fast as it appeared yet its light had been so strong that its image seemed to hold in my eyes for a few seconds longer. I doubted I would see anything more amazing tonight and I called to my servants to prepare me for bed.

I lay in bed alone and despite the sleep that had called to me while I sat looking at the heavens I now lay wide awake as my mind recalled the disastrous way I had dealt with the evening. My drapes were drawn closed, but a shard of moonlight broke through between them cutting the room in two. Its sharp peak hit the end of my bed touching where my feet lay. I once again heard Beketamun's words as she stood before me raw with hurt. In all my life my words and actions had never failed my intentions as they had tonight. I made a silent prayer to my mother and father for guidance, calling to them in paradise to help me heal what I had done tonight. I heard no words of wisdom though--instead all I heard was laughter. It was not my parents' laughter. I knew that immediately. It was Hatshepsut.

I sat up in bed and my chest pounded as much with fear as anger. I jumped out of bed and paced my room. Perhaps I had dreamt I heard her, after all I was so close to sleep. My mind raced but I knew what I had heard was no figment of imagination.

"Be gone you vile jackal!" I screamed out to the darkness.

Within seconds my night guards were in the room, brandishing swords and surrounding me.

"It is nothing," I gasped to them. "I think I heard an animal at the window."

The chief guard walked towards the window scowling as fiercely as he could. Animal or otherwise, a disturbance on his shift was a serious matter. He quickly gathered reports from the guards scattered in the gardens and only when he was satisfied that there was nothing to threaten me did he accept my dismissal.

I fell back into bed but the pounding in my chest had now turned into a deep ache and I felt it creep its way into my arms. My breath was short and the room seemed to be moving despite me lying still. Then I felt a weight push on my chest and my arms grew limp. For the first time in my life my body felt weak and helpless. The fear that came with this pain overwhelmed me and I felt I like I was drowning. I don't know if I would have had the strength to call out for assistance but I wouldn't have anyway as I knew there was no one who could help me. Instead I called out silently to Hatshepsut and demanded that she leave my life once and for all. I probably fell unconscious at that point but it was the same as falling asleep. Either way I finally found some rest.

It took me some time to wake in the morning and I asked that I be left to lie for a while as my servants fussed about my room, pulling back curtains and sprinkling oils to freshen the stale air. My butler came to my side asking if I was ready to rise, holding my robe to cover me. I sat up slowly and a sharp reminder of the pain from the night before grabbed at my chest. I could not help but grimace and grabbed the edge of the bed to steady myself as the shock of such pain shook me.

"Sire, what is it?" cried my butler.

I sat silent for a moment gasping, one hand still gripping the edge of the bed while the other clutched my chest. "It is nothing, just an old battle ache coming to visit," I tried to smile as I spoke but the pale colour of my face and the desperation in which I hung onto my bed spoke much more.

"Sire, we must call a physician," he stated simply.

I fell back into my bed, simply lacking the strength to even argue with him. Never had a malaise or illness held its grip on me overnight. I had always awakened fresh and revived. That part of my life was now long gone and as I lay and looked at the ceiling above me I realised that my youth was well and truly in the past. This did not trouble me so much as I had faced the reality that my end days were nearing many times in recent years. It was this awareness that had led to the previous nights events. What troubled me was that this illness that had burrowed inside me might steal me away before I made right with all my children, especially Beketamun.

As I lay still, wondering what fate this illness would bring me I heard murmurs and movement about me. My butler ordered someone to fetch the royal physicians while others were sent throughout the palace with messages of my illness so that all might rearrange their day accordingly. As the news made its way it was met with raised eyebrows as never before had I cancelled my duties due to illness.

When the news reached the court Beketamun and Siamun were busy checking records with a vizier of the south. Siamun thanked the messenger then turned and looked to Beketamun who had grown pale as she heard the message.

"This is most unusual," he whispered to Beketamun. "Do you suppose he knew of an illness about to beset him and that is why he called us all together last night?"

Beketamun shook her head. She knew much better as to the cause of my illness but she could not say anything to her brother. "No man can predict such things Siamun. Not even a high priest," she muttered back. Her head began to swim as she remembered the way she had spoken to me the night before. "Perhaps we should stop by his rooms to see how he is doing."

"We have so much to do here," he said. "If it was serious we would have been summoned. I imagine our father has just had a taste of old age and needs some extra rest for once. He thinks he is still like Menkheperre most days. Why don't you go? He loves when you girls dote upon him. If I were to go he would just want to talk business anyway."

"You do not think it may be caused by the meeting last night?" she asked.

Siamun burst out laughing, "After all that Father has dealt with in his life do you suppose having Menkheperre yell at him would do this?"

Beketamun had no answer, for to explain her fear she would have to tell Siamun of her visit to me the night before and she was simply not willing to admit her behaviour to anyone. As much as she was glad that she had the courage to speak to me she was not proud of how it ended. Her emotions had gotten the better of her and she knew that she had hurt me. She excused herself and made her way through the corridors to my rooms. Along the way she imagined all the possible scenarios that would greet her. I might be recovered and walking my rooms, holding my arms out to embrace her, or it could be the worst scenario; seeing me lying, weak and frail, only to turn my head as she entered, rejecting her.

When she did make it to my rooms a priest and physician were leaving my chambers. They bowed their head to her as she approached and when neither offered any news she did not bother to ask and continued on. The doors to my private chambers were open and there was much movement within. Servants were cleaning as usual and several priests were milling about speaking in hushed tones. The doors to my bedchamber opened and Satiah walked through looking concerned but calm. Seeing her mother composed eased Beketamun's mind and she raced towards her before the priests could converge upon Satiah asking for news.

"Mother, is he alright?" she cried.

"Yes, yes," she said, taking Beketamun's hand. "He just needs some rest."

Satiah led Beketamun by the hand away from the bedchamber doors. As she did so she turned to the priests and simply nodded signalling that they now could enter to witness my condition. Ironically, she too thought she was responsible for my condition knowing that her rebuff of me as I went to kiss her would have crushed me. She had been one of the first to hear of my turn and rushed to my room, scared that it was far worse than she had been told. I will admit there was something quite satisfying about having my wife burst into my room, then run to my side, grabbing my hand, kissing it fervently while crying out, "My beloved, my beloved…" As the priests entered to check upon me I saw Beketamun through the doors standing with her mother. Then for the first time that day I was able to take a deep breath without it feeling as though my chest was being torn to shreds.

By the afternoon I was restless and bored from having lain in bed all day. The pain and heaviness in my chest had lifted giving me the confidence to once again attempt to get up. I swung my legs off the side of the bed and sat upright. The only servant in the room at the time, a young boy fanning me with a mass of white feathers, froze in place, the fan suspended above him as he watched me, undecided as to whether to call for my butler or not. I too had frozen in place, my head swirling with the dizziness of sitting up after so long on my back. I looked to the boy, "Go fetch my butler."

Within seconds the fan was dropped and the boy raced out of the room. I did not need my butler or anyone else. I just wished to have the room to myself to test my strength without witness and my pride would rather have my butler enter and to see me lying back upon my bed once more than have him witness me stumble.

I stood slowly, taking notice of every sensation within my body as I did so. My legs while a little shaky lifted me to stand without the return of the pain in my chest, making me smile. I took one step and when my body seemed quite happy to do so I took another and then another. By the time my butler walked through the doors I was walking around the room.

"Sire, the physicians have told you to rest all day," he stated firmly.

"I have rested enough and my vigour has returned," I answered just as firmly. "I now wish to bathe and be dressed. There is much that needs to be done this afternoon." I then added to myself, *"Else this illness will return."* I had indulged this weakness long enough.

After bathing and having fresh clothing upon me I was renewed. As the clear water washed over me I imagined it washing off the last tendrils of the condition that burrowed into my chest. I kept breathing deeply, testing the strength of my muscles as much as to see if there was still pain. Each breath grew larger and seemed to push the last remnants of pain away.

As I was dressed I looked over the shoulder of my butler into the mirror and was shocked. I looked at the man staring back at me and for a moment saw my father as I remembered him. It was not my father though it was me. I saw lines I had not seen before--there was darkness under my eyes whilst elsewhere my face seemed pale. I may not be feeling pain anymore but my face showed what my body had endured.

I sat and was eating my first substantial meal since the dinner with my family the night before when Satiah arrived and asked if she might join me. I smiled and nodded, grateful for the company and the obvious warmth she always brought.

"How do you feel now?" she asked gently, stroking my arm with the touch of a feather.

I looked to her smiling, swallowing the last of my meat. "I am much revived Satiah. Do not let the colours or lines upon my face tell you otherwise. They too shall leave me soon," I laughed as I finished as though this would convince her more.

"Thutmose," she barely whispered my name as she spoke it, "I cannot but help believe that I aided your illness with my behaviour last night. I was not the supportive wife that you chose me to be."

I could not smile as I saw a tear fall down her face. Grabbing her hand firmly I held back my own tears, leaned close to her and whispered, "My love, no one is the cause of my illness."

Satiah looked deep into my eyes. "What happened last night Thutmose? It was like another man sat before us. It was as though I did not know you."

I wiped my mouth and sat back in my chair. It had been like I had not even known myself last night and I truly was not sure of how to answer this. Rubbing my chin with my hand I shrugged my shoulders.

"My beloved, in all my years as Pharaoh, even with Hatshepsut beside me, I have never had my choice of actions fail me as they did last night. I truly thought I was acting for the good of our family," I finished with another shrug of my shoulders.

Satiah kept looking at me and I could sense some frustration. She raised an eyebrow. "Nothing that is decided from honour would divide a family as it did last night," she said sharply and I froze in my seat.

Never had Satiah said something with such conviction but there was something beneath what she said that suddenly struck me. I slowly nodded my head and I felt my stomach tighten as I understood just how foolish I had been. I had acted pompous and self-righteous, succumbing to ill-founded fears. I had acted as Hatshepsut had all her life and that realisation made me feel sick. The tightness in my chest once again clenched its fingers and I grabbed the edge of the table.

"Thutmose!" Satiah cried.

"It is okay my beloved," I said, loosening my grip and resting back in my chair. "I now know my folly."

That madness had crept upon me so stealthily that I not only reviled its talent for doing so--but also admired it just as much. I returned to my room and as I rested once more I smiled. It can be so easy to lose oneself in games of fear and paranoia. In fact some get so embroiled they know of no other way to enact their life. Last night I had given myself a taste of what playing such a game was like and in return received the bitterest aftertaste. I prayed that I could now heal this and rose from my bed to walk the palace and conduct three of the hardest meetings I would ever attend.

I found Menkheperre first within the war rooms meeting with generals. The men all stood to attention, but while Menkheperre stood he remained with a slack posture, his arms crossed letting me know he was still displeased with my treatment of him.

"Come Menkheperre, I wish to speak with you in private," I said, and gestured to the gardens outside the meeting room.

Menkheperre followed without one word and as we entered the grounds he remained standing despite my seeking a chair. I panted a little as I sat and took a moment to catch my breath. This made my son uncomfortable and as I looked up he frowned even more. "Father, you are still unwell," he said sternly. "You should have summoned me to your rooms."

"No, my son," I strained a smile back. "Today I must be the one who walks to meet with you."

My apology was short and sweet and all that Menkheperre needed. Not only had he inherited a carbon copy of my looks and physique--so too did he have my distaste for flowery speeches. As I finished he stepped forward and dropped to one knee taking my hand firmly as any noble soldier would do to honour his commander's words. He rose and squeezed my shoulder.

"Now wait here and let me call for your sedan," he smiled. "You may have impressed my by walking here after being so ill but I will be just as impressed to see you leave as any Pharaoh is entitled to."

"No, Menkheperre," I began to beg.

"Oh hush," he cut me short. "Are you in that much of a hurry to see Amenhotep succeed you?" he finished with a laugh and I joined him as he called out to my guards to fetch the sedan.

In truth I was grateful as even though I was feeling better, the long walk of the palace did make me tired and I was becoming wary of inviting another turn. Menkheperre helped me seat myself upon the sedan. In fact I believe he may have even lifted me onto it had I let him. I gripped his hand one last time as a thank you. He smiled then leant over and kissed me, then I was raised and on my way to the courts to find Siamun.

Siamun was just leaving the main courtroom having met with the northern viziers and gasped as he saw me approaching the court upon the sedan.

He ran forward to meet me.

"Father, how are you?" he almost shouted. He didn't wait for my answer as really the sedan answered that for him. "Surely you should be resting. The meeting with the viziers is complete and successful. Let us return to your rooms and I will tell you all that occurred. The wheat of the delta region has slumped but the fish trade has been…" He began to ramble and I held my hand up for him to stop.

"I have no concerns about trade today Siamun," I said. "Let us go to the private courtroom and speak."

He appeared puzzled at this but followed alongside the sedan as we made our way back into the room where the ill-fated meeting had occurred just the night before. It looked different though as we entered, the row of chairs that had cut the room in two were all now back against the walls of the room, leaving just those that myself, Amenhotep and my wives had sat upon still in place with their backs to the windows. I gestured for the sedan to be lowered as soon as we were in the room and walked towards my chair, the largest one of course--its high back throwing a shadow across the room as the afternoon sun speared inside. I gestured for Siamun to follow me and then pointed to Amenhotep's chair.

"Come sit with me," I said.

Siamun paused and looked at the chair not sure if he had seen my gesture correctly. He turned and looked to the chairs circling the walls and was about to call for a servant to bring him one when I realised what he was doing.

"Siamun, you may sit here beside me today," I said, once again gesturing to his brother's chair.

He responded with a nod and I saw him swallow as he stepped forward and sat down. I could see he sat awkwardly as though he was too scared to place his full weight upon it. Perhaps he just didn't want me to think he was too comfortable sitting there--which in fact he wasn't. I allowed him one final squirm and began my apology, only to have Siamun begin shaking his head and raise his hand. "Father, please stop," he interrupted. "I do not need nor ask for your apology. You acted as you thought necessary and whilst I may not fully understand I will always honour your right to do so."

Siamun finished and looked away but I could see his chest heaving. He would have been happy to have just forgotten about last night and let all go on as though it hadn't occurred. Siamun did not identify with the notion of a grudge or resentment. A slight against him could be washed away with his next bath, but I knew that some things could return no matter how far away you pushed them.

"Siamun, perhaps instead of an apology I can explain myself then," I offered.

"You have no need for that with me either, Father," he responded shaking his head once more

"I have no need, my son, but my old age has shown me that understanding can bring much relief to many. It is not so often that we are able to hear the truth from the perpetrator's mouth and it can bring much peace and clarity with it," I said.

Siamun looked to me once more and nodded so I began. I explained my fears, those of Amenhotep's and how I had allowed both to lead me to call that meeting. Siamun nodded as he listened and he finally seemed comfortable in his seat. "So there was no talk from anyone in the palace that there was a plan to contest the throne?" he said quietly as I finished.

"No Siamun, there never was or has been such talk," I answered. "In fact I am sure that I would only hear of your and Beketamun's honourable behaviour if I did question anyone in the court."

Siamun raised his eyebrows, "What of Menkheperre then?"

I shook my head and then smiled. "I think we both know that your young brother is far too busy with the army and women to even have the time or energy for such things."

Siamun burst out laughing, "Oh I did not know that you were aware of his--umm--extra activities."

"Son, I am Pharaoh! Do you think there is much that happens in my empire that I am not aware of?" I smiled but Siamun no longer did.

"No Father, I imagine that there isn't much at all that you do not know of," he answered no longer laughing and quite solemnly.

I nodded, somewhat disappointed that we had ended on a more serious note but that was the way of Siamun, the consummate professional when within the walls of the court no matter who was before him.

"Now then, I would like to hear how your meeting with the viziers transpired," I said.

Perhaps I should have gone to find Beketamun instead of listening to business, because an hour later when Siamun had finished with his report I was tired beyond words. I was so grateful that my sedan was close by and as I climbed upon it all I could think about was getting back to my bedchamber and resting. I could find Beketamun later; the day was far from over. In my bed I fell back upon the soft feathers that filled my pillows and mattress to drift into sleep unaware that matters with Beketamun were about to become worse.

Beketamun had actually been nearby in court when I met with Siamun and word soon reached her that I was in private audience with Siamun. The spark of relief that I was well enough to have left my bed was just as quickly dampened with a feeling of jealousy. She knew just as much as Siamun, why had he not sought her or invited her to attend as well. Then she realised why. Siamun had not confronted their father the night before as Menkheperre had in court and he most certainly would not have in private as she had chosen to.

Beketamun now had to face the very high probability that she would no longer be shown any favour from her father.

Beketamun was actually watching through a doorway as I was carried away back to my rooms and she then walked towards the small courtroom to see if Siamun remained inside. As she stepped into the doorway she saw Siamun still sitting in Amenhotep's chair, slumped to one side and looking off at nothing in particular.

"Siamun! Why are you sitting there?" she exclaimed.

Siamun jolted in his seat, abruptly pulled out of his thoughts.

"Father asked me to," he answered defensively and then jumped up from the seat, suddenly remembering exactly what it was he sat upon. "I know it seems peculiar but it was quite a peculiar meeting."

"Oh really? How so?" Beketamun's suspicions now seemed to have some foundation.

"He came to apologise and explain about the meeting last night!" Siamun screwed up his nose as he spoke.

Beketamun froze. "You received an apology from him?"

"Oh Sister, I am sure he will seek such a meeting with you too," his eyes grew wide as he realised the offence he had just offered his sister. "He is just so tired from his illness he needed to rest."

Beketamun shook her head, "Siamun he was with you for almost two hours. Do you truly expect me to believe an apology took that long?"

"Well no, of course not. He wished to hear of the meeting with the viziers also," Siamun stopped short. He saw Beketamun's face grow red and then tears began to fill her eyes as she heard that I had chosen to discuss business and didn't call for her as well when she was only a few rooms away. Her heart suddenly felt heavy and she put her hand to her chest.

"Beketamun, I am sure he will call upon you also," Siamun said once again softly.

"I am not so sure Brother," she barely whispered and then turned to leave.

Beketamun forced back tears as she walked back to her private rooms. She wished now that her mother had allowed her to enter my bedchamber that morning and then she could have apologised to me. Everything could have been made right again between us that morning. Instead now the sun was dropping fast in the sky and she still carried her regret. She was almost to her room where she hoped Kamankh would be resting and ready to dine with her. As she turned one last corner Menkheperre appeared before her, also heading to his rooms.

"Ah Sister, how are you?" he smiled.

"I wish I could say well but I am looking forward to the sanctuary of my rooms," she replied dryly.

"As we all do!" he said loudly.

"Menkheperre, have you visited with Father today?" Beketamun asked, hoping her simple question would reveal if I had met with him also.

"I did see him but he actually came to me at the army rooms," he answered and then stepped close to his sister and dropped his voice as low as he could. "Did he also seek you to apologise?"

Beketamun's wide eyes answered this for him and then she shook her head as tears filled her eyes again.

"Oh Sister, I am sure he is yet to find you also," he said, and touched her shoulder.

Beketamun kept shaking her head, "He also sought Siamun for the same reason when I was close by, but he has not chosen to do so with me."

Menkheperre repeated his belief that she was simply next. "He is far more ill than he imagines. I had to insist that he use the sedan. He is probably just sleeping to make sure he is rested enough to meet you."

Beketamun remained unconvinced and bid Menkheperre goodbye and continued on to her rooms. She found Kamankh freshly dressed after bathing and relaxing with some wine. He jumped up as his wife entered and crossed the room to greet her with an embrace as he always did. Beketamun fell into his arms and cried great sobs until he felt the tears wet the shoulder where her face rested. He rocked her gently, not saying anything knowing the hurt that she had been carrying since the night before and could only imagine what may have happened to inflame this today.

When she finally settled he pulled back, kissed her forehead, then walked her to the bedchamber. He made her lie upon the bed and then lay beside her, stroking her hair gently. "Beloved, do you wish to share with me and lessen your grief?" he whispered.

Kamankh had no idea that Beketamun had visited me the night before. Beketamun had merely said she wished to check upon her mother before she slept. He was in a deep sleep by the time Beketamun returned. So as his wife lay there and now recounted what she had said to me the night before and the meetings I held with my sons, he suddenly found himself somewhat bemused.

"Well my dear, I can't say I am surprised that you had the courage to speak up to your father but to speak to a Pharaoh so!" he said and burst out laughing. "And now a full day later you are still alive and our children and I are not in exile. I would somehow accept that as an apology. I dare say he is avoiding you lest he receive another scolding."

Beketamun could see Kamankh's reasoning but failed to join him in finding the humour. As her husband continued to stroke her hair she slept lightly, escaping from her hurt and remorse. She heard a servant tap at the door and felt the bed rise slightly as Kamankh stood up to receive a message. He was soon beside her once again and he gently shook her. "Beloved, your father has summoned you to his rooms," he said quietly.

Beketamun sat up quickly, her eyes wide and her chest pounding, "Will you come with me?"

"I will walk with you but I cannot enter," He shook his head and another grin crept across his face. "You began this alone, you can end it alone."

Beketamun bathed quickly and dressed, her mind racing the whole time. One moment she smiled with excitement that now her time for an apology had also come, then her heart would sink as she considered she may also be called for a reprimand. As much as she wanted to get to my rooms quickly and have this curiosity satisfied she also wished she could delay it forever. She walked the corridors with Kamankh by her side but he was little comfort, grinning away and making small talk with the guards sent to escort them. His voice was buried beneath the noise in her head and as she saw the doors to my rooms grow closer this clamour was replaced with the heavy thudding of her heart. A few paces from the doors Kamankh grabbed her arm stopping her steady approach.

"I will bid you goodbye here," he said and kissed her cheek, "and here I shall also wait."

Beketamun nodded and as she turned to continue the guards that stood eternally by my doors opened them. I believe she hardly knew how she managed those last few paces to stand in my doorway and my first sight of her showed a face I had seen only few times--that of a woman about to faint.

"Come and sit with me Beketamun," I called out to her. "You must forgive me not rising to greet you but I am terribly fatigued from my turn."

Indeed I was and my face showed it even more than when I was dressed that afternoon. Beketamun walked softly and sat across from me. She dropped her head and looked to her hands sitting in her lap. I suddenly remembered Neferure sitting across from me that night Hatshepsut had dragged her in here to sleep with me.

"There is still some light outside, let us be seated in the garden," I said, and slowly began to lift myself out of my chair.

Beketamun forgot her own fears as she watched me using the table edge to help push myself to standing. She said nothing even though she wished to. She also resisted the urge to run to my side and hold my arm to support me as I walked stiffly, instead remaining one pace behind me. We sat in the chairs that looked across the whole garden and traces of pink and red were now in the sky just above the top of the walls. I sighed, grateful we could meet somewhere away from the courts and the wide ears that were around every corner.

I reached over and touched Beketamun's hand as she sat beside me and she jumped but I did not pull my hand away; I kept it in place and looked to her. Her face was once again down but I held my gaze knowing she would have to look up soon and she did within moments. I know it would have been hard for her and as our eyes met I smiled tenderly. Within that smile was all that my daughter needed to know and she began to cry. Tears filled my eyes also for just having her walk through my doors once again was all that I needed also.

We sat quietly and soon both our tears were dry. We continued to sit hand in hand looking across my beautiful garden that was disappearing within its own shadows that grew by the minute. As the plants disappeared though the sky grew more spectacular and we both looked up as the colours swirled and played with each other.

"So beautiful," I said quietly, "and never will we see two evening skies that are ever the same." Beketamun nodded beside me and finally I saw her smile. "I like that this is so--that no two days are alike for it means that days that we regret are lost and will not occur again. The sun will rest and then so do we, to start fresh again when it rises."

I paused for a while as we watched the colours now pale and the first faint sparkles of stars began their show. It was so nice to sit quietly with my daughter and admire the simple elegance of the evening sky. I looked around me at my lovely garden now lit by the faint glow of lamps and candles set upon the windowsills of my rooms. I looked through the open doors that led to my rooms and all that was there within them. I saw the lush fabrics draped everywhere, the elaborate furniture, golden ornaments and a servant waiting around every corner waiting to serve me. There it all was every day, as natural and expected a part of my life as waking in the morning. A peasant would walk these rooms in awe, astounded at my wealth, but I walk these rooms as though they are my right. I suddenly wondered what my life would be like if I were to lose all of this. As though Beketamun heard me pondering I felt her squeeze my hand. I looked at my daughter and I suddenly saw in her face the most profound beauty that made everything around us disappear.

I smiled at her, "Come join me for dinner. It will be my honour to have you as company tonight."

This time as I slowly began to lift out of my chair she was by my side offering her hand and I took it. When the doors to my rooms opened once again Kamankh was still in his place as he had promised to his wife. Beketamun now walked towards him arm-in-arm with me and he smiled as he saw us, then stepped forward and bowed as graciously as he always did.

"Your Highness," he said. "I trust you are feeling much better?"

"Yes I am Kamankh, and now that my daughter has visited with me I feel all the more revived," I said smiling.

"Wonderful!" said Kamankh beaming at Beketamun as though his smile could say "I told you so!"

"Father has invited us to dine with him tonight," she said smiling back.

"Wonderful!" was all Kamankh could say again and he was so right--it was wonderful.

I lay in bed that night with Satiah once more by my side and felt that order had been restored. My ears searched for any sounds that might be there to haunt me but I could hear no laughter tonight. All I could hear was the gentle sound of Satiah's breathing as she slept beside me. I had finally heard the last of

Hatshepsut; I knew it in my core. If only I could now wipe her existence from the country itself, but this was a much larger task and I could never imagine destroying her mortuary temple or dismantling the temple structures that she had commissioned. I would find a way to correct her heresy at being crowned a Pharaoh though. This simply had to be done, not just to heal my family dynasty, but also to make sure this never happened again.

Amenhotep had not seen or spoken to any of his brothers or sisters that day. He had returned to his rooms the night before and sat staring at the floor for sometime. He simply could not believe that I had handled the matter so badly. Now his siblings seemed to hate him. If ever his role as eldest male set him apart from the others now it was ever more so. He believed this divide would always remain and he now felt more wary than ever.

Menkheperre's words still stung his ears. To hear his younger brother declare his delight at not being successor ripped at something inside him. He wished he could be the one to say such words and he actually sent a curse to Amenemhat for leaving him in this position, and then just as quickly prayed in the hope of cancelling it. Tiaa entered the room; still just a consort despite having bore his successor and other children she had not been invited to the meeting and was curious as to how it had gone. She could not ask outright as this was also not a consort's place to do so. Instead she fussed about Amenhotep as she always did, offering him wine and wiping at his forehead with a cloth. When he did not speak she stepped away. "Sire, I would seek to retire if you do not require any more from me this evening," she said bowing her head.

"I would like for you to sleep beside me tonight," he said, looking up to her from his chair.

"As you please, Sire," she said, bowing her head once again and made her way to the bedchamber.

There were many ways in which a consort could have her patron request their presence in bed but the way Amenhotep had asked was the first time Tiaa had heard it worded in such a way. This was because this is what Amenhotep truly just wanted of his consort tonight. He just wished for some gentle company from someone he believed cared for him. Tonight the only person who was that to him was the mother of his children and he wished to have her as close as possible. When he climbed into bed Tiaa began to lift her night shift ready for Amenhotep to begin.

"No, Tiaa, leave your robe in place, let us just rest together tonight," he said softly.

As nice as it would have been to forget about the evening in that way he knew his body would never respond tonight as it needed to. Tiaa lay there quite confused, not sure what she should do now. Amenhotep only made this more puzzling when he slid across and pulled her against him, wrapping his arms around her and nuzzling her hair.

"You are a wonderful comfort to me tonight Tiaa," he whispered.

She waited for him to begin moving against her, to have his hands start moving around her body, but he lay as he was, against her side, his arms wound around her and soon she felt his breath fall into the rhythm that she knew accompanied his sleep. Tiaa smiled, her confusion melting into a sensation that she had only felt as she nursed her children to sleep. She gently turned her head and kissed Amenhotep on the forehead as he slept and soon she too was asleep.

The next morning Amenhotep rose at dawn as he always did. He knew there were viziers attending court today but Siamun and I could deal with that. He had heard there was battle training on the plains outside Thebes and told his butler to inform all that this is where he would spend the day. Moving quickly through the palace in order to avoid anyone he was soon upon his horse and passing through the boundaries of the city. As the city grew smaller behind him and the desert plains opened up before him he let out a great sigh.

"Sire, is all well?" asked one of his bodyguards riding up close.

"Yes, yes," Amenhotep replied. "It just feels wonderful to be out in the open."

"Yes, Sire," he nodded and dropped back again.

Amenhotep's retreat to the desert worked for him just as he intended and he managed to forget all about the dreadful meeting. He spent most of the day training and consulting with the commanders at the site, barely thinking of anything happening at the palace. There was even the delight of a chariot race--something he had not indulged in for years. As the sun began to fade he knew he must head home and he sighed once more. Hopefully things would have smoothed out somewhat with the passage of time.

As he entered the palace he felt the answer to that. There was quiet and calm, not entirely unusual for night time in the palace but somehow it had settled a lot earlier tonight. His butler greeted him at the door of his rooms as expected with the usual affectations and then added, "Your brother Prince Menkheperre waits to see you Sire."

Amenhotep froze in place and then rolled his eyes. He was exhausted and filthy, all he desired was to bathe, eat and then sleep. Something within him was not surprised that what he had avoided all day now waited to greet him. He just wished it wasn't sitting in his rooms and with Menkheperre's temper.

"I need to bathe," he said abruptly. "I will be with him shortly."

Menkheperre snorted when he was told, not that he minded waiting for his brother, it was just that his favourite priestess was waiting for him to hold a special "prayer session" and he wished this part of his evening with his brother to be over. He was slumped in his chair from boredom when Amenhotep stepped into the room. He barely sat up but grinned widely. "Brother, I imagine you weren't expecting to see me this evening," he said half laughing.

Amenhotep was not amused at all. This was typical of Menkheperre to come here and begin another argument by trying to be funny.

"No, I was not, Menkheperre," he said dryly. "I am fatigued from serious training and wish to rest. What brings you to my rooms?"

"Well I would have liked a warmer welcome, but I suppose that is understandable given my recent behaviour," he said trying not to laugh again.

"Please Brother, I am tired," Amenhotep rolled his eyes. "If you are here to simply mock me then get it over and done with that I may rest."

"I did not come here to mock," Menkheperre said. "I wish for us to make amends."

Amenhotep was still walking to sit as they began speaking and he stopped and looked at his brother, expecting to see the smirk or grin that would let him know that this also was said in jest. He saw neither; for once Menkheperre was actually serious. Amenhotep sat and smoothed his kilt over his legs. He then nodded to his brother to speak.

"Father came to see me in the army rooms today," Menkheperre informed. "Today he did something I never imagined a Pharaoh would ever do; he apologised. I believe that if a king can find it within him to do so despite believing he acted with noble intention then so also can I." He paused for a moment searching Amenhotep's face, but Amenhotep sat still and blank so he continued on. "I hope that we can let the events of last night vanish and not remain between us. I ask that you forgive me the brutish tone in which I chose to speak with you."

"Of course Brother," Amenhotep said nodding his head. "It is apparent to me now that we all wish the meeting never occurred." He leaned forward in his chair. "Menkheperre, can you now forgive me for having such thoughts of you?"

"Of course!" he beamed back. "How could you not think such things of your more handsome younger brother, especially when I am a better swordsman than you!"

Amenhotep was too tired to laugh but smiled back. "What of Siamun and Beketamun?" he added soberly.

"Father sought Siamun also. As I made my way here I heard that Beketamun was dining with him so I imagine he also made his amends with our sister," he said smiling still.

Amenhotep sighed, "I sometimes wish we were all young again Menkheperre. Remember when it was that we could spend our days playing?"

"I still play, Amenhotep," Menkheperre said without hesitation. "Perhaps if you found ways to still play in your adult body then maybe you would not find life so serious. You make your place in life so...*heavy*." He shook his hands as he said this. "When was the last time you rode for fun? I know each time you pick up a sword now you are thinking that you need to be perfect for Father. Let me tell you, the very fact that you breathe makes you perfect to him. There is not one person who doubts your abilities to rule

Amenhotep. Maybe when you can see this also then you will enjoy the path the Gods have given you."

Amenhotep nodded as Menkheperre finished. "Now Amenhotep, I believe my apology has been successful and you have had the bonus of me sharing my view of life with you. I shall be on my way. I have a priestess waiting to bless me," he said as he rose from his chair, smoothing down his kilt and straightening his collar.

"Menkheperre! A priestess?" Amenhotep grimaced. "Have you no boundaries?"

"No I don't, Amenhotep. Perhaps you might try letting go some of yours," he answered laughing and then made his way to the doors. As he was about to step through the doorway he turned and then laughing once more he added, "I highly recommend you try a priestess. It is the closest that you will get to tasting a Goddess." And then he was gone, his laughter echoing behind him.

Amenhotep sat and suddenly felt lonely. Despite his tiredness he had enjoyed his brother's company and wished he were still here. In fact if Menkheperre hadn't his liaison with the priestess he would have called him back. Suddenly Siamun came to mind and he decided to seek him for company with the perfect excuse that he now could apologise to him.

Amenhotep made his way through the corridors and as he neared Siamun's rooms he saw the doors were open. He could hear noise and some movement so made his way quietly that he might see what was happening without disturbing them. He approached the doors and gestured to his own guards to move to the side of the hallway and then he too stood against the wall so he could watch inside without being seen.

There in the huge room sat Siamun with his wife by his side. Before them their three daughters and two sons were acting out a story about the Gods. Each child yelled out their line and moved dramatically when it was their turn. Siamun and his wife would clap and cheer every gesture and sentence, often wiping at their eyes, as they laughed so hard. Then finally the play ended with the youngest daughter as Isis stepping forward to declare peace and harmony. Siamun and his wife jumped from their chairs madly clapping then grabbed each child in turn, hugging them tightly to congratulate their performance. Amenhotep watched and his heart ached. Now he knew the truth of Menkheperre's words.

He was contemplating turning back to his own rooms when Siamun's youngest son saw him within the shadows of the doors.

"Uncle!" he cried, and they all turned to see him standing in the door.

Immediately they all stopped and turned to face him, bowing their heads.

"Welcome Brother. What a shame you missed our little play," Siamun said, stepping forward to grasp his brother's hand.

"I came to speak with you but I shall call again another time," Amenhotep said softly, hating himself for disturbing their fun. "I do not wish to disrupt your family anymore."

"You disrupt nothing, Sire," Siamun's wife answered. "The children were finished and now must make their way to sleep."

This of course was met with the usual symphony of sighs and pleas soon cut short by their father supporting their mother's decision. "Goodnight my children," he said sternly. "Now is my time to spend with my brother. Go!"

They shuffled out of the room, herded by their mother and suddenly the room was decidedly quieter with just the two brothers standing opposite each other.

"Come," said Siamun. "Let us share some wine." He made his way to a table and called for a servant to bring some wine. "What a pleasure to have you here. I do believe this is the first time you have been to my rooms."

"It is indeed, and much delayed. I should have been here many times to seek my brother's company," Amenhotep replied. "I wish it was for some other reason than to apologise to you for being the cause of the meeting last night."

"No, no, STOP!" Siamun waved his hand and put back down the glass of wine that he had just picked up. "I have already endured one such unnecessary meeting with Father today--do not make me repeat it with you!" he almost begged, screwing his face up as though his wine had been sour. "Amenhotep, I do not begrudge you or Father's actions but I cannot endure such continued talk of it. In fact the sooner we can stop discussion about it then the further it is from us. Now," he raised his glass, "*please* let us simply enjoy being brothers drinking wine."

He paused, holding his glass in mid-air waiting for Amenhotep to hopefully agree. Amenhotep raised his glass also and nodded.

"Yes Brother," he said softly, "that is a much better idea." Then they made their agreement firm as they both drank from their glasses.

Siamun beamed as he gulped his wine, watching his brother over the edge of his glass mirroring his actions. He put the glass down and reached over the table to where a low box sat. It was painted in gold with lapis and other stones making a pattern on its sides. On the top was carved a grid, also painted but now chipped and scuffed from much contact.

"Shall we play a game or two of Senet?" Siamun asked lifting an eyebrow.

Amenhotep nodded. "Yes, let's play."

The one or two games of Senet became many more than that and as the evening grew into deep night the bottles of wine also matched the number of games. Suddenly the tiredness that Amenhotep pushed aside to be with his brother was well upon him once again and now with a decidedly thick layer of drunkenness added to it. He bid his goodbyes to an equally drunk Siamun and dragged his feet to his rooms, thankful that he had guards to accompany him should he not make it. Amenhotep collapsed upon his bed as his butler undressed him and he fell asleep with his arms and legs spread over the bed and a smile spread across his face.

The next morning when Amenhotep woke his head was heavy and his stomach was moving in that uneasy way it always did after he drank too much. He called to his butler to fetch a bowl to keep nearby as he was bathed and dressed. Amenhotep walked to the court and smiled the whole way as he remembered his evening with Siamun. Amenhotep was still smiling as he entered the record room where Siamun sat.

"I see by your smile that you are not as afflicted as I am this morning," Siamun laughed and then stopped suddenly, putting his hand to his forehead. "My wife was not so pleased with me when I climbed into bed smelling of wine."

"Oh trust me--I am quite as sore as you," Amenhotep laughed. "I am just glad it is from having some fun instead of battle." Amenhotep looked at the scrolls surrounding Siamun. "As there is no audience today I thought I may join my sons in their training."

"That is a wonderful idea, Brother," Siamun answered. "My sons are with them too so you can show your influence over all the princes."

Amenhotep nodded and grunted, as he liked the sound of that, then made his way to the large courtyard near the army rooms where Menkheperre had felled Suresh all those years ago. Three targets were set up and the young princes were all getting their bows and arrows ready for their archery training

As Amenhotep approached young Thutmose took aim and his arrow flew across the courtyard, hitting the target so hard that it shook upon its stand. His tutor clapped hard. "Well done Your Highness, a fine example to the other princes!"

Amenhotep's chest swelled as he saw and heard this. "Yes, a fine example to set indeed!" he bellowed to make his presence known. The tutor and all the princes turned and bowed. Young Thutmose blushed slightly as Amenhotep walked towards him now realising that he had been watched.

"You are quite the equal to what I was at your age Son," he said to Thutmose warmly, "I believe you may even grow to rival me." Amenhotep laughed as he grasped his son's shoulder.

"Father, now watch me," cried Ahmenmose his second son, barely able to lift his bow and arrow at the same time, intent on also impressing his father.

The tutor quickly stepped behind him to support the bow so the young boy could use all his strength to launch the arrow. Ahmenmose's hand let go of the arrow and it sailed across the yard landing just shy of the target. The boy hung his head and kicked the ground. "I am not as good as Thutmose."

"Pah! You are perfectly fine for a seven year old. One more year and you will hit the target as hard as your eight year old brother." Amenhotep was relishing every moment of this. "Now perhaps I could show you a few of my tricks. That is of course if your tutor will allow me to join you all?"

"Sire, how could I deny the princes the chance to learn from Egypt's greatest soldier!" he beamed and bowed. Amenhotep nodded, accepting the praise he knew was true.

"Did you hear that, young princes?" Amenhotep said smiling as brightly as he could. "Now let me see what we can do about making you all as great as I am," he finished with a laugh.

I had always hoped that my actions would teach my children as much as any words I spoke, but I never imagined my talk to Menkheperre would lead him to seek such an audience with Amenhotep and then for Amenhotep to seek Siamun. When I did find out my heart swelled and my pride in my children expanded beyond all that it had been.

Amenhotep was different from that day. He walked lighter, smiled more often and his sense of servitude became matched by the joy of nurturing his children. In turn his children flourished and I was soon hearing word from the war rooms that young Thutmose was becoming as grand a soldier as any man in my family. My intentions in calling that meeting may have begun in a less than noble way but I will never regret the events that it in turn led to.

When the day of my mother's funeral arrived it was a very different family that rode from Karnak to the Valley. Not the least changed was myself thanks to what you would call having suffered a heart attack. I would never call it a suffering though. Sure I was not as robust as before, I now tired quicker and my sword felt heavier but my mind was clearer than it had ever been. Riding into the Valley to place my mother's sarcophagus with my father's made me aware of just how clear I had become. On this day as we passed Hatshepsut's temple I did not feel consumed with anger or some inflated superiority. This time I felt nothing. I just saw a monument. However it was still a monument that carried images of a woman dressed as a Pharaoh.

CHAPTER TWENTY-FIVE

Mourning was over once again and we were quickly celebrating the arrival of Meritamen's second child; a beautiful girl that we all agreed would be named Isis. It seemed so natural that our loss should be replaced. I held my granddaughter in my arms as she was blessed at the altar of Karnak and looked up to see my children surrounding me, in turn surrounded by their children.

"Come young Thutmose," I called out to my eldest grandson. "Stand close so you may know what to do when your grandchildren arrive." He ran to my side and I grabbed his hand, keeping my other arm curled around the baby. "Look at our family young prince. Today I shall also ask Amun to surround you with family when you stand here as Pharaoh."

There was one person that I considered family who was not there though, my priestess Arisina. Her apologies had been sent and the priests relayed to me that she was resting in bed unable to leave. It was not something I was surprised to hear so with the ceremony over I made my way to the priestess's quarters to see her. It was highly unsuitable for any man to enter the bedchamber of a priestess and several priestesses actually began to speak of moving Arisina as I approached.

"Nonsense," I cried out while inside Arisina was saying just the same to those around her. So I walked in to see my beloved teacher resting upon high pillows on her bed. Her face did not reflect her discomfort and she assured me she was in no pain but I knew how powerful she was. She could have laid there with a broken leg and still found strength to smile and then counsel me if needed.

"Have you everything you need?" I asked.

"Yes," she said softly and smiled. "Just as I always have had."

"Let me bring you to the palace," I said. "You can recover there."

I choked on the word *recover* and Arisina smiled as she heard it.

"Oh my dear Pharaoh," she said. "We both know the only recovery for me involves Osiris."

I wanted to laugh but I just couldn't. "Then come spend your last days in the comfort of the palace," I choked. "Let me return to you that which I owe you. You oversaw my first days, now I can make sure your last are grand."

"They are already grand," she said and sighed. "No Thutmose, I shall spend my last days here at my temple. This vocation has given me grandeur beyond words. I wish to stay close to my Gods."

I knew there was no changing this so instead I would make my way to see her each day, always with at least one daughter carrying some flowers or fruit from the palace gardens. Her smiles remained so that seeing her each day made it hard to witness her fading as I imagined she would simply remain as she was forever. Then one day when I entered she was not lying propped on her pillows as always--instead she was lying flat.

"I just feel more comfortable like this," she said matter-of-factly. "Now come close so I do not have to strain my voice." I sat on the edge of her bed and took her hand in mine. "I was with you on your first day and now here you are at my last," she sighed.

"How do you know this is your last?" I asked.

"After all I have taught you, you now you choose this moment to doubt me?" she strained a smile and I had to return it with my own smile.

"Thank you," she said. "I thank the Gods for sending me to be part of your life. Now you need to go and continue living while I begin my afterlife."

I furrowed my brow but stood to leave believing she just needed rest and said my farewells. "I shall see you again tomorrow." I said as I kissed her goodbye.

"No, you will not Pharaoh," she said firmly.

As she had always been in the forty-eight years I had shared with her, Arisina was right. That night with only a sliver of moon above the temple, when all was still and quiet, she took her last breath. She had refused a grand tomb in the Valley close to where mine was carved, deciding instead to make her final place in the temple mausoleum near her beloved sacred lake alongside all the other Karnak priests and priestesses. Of course I would honour her decision.

I finally farewelled my second mother, my grandest teacher and my most loyal friend and it felt strange to now stand as a Pharaoh with no official elders. There were no parents, no tutors, no priests or viziers who had known me from birth. All that had guided and nurtured me were gone. I stood on a balcony of the palace the morning I received the news of Arisina's death and looked over Thebes and to the temple at Karnak. As I stood I realised all the pillars of my life as I knew it were no longer. I thought about this, breathed in deep and felt there was no sense of grief or reluctance to acknowledge this. I called out to my butler and asked that my children be summoned so I could tell them the news of Arisina's passing.

Prince Thutmose turned ten and I ordered a grand feast to celebrate. Everyone was puzzled as to why I should choose this age to celebrate as it did not mark any usual milestone for a young man be him prince or otherwise. Thutmose had not been made a soldier yet, nor had he began to show the signs of manhood. I can admit now that it was more a celebration for myself. As you will recall I became a Pharaoh at age ten and I was beyond delighted that my grandson, and successor to my own successor, had reached this age with no need to be anything other than the child that he still was.

The entire family and palace rode to Karnak and we all prayed for Thutmose to grow and prosper, for him to remain vital and strong and for him to gather the wisdom of the Gods so that when his time came he could rule as worthy as any of his forefathers. Young Thutmose was quite amused by all the ceremony and I could see that he hadn't quite yet grasped the immensity of his role. That was fine by me, as I knew he had many years in which this could be realised. I watched him smile as the prayers were recited and the priests dabbed oil upon his hands and feet. He could hardly believe the attention he was getting and with his grandfather the Pharaoh by his side. The priests finished their incantations and stood upon the altar before us with their heads bowed--then a high priest stood forward.

"The Gods will now call upon Prince Thutmose so that he may speak to them," he said with that wonderful solemnity required of a royal ceremony.

I nodded to my grandson. "Go to the altar and pray to Amun."

Thutmose rose from his chair and walked slowly to the altar. I could sense his nerves and held my breath. All the court officials were here, the highest priests of Karnak and the most important viziers. Each one would be measuring my grandson's performance and words as indication of how capable the future Pharaoh was. Every gesture or phrase would be tomorrow's gossip; even the way he now stopped to kneel before the priests was being made note of. I prayed to Amun to help my grandson speak strongly and then he began.

"I call to Amun to give thanks for my life. I call to Amun to thank him for making me my father's heir. I call to Amun to give thanks for all that the Pharaoh has done for our country. I call to Amun to give thanks for the prosperity of our people." He paused to take a breath and finally so did I. With the thanksgiving said he could now continue on with prayer. "I pray to Amun to keep me strong so that I may ride with the army and protect Egypt. I pray to Amun to grant me wisdom to rule the courts justly. I pray to Amun to make my seed strong to provide future kings to Egypt. I pray to Amun to protect my family. I pray to Amun to protect the people of Egypt and her allies. I pray to Amun--to--to…" He stopped and I saw him wince as he tried to remember his words. "To make me as powerful as my father and grandfather and their forefathers that I may rule as noble as they have. I pray to Amun to keep the order of Ma'at pure for Egypt. I pray to Amun for the souls of my ancestors to be granted eternity in paradise. I pray to Amun to grant strength and wisdom to my brothers and sisters that they may make my rule more glorious."

His voice had wavered on the first few words but it grew strong as he continued. I almost wanted to applaud at the amazing job he had done. Tiaa and Matreya had tutored him well, making him recite the prayer over and over for weeks leading to the ceremony. No one could honestly speak any criticism of Thutmose as no child his age could have done better.

As he climbed onto my chariot to ride with me back to the palace he looked up. "Grandfather, I spoke well didn't I?" he asked.

"You were magnificent Thutmose," I said with all honesty.

"Grandfather, as I finished I added a silent prayer that Amun make me as good an archer as Father. Was that wrong?" he asked quietly.

"Very wrong, Thutmose," I said, with a stern face and he cowered. "You should have prayed to be as good an archer as I!" I laughed and he smiled up at me. "Now stand before me so that all of Thebes can see you."

We had a wonderful ride back to the palace with Thutmose standing tall and holding the front of the chariot as I flicked the reigns on either side of him. The commoners lined the streets with the hope they would see me as they always did when I rode the streets, but today I decided not to take all the glory.

"Wave, Thutmose--they come to see you today," I said loudly so that he could hear me over all the noise they made.

That night I sat Thutmose between Amenhotep and myself at my table overlooking all others in the grand dining hall. This was a very high honour and my grandson knew it. He lapped up every second and as we were well into the meal he sat back against his chair, his stomach swollen from too much food. He was holding his cup in both hands and grinned as he looked to me.

"This has been the most wonderful day," he said.

"Yes it has," Amenhotep answered, "You must thank your grandfather for such a celebration," he gestured with his head towards me.

"Thank you Grandfather," he said still grinning, holding onto his cup as though for dear life. "I wish I could summon a day like this for you."

I leant forward to Thutmose. "Look to your left," I said. "Who do you see?"

Thutmose turned his head. "My father?" he answered and I nodded.

"Now who is to your right?" I asked.

"You?" he answered and I nodded again.

"Who else of your family do you see?" I asked and sat back in my chair.

"Mother is here, Grandmother and Satiah, my uncles and aunts, my brothers and cousins," he said looking over them as he spoke.

"Thutmose when I turned ten the only family I had here was my mother. I also had an aunt and cousin in the palace but they despised me so much that they may as well have been strangers." I said plainly. "That you can sit here and have so many people around you who love you is a triumph for me as well as you. So you see you have summoned this day for me as well. I pray one day you will sit here and celebrate your own grandson with just as much family surrounding you and then you will know my joy."

As the following decade passed all was well in my kingdom. Canaan remained calm, the crops in Egypt were once again plentiful and my grandchildren grew stronger. My beloved Satiah though continued to fade beside me. Her demise after losing Nefertiry had been sudden and harsh and everyone who knew her saw the changes in those first few weeks following our daughter's death. It was now ten years later and her decline was being measured out in small doses; so small each day that not even I who spent each night with her by my side noticed. Then we would be sitting in the garden and the sunlight would show the lines in her face and the darkness under her eyes. I would then see how fragile she had become.

Old age was more rapid in our time with people rarely living beyond fifty years. Despite the skills of our physicians, many illnesses or diseases carried out their intentions without any significant impediment. We cared not for the longevity you seek as we knew another grand life awaited us in paradise. However the pull of life can be great and we often wished for those around us to remain to keep our lives full. I always knew I would have to face the day that I would be separated from my beloved. It is just that I always imagined it would be she that would say goodbye to me as I left. This had been the way of all men in my family, but just as I had changed so much in my time, this would be another pattern that I would break.

I slept soundly but always aware of my surrounds. This is the way of a Pharaoh, always needing to be alert to protect my land and myself. When Satiah slept beside me I felt every turn she made and could hear the soft murmurs she sometimes made as she always rested so peacefully. I would watch her sometimes and smile knowing that she deserved to sleep so soundly as any virtuous person should.

One night though I felt her turn more than before and her murmurs turned to moans. I woke and as I reached over to her I could feel the sheets damp around her. I shouted out to my servants and within seconds the room was full of guards and maids waiting for instructions. "Call the physicians" I shouted, "and get wet cloths for the Queen." I lifted Satiah in my arms and her eyes tried to open but fell closed again. "Fear not my beloved," I whispered to her as chaos erupted around us.

Satiah though had no fear that needed consoling. She was ready to go. My wife had lived a full life with integrity, honesty and purest love. I was the fearful one holding onto her.

The physicians came and started to grind herbs and brew teas in my chamber whilst the maids wiped her body. Neither did any good though, and anything we poured into her was soon coughed out and her skin glistened with sweat within minutes of wiping her. Her chest heaved and her hands would grasp at the sheets occasionally. I stayed on the bed beside her but as the second hour showed no sign of her recovery the chief physician stepped forward.

"Sire, I suggest you leave the bed and sit upon a chair," he said cautiously. I did not rebut him though as I knew what he inferred. The last thing needed now was for me to join my wife in illness.

So I sat upon a chair just as close anyway, stroking her hand whenever she moaned. "I am here beloved," I said softly, "I will not leave you."

When dawn made itself known and Satiah's fever had not abated the chief physician stepped forward again. "Sire let us call for the priests," he said plainly and then we all knew that higher help was needed for Satiah now.

I shook my head though. "No--not the priests. Call the priestesses of Isis for her." My beloved would have her favourite Goddess with her. The physician nodded and my butler who had heard this left the room to summon the priestesses. "Call for Beketamun and Siamun also," I said when he returned.

Beketamun had foregone her eye makeup to get there as soon as she could which was a good thing as her tears when she saw her mother would have had sent kohl streaming down her face. When she rushed to Satiah's bedside and cried "Mother!" Satiah actually softly opened her eyes and we saw her smile just for a moment. Siamun followed soon after and once again Satiah opened her eyes and smiled.

We arranged ourselves in chairs beside her bed so that we were not only close by but so Satiah could see us should she open her eyes again. The priestesses gathered in a corner and begin their soft chanting, occasionally stepping towards the bed to blow incense smoke over my wife or to dab oils on her hands, feet and heart. It may have been my imagination but I am sure her chest did not heave so much as she heard their prayers and smelt the oils and incense.

Our vigil remained in silence by the bed and we watched for any sign that her illness was receding but it would not. "Sire should we move the Queen to her chambers?" my butler asked. I just shook my head, scared that the slightest change to her now would just take her quicker.

Isis came to the door, heavy with her second child. I looked up, shook my head and held my hand up to stop her coming closer. She understood my concern for her and the child so she nodded, burst into tears and left immediately. The others also came but having heard of Isis' reception they too came no further than the door, said a quick prayer and left. Then Matreya, the one person I did not expect arrived. When I looked up and saw her standing in the doorway I half expected to see her smiling, gloating that finally her day to be chief wife in every way was near. She was not smiling though and she cried tears like all of us.

Matreya did not stop at the door and walked straight to Satiah. Matreya bent over and softly kissed her upon the cheek and then whispered something that none of us could hear, "Peace to you my sister." As she stood up straight I once again saw Satiah try to smile. This was not lost on Matreya who cried new tears as she turned to us sitting beside the bed. She walked to us and kissed Beketamun upon the cheek. She turned to me but hesitated. "Thank you for coming Matreya," I said softly and took her hand in mine and kissed it. She nodded and stared at her hand for a moment--the only affection I had ever shown her. Matreya looked at me, bowed her head and then was gone.

The praying continued and the fans of feathers continued their rhythm to try and cool Satiah. The sun continued to climb in the sky and as it reached its peak everything changed. Satiah opened her eyes and turned her head to see us sitting beside her and smiled.

"Oh Mother!" cried Beketamun.

Satiah reached out her hand to me and I left my chair to take her hand in mine as I sat upon the bed once again. "You have been most brave, my beloved," I said, and kissed her hand gently. Satiah smiled once more and turned to look at her children. I could see tears in her eyes. "No tears now my love, rest some more so we might dine a fine supper tonight," I said. She smiled once more but now the tears spilled over her cheeks. I saw her chest suddenly rise sharply. It dropped just as suddenly and rose again. Satiah's eyes were wide and clear. I felt her hand tighten around mine and then her chest dropped down again. This time though it would not rise again and her hand went soft.

Within the bed where we had consummated our marriage, become lovers, conceived our children and held each other in comfort I had now held my wife's hand as she took her last breath. I could hardly comprehend it as I sat there. I had watched many men on the battlefield as their *ka* left their body with blood gurgling in their throats and their hands grabbing at wounds. Never could I have imagined it could be as peaceful as this. I should not have been surprised that Satiah would leave like this though, as graceful as she had lived.

I stood as the priestesses rushed forward realising what had occurred and then I collapsed back into my chair. Beketamun grabbed my hand and was sobbing, crying "No" over and over, while Siamun leant forward and buried his face in his hands; soon his body began to shake with tears. I looked at my wife's frail little body and wished I could relive our time together. It had been too quick. I wanted her to be fourteen again, with me leading her by the hand through the palace. I thought of all we had been through together as the colours of her body rapidly faded into grey before me. Then a blur of maids and priestesses suddenly swept like a curtain before me and Satiah's body was lost behind them.

The next two months as we prepared her funeral was the strangest time for me. I would actually forget that Satiah had died. I could wake in the morning and be surprised she was not beside me. I would sit at my dinner table and wonder why her place had not been set. Once I was speaking with Beketamun about her children and said, "Let us ask your mother what she thinks." Beketamun could not answer and just stared at me wide-eyed. I grabbed her hand in mine. "I am sorry. She was with me so long I still cannot believe she is no longer here." This did not stop the tears in Beketamun's eyes nor her concern that I was showing signs of the mind illness that signalled when the viziers would retire.

I truly was nowhere near senility or dementia. I was just readjusting my life, which may seem weird, as I had lost my mother and Arisina already and they had been just as much a part of my existence and for even longer. Satiah's place though was more intimate than I ever imagined it would be. To lose the person who lay beside me at night, who shared the love of my children as equally as I loved them, was like losing a part of my physical body. It was just too hard after thirty-four years to imagine this part of my life had ended.

Satiah's tomb had been prepared as mine was many years before. As her coffin was placed within the sarcophagus I stood with my hands upon the crown of her head and watched as Matreya, the children and then my grandchildren made way to say a final prayer and farewell. Then what remained of Satiah's family entered the tomb. Her parents had passed many years earlier so it was her brother General Ahmenmose that led her family in for their goodbyes. He knelt by the sarcophagus and said a prayer, then rose and bowed to me.

"To imagine that I brought her to the palace as a young girl and now we farewell her as a Queen," he said softly before he made way for his younger brothers with their wives and children.

When all were done, the priests stepped forward and motioned for me to make my way back out but I could not move. Instead I asked that they leave instead and they looked at me not knowing what to say. Beketamun, who had stayed behind to watch over me and walk with me back into sunlight, once again had her fears for my sanity tested and walked to me touching my arm.

"Father we must go now," she said gently.

I stood still and shook my head. "No it is not time yet," I said quietly.

"Sire, we have done all that we can to ensure her passage," the eldest priest said.

This was true but there was more that I needed to do. I looked up and squared my shoulders, then spoke as clearly as I would in court. "You shall all leave me to say my final farewell to my wife."

The priests looked to Beketamun who nodded and gestured with her hand to the corridor that led the way out. They all bowed and left--not happy at all to have their ceremony altered. I watched them all leave with a stony face, while Beketamun watched me. When the final priest was well within the corridor she turned to me. "Would you like me to come for you in some time Father?" she asked.

"No," I said firmly. "I shall make my way when I am done."

Beketamun touched her mother's sarcophagus one last time. Even in the torchlight I could see her lip tremble as she whispered one last farewell. Then too she was gone and it was just Satiah and I deep within the stones of the Valley. I walked around so I could see her face carved in gold and traced my fingers in the beautiful lines the goldsmith had made. I smiled a little, as I knew she would have hated to be painted or carved so perfectly.

"My beautiful Queen. You made me who I am. When I met you my heart began to beat with love that I had prayed for. I was not truly a King until you were beside me as Queen. Our love made me a father." I started to cry as I thought of Amenemhat, "You gave me an heir to make my family strong and that let all know our love. You stood beside me and never faltered, not once, with nothing but love and honour for me. I thank the Gods for every minute we shared. You are the reason I am a grand Pharaoh and I will honour you with every remaining breath in my body."

I bent over and kissed her carved gold mouth wishing I had spoken those words to her before she had left. I knew she heard them anyway. "Farewell my love. I shall see you someday in paradise."

I imagined Satiah walking through the final gate of the afterlife to be greeted by her parents and mine, and then our grandparents. Then there behind them all would be Amenemhat and Nefertiry, their arms outstretched to greet her with all the joy you could imagine. My heart ached as I pictured this and suddenly I wished I were there also. I slid to the floor beside the sarcophagus and wept.

Everyone waited outside patiently despite the sun bearing down on them as it always did in the Valley. It had been over thirty minutes of people standing in silence when mutterings and murmurs began amongst those gathered. Beketamun looked up and frowned, already concerned for her father, now she had to stand here and see her mother's funeral treated with disrespect from the mourners. Amenhotep saw the look upon his sister's face. He knew he could not yell out "Silence" as he wished to. Instead he climbed aboard the closest carriage, stood above everyone and stared fiercely at all those present. His very action had stopped the chatter--but his look made them all know that they would not begin it again.

Almost an hour later I walked out into the sun, my eyes squinted already sore from my tears and now being hit by the bright light. Beketamun rushed to my side and put her arm around my waist to guide me to my carriage, whilst Amenhotep gestured for the priests to return to the tomb to place the final granite lid on the sarcophagus. I sat in the carriage waiting for them to finish with Beketamun holding me, her head resting on my shoulder. "I just needed to say some things in private," I said quietly hoping only she would hear.

Beketamun lifted her head, looked at me and nodded. "Of course Father," she said.

"Do not fear for my mind Beketamun," I said. "I just need some time to readjust my ways without her by my side."

Beketamun nodded and placed her head back upon my shoulder.

The next morning when I woke I dressed and made my way to the stables. I planned to ride back out to the Valley. I entered and saw Menkheperre was there waiting for his steed to be brought to him. He jumped when he saw me, clearly surprised to see me there so soon after the funeral.

"Father, what brings you to the stables?" he asked hesitantly.

"I do believe that is the first stupid question you have ever asked me

Menkheperre!" I exclaimed. "Why else would I be here but to gather my horse to ride."

"Of course Father," he said, and bowed his head. "And where are you planning to ride?" he continued narrowing his eyes.

I looked at him and tilted my head. "So many questions from my prince. I plan to ride to the Valley to oversee progress upon my tomb."

Menkheperre continued to stare at me, his eyes measuring me from head to toe. I was about to snap at him for his disrespect when I realised what lay behind the questions and the examination. "I see your sister has spoken with you as to my fragile state," I said brusquely as Menkheperre looked away awkwardly.

"She was just concerned for you," he said simply. "Please let me accompany you."

"I have my guards Menkheperre," I replied bluntly.

Menkheperre sighed and then took another tact that he knew would be hard for me to refuse. "Fine, I acknowledge you don't need me or anyone to act as your nurse, but we have not ridden together, just the two of us, in so long. That in itself would be nice, wouldn't it?"

My son played me perfectly. He knew I had a soft spot for him. Apart from his indiscretions with women, Menkheperre was a walking replica of me in every way. I would never use the word favourite but I did enjoy his company just that bit more than my other sons. I thought for a moment and decided that he would also be help for the true intentions of what I planned for today.

"Fine, you shall join me," I said, and then smiled. "On our return though you shall go immediately to Beketamun and tell her that her concerns are unfounded."

"As you wish Father," he said and laughed.

As usual to get to the Valley, we rode to the edge of the Nile to the pier used exclusively for my family or palace duties. We led our horses upon the barge and dismounted before we began to float across the waters. When we reached the western bank we climbed upon our horses once again and rode into the Valley. There, as always, Hatshepsut's temple stood to greet us. Sand still continued its climb against its stones. I stopped my horse in line with its huge ramps that swept up bridging between each level while Menkheperre rode to my side, watching me closely. I was yet to truly convince him that he had nothing to be concerned about.

"My son, I had no intention of visiting my tomb today," I said, and turned to him. "Today you shall join me in beginning the next chapter of our family history."

Menkheperre looked at me puzzled. I could tell he wanted to speak but he didn't. Instead he followed me in silence as I kicked my horse and began to make my way towards the temple. I stopped my horse as close as I could in the drifting sands and turned to my entourage. My four guards who were with me at all times were today joined by a scribe, hand chosen in secret by me. He did not know the complete reason for being summoned, but he did know that his discretion would be rewarded. I nodded as I looked at the six men with me. Apart from my two absent sons there were no others who I trusted more

I dismounted and then for the first time since I came here with Salas by my side I began to walk the ramps to enter Hatshepsut's temple.

I had not stepped upon it since that day, as there had been no need to. Hatshepsut had even chosen to consecrate it when I was away from Thebes, which I always believed was to avoid me pointing out the errors of the history recorded on its walls before everyone present. Not that I ever would have as such dramatics were never my way. I also had no need or desire to worship here since I had my own mortuary temple erected, in far more modest means of course. Menkheperre followed close behind me and I know his eyes watched my every facial expression and gesture. I did not pay that much attention to it though as my task at hand was too important to be distracted from.

I walked up the first ramp and stood within the first courtyard. My men following silently behind me, waited for orders. I looked about me while two guards rushed ahead to make sure all was clear to go further. As I glanced around I saw just how sad her plants were in their decaying clay pots. Suddenly I considered that maybe I would not need to do what I came to do as time itself would achieve the same thing. Then I peered up at the row of columns on the top terrace, each one with a statue in front of it. I had seen these so often from a distance but now only one terrace away they were so large and their details amplified. There stood dozens of Hatshepsut dressed as Pharaoh or as a God all lined up and smiling down on me. My resolve was returned. As soon as my guard emerged from between the columns before me crying "All safe Sire" I made my way towards the walls of paintings behind them.

"Come stand by me to make note as I call out to you," I called to the scribe. He became my shadow, following every step and looking to where I did, all the time with his charcoal ready to scratch whatever I would say upon his papyrus. I quickly scanned the wall before me searching for the lies of Hatshepsut that I now sought to correct by erasing them. However, as determined and prepared as I was I did not expect what I would see before me. There in the midst of her memoirs, for all to observe upon her departure, she had chosen to portray me dancing with the God Min, the god of fertility, the one summoned to make a man's seed strong and to help him create heirs. I froze in my tracks.

Menkheperre was close by and saw it also. "Well Father, that could explain the size of your family," he said and laughed. When I did not laugh as well he stopped. "You did not know this was here did you?"

I shook my head slowly. "Let us move to the next area," was all I could say and led everyone back out into the sun. We moved onto the colonnade to the right of the ramp leading upwards. Here was painted the day to day life of

Egypt as the people hunted and fished albeit led by Hatshepsut. It could not be faulted, even though my aunt had never touched a fishnet, and my scribe's papyrus remained blank. I stood at the base of the ramp feeling somewhat defeated. Perhaps Beketamun had been right to worry about my mind. I looked back up at the statues with their rigid smiles, somehow more like smirks now, and began to walk up the second ramp.

Now I stood before the statues and they towered over me. I could see the lines upon the fake beards, as Hatshepsut stood dressed as a Pharaoh in her male kilt. I turned to the scribe, "Note those that depict the queen dressed as pharaoh," I yelled to him and began calling out the position in which they stood. She could keep her statues of herself as a God but she would not remain staring over the Valley as a man. Now I remembered why I was here.

We moved inside and made way to the temple of Hathor. I called out the positions of two carved columns to be recorded. Next behind the colonnade was the story of her journey to Punt; the one she had never actually been upon. I scanned its images now full of colour unlike that day when Salas and I watched it just beginning to be scratched in charcoal. Menkheperre looked intently too and I saw he was quite entranced by it all. It was hard not to, it was a magnificent piece of art and record keeping combined. Then I saw him screw his face up tight, "Urgh, look at this poor ugly soul," he said.

His finger pointed to a small figure with a deep sway back, a rather large behind and folds of extra skin on their belly. Their hair was certainly in no organised manner nor were the features upon their face.

"That my son is the Queen of Punt, one of our most noble and loyal allies," I said dryly.

"Oh," he said. "Well Father, loyal she may be--but if she is an example of her local women then I am glad you have never sent me on mission there." I laughed along with him and it echoed through the colonnade.

We walked along the colonnade toward the wall painted with her birth story. A grand story it was, supporting her claim to the throne just as she always claimed she was entitled. Within its details were dozens of depictions of my grandparents, the first Pharaoh Thutmose and his most noble Queen Ahmose. If I were to touch this I would also touch them. It would be upon my very soul if I were to alter this in any way. I turned quickly and almost pushed my scribe over as I brushed past him.

Menkheperre followed tight upon my heels as I entered the Temple to Anubis, the guardian of the afterlife. I looked about at the images, drew a deep breath and waved my hand to the scribe. "Pull a fresh sheet of papyrus and stay close. There is much to record here," I said smiling. With that I looked over each wall pointing to image after image of Hatshepsut painted or carved as Pharaoh and the scribe soon needed yet another sheet of papyrus. Menkheperre watched from a corner with his arms crossed.

"Do you understand what I am doing?" I asked without even looking at him.

"I am not sure Father," he said. "Do you not fear that this will be viewed as desecration?"

I turned to look at him. "No, I do not. For this is not desecration this is correction." I could see he did not completely understand. There was general concern upon his face but still he nodded and softly replied "Yes Father" before turning to leave the temple and wait for me in the sunlight.

There were a few more carvings to be noted in the last sanctuary but here she had also interplayed her story with Neferure and myself. These too could remain untouched as no one was allowed into this space anyway. The more obvious ones would be dealt with and that was all that mattered. As we finished we passed through the small corridors beside the sanctuary which once acted as storerooms for the priests who had attended here. "Shall we check inside these also Sire?" enquired the Scribe. I looked at the cedar doors and shook my head. "There would be nothing of note within them."

However, you see, there was. Senemut had been cleverer than I knew for he loved Hatshepsut more than I ever could have imagined. His hunger for recognition would have ached as he built this temple, ordering images of a daughter and nephew who hated Hatshepsut, while he would not be recorded at all. He did find a way though and in the darkest wall of one of those small rooms in the furthest corner of the temple he carved himself kneeling before Hatshepsut. It was his version of a heart carved in a tree holding their initials forever and my indifference would mean it remained intact. I do not regret this as it has given your archaeologists so much amusement in piecing together their love affair.

I walked back out into the sun content that I had achieved what I had set out to. Menkheperre was standing looking out over the Valley and turned as I made my way out. "We are done Son," I said and he nodded, waiting for me to lead the way back down the ramps.

We were about to climb back on the horses when I saw the pile of rock that I knew covered the entrance to Senemut's tomb. I began to walk towards them and Menkheperre was instantly by my side. "Father, where are you going?"

"You were too young to remember him Menkheperre," I said as I walked. "But behind these stones lays the man who made your aunt a Pharaoh." I stopped at the rocks. There weren't so many when you were up close and you would only know what they hid if you had been told. I looked to the men surrounding me. "We need to clear these," I said plainly and bent over to move the first one.

It took us close to an hour but we cleared the entrance. We all stood covered in dust and sweat and I felt my chest twinge with the pain it always did now when I did too much. I didn't care though, the narrow doorway was clear and I wanted to laugh at the warning carved over it as I stepped inside.

The musty air made me cringe and I was thankful that the smell of the torch my guard soon had next to me masked the stale air. The corridor opened wider as we entered and I waited until all had joined me, except of course for two guards who would stay watching the entrance. I heard Menkheperre sigh as he moved beside me.

"You do not need to join me here," I said and held up my hand.

"No, I shall come with you," he replied. As concerned as he was to be stepping into a tomb he was also curious to do so, and besides he needed to see just what I planned for here.

We followed the long narrow corridor as it travelled down and then turned left *"Ah towards her temple and tomb,"* I thought. Most clever indeed of him to make sure he was as close as could be to her and his monument to her

We finally arrived at the cold, dank burial chamber. There was water upon the floor that had seeped through its rock walls and I smiled that the grand architect's plans had not been so flawless. I took the torch from my guard and waved it from top to bottom of each wall, scanning the hieroglyphs and seeing how Senemut chose to record his life. It was all standard, recalling his duties and achievements, not exposing his true link to my aunt. Then in the middle of one wall, level to where Senemut's heart lay inside his mummy in the centre of the room, Senemut chose to make his love known. Two small figures were painted; Hatshepsut sat while Senemut was before her, his hand reaching out to touch hers.

I reached down to my waist, took my dagger from its sheath and turned to look at Senemut's sarcophagus. "Father!" Menkheperre shouted, or perhaps not. The small solid room made every slight noise seem loud. "Please do not do anything you will regret," he pleaded and stepped close to me putting his hand out to take the knife.

"It's alright my son," I said nodding. "I will do nothing to harm us." I then turned back to the wall and with the tip of my dagger I scratched away at the face of Hatshepsut and then of Senemut before her, all the while Menkheperre breathed heavily beside me. I replaced my knife in its sheath and brushed away the crumbs of stone and paint that had not fallen, smiling at the empty gouges that remained. "You shall never kiss again," I said to them both.

"Are you done Father?" Menkheperre asked sharply and I nodded my reply. "Good then let us make our way lest this water rises anymore." He grabbed my arm and began to push me towards the corridor.

I am sure that was one time Menkheperre truly hated having to follow me as he would have sprinted out of the tomb if he could have. When we reached the surface he sat upon a rock and I saw his chest heaving. I ordered the guards to recover the tomb and as they began replacing the rocks I sipped on water from my canteen. I walked to Menkheperre still sitting on the rock and offered it to him. He looked up, snatched it from my hand and gulped from it. As he handed it back his eyes narrowed. "What have you involved me in today?" he asked.

"I told you before son. Correction," I answered and took another sip of water.

Menkheperre did not speak on the journey back to the palace; he rode a distance from me and on the boat sat a distance also. I knew that he kept watching me though as often I would turn to look at him and catch him doing so. I invited him to join me for lunch but he declined with an excuse that was quite transparent and I said my thank you and farewelled him. I envisioned that he would head straight to Beketamun's rooms and this is just what he did. When he arrived Beketamun was sitting and watching a maid brushing her eldest daughter's hair.

"Good day Sister," he said as he entered and nodded to his niece and the maid.

"How goes it Brother?" asked Beketamun. Then her eyes dropped down and she saw his kilt was a decidedly light brown rather than white, and as her eyes came back to his face she realised that too was streaked in dust. "I see you come to me straight from riding."

"Yes," he answered before she could say anymore. "I have been riding with Father in the Valley of the Dead." He said this slowly and finished by raising his eyebrows. Beketamun understood immediately and rose from her chair.

"Come, we shall talk on the balcony," she said, and nodded her head for him to follow her.

"Can anyone hear us here?" he asked in a whisper as he looked over the balcony and to the windows nearby.

"No, we are fine," Beketamun said anxiously. "What happened today?"

"You asked me to observe our father when I could," he said.

"Yes, yes, Menkheperre, that I did," she said quickly. "Please tell me what has happened! Do you also believe his mind is weakening?"

Menkheperre shook his head. "That is my dilemma Sister. I cannot decide if he is now acting as a true Pharaoh or if he has completely lost his mind."

"What?" snapped Beketamun.

"Hush," he said. "The last thing we need is for the rest of the palace to hear this any sooner than they need." Menkheperre took a deep breath and told Beketamun all that happened.

"By his own hand? With his own knife?" she asked and Menkheperre nodded in answer to both questions. "This is so unlike him," she said.

"I know! But it is not unlike the stories we have heard of other Pharaohs," Menkheperre continued. "It has been at least twenty years since she died. Why now? Why would he choose to change his actions this way so far into his rule and at his age?"

Beketamun dropped her eyes, as she knew why it would happen now. As Menkheperre saw her reaction he too knew. "Oh dear Sister, it was your mother," he said and he too looked down. There was silence for a moment and he looked up. "Arisina is gone too. He would never have touched a tomb while she was alive."

Beketamun nodded and closed her eyes. "We are no match for either of them," she sighed.

Menkheperre left after agreeing with Beketamun that they would keep an even closer eye upon me. He made his way to bathe but not even the soothing waters could distract him from replaying over and over what he had seen that morning. It was no surprise when a few hours later Beketamun sent a messenger from the court asking that he make way to the hall of records. Menkheperre practically ran the entire way, as curious as he was scared of what he would find. As he turned the last corner he heard my voice calling out orders.

Menkheperre stepped through the door and saw what at first looked like chaos. The large tables that sat in the middle of the room were strewn with scrolls and scribes were carrying scrolls back and forth from the shelves that lined the room. Beketamun was standing at one wall, watching the scribes with her arms crossed. When she saw Menkheperre she put her finger to her mouth letting him know not to say anything.

At the furthest end of the table I sat. I grabbed at the pile of scrolls before me, uncurling a scroll and scanning its words. Siamun stood to my right and also read the scroll from over my shoulder. I hit the scroll with my hand making Siamun jump. "Pah! Here she has written that *she* oversaw the expedition to Mitanni," I spat. "That was me and your uncle Ahmenmose!"

Without even rolling the papyrus back up I flung it over my left shoulder to join other unfurled scrolls gathering in a pile behind me. These were the scrolls to be discarded, while those I approved were now upon the other table waiting to be placed back upon the shelves. I reached over and grabbed another scroll to check over not even noticing that Menkheperre had entered the room. He walked to where Beketamun stood. "What is happening?" he said quietly.

Beketamun sighed, "He is correcting the records."

Amenhotep burst into the room, nodded to Beketamun and Menkheperre then strode quickly to my side. I barely noticed him arrive until he said his customary "Father".

"Ah, finally you arrive!" I said loudly. "I cannot believe you took so long."

"Father I was on my way to Memphis to meet with the viziers. You arranged the meeting yourself," he answered defensively.

"Oh." I put down the scroll I was reading and looked up. "So I did--I forgot that. Never mind this is far more important. Sit by me." I pointed to a chair close by and picked up the scroll again.

Amenhotep looked to Siamun who simply turned back to reading the scroll with me. "Might I know what it is that we are doing?" Amenhotep asked with more than slight agitation in his voice.

"My son we are correcting the records so that Egypt's history will be stored with truth and integrity. This will allow our family to continue on without question or reason to challenge our rightful place." I said bluntly. "When we are long gone there will be nothing here that will cloud the right of your son, or his, or those that come after."

Amenhotep smiled at this. He knew every family wrote their own history as they took the throne to legitimise their claim. There were endless reliefs and carvings that heralded pharaohs and queens as God-chosen beings. Siamun saw his smile and glared at him. Suddenly Amenhotep knew this somehow was different. "Yes Father," he said simply and pulled his chair close by my side.

Four hours later even I joined the scribes and my children in yawning. Menkheperre was long gone; bored within thirty minutes he had dismissed himself to return to the war rooms. Beketamun faithfully guided the scribes to restore those scrolls that were deemed truthful and soon the tables were mostly clear. Behind me though lay a pile three feet deep, and just as wide, of scrolls to be destroyed. They were a great big pile of lies and propaganda that I am sure was mostly written by Senemut--all with Hatshepsut's knowledge of course. No longer could they kiss and now no longer could their words be read.

"Amenhotep, I trust you sent word of your delay to Memphis?" I asked as we finished.

"Of course Father," he answered.

"Good. I shall also send my own apology. It is easy for men to be respectful when they are given respect," I said smiling. "You will leave tomorrow and attend the meeting but you shall return in ten days. I need you back then to be with me to deal with the records at Karnak."

"There are no such record scrolls at Karnak, Father," he said puzzled. "There are only the scrolls of the priests which we surely cannot touch."

"I know there are not such scrolls to correct there Son," I said smiling and put my hand on his shoulder. "There are carvings."

I called all my family together for the evening meal that night and Matreya, relieved to be officially out of mourning clothes, sat beside me now as my chief wife. I actually turned to her once and jumped as I realised it was her and not Satiah beside me.

"What is it Thutmose?" she snapped when she saw my surprise.

"Nothing," I said, and quickly filled my mouth with food to avoid talking.

The meal continued on with small talk and some laughter. It could have been any ordinary meal despite Menkheperre constantly monitoring me and then exchanging glances with Beketamun. These looks soon were gone though as he drank some more wine and joined in some spirited talk with the other men

I tired sooner than them all, which was not unusual these days, so I bid my goodnight to the table and they all stood as was required until I left the room.

"Father, let me walk you to your room." Isis came to my side and placed her arm under mine. "I have seen so little of you lately."

I nodded. "That would be lovely." Taking her hand in mine, we made our way to my chambers. "How goes my new grandson?" I asked as Isis had just delivered her son the month before.

"He is well, strong and so hungry he requires two wet nurses," she laughed.

"How wonderful," I said. "We are blessed to have new lives join as others depart. Are we not?"

We were now far from the dining room and deep in the corridors of the private apartments of the palace. "Isis, my dear--did they send you to watch me?" I asked, leaning to her and smiling.

Her look answered my question enough and then she shook her head. "No one did--I simply wanted to walk with you."

"Ah, I see." I smiled again. "You do know they will be talking about me when you return."

Isis shook her head. "Father, you need to rest and let such thoughts out of your head."

I was right though. They all stood quietly and watched me leave only sitting down when I had stepped through the door. Menkheperre listened with a soldier's ear for our footsteps to fade and then turned to Beketamun.

"He seems a lot better tonight," he said.

"Well of course he does. He has done what he wanted to," she replied sharply.

"What are you talking about?" cried Meritamen. "Has Father been ill again?"

"No--well not of his body," huffed Menkheperre.

"Well what is going on then?" Meritamen yelled. "I'm sick of the way you older ones keep things from us just because we don't serve in court or the army." She sneered at Menkheperre as she mentioned the army.

"Nothing has been hidden from you," Siamun reasoned as soberly as ever. "It has only occurred today." He then relayed what had happened in the record hall while Menkheperre added his tale from the morning to complete the picture.

"Just how far is he going to take this?" Matreya said as she turned to her son Amenhotep. If he were to erase Hatshepsut completely then there would be no merit in the honour that she had granted her to be known as Matreya-Hatshepsut.

"Not so far that she will disappear completely," Menkheperre answered her. "He was quite selective at her temple. She will still be recorded as a queen. Father knows that there are some boundaries to what he can do."

Matreya sighed with relief. "I do believe this is just the stress of his grief. Perhaps you princes could find a way to delay him. Then he may see how irrational this is when his mind settles."

Menkheperre shook his head. "The scrolls would have burnt while we ate. The damage to Senemut's tomb has been done. These are not the ways of a man who can be swayed."

Isis entered the room as more talk of my behaviour continued. She stood and watched over her family as they discussed me, her face growing sad as she realised I had been correct. "He knows you are speaking of him," she snapped as she sat down.

"How?" Menkheperre screwed up his face. "We made sure you were well away before we began."

"He just knows--like he always does," she said and looked over us all. "He is our Father and he is Pharaoh. We should not discuss him as though he is some diplomat from Canaan."

"Isis, this is no talk of treason or coup," Amenhotep explained.

"I do not care," she said firmly. "This is disrespectful and I will not be a part of it." She turned to her husband. "I shall return to our rooms to check upon our son."

"I shall come with you," he said. As curious as he was to stay and continue the discussion, he knew to honour his wife.

"Good evening to you all," she said and left the room with her husband close behind.

The next morning I was taking time in my private garden, enjoying some quiet before an audience session of court. Isis appeared at the doorway and it seemed like only yesterday that she used to sit here with me as a young girl. "Come Daughter." I gestured to her to sit by me. "Have you come to walk me to court? I could get used to having my beautiful daughter escort me through the palace and dismiss my guards."

"I need to speak with you," she said seriously and sat beside me.

"Oh, well speak," I said.

"Last night when I returned to the dining hall the family were indeed talking of you," she said quickly.

"So you see I was founded in my thoughts," I laughed.

"Father, they are concerned for your mind--especially in light of what you did yesterday and what you plan for next week," she said this slower watching my face as she did so.

I leant in close to her and dropped my voice. "Do they plan anything against me?"

She shook her head and tears fell down her face. "No," she cried, "but please tell me they are wrong. Please tell me you are well and sound."

"Of course I am," I answered confidently and straightened my back as I said this. "They just do not understand. When this is done they will. They think I am changed Isis, and I am. You cannot live your life and stay the same as you began. The last time you sat here with me you were a young girl and now you are a wife and mother. Can you say you are the same person?"

Isis blushed as she remembered herself as she was all those years ago sitting here watching the gardener and daydreaming. "No, Father, I am much changed," she said.

"Do I see you as unhealthy or flawed that you are not that young carefree girl anymore? No!" I answered myself. "Quite frankly I would be concerned if you had not changed. Maybe I should have been harsher upon you all as children, then my actions now would not seem so shocking." I actually smiled as I said this and even Isis laughed a little. "Fear not of what is spoken of me. This will all pass soon." I took her hand in mine and kissed it.

CHAPTER TWENTY-SIX

The following week I rode to the Great Temple of Karnak in my chariot while my sons followed behind me on their horses. As we approached the temple the sound of chisels and hammers hitting the rock echoed out to us. The stonemasons and scribes had begun at first light so that when I would arrive there would already be much for me to oversee. We all dismounted before the first pylon and made our way into the temple complex. The sound was even more intense within as it bounced off the walls, repeating so that it seemed a thousand men were here rebuilding, rather than the dozen or so that simply hacked at the walls to rectify history. Scribes walked back and forth unrolling scrolls and looking at walls, then pointing and giving direction to a stonemason. When the stonemason began their work the scribes would move on to check on those walls already started. Other men walked the temple carrying buckets and swags of chipped and broken stone to dump in a pit beside the temple.

A high priest came running towards us as we watched the men working. "Sire," he said quickly and nervously, almost tripping as he bowed. "The work progresses as you desire and most efficiently."

"I can see and hear that," I acknowledged. "Thank you for your attention to this matter." I smiled at the man and he could not help but smile back. Later when I was gone leaving them to work without their Pharaoh watching over them, he would walk to the temple gushing that "the Pharaoh is most pleased with our work" to all the men involved. For now though he would be as professional as his fear and nerves would allow him.

"Shall I show you through to the other work done so far Sire?" he offered.

I nodded and soon we were taken upon a guided tour amongst the striking hammers, the mist of stone dust and the occasional chip flying like a missile past our ears. I kept nodding as we walked through and the priest would point out another image of Hatshepsut being scraped away. We came to yet another pylon where ten stonemasons laboured. A rough scaffold of wood was in place and they worked at different levels to clear the wall. Stone chips fell and bounced off the scaffold and I loved the sight of every one of them, but not so much as the sight of that wall slowly being wiped clean.

I turned to my sons and they were standing in awe at the sight of this. Siamun with his mouth open taking in the amount of work, Menkheperre with his arms crossed looking bemused as always, and then Amenhotep hands on hips, feet apart like a soldier surveying a field before battle.

"What are you thinking Amenhotep?" I said loudly over the hammering.

"I am wondering what marvellous tribute to your achievements shall now fill this," he said not taking his eye off the wall for a moment.

"I shall be placing no carvings here Son," I said. "This wall is now blank for you."

Amenhotep looked to me and for a second his face froze as he hardly believed what he heard.

"I did not make this temple so grand and large as monument to me alone," I said. "Here you shall make known before all the Gods your worthiness to be Pharaoh so that all others who come after you shall know also."

Amenhotep nodded then he shook his head. "Father, what if those after us would choose to erase us as we have erased Hatshepsut in seeking their own glory here at Karnak?"

"That will not happen," I said and I was most sure of this. "We are correcting the history of Egypt. No Pharaoh would defile the laws of Amun nor risk his curse in doing any such a thing. The pyramids have stood a thousand years and no Pharaoh has laid claim to them being of any Pharaoh but Khufu. Karnak and all within it shall be the same."

We then made our way to the Valley to see how the correction of her mortuary temple was progressing. I almost wanted to clap and yell with delight as we rode towards it and I saw the swarm of men climbing over the temple. Meritamen and Meryt's husbands, both now generals of the army had been sent to supervise the work here. They saw us approaching and made their way to greet us.

"Sire, all is progressing well as you can see." Meritamen's husband waved his hand to the massive pit in the sand that was being filled with the results of their work so far.

I looked and I saw that the large statues of the high terrace were still in place though and this did not please me. "Why are the largest pieces still in place?" I scowled sure that I would now be fed some lame excuse for their poor organization.

"Why, Sire," he smiled deep and wide. "I imagined that you would like to be present for that momentous act!"

I laughed so loudly when he said this. "True, true my son," I chuckled. "You have learnt the ways of your new family well."

When we made our way to the top terrace I saw that each statue marked for destruction was bound and tied with ropes in place ready for them to topple and smash upon the ground. Meritamen's husband called out to the workers to ready themselves at the ropes of the first to pull it down. They had all been primed with how this would be, as though they had prepared a performance to entertain me. They ran to the ropes and began to pick them up, twisting them about their bodies ready to use all their strength. Meritamen's husband raised his hand to signal that he would begin the countdown for them to pull but before he could start counting I stepped forward.

"Stop," I cried and walked towards the workers. I pointed to the four who held the ropes that encircled the top most part of the statue. "Drop your ropes and join onto another. Siamun and Menkheperre, take place on the left side. Amenhotep, I want you by my side here on the right."

My sons ran to take up the ropes that had been dropped and soon all four of us stood with the ropes around our waists, our arms twisted into them and our sandals gripping the stone terrace beneath us.

"Bear upon your ropes men and when I cry then pull with your might that this heathen shall return to her rightful place," I yelled out. The men all braced and as I cried "heave" we all pulled upon the statue--muscles bulging and feet slipping. We all felt the statue shift but it was not enough to fell it. I quickly yelled again and the statue began to move. I saw the head falter and knew its centre of balance was lost, one more pull and she would fall. "Heave!" I cried once more and then the statue gave way. It fell with a crash that echoed through the Valley and I was sure it could have been heard at the palace. The statue smashed as she fell, sending the workers scurrying from their ropes to escape the debris.

I stood still though with her fragments bouncing around me and my ears rang from the noise. I eventually heard coughing as some of the men had taken in dust and then I heard Siamun's voice. He stood on the other side of the rubble and he was pointing at me and saying something.

"Father! Your leg!" he shouted.

I looked down and saw blood upon my left shin. I had been so delighted at felling the statue I did not even feel when a rock fragment hit me taking a nice chunk of skin and flesh with it. It was not so bad an injury and I am sure the men involved with the work would suffer far worse before the day was out. However I was rushed towards by guards, sons and priests alike, swept off my feet, and carried to sit in the shade inside the temple. There I was dabbed and fretted upon, but I could not join them in their concern. Instead as the blood was staunched and a prayer was muttered behind me I just smiled as I heard another statue fall and smash outside. A piece of rock flew into the temple, landing at my feet. How it managed to miss everyone I do not know nor care. All I could do was laugh as I looked down upon it while everyone else looked at it horrified.

A high priest ran back out upon the terrace and shouted, "HALT! There shall be no more statues felled while the Pharaoh and princes are here!" I heard some sighs around me as all became silent outside.

Amenhotep stepped before me. "Perhaps we have seen enough for today Father. Let us make our way back to the palace," he coaxed and gestured to the guards to carry me.

"I will not be carried!" I shouted and my voice boomed inside the stone walls making everyone around me take a step back. "I am far from injured. I shall walk back to my chariot."

There simply was no way that I was going to be carried from this temple like I was an old or weak man defeated by a stupid chunk of stone. I would walk out of this temple as defiant and strong as I had entered it. I stood up and there was merely an ache in my leg. "Pah!" I cried, "I have suffered worse." With that I strode back out onto the terrace and made my way down to my chariot.

The remaining statues fell soon after my departure with many more rocks cutting the flesh of my workers. They wore the scratches and cuts with pride though knowing that they now carried a mark from their work just as their Pharaoh did. The debris from their task filled the pits dug into the sand and as I had ordered the pits remained open, free for anyone to pilfer or lay claim to the rocks should they require the fragments to recycle for their own needs. The stones within though were never touched. Those that believed I had desecrated a sacred place were too scared to touch them lest they carry that sacrilege with them, while those that supported my actions did not want stones that carried Hatshepsut's memory. So the pits lay as they were on the day they were created, eventually filled in over time by the ever-hungry sands that crawled over and buried anything that lay in its path.

That night we had a grand feast at the palace. Every priest, scribe, stonemason and worker who had assisted with the correction was invited. It was my way to celebrate a grand occasion and thank those who had helped it happen. We began the evening with a high priest of Karnak reporting to me that the work was now finished at the Great Temple, then another high priest who had been in the Valley said that the work at Hatshepsut's mortuary temple was complete. Others also lined to speak of the corrections made at smaller temples across Egypt. Each announcement was met with a roar and applause from everyone present.

I stood up from my place at my table and immediately all those within the Great Hall rose too. I raised my glass, "Today each one of you helped to make Egypt's history right. Together we have removed the scars of a pharaoh who should never have been. I thank you all from the core of my heart." My voice faltered a little but only those nearby would have noticed. I swallowed hard and pushed my emotion aside. "Now eat and drink until you are full!"

This they did indeed and few dishes were returned to the kitchen with anything but mere scraps of food upon it. The cellars were constantly busy with servants filling jugs of wine from the barrels to bring to the dining hall and I imagine there were many sore heads the next day. Most of the men who sat at that feast knew the privilege of being there and that they most likely would never sit within the palace walls again. They knew to enjoy as much of Egypt's finest wine and food before they returned to their more modest lives. I would have been happy for the day to end with my kitchens and cellars emptied and rumours actually crept through Thebes that this indeed happened. Tale after tale was told of the feast within their homes and along the streets. Within the descriptions of the dozens of different meats, exotic sweets and rich wines the people heard much more. They heard of a Pharaoh who was generous and kind.

When most of the food was eaten and there were just a few people lingering on eager to dry the last drops of wine from the tables, I gathered my family and made way to my chambers. I wished some private time with them before the day was over. We did not talk too much of what occurred as that had happened over dinner. It was just nice to relish some time with them all away from the noise and clamour of the feast. Nebetiunet had come from her temple for the celebration and I gestured for her to sit beside me and held her hand. She smiled and then her eye caught sight of the mark upon my leg. As a priestess she was called to pray for people in many conditions. She had seen so many injuries and illnesses that she knew when prayers for healing would not be as powerful as prayers to simply end suffering. As Nebetiunet looked at the gash on my leg she saw the redness and swelling that so often was the beginning of far worse.

"Father, have the physicians seen to your injury?" she asked leaning forward and looking at it closer.

"It is hardly an injury Daughter. I have suffered worse in battle training. It is merely a scratch." I brushed off her concern but she shook her head.

"Father, you have not the vigour of youth to heal such things," she said firmly. "This wound is open--the flesh will become proud and if it begins to turn then it will carry its poison through the blood and claim more of you." Amenhotep stepped forward to hear what was being said and Nebetiunet looked up at him. "Are there any physicians who are not drunk?"

Amenhotep nodded and called to a butler to fetch a physician. He did not look away from my leg though. It looked far worse than it had earlier today and now he was more than concerned. He was also feeling guilty that he had not insisted upon more attention to it sooner and Nebetiunet's scowls only added to this.I sat quietly for as proud and brave as I wished to be I knew her concerns were founded. During the meal a dull deep ache had set into my leg and now after walking from the dining hall to my rooms the ache was accompanied by a burning feeling. As much as I tried to dismiss this as simply being because I was tired, it was showing no signs of abating now that I was resting.

Nebetiunet grabbed a stool and dragged it in front of me then lifted my foot and set it upon it. "Gather some water and cloths," she called out to no one in particular as she pulled over another low stool before me to sit on. Then with a bowl of water below my leg and a cloth in her hand, she gently drenched the cloth and began to clean my damaged leg, letting the water flush over it and fall back into the bowl. Everyone became silent; fascinated with watching their sister care for me. Isis sat in the chair beside me and took my hand in hers then a voice broke the quiet.

"Nebetiunet--that is no task for a princess or a priestess," Matreya said coldly. "Sit back upon a chair and wait for the physicians as the rest of your family do."

Nebetiunet did not look up from my leg, still concentrating on cleaning my wound as delicately as she could. "The gash needs to be cleaned without delay. Another hour could see this being beyond poultices and tonics," she said plainly and then glanced up at me and smiled. "I do believe this is quite a suitable task for a daughter to perform for her father." She looked back down and continued her washing. All was quiet again except for the gentle sounds of the water trickling back into the bowl and the clatter of Matreya's bangles as she stormed out.

I loved that moment with Nebetiunet so much. My daughter who I knew so little of, who had left the palace so young to make her own way, yet she could sit here now and show me so much love and care as though she had spent every second of her life by my side. I could have cried from the love I felt but I feared it would be mistaken for pain and I certainly wasn't about to let my sons think that this wound would bring me to tears. Instead I mused upon the fact that Matreya had been outwitted by her own daughter with all the strength and determination that Matreya prided herself on. So I sat and smiled instead.

When the two physicians arrived Nebetiunet did not move from her stool in front of me. "Pharaoh needs a poultice of wheat and honey to seal the wound," she spoke with confidence and the physicians nodded. "Have you fir oil?" The physician opened one of the boxes they carried with them, pulled out a small alabaster bottle and handed it to Nebetiunet. "I shall prepare the wound for the poultice," she said with authority.

I remained still while Nebetiunet called upon servants to remove the water and bring her fresh cloths and another empty bowl. She dabbed at my leg gently to dry it and then slowly poured the fir oil over the wound. I jumped slightly as the oil hit my flesh, but she acted as though she did not notice even though I saw a slight smirk on her lips. The physicians nearby at a table ground the wheat and then poured honey over it, blending it into a smooth paste. The smell caught Nebetiunet's nose and she looked up. "Do not mix anymore or you shall crush the essence of the honey."

The physicians stopped and looked at one another. They could not question the Pharaoh's daughter and especially not in front of me. So they carried the bowl over to apply it to my leg. Nebetiunet reached out for it and the physician instinctively pulled it back to himself. "Madam, surely you have done enough," he said feigning a smile. "As His Highness's physician I should be the one to apply it."

"Give it to my daughter!" I snapped and the bowl was finally placed into Nebetiunet's outstretched hand. When she reached out again for the brush to apply the poultice it was immediately handed over. She dipped the brush into the poultice, coating its bristles with the syrupy potion and then held it over the bowl.

"Let us call Amun to infuse the poultice," she said softly and the physicians dropped to their knees beside me and bowed their heads. Everyone else in the room bowed their head also as Nebetiunet closed her eyes and began the prayer.

"Oh Grand Amun, true and faithful guardian of Ma'at and all that is, we call upon you to enter this poultice to heal our Pharaoh," she said loudly. "Bring with you Imhotep and Sekhmet to close this wound and restore Pharaoh's leg."

She opened her eyes and began to daub the mixture over the wound sealing it. With each new dab of poultice she offered a fresh prayer to Amun for my healing. When the wound was covered, she smoothed over it with the brush making sure the poultice was evenly spread and then wiped away any that she had dripped on the nearby healthy flesh. She tipped her head from side to side as she assessed her work, nodded and then looked up. "This should see you healing within days," she said to me reassuringly and then turned to the physicians. "Bandage this now to bind the poultice in place and prepare a tea of chamomile to calm Pharaoh's blood."

Nebetiunet stood now to make room for the physicians to bandage my leg. As they did she continued with her instructions. "A fresh poultice will need to be applied each morning and night. The leg will then be rewrapped in fresh bandages."

Too scared to say anything the physicians merely nodded and answered, "Yes Madam" as they bound my leg. I sat still and silent though highly entertained with the whole scene. Not only had my daughter quieted Matreya but now my physicians who would normally have been muttering grand dramatic diagnoses and ordering complex remedies were sitting upon stools with their heads down and working silently. When she announced she would be leaving for her own home all I could say was "Oh" as I would have loved to see what else she might have done.

"All is organised Father," she said. "I have no doubt that you will heal admirably. Amenhotep and the others have heard what is needed. I know they will make sure all is a carried out as necessary."

One of the physicians shot her a quick burning glance that I did not miss.

"All will be fine Daughter," I said. "I thank you for your care. I almost feel that tomorrow when the bandages are changed there will be no wound to speak of."

I am sure one of the physicians grunted when I said this but it was lost beneath the chorus of farewells as Nebetiunet bid her brothers and sisters goodbye. When she reached Amenhotep she said quietly, "Will you walk with me?" and he nodded and followed his sister and her husband out into the corridor.

"What is it Sister?" he asked when they were away from the room.

Nebetiunet stopped. "Go ahead without me," she said to her husband

Nahkim, who understood his wife needed to speak privately. When Nahkim had left them she locked eyes with her brother, "Are you ready to rule?" she said bluntly.

Amenhotep jumped in shock at the last question he thought his sister would ask him. "Why do you ask me that?" he snapped. "Is Father's leg worse than it appears?"

"Father's leg will be fine," she said.

"His mind then?" he asked.

"That is fine too Brother," she said and sighed. "It is far stronger than we could imagine. His body cannot match it anymore though and his inability to see this is his weakness. Today he was reckless but with you by his side to curb anything worse happening. We cannot be by his side every moment to watch him like a child and who has the power to tell the Pharaoh what to do. Even if they dared he would not listen."

Amenhotep nodded as she spoke as he had thought these things himself.

"Amenhotep, you must begin each day as though it is your last as a prince. Only the Gods can know what day our father will choose to leave." Nebetiunet breathed deep. "But we now must face that it may well be some day soon."

I sat in my chair after my family left sipping on sour chamomile tea and wishing it were wine. I stared down at my leg wrapped in its bandages. *"It is almost like a part of me has become a mummy already,"* I thought. My heart panged suddenly as the image of Satiah lying with layers of bandages over her jumped into my mind's eye.

I suddenly heard the question, *"Are you ready to leave also?"*

I do not believe it was Satiah, nor do I believe it was a voice of the Gods. I now know it was my own voice asking myself the question that we all avoid so well. I could not go. I was Pharaoh. I had so much to do and my mind went through an endless list of duties and responsibilities. Then my heart chimed in, *"Ah it would be so nice to not worry anymore--to be with my beloved in paradise."*

I sighed and still looked down at my bandaged leg. Nebetiunet was right; my strength and vigour that had served me so well was now fading. I had lost my love and now my health was leaving me also. I had achieved so much and all was prepared for Amenhotep and my family to continue. So why did I feel such a pull to remain here. I could not answer my own question and this frustrated me.

"Oh well," I thought to myself. *"You are either alive or dead. Right now I am still alive and shall simply continue to be so. Death will come soon enough and when the Gods know that it is my time to go."*

I slept quite well that night even though I woke a few times as my wound made itself known from time to time. Once though I had looked down, saw the bandages turn a dark colour and convinced that I was bleeding to death called for my butler. It was just the poultice that had seeped through the bandages rather than blood and so I fell back asleep quite relieved.

The next morning the physicians were waiting outside my bedchamber. I was somewhat surprised that they had brought with them their full collection of herbs and oils after Nebetiunet had used only three components. My physicians though were armed and ready to prove themselves. They had walked the corridors to my chamber speaking in hushed tones between them that they expected to find me declining and now with "Princess Priestess" gone they could finally perform as they knew how to.

So when I walked out of my bedchamber refreshed and with a healthy colour on my face they were actually quite disappointed.

"Sire, you are walking straight," one gasped while the other stood with his jaw open.

"Well of course I walk straight," I said. "I am healing wonderfully."

I sat myself down upon the same chair as the previous night with its stools still around it. I placed my bandaged leg upon one. "Now unbind me so that we can see how superbly my daughter did last night." I smiled straight at them so they had no choice but to smile back even though I knew they hated the fact my daughter had usurped their authority over my care.

The bandages began to be unwound and my leg actually felt some relief as they came off and the fresh air touched it. They were just about to reveal the wound when Meryt and Isis walked through the door and I saw the shoulders of one physician rise and drop as he exhaled sharply.

"Father, we promised Nebetiunet we would visit with you this morning," Isis said quickly and sat beside me once again.

Meryt saw that the bandages were almost completely off and made a hasty retreat to the window away from me and sat upon the sill. "Isis--I will trust you to see how this goes," she grimaced and put her hands to her eyes.

The last of the bandages came off and the physicians' heads both leant in so close that I could not see anything. They seemed to stay that way for much longer than they needed to and then slowly they both looked up. Their mouths were both open and their eyes were wide. "Remarkable," one said so softly I almost didn't hear him.

Now Isis and I both looked down at my leg. The wound was still there but all the redness and swelling around its edges was gone. This was not so impressive but as I looked closer I now saw what had made the physicians gasp in awe. There was new flesh starting its way inwards, preparing to close over the wound. It was only slight but still remarkable, something that should not have happened for days. I fell back into my chair with my eyes wide now matching the physicians.

"What is it?" cried Meryt and she jumped up off the windowsill.

"Your sister is a most powerful healer," was all I could say.

Needless to say the physicians repeated all that Nebetiunet did the night before including the prayers over the poultice. As the physician finished the prayer the other turned to him and hissed, "Are you sure that's what she said?"

"Yes, that is just what she said," Isis answered.

"Fine, I shall speak the prayer again. This time *without* interruption!" he glowered at the other physician as he said this.

So each morning and night we would repeat this little ritual. I grew quite accustomed to the smell of honey and its occasional sticky dabs that I would find around me. I was however quite relieved when the day came a week later that the poultice and bandages were not needed. This was yet another milestone that was considered quite miraculous. So much so in fact that when Nebetiunet heard this in her daily report sent by messenger from Isis, she immediately made her way to the palace to make sure it was true and not some fancy ploy created by the physicians.

Even she looked upon my leg in awe and I saw tears in her eyes as she spoke to me. "Father, we have always known that you are truly loved by the Gods. Now today we have all seen it."

"I am truly loved by the Gods to be sent a daughter who not only conjures mighty prayers but also found the knowledge of healing," I said and Nebetiunet shook her head. I raised my hand. "There are many wonders to recognise within this, Daughter. Do not diminish your grandeur by denying those that you have created."

Nebetiunet didn't shake her head or cry through any disregard for her work. She did so with remorse for being so hasty with her thoughts. When she returned to her temple she sat in her private room and cried for a few minutes, then gathered herself and made her way to the altar. There she gave thanks to Amun, Imhotep and Sekhmet for aiding my healing. Then she followed with prayers to Isis to keep her mind clear of thoughts that served no one. A small group of women had gathered to hear prayers with Nebetiunet but she asked them to wait just a few minutes more. She went to the scribe's room and took a small piece of papyrus. Upon it she wrote a simple note to Amenhotep and called a servant to carry it to the palace. She was direct but discrete lest unwelcome eyes should read it.

It simply said, "*I was wrong.*"

When word spread through the city and then beyond of my miraculous healing and Nebetiunet's part in it the people began to swarm to her temple to receive her prayers and guidance for treatment. She never turned anyone away even when their ailments were beyond her. Nebetiunet would call upon the women who lived around the temple--the very ones who had shown her the way to treat my wound. She had always known the knowledge that they possessed handed down through dozens of generations should be known by more and my leg had now served to make this happen in a way grander than she ever imagined. Most days the temple would be so full that the people would end up spilling onto the streets where they would wait in the sun until there was space for them also. People would pass and ask why there was such a gathering and when they were told would often join the crowd to wait for their own turn, or they would carry the news back to their village to return with all there that needed healing.

When they made it inside they would simply find a free space to sit or lie and wait. Then a priest or priestess would come to them to offer prayer and counsel while one of the local women would decide upon what herbs or treatment was necessary. It was spoken that miracles occurred instantly, including the usual wonder of the lame walking out of the temple after having to be carried in. They were never denied by anyone and I believe this helped add to the power of the healing there. Word carried fast in Egypt and if these miracles were not founded the crowds would have diminished as quickly as they had gathered and they never did. Soon those that needed healing were joined by priests and commoners wishing to learn the ways of healing so that their temples and villages might aid people as Nebetiunet's temple did.

At the end of the day those that were not seen to were made welcome to sleep within the temple to wait for the next day. The servants of the temple would wander amongst them handing out bread, meats, water and blankets. Nebetiunet sat upon the stairs of the altar rise each evening to make sure all were made comfortable. To sit on these stairs with your back to the altar was most unorthodox for a priest or priestess but this temple had forgotten its rules. A young woman sat against a wall relief of Isis and breastfed her child, while a man nearby was curled under a lesser altar ready to sleep. Every space was made use of and many would awake claiming they were healed from simply experiencing this sanctuary. As Nebetiunet sat and looked upon the massive room filled with so many needy people each night, she knew the temple had been transformed into much more than it had been built for.

When word travelled to Karnak as to what was happening within Nebetiunet's temple she had received serious caution. The high priests warned her that she was turning her temple into an incubator for small pox or, even worse, the plague. Nebetiunet never paid them heed and continued on. She knew the Gods had chosen her temple to begin this work and true to her beliefs not one disease made its way from one person to another within her walls. Nebetiunet did not fight with nor seek approval from Karnak; she simply kept going, knowing that what they all achieved here would teach far more than any preaching or sanctimony.

The high priests finally arrived one day, unannounced in the hope of catching her off guard and ill prepared to cover her methods, Nebetiunet received them with a smile. They were allowed to wander where they pleased and did so without a word or a glance, despite their horror at finding a temple filled with illness and injury, where children walked freely upon the altar space to only receive a smile and a gentle hand to guide them back to their parents. The high priests though could not deny the great acts that were occurring and the scrolls they carried with them to demand the temple be restored to the laws and rules of Amun were never removed from the sleeves in which they were carried.

"We will continue to allow you your *interesting* methods. However heed our warning that should plague break out here, we shall close your temple," one of them said as Nebetiunet and Nahkim walked them back to their carriage to return to Karnak. As the high priest was about to step up on the carriage he turned one last time and feigned a smile. "I also pray you do not petition your father to bring your methods to Karnak. Let us just say that if the smallest word reaches me of this then we will return and most certainly find plague within your walls. Do you understand?"

"We understand completely," answered Nahkim. He quickly bowed his head while he reached for his wife's hand squeezing it in the hope she would follow his lead.

Nebetiunet did not answer and kept her eyes straight, locking them with the high priest's in the only act of defiance that she knew she could get away with. The high priest kept his eyes upon Nebetiunet's waiting for her answer. "I bid you safe return to Karnak," was all that she would mutter to him after his threat. She then swiftly turned her back and walked towards the temple.

Nebetiunet walked back amongst the crowd of people saying quick prayers as she walked by, touching the hands that reached out to greet her. When she made it to the doors of the temple she stopped for a moment to let her eyes adjust to the drop in light before she walked any further. As her pupils widened and the interior became clear again she saw the same scene she saw everyday and her anger at having it threatened made her blood pulse faster. Nebetiunet looked back outside to the hundred or so people who waited so patiently in the sun. When she looked back inside, the small altar that sat towards the side of the temple hall caught her eye, and she called for some male servants.

An hour later the altar had been pulled apart and reconstructed outside. Within minutes of this being completed Nebetiunet began offering prayers upon her new outdoor altar much to the delight of those waiting in the sun. It was soon surrounded by offerings and many people began their passage home saying that this beautiful priestess had healed them though her love and dedication alone. Nearby Nahkim watched with his brother who also served within the temple as a priest.

The brother turned to Nahkim and chuckled. "Shall we prepare for another visit from Karnak?"

That evening as Nebetiunet sat upon the altar stairs and watched the people settle for the night her husband came to sit beside her. He took her hand in his and kissed it. "Just how far do you intend to try your luck with the priests of Karnak?" he said gently.

"I will do whatever I need to do to help these people until they no longer need us," she spoke strongly but smiled as she did so. "This is how a temple should be Nahkim. It should be a place people come to for help and guidance, not to be scared that if they break some silly rule they will be punished. The Gods love us and wish us grand lives yet why do the high priests teach so much fear?"

Nahkim sighed, "Because that is the way to stop people doing wrong." He reached out and stroked her arm. "You want to be their mother. That is what they don't understand."

Nebetiunet turned to him sharply. "No, you are wrong. I just want them to see the beauty of life and for them to know they are protected and safe."

"As every mother does her child," her husband laughed.

"Do not mock me tonight!" she tried to say sharply but smiled back at her husband. "We will continue on. How could anyone stop this without carrying weight within their heart?"

CHAPTER TWENTY-SEVEN

With the statues, images and records of Hatshepsut now crushed, cleared or buried, I felt a wave of calm and clarity settling upon my life. The pain of losing Satiah was still ever present but I did not wallow in my grief. Even though I missed her terribly I had accepted that she had moved to paradise and now simply looked forward to joining her someday. I looked about my life now at fifty-three years of age and would literally breathe in the wonders around me. My fifties were the smoothest ten years of my entire life. Something I attributed to resolving Hatshepsut's memory.

Beketamun and Siamun kept my courts running seamlessly and with rare ill incidents. Amenhotep travelled the lands of Egypt and acted as thoroughly as if he actually ruled. He was well supported in the army by Menkheperre who now oversaw campaigns and tours of Canaan. Meritamen and Meryt continued their quest to create new palace fashions, which Isis observed with much amusement, occasionally being swept up in their "experiments". Nebetiunet pressed on with her temple that now saw people travelling from as far as Kadesh to observe their methods.

My days were spent mostly within the palace with only short rides to the Valley to oversee building or simply for the pleasure of riding through Thebes to let my people see that I had not become frail or a recluse. I granted more audiences in court and spent more time in the war rooms, which delighted me no end. My "palace days" as I like to call this period should have been quiet but with a steady stream of grandchildren arriving over the years this was far from the case.

Even though they were generally confined to one wing of the palace, some days it felt as they could be seen or heard everywhere. I hesitate to use the word "rats" to describe these children that I loved so much, but it gives you an idea of how they got in everywhere and into everything. They could be found in the kitchens grabbing at fruit or asking for sweets. There were always two or three running through the gardens and playing. Thankfully as they got older and began tuition and training they fell into a more disciplined routine but this seemed to take forever. My own children seemed to grow up overnight but this gaggle seemed intent on holding onto their youth for eternity. I decided that these years would be the perfect opportunity to impart my experience and wisdom directly to this third generation.

The occasion to do this occurred often and sometimes more dramatically than I hoped for though. One such day I was resting in my rooms when I heard an almighty cracking sound, followed by a symphony of screams and shouting. I ran along the corridors to where I believed the sounds came from and soon found myself rushing towards Amenhotep's chambers that were beside my own. The screams and crying were coming from his bedchamber and I entered to see a flurry of maids and mothers--all hysterical, surrounding Amenhotep's bed that was now a soup of split wood, twisted linens and contorted children. Amenhotep's sons, all eight of them, ranging in age from two to Thutmose at fourteen years had entered their father's bedchamber and decided it might be fun to climb the drapes that framed it. Thutmose of course made it more interesting by making it a race. The frame unexpectedly added to the excitement by collapsing under their weight, sending the lucky ones onto the feather stuffed mattress while most hit the relentless solid stone floor.

The women pulled at the wood and linen to uncover and retrieve the screaming children who soon formed a line beside me where they wept with relief and rubbed at their sore arms or legs. Then one maid shrieked above everyone. There on the floor lay four year old Nedjem with an extra bend in his right arm. The poor thing was calling for his mother while he lay buried under the pile of drapes, drowned out by the clamour around him. His mother, one of Amenhotep's consorts, rushed to gather him but I quickly stepped forward and stopped her.

"You will make the injury worse," I said sharply. "Call for the physicians."

I walked to my little injured grandson and seeing that it was his right arm, the arm needed for archery and swordplay, I shook my head. I had seen many broken bones in battle and was sure I could set it but I did not have the feel to make sure I would do so with the finesse needed for a young prince to heal as though it had never occurred. Tiaa began to usher the boys out of the room in readiness for the physicians to arrive and also to stop their distress at seeing their brother in so much pain. I stopped her though. "Take the youngest but leave the rest here so that they might see the consequence of their actions today." I turned to the boys directly. "One day you boys will be soldiers and see far worse on battlefields."

So the remaining boys stood and watched as the physicians rushed into the room and knelt beside Nedjem, hearing his fresh screams as the healers touched his arm to decide what to do.

"It is a clean break, Sire," one said to me. "It shall reset easily, but perhaps the children should be elsewhere."

"Proceed," I said. "The children will remain."

The physician knew just how painful this would be and while he anticipated the screams that accompanied resetting a bone he knew the children weren't. He also knew he couldn't question the choice of the Pharaoh.

"I will steady his legs for you," I said, and knelt down at Nedjem's feet placing my hands upon his little thighs and then nodded for the physicians to go on. One grasped at Nedjem's right elbow while the other held just above the wrist. This alone was enough to make my grandson scream afresh but nothing compared to what would follow as the physicians pulled and twisted at the arm. They reset the bone within seconds but the child's screams echoed far longer, then suddenly he fell silent and his body went limp. The boys now aghast at the sight of their brother, lying quiet and still, were convinced he was dead and began crying again

"Hush!" I shouted. "Amun has just taken his spirit for a short time to relieve his pain."

It also relieved the physicians who could now splint and bind the arm without their ears ringing or his small frame squirming. Nedjem soon came to as they finished and looked down at the bandages, whimpering at the ache he must have felt.

"You have been most brave Grandson," I said and turned to his brothers. "Do you see how brave your brother has been?"

They all nodded and some murmured "yes". The physicians gave Nedjem some tonic for the pain and even though he pulled back at the first taste he soon swallowed with my encouragement. I gathered him up in my arms and made way to take him to his own intact bed with everyone following me. Leaving him to be fussed over by his mother and servants I turned and grabbed Thutmose by the arm and pulled him to the salon next door.

"I trust you will show more sense in future when leading your brothers," I said with my back straight and my arms crossed. It was not a question and my grandson knew it. He looked up with eyes red from crying, mostly from fear, and nodded his promise to me. Thutmose never did coax any of the other children into such foolishness again.

While Thutmose may not have intentionally instigated any more injuries or lectures for misbehaviour, the remaining children continued on with being children. Part of me quite loved that some of them could outwit their nurses and then slip away through the palace. The moment came though when the novelty of this wore off quite abruptly.

I was returning to my room for a rest after a morning in court. I sighed as I walked the corridor, looking forward to the cool quiet of my rooms. As I entered I heard some noise from the garden and walked to the windows curious to see just what was going on.

"Sire, they told me they were allowed..." my butler's voice trailed off as I looked out into the garden and saw one of my granddaughters plucking jasmine flowers, crushing them in her hand to release their perfume and then simply letting them drop to the ground. Nearby another granddaughter was standing ankle deep in water along the edge of my lotus pond. In her hand she held a lovely bunch of my lotus flowers that I had waited all week to see open. This wasn't the worse though--as across the courtyard one of the boys was swinging from a branch of my beloved persimmon tree. Like Amenhotep's bed I could not imagine it was going to hold his weight much longer and the creaking sounds coming from it only reinforced this.

I ran forward screaming, "STOP! Get down from there!" I pulled at his waist until he let go, dropping him on the ground. The two girls froze in place but they did not realise they were in trouble too.

"Look Grandfather, I have picked some flowers for you," said the one in the pond holding out her bouquet.

"This is not your playground!" I bellowed as I walked over and grabbed her about the middle lifting her under my arm. While gathering the other girl under my other arm I continued, "This is my private garden! The private garden of the Pharaoh! You shall not play in here again." I turned to the young boy and nodded my head to the doors that led back to my rooms. "Out--NOW!"

As he got close I pushed him with my foot to make sure he knew I was serious. I followed closely behind with my two granddaughters still tucked under my arms and now both crying, while I occasionally gave my grandson another push with my foot. When I reached the massive doors that opened to the corridors of the palace I dumped the girls unceremoniously on the floor. I stood straight with my back aching and pointed in the direction they all should go. "Leave! Do not enter my rooms again unless I invite you."

With that the three whimpering children walked off to where they should have been. I turned back to my room and saw a trail of lotus flowers that my granddaughter had dropped as I carried her. It was accompanied by a trail of water that had dripped from her feet and dress. Before I could say anything a servant was gathering the flowers while another wiped at the water. I looked back out to the garden and sighed with relief as I saw my persimmon tree was intact, and then I looked to my lotus pond. Cleared of its few flowers it was back to its simple green, as was the lower three feet of my jasmine vine. I shuddered to think of what else they would have done if I hadn't arrived.

Tati appeared with my lunch and I turned to him. "How were they allowed in the garden?" I was quite stern and the butler knew he was in trouble but he was ready for this conversation as was most of the palace staff.

"Sire, the boy told me that you gave them permission," he simply stated and even though he lowered his head with the pretence of serving my food I am sure he was trying not to smile

"And you believed him?" I continued.

"Sire, you have not said otherwise," he said without a trace of smile.

"Would it not be obvious that I would not allow that?" I pushed.

"Sire, if I may be bold," the butler placed his hand on his chest to indicate he would speak honestly and I nodded for him to continue. "Your grandchildren are granted access to the entire palace. They move about without boundary so it makes it awkward for serving staff to impose any limitations upon them."

I rubbed my chin as I pondered this but I immediately knew it was true. "Is this how all the serving staff feels?" I said.

"Yes, Sire," he said, "but please know we are all most fond of the children."

He bowed and left me alone to eat and rest. As I lay upon my bed that afternoon I came up with a brilliant idea and when I rose I called to call my butler, "Summon a painter."

"Do you mean a scribe, Sire? One who writes glyphs or script?" he asked.

"No, it need not be anyone that skilled. Just someone who can paint a line," I answered, "and tell them to bring red paint."

Within an hour I had my painter at my door with a small bucket of red paint hanging in one hand and a paintbrush in the other.

I walked to the doorway. "Wonderful! Now," I said as I pointed to the threshold of my doorway, "paint a line across here."

I stood and watched as he painted with utmost care a simple thick red line marking where my rooms began and where the corridor finished. It was thick enough not to be missed yet not thick enough to detract from the patterns in the tiles of the floor.

"Is this as you desire Your Majesty?" the painter asked looking up while still upon his knees.

"It is perfect," I said and clapped my hands. "Now walk with me through the palace to make some more."

The painter got up and trailed me through the palace. Red line after red line was painted. They appeared across the doorways of the court, the corridors that led to the treasury, and even formed a square within the doors of the kitchens. It took us three hours to walk the palace like this but when it was completed I knew the task had been executed as thoroughly as I desired and would provide a most apt solution. I finished by asking that my butler send word that all grandchildren residing in the palace would gather in the nursery the next morning.

When I arrived at the nursery the next morning there was the usual bedlam whenever the thirty-five grandchildren who lived within the palace were gathered. They were running and squealing as always with an endless stream of nurses fluttering about the room attending to them. When my guard bellowed my arrival it was only the elder children who sat and were quiet. The rest kept talking; some ran to greet me, while others continued on as though I had never arrived. So the guard bellowed again in the hope the nurses would understand this as a cue to quiet them, which fortunately they did and reduced the noise a little more. Finally at the end of my patience, I clapped my hands and yelled, "Quiet!" Finally there was silence and all eyes were upon me.

"Now, my precious little ones," I started and smiled. "You all have the joy of having the grandest home in all of Egypt. You have also had the joy of being free to enjoy this home however you chose. Time has moved on and as you grow older you must now become aware of just where your place is within the palace. For this palace is not just a home, this is where the power of Egypt begins and all must run smoothly here. Learn this now and you will learn much of the ways of not only the palace but your empire."

The older children understood this but many of the younger ones looked at me quizzically while the babies remained content chewing on whatever they could grab.

"Now you will all follow behind me. Thutmose as eldest you will walk beside me. The rest of you follow by your ages. The nurses shall carry the babies," I ordered and turned to the door.

Thutmose ran to my side smiling. He relished the attention of being the eldest and since his feast at turning ten this was even more so. As we began walking he knew to fall slightly behind me, respecting that I should walk ahead. Of course within minutes of us walking the corridor one of the boys decided he would race ahead and Thutmose hissed, "Get back behind. No one walks ahead of Pharaoh but his guards!"

Immediately the boy fell back into place and I smiled at Thutmose. "Thank you--and well done!" I said and young Thutmose smiled and squared his shoulders.

We came to the first red line painted across my chamber doors.

"See this line!" I spoke loudly so they would hear clearly. "This means that you do not pass. This means you are not allowed within this room! You will not cross any line like this within the palace unless you are doing so with an elder." I kept my voice firm and the older children nodded as I spoke. "I am entrusting you older ones to remind the younger ones of this and help them learn this new way." They continued to nod and now the nurses joined them, as they understood it would also be their duty to enforce this as well.

I continued to lead the tour through the palace pointing at red lines that stopped them entering the wings of the palace that led to the court and war rooms. Then we arrived at the kitchens and any amusement that the children were having with this excursion soon ended. I walked into the massive room of the kitchen, which did not have a red line across its door. Instead there was an area enclosed by a red line to the left of the doorway.

"This is the only part of the kitchens that you shall enter," I said pointing to the spot. In the middle was a table laid out with bowls of fruit, breads and jugs of water. "There will be no more getting in the way of the cooks. No more pilfering of food *and* no more wine during the day for children. Wine for children is just for meals. If these bowls are empty then you may call to the cooks to bring some more."

Many of the children now lost their smiles and looked down. Here was one of the most fun places within the palace. They could sneak in here in-between meals to steal sweets or persuade the cooks to cut them some meat, which they always were ready to do. They needn't have worried too much as the cooks never followed this new rule. They took too much delight in feeding the royal children and within days the line may as well have never been painted there. The rest of the lines though were followed and respected. My butler soon reported that the palace staff was most relieved and happy to have this system to work with.

It was just over a week later and I was sitting in my chambers writing in the afternoon sun. I heard my guards say "Good day Sire" which was curious, as I had not heard the customary footsteps of any of my sons approaching. I looked up and saw Menkheperre's five year old son Waset just outside the open doors of my chambers. In one hand he carried a small wooden toy sword and in the other a wooden horse. As he walked he kept his eyes down and when he reached the red line across my door he stopped, sat down and there he began to play. I watched him for a few moments as he played, oblivious to anything around him. Once though his sword fell, landing upon the red line and he quickly reached and pulled it back towards him, clear of the red paint.

Finally though I had to say something, "Good day Waset," I called out from my chair.

He looked up at me as though I had just appeared. "Good day Grandfather."

"Grandson, should you be playing here?" I asked. My tone had more than a slight suggestion that the answer should be no.

He looked me in the eye. "Grandfather, I have crossed no red lines to be here," he replied plainly and continued playing.

I could not rebuff such simple reasoning. I had created the system and here sat a five year old who understood it completely. To reprimand him and send him away would make my system worth nothing. I turned and continued on with my writing whilst outside my guards, who had heard the entire conversation, were glad that I could not see that their faces were now red from holding back laughter.

CHAPTER TWENTY-EIGHT

Spending more time at Thebes also let me oversee the final stages of many construction projects that had been started over the years and that were now finally heading towards completion. The additions and alterations to Karnak were finished during this time, as was my tomb across in the Valley. I revelled in the joy of adding to Karnak, as had my father and grandfather. My construction here not only carried on the majesty of my family but let all know the power I held as Pharaoh. This construction served to provide the people of my time with this knowledge and helped make my mark in history for all peoples of all times to know. I would breathe deep with pride every time that I entered the temple. I would look at the fresh carved sandstone with its bright new paints upon it and smile knowing I had helped create a place for the Gods as magnificent as the life they had created for me.

The priests also delighted to work amongst spectacular surrounds that verified the importance of their duties here. Every new pillar that was built, every altar that was refurbished and every painting that was marked upon the walls reinforced their dedication to my family. As we all knew by now a smooth relationship between the high priests and the Pharaoh meant a smooth time for Egypt. Every gold piece that I spent upon Karnak was returned to me in ways that could not be measured and that would benefit my family for generations to come. That was until my notorious descendent Akhenaten came into power.

Few temples outside of Karnak received the attention that the Great Temple did but that was understandable as it was basically our equivalent of the Vatican. Smaller temples through the country although funded by myself to be built could often fall into disarray as they were forgotten or pharaohs simply did not have the riches to support them. Many temples to different Gods also fell away as their God fell out of fashion and pharaohs simply chose to focus upon the temples of the Gods they did favour. I had hoped to never fall prey to either of these follies while I reigned, and if I came across any temples in less than pristine condition upon my travels, I would order that they be sent funds and workers immediately. This is where my attention to Karnak also paid off, for when it came time for the priests of Karnak to open their treasury to make this happen, they did so without resentment knowing that their own temple did not lack in anything.

The only flaw to this way of sending help to the lesser temples was that it was the ones mostly along my path north and east that received this favour. All the temples on my way to Canaan prospered much during the first half of my reign when I was constantly enacting campaigns to this region. Unfortunately the temples south of Thebes weren't always so lucky.

When young Thutmose turned fifteen I decided to take him upon a trip to the south of Egypt. I would have loved to make my way upon my chariot with my grandson beside me in his, especially as he had now mastered driving his own. What an amazing sight that would make for my people as we rode by. When I announced to my grandson that I would take him on a journey to see the south his eyes lit up. "Oh, shall we go by boat? I have never been south upon the boat!"

When I saw the excitement in his eyes I could not say otherwise, besides the boat would be a bit easier on my aging frame as well. "Of course we shall go by boat," I said.

Each day of our trip I silently thanked my grandson for choosing the waterway. I could spend my days relaxing as we drifted up the river. I could talk to my grandson as we travelled and we weren't constantly filthy. In my younger years I loved the feeling of being covered in dust and dirt after a ride, these days were quite different though. I would sit on the deck of the boat feeling the breeze off the water while Thutmose ran from side to side, pointing at landmarks and calling out their names to impress me.

"Well done, Grandson," I would respond each time.

Locals would line the shores near villages to wave and some would even venture in boats to get closer. Gifts would be thrown aboard and my guards would rush to them to make sure that a cobra or something just as harmful hadn't been tossed in whilst other guards stood with swords and spears drawn making sure that common boats didn't get too close. I would sit and smile, occasionally raising my open hand in the simple dignified gesture that acknowledged them. Most times Thutmose would stand and watch, amused at the reception we would receive. By the third day though he enjoyed to sit beside me and raise his hand just as I did.

"I should practise for when I am Pharaoh," he said and my heart could have exploded with the pride I felt. I spoke many times with my grandson as to what his future held but I never pushed him beyond what was necessary. His own father was yet to succeed me and his responsibilities lay years ahead.

I often wondered if all the knowledge and skills I had gained so young had in fact sped up my ascension to the throne. I had never pushed my sons to learn as fast as I had and here I still sat as Pharaoh with two more generations below me and I was over twenty years older than my father had been when he died. Perhaps the Gods just helped me to learn more quickly knowing that I would reign younger, and perhaps the Gods protected my grandson by letting him be a child for longer.

As the boat drifted farther from Thebes and the towns grew smaller and quieter I could almost forget I was Pharaoh. A peace and calm surrounded the boat and I sensed that relaxation that one would get if they were on vacation. I even admit there were moments when I would have been happy to never return to the palace and just keep floating on. Perhaps this was what it felt like as you made your way to paradise in the afterlife.

Of course the relaxation was still dotted with duties as we stopped each day to hold audience at the many temples that were upon the river edge. I would also note the state of each temple as we passed and my heart would sink a little when I saw one in a state that was less than it should be. Time had been kinder to some but they all still were fading or slowly being lost in sand. Many of the priests tried to hide the decay with drapery that made many of the temples glow in the sun and the movement of the cloths in the breeze made them seem alive. I saw that this was their attempt to make the temple presentable and I soon learned that the more fabric that festooned a temple, the more likely it was that it needed care. The scribe that travelled with me on this trip would return home to Thebes with dozens of scrolls containing orders for funding and repairs to be carried out on such temples.

Several days into our trip we entered the area now known as Aswan. This was an amazing part of the river so wide that it holds a collection of islands within it. Each island was its own vibrant community, enjoying its separate existence as though it was its own country. The commoners here were still fiercely loyal to me though and as we wove between the pockets of land they would stand, waving and cheering in the hope I would choose their island to stop at. Of course there was only one island that I would dock upon and that was Philae.

Philae was a known meeting place where dealings and exchanges had occurred for generations. At this time it did not hold the buildings that it is known for now and of course it was much larger before the Aswan dam waters stole its lower ground. Here traders from Punt would meet with those from as far north as Alexandria. Sometimes they would not even dock but simply bump their boats together forming their own private meeting ground.

As my boat glided towards the small island we pushed and jostled smaller boats aside amid all the noise of traders yelling out to each other. Not even my presence would slow this activity down. Thutmose ran to the side of the deck smiling at each boat we bumped aside as he figured out just what goods they carried. My boat captain was on the stern now yelling for the dock to be cleared and letting all know his displeasure that it had not already been done so. I too would have been upset if I did not have the distraction of seeing my grandson so entertained by the entire scene.

Finally we were on land again and we made way to the pavilion in which I would receive people when I journeyed here. Thankfully that was prepared and ready for me. They had even made sure to have a smaller throne for Thutmose to sit beside me so I was most pleased. We soon had a procession of foreign traders, all from the lands south of Egypt lined up before us. In their hands they held small chests to showcase their goods or bundles of skins or fabrics slung over shoulders of servants beside them. When it was their turn they would bow and open the chest while they held it close to themselves, or have their servant hold up a sheath of fur or fabric while they talked about the merits of their goods. Only when I put out my hand to indicate I wished a closer look would they then hand it to a guard who would hand it to me.

I would then finger its contents, sometimes lifting a sample up to see it in more light, or put it to my nose to smell it closer should it be incense or food. All the while the trader would continue on speaking of its superiority, the care in which it had been grown or made and the honour of showing it to me. I would keep a plain face, even when I held something of quality beyond anything I had seen. If I did not like the product I would simply shake my head and the vizier of this region who also sat beside me would dismiss the trader and announce the next. This was a crushing blow to the trader and now they would have to join the melee of boats in the waterway in the hope of selling their goods there.

If the chest held something I did like then another game commenced. I would still remain with no expression but turn to my vizier and nod. Then my vizier would turn to the trader and make him an offer. Of course this was always much less than the product was worth and the expression on the faces of traders who had not experienced trade with the Pharaoh before was always one of shock. Some would give in at the first offer through sheer inexperience, fear or just the desire to say that the Pharaoh had bought their product.

The more experienced though were not so easy to bargain with and they did not seek or need my approval. They simply sought good value for their precious goods so that when my vizier would start with the usual ridiculous offer they would shake their head firmly and speak their case. "That is not a suitable price. Lesser quality incense is receiving double that from your noblemen," many would respond. This of course would always be correct and bargaining would continue until a price was agreed upon. Of course if the trader got too greedy then they would be sent away. My viziers knew trade too well to be duped by anyone, let alone a foreigner, and my coffers did not stay full by indulging traders their whims.

Thutmose stayed by my side quietly taking all this in. He even copied my facial expressions so that he matched every posture I held. Of course I did not turn and look at him today as I had to appear as stern as possible, but the priests who accompanied me told me so later. "Sire, the young Prince is a fine figure of royalty. The Gods shine upon him," they said, and I nodded for I knew indeed they did.

When the line of traders was finally diminished and we had indeed bought enough goods to stock the palace and Karnak for many months to come I called an end to the official audience. The sun was starting to dip close to the horizon and I desperately needed to stretch my legs before we reboarded the boat.

"Come Grandson, let us walk Philae for a time and let the blood move through our legs." I put my arms behind me, grasped my left wrist with my right hand and pushing my chest outwards began to walk. I cast a glance beside me to see that Thutmose was walking the same way.

Philae could be fully walked then within an hour but we took longer as I stopped to talk to my grandson about the various pavilions and altars that dotted the island. Some were for business whilst some were for worship. There was even the carved stone at the waters edge that measured the height of the Nile waters. The higher the water, the more abundant the crops and therefore the more income for the farmers--so then my viziers collected more taxes. You could call it the precursor to the big flashing boards in your stock exchanges but just a whole lot simpler.

As we made our way to the opposite side of the island the sounds of the busy waterway faded into the distance and we finally had some quiet, apart from the gentle sounds of the water lapping at the shore and the rustle of palm leaves whenever a breeze came along. Thutmose was busy shimmying his way up a tree while my guards stood nervously below him ready to catch him lest he fell. I decided to leave him to his play and keep wandering when I saw a small temple on a clearing close to the waters edge. It had a small dock nearby that was kept clear for boats that carried people here specifically for the temple and there was a well-worn track from its wooden platform to the small stone building.

The priest saw me eyeing the temple. "Delightfully quaint is it not?" he said quietly and I nodded while I continued to stare at it.

Then I heard them. The soft sounds of women praying began to reach my ears. "So beautiful," I murmured.

"Indeed it is a fine example for a temple its size," the priest answered.

"Not the temple. The sound of the women praying," I said.

"Sorry, Sire, but I cannot hear anything," he answered and I saw him strain his head as though trying to hear also.

I started to walk to the temple and the voices while still soft grew stronger. There was something so familiar about them yet they all blended together so that they created something new. I turned again to the priest. "Do you hear it now?" but he only shook his head somewhat embarrassed that he could not agree with me.

As I stepped before the temple entrance the swirl of voices grew again. I suddenly felt dizzy but I knew this was just the power of the women's prayers and now I wanted to see them. The priest followed me into the darkness of the temple and we stood still for a moment while our eyes adjusted. I expected to now see a group of women, maybe up to fifteen of them here, burning incense and kneeling before the altar while they recited their words. I even smelt incense smoke wafting past me. When the shapes within the temple became clear I could see no one and upon the altar there was only the grey ash from incense long finished. The voices though continued and as I looked at the priest I knew to not even waste my time asking him if he heard them now.

Instead I simply asked that he leave me alone for some time to give thanks for the successful day of trading and for our safe journey so far. He was reluctant but he quickly scanned the temple and left happy that there was no one here to harm me. I felt completely surrounded though as the voices of countless women grew even stronger now I was alone.

I closed my eyes and breathed deep, then reached my arms out so that I might feel them. The sounds grew louder and I now knew that it was not prayers that they chanted. Their words were the wisdom of generations of women spoken here for anyone ready to hear them. Within seconds I heard tales of compassion and nurturing, then I heard messages of pure love as they asked me to see my grandeur. I heard my mother's voice offer me protection, I heard Satiah thank me for her children, I heard Neferure offer her lessons of self-love and I heard Nefertiry speak of joy. One by one they rose above the other voices and spoke, wrapping me with their love til every fibre of me was glowing with a warmth that the sun itself couldn't offer.

Then they melded into one. The words dissolved, but their energy grew stronger and I saw them all blend into a single figure--the Goddess Isis. I now heard her as the voice of all women, as the embodiment of all that was feminine and I knew the depth of her wisdom. The eternal mother reached out to me and stroked my face and I felt that touch until I returned home to Thebes.

"Sire," called the priest who had come back inside. "The light is now fading. We must make our way back to the royal boat."

I kept my eyes closed and Isis smiled at me one last time. The low murmurs of her teachings though continued on and I could hear them until we left the island.

I resisted the initial urge to flood the temple with funding so that it could expand. Bigger temples attracted more people but it did not guarantee their dedication. I knew that by leaving the temple as it was that only those that heard the voices or knew the truth of Isis would make their way there. It was a truly sacred space and I quite liked that it was upon an island so heavy with the masculine ways of trade as though it seemed to offer balance.

I know I was not the only one who had heard the voices as the trail carved from the dock attested to this. I also know that I was not the last one to hear them either. As time passed the temple would grow as other pharaohs heard the voices when they visited and were overcome by the beauty and wisdom within them. Some would not hear but they would be drawn here anyway and know this place was important.

It was our final kingdom of Ptolemy's family that would be the most responsive and create the majesty you see today. As the rest of Egyptian ways crumbled around Cleopatra, Philae held our religion the longest and it is here that the last hieroglyphs were ever carved. Isis and her wisdom touched even those that chose to wipe away our culture in order to dominate our land. Isis was carried back to Rome and her image became that of Holy Mother Mary, she travelled east and became Kuan Yin. She is every image of women in religion and worship because they are all one, holding unlimited compassion and love for each person here. She is eternal and divine and it should be no surprise she has found her way to every culture in some form.

CHAPTER TWENTY-NINE

With young Thutmose now reaching fifteen years of age and having experienced several excursions away from Thebes with his father and myself, he could now take part on such journeys on his own. As had his uncle Amenemhat and his father, he would mostly spend time at Memphis learning the ways of trade and greeting travellers from the north. It was hard for us all to farewell him the first time he left but everyone knew this was the way of a successor to learn his duties and to serve the kingdom. It also helped to lessen his dependency upon people such as his mother and childhood nurses who were slow to let go of what they knew as nurturing--which for a young man might soon become unnecessary coddling. A young prince could also use this time to become comfortable addressing his entourage without other elders around to do it for him.

Within a year Thutmose returned to the palace to visit our family and he walked and talked like a man. Not surprisingly I also heard that two consorts now were part of his entourage and I delighted at the thought of great grandchildren arriving. I imagined having four generations within the palace and promised myself that would be something that would be celebrated throughout the empire so that everyone knew of the good fortune of their Pharaoh.

Rarely had a Pharaoh had the opportunity to know that not only his own son was worthy and capable to follow him but also to know that the generation after was established and just as strong. My palace years were now a time of completely enjoying all that I had created and watching all before me continue to flourish. My remaining children stayed loyal and supportive while my grandchildren took on their ways and attitudes without one faltering amongst them. The ways and laws of Egypt were made solid in how we lived and my family were the example for all of my people to follow.

The only restlessness that was present within the palace belonged to Matreya. That single moment of softness that we had shared beside Satiah's deathbed had long evaporated and I will concede that this was entirely due to my actions with Hatshepsut's memorials. A significant part of her own glory had been extinguished that day as well as my aunt's. My aunt's permission for Matreya to carry the name Hatshepsut along with her own no longer tied her to the only woman to be crowned Pharaoh. She was now tied to a woman who was recorded merely as a queen and barely grander than herself. There was one part of Hatshepsut that did remain to attest to her grandeur and that was the mortuary temple in the Valley. Matreya had her sights set on something just as impressive and now that she was a Great Wife as well as mother and grandmother to my successors, she believed she could match this monument with her own.

Building had begun on her actual tomb years ago and as with mine it was all but completed. Of course final touches could only be added when we actually died, as our final years could not yet be depicted when they had not occurred yet. Matreya would make her way to mine often to compare and make sure that she would match anything I had created. She requested a cartouche shaped room for her sarcophagus as I had, but the priests refused her stating that it was a sacred shape reserved for pharaohs only. As always Matreya did not take no for a first answer and made her way to me.

"This is ridiculous!" she shouted at me. "How dare I be denied *anything*! I am the mother of your heir and grandmother to his heir. My tomb should reflect this!"

"Matreya, there are many queens buried in the Valley who have contributed to as many pharaohs as you have or will," I said bluntly. "You shall follow their ways."

Matreya breathed in sharply. "Then allow me to make my burial chamber bigger."

"Whatever for?" I asked incredulously.

"I wish my maids to be interred with me when they too pass," she said. "I have promised this."

I wanted to shake my head and refuse her again but somehow I knew that if I made this concession for her then she might be satisfied and stop. So I nodded. "Fine, you may expand the burial chamber."

Matreya straightened and smiled which was the closest I would get to a thank you. Then she spoke again. "I also require that you approve the funding for my own mortuary temple."

My mouth dropped at how ludicrous this was. "Matreya, our family has a temple in the Valley. There is no need for your own."

"That is made mostly of wood and will disappear with time," she sneered. "I should like to build one completely of stone."

I knew exactly what she was up to and I actually smiled at how transparent her excuse was. "You shall not have funds for your own temple, stone or otherwise," I said calmly. "Those funds will be better spent on tombs for the rest of the family. Unlike the queen who sought to build such things you have children and grandchildren to consider."

"That is ridiculous! You have more tribute and taxes flowing to the treasury than you need," she spat. "You spend it on temples for peasants while you could build monuments that will let eternity know of your wealth."

"My dear, you seem to have forgotten that I have made Karnak greater than it has ever been," I said firmly. "My people speak of my generosity and share my wealth and I will not compromise them or my family's future with the building of a temple for the sole purpose of your glorification."

Matreya's eyes grew dark. "I will never be more than the mother of your children will I?" she said dropping her voice.

I was not about to be pulled into this game with her. There was no need to state the obvious or to rehash the past. Things were as they were and despite Matreya's constant desire to push the limits of her position it just was not going to happen.

"Matreya, please go and leave me." I said softly. "You made your case and you received my answer. Do not make more of this than needs be."

Matreya knew she would now have to settle for my refusal but as always she was not going to let me feel that I had won. She stood up and her sly smile curled her lips as she looked down on me. "Fine, Thutmose, don't allow me my temple. There will be pharaohs to follow who will. I will just wait for them to take the throne." With that she threw her head to the side and left the room leaving me relieved to see her go as well as bemused that she would think that she could persuade Amenhotep to allow her such a decadence to be built.

It also left me to picture the scenario that Matreya would outlive me and be a possible influence upon Amenhotep. What if she did manage to persuade him to allow the funds and once again a woman undeserved of such monuments made her place in Egyptian history? I had already negated Satiah's place by having to now call Matreya my Great Wife due to her being the mother of my heir. If Matreya now continued her campaign through Amenhotep then Satiah would die all over again. This was made worse by the fact that Amenhotep had yet to make any of his consorts into wives despite them having bore him twelve children so far. This included Tiaa who had bore him Thutmose, his successor. If I passed away before he declared a wife then Matreya remained Queen. What that would make her capable of while Amenhotep found his way as a new Pharaoh made my blood run cold.

Amenhotep arrived a few days later from his latest trip to Memphis and as always made his way straight to wherever I was to report on how things had transpired. I was in court that day so he sat beside me on his own throne and re-told the latest trade details before the viziers as well. When session was completed for the day I invited him to dine with me and I dismissed my servants as quickly as I could.

Amenhotep sensed something serious immediately. "What is it Father?" he asked. "I could see the concern on your face the moment I arrived at court."

I sighed deeply. "Amenhotep--you must make Tiaa your wife as soon as possible."

He put his food down and wiped at his mouth. "Why the sudden concern for this? Has she approached you?"

"She has not approached me," I answered. "I just believe it to be in the best interests of your son to do so."

Amenhotep smirked at this. "Father, coming from the son of a consort himself I find that hard to believe is your true fear. Perhaps you could be more open with me.'

Amenhotep was right; if I could not be honest with my son and heir then all was lost. My concerns that I would upset him by speaking ill of his mother would just have to be set aside.

"Your mother has approached me with a request to build her own mortuary temple in the Valley," I began and was quickly interrupted by Amenhotep.

"Like Hatshepsut's?" he said, and raised his eyebrow knowingly.

"Yes, just like Hatshepsut's and in stone," I answered dryly.

"And how does Mother's desire for opulence affect me taking a wife?" he asked.

"Because, my son and successor, if I pass and you have not declared a Great Wife then your mother remains Queen," I said bluntly.

The look on Amenhotep's face signalled that he understood perfectly and he looked down at his plate as he took this in.

"Whilst she knows she cannot influence me, she believes she will be able to do so with you," I said.

Suddenly Amenhotep started nodding. "I know," he said, looking me in the eye.

"How do you know?" I asked as I sat straight in my chair. "She has spoken of this with you already? I believe it is now your opportunity to be open with me."

"She said such things back when…" he hesitated to finish. "Just before my first trip alone to Memphis."

This was Amenhotep's polite way of saying, "Just after Amenemhat died," and just as he knew it would my bile rose.

"She did not speak of it again though," he added hoping to lessen the anger he could see in my face. "I made it quite clear that I would not be influenced by her."

I nodded as he said this but I soon stopped. "And just how sure are you of avoiding this once I am gone?" I asked.

"Quite sure, Father," he said plainly.

"And what do you imagine would happen if you were called to Canaan for several months of battle as I was at Meggido?" I raised my eyebrows as I said this and Amenhotep sat back in his chair. "She would only need one high priest to listen to her with sympathy to begin her influence."

Amenhotep nodded as I spoke. "So you will agree to make Tiaa your Great Wife?" I asked and he nodded once more. "Good, we shall find a suitable time for this and when you do I shall also declare our co-regency."

Now Amenhotep shook his head. "No, Father, that is not necessary," he said firmly.

"I know it is not necessary nor is it customary, but then few things of my rule have been so and it does not seem to have faltered so much," I said smiling.

Amenhotep knew I was serious and he shook his head. "I will appear to have forced you, or it will appear that somehow I am questioned as your successor that you need to make such declarations and actions," he said still shaking his head.

"Now where has this come from?" I said loudly. "Your paranoia has returned!"

Amenhotep smiled and looked up at me. "Yes it has and I barely noticed. Thank you for reminding me that it is not necessary." He laughed a little as he finished, but then he stopped. "I will agree to this co-regency but only when you begin to grow weak with old age."

"I am already grown weak, Son," I laughed.

Amenhotep did not return the laughter and his face stayed sober as he shook his head once more. "Father, you may not be the vigorous warrior that made his way to Megiddo but you are far from weakened."

Matreya did not take lightly my refusal for her temple and any civility in our relationship was now completely gone. She would sit beside me in court or at temple as she knew she deserved to, but our eyes would never meet. We now simply acted out our partnership with the least amount of civility needed. Matreya consoled herself by spending as much funds as she could without having to seek my approval. Those at the treasury became accustomed to her visits to gather what gems and gold she could convince them to give her in order to make herself more jewellery and adornments. If I would not allow her a temple to make known all of her grandeur then at least they could all see it as she walked past covered in such opulence.

I would just sigh as I saw her wearing another new piece. I was not concerned at her depleting the treasury, as my men there were cleverer than her. They would stash jewels in areas that they knew they could refuse her entry to. Thankfully, they were also then brave enough to stand up to her with the simple phrase "You cannot access that room without the Pharaoh present" when she did attempt to enter--which instantly made her blood boil. She would fake a smile though and continue on towards the rooms that she was allowed access. I did not make any attempt to curb her behaviour as I knew my wife too well.

Each new piece upon her was a relief to me, as I knew that it signified time not spent speaking to priests or viziers to build some form of allegiance. Each new piece being paraded before me also meant that those jewels were remaining within the palace where I could see them and they were not being handed to priests and viziers in return for favours. So the more jewellery Matreya wore, the more I was actually relieved and quite happy.

In the meantime Matreya's new ambition became to simply outlive me. She knew she was more robust than Satiah and she knew that my family did not have the history of longevity that would keep me here into significant old age. However I was proving this part of my family history quite wrong so instead she was banking on my recklessness to hopefully lead to an injury and hasten my end. Each time a maid reported that I had left the palace upon my horse she prayed that it would throw me and I would return upon an ox cart ready for the mortuary.

I continued on though and my burst of carelessness after Satiah's death had not been repeated as each day my body made known its limits. However one morning I awoke feeling robust and strong which I foolishly mistook for a return of strength and decided to ride on horseback out to the Valley to oversee some new tombs being built. As soon as I saw that wonderful stretch of sand that lay so open and still I just had to kick my horse and gallop fast along it. I swallowed the dust as my horse stirred it up all around me and soon had sweat pouring down my face. It was just like I used to ride as a boy. I stopped the horse near the area I was inspecting to catch my breath but my breathing refused to slow and I sensed something was wrong immediately. Then suddenly I felt that familiar tightness hit my chest and realised I had exerted myself too much. Those around me knew it also as I suddenly grabbed at my chest and lunged forward on my horse.

Within seconds there were priests screaming while guards pulled me down from my horse and carried me to what little shade the site offered. The pain was so overwhelming that I could not even answer as the priests asked me what I was suffering. I decided that all that could be done was to lie back and wait for it to pass just as I did on the first night it visited me. Soon the priests agreed also and they huddled near me to discuss how best to transport me home to the palace. I heard mutterings about a sedan but they knew I could not sit up and would need to return home lying down so as not to stress my heart anymore. Unfortunately this had never occurred before and there wasn't exactly a royal stretcher on hand at the Valley, or an ambulance that could be called for such occasions, so the dilemma became how to transport me in the manner of royal grandeur that was necessary.

There were ox carts nearby but how could they even consider transporting a pharaoh upon such a vehicle as though he was some sort of commodity being shipped--and by such common beasts as oxen? So they discussed changing the oxen for horses but that was not possible as the cart's bridles and harnesses were too big for the horses. So the oxen would remain but then how would they dress the cart to make it befitting for me? In the meantime I lay still and quiet, feeling the pain slowly subside and my breath grow deeper. The talk continued and I now heard a priest decide to send someone to the royal barge to collect silks and other cloths to line the cart for me.

"The cart will do just fine as it is," I spoke suddenly and loudly so that the priests all turned and looked at me as though they had forgotten I was even there. "The sooner I am returned to my bed the better. Silks will not help me heal," I added.

I made motion to sit up and they immediately surrounded me and pushed me back down. "Sire you must not exert yourself or put any pressure upon your heart. Lie still that your blood will ease its way through you," one spoke as sternly as he thought he could get away with. He then flicked his hand towards the guards. "Come, carry the Pharaoh--but keep him as though he is upon a bed."

So my four guards came and lifted me as though I was the most precious treasure ever. They kept me as flat as possible and I looked up at the sky over me. It was completely clear apart from the sun and not one wisp of cloud made its mark upon it. It was just a place of purity and while I at first thought it was empty I knew it was also full because here sat the sun feeding all down below it. I sighed deeply and the guards stopped and peered down at me, fearful they had hurt me.

"It is alright," I said. "I was just admiring the beauty of the sky."

They looked puzzled but as always continued on with their task as professionally as ever. I was soon upon my cart which cloths had been hastily thrown over to cover the rough wood below me. I wondered where the cloths came from and as one of my priests leant over me I saw his bare chest and looked down to see he had only his loincloth tied over his groin. Soon another almost bare priest was on my other side. A third priest's robes became like a sail held over me to keep off the sun as we made our way back to the boat. I smiled at this sacrifice and was thankful none of my daughters were here to see this though.

When we reached the barge I was once again carried so preciously aboard to lie upon one of the benches while we crossed the river. The priests hastily retrieved their robes and redressed while servants gathered more suitable dressing for the journey from the pier to the palace. Another cart was gathered at the Thebes pier and dressed in whatever had been collected on the barge. There was not only a makeshift mattress for me to lie upon but great swatches hung around the cart also and then around the oxen's necks. Priest robes were sufficient to ride through the Valley and past its workers but my entourage now made sure that I would be carried through my city in grandeur.

As always word spread quickly through Thebes that I was about to make my passage back to the palace so the usual throngs gathered. However many more gathered today when news was shared that the Pharaoh was making his way on his back and within a cart. My people crowded the streets believing I was dead so that as we rode through I heard crying and prayers called out for my soul.

"The Pharaoh is alive!" shouted a priest. "Pray for his recovery from a minor illness."

"We don't believe you!" shouted someone in response from within the anonymity of the crowd and I was proud that my people would not accept a priest's word about me so easily.

I wished to sit up and show them but knew I was not quite that strong just yet. Instead I pulled my headdress from my head and raised it into the air so that all that came to see would know that it was I upon the cart and that I was alive. The roar from the crowd as my hand and headdress first appeared above the wooden edge of the cart was magnificent and gratifying. So much so that I enjoyed repeating this every minute or so as my strength allowed me just to hear the reaction. I was quite fatigued as we finally entered through the palace gates and made our way to the doors closest my chambers.

Matreya was standing ready at the doors, not that I could see her from my place upon the cart. She had been preening herself as she did most days when her chief maid came to her and said, "Madam, the Pharaoh is returning to the palace upon an ox cart." Matreya did not ask anything more nor did she seek any additional information as her own heart began to burst within her chest at the thought I was possibly dead. As she stood and watched the procession pull to the doors of the palace she noted how sombre my guards and priests were and Matreya fought back a smile as she imagined this to be due to the fact that their Pharaoh was dead.

As the guards slowly slid me off the cart cloths fell from the cart as they did so and gathered below me as a priest ran forward crying, "Be careful, be careful!" He turned to Matreya. "Most unfortunate event Your Highness--and to happen in the Valley so far from the physicians."

Matreya was now sure that the priest spoke of my demise and she braced herself as the guards carried me towards her to take me inside. As they passed beside her she looked down upon me and saw the colour of my skin was far from grey.

"Matreya, I do believe I should not ride my horse anymore," was all I could say as I was carried past.

Matreya stood still for a moment and her face grew red from anger.

"Damn you!" she yelled then pushed past the men carrying me, her fists clenched as she stormed her way back inside the palace.

I once again lay upon my bed and was immediately surrounded by my physicians. One asked endless questions while two others poked and prodded me. Three high priests stood behind them watching on silently taking their own notes.

"It is merely my heart again," I said exhausted and the physicians looked sternly at me as I passed upon them my own diagnosis. "I do believe I know my own body and all too well this pain that I carry within it."

The chief physician nodded. "Of course, Your Highness," he conceded. "Do you wish to continue with the usual prescription?"

I nodded and once again was handed the standard tonic which I sipped while being lectured on bed rest and not seeking activities that would invoke another episode. "I suggest you only make short journeys from now on Sire, and that when you do it is upon your chariot and at a sombre pace," he recited as the other physicians and the priests all nodded along. "Sire, I would also suggest that you--um--limit any activities with the royal consorts."

I burst out laughing so loudly that they all jumped and the chief physician's eyes grew wide with shock. "That should be of no concern to any of you," I laughed as I spoke. "That particular activity has long been abandoned."

I did not joke or lie about this. I had stopped lying with Matreya when Isis was conceived which had been a great relief to us both. My intimacy with Satiah had remained until she left but that had rarely involved lovemaking in her later years. I had no desire now to be with any woman and any occasional physical urges dissolved quite quickly as I learnt the art of distraction. Unfortunately now I had lost my best distraction; that of horseback riding. I doubted my chariot would be as satisfying but it would have to suffice and, besides, if anyone knew about adapting to circumstance it was I.

The physicians and priests were soon gone only for my bedside to now be surrounded by my children. As each one arrived and discovered what had actually happened they begged me to give up my horse riding and I promised each one that I would as though I was being asked for the first time. Grandchildren were ushered in, their hands clutching precious toys and full of promises to be quiet. I greeted each one as enthusiastically as I could but I was growing so tired. When the last one left the room I sighed with relief and closed my eyes savouring the stillness and quiet.

I finally drifted into a delightful sleep that came so gently I believed I was still awake but I was in fact dreaming. My dream began where I was in my bedchamber and I could even hear the sounds of my servants within the next room. I rose from my bed and walked to the door to see them cleaning and tidying the salon. They continued on as though they did not notice me, for if they had they would have stopped instantly to acknowledge me and make sure their backs were turned away from me. I heard them speak of my latest turn and I felt their concern.

"I am fine," I called out but they continued on as though I had not spoken so I walked close to my butler. He did not even turn and continued on as though I was not there.

"Can you not hear me?" I spoke again and still there was no response. *"My, this is interesting,"* I thought, and made my way to the corridor.

As I passed through the massive doorway I expected to hear the loud thud, as my guards on either side of the doorway would snap their spears into position before them to await my orders. They remained at ease though and one scratched at the shadow of his beard. I stepped before him and pushed my face close to his but still there was no reaction. He turned to the other guard. "Aren't you glad we weren't the ones who escorted Pharaoh to the Valley today?"

The other guard snorted and nodded. "Very glad. Now hush lest we are heard talking. I do not fancy one of the butler's lectures today."

"Tati lectured my guards?" Well this was news to me I thought and

carried on down the corridor. If no one had seen me so far I would not need my guards and what a wonderful opportunity to walk the palace without anyone by my side. I stopped nearby at Matreya's room to find her lounging upon a seat by her window. She did not speak but I could feel the pulsing within her as her heart still pounded and her mind raced with anger after her disappointment this afternoon. I laughed out loud at her but then stopped as she suddenly looked so sad to me. Her eyes dropped down and I almost thought she might cry--then her head snapped up and she locked eyes with me.

"Can you see me?" I asked.

She turned her head back to look out the window, which could have been "yes" or "no" from Matreya. Ignoring me was one of her favourite games these days and I simply could not be bothered to find out her answer so I moved on.

I then passed through the rooms of my children. I saw Isis cradling her young son in her arms while she gently whispered against his soft hair. She kissed him so gently and I saw her eyes grow teary which made me want to cry also. I knew her tears were about me and I hated myself for causing her sadness.

"I promise I will not ride again," I whispered.

I wandered into court and saw Siamun and Beketamun sitting with some viziers. My children were assuring them of my health and the viziers nodded. I nodded too as I watched this scene so proud that they could sit here and address these men as such. I was enjoying my invisible journey so much and walked through the kitchens, the treasury and wherever my feet seemed to carry me. I saw everyone carrying out their duties as perfectly and diligently as though they knew I was there. I stood and nodded over them occasionally calling out but of course gathering no responses at all. My bemusement at all of this only made me want to explore the palace more.

I turned a corner near the war rooms and heard Menkheperre's voice. It was not its usual loud tone though, seeming hushed and quiet. I then saw him standing within a small alcove along the corridor that was formed by a column near the wall. Before him against the wall was the daughter of one of the viziers and Menkheperre was leaning in close as he whispered to her. His right hand stroked her face while his left hand gently traced the curve of her breast. I could see her breath quicken and she trembled as he leaned in closer and brushed her lips with his.

"Oh my," I sighed.

Menkheperre pulled away from her and his head turned to face me.

"What is it?" whimpered the girl.

"I thought I heard someone," he answered and stepped away from her while he scanned the corridor. When he was assured that no one was there he resumed his position against the girl and kissed her once again.

"I never planned for these corridors to be used in such a way, my son," I muttered and laughed.

Menkheperre jumped back once again and looked around him. "Who is there? Make yourself known!" he cried.

I felt myself freeze in place, astounded that he had heard me when none others had. Perhaps the magic of my adventure was wearing off? Menkheperre could not see me though and as much as I would have liked to toy with him a bit more I decided against it.

Anyway I had spooked him well enough. He turned back to the girl. "You should make your way home lest someone does make their way here," he said, as he walked away from her still scanning the corridor as he did so.

I had seen and heard enough now and decided to make my way back to my bedchamber. I did not wander back in the same way that I had set out through the palace. Instead within that second that I decided to end my journey I was instantly back within my bed. I then felt that familiar pull as my body awakened and my eyes grew accustomed once again to the light in my room and the heaviness in my chest made itself known again. My mind tumbled with thoughts for a moment as I realised my walk had been just a dream and there was a mix of confusion and disappointment as my dream state dissolved away. It had all felt so real it seemed impossible that it had not occurred, yet now as I opened my eyes it slipped away.

I sighed and closed my eyes once again as though I could call it back but it was most definitely gone. So instead I called for my butler to add some more pillows behind me so I could sit up a little. As he was doing this Menkheperre, having just heard about my illness, appeared at my door to visit. As he walked towards me the scene of him and the girl in my dream came rushing back as though I had just freshly seen it. My look must have been quite odd as I did this for Menkheperre smiled while he cocked one eyebrow.

"Are you still sleepy Father? Perhaps I should come back when you have awoken more?" he asked.

I shook my head and tapped the mattress, indicating for him to sit close by. I waited for my butler to leave then beckoned with my hand for him to lean in close. "Were you just with a vizier's daughter?" I asked matter-of-factly.

The look on Menkheperre's face and the stiffening of his spine answered my question. He nodded and then stammered. "So it was you. How much did you see?"

I laughed and hit his shoulder. "I saw that her breast fit in your hand comfortably!"

Menkheperre shook his head and said, "But you were here asleep. This is impossible." Menkheperre also knew it could have been a lucky guess, not many days passed without some woman being pressed into a dark corner of the palace by my son. He still felt that sensation that he had been watched though and was curious as to what I would say.

"I had such a vivid dream," I began and sank back into my pillows. "I walked the palace and saw everything. No one could see or hear me, except for you."

"Were you pleased with all that you saw?" he asked.

"Yes, I was," I smiled. "Although I would rather you choose more suitable women to woo!"

"Well I am glad that only my indiscretion spoiled your walk," Menkheperre joked. "Perhaps if you can travel like this then you won't miss your horse so much now."

I nodded at this thought, for if I could finally sleep so deeply as to allow this to occur again then my depleting vigour really was no limitation upon me. I imagined travelling at night to survey Canaan, or to the south to check upon trade with Punt. I knew I could trust what I saw for I had just been offered proof of this through my son. Admittedly it was a most unusual way to confirm such abilities but there wasn't another of my children so in tune with such ways so this would be how it was made known to me. I was not the first to learn such a way as the priests had used dreams to prophesise or analyse for centuries. I had always just imagined that it was yet another dramatic method to express some insight or to make their personal opinion more acceptable. Now I too had been given a taste of this experience and understood it completely.

When the next dream priest came to me in court kneeling before my throne, begging to share a message he received as he slept, I did not remain back in my throne with one eyebrow raised as I usually did. This time I truly listened to the words. I saw the priest close his eyes as though this would help him recall the dream clearer, just as I would when I wanted to revisit the experience. When he finished he looked to me waiting for my usual acknowledgement of a nod so that he could leave. This time though as he looked up he found me leaning forward in my chair.

"Does this dream displease you, Sire?" he asked nervously.

I shook my head. "I wish to know more. Do you feel that you are actually there when you have such a dream?" I asked.

"Why yes, Sire. It is as though I am not asleep at all," he answered smiling at my interest in his ability.

"And tell me, are you sometimes as though invisible and silent when you have these visions so that no one can see or hear you?" I continued still leaning forward.

"Many times Sire," he answered again.

"And when you awaken, do you feel confusion as to where you are?" I continued.

"Oh yes Sire," he gushed. "It is as though my spirit needs to re-enter my body but I am much used to this now."

I sat back and nodded, happy to know that what I had felt was indeed a "normal" part of the process. "Thank you for your service and message. You may go now," I said satisfied that I had understood enough for now.

The priest nodded and started to walk away then turned back. I raised my eyebrows as this was quite disrespectful to do so--but I sensed he had some more to add to his answers.

"Sire, those that wish to develop this talent are best to seek the guidance of Horus," he finished as quickly as he began, bowed once more and this time turned and did leave

My clever priest had indeed worked out the motivation behind my questions though I hoped that others around me were not so attentive that afternoon. When I returned to my chambers for rest I called Tati. "Have our goldsmiths make for me a likeness of Horus to place beside my bed," I asked casually hoping he would not ask any questions.

"Yes, Sire," he answered. Tati knew all too well how soundly I slept these days and even caught me murmuring as I now also spoke in my sleep. He knew that a God to guide me during my dreams would be most useful and ease my sleep.

When the goldsmith arrived with the small crate just over a week later Tati gathered beside me just as anxious to see the new icon as I was. The goldsmith clicked his fingers at his apprentice who came with him and the young boy pulled from his belt a flat tool and pried open the lid of the box. Shreds of hay sprung up as the lid lifted and the boy gently pulled off two great handfuls of it and stood back as the goldsmith stepped forward to lift his creation out for me to see. He cradled the base in one hand and the head in the other as though it was a newborn child--which to him it was.

"Your Highness, I pray this is to your liking and as you envisioned your commission," he smiled as he spoke, knowing very well that it was as magnificent as it could be and ever so slightly rocked it in his hands so that the light continually glistened and bounced off the gold and jewels upon it.

All I could do was nod and smile for it was truly glorious. There was something familiar about it too and then I realised it reminded me of the statue of Isis that I had made for Satiah when she first came to the palace. It was the same size and of solid gold worked to perfection with each gem placed delicately and precisely.

"It is a most superb piece," I said and smiled at the goldsmith. "The Gods truly work through your hands."

This was the highest accolade that he could have wished for from me and as Tati took the statue from his hands the goldsmith and his apprentice bowed low to accept my praise. As they stood back up I believe I saw tears in the man's eyes and I felt his pride at having his work received so graciously. To be asked to sculpt for the Pharaoh was one thing but to be praised so openly was another honour again.

# CHAPTER THIRTY

When I went into my bedchamber that night Tati had placed Horus upon the small table near my bedside. However in doing so he had removed Satiah's statue of Isis that I had kept close by me since her death. Tati had placed Isis upon a table across the room where I could still see her but I did not like her distance. I immediately walked over and gathered her to return her near to my bed. Tati watched and ran to take her from me to carry but I pulled her in close to me.

"I shall place her Tati," I said plainly and he stepped back.

When I reached my bedside I placed her beside Horus and took a deep breath. They were a perfect match in height, the gold was the same tone and the patterns of jewels upon them reflected each other also. I sat upon my bed and was mesmerised at how they were so alike as though I had commissioned them at the same time.

What I did not realise was that the goldsmith before me today had been the apprentice to the goldsmith who had created this beautiful Isis. He had sat transfixed as his teacher worked the gold, heating it and shaping it, then carving the indents to hold the gems and stones. He watched intently at how his teacher's hands worked. He quickly understood how the tools could be held at different angles to achieve different effects. Sharp lines and deep grooves could be made with the same simple tool depending on the angle you held your hand and how you pushed or pulled.

His teacher rarely spoke knowing that a goldsmith learnt through his eyes but grew through his hands. The apprentice knew this also and he ached to make something as magnificent as this Isis that he saw form before his eyes. He continued on diligently each day with his more menial tasks. He swept up the floor and sifted through the mess making sure no shavings of gold or small gems were lost in the debris. He washed brushes and mixed paints and he did so knowing one day he would have an apprentice doing this for him when he became a great goldsmith.

Each night when the senior goldsmith was finished for the day he would wrap the incomplete statue in silk and leave her upon a table for the apprentice to put into the guarded storeroom. After his teacher was gone and all his chores had been completed the young goldsmith would unwrap Isis and study the work that had been completed that day. He had a scroll of papyrus and upon it he sketched every detail and made notes. He wrote of which tool had created each line, which gems had been used for which colours and what shape they were.

When the old goldsmith finally finished Isis he lit three lamps upon his workbench and sat them close together in an arc before him. Then he leant close into the light with Isis in his hands, his eyes scouring every part of her looking for the smallest flaws in the gem settings or for the slightest mark within the gold. His fingertips would trace over the surfaces hoping to catch what his eyes would miss. Every so often he would stop and grab for his file to rub at the gold or he would take another tool to push at a gem to align it with its neighbours. For two hours he did this, never losing his focus while his apprentice sat nearby hardly taking a breath lest he disturb his teacher and cause him to miss something that would allow Isis to leave their workshop anything less than perfect.

The sculptor took a deep breath and turned to the young man, "I do believe I need some wine," he said, and as the apprentice had been expecting an order from him he jumped up to fetch this for his teacher. "No, no, I shall go," he said to him and beckoned the confused boy back. "I need some time from this bench. Here," he held Isis out to the young man, "you continue checking the Goddess."

The young man merely nodded and was within his teacher's chair, leaning into the light with the statue before the old man had even left the room. Of course he knew every inch of the statue with all the intimacy of her creator. He had seen the tiny flaws before the old man had and was delighted in seeing his teacher correct them. So when he sat now he immediately went to a small line of rectangular lapis stones that he had looked at only the night before. Only the most trained of eyes would have known that the small pieces of the blue stone were not sitting against each other as tightly as they could. The young man began to write this upon the sheet of papyrus so that he could tell the old man when he returned but then he put down the quill and took up a copper tool with the finest tip imaginable. He knew the old man would be some time and the temptation to correct this himself was simply too great.

The apprentice gently tapped at the stone just as he had seen his teacher do, first upwards, then to the left and the stone slid within its place so that you could not see where it ended and the next stone began. He smiled down on his work and was just about to start tapping upon the next when he heard a noise behind him. Of course it was his teacher who had been there some time. He had intentionally come quietly back into the room to observe his student and to see how he worked. He had hoped to find him slowly looking and touching over the surface, with a list of faults noted. He also prayed that he would not find him quickly turning the icon, a blank piece of papyrus next to him and the apprentice merely shrugging his shoulders saying he could not find anything.

When he crept back to the doorway he never imagined that he would find the young man with a tool in his hand gently guiding a stone to its perfect position. He stood still and watched for a while then slowly crept forward to watch him closer. The young man had been so enraptured with finally touching Isis with a tool that he was completely unaware of his teacher so close behind until that final moment when the old man had scraped his sandal on the floor.

The apprentice looked up and stammered, "I--I..."

"It is alright," said the old man smiling. "Continue on." He pulled up a chair and waved his hand at the statue. "Show me what else I have taught you."

The young man hesitated, as scared now of displeasing his teacher as he was of not making the statue as perfect as she should be. However when he once again raised the copper tip to the lapis his hands did not tremble at all and his teacher noted this as much as he did the angle and the strength of the young man's touch. Another line between the lapis disappeared and as the young man looked up for approval the old man nodded and he continued on. When he finished the line of lapis he imagined the old man would resume his work but instead he stood up. "I shall begin some other pieces the Pharaoh has commissioned. You continue on with this. When the gems are aligned then polish the gold. Do not stop until you are satisfied that it is worthy of our Pharaoh and his new bride."

So the young man continued on with all the dedication he would have given something he had created from its very beginning. It was over four hours later that he was satisfied that the gems were perfect and he began to polish the gold. Three times he refilled his lamps to keep his light as bright as he needed. He barely noticed when the old man left for the day nor did he even notice as his stomach called out for food. All that existed was this statue. Finally she was complete and the finest silk dragged across her surface did not catch upon anything and as the young man satisfied himself with this test he finally let out a yawn. After wrapping her for the last time he finally made his way outside to walk home. As he looked up he saw the stars were not where they usually were on his walk home as it was now long past his usual departure time.

It was only a few hours before dawn when he finally rested his head upon his pillow and no wonder that he slept beyond the time he should have awoken the next morning. He grabbed some bread from his mother as he rushed from his house, chewing as he ran through the streets back to the workshop. As he approached the workshop he saw the old man with another goldsmith standing outside in the sun. He held the statue of Isis before him and both he and the other goldsmith were turning it over and over rubbing their hands along its surface. Their brows were furrowed though and this made the young man's stomach sink to think he had not completed his work properly. He slowed his pace and arrived in front of the men and called out his greeting.

The old man looked up but did not return the greeting. Instead he asked, "Who helped you finish the piece?"

"No one, Pareen," he answered respectfully.

"He is lying!" spat the other goldsmith.

"He does not lie!" protested the old man and waved his hand at the young man. "Come inside."

"No apprentice works like this," the other goldsmith insisted as he huffed after them.

The old man turned. "Yes they do when they have an able teacher and they are a willing student!" he declared.

He placed Isis upon the workbench where she had spent all her days while she was created. The young man looked upon her and she was even more beautiful than when he had left her last night. All night he had dreamt of her as even in his sleep he had continued to work upon her. He was sure that today the old man would find something that he had missed but indeed he couldn't. Instead the old man walked to him and grasped the young man's shoulders and shook him.

"No student of mine has ever learnt so quickly and none have ever finished a piece for me better than I could have," the old man smiled as he spoke and continued to shake the young man.

The young man smiled. *"Better? Did he really say better?"* was all he could think. He was so exhausted physically and emotionally that he couldn't decide if he wanted to just sleep or cry.

"It is bad enough this one here has seen your talent," he nodded his head to the other goldsmith, "for when word gets out every workshop from Thebes to the sea will try and steal you from me." The old goldsmith leant in close, still gripping the young man's shoulders. "So as of today you are no longer an apprentice."

The young man's exhaustion didn't quite know what to make of this statement and he just looked blankly at the old man which only made him laugh.

"Hah! You are too tired to even know what I am saying. Look at her!" he shouted pointing at Isis. "When the Pharaoh sees this he will favour our workshop above all others. Now go home and rest. You did two days work in one night. When you return, there will be a new apprentice to learn from us both!"

With that he began to push the young man towards the door but as they both stepped back into the sunlight he grabbed him one last time. "Wait!" he cried, and reached into the leather purse that hung from his belt. He pulled out five coins and pressed them into the young man's hand. "For the love of Amun buy some decent clothes. You are no longer an apprentice. You are a royal goldsmith--dress like one!"

The young man walked back to his home in a daze trying to take in what had just happened. As he stepped back through the front door of his home his mother came to see who was there. "Why are you home at this hour?" she cried her face twisting, ready to hear bad news.

Her son looked at her with his eyes glazed over and said quietly, "I am no longer an apprentice." With this his mother began crying at the thought that her son had lost a most prestigious job but he shook his head, "I am now a royal goldsmith." His mother's tears now turned to those of joy as he stumbled to his bedroom and collapsed upon the bed still clutching the five coins in his hand.

When that statue of Isis arrived at the palace I was too young to know or appreciate the craftsmanship that was within it. All I saw was something beautiful that I hoped would touch Satiah in some way, which of course it did more than I ever imagined that it would. Now here sat Isis beside the image of her son as though they were always meant to be together. It had been over thirty years since her birth but when Tati arrived at the workshop to commission this new icon of Horus to sit within the royal bedchamber the goldsmith's mind raced back to the statue of Isis. He remembered that she too had been commissioned for a royal bedchamber. As soon as Tati left his workshop he made way to where he stored his scrolls of sketches and climbed upon a chair to reach the very highest and dustiest shelf. He knew exactly where to reach and was soon down upon the floor with that precious scroll he made when he was an apprentice.

When he unfurled the scroll he smiled at her once again and stroked the notes and colours upon the page. "Soon your son will join you and he will be as magnificent as any child of yours should be."

With that he put aside all other pieces that he was working upon and began. He only stopped for quick meals that his wife carried to him and even slept upon the floor of the workshop so that his days became more efficient. It was late at night once again when he slid the silk over the statue's surface and he laughed as it slipped with ease never stopping for a second. There would be no hard floor to sleep upon tonight and he left the workshop with the moon starting to drop in the sky, *"Just like when I finished Isis,"* he thought.

When he crawled into his bed his wife roused slightly and turned to him. "It is done?" she murmured.

"It most certainly is," he whispered back and curled up against her to sleep.

Within minutes he was snoring so loudly that his wife wished Horus was far from complete.

The next day he dressed in his finest clothes and gave Horus one last polish before he asked his apprentice to pack it within hay to make its journey to the palace. All those years before when Isis made her way to the palace, he had been sleeping which in its own way had been reward for his hard work. He had always regretted that his teacher had not taken him along to meet me and to see my reaction when I first saw Isis.

Over the years though, he had met with me many times and delighted in my reactions when he delivered new pieces. Of course when he would recount our meetings my reactions and remarks were always somewhat exaggerated by him for dramatic effect but for those who would never have the honour to speak with me they were delightful stories to hear. My compliment to him as I did see Horus for the first time would need no exaggeration and when he left the palace he smiled so hard on the way back to the workshop that the apprentice that had accompanied him eventually burst out laughing.

"I do believe your face will begin to ache soon if you do not rest it," he said to his boss.

The goldsmith turning to the apprentice and smiling even wider replied, "I hope one day you too have reason to smile like this."

As I sat upon the edge of my bed now as my servants bustled about the room I looked at the two statues and I knew that it was no accident that they were together. Horus with his eagle head stood beside his mother, the eternal mother of us all, and I knew that the two together would guide me more powerfully than if either had stood alone. Somehow the Gods had called them together for me. I drank in every detail of each one; Isis's open palms offering me succour, Horus' eyes that saw all. Both stood with their feet planted firm and strong. I reached out and let my fingers glide along each one in turn. As they ran along the surface I smiled as I could not feel where the gold made way for the inlaid gems; each piece of stone sat as though it was a natural part of the gold and not something added by a man.

Tati began to extinguish the lamps that were placed around the room and I stopped him when he started on those nearest my bed.

"Leave these two." I pointed at the lamps closest to the table that held the statues.

Tati nodded understanding perfectly and clapped his hand signalling for the other servants to finish what they were doing and leave me to sleep. He turned to me and bowed as he did each night as he left the room for the last time.

"I pray you sleep well, Sire," he added his customary farewell and I caught him glance one last time at the statues before he left.

I breathed deep and finally lay down upon the bed. I lay on my side so that I could look at Isis and Horus as I fell asleep. A pharaoh always lay upon his back and it was unthinkable to lie like this with my back exposed but I had never felt safer. The lamplight flickered upon the gold and gems, sending a spark of light off them occasionally. As I slowly let sleep come upon me I sometimes thought I saw their chests move as though they breathed and I even thought I saw Isis turn her head slightly. I knew they too were preparing for whatever they would teach me within my sleep.

Finally I was deep in sleep but once again it was as though I was awake as I looked about my room. I looked upon the table to connect with Isis and Horus but they were gone and I jumped from my bed horrified that they had been stolen.

"We are not gone," a gentle voice behind me spoke and I turned to see Isis and Horus standing within my room, no longer as statues but alive and as tall as I was. Their chests moved with breath and Isis' hand reached out to me. I fell to the floor before them, prostrating myself to declare my obedience.

"Rise Thutmose," Horus said in a strong, deep voice. "You called us to you so now we begin."

I stood up and they came towards me with Isis taking her place on my left while Horus stood to my right. Horus gestured with his hand for us to walk and we left the room, moving out into my private garden but as we stepped through the doorway I saw that it wasn't my garden at all. The sun was shining brightly as we left the night behind within the palace and I saw before me a great gate made of gold that glistened with millions of jewels and gems. A lone figure stood before the gate and when we walked closer I saw it was Osiris. I now knew the gate was the entry to the afterworld and my heart raced with panic that in asking for this experience I had in fact simply called upon my death.

I turned to Isis and Horus to beg them to take me back to my bed but they did not look at me and kept their eyes ahead and upon Osiris, their husband and father. I turned to look at Osiris realising it was him that I would need to reason with and I saw him smile also--though I assumed it was at his wife and son. I wanted to stop but suddenly I was before him and so close to the gate. Osiris reached out to me but I pulled back, scared that if he touched me then I would be pulled to the afterworld.

"Thutmose, it is your choice to stay or join me," he said with a gentility that surprised me. "I cannot take you unless you are ready? Are you ready?" he asked, and I realised this was simply a test.

I shook my head too scared to speak with this God but just as suddenly I realised that beyond these gates was Satiah, Nefertiry, Amenemhat and my parents. I looked over Osiris's shoulders as though maybe I would be able to catch a glance of them before I moved on but Osiris knew my thoughts and shook his head.

"This cannot be done in parts," he said. "You are either one place or the other."

"But where am I now?" I asked. I knew I was neither awake nor dead-- so what was this space that I was playing with.

"You are within," he said plainly.

"Within what?" I asked but Osiris did not answer and suddenly the scene dissolved and I was standing upon a rise looking over a great open plain of Canaan. Isis and Horus remained by my side so I turned to them. "What is it I am within?" They did not answer either and looked straight ahead as they had when we stood before Osiris.

When I looked before us I saw two armies had gathered on opposite sides of the plain. To the south I saw the flags of Egypt flying but it was not my cartouche upon any of them. The flags were marked for Amenhotep and as I looked closer I saw him at the front of his men upon a chariot now bearing the symbols of Pharaoh. Nearby Menkheperre was upon his and I saw him drawing an arrow to ready it upon his bow. My breath quickened as I could sense that they were about to begin and I prayed that they remembered all that they had been taught.

Isis grasped my hand. "Slow your breath Thutmose."

I don't know how I was able but I did and as I looked back to my sons I saw clouds of colour around them and all the men. Amenhotep had swirls of green and blue while Menkheperre was bathed in reds and oranges. I looked amongst all the men and saw swirls over them also. Most were colours similar to those nearby but sometimes one would stand out; his colours contrasting to those around him.

Amenhotep pulled his sword and nodded to Menkheperre who nodded back. This was their signal that they would soon begin and I wished that I could run and join them. Horus grabbed at my hand though and I knew to stand and watch, while another gentle touch from Isis reminded me to keep my breathing slow. I watched intently as I saw the generals and commanders let the soldiers know they were about to commence battle and I saw that the same colour began to envelop all the men and suddenly they were all clothed in the same tone of red that seemed to start from Amenhotep and cover them like a cloak. There was the occasional spark of different colours but the colour held firm as I saw Amenhotep raise his sword just as I always had when I began battle. Then with the same cry that I had always used, the army charged ahead with Amenhotep leading the way.

I watched with delight as their arrows hit the other army and I saw their men fall but so did some of my men and my emotions bounced from pride to concern. I saw that the other army were slowly being pushed back and I smiled as I knew Amenhotep would soon taste victory but then suddenly things changed as from the side of the plain rode another section of the opposing army. They had waited behind the small mountain range that edged the plain waiting for their moment and attacked our army from the side. I cried out and stepped forward wanting to call out to Amenhotep and race to his side to help him but Horus grabbed at my shoulder stopping me.

I saw the colours of the army change within the panic. There was a kaleidoscope of every colour imaginable as they realised what was happening. I saw men fall and our army was suddenly being pushed from both sides as the enemy tried to surround them. My heart raced as I stood here about to watch my sons be killed in what seemed like inevitable slaughter

I turned to Horus crying, "I cannot watch anymore. Please let me return to my bed."

He kept looking ahead and did not falter and I wanted to hit him, to push him into the battle so that he could die alongside our army. I did not want to watch but I did not know what else to do--so I did with tears, praying for a miracle to help my army. As I kept watching I saw the Egyptians stopped moving back and suddenly they were once again pushing forward, their colour was going back to a single solid colour as the men had rearranged themselves and regained their strength. Once again the opposing army was being pushed back and suddenly all movement stopped and the Egyptians all screamed the guttural cry of victory while Amenhotep in the centre of the carnage stood over the dead body of a Canaan king, his sword held high in the sky. Menkheperre made his way to his brother's side dragging the dead body of yet another tribal leader to dump beside the king and then he too joined in the screams while I sat down upon the dirt and cried with relief. My tears poured from me more deeply than they had ever done when I was awake and as they subsided I felt Isis reach down and touch my shoulder. I looked up at her and she smiled down upon me then gestured with an open hand for me to look ahead again.

I stood up and as I looked before me I saw that all the soldiers were long gone and not even the stains of their blood remained. The small mountains that the surprise attack had emerged from throbbed and suddenly their curved sides grew straight. Their rounded peaks sharpened and I was now looking at the grand pyramids of my forefathers. Around their bases sand had gathered and I saw men sweeping it away as best they could.

Before the pyramids, in the place where Amenhotep had stood claiming victory, the Sphinx lay buried with only its head peering out of the sand. The men were paying this no heed and I could see another layer of sand being blown upon it. The sound of horses was reaching my ears now and I could see a cloud of dust following a small group of men as they rode towards the pyramids.

It was a royal party for I could tell by their dress, but it was not a pharaoh. I saw a young man wearing the headdress of a prince jump from his horse and his face became clear. It was my grandson Thutmose, no longer budding with manhood but fully a man, strong and fit just as his father and I were at that age. My heart swelled to see him still dressed as a prince for this meant Amenhotep was still alive. Then I heard his voice deep and powerful. "Father, told me that he visited here with Grandfather when he was young," he said, and once more I felt tears remembering that day.

I watched as Thutmose walked to the base of the pyramids taking in their size and I could hear his thoughts. He was in awe of their grandeur and the precision in which they had been created. Then I felt his mind assess the cost and how much else could have been achieved with the time and resources spent here. I laughed as I realised he had inherited my economic reasoning and decided to walk to him so that I could see more closely what he was doing.

Horus and Isis did not stop me and I felt them at my side never missing a step as we followed younger Thutmose as he walked about the monuments. He climbed upon the rise of sand to the Sphinx's head and stood within the shadow that it cast. I could feel he was tired and watched as he sat within the shade to rest his eyes while his guards observed from nearby. He was soon asleep as he leaned against the stone head and I could see his eyes move as he too dreamed and then suddenly his eyes flew open.

"Grandfather," he cried and he looked directly at me.

I quickly looked around but no one had heard him. "You can see me?" I asked quietly.

"Well of course I can," he laughed. "You are right here before me. Although I wish this were real and not a dream."

"As do I," I nodded. "Do you realise what it is you sit upon Grandson?" I asked but I did not wait for an answer. "Below you lies the great Sphinx, as magnificent as anything built by any pharaoh including myself, yet it lies buried and forgotten when it should rise free to protect the pyramids and our forefathers as it was built to. Uncover its beauty, restore its colour and let it sit with all the glory and majesty it was created with. Do this and all shall know your grandeur and your dedication to your land. You shall become Pharaoh with as much might as if you built this yourself. Our forefathers will bless you and your successors will follow your example."

Thutmose nodded, took in my words and then he gently closed his eyes as though he was returning to sleep. Moments later he opened them again and stood up, dusting himself and then stretching. I knew he could no longer see me and I did not try to speak to him again.

As he walked back down the sands he was met by the high priest who travelled with him. "Do you rest enough Prince?" he asked.

"Yes, Wajeb," he answered. "But while I rested I had the most amazing dream. Horus arrived with my grandfather and they told me to uncover the Sphinx."

"Oh my Prince," cried the priest. "This is most prophetic for you. To act upon the message of a God and a forefather would most certainly affirm your position as successor."

"That is just what they told me," said Thutmose as the priest nodded and beckoned to another priest.

"We must record this Sire and let your father know," he said quickly. "I beg you to sit and recall as much detail as you can for dreams can dissolve when we return to the awakened space."

I watched as Thutmose told in detail his dream to the priest who marked it all upon a scroll. I thought it interesting that in his recollection it was Horus who spoke while I stood by silently, but I was happy that the meaning would be preserved and that my grandson would indeed act upon my words, regardless of who he thought spoke them. As I watched the message being scratched upon the papyrus I saw how what had happened within this strange space could be pulled back to the awakened state and made as real as though it had occurred there. Memories are so fragile and malleable, they can be tainted by time or a mood, but when something is recorded in writing, then it is not so easy to change alter.

Soon the priest and Thutmose were finished. "It is most impressive that you have inherited your grandfather's skill," he said, nodding as he rolled the papyrus and wound a ribbon around it. "Perhaps you could study with the priests of Horus to develop this more when you return to Thebes."

"Do you really believe that I could be as powerful as Grandfather?" Thutmose asked.

"Of course you can for you have his blood in your body," the priest said, "and he did not develop this skill until late in life. Imagine if you work on this before you take the throne!"

"*Pah!*" I thought, "*I always had this talent. I just never played with it much until now.*"

I had seen enough now though and as Thutmose climbed back onto his horse and rode away I turned to Isis and Horus to let them know this. Horus nodded to me and within a blink I was back within my bed with Isis and Horus standing on each side of the bed. I lay back and felt the soft feathers beneath me. Through the window the first soft pinks of the sunrise were cutting between the drapes and I could hear the servants begin to move in the salon getting ready for when I would awake. I decided to rest and closed my eyes to truly sleep for a short time before Tati would come to dress me.

# CHAPTER THIRTY-ONE

When I next opened my eyes the room was bright and I knew it was well past sunrise and the time that I would normally awaken. Tati was standing by my bed looking down upon me. "Sire, are you not feeling well? You have slept the longest you ever have."

I sat up too quickly and my head swam with dizziness so that I immediately lay back down which only confirmed Tati's fears for me.

"I shall summon the physicians," he said firmly and gestured to another servant to go and call one.

"No Tati! There is no need," I urged lifting my hand. "I had the most intense of dreams and feel as though I did not sleep. That is all that should concern you."

"Then Sire perhaps after breakfast we should call for the priests of Horus to interpret and record your dream?" he offered.

Once again I sat up straight as I recalled some of the same words spoken to my grandson as I dreamt. "Call for them now Tati," I said. "I believe I need to record this before the sun fades my memory."

The message was sent immediately and I began to dress, but I knew it would take time to fetch the priests. When I finished dressing I asked for my writing set and sat at my breakfast table eating and writing so that when the priests arrived I had begun what they had been sent to do.

A young scribe had come with them and he sat cross-legged on the floor beside me and unfolded his low table across his legs to continue on as I spoke. The two priests sat across from me at the table and listened intently as I dictated all that I had seen. I watched their faces as I re-told the dream but not once did they show the slightest expression upon their face. They remained still and quiet until the very end and even then waited for me to ask their thoughts.

"Most extraordinary, Sire," said one quietly while the other nodded.

"Can you see any meaning within what I saw," I asked, hoping they could expand this even more.

"Sire, these are prophetic dreams," said the second one slowly, looking at the other priest to affirm his interpretation. "You are being offered glimpses into the future of your family perhaps for the opportunity to guide them."

"These dreams were so real. It is as though I am there," I said.

"Well yes Sire, you offered your *ka* and inner sight the opportunity to travel and they did," he answered. "You are most blessed. Only the most talented of priests can experience such dreams. Of course it is no surprise that our Pharaoh, who is chosen by Gods, should have such ability." He finished with a bow of his head to show his sincerity.

"Am I to dream like this every night now that this has been awakened within me?" I asked, hoping that they would say no. If I was to dream like this every night I would be continually exhausted.

"Ah well, Sire--did you perform any prayers to conjure the dream?" the priest asked.

"I just prayed to my icons of Isis and Horus before I slept." I saw their eyebrows rise and immediately I knew that I had done something wrong.

"To both Sire?" one asked without waiting for an answer. "This is a most potent combination of prayers Your Highness. It is not surprising that your dream was so vivid and lucid."

"It also explains why they both accompanied you also," added the other and they both nodded.

"Yes," the first priest continued, "and that Osiris, the father, would appear to you. To have the entire holy family in one dream would be a very rich experience for even the highest dream priest to endure."

"So if I wish to have a night without such dreams I would simply not pray to the Gods before I sleep," I asked.

"Yes, Sire," one answered and the other continued his nodding.

"And will they always be so lucid when I do pray?" I asked.

"Perhaps Your Highness would consider praying to just Horus," the priest said, and tilted his head as though he was speaking to a child.

I knew the priests too well and could feel how patronising this was. Apparently he considered me too ignorant to deal with whatever prayers I chose to say and I actually got quite angry that he would ask me to dismiss Isis as though she was to blame for how intense my dream was. I knew better though for she was as valuable a teacher and guide as Horus was to me last night. No, I would not set aside Isis as I explored this dream state--besides to reject her would be like dismissing Satiah or my mother. I also suspected that this was their way to bolster their own interests, for the more I prayed to Horus, the more I would supposedly favour the Horus priests. They were hardly likely to support the Isis priestesses if they didn't need to. I would simply find a way to wake in the morning without carrying the experience with me beyond relaying it in words.

"Fine," I lied to appease them and avoid any further lectures and then slyly added, "Do either of you awaken fatigued from the more lucid dreams?"

"Only in the beginning Sire," the patronising one spoke again. "A truly talented priest soon finds it does not affect them."

"Ah so it may just take time for me to adjust to this," I thought as I nodded to the priests.

My curiosity was now appeased and I believe the priests were satisfied that they had achieved what they were summoned for, so I bid them good day and dismissed them. I was still somewhat unsettled from my night's adventure though as I headed to court, and found myself constantly distracted by remembrances of what I had seen. I was not too concerned as Siamun was nearby listening as intently as he always did and I knew that anything important would not be missed. I was now so skilled at presenting myself to the public that no one could even notice when I wasn't truly listening, that is except for Siamun, so that as we walked to the dining hall to have lunch I caught him smirking as he glanced at me.

"Siamun, would you care to share what you find humorous," I joked.

"I am wondering just how little of today's session you actually heard," he said quietly but laughed as he finished. "The viziers may not know how to tell when you are bored but I most certainly do!"

I stepped closer to him and lowered my voice, "You would be lacking concentration in court too if you had the night I had."

"I thought you were told to no longer call upon consorts?" Siamun said concerned.

I burst out laughing. "Oh my Son, they were no consorts who I spent the night with."

Siamun was the first of my children to hear of my new dream experiences but word soon spread amongst them and they all came to me eager to know if I saw anything about them. Of course what I had seen was for Amenhotep and young Thutmose who were both away in Memphis. When I had no news for them the questions then turned into requests. "See if I will have more children?" "What will my sons achieve?" and the list of trivial curiosities went on, only stopping when I declared that dreams could not be forced and that it was up to the Gods as to what I was shown.

I would not pray to Isis and Horus each night, in fact some nights I craved truly restful sleep so I would actually ask them to leave me be and they would. I developed a wonderfully respectful relationship with them and my dream abilities soon filled my days that had become to feel so empty now that I could no longer ride or battle. I would consult with the priests of Horus when I had any queries to settle or had seen something I did not understand and they revelled in their new importance to the palace. I would also consult with the priestesses of Isis and was quite amused at how differently they dealt with me. There was none of the pomp or drama as they listened and then gently guided me with their advice or counsel.

My bedtime and awakening routines were now quite different for my servants and myself. Now as Tati come to perform his final duties for the night he would ask, "Sire shall you be praying to Horus and Isis tonight?" An answer of "yes" would mean that the lamps near my statues would remain lit and then a scribe would be waiting in my salon the next morning to record what I had seen. Over the next year I created quite a library of scrolls and eventually I had a small room near my chambers converted with shelving and tables similar to the Great Hall of Records to store them. The priests of Horus had insisted that they store the scrolls within their temple but somehow I could not trust that they would do so without resisting the temptation to alter them. I steadfastly refused and they could not offer any argument that could match the safety of the palace nor the right for my family and myself to access them with ease.

Eventually there was a scribe assigned full-time to the library and he came to live within the palace. He scanned and checked for any mistakes and if he found any then he would rewrite the entire scroll so that each one sat in its place perfectly edited. As the stories gathered he would also organise them meticulously and created scrolls which listed the dates and contents of each scroll so that anyone would know where to look for a particular story. As if this was not thorough enough, he then created more scrolls that collected the stories of battles, or dreams about a particular child of mine. Soon one wall of my dream library held scrolls according to when I had dreamt them while the other held scrolls sorted by category. It was done with the utmost care and attention and I loved to stand within it admiring not only what it kept but also the immaculate way in which the very words themselves were being held.

My scribe would not sleep at night until Tati came to his room to let him know whether I intended to call upon Isis and Horus that night. If he knew I was then he would awake well before daylight to clear his own mind of anything that he had dreamt and would be standing at my chamber doors with his writing tools before Tati had even begun his own work. He would sit patiently within my salon to wait for me, thrilled that his work allowed him into the most private rooms of my palace. Even more though he loved that his work had allowed him to know what was possibly the most intimate of my experiences.

It was not with ego that he delighted in this but a pure fascination with what he recorded and the joy of knowing he was helping these words become permanent. This pride showed in his work and I soon developed an amazing respect for the scribe. It was this respect that led to my absolute trust in him so that when he offered to create the new scrolls pulling similar stories together I agreed immediately with the knowing that he would not succumb to the tampering that I was sure the other priests or scribes would.

The library grew and Amenhotep honoured the work within by keeping it exactly where it was. His son also maintained this honour so that four generations following me could come and read the scrolls. Some did with pure curiosity to see if they were mentioned or could interpret a story that they could see themselves within. Others came to study them as though they were lessons, hoping that my insights for others may help them also.

Their wisdom and magic soon grew beyond the palace and my family when the dreams I had actually began to occur and the foresight that I had provided guided my family and Egypt. Amenhotep did indeed mount a great battle upon a field within Canaan and as soon as he arrived and saw the small mountains to his left he knew what was in store. He rearranged his men to strengthen his left flank and when the ambush occurred during mid-battle his men barely faltered; never losing even an inch of the ground they had gained.

Young Thutmose did indeed rest within the shade of the Sphinx and dreamt of being told to uncover it. He had long forgotten the story I had told him but Amenhotep had not. When he recounted the story to his father, Amenhotep took him to the scroll room and found the original scroll on which I myself had begun to write that first night's story.

"How strange that I should experience it then within his dream, but then I experience it now as my own," muttered Thutmose as he read the scroll.

"It is not strange at all," said Amenhotep. "It is simply a sign of your grandeur to communicate in such a way."

Thutmose understood this perfectly and soon left to return to Giza where he oversaw the Sphinx being uncovered. He commissioned a new block to stand before the great guard celebrating his dream and the dedication he showed to Egypt in restoring the Sphinx and establishing his right to the throne. I quite like that thousands of people each year walk before this memorial which lies within the very place that we once connected by a dream and read about it.

CHAPTER THIRTY-TWO

I am also grateful that something more lasting recorded at least one of the stories I dreamt, for my scrolls would eventually perish. It would be four generations later when they would be pushed away and lost. Ironically, I had even predicted this happening and it was the very account of this dream that saw to their demise.

I had been playing with my dreams for some years now. It was as familiar to me as it had been to climb aboard my horse and ride when I was younger. I would sit upon my bed after the servants had all left and I would speak with my statues. Sometimes I would hear them speak back before I was even asleep. Some nights my dreams would answer questions or curiosities that were upon my mind whilst other nights I would simply be surprised with a vision that I could not explain. On one such night when I did open myself to receive a dream I saw the end of my family's reign. It was the only time that I doubted what I had seen, but a part of me knew that someday this could well be inevitable. Not all future pharaohs would have the riches of sons and grandsons that I now possessed within my life.

The dream began as it always did within my bedchamber with Isis and Horus standing as full sized beings on either side of my bed ready to escort me. We walked as we always did with Isis to my left and Horus to my right and stepped through the doorway that led to my garden. When we stepped through this door and left the palace was when I entered whatever scene I would watch for the night. Tonight as I stepped through the door I was immediately returned back within my chambers and stood within the main salon. The doors opened and Amenhotep walked in wearing the crown of Pharaoh. He stood still and silent as Tati came forward to lift the crown and then the heavy collar off him.

"Sire, we have water ready for you to bathe," Tati spoke quietly and with an unease that I had never heard from him.

Amenhotep shook his head. "I would like to sit for a while. It has been a most intense day."

"Of course, Sire," said Tati bowing as he had done when he first started serving me. "May I fetch you some wine in the meantime?"

Amenhotep nodded and I saw him sigh as Tati walked away. He stayed in place and looked about the room, rubbing his chin just as I did. He looked exhausted but there was a heaviness also that I could not quite understand until Tiaa walked in. She was dressed as Queen but her clothes were ones for mourning.

"Tiaa," Amenhotep reached out to his wife who put her finger to her mouth letting him know he didn't need to speak. She walked to him and gently wrapped her arms about him.

"It has been a hard day for you," she said, and I saw Amenhotep's eyes begin to water as he looked into hers.

"I always knew this day would come but that knowledge does not ease the ache in my heart," he said so softly.

"How wonderful though that your Father could leave knowing you are here to carry on for him and your family," she answered gently wiping away the tears that fell down his face. "I am sure he would be most pleased with how your first day as sole Pharaoh was performed."

Then the room was empty once again. I heard crying from my bedchamber and moved to that door. Amenhotep was now an old man lying upon the bed. He was pale and tried to open his eyes but could not. Tiaa held his hand and whispered prayers for him along with the children and grandchildren that had crowded the room to be with him. Priests moved about them leading the prayers and keeping an ever-watchful eye upon Amenhotep whose breathing was growing shorter by the minute.

"What is happening?" a male voice behind me spoke. It made me jump as I knew it was not that of Horus and I turned to see Amenhotep standing behind me. I quickly turned back to look at the bed and he was still there also, but now Tiaa and the others in the room were crying as the priests began to wipe Amenhotep's body with oils making it ready for the mortuary.

"It is done?" asked Amenhotep and I nodded.

We watched as his empty shell was carried out of the room and the bedchamber slowly emptied to now be filled by servants who stripped the bed replacing the linen with new sheets, pillows and drapery. As always the bed was renewed to make way for a new pharaoh. There was noise within the salon and Amenhotep joined Isis, Horus and myself as we walked to see what was happening there.

Through the doors of the salon stepped my grandson Thutmose now wearing the Pharaoh crown and collar. A new butler came to him to take his adornments.

"Sire, I trust I shall serve you as well as I did your Father," he said to Thutmose.

"I have no doubt of that, Mentiywy," Thutmose answered and smiled. "You have always been a most loyal servant of the palace," He then sighed as he looked about the room. "I wonder what my father and grandfather felt when they entered this room for the first time as Pharaoh?"

"It is a true mix of honour and sadness," offered Mentiywy.

"That it is," agreed Thutmose. "You know my grandfather was only ten when he was crowned. I am truly gifted that my father should have lived to his grand age. I shall miss him though."

"As we all shall," added the butler.

Once again the room emptied and I heard sounds from the bedchamber. Thutmose was now in bed and surrounded by wives, children and priests all praying over his body as it slowly released his *ka*. He was not that much older than when he entered the salon and I saw his skin looked the same as my father's had when he fell ill. Then I saw Thutmose slowly step through the people holding vigil and look down upon his body in the bed.

"I never wanted to leave this soon," he said, as though he was apologising to himself. He then looked up at his father and me. "I wanted to live as long as either of you."

"These things cannot be planned," Horus answered firmly and Isis reached out her hand to invite him to join us.

The room once again emptied and servants cleared, cleaned and renewed the bed once more. I led us now back to the salon to wait and see what would occur next and was truly curious to see which pharaoh would now claim these rooms. As the next Pharaoh stepped through the doors his family likeness was indisputable. Every detail on his face replicated Amenhotep's so much so that he was even more like Amenhotep than his own son Thutmose was.

A young woman walked behind him closely followed by two young boys. "Amenhotep, our sons wish to bid you goodnight," she said and I felt strength in her voice.

"Of course," he answered, as his butler carried away his crown and collar. He took a seat and the two boys walked to him.

They seemed close in age but one was taller than the other and I assumed he was the eldest but it was the smaller boy that the Pharaoh grabbed by the shoulders and pulled close to him first.

"Thutmose, one day you shall walk in here as Pharaoh," he said. "I pray I will leave you as well prepared as my father but not as soon as he did."

He pulled the boy close and gently kissed his forehead while behind them I could see the other boy watch with harsh eyes that spoke of jealousy.

"And you Amenhotep, shall be there to support your brother as any royal brother would," he continued and kissed the other child in the same way.

Amenhotep pulled away as fast as he could and his father looked at him puzzled. "Son, I know it has been a strange time for us all--but do not forget your affections with me."

Amenhotep looked down and muttered "Yes Father" but I could feel the insincerity and something about this boy troubled me.

Once more we were within the bedchamber to witness the Pharaoh's last breath. The room was not as full as it had been for any of us already passed. There were the priests moving about and praying and a few viziers had come to pay their respects also. His wife sat close by crying as she prayed and I looked about to see where his sons were. In the corner slouched against a wall stood one that I immediately knew was Amenhotep as his eyes still held that darkness I had seen in his child eyes. Thutmose though was not here and I assumed that he was away on a campaign or business. Amenhotep crossed his arms and yawned without the barest of intentions to hide his boredom and how tedious he found the whole scene.

When this Pharaoh crossed there were the usual tears from his wife and as he walked across the room to join all of us he shook his head. "I am sorry that I did not leave as able a successor as you all did," he said quietly.

We all watched as Amenhotep suddenly stepped forward and smiled as he realised that his father had passed. He did not wait to see his father's body prepared and was the first to leave the room. I could not help but follow him as he made his way into the salon. There upon one of the lounges sat a young woman dressed as a princess. Her features were fine and delicate and she sat with such poise that she reminded me of Matreya, even in the way that she tilted her chin upwards. When Amenhotep entered the room she jumped from her chair.

"Is he gone?" she said quickly.

"Yes," was his reply and he smiled so broadly that I thought his face might tear. "Come let us go and dress as the Pharaoh and Queen that we now are!"

"Where is Thutmose?" I asked to no one in particular as the young couple left the salon.

"He died in a riding accident only a few years ago," answered his father.

"Just as my son and successor," I thought and then realised that the name Thutmose in our lineage was now gone.

When Amenhotep and his wife re-entered they were indeed dressed as Pharaoh and Queen and with so much finery that one would hardly know they were in mourning. As they stepped into the room Amenhotep grabbed his wife, lifted her off the floor and swung her around so that she giggled.

"Nefertiti, we have waited for this and the Gods have rewarded us," he said loudly. "We shall rebuild Egypt and make her new. We will be remembered for all eternity for ending the domination of the Amun priests. From now on pharaohs shall rule as the leaders they were meant to."

All of us standing together and watching this gasped with horror. Only Isis and Horus remained steady as this new Pharaoh spoke with such heresy. When his butler entered and addressed him by his new name we all knew just how far he would take this.

"Pharaoh Akhenaten, shall I take your crown and adornments?" he said timidly.

"No," Akhenaten replied without even looking at the butler. "I do believe I shall wear it for some time longer," he said smiling at his wife while she continued to giggle.

Then the new Pharaoh and his Queen were gone and I saw servants carrying out trunks of clothing and then even the furniture. Some remnants were left behind and I saw thieves climb through the windows and wander about collecting what was left. Dust settled upon the floors and when I looked out the window I saw my garden was dry and brown.

There was silence for what seemed an eternity and I turned to Horus.

"This surely is the end. What else could there be to see?"

Horus nodded his falcon head at the doorway and I turned to see the doors open again. The floors were clear of dust and servants were carrying in trunks and furniture. A young boy walked into the room wearing a crown and I smiled as he looked exactly like me at that age. In fact for a moment I believed I was seeing myself newly crowned at age ten.

The young king walked into the room and looked about at everything taking in his new home. His young eyes seemed curious but wary as he examined the room. A priest stood close by him watching his every expression. I saw that the priest wore the robes of the Amun priests of Karnak and I felt relief sweep over me.

"Sire, these are the very rooms that your forebears occupied when they too ruled," the priest said waiting for the young Pharaoh's reaction but all he received was a nod. "Can you not feel your family here?" the priest pushed hoping for just something a little more from the boy.

"Of course I can! It is as though they are watching me enter here yet I am a stranger to them. This is where I should have been raised, not out in the desert like a camel herder!" he spoke so loudly that he almost yelled and the priest smiled to see this fire within him.

"We all agree, Sire," the priest said bowing as he did so. "We thank you for returning Egypt to the ways that serve the Gods best. We are all most assured that they will in turn favour you."

"I want my name changed," said the boy firmly. "I refuse to carry anything from my cousin that will remind people of his heresy and disrespect."

"A most wise decision Sire," smiled the priest. "Shall you take on a name from your forebears to honour them?"

"I will replace Aten with Amun so that all will know this great God is once again restored," he said,

"Most honourable and wise Sire," bowed the priest who could not hide his smile of delight. "We shall hold a grand ceremony at the Great Temple to declare this and all shall know the name Tut-ankh-amun reigns over them."

We watched as the palace was restored and my garden once again grew green and lush. Things were not quite as majestic as they had been but at least this was once again home to our family. Then I heard screams from the corridor and the doors burst open.

Guards carried Tutankhamun and he was writhing and crying out in pain. Blood was dripping from him and I could see that it was coming from his left leg. Priests and physicians followed the stretcher as it made its way to the bedchamber and the guards lifted the still so young Pharaoh upon the bed making him scream anew as they moved him. The physicians moved in immediately while the priests hovered over them.

The bleeding was eventually stopped but the blood loss for the Pharaoh was traumatic. He was weak and the physicians and priests manner was now one of utmost concern. Prayers were begun and the salon filled with generals and viziers waiting to hear as to their ruler's condition.

"It has only been eight years," one muttered under his breath. "He does not even have a successor."

We all watched as the young King became weaker and then fever set upon him as the wound now festered. I looked about for what family there was but there was none. All that this boy had was courtiers and priests. His life was literally in their hands. A physician tried to pour tonic into Tutankhamun's mouth but he just choked and spluttered so that most of it ended upon the bed sheets or his chest. The physician turned to the priests and shook his head.

The highest of the priests walked back to the salon and found the most senior of the viziers and gestured for him to walk to a corner of the room where they could talk in private.

"The Pharaoh fails more each second and he cannot swallow his tonics," the priest spoke matter-of-factly. "There is more that could be done but the physicians wait upon my direction on whether to proceed."

The Vizier's face was stern but he nodded with full understanding as to what the priest was implying. "Perhaps it is best that this bloodline should finally leave the throne. It seems clear that he carries some curse set upon the family by Akhenaten," the vizier answered plainly.

The priest tried unsuccessfully to hold back a smile. "A very wise observation Huy and one that would be hard to argue with. The question now arises as to whose blood will replace his?" he asked slyly.

The vizier locked eyes with the priest ready to fight for what he knew was his. "The question should be who is the strongest to replace him," he answered boldly. The priest's eyes dropped as the vizier continued. "Support my claim and I shall restore the priesthood to all the glory that was when the great pharaohs of his family ruled."

The priest looked back up and nodded. "So be it," he said, and turned his back to return to the bedchamber as the vizier took a deep breath and squared his shoulders.

Within the bedchamber I saw the priest call the physicians away from the bed and whisper to them. They nodded and left the room but I saw one frown as he looked one last time at the bed. Tutankhamun grew redder with fever but then eventually his skin went white as his breaths grew shallow until finally his body lay grey and still. The last of our family to sit upon the throne had all but been murdered and I felt the grief from every one of the men surrounding me.

"I am glad to be finished," I heard Tutankhamun say as he stood beside me. "What sort of life was that to spend amongst men so willing and ready to see me die. They have what they have wanted from the moment of Akhenaten's death and I am finally free of a life that I hated."

I shook my head and turned to Horus. "I have seen enough" was all that

I needed to say to return to my bed.

When I awoke the next morning my dream seemed to be with me as a weight upon my chest and I felt it would crush me with the pain that it knew conquered me. The images of my dream flooded back and with it the reality of what my family would become. Even though it would be another five generations and almost one hundred years after my death I was overcome. When Tati came to wake me and prepare me for the day he found me sobbing.

"Sire, what is it?" he gasped.

"My dear Tati," I choked through my tears, "I have seen the end of my family and it pains my heart."

My tears continued as the scribe recorded the most detailed and lengthy scroll that we would ever write together. Even he and Tati wept as I re-told what I had seen.

"Let us all pray that this dream is a falsehood and shall not occur," I asked of them both.

That night as Tati came to undress me and extinguish his lamps he stopped as always at the ones closest to the statues. I looked to the statues and then to Tati. "Extinguish all the lamps and please take Horus and place him within the salon. I have no need for him within my bedchamber anymore," I said, trying to hold back tears.

My Gods had served me well and taught me much. I had explored beyond the world that I walked when I was awake and I cherished that I was able to do so. I had seen things that soothed my heart and also those that made it hurt, but last night had been the most painful of all. There truly was no more to see now that I had witnessed the fate of my family. To keep playing in this dream world served me no longer. From now my nights would be for the rest that they were intended and I would leave such rigorous dream states to the priests of Horus.

The scrolls stayed within their area and my scribe remained also as his work continued even though I recorded no more. Each generation that passed came to that room to read and be either warned or comforted by what I had seen. Scribes were assigned to study what was within them and priests would use them to support claims by each pharaoh in turn. Some priests would say the writings were perfect prophecies while others would interpret new meanings to what was written. Either way the scrolls remained preserved and respected.

Then eighty years later a tall young prince came to the rooms. He was still known as Amenhotep at that time and his vanity called him there to see what had been recorded of his name. He knew of the most revered scroll that held the names of all the successors and their fates but, unlike other Pharaohs, his father had not discussed this with his sons. It took some convincing by Amenhotep to make the scribe show him the scroll for the Pharaoh had instructed that it be 'misfiled' in order for it to be hidden. Amenhotep though knew of all the priests' love of gold and this scribe was no exception. The scribe took the gold piece even more quickly than Amenhotep had imagined he would, so that the Prince sneered at him as the scribe turned to find the scroll for him.

Amenhotep's eyes scoured the scroll racing ahead to the part that dealt with his family. His bile rose at how I described his dark eyes watching his father and brother but soon he smiled when he saw that it was he, not his brother Thutmose, who would take the throne after his father. He delighted to read of the changes he would make including the desertion of the palace. These were things deep within him that he ached to do should he one day rule and to now know that they were more than just a fantasy only made this ambition brighter within him.

Ambitions can be quickly raised and then just as quickly destroyed. Within moments of having the joy of knowing that he would be a maverick among Pharaohs, Amenhotep learnt of not only his personal demise but also that of his reforms. The bile rose within him once again and he felt his temples throb. He threw the scroll upon the table and a gold piece soon followed it.

"Find a new place for this scroll," he demanded and stormed from the room.

When the day arrived that the packing of the palace contents was begun for the move to the new palace of Amarna, the current scribe of the scrolls made his way for audience with the Pharaoh and his ever present Queen.

"Sire, shall I begin packing the scrolls for the move?" he asked.

Akhenaten looked to Nefertiti and they both laughed. "There is no need for these scrolls anymore," he said still laughing. "Your only task now is to burn them and come to Amarna to write the new scrolls that Nefertiti and I will now create. Is that not right, my love?" he finished and turned to his wife taking her hand in his and kissing it.

"Yes, my Pharaoh. In fact I had my first dream last night. I dreamt that finally the Pharaoh ruled Egypt without priests interfering. The land was green with crops bigger than ever before and the Nile so full of fish they jumped upon the boats with no need of nets," Nefertiti said, and her eyes grew wide as she spoke to her husband. "Perhaps this could be the first that we record!"

When the scribe did return to the small library he began to pack the scrolls within sacks to carry them to be burnt--but halfway through filling the first he paused. He was not sure what it was that stopped him but he knew he could not be the one to allow their destruction. The scribe waited until the following day to see if Akhenaten would send guards to ensure that his orders were being carried out, but when none had arrived by noon, he knew that the scrolls had been forgotten and that the Pharaoh's order was lost within all the other activities of the palace move.

It was quite easy to smuggle them from the palace unnoticed. There was so much confusion that no one could have kept track of each and every trunk and what they contained. The scribe also knew too well that he could bribe just about anyone to help him. So a trail of gold coins ensured that guards did not question what the twenty trunks contained and where they were going. The coins also ensured that a driver and cart would detour to the Temple at Karnak and not head straight to the pier to meet with one of the fifty boats collecting the palace's goods to sail south.

Karnak was all but deserted when the cart pulled up. The priests of Amun that had not converted to serving the order of Aten were long gone having chosen one of three fates; to be killed when they refused to denounce Amun as their ruling God, to have escaped into exile in order to remain alive or lastly, to simply hide within Thebes to continue to serve the people who wished to continue praying the old ways. Word had reached these priests still within Thebes and they hid amongst the most obscure recesses of the temple complex waiting for the appearance of the cart.

When the scribe arrived in the late afternoon the shadows of the temple fell long and solid across the dust. *"Perfect,"* he thought, as he knew this would make it easier to move about without being seen from a distance. As the cart stopped he looked up to see my grand carvings as I stood in my glory before Amun. "I hope I have honoured your soul old Pharaoh," he whispered to me. The priests scuttled out of their hiding places to greet the scribe. "Do you have the place ready?" he asked them. They nodded and began to unload the trunks from the cart hauling them to the small temple at the rear that I had built during my time.

When they entered the temple only a small lamp was already lit within the dark space and the scribe could barely see ahead of him. One of the priests went behind the altar and knelt down beside a large square block of stone. It had once been the base for the most beautiful statue of Amun that stood proud and tall before my family as we prayed here. It was long gone now, desecrated as part of Akhenaten's reforms and even the carvings around the block had been scraped away. A second priest knelt also and they pushed upon the block until it slid from its place to reveal what looked like a black square. The priest asked for another lamp and as he held it over the square the scribe saw that it was actually a hole. The priest carrying the lamp balanced himself and made his way down into the space by a ladder propped up from below.

When he reached the opening, the scribe looked closer, and could see there was a room below full of scrolls as well as statues of all kinds. All had been gathered as the reforms began to protect these precious things from the destruction that had begun to sweep the temples.

"How long has this been here?" asked the scribe. "Did great Thutmose build this?"

A priest shook his head. "No. The old priests had this dug during the reign of Pharaoh's father. They knew of the prophecy within the scrolls and made ready to protect what they could."

So my grand scrolls survived Akhenaten's rampage but they were not returned to the palace when Tutankhamun did. The young King never heard of my scrolls and the priests of his time were too consumed in restoring Amun's dominance as well as their wealth to bother with such records. Besides they saw no need to warn the young Pharaoh of his premature death or the way that it would come about. Those after Tutankhamun had no need for them as they did not mention anyone past his time, so they remained in the crypt and eventually dissolved over time, as did most scrolls.

I still ponder upon how the scrolls affected our family history. I know some events were made easier but others occurred as though no knowledge of them existed at all. Even Akhenaten being able to see that he would fail did not alter his actions--in fact it only made him more determined to exact his reforms. Perhaps this in itself cemented his downfall. The knowledge of what lies ahead can be a blessing or a curse to those that seek it and for my descendent Akhenaten it was both.

# CHAPTER THIRTY-THREE

For me the knowledge of what lay ahead changed nothing for my present. It simply made my resolve to strengthen my family and to make sure the successors that I could influence here and now were ready to take to the throne with the strength and wisdom they needed. It was six years later at the age of sixty-three and well into my old age that the dream began to weigh upon me again. I sat with Amenhotep and when I reminded him of what I had seen that night he spoke the very words that I knew were true.

"Father, we cannot rule beyond our deaths," he said plainly. "All that we can do is rule with strength while we are here and have faith our sons will carry on."

"Does it not bother you that our family rule shall end?" I asked somewhat disheartened at his dismissal of my dream.

"Of course I am upset to know this," he said strongly. "But each pharaoh rules in his own way. He either reaps the rewards of a just rule, or suffers from his incompetence. Life has its way of being its own judge."

I slumped back in my chair. "Do you not think that we can do anything to alter this?"

"All we can do is teach those that stand before us," he said. "Do you truly wish to worry about someone you will never meet when you have enough before you to contend with?"

I sighed and grunted under my breath to respond.

"Father, families have come and gone from the throne," Amenhotep continued. "Let us just rejoice that it is not you, I or young Thutmose, or his son who will be the demise of ours." He stood and squeezed my shoulder. "Let us enjoy our time. The Gods have rewarded you and I know they will reward me when my time is come."

I looked up at him and nodded. "Your time has come Amenhotep."

Amenhotep furrowed his brow. "What?" he said quietly.

"It is time I make you co-regent."

Amenhotep fell back into his chair. "Father, are you sure of what you are saying? Surely this dream does not affect you this much?"

"We have discussed this before," I answered. "Why are you acting so surprised?"

"Because we agreed it would occur when your health had begun to fail and it is far from that," he said.

"Amenhotep, my health has been failing for some years," I said bluntly. "My horse is long retired and you know this is the reason."

Amenhotep nodded but then slowly shook his head. "It will make people think you are frail."

"It will make people know you are ready!" I said loudly.

Amenhotep was not worried about what people thought of a co-regency being declared, as he knew it would serve the family well. My son just hated to be that step closer to the throne as it meant he was closer to losing me. Death had not become any easier for him to deal with since losing his brother. We had discussed and agreed to this style of rule when Matreya had made waves nine years before. It had been the plan we made to subdue her before my death. If Amenhotep was indeed a Pharaoh before I left then he could declare a wife as queen and that woman would be the ruling Queen when I died. However Amenhotep had pictured this being declared when I was bedridden, made from necessity to grant him greater powers to support my diminishing capabilities. He never imagined it would happen when I was still upright and the only thing I was incapable of was horse riding.

"Let it be done then," he said, and I could see him trembling. "But please can we announce it to the family before any priests or viziers know?"

"Of course," I answered.

The next day I called my children to eat together at the midday meal. I did not forewarn them of what was to be discussed and none even suspected that this was in fact a meeting. It was not unusual to gather my children together for such a meal and I would do so whenever all of them were in Thebes and home from visiting in-law families, military campaigns or business. We would sometimes discuss family and palace affairs but it was far from formal or serious with much chatter and laughter. This was how I would let them know of the co-regency. I had learnt the mistake of treating my family with the formalities of court and I would not repeat that offence again.

Eighteen of us sat along that table and while it pained me still that Amenemhat and Nefertiry were missing my heart would swell to see my remaining children together. Tiaa, still simply regarded as Amenhotep's consort, was included today--the first time that she had been summoned to take part in a family gathering as such. She fought to hide the smile on her face but was most unsuccessful.

Matreya sat by my side and would shoot a smile at the children every now and then but kept her eyes away from me. She had tried to escape inclusion but I did tempt her with the message that there was something important that needed to be discussed. Matreya sat and ate, anxiously waiting to hear just what this was. She was patient through the first dishes of duck and pork; she even managed to remain calm when the main dish of roasted veal was presented. However when the platters of sweets and fruit arrived her humour was worn thin.

Matreya looked up and turned her head to me so quickly that her earrings jangled as they played against the beads of her wig. "Well Husband, we were brought here with promise of great discussion. The meal is almost over and yet we hear nothing. Perhaps your memory is failing as quickly as your heart," she spoke loudly and received the desire effect as those sitting closest abruptly stopped speaking and turned to look at her then me.

I froze for a moment, first with anger and then with the embarrassment that my children had to hear my intentions spoken from Matreya's mouth. I turned and looked at them all and was grateful that it was only the elder children who had heard. My younger daughters and their spouses at the other end of the long table were still deep in talk and oblivious to what had happened. I cleared my throat and called for their attention also. When all eyes were upon me and the table was silent I began.

"My beautiful family, what a joy it is to have you all here to dine with me," I smiled as I spoke but suddenly I felt a catch in my throat and felt tears begin in my eyes. This I had not expected and the words that were ready to be spoken now seemed caught within me, but the loving eyes of my children melted this pause and I carried on. "I am so proud that today I can sit here and let you know that our family will begin its next phase of rule," I extended my hand gently towards to Amenhotep. "I have decided that I will declare a co-regency with your brother."

I would have said more but the quiet of the table was soon replaced with applause and congratulations were being showered upon Amenhotep. Now the tears could not be held back as I watched them all embrace this decision with love and honour. I thanked the Gods that this was all being received so well. Of course Matreya was the happiest of all. She had suspected this for sometime and was delighted to finally hear it--which of course was quite ironic given that her suppression was part of its conception.

Matreya sitting at the head of the table beside me leant towards Amenhotep who was sitting to the side of her. "How wonderful my dear son," she drawled. "I guess I will have to give up my seat now for you," she finished and sat back smiling as slyly as a cat waiting for some morsel of affection to be thrown to her.

Of course Amenhotep would not and simply turned back to look at his brothers and sisters who were still smiling at him. Matreya's smile slid off her face but it would even more when I asked Amenhotep to now announce his other news.

"I have chosen Tiaa to be my Great Wife as is deserving of the woman who bore our family a successor," he said strongly looking down the table to avoid his mother's eyes and her reaction.

"How wonderful Tiaa," beamed Beketamun. "You will now be a grand Queen for our family and most deservedly."

"Yes," agreed Siamun and raised his glass. "May the Gods bless our new Queen."

The rest of the table joined in his blessing for Tiaa and her face blushed bright as she smiled back at them and then grabbed Amenhotep's hand as though thanking him. One person though did not raise her glass nor offer her blessing--Matreya remained firm within her seat although I did hear her take a deep breath ripe with frustration. Our son had spent over twenty years with no need to declare his heir's mother a queen and she now knew exactly what all this meant. My betrayal and manipulation was expected and somewhat tolerable but to have her son join me so decisively was so completely insulting that she felt paralysed.

We all continued on discussing the new arrangements with much excitement. Questions and jokes bounced around the table amid laughter and I felt relief sweep over my children. Matreya though sat still and stiff. The glass in her hand never moved again to her mouth and yet she did not let go it. I glanced quickly to my side to see what demeanour she carried and what I saw shocked me. Her eyes were downcast and her face looked as though it was falling from its bones. Her mouth turned downwards, not so much in a frown but in a look I knew too well. It was the look of abject defeat and one I had seen on the faces of the kings at Megiddo and then many times over on the faces of other leaders conquered in battle.

I would have thought this moment would be like any great triumph that I had achieved on the battlefield but it wasn't. As I looked at Matreya now I saw an aging woman who was lonely and lost. My heart could not rejoice to see her like this and for a moment I was tempted to grab her hand and assure her that all was right. A quick burst of laughter from the table caught my attention and I looked to see Isis and Meritamen in a fit of giggles that soon had everyone smiling or joining them in laughter. I remembered now why I had enacted this plan and I saw no need to turn to Matreya. In fact I never even so much as glanced upon her again that day.

Three months later we held a glorious coronation ceremony for Amenhotep that combined the declaration of Tiaa as queen so that they both emerged from the Great Temple as husband and wife as well as Pharaoh and Queen. I sat upon the altar amongst the high priests as all was performed and delighted in every chant and cloud of incense.

"This is how all Pharaohs should begin," I thought to myself. Imagine if my father had been able to watch me be crowned and had sat by my side as I began my rule. Yes, this is how all reigns should begin; with the blessing and loving witness of the forefather.

The feast we held that night was the grandest that had ever been held at the palace. There had not been a coronation since Hatshepsut became Pharaoh fifty years before and this alone made me determined that my son's ceremony would be so grand as to make hers pale in comparison. The palace was attended to so that its every detail was fresh and sharp as though it had just been completed, as was Karnak. The cooks toiled for two weeks to prepare the feast and the meal was flawless and spectacular. I even had fruits shipped from Punt and Minoa. Each dish was carried in upon great trays that needed six men to carry them and all the guests would meet them with applause. Of course the wine flowed as easily as the Nile so that the palace and indeed all of Thebes was somewhat cloudy for some days following. Even Matreya joined the merriment and rejoiced in her son's crowning. I knew it was mostly a performance for the guests but I also knew part of her truly celebrated seeing her child finally recognised this way.

My younger grandchildren ran about the Grand Hall, sliding under tables and copying the dancers as they performed, entertaining everyone as much as the official show. Amenhotep's sons, now all men well into their teens and early twenties, stayed close to the main table, wanting to be by their father. They were in awe of his new adornments and would find excuses to approach him to see them closer and steal a chance to touch them. They were all old enough to understand just what this day and their father's new clothes meant but none more so than Thutmose. Several times through the day I would check upon him to see that he was behaving appropriately and each time he made me proud. Today now saw young Thutmose as the next Pharaoh.

Every time I did survey my grandson I noticed more than just suitable poise and mannerisms. I could see his eyes taking in everything. I saw it first during the ceremony at the temple. When I initially looked upon him I was disappointed thinking that he was distracted as he was scanning the crowd as though bored with the ceremony. I was about to instruct someone to address him when I stopped as I suddenly realised what he was doing. He did not turn his head in such an obvious way for instead he was most delicately viewing everything and everyone. His face was stoic and strong so that if anyone did meet his eyes they would have turned away in an instant. I saw it again during the feast and even though he did not have to be so subtle with his actions now that he was within the palace he was still just as discreet.

I knew exactly what he was doing for I myself did this often and I wondered if he had learnt this from me or if he instinctively developed this. Thutmose was taking in every detail around him. In those observations he would be noting every person's actions and manners; he was noting who was with whom and how they seemed to interact. He would watch how things were occurring and the details of every ritual from how a priest's hand fanned over incense to feed its heat through to how meats were sliced upon a platter. I had noticed my grandson sat quietly more often these days and when I realised this I grew most happy for I knew my grandson had found a key to great wisdom. Just as I had found in my very early years Thutmose had found the power of deep observation.

I knew he was watching even myself, taking in how I spoke to my servants and how I carried myself in temple. My grandson was well tutored but he knew that his true education would be from observing his father and I if he wished to carry on as we did. He sat and watched his father now dressed as Pharaoh and Thutmose wondered if he too would ever be declared a co-regent with his father. Just as quickly he changed his thoughts for to think that far ahead meant also to think of my death. Such thoughts jarred his spirit and like his father he hated to think of death in anyway.

I was relieved when the sweets were served for this meant the meal was drawing to a close. I was nearing exhaustion and ached to be upon my bed resting. It had been a long day and already many of the younger grandchildren had been carried off to their beds and now that the meal ended the older guests too began to say their farewells. Soon came the time for me to bid goodnight also and I rose, thus making the entire room also stand from their chairs. I stood still for a moment and was overcome at the sight of this room full of people all upon their feet simply because I had chosen to stand. I looked upon them and saw smiles, belches being subdued and eyes hazy from too much wine. I smiled also as these were all signs of a most successful celebration.

"My dear family and guests," I spoke as loud as I could so that every corner of the room would hear my words. "I thank you for celebrating my son's coronation."

I should have said more but I couldn't as words once again caught in my throat and I would not force them. To the guests these words were more than enough and my children all sitting close to me saw the emotion upon my face and didn't need to hear anymore. I bid a simple farewell and made my way to leave the hall when Amenhotep began to say his farewell also but I stopped him.

"You do not need to leave Pharaoh," I said to him. "Stay. Enjoy your celebration longer."

"Father, but if you leave should I not do so also?" he asked.

"Pharaoh, we are only equal in title," I laughed. "I believe our ages and need for rest are another matter altogether. Stay!"

Finally upon my bed I looked up and watched the dance of the flickering lamplight upon the canopy of the bed. I thought back to that moment when I stood before everyone in the dining hall and the words that I did not speak. I knew why I could not speak them for how does one put into words all the love, pride and gratefulness at having your family safe and prosperous. I am glad that I did not push myself to try to do so as my speech would have been a blubbering mess.

Tears fell down my face as I thought of everything I had done to have my family as it was today. All the army training, the battles, the court sessions, the building and the ceremonies flew through my mind. I counted the blessings that the Gods had sent me in the way of the people in my life, from my parents through to the youngest grandchild as well my noble viziers and priests. I thought of Arisina and Satiah, I even thanked them for my aunt Hatshepsut. I pictured Amenhotep now dressed as Pharaoh as able as any of the greatest kings to rule and continue all I had created.

I felt complete and satisfied so that when I cried out to Osiris my words were honest and true. "Osiris, I am done. If you should take me anytime now I will be most ready to walk with you."

Now I imagine you are all thinking my call to the afterworld would see me pass peacefully within my sleep but this was not the case. Yes, I was truly ready to leave and the thought of joining those that already crossed made that decision all the more easier. However, I was still in love with life and that would keep me breathing for a few more years to come no matter who or what awaited me in paradise. I awoke the next morning refreshed and ready to continue on ruling with my son by my side.

CHAPTER THIRTY-THREE

Amenhotep rose to his new ruling status effortlessly and with a strength that made me even prouder of him. The solidity of the co-regency sent waves across the empire. Within Egypt my people rejoiced to know my family's progression was firmly decided and they spoke of the blessing to be led by two strong Pharaohs. Their land was now overseen by four eyes and four hands. This only ensured their safety and prosperity and while the outer regions missed my journeys to their locales they would celebrate the arrival of Amenhotep wearing his headdress as enthusiastically as they ever did for me. A Pharaoh was a Pharaoh no matter his name or circumstance.

Outside of Egypt the regions under my rule took a collective sigh of resignation. There would be no transition period following my death allowing them some window of weakness in which to penetrate or weaken Egypt's hold upon them. A mature and able Pharaoh was already in place to continue on and the stories of Amenhotep's skills as a soldier were well-known throughout the lands we ruled over. This did not quash their desires to remove our rule though so they continued to train their men in the hope that one day they would indeed reclaim their sovereignty. Amenhotep stamped upon their ambitions quite decisively though after I was gone and earned himself the title of "Warrior King" most deservedly.

I was sitting within my private garden one afternoon taking in its beauty with a peacefulness that came easily to me these days. Someone caught my eye and I turned to see a woman standing in the doorway that led from my salon to the garden. It was Satiah as beautiful as ever and smiling that gorgeous smile that melted my heart and made me thank the Gods for sending her to me.

"I am dreaming aren't I?" I said to her but she shook her head and kept smiling. "Then you have come to walk me to paradise?" I asked.

Once again she shook her head but she did not speak. Instead she beckoned with her hand for me to follow her and turned to go inside. I got up from my seat as scared as I was curious but there was no way I could not follow her regardless of whether this was a dream or a hallucination. As I entered the salon I saw her walking into my bedchamber and when I walked into that room she was standing by a small chest that sat in the corner. Satiah pointed to it and smiled.

I had not opened this chest in years. It was the chest in which I kept all my most precious reminders of Satiah. These were the things that I collected after her death as we prepared her tomb and then could not let go of. I gathered them within one of her personal chests and had them kept within my room but had never had the strength to open it--not even once since her burial. It was so wonderful to have them so close to me yet I could not bear to look upon them. Now here stood Satiah and I knew she was asking me to finally open the chest again.

Kneeling before the chest it felt like it took forever to reach out and just touch the latch that held the lid closed. I had fastened it myself in her room when I felt I had everything that I needed but now as I reached out to open it the hands before me appeared to belong to someone else. Finally I slipped the pin from the latch and I took a deep breath as I lifted the lid. Its musty smell floated up as I leant over and looked upon its precious contents for the first time in twelve years. Everything had been wrapped in silk to protect it so in fact I saw dozens of small bundles, bound within small pieces of bright coloured silk and tied with equally colourful ribbons. They sat nestled together like tiny mummies each one preserving a memory as much as the object within it.

I could still see Satiah beside me. Her sandalled feet were right next to the chest and although she still did not speak I could feel what she wished me to hear. I nodded and reached in to take into my hand the bundle that sat the highest. Even though I could not remember what exactly lay within it a lump formed in my throat as it sat within my hand. I saw my fingers were trembling as I pulled at the ribbon letting it fall away from the silk it held closed.

I gently peeled back the cloth and there was the beautiful ruby heart necklace that I had sent her from Megiddo. As I looked upon it a flood of memories came back to me as vividly as though they had just occurred. Once again I was a robust young soldier seeing this necklace for the first time. I could even smell the sweat and dirt upon me. I felt the ache in my heart to return home to my family and the joy at my success. I then saw Satiah wearing it to welcome me home and then smelled the scent of her perfume as I pulled her towards me to hold her once again. I recalled how she wore it to each of our children's weddings and the celebrations as each of our grandchildren were born. Each time she wore this she had carried her beautiful smile. I lifted its priceless gemstone to my lips and kissed it tenderly, thanking it for carrying so much more than its own beauty.

I imagined that I would cry but I didn't. I placed the necklace with its silk wrapping on the floor beside the chest and I reached into the box once again to see what else I would rediscover. The next bundle held the earrings from our wedding day and I grimaced to think of the first time we had sex, but then I remembered the first time we made love and my smile returned. I pulled out bundle after bundle and when I finished reminiscing over each treasure I lay them upon the floor around me so that each one, lying upon its silk wrapping eventually surrounded me. As each package left the chest to be remembered and adored I delighted to see them all together but open and wished I had been brave enough to do so long before this day. "*I should have done this over and over*", I thought and I looked up to see Satiah smiling and nodding.

"You don't need to hide anything away," she said gently and with those words, the only ones she would say to me, my wife turned and left the room.

I knew not to follow her and I did not cry to see her leave me once again. I looked down and she was here with me as a kaleidoscope of memories that I would never hide away again. I knew now what I must do and called out for Tati. When he entered the room I was still upon my knees fussing over my collection of treasures and he stopped in his tracks unsure as to what to make of this scene.

"Ah Tati, please call for Beketamun," I said glancing up at him briefly before looking back at my collection and continuing on with arranging them upon the floor around me.

Beketamun did not take long to arrive as she was within her chambers nearby so that when she walked through the door to my bedchamber she found me on the floor still amongst the trinkets. She paused for a moment and smiled as it reminded her of her children when they were small and would play upon the floor surrounded by their toys. Then as she stepped closer and she saw just what it was that I was entertaining myself with her smile dissolved into concern.

"Father," she called out gently as I was yet to even hear her enter. "You called for me."

I looked up at my daughter--now so much like her mother as she grew older. *"If only she would smile some more,"* I thought as she walked towards me and squatted down to be close to me.

"What is it that you are doing?" she asked trying to smile at me.

"Beketamun your mother came to me," I said quietly and immediately seeing her attempt at a smile was washed away I hastily added, "in a dream of course."

This seemed to ease my daughter's mind and she slowly nodded. "Of course," she replied.

"She told me to take these things out and enjoy them each day," I continued and picked up the ruby heart necklace, "Look at how beautiful this is Beketamun. Do you remember when your mother used to wear this?"

Beketamun nodded and I saw her eyes grow red and watery. "Yes I do Father. She never looked more beautiful than when she was wearing it."

I reached out and took Beketamun's hand in mine and then with my other hand pressed the necklace into her palm. "It is now yours. Wear it often," I said strongly and closed her hand around it. Beketamun dared not open her hand again until it was held close and then she looked down in awe at the necklace. She did not speak for a moment or so but I could tell that she too was letting her mind travel through all the memories that she had of that necklace.

Beketamun was barely eleven when I left to fight at Megiddo. She did not understand completely the politics or dangers of the battle but she knew the sadness of saying goodbye to her father. That morning when she had been dragged from her bed before dawn to say goodbye to me she stood hazy from being woken so abruptly and waited for her turn to hug me and bid me farewell. She tried not to cry because no one else was and she wanted to be as brave as everyone kept telling her I was. So she remained composed and as I came to her and leant to kiss her, Beketamun smiled as hard as she could.

"My brave princess," I had said to her as I stroked her face. "I will see your smile again soon." Then just as quickly I was on to my next child for their farewell.

When the nurses began to gather the children to return to their rooms Beketamun pulled at the nurse's hand. "No, not yet, he is not gone!" she cried.

"Come young princess, you have had your farewell," snapped the nurse and she dragged my daughter away.

Once again in her bed Beketamun could not sleep and she wept silently as she thought of me riding away without her to wave to me. A few hours later when she was up and dressed for the day she wandered to her mother's rooms hoping that being with her would help lessen the ache from saying goodbye. However when she walked in she found Satiah by a window weeping. The second that Satiah saw our daughter though she stopped and wiped at her eyes.

"Beketamun, you are dressed. Have you eaten yet?" Satiah asked.

Beketamun did not answer but ran to her mother, grabbing her waist and burying her face into Satiah's gown she began sobbing.

"Hush, hush my princess," Satiah said softly as she stroked Beketamun's hair. "He will be back soon."

Beketamun looked up at her mother and choked through her tears, "What if he doesn't come back?"

"He will, Daughter," she said softly with her tears flowing fresh. "He has promised us and your father always keeps a promise, does he not?" Beketamun nodded and Satiah wiped away our daughter's tears. "We must be strong and patient. The Gods will protect him and return him to us."

Beketamun was soothed for the time being but each time she caught Satiah with a tear in her eye she was not so sure that the Gods were watching over me. The days turned into weeks and then it was months that I was still away and her faith in my promise wore thinner each sunrise. Messages returned of my triumphs but they did not help my daughter. Beketamun would only be appeased by the site of me walking into the palace and she would often dream this was so to only awake to her much harsher reality. All that changed though in one afternoon.

Beketamun and Nefertiry were spending some time with Satiah within her rooms. Satiah loved to talk with the girls quietly and away from the bustle of the palace. She would speak of the seasons and nature, tell stories of their ancestors or teach them the legends of the Gods. On this day Satiah was speaking of Isis to the girls when a young soldier was announced at her doors wishing to speak with her. Beketamun saw the puzzled look upon her face as

Satiah rose to greet the young man as he entered the room.

"Your Highness," the soldier bowed but they could see that he blushed with embarrassment.

"Good day to you," she said but Beketamun heard a tremor in her voice. "Do you bring news from Megiddo?"

"Not exactly Madam--umm--except I could tell you that the Pharaoh still reigns victorious," the words stumbled out from the poor boy. "I am in fact here to present you with a gift sent from Pharaoh to you. I was given the honour of carrying it back and was told to make sure that you received it."

With this he stepped forward and presented Satiah with a small bundle wrapped in silk along with two smaller ones. "There are also presents for the princesses Your Highness."

Satiah looked upon the bundles now within her hands too relieved that this was all that the soldier carried for her to even wonder what may be within them. She sighed and looked up realising that the soldier was waiting to be dismissed.

"Have you eaten since your return?" she asked.

"Ahh--no Madam I have not," he answered awkwardly.

"Then I will make sure you are taken to the kitchens before you leave," she said signalling to a maid to escort him. "You have been most loyal and true. I will ensure the Pharaoh knows of your dedication."

The soldier bowed low and could not help but smile broadly as he stood back up. "I am most honoured by this Madam. I wish you well." Then led by the maid he left the room.

Satiah turned to her daughters. "Come let us sit and see what treasures your father sends to us," she said as she went to sit upon a lounge where the girls could sit on either side of her. "Which shall I unwrap first?"

"Yours!" shouted Beketamun simply because it was the largest and she knew it would be the grandest.

Both the girls leaned in so close Satiah could hardly see what she was doing as she slowly untied the bundle and she heard the girls gasps before she even saw what was within it. All three of them sat silently mesmerised by the ruby heart for a moment and then Satiah lifted it from the cloth and let the light play upon it.

"It is so beautiful, Mama!" Beketamun cried out.

"Yes, it is Beketamun," Satiah replied softly.

"May I hold it?" Beketamun asked expecting to be told no.

"And then me?" jumped in Nefertiry.

"Yes, yes, but be careful," Satiah said as she slowly placed the necklace into Beketamun's hand.

Beketamun sat with the heart resting upon her palm while the rest of the necklace cascaded over her hand. Like me she felt how solid that main gem was and she was astounded at how something that looked so delicate could feel so heavy in her hand.

"Mama, it is so heavy," she called out but Satiah did not respond so Beketamun turned to her and called again, "Mama?"

Satiah was looking down at the cloth from which she had lifted the necklace where now uncovered lay the piece of leather I had cut from my battle kilt. She lifted it up to her mouth and gently kissed it as a single tear fell down her cheek.

"Mama, why are you sad?" Beketamun asked.

"I am not sad, Daughter," she said smiling. "I am happy for I know your father will soon follow these gifts home."

That tear was the last tear Beketamun would see fall upon her mother's cheek while they all awaited my return. My daughter now would only find Satiah smiling and humming whenever they were together. In fact the whole palace was a place of rejoicing as the first carts of tributes arrived at Thebes. Beketamun overheard stories from Megiddo that spoke of my bravery and leadership as she walked the palace. Even her nurses spoke with eyes wide with awe when they spoke of me. Now when she went to sleep at night she knew it was yet another day without me over and each new day that began was another closer to my return.

It was a week after the necklaces arrived that Isis was born. Satiah gathered Beketamun and Nefertiry. "Come. Mother Matreya has given birth. It is time to meet your new sister," she told them.

Satiah walked the girls to the birthing room and they were all excited to meet the new baby. When they entered Satiah kissed Matreya and congratulated her with the girls bowing. Isis lay beside the bed in her crib and as Satiah spoke with Matreya about the birth, Nefertiry and Beketamun wandered over to see their sister.

Nefertiry held the edge of the crib and lifted herself upon her toes so she could see Isis. "She is so small!" she cried.

"As you all were once," Matreya called out. "Thanks to Amun you do not start any bigger or we women would never survive to repeat the act."

With this Isis began to stir and was soon bellowing for her wet nurse. Beketamun reached out to her new sister and gently stroked her head. "Don't cry little one. Father will be home soon," Beketamun said.

Satiah was now behind Beketamun and kissed the top of her head. "Yes he will be home soon," she said.

The following weeks passed quickly. Word travelled to Thebes that I was returning so the entire city went into preparations to celebrate my return as the victorious event that it was. The temple at Karnak was cleaned and paint was retouched while the palace became a literal beehive of activity also. To Beketamun it seemed that a hundred extra people walked the corridors and she was quite happy when she was told to stay within the nursery and keep her younger sisters company. Beketamun walked to the window hoping to see what was happening outside but all that she could glimpse was a quiet and empty garden. Beyond its walls though, she could hear much going on. She grabbed a chair and pulled it to the window and used this as her step so that she could climb upon the wide sill of the window. Once upon the sill Beketamun could now peer over the garden wall and within her sight was one of the gates of the palace.

"What are you doing?" asked Nefertiry with Meritamen and Meryt by her side.

"I am looking to see when Father will arrive," Beketamun answered never taking her eyes from the gates.

Beketamun held this vigil everyday for the last week of my return and it was where Satiah found her when she went to gather the children as soon as she heard I was only hours away.

"Come daughters," Satiah called breathing heavy from excitement.

She gathered all the girls in her rooms, even Matreya's as she remained in the birthing room. Their maids fussed over them with new dresses and hair brushing. Their eyes were decorated and then Satiah took great delight in placing upon each girl the necklace that I had sent them from Megiddo.

"Oh, your Father will be so happy to see you wearing his special gifts," she said through the brightest smile. "All his beautiful princesses, the most special girls in all the land!"

Satiah asked her maid to help her with the ruby necklace and when she turned to stand before the girls, now also ready for my arrival, they all cooed and gasped. Beketamun was in awe of her mother's beauty in that moment but it was more than her dress and adornments. It was her mother's smile that made her so beautiful. It soothed my daughter and made her feel safe, and Beketamun knew that it was the ruby necklace that had made her mother beam again. Every time Beketamun saw this necklace she did not just see a beautiful piece of jewellery, she saw my promise to return home.

As Beketamun knelt upon the floor holding the necklace in her hand once more she could not let any tears fall, for this necklace was also her mother's smile. So she too beamed as she looked back to me and thanked me so gently I barely heard the words.

I gathered the other pieces of jewellery and gave them to Beketamun also. "Wear them often and when you are done with them then your daughters shall wear them," I all but ordered of her. "Now help me arrange the rest of these."

The remaining collection of statues, hairbrushes and perfume bottles found a new home on a table against the wall of my bedchamber. Each day the sunlight would touch them and each day I would awaken an old memory through one of these treasures.

Two pieces would remain separate though. Upon my bedside table and next to the feet of Isis sat the two most precious items--the piece of leather from my battle kilt and the lock of Satiah's hair.

CHAPTER THIRTY-FIVE

I did not see Satiah again as clearly as I did that day, although I did still feel her close by at times. I would be sitting in my room and feel someone behind me and turn to find no one, or see a glimpse of her robes disappearing around a corner. She would float into my dreams and I would reach out to touch her but she would step back, smiling as she turned and walked away into a mist. I would awake grateful to have seen her and would then go to sit in front of my treasure table touching one of her hairbrushes or statues, recalling a moment I had spent with her.

These were quiet private moments that I shared with no one and as my days now progressed I seemed to need them more and more as there seemed to be a space growing around me, separating me from everything that I lived within. Perhaps it was my mind playing tricks upon me but I felt that everything within the palace now operated despite me instead of because of me.

Understandably the army was no longer my concern as Amenhotep and Menkheperre were more than fit to carry its duties upon their shoulders most admirably and efficiently while Siamun and Beketamun were managing likewise within court. Since the co-regency was announced most of our viziers and courtiers seemed to have assumed I had chosen some form of retirement. Many sought out my children to discuss matters believing that I wished not to be approached so often as before.

They did not respect me any less though nor feel any diminished allegiance to me or my powers, they just now all saw me as an aging pharaoh who well-deserved to spend his final days in peace and relaxation. Court sessions saw me speak less and less as Amenhotep now spoke as my equal and shared the conversations with viziers, while Siamun would often address any issues between sessions thus reducing my need to sit upon my throne in court more and more each week. My days grew slower with the quiet spaces within them spreading over time so that soon most of my days were filled with voids that I struggled to fill with activity. This should have been the wonderful time of leisure that my family and subjects desired for me but to a man whose days had been crammed with duties and responsibilities since his childhood they felt like desolation.

I would walk the palace and all would bow and greet me as they always did but I saw that they all carried on their duties without need for direction or supervision. This most certainly was due to years of my leadership and the loyalty of my servants, so that these days the palace ran like a well-oiled machine. No questions were asked of me because they all knew what to do and exactly how it should be done. I however could not see it like this and as I watched them moving about all I could think was, *"They do not even need me anymore. If I disappeared this very moment all would continue on without the slightest hiccup."*

One day after such a walk and the usual internal dialogue of my ever growing obsoleteness I sulked back to my room. When I entered I walked to my statue of Horus and declared, "I am not only ready to go to your father but I believe all around me are ready also!"

Tati was only through a nearby doorway and heard me speak but didn't quite hear my words. "Sire, sorry but did you need for something?" he asked.

"I need nothing Tati," I cried, "and it appears no one needs me!" Then with fists swinging by my side I stormed out to my garden and fell into the nearest seat, crossing my arms and pouting as I looked upon my plants.

I did eventually calm down and for the first time since her death I thought of Arisina. I so would have loved to talk to her now, as she would have known how I could deal with this frustration that grew within me. I looked up to the sky and wondered what she would have said to me. Some wisps of clouds swirled above me providing a momentary distraction but these soon bored me and I was back to my thoughts. Arisina may no longer be here but the temple was and I felt happy to know that I could fill my afternoon with some prayers at Karnak.

I was received with all the fuss and attention that I deserved with twelve of the most high priests escorting me to the private temple. They all surrounded me in silence as we walked with only Sennefer, the highest of this group of priests speaking with me. "Sire, you honour us with such an unexpected visit. I hope we can assist you with whatever it is you seek us for this day."

I stopped in my tracks and turned to the priest so abruptly that I saw his shock and nerves at what I might now say. My mouth opened ready to yell my frustrations but I closed it just as quickly and continued walking to the altar.

Several priests rushed to help me kneel and my hands flew out, hitting them roughly making them step back to their official positions. It was bad enough to be thought of as old, I was not about to be treated like I was frail. Sennefer watched this and sighed, knowing that this was going to be anything but an ordinary prayer session.

As I settled myself in front of the altar Sennefer watched me intently. He could see the frown upon my face and after the awkwardness in the corridor leading here he did not feel that he should ask of my needs again. So he stood and waited for me to address him, while the other priests tried to keep their eyes down but were soon glancing between themselves and then to Sennefer as the silence grew longer. I remained still and with my eyes downcast. I hardly noticed the silence as my mind was quite busy with an assortment of thoughts.

"How dare they treat me like a cripple? The old priests would never have acted like this," I stewed with these thoughts in my mind and then suddenly I became aware of the silence, which gave me a whole new set of frustrations to churn through. *"Why haven't they started the prayers? Are they so stupid that I need to tell them to start?"*

This last thought made me smile for they did in fact need me to tell them to start and I could have almost laughed at how good this made me feel. Poor Sennefer watched as my frown dissolved and within a second I was almost laughing as I looked up to him and announced, "You may begin."

Sennefer nodded and walked to the altar and lit the first pile of incense as he began the chanting. He led the prayers most diligently and as stoically as was expected of him but all the while he stole glances at me to monitor my state. He did not get much information from me though as I kept my head down and remained as still as I had always done in temple since my childhood. I did tune into the chanting from time to time but most of the prayer session I was lost in thoughts of my family as well as searching for what I could find to entertain me once I was finished at temple. I suddenly thought of my tomb and realised I had not checked upon it in some time. This would fill at least half a day if not more and I was so excited at realising this that I almost laughed out loud. I didn't even notice that I nodded my head as I thought of this and luckily Sennefer did not see this, however one of the other priests did.

Two hours later the prayers were finished and I was upon my feet the second that Sennefer spoke the last word. "Sire, I trust we have satisfied all that you sought this day," he said bowing low as I turned and began walking away.

"Yes, yes," I called back over my shoulder and chuckled. "More than you could have imagined."

Sennefer and the other priests scurried to form a procession behind me to escort me out of the temple as was expected and once again we walked in silence. I was barely out of view when Sennefer turned to the others, his face as serious as they would ever see it, "Come, and let us gather in the main temple and offer prayers for the Pharaoh."

Sennefer did not need to explain why, as they had all seen my sudden unexplained smiles during the most serious of prayers and some were still shocked from having been hit by me. If there had been a God to oversee mental health they would have prayed to them, but instead they prayed to Amun as was their vocation, and he answered all anyway.

Thus the agitation aroused by my abject boredom was evident but none understood my change other than my children. Having seen my behaviour after Satiah's death they saw nothing new nor expressed any concerns. They did not see the old temperamental man that my courtiers or priests did. They just saw their father readjusting once again to a new phase in his life. There were the occasional whispers amongst themselves but they would remind each other of my strengths and any concerns would be allayed so that they soon formed a unity that spoke more than words to all the servants and officials. If my children held no concerns for my state than neither should they and soon all carried on as though this was how things had always been.

I did test my priests before we all settled into this new pattern. It was only a few days after my session at the temple that I announced a visit to see my tomb. Tombs can take years to complete and are often begun as soon as you become Pharaoh so as to be ready well before they are needed. Those of us who survived battles and illness to actually die of old age were allowed the indulgence of being able to remodel and even make larger our resting place as the years went on. Decorations could be added quickly and even within the months of funeral preparations and of course the treasures to accompany us arrived with our mummy as we were placed.

I was carried to my boat upon a covered sedan which I hated, but I could no longer ride horseback as you know and even my chariot was now considered beyond my physical limits. I cringed as the sedan was brought before me at the palace doors with all its bright coloured drapery hanging from a frame that formed a canopy over the seat inside that was in turn covered with a pile of silk covered pillows. This was the transport of women, adorned and soft just as they were, not the vehicle for a man who had fought upon the sands of Canaan. This particular sedan was one that my daughters would sometimes use and as I climbed aboard I smelt the traces of their perfumes within the fabrics. I fell back upon the pillows and sighed as the wafts of oil reminded me just why I was not upon my horse or chariot testing my health anymore.

A guard stepped forward to close the drapes and seal me inside. "No, no, no!" I snapped with frustration. "How will the people see me if you close those? Open them all!"

The sedan was immediately surrounded by a dozen people grabbing at the drapes and pulling them as tight as possible to the four poles of the frame, binding them so that that I was as exposed as possible. They stood back waiting for my approval, which they received as a grunt and a nod, before the bearers stepped forward in place ready to lift me. They raised and carried me so smoothly that I could have literally floated off to sleep in this little cloud of softness. Thankfully the usual crowd gathered along the streets of Thebes to wave and shout their blessings keeping me alert.

"Slow down!" I shouted to my bearers and guards.\

The pace of the sedan was slower than my usual passage by horse and I could see that the people enjoyed seeing me clearer and for more than a fleeting glance. I decided to indulge them just that bit more and besides I did not need to rush. It took us almost an hour to make our way to the Nile bank, more than double the usual time and though my bearers would never complain I did catch a few of them stretching their arms and shoulders once we were on board the boat. The sail across the river was enough time for all to rest and soon we were making our way into the heat of the burial valley. Hatshepsut's temple was now in even more disarray since my correction and I saw that the elements too continued my work as its colours had faded even more since my work here.

My tomb is only a short distance from there with its entrance set high within a cliff face. A huge stone staircase led to the cut in the stone and this would be dismantled upon my eventual internment making my tomb completely inaccessible--or so we had all planned. The priests I consulted for my tomb were waiting for me and they rushed forward bowing as the sedan was carried to the base of the stairs.

As I stepped out of the sedan the eldest stepped forward. "Prepare to carry the Pharaoh!" he barked at my guards. Knowing the stairs and interior were too narrow for the sedan he pointed to two of my guards, waving them forward.

"There is no need!" I said strongly. "I may not be able to ride but I can still climb stairs."

"Sire, there are many stairs also within," the priest reasoned. "I think you should consider that they may fatigue you."

"Your fussing will fatigue me far quicker than any stairs," I said plainly. "Now let us proceed with discussing my tomb as I made this journey for."

I am sure my guards and bearers would have stifled a laugh once we had left them outside, as this was the response they expected of me nowadays. So this is exactly what they did as soon as I reached the top of the stairs and made my way inside. Sitting down to take rest within the few shadows of the cliff face they sipped their wine and broke bread while they laughed at the way the old priest had shrunk back a pace as I declared the last remnants of my independence.

The chief guard having finished his small meal stood and brushed the crumbs from his face and then from his kilt. "My grandfather also believed he was still strong despite his years. He was found lying amongst the grasses of his fields while the oxen ate the grass away around him," he smiled as he said this to the others but they saw that he was serious. "I will enter the tomb's passage so that I may hear if we are called for. Two of you will wait at the entrance to hear my call and then join me if needed. The rest of you remain vigilant by the sedan ready to return the Pharaoh to the boat within a moment of notice." He turned and started his way up the staircase while the others finished eating and then placed themselves ready also.

Within the tomb the eldest priest walked ahead of me with a torch to light my path. We made our way down the first stairs and the coolness that had washed over us as we stepped out of the sunlight now became decidedly colder. The rocks here had been cut several times as my lengthy reign had allowed the passages to be made wider as work had continued. The priest leading the way pointed this out as well as making sure that I noted the exceptional work of the stairs. I would have loved to carry my own torch but my hands running along the walls as I walked showed me how smooth a job had been done in carving them, while my feet did not stumble upon the slightest bump or dip in the floor.

Down we walked again by another set of stairs and the temperature dropped yet again. Stepping into the stillness and darkness here was how I imagined those first moments of death to be like before the Gods arrived to escort you on. The priest ahead of me babbled as he pointed to walls reminding me of what would be carved or painted at different places and even though he could not see me I nodded as he spoke. Then he came to a stop in front of me so suddenly I almost pushed into him.

"Sire we have reached the well shaft," he said and swept his torch ahead of him and then lowered the flame so that I could see the huge square of darkness before us. "It has now been dug deep enough that no man can exit its depths without the longest of ropes to pull him, and that is if he has survived such a fall to do so."

The priest smiled as he said this and I nodded my approval. Looking down one more time I could see that the torch light did not even allow you to see the floor of this space. Only a fool would attempt to continue further and even if they did somehow cross over this hole they would have a most difficult task in returning with anything significant. It was a simple but most ingenious form of security and while I hated that I even needed this within my tomb I was grateful to the architect who had the creativity to design it.

Across the well shaft were laid several thick planks of wood forming a strong bridge to allow builders access and eventually my sarcophagus and treasures to be carried into the final chambers. We now continued on across these and our footsteps upon the wood echoed deeply below us into the dark void below. When I stepped off the wood and once more onto stone I now stood within an open area. The lengthy corridor that carried us down now opened into the first chamber, a room that would celebrate my life and call upon Ra to protect me and guide my journey in the afterlife. When the priests behind me entered they moved about the room so that their torches glowed evenly and I could see clearly. Only two large pillars threw shadows to break up the glow from the torches.

I walked around the space looking at the smooth walls and nodding. It was wonderful but I was now anxious to see the most important part--my burial chamber. The passage out of the first chamber was to the left so that we now travelled at a right angle to the entry passageway and once again we walked down another flight of stairs to climb even deeper into the stone.

The priests moved about this chamber as well so that their torches revealed the room to me in its entirety and I gasped when I saw just how magnificent the space was now. It had begun as a simple rectangular box, enough for my sarcophagus and treasures. Now it was twice that size and its corners carved away so that the wall curved in one continuous flow. I walked and touched the wall, and it was so smooth that for a moment I believed it had already been plastered ready for the glyphs to be painted. The only disturbance to this wall was four doorways, two on each of the longest walls that opened into four small chambers to house my much needed treasures

"It is far grander a burial chamber than I could have imagined," I said to the priest softly.

"Yes Sire, the cartouche shape is most majestic," he replied.

It had indeed been a cartouche that my architect had intended to invoke when he drew the plan and presented it to me. 'Sire, your name is held in this sacred shape," he had said nervously as he presented the plan. "Let us hold your burial within this shape as well so that the Gods shall have no doubt as to who lies within it."

I had loved this idea as much as the joy of being the first to do so but standing here now within the oval shape it was not a cartouche that came to mind. As I looked upon the wall all I could think of was a papyrus scroll unwrapped and ready to be written upon. I was about to say this to the priest but the torches were beginning to dim and I knew that we must leave soon lest we have to climb out in the dark. The priest babbled as we made our way out of the tomb and I nodded as though I was listening but I didn't hear anything he said. The image of a blank papyrus scroll played upon me so much that no other thoughts could enter my mind.

Finally back within my sedan I did truly feel weary. As the excitement of seeing my tomb wore off my legs now suddenly felt tired and I was quite grateful for the soft pillows beneath me and the legs of my bearers beneath the sedan itself. The gentle swaying of the sedan as they walked was so soothing that I actually dozed off as we made our way back to the boat. The rocking of the boat continued this so that I slept most of the river crossing also. Upon our arrival at the Theban dock the sounds of the boat landing woke me and I made sure I was roused enough to greet my people without any trace of sleep in my face.

I did not slow my bearers or guards this time and asked them to keep a steady pace. All I could think of now was my bed and a lovely afternoon sleep. When I was finally upon the mattress my mind kept going over the sight of the curved wall of my burial chamber and I began to even see it the colour of papyrus as I recalled the red glow of the torch light upon it. As sleep did begin to come over me I prayed that it may reveal to me more of why this image could not leave me. I slept soundly and did not dream at all so that when I woke I had a blissful few minutes of feeling refreshed then recalled I had dreamt nothing. Falling back upon my pillows I decided that something would reveal itself to me soon enough.

It was only two days later that this something was indeed revealed to me. A great scribe of Karnak had been appointed to create my "Book of the Dead" to be placed beside me within my sarcophagus. This scroll would be my travel guide once I began my journey, containing an outline of what to expect as well as the chants, prayers and incantations I would need to recite in order to make safe passage through each of the regions. The scribe arrived with the scroll and I saw his hands were shaking as he opened it upon a table. As it unrolled before me I was so struck by the artistry in which it had been marked upon the papyrus that I inhaled deeply and sat straight within my chair.

The poor scribe took this for disappointment and his hands shook even more. "Sire, of course this is merely the initial draft," his voice trembled. "There is much more embellishment to occur upon your approval of this layout of glyphs."

This was indeed a first draft with glyphs simply struck in just the deep dark browns of ink against the soft brown of the papyrus. Their forms were the simplest you could mark them while still making sure they conveyed their meaning. It was not done roughly by any means and each stroke was purposeful and strong, so much so that it was as detailed a work of art as any scroll that burst with colour and intense detail. Its simplicity made it all the more powerful and I felt it made the meaning of its content all the more potent.

I looked up at the scribe. "There is no need for any further work. I will accept this as it is. No amount of colour or embellishment will make these words any more powerful."

The scribe was confused but nodded anyway. "As you wish Sire, but surely we could just add some colour to the images of you within it?"

I put my hand up to stop him. "It is perfect and complete," I said, hoping to halt any further questions which it thankfully did.

I asked that the scroll be left with me to look over some more before it was taken back to Karnak for its final prayers and blessings and stored ready for my burial rites. It sat upon my table in my salon and I looked upon it now flattened out with weights as I sipped my wine. A breeze came through my window and it lifted the papyrus slightly pulling one corner from under its weight so that it tried to curl back upon it self. As I looked upon that curled corner I suddenly recalled my burial chamber and its rounded wall. A smile spread across my face as I now had the answer.

When I sat with the high priests to tell them that my burial chamber wall would become a replica of my scroll they nodded but I could feel their hesitation.

"Sire this is most noble of you to shun more elaborate records in favour of the holy words but surely you diminish your grandeur and deny your status in choosing this style?" one said to me.

"There is plenty more wall space for such grandeur and exaltation of my achievements," I said firmly. "Besides what other pharaoh has given himself the honour of the entire *Amduat* to surround him in burial. The Gods will relish this dedication and its simplicity will only confirm my devotion to the words."

The priests all nodded but they were far from happy and I knew why. There was no concern that my passage would be hindered by the spartan decorations for they knew the power of the words that would be marked upon the walls. They had now lost the opportunity to make their own involvement as grand as it could be. A pharaoh's burial was a reflection of the priests who oversaw it and Khufu's priests were as celebrated as his pyramid was during their time. My priests now would have to settle for making the most of the fact that I was the only pharaoh so far to have a cartouche shaped chamber that held the complete *Amduat*.

The propaganda began almost immediately as word spread about my choice. They embellished the story with such words as majestic and honourable. Within months it soon had its desired effect as priests from all over Egypt came to Karnak to see the very scroll that had inspired this decision so that they could recreate it for their own nobles and commoners. Thousands of scrolls replicating my own were tucked alongside mummies all over Egypt long after my death and it was only the succession of new priests at Karnak that changed this.

CHAPTER THIRTY-SIX

With my tomb plans finalised I felt all of my life from beginning to end had been put in order. I had married and raised children including a successor who was already crowned and ruling by my side. He too had already bore his own successor with another nine sons lined up behind him. Everything that had been asked of me when I was born into my life of royalty had been met and some days I wondered why the Gods still kept me here. Not that I was in any hurry to go but just that I wondered what else I had to achieve during my time.

Some mornings I even awoke and upon realising I was still alive I would wonder what this day would hold for me. There were always the trivial dealings of the palace such as which wines would be served that week and I still did attend more serious court sessions to officiate. In all honesty any days of boredom and the frustrations that I allowed that state to perpetuate were of my creation. A man with eight living children, forty-one grandchildren and an empire to rule had endless ways to fill his days.

One day I wandered out to the training arena to watch my grandsons practice their riding. While it made me so proud to see them all developing their skills it also made me acutely aware of the fact that I could no longer climb aboard my horse and join their tutors in teaching them. I stood along the edge of the track that they rode around, smiling and waving as each one rode past me, occasionally yelling out a directive or encouragement, but my legs soon grew tired and I made my way back to the palace.

I wandered down to the rooms that my daughters spent most of their days in. As I approached I heard Meryt's voice re-telling a story she had heard from one of the silk merchants at the markets. It was some gossip about one of the princesses from Greece and she laughed as she divulged what had been shared with her, while her sisters laughed or gasped in shock. As I came closer to the door I could see that as they spoke their maids were brushing my princesses' hair. The maids too joined in the gossip contributing anything they too had heard. I stood silently in the doorway for a moment enjoying this lovely carefree scene of chatter and preening. For a fleeting moment I felt some envy for how relaxed they all were but I soon shook this off, as I could not imagine a life filled this way. Of course my observation was short lived as a maid saw me and jumping up and bowing notified the others of my presence.

"Ah Father, have you come to be preened as well?" cried out Meryt.

"Yes, we have a lovely wig for you," laughed Meritamen and held up a wig that was sitting beside her.

"Leave him be," cried Isis who stood up and came to kiss me before taking my hand. "Come sit with us a while."

So I sat amongst the women but there was an awkward silence for some time as this was most unusual for a man to sit amongst them here. The maids kept their heads down and would not speak, suddenly reminded of their ranking.

"Keep talking please," I begged.

"As you wish Father, but you must know we do not speak of army or court here!" laughed Meryt.

"As I am aware from what I heard as I approached," I nodded. "Now let me hear just what is it that Princess Marina asks of her servants."

"Oh you would not believe it…" Meryt continued and finished relaying the story. I have to admit even I was wide-eyed at what I heard even though a part of me wondered just how much was fabricated or exaggerated as it had passed from mouth to ear and made its way across the sea and down the Nile to Thebes. I had always known the power of rumours and hearsay as I had used these in campaigns to forewarn and scare my enemies. I never imagined that such idle gossip though could travel so far and so passionately via the mouths of women.

I soon tired of listening to the stories and when the discussion turned to current fashions I left for the sanctuary of my own chambers. Tati was moving about making sure the servants had cleaned as thoroughly as he demanded and as I looked at him I was grateful that he did not feel the need to share with me any gossip that might reach his ears. My rooms always were and still remained a sanctuary from unnecessary words. I sat upon a lounge and my head was actually aching from the loud and fast talking of my daughters. Women may be saved the rigours of battle but their voices could be as punishing as any sword or fist. I decided once again to be thankful for being a male and made my way to my bed to rest.

The sense of completion within my life grew with each sunrise and I actually became content to spend my days relaxing within my rooms and garden. I would receive visitors including my daughters but somehow all knew that the rooms here did not tolerate idle talk. We would sit and talk gently about matters that were tangible or valuable. Even when I ventured from my chambers those around me spoke gently and simply so that the brutality of the battlefield and the dramatics of the court soon felt like they had occurred a lifetime ago.

Soon there came the day that I simply could not wander from my rooms. I sometimes felt that my legs had forgotten what they were capable of and it was as if the less I did the faster this occurred. The sanctuary of my rooms now became my world and when people came to visit or seek audience they were even quieter.

As much as my pride hated it I even succumbed to having servants aid me in walking from my bed to my salon and garden following a fall as I walked the shortest distance upon the level floor of my rooms. I was upon the floor before I had even realised what had happened and I lay there helplessly shaking as Tati ran to me shouting orders to the other servants.

"What happened, Tati?" I said through struggling breaths.

"You slipped Sire, there must have been some water upon the floor," he answered but I could see the lie upon his face.

There had been no water, not even a join between tiles had been under me as I had taken that step. I was carried to the bed and as I lay waiting for the physicians I closed my eyes and asked for the Gods to take me before I grew any weaker. Longevity meant nothing to me if it meant existing like this.

The physicians arrived and satisfied there were no broken bones administered the tonics for the obvious shock and dismay they saw upon my face. They were just finishing and were about to leave when I grabbed one by the arm so suddenly that he jumped.

"Sertakh, you have been a most noble and loyal physician," I said, but it did not come out as the compliment I intended and he nodded, his eyes wide and I felt him tremble. "Tell me do you have the herbs on hand should I choose to make my way to the afterlife?" I asked.

I did not think his eyes could grow any wider but they did and he leant in close to me. "Sire, you must not say such things!" he hissed. "It is heresy to even contemplate such an action and I could never aid you in doing so."

Everything he spoke was true and his fear as he spoke to me was palpable. He looked around as he stood back up, hoping that only the other physician had heard my request. To have a pharaoh consider suicide was serious enough a matter but to possibly be implicated in this was even worse. I had now sentenced both these men to a sleepless night, as they lay awake praying that I did not pass so soon after their visit to me lest they be linked to my death.

The next day I awoke and as soon as I made to move from my bed the aches and pains reminded me of the day before. I reluctantly informed Tati that I would be spending the day in bed and he nodded, relieved that he had not even had to suggest this. Not that I rested so much as I received an endless stream of visitors all intent on entertaining me or simply making sure that I was resting properly.

Isis's daughter brought me a drawing and as I held it before me she climbed upon the bed beside me and pointed out all the details. It was a battle scene and she pointed to a chariot before a massive army. I saw the soldier in this chariot was wearing a crown and realised it was me.

"I was telling her all about your grand victory at Megiddo as well as all your other campaigns," Isis said as she watched us.

I nodded and tears filled my eyes.

My granddaughter put her arm over me as a hug. "It is no wonder you are so tired now, Grandfather," she said quietly and then the tears fell down my face.

The gentility of being visited by my family was instantly quashed by the arrival of the Karnak high priests. As soon as I saw their figures at the door with their animal skins hanging over their shoulders I knew this was no mere obligatory visit to check upon my status. The physicians had run to them at dawn as much from concern as with the intent of covering their own backsides.

Five of them stood around my bed refusing to sit knowing this would make their presence as formal and formidable as they intended. I sighed and surrendered to the inevitable lecture warning me of the perils of suicide. In truth it was a good reminder of the terrors that followed this choice but that impulsive thought made in the midst of shock and frustration was long gone. I nodded as they spoke and assured them that such talk would never be spoken from my lips again.

"Sire, we do not question your word," said the highest priest gravely, "however such words from a man who has lived life so richly and with no cause for regret can only lead us to believe that demons have carried these thoughts to you!" With this he clapped his hands and another ten priests entered the room. "We shall administer the rites to remove these demons and clear your mind so that such ideas cannot return," he said dramatically.

I took a deep breath and sunk back onto my pillows. There was no stopping the priests of Karnak and what they believed they needed to do to protect a pharaoh. After an hour though, with the room thick with incense and repetitive chants that made my head ache I once again wished I were dead. I chose the next best option and escaped by falling asleep.

Menkheperre appeared as my first visitor the following morning and I saw him screw his nose up at the stench of incense that still hung in my room as he entered the bedchamber.

"How goes it today, Father?" he asked as merrily as he always spoke.

"I do not know yet," I answered truthfully as I was yet to even sit up that morning. "Wait a moment and I will answer you."

With that I pulled back my sheets and Menkheperre rushed forward to help me. It was then I saw what he carried in his hand. It was a long stick made of gold beginning at a curved handle and then tapering down to its end. The handle was wrapped in the soft fur of a lion and the space where the handle met the main length had been carved with a cobras head with its body winding down to the ground. Jewels were embedded within the cobra's head so that it glistened. I let him help me sit up with his free hand but I did not take my eye off the stick.

"There now, how do you feel sitting up for the day?" he asked.

"What is that?" I ignored his actual question and even what pain I was feeling as I was too curious as to what he carried.

"It is a gift for you," he smiled and held it towards me. "I had it made for you after your fall so that you can use it to help you walk."

I looked my son in the eye and raised my eyebrow. "Do you seriously expect me to believe you could have this commissioned and created in less than

411

two days?"

Menkheperre took a deep breath and smiled. "Fine, I commissioned it a few weeks ago when I noticed you walking stiffly," he said. "I should know better than to lie to you."

"Yes you should," I snapped. "Just because my body is failing does not mean my mind is joining it."

Menkheperre nodded. "Well would you like to try it?"

"Yes I would," I said, and wrapped my right hand around the handle that felt as though it had been carved especially for my hand. I pushed it down onto the floor and lifted myself to standing only to fall immediately back upon my rear on the edge of the bed.

Menkheperre rushed forward again but I assured him I was okay. "I just stood too quickly."

I took a few deep breaths and prayed that my legs would this time remember their duty. When I lifted myself finally I could stand but Menkheperre saw the wobble in my legs and came to my side. "I will support your left side," he said softly and let me rest my left arm upon his right. I suddenly felt safe and took my first step for the day.

That walking stick became a permanent fixture by my side from that day on. Most of the time I would still need another person by my side for extra support and this was usually a son, daughter or older grandchild as my family rarely left me on my own now. On the few occasions that I was alone my stick helped me retain the last vestiges of independence I had and I was able to take a few steps on my own should I choose or need to.

Unfortunately the days that I could walk alone grew fewer and soon not even a second walking stick allowed me to walk unaided. The loss of pride in allowing myself to be carried was no match for the indignity of being collected after a fall and so I surrendered to the help that I needed. I would be lifted out of my bed and carried to my salon to sit and receive people or outside to my garden to relax, then returned to my bed as soon as I fatigued.

My children would bring to me news of the court and all seemed to be flowing well so that my mind could rest as well as my body. Of course my children would never bring anything other than harmonious news to me and I was somewhat glad that they knew to lie and help my final days be as gentle as possible.

Yes, I did know these were my final days as did all around me. I knew the lies about the court fed to me by my children were joined by the hushed tones of the servants who worked within my chambers. A granddaughter succumbing to some gossip before me was hushed wide-eyed by her sister and it was then that I realised that my chambers were now my cloister.

I sat within my garden one day as my gardener entered. These days he could not delay his work as I was always nearby so he simply appeared each day at the same time. He bowed as he should and asked after my health to which I supplied my customary response. "My heart beats and my lungs breathe." He would smile and then go about his work. It was a pleasant routine that we played out and one that we both enjoyed. Most days I would leave him to work quietly unless I wished to ask him about a certain plant or make small talk as to the weather. Occasionally too he might speak with me to seek approval for something he was considering within the garden.

This day I watched him working as diligently as ever, enjoying his attention to my plants. He walked to my precious persimmon tree and I saw him look closely at its leaves turning a few as though to look behind them. As he did so his face grew grave and I saw lines appear upon his brow.

"What is it, Mahu?" I called out.

"I would have thought your tree would be bearing the signs of fruit by now but it has no buds forming at all," he replied and turned back to examining the tree. "I don't recall it having done so before."

"No it hasn't," I said, as I too scraped through my memories. It had always been the most healthy, abundant tree with the sweetest of fruit and never once showing any signs of disease.

"It has received plenty of water and I cannot see any indication of pests or illness," my gardener began as though wishing to convince me it was not due to his care but I knew his reasoning was genuine. "It must be the soil," he said and looked down. "I shall gather some oxen manure to feed it. It may not be too late for this season."

I nodded at first but the thought of the stench of manure wafting through my chambers came to mind and I shook my head instead. "No, Mahu," I said. "Perhaps this year my tree can rest. It has produced most nobly and earned itself a respite."

Mahu looked to me and I caught him quickly glance down at my legs before looking back up. "Most wise words Pharaoh. It has indeed earned some rest."

CHAPTER THIRTY-SEVEN

It was my sixty-sixth year when the hours I spent within my bed outnumbered those that I wasn't. No male of my family had survived to this age whether due to disease or battle wounds. True, I did carry the skin lesions that have been found upon my father and grandfather but these were simply the way the sun wore upon us. I had evaded the insipid illness that struck my father and the cancer and arthritis that had eaten away my aunt. The biggest enemy that my body had now was the fatigue and pain of old age. Some days it would have been a blessing to have something more substantial to blame my limitations upon.

The physicians now visited me daily to administer or leave potions to strengthen me or alleviate pain. I truly felt they did nothing but I took them anyway for the one day that I did refuse the high priests arrived within the hour to once again drive away the demons that were interfering with my thoughts. Even when the priests were gone the incense that hung in the air reminded me that it was simpler to comply with the physicians' orders.

Within the confines of a bed there are few things to amuse you apart from those who come to visit, so I sought my own enjoyment in-between these times. A second smaller bed was made for me to be placed near a window or even carried out into the garden should I choose. I could sit up against a mountain of pillows and thankfully see more than the roof of my bed canopy

I would even sit up as dark fell waiting for the moon to make her way in the sky and to watch the stars glisten. As long as I could see the sun and the moon each day then somehow I was still connected to the world and the Gods would not forget I was here.

While I do brag that I did not have the cancers or arthritis of my father or old Hatshepsut I did have one ailment that was always there like a ghost and that was my weakened heart. Having chosen this quieter life I had developed a respectable relationship with my heart. I did not test its limits and it remained quiet and well-behaved, functioning within its abilities, as too did I. However even the most refined and sturdy machines eventually find their mechanisms cannot continue. No matter how rested I was, this little red pump in my chest was slowly struggling to provide me with the life force I needed.

It was late one night well after I had been placed upon my bed to sleep that its weakness made itself known to me once again. Even though I was lying flat I could see a slice of the moon through the curtains and I smiled comforted that she would show herself to me one last time before I slept. As I closed my eyes the pleasure of that glimpse was washed away as I felt that tightness in my chest that had been absent for so long. I am not sure if it was simply my memories of the pain that had faded, or if it was my more fragile state, but it was the strongest most intense pain that I had ever experienced. As it travelled down into my arm and my neck tightened I knew that this was my last night within this body and yet no matter how ready I had told myself I was there was still that last cry within me, "I don't want to leave!" Then just as quickly as the pain had entered me there was nothing.

When I opened my eyes I saw a great wave of light fall upon me and a voice called out, "Good morning, Sire." It was Tati drawing my drapes as he did every morning. I tried to call out but somehow my voice was trapped in my throat and could not leave. I felt a heavy weight upon my chest and tried to reach it with my right hand but I could not feel my hand. As I reached with my left hand, I realised the weight was in fact my right arm slumped across my chest—dense and lifeless. Tears fell down my face as I discovered I could not feel my right leg either.

I looked up and Tati was standing over me with an expression of sheer horror upon his face. I wanted to tell him of my heart and now my paralysed arm and leg but all that could come from my mouth was gurgling. He turned his head and screamed out to the servants. "Run and call the physicians! Do not hesitate a moment!" Then looking back to me, "Sire I have sent for help, please try to rest." He tried to maintain his usual composure but his eyes and voice betrayed him. "I will send for your children," he said softly and I saw his eyes grow moist. As much as I did not want my children to see me like this I knew somehow that I had survived the night so that we could all see each other once more.

Thankfully the physicians arrived first, breathless and with chests heaving from having run the entire way. They gathered themselves as best they could but as soon as they looked down upon me and saw the muscles on the right side of my face hanging limp along with the paralysis through my body all they could do was confirm what Tati and I already knew.

Beketamun was the first to arrive and stood in the doorway waiting for the physicians to finish at my bedside. When they turned to see her there they waved her to my salon to speak.

"Your Highness, the Pharaoh's body is failing," they said simply hoping she would not press them for more information than they could provide.

"Have you potions for this? Surely you have something?" she begged of them.

The physicians just shook their heads before one stepped forward and spoke. "He cannot swallow, Madam. Should we try to administer anything we risk him choking. We have balms for his paralysed limbs but truly the only thing to heal now is time." At this the physician stopped for a moment before adding, "But I will be honest Madam and tell you that this is something rarely recovered from and at the Pharaoh's grand age this may simply be the God's method to begin his transition."

It was a most theatrical way to tell my daughter I was dying but it answered the one question she could not bring herself to ask. She nodded slowly and knew that she would now enter my bedchamber not just to visit me but also to begin a bedside vigil. As the physicians left, Meritamen and Meryt arrived at the door already in tears and ready for the worst. Beketamun told them solemnly that this was most likely my last day and made them hush their sobbing before stepping further.

The three of them came to my bedside, their faces wet with tears and when they saw my twisted face all three cried anew. I tried to comfort them but my strangled voice only upset them more. "Please Father, try to rest," said Beketamun as she grabbed my hand. "We know what to do." I wanted so much to at least squeeze her hand to respond, but Beketamun lifted my right hand in hers. As she felt how lifeless it was and realised this was my paralysed hand her tears fell even harder.

The girls arranged their chairs and began their vigil. They were soon joined by Isis who refused a chair and instead curled up on the end of my bed like a cat. Every so often she would sob into the sheets and no one dared ask her to get off and sit as her sisters did.

"Where are the men?" hissed Meritamen after an hour.

Siamun was in fact finalising court matters and was on his way, arriving just as Meritamen asked the question. Amenhotep and Menkheperre were on the outskirts of Thebes overseeing army training. Messengers had only just found them to let them know of my condition. Beketamun knew all this and relayed it to her sister but bit her tongue at another response that she wished to say, *"Where is your mother?"*

Matreya was within her private chambers as the news arrived to her. She asked if the children had been informed and when she was told that our daughters were already with me and our sons on their way her instant reaction was to fume that she hadn't been told first. "Always the last to know anything," she sighed as she heard, "I suppose they will tell me of his death when his mummy is ready!" She sat firmly in her chair. "I will wait for my son the Pharaoh to call for me," she declared and then asked her servants to air her mourning clothes to be ready. As they pulled the clothes from the chests and hung them about her bedchamber she looked upon them and smiled. Usually she hated when these garments saw light but today she quite liked them.

Amenhotep and Menkheperre arrived at my bedside just before midday. They were covered in sweat and dust from their swift ride back to the palace and as they came to stand over me their hearts sank as they saw that the message they had received had not been exaggerated. Amenhotep turned to the physicians who had returned to monitor me, "Have you done all you can?" It should have sounded like a command but it didn't. It was more the plea of a child and the physicians nodded and murmured that this was in fact the case. Amenhotep then leant in close to me. "We will not leave you Father," he said earnestly.

As I nodded my thanks to him I looked fully into his eyes and I felt such deep fear in them because I too knew that fear once. It was the fear I had felt when I left Hatshepsut's deathbed and realised that my time to rule alone had finally come. I wished I could have told him he had nothing to fear, that he would rule as grandly as any of the men of our family but I could not bear to hear my tortured voice again and instead I shared with him a crooked grin. He caught my face changing and he saw my mouth try to form my old familiar smile. Amenhotep nodded before he turned to sit within the chair closest to me.

My children sat in silent vigil all day. I would drift in and out of sleep, or perhaps it was consciousness. Each time I opened my eyes there would be another priest or vizier come to pay his last respects. I tried to nod or smile as each one came forward but as the hours passed even these simple gestures required massive effort and so I just lay still. The priests began their chanting in the early afternoon and I heard Nebetiunet's voice join them as she sat in her chair with her sisters, having made her way from her temple. It suddenly felt right to no longer try to open my eyes and instead just listening to the voices recite their prayers was enough for me. Occasionally I would hear a whimper from one of the girls and I would try to look for them but I now simply couldn't.

Everyone knew this extended time of "sleep" for me was just my final hour drawing closer and the chanting became more intense as the priests began the stronger prayers for my spirit. Isis still upon the end of my bed would every now and then look up to see that my chest did move and then when this became so shallow that her eyes could not see, she would place her hand upon me until she felt the subtle movement. I tried once to touch her and thank her for her care but I could not. Instead I cherished every time I felt her warm hand upon me.

The sun set and as usual in Egypt the temperature plummeted with her departure. The drapes had been pulled long ago, as is the custom in a room where death is about to visit so that the darkness of the night sky was barely noticed by the people around me. I could feel it though and I wished I could see the moon one last time. It took all my energy but I opened my eyes and hoped I would be able to see out the window to the night sky.

Of course all I saw was a blur of people and their faces were like a wall surrounding my bed. I looked upon the faces of my children and I ached to speak to them one last time, to tell them I loved them and how proud I was to leave Egypt in their hands. Amenhotep and Beketamun sat the closest to my side, my strongest and most clever, ready as always to do what was needed for me. Beyond them stood the only other faces apart from my children that I could have wished to see. Behind Amenhotep stood my father and behind Beketamun was Satiah. They both smiled at me and I knew they were here to walk me away from this life.

I looked to them both and suddenly I could smile. Beketamun and Amenhotep both saw this and sat forward. Amenhotep with a sudden glimpse of hope called out to me, "Father."

Beketamun though knew this smile as she had seen it once before, upon her mother's face just before Satiah's last breath.

"He is leaving!" she cried and rushed forward to take my hand.

Satiah and my father disappeared as all of my children rushed forward upon hearing Beketamun's cry. This is how I took my last breath, with the faces of all my children looking down upon me. It felt like it lasted an eternity and yet it was over quickly and so simply.

CHAPTER THIRTY-EIGHT

Everything had turned black but I could still hear their voices and the crying. Then suddenly it was like my whole body twisted but it was beyond a physical sensation. It was like stepping out of a deep pool of syrup, leaving behind the heaviness of the liquid and letting the cool air fall upon you. I played with the rush of sensations and this immaculate sense of freedom but the sounds of my family pulled my focus back to the room. The darkness cleared and I was now watching the room just as I had in my dream so long ago. My daughters were all now upon the bed holding my body and crying while my sons stood watching, also with tears upon their faces. The priests too had rushed forward but they had no chance of getting to my body.

One priest ran to the door of the bedchamber and announced my passing to the spouses of my children as well as the viziers, priests and generals that also waited there. Some sat quietly and wept whilst others rushed into the corridor to inform messengers to carry the announcement to their charges. A scribe sat and scratched the official declaration as dictated by a high priest and then left to replicate the parchment a thousand times over with the other scribes at Karnak so that every temple in my empire would carry the news. In the corridors servants from the kitchens, the stables, the nursery and all the private chambers had lurked waiting for news and as they saw the messengers leave my chambers they did not have to hear the words and within ten minutes the entire palace joined in the tears of my children.

Word reached Matreya's chamber as quickly as it did everywhere else. She had sat within her room waiting for Amenhotep to call for her but he hadn't. When Amenhotep had arrived at my chambers Tati relayed to him the message sent by her chief maid that his mother awaited his personal request to attend the vigil. "The Queen Mother will wait for some time then," was all Amenhotep offered and the usual anger he felt for his mother found a whole new level of hate that day. "How dare she choose today to play her games," he whispered to Beketamun.

Beketamun said nothing but took Amenhotep's hand in hers. She wondered if her own mother was alive what she would be do right now and pictured her wiping my brow or sitting gracefully in her chair quietly praying. Beketamun felt someone close behind her and turned quickly but saw no one. As she turned back straight in her chair she caught Menkheperre's eye. Sitting in a chair at the foot of my bed he had been looking over Beketamun's shoulder and now smiled at her.

"I believe our ancestors' spirits are here to guide him," he said.

Isis still lying at my feet lifted herself from the sheets. "Can you see them?" she asked softly and looked around the room

"No, but I can sense them," he answered.

Beside him Nebetiunet nodded. "That means his spirit is now ready."

Isis lifted herself on the bed and looked at me. "If you are ready Father, than so must we be also."

This awareness though did not make my passing any easier for my children and the priests thankfully allowed them their grief. My daughters soon gathered themselves and let go of my body. As they stood back I was able to see my shell completely for the first time and I was shocked. There it lay, so small and fragile; it was nothing like the young man who led the army at Megiddo. So much had passed and I had not even seen how old my body had become. I thanked myself that my records would remind my people of the man I had been, as my mummy certainly would not be indicative of my vigour.

The priests moved in and began the initial rites, chanting as they straightened my body and arranged my feet, arms and head into the Pharaonic burial posture. My children had stepped away from the bed to allow this and now their spouses arrived to comfort their partners and unite in the mourning. One other person also joined the children and as Matreya appeared in the door Tiaa felt Amenhotep freeze beside her and saw his jaw clench as he kept his eyes upon my body. Matreya walked towards her son and while the others offered a cursory head nod the now sole Pharaoh refused to acknowledge her. She stood for a while and watched also as my body was fussed over by the priests who were now daubing me in oils, but finally she could not resist the urge to draw a response from her son.

"I did not realise it was so serious else I would have been here sooner," she pathetically offered.

Amenhotep's face grew red and I am sure it took all the strength he had to hold back from causing his mother's body to join mine in having its final rites. Instead he sighed and spoke softly so that only his mother and wife heard him. "Have no regrets, Madam. You were neither needed nor missed."

These were the first words my son spoke as sole regent and I have no doubt there was few times during his reign that he said anything that was as potent or powerful.

CHAPTER THIRTY-NINE

I felt no need to leave the surrounds of the palace just yet and besides until my funeral rites were complete it was not expected that I would begin my passage to paradise. The sensations of my death were immediately familiar to me and I revelled in no longer having the limitations of a body. I did hate though that the lines of communication were now no longer intact, as though I had to trade one for the other. I would have loved to have actually lived like this, with the freedom to immediately be anywhere within seconds and to hear everything that was spoken. However this was the order of things and I accepted them.

My time, for want of a better expression, was spent wandering the hallways watching over how all was continuing on, and just how my funeral was being prepared. I saw everything from the tears upon the faces of minor servants as they spoke of me through to talks in the war rooms of fortifying the borders lest this time be seen as ripe for a challenge. I heard my daughters crying as they lay in bed at night while their husbands comforted them and I heard the questions from my grandchildren as my death formed part of their education.

One afternoon soon after my death I stood nearby Amenhotep as he discussed with the goldsmiths and the high priests the adornments to be made for my burial. We were within the salon of my chambers that now should have been his but Amenhotep refused to move in until my funeral was over. "It is still his home until then," he had said to Tati. He would use the salon for private audience but couldn't bear to even think of sleeping within a room that I had only left days before.

He was as dignified as I expected a new ruler to be but I could see that his eyes were washed with the haze of grief and each word he had to speak seemed painful. The goldsmiths noticed this also and spoke quietly and simply, hoping to end the meeting as soon as they could as much from respect as the need to begin their work. They discussed my funeral mask and the amulets to be bound within my wrappings. All seemed to be final and the goldsmiths began to roll the sheets of sketches that had been approved when Amenhotep looked up suddenly with his brow creased. "We did not discuss his crook and flail. Or did we?" he looked to the priests for confirmation.

"Sire, it is tradition that the Pharaoh is buried with the actual crook and flail that he ruled with," offered one priest as explanation.

Amenhotep looked to the floor and thought about this. I had ruled for fifty-six years including my time with Hatshepsut. The crook and flail handed to me at my coronation had been those that I had held my entire reign. Embedded with the blessings of the grand ceremony to begin my rule they were considered sacred and powerful, as though Amun had touched them himself. The longer they were used the more potent they were. I had seen the colour drain from many a face when they stood before me and saw these symbols held in my hands. Fifty-six years on, despite their maintenance, Amenhotep believed them to be old and tarnished, and he hated that his were still glistening while the handles of mine were dulled from my grip. It was a shame he never saw the beauty of that tarnish.

"They are old and worn," he said. "I wish to commission a new set for him to hold."

The priests' cried out in shock and Amenhotep heard a chorus of gasps. "Sire, we truly advise against this! They were created for Pharaoh Thutmose alone. We hope you are not considering using them for your rule?" one of the priests cried out.

"Of course not," snapped Amenhotep. "They will still be placed within his tomb but I should like that he will hold a new set. Surely he should meet the Gods in the grandest way possible."

"The Gods may not recognise him!" begged the priest.

"Yes! Listen to them!" I tried to scream out. I couldn't believe my son would change such a fundamental part of my burial. In my frustration I turned to the table beside me and grabbed at a vase smashing it on the ground. Of course that didn't actually happen as I could not do such things anymore but the intention was there with such force that the vase fell to its side. Amenhotep and all the men looked up as the alabaster thudded against the wooden table and they all watched as it rolled to the edge of the table and fell, smashing upon the tiled floor. Amenhotep's face had gone white and I saw the priests eyes grow wide as they all knew there was no possible way that this could have happened without someone's involvement and there was no one near the table.

There was silence for a moment then the inevitable scurry of servants to clear the mess. Amenhotep turned back to the priests and looked to them as a child about to confess a misdemeanour to a parent might appear. He cleared his throat. "There will be no crook and flail made. My father shall be buried with his customary set."

The priests all nodded with relief and Amenhotep now wished them gone so he could leave my chambers. My son knew I still walked these rooms and he hated to be in here as he felt my presence as soon as he crossed the doorway. He would never admit to it though and while the other children would speak of signs that they believed were sent by me, Amenhotep would remain silent. He had a country to run, an army to command and a Pharaoh's burial to oversee--there was no way he was going to be distracted by mystical fantasies.

Now today he had experienced something that could not be denied and in the presence of others. The priests would spin this into some myth and it would spread through the priesthood. It would begin as a tale of my great might and how I supported the priests in their admonitions to the Pharaoh but underneath that was the implication that Amenhotep had almost led my burial into some heresy. My longevity had many gifts for my family and the foremost was that my successor had many years to learn and know the machinations of the priesthood, as well as the burn of loose talk if it spread unchecked. Amenhotep knew he could never stop gossip completely but he could control what was officially said and recorded.

My son turned to the priests and goldsmiths. "The incident with the vase shall not be spoken of *ever*. If I hear word of it beyond these walls or beyond this day I shall know it was from one of the five mouths before me. I will ask no questions nor offer any mercy. You shall all be punished."

His words were cold and clipped, even Amenhotep himself could not believe that he spoke them. However it was necessary and he felt some relief at having delivered them. The priests nodded as did the goldsmiths and Amenhotep dismissed them, rising from his chair to leave these rooms also. The sooner he was out of here, then the sooner he could avoid any more incidents; the very thought of which made his flesh crawl.

It always amazed me that Amenhotep should find my presence so disturbing. He loved me and watching his actions after my death only confirmed this. We had been close and I do not believe we had any trace of unresolved issue and yet to sense my energy he responded as though I was a demon there to harm him. I chose to leave Amenhotep alone after that day, and even though there was much more to be done for my funeral, the major things had been decided so I did not care so much as to what else was done. Besides Amenhotep was too scared to try anything new after I smashed the vase that day. In fact the poor man was very nervous around vases until the day of my funeral. Even when that too had passed he would sometimes go by one upon a table and the sound of alabaster shattering would ring in his ears like it was yesterday.

He was about to leave the salon when he heard some noise from the garden and went to look. It was just the gardener tending to the plants as he still did every day. Mahu looked up and saw Amenhotep standing in the door and immediately turned to him, bowing his head. "Good day, Sire."

"Good day to you also," Amenhotep replied as he stepped outside and walked towards Mahu. "You have always taken such good care of this garden. I trust this will continue."

"Of course, Sire," he replied bowing again. "This is now your garden. I look forward to serving you as I did your father."

Amenhotep smiled and nodded as he looked over the little paradise. He had rarely been in here even as an adult and never without me. Standing there he now felt like he was discovering it for the first time. "He loved this place so much. He never even let us in here as children lest we damage anything. Now I think I know why he cherished it. You can pretend nothing else exists for a while," said Amenhotep.

"Indeed Sire," answered Mahu. "It is a very special place."

Amenhotep was now standing by the persimmon tree and he reached out to touch its leaves. Beneath them he could see the first round promises of new fruit. *"These are mine now,"* he thought then said aloud, "This tree will soon be orange with fruit."

The gardener looked up and realised which tree Amenhotep was speaking of and a lump formed in his throat. He swallowed hard as he knew he must answer. "Yes Sire, it is going to be a most abundant season," he finally said. Mahu continued on with his work but a part of him ached to share with him that the tree had missed a year and my words about this. He remained silent though, unwilling to test his new relationship with the Pharaoh so soon.

Amenhotep looked once more over the garden and left quietly. He passed the place where the vase had smashed and stopped. He looked up and sighed. *"It will be different when his things are gone and mine are here."* He didn't so much just think this as pray it. I was so tempted to do something else to him but I saw his shoulders slump and knew he had been tried more than enough. I let him go and went to watch my gardener at work. He would be much more fun to play with.

I did venture from the palace to see my body being prepared and quite beautifully I might add. I saw my adornments being made and the paintings being finished in my tomb. The attention to details and the care with which every person assigned a task took to make my last rites as grand as they should be was overwhelming. As I watched them all I felt the first tugs of regret at leaving and longed to return to feel the adulation once more as I did when I lived. Then I would hear the prayers at Karnak or the whispers of those waiting for me and I would remember where it was that I was going and those longings would disappear.

In fact the closer it got to my funeral the more anxious I was to be moving on. The initial amusement at being somewhat omnipotent had faded into a sense of transience. I was no longer truly part of this life that I was now observing and was yet to journey to my final destination. This space that I was in was of neither world and there was nothing to achieve here.

Finally it was the week of my funeral. My body was ready and as the final rites of the mortuary priests were spoken over my mummy others were within my tomb consecrating the space that was now embellished and ready. The high priests of Karnak gathered within my rooms along with a team of servants to begin gathering the belongings that would be placed within the annexe rooms to make their way with me. Amenhotep asked Beketamun and his sisters to oversee this part of the formalities excusing himself with matters of court and army to address but I know there was far more to it than that.

Beketamun was walking the rooms watching as the vases and statues were begun to be packed in boxes padded with straw when Meritamen and Isis appeared in the door. "Meryt could not bear to come. She says it will be like having father die another death," Meritamen said softly and her eyes filled with tears as she watched the first piece of furniture being carried out.

"Come, let us sort the things in his bedchamber," said Beketamun who had been avoiding this until her sisters arrived.

When they entered Tati was standing by my bed, folding clothes and sorting them into piles before him. He moved slowly and deliberately as though each garment was as delicate as fine glass. Beketamun swallowed hard. "Tati, we have come to help sort Father's most personal belongings."

Tati turned and bowed his head. He opened his mouth to speak but no words came out. Beketamun nodded. "You are doing a most wonderful job with his clothes. Sisters, perhaps you can help Tati."

Beketamun was both clever and diplomatic in her directions for this allowed her alone to pack the table that held my mementoes of her mother. She dragged the chest that had housed them from beneath the table and smiled as she opened it. Inside it the pieces of silk that had wrapped them all so wonderfully before were still there and Beketamun unfolded the first piece to lay a small perfume bottle inside it.

She was just placing it within the chest when a small bird flew in the window and landed on the edge of the opened lid of the chest. Beketamun jumped but the bird did not fly off and sat turning its head in gentle consideration of my daughter as she stared at it with amusement quickly replacing her initial shock. Isis looked up and smiled when she saw it also making Meritamen and Tati look. The bird then flew to the bed, landing on the rail over their heads looking down upon them, still turning its head as though addressing each person in turn. Meritamen shrieked and threw herself over the piles of my clothes. "Oh don't let it soil Father's clothes!" she cried out to which the bird chirped loudly and flew back out the window. All four of them laughed, even Meritamen as she stood back up and straightened herself.

"Do you suppose that was Father?" said Isis still smiling.

"I am sure it was," answered Beketamun grinning as she began to wrap another ornament.

I wish I could say that it had been me for the atmosphere in that room lifted considerably after the little visitor. My daughters and Tati now smiled as they continued on. Gentle conversation allowed itself to happen and the women begged Tati to share stories of his time with me, which he did with much love and humour. The priests in the salon would occasionally turn their heads to the bedchamber door as my daughters burst out laughing during the tales. One priest shook his head, "This is why women should not be involved in such things. It is just another chance for them to be frivolous!"

When the day of my funeral arrived I was grateful and felt a surge within me as I prepared to truly move on. My entire family gathered at the grand gates of the palace to board carriages to make their way to Karnak. Amenhotep led the way upon his chariot and he requested that his brothers and young Thutmose also ride upon theirs to lead the family procession.

"We will show that the strength of this family continues and ride before all of Thebes as the warriors our father was," he said solemnly to his brothers when he asked this of them. Menkheperre and Siamun nodded silently agreeing wholeheartedly with this tribute and declaration. They also knew this would be an opportunity to show Egypt their support for their brother by riding behind him so.

Amenhotep climbed aboard his chariot and looked back upon the family. The first carriage held Matreya and Tiaa as was fitting for the royal mother and the current queen, then the carriages with his sisters and their spouses, followed by more carriages for the grandchildren. Viziers, generals and butlers were next on foot, while lesser palace staff trailed behind them. A line of guards flanked either side of the stream of family and officials. The only ones who would not leave the palace today were those making ready the grand feast to finish the day.

Amenhotep felt a lump as he looked upon those behind him. Here gathered before him were those most important to his heart and to his rule. He stood still for a moment as this realisation set in and then he nodded and turned to his brothers and son.

"Let us farewell our Pharaoh and father," he declared and with a flick of his reigns Amenhotep began my funeral.

Any royal funeral day was unofficially a holiday in Egypt. Market stalls and business would stop for the day, while farm tools were downed and fishing boats were docked. It was partly out of respect for their deceased leader but mostly so that vendors, farmers and fisherman alike could leave their work to attend such a grand occasion. The streets that were always lined to greet my family or myself were today crowded thicker than any time when I had lived. The people cried out their condolences to my family who did not wave or acknowledge but kept their heads down as was expected of any family in mourning. Matreya satisfied the women in the crowd by weeping and letting out an occasional wail as was befitting a widow, but my daughters remained stoic, the worst of their grief was long gone by this day.

My body waited for them at Karnak. It sat upon the altar within its three coffins, the most outer one being wood gilded all over in gold, polished with silk so that it bounced even the smallest ray of light off it. It was as though it had ten spotlights upon it when my family entered the main hall of the temple to take their places before it. The priests did not wait for the rest to assemble and began as soon as the last of my grandchildren had entered. They could not wait for the rest as there was simply too much to do and the loud chanting drowned out the sounds of their footsteps and rustling gowns as the mourners scattered amongst the columns to find a place.

Three hours the chants went on and I watched everyone as the priests performed ritual after ritual. I nodded as I counted off the royalty and dignitaries sent by our neighbours with even Minoa and the region you know as Rome represented. The young princes taught so well by my palace knew precisely what such a day meant and what having a symbol of their territory would buy them in the way of peace and trade. Suresh, now King of Mitanni knew more than most. He stood at the front of all the foreigners in his finest regalia and I saw his lips move to many of the prayers. He bowed the lowest when my sons entered and I caught a small smirk on Menkheperre's face when he realised just who this king was.

I saw courtiers fall asleep against columns, some younger grandchildren begin to fidget and many more people hide yawns behind their hands. Then suddenly it was over. The mortuary priest who had overseen my embalming came forward wearing the jackal head of Anubis and all within the temple stood straight and alert as though the very God himself was there ready to usher any one of them. He walked to my coffin and raised above his head his own crook and flail, summoning me to follow him. As Anubis turned and walked down the steps of the altar, twenty priests lifted the coffin to carry me down the stairs to be met by twenty pallbearers who would now carry me to my final place. The family parted and made way for Anubis to lead me from Karnak and to my tomb.

When my coffin was carried through the grand pylon that formed the gate to the temple it was met by all the commoners who could not fit inside. It was the first time they had seen my body and they began to shriek and wail to show their grief at losing me as well as their sympathy to my family. Flowers were thrown before me and they formed a path of such colours it was magnificent. It was also slightly dangerous and several pallbearers had a foot slip upon a stem or flower head and were thankful that the other men could take on the weight as they gathered themselves.

As their feet crushed upon the petals, an incredible perfume rose up and around my coffin. It continued on as the chariots and carriages of my family rolled their wheels over the carpet of flowers. The wind carried that rich perfume with it through the streets of Thebes and beyond. On the far outskirts of my city a group of farmers, too busy with work to stop for the day were suddenly awash with the mix of roses, jasmine and lotus. They looked up from their ploughs and hoes towards the city as it touched their noses. The pallbearers' sandals would wear that scent for days until the oils they had crushed into them dried out, as too would the wheels of the chariots and carriages. Several of my grandchildren would recall that scent well into their old age and would speak of it when re-telling the day to their own grandchildren.

Even though the flowers upon the ground stopped at the barge the scent carried with us across the water. A dozen boats carrying my family followed the funeral barque and we were flanked by a hundred fishing boats calling out prayers and also throwing flowers that floated in the water. Those in the procession were grateful for the dry air of the Valley to clear their noses and heads as many of them now had headaches from all the perfumes of the flowers.

They continued on silently finally stopping at the staircase that lead to the tomb entrance. Anubis continued to lead the way beginning his ascent up the stairs and the pallbearers braced themselves for the final but most difficult part of their duty. My family waited as the coffin made its climb and then disappeared inside to make its way to the burial chamber and be laid in its granite sarcophagus. The pallbearers made their way back out and a priest standing at the entrance nodded to Amenhotep and my son led my family in for their final goodbyes.

Lanterns were hung from the ceilings of the passages to light the way and priests lined the chambers with torches to illuminate those spaces. The men held the hands of the women to ease them down the stairs and across the planks that bridged the cavern of the thief trap. The antechamber provided a waiting space as my family entered the chamber one at time to kiss the sarcophagus, say a final prayer and place a tribute. Amenhotep and Beketamun remained at my head and observed as each person entered. They stood gracefully watching over every mourner that had made their way to the burial chamber.

Matreya was first and the quickest, her last contact with me was as brief as she could make it but Amenhotep saw her eyes drinking up every detail that she could as she entered and left--no doubt making notes for her own tomb. My daughters had one last cry as they placed small statues, except Nebetiunet who placed an ointment made only that morning. "For any scratches you may give yourself as you run through the fields of paradise," she whispered to me.

Beketamun looked about the tomb also as the mourners filed in and out. The burial chamber had few possessions within it as I had asked to leave the walls with their prayers unobstructed. The four doors leading from the curved room were now filled with the treasures I needed to take with me. My chariot, now disassembled lay in pieces within one, surrounded by my battle armour, shield and weapons. Another room held my furniture and ornaments from my chambers as well as chest upon chest of my clothes, bundles of linen and even my pillows. The other rooms were filled with endless treasures collected from the palace or newly made.

As the final mourners left, a priest followed the last one to ensure that no one was within the tomb before the final rites were performed. Amenhotep announced he would remain and the priests nodded. "Sister, would you like to stay also?" Beketamun nodded and smiled a thank you to her brother. He was not obliged to invite her and could have demanded she leave but somehow I think he needed her there for himself as much as he knew she would like to stay.

Beketamun walked the room as the priests waited to hear that all the other mourners were now gone. She read the prayers upon the wall and smiled. *"I am sure you will find your way with or without these words. How could anyone deny such a wise and brave man,"* she thought. My daughter passed the open doorway of the annexe that held my chamber belongings. She smiled as she saw them all stacked up, memory after memory piled upon each other with the lamp light from the burial chamber flickering upon them.

She began to step forward and as her shadow moved it let more light fall upon the collection and the warm glow glistened off my statues of Isis and Horus. They sat tucked within the legs of a chair at the base of the tangle of furniture and ornaments. She smiled at first as she looked at them but then she frowned. Beketamun knew the history of the Isis statue and it pained her to see it shoved amongst other things as though it meant nothing more than anything else. She knew it had been a wedding gift and Satiah had even used it to teach the children about Isis. Beketamun's first prayers had been said before this statue. She reached down and pulled at it to test that the rest wouldn't also shift if it were removed. Nothing did and so Isis was soon tucked within her arms. She looked back down at Horus now alone. "You can stay here for now!" she said quietly and turned back to the burial chamber.

"Madam, what are you doing?" hissed a priest. He was thoroughly disgusted to see someone tampering with the tomb already, "That must remain there!"

"It shall remain here," she answered calmly and walked to my sarcophagus setting it beside where my head rested and amongst the small gathering of statues that my daughters had placed. Beketamun looked at Amenhotep as she stood up. "He needs this close by." Amenhotep nodded for he knew this statue had been by my bedside since Satiah's death. His sharp look at the priests let them know his decision was final.

The priest sent to check that the tomb was clear now returned. "They are gone," he said short of breath.

"Let us finish then," Amenhotep said as strong as he could but all heard the tremor in his voice.

My Canopic jars were given their final prayers and lined up alongside me now joining Isis and the other statues to form a line. There was a simple chant said over my coffin and then the priests began to lift the granite lid to seal my coffin within the cold stone. Amenhotep joined them helping to make the weight easier and the sound of the stone closing upon itself echoed loudly within the chamber. When it finally faded the men heard the gentle sobs of Beketamun behind them.

Amenhotep held his sister as the very last prayer was said while rose oil was poured over the sarcophagus. Finally the priests were silent and my son found it hard to believe that it was finally all over as he stood with his arms still around Beketamun, not sure of what to do.

"It is done Sire," said the high priest whilst the one wearing the Anubis head lifted it off his shoulders. Amenhotep nodded and took Beketamun's hand to walk with her back out to the sunshine.

I almost began to walk with them back to the palace and join the feast. It just felt like the next natural step but I looked upon my sarcophagus and remembered what I must do. I stood and watched my children's backs as they walked out of my burial chamber followed by the priests. The torches were carried out with them and the darkness closed in around me. I could still see a glimmer of lamplight as it bounced down the passageway and into the antechamber. I heard the scrapes as the planks were withdrawn from across the well. Soon after those sounds the last ripples of light were gone.

I was now alone in the deep silence and enveloping darkness. I lay upon the lid of the sarcophagus and waited for Osiris to come for me.

CHAPTER FORTY

It could have been an eternity and it was also the blink of an eye. The infinite dark with nothing within it as a marker or sign was not only boundless physically but finally the constraints of time were also gone.

I felt them coming before I saw them. The calls to the oarsmen to push the boat along met my ears first and then I heard the oars as they hit the water. I sat up upon my sarcophagus and saw a faint light in the distance that grew steadily. I heard something below me and now I could see some movement. Silver threads twisted around me and I realised it was the tops of small waves as water now lapped around the edges of the floor upon which my sarcophagus laid. I jumped down from the sarcophagus and checked that Isis and my jars were safe, which of course they were, but I lifted them upon the granite anyway.

The light was now almost blinding and the voice was clear and strong. As it lit up all around me I could see my tomb was gone. There was nothing but the small island I stood upon with my remains beside me. The light suddenly softened and a shape appeared in the middle of it. A magnificent boat emerged illuminated with a thousand torches and lamps and with a thousand oarsmen below its deck to power it. Their oars emerged from the sides like wings, fanning out into the water making the boat look even larger. I could have walked upon their stems they were so many.

I drank in every detail as the boat slid along the water and arrived before me. The grandest was the figure stationed at the bow of the boat. It was Osiris standing tall and strong--in one hand he held a staff and the other pointed forward towards me. "*Finally!*" my heart cried out and then almost exploded with a mix of elation and fear.

The boat stopped abruptly and the water slapped against its sides as some sailors ran to drop a gangway over the side next to where Osiris stood.

"Thutmose!" Osiris's voice boomed, but I did not see his mouth move nor did it seem like his voice travelled to me. I heard it within my head as though I had spoken it myself. "Are you ready to leave?" he asked, his hand dropping by his side now.

"Yes I am Great One," I shouted out as though he might not hear me.

Osiris raised his hand once more and gestured towards to the plank that led onto the boat. "Then come aboard and let us begin your journey."

So determined and so ready, yet I hesitated before I lifted my first foot upon the wooden gangway. There would be no turning back once I stepped from this existence. I looked about me and saw the endless black and thought of seeing Satiah and bounded up towards the boat. Halfway though I stopped, "Wait! I forgot something," I cried out to Osiris. I wanted to carry Isis with me and I had forgotten my scroll of prayers. As I turned though my little island was gone, even the gangway I had walked upon so far had been eaten away by the black that lay over everything except this boat and where I stood. I heard a laugh from the boat.

"Come aboard Thutmose," Osiris said amused. "All is here for you."

I continued my way upwards and as the deck of the boat come into view I could see my treasures were already loaded and ready to travel with me. Osiris walked to greet me and handed me my scroll of prayers. "Do you imagine that we would not care for one of our own?" he said, and chuckled again.

All I could do was shake my head as I looked about the boat now even larger that I was aboard. It glistened with all the gold and jewels of my belongings. Osiris now pointed to the bow of the boat where he had been standing and I saw my throne waiting for me. Osiris led the way and as I took my seat he stood beside me. He lifted his staff and hit it back against the deck, then pointed ahead. This was all the instruction that was needed and once again the oars hit the water and I felt the boat surge forward.

I settled back within my throne, my scroll held in my right hand ready for what lay ahead, when I felt something at my feet. It was Isis, placed there close by as I would have wished her to be. I lifted her into my arms and let her sit upon my lap as the boat glided on.

There was nothing to see before me or beside me, just the darkness that we began in. Osiris though seemed to see much more and I saw his eyes scour from side to side. Occasionally he would point a different direction and I would hear a cry from below the deck and the oarsmen would pull the boat towards a new course.

We seemed to float in this void forever when I saw Osiris lean forward and thrust his hand forward. The great cry I heard as the boat approached me in my tomb rose up all around me once again and I knew we were nearing something. I sat forward in my chair and looked out ahead but I could still see nothing.

"Your eyes will adjust soon Pharaoh," Osiris said looking ahead, "then you will see much. Now open your scroll and prepare your first prayer."

I unrolled the papyrus, balancing Isis in the bend of my arm as I did so. I read over the glyphs and began to recite them in my mind when I felt the boat heave. I looked up and saw my first stop on my journey. It was a temple as grand as Karnak but it did not have the warmth of the temple I helped to build. This one stood as though its very stones would judge me and I knew that if I did not satisfy the test that lay within its walls then I would journey no further. The words of the prayer continued within my mind as I stood and placed Isis upon my throne. Osiris walked before me as my guard and my guide, and we made the descent down the gangway and walked to the temple.

The strength of my prayers, the power that I carried within that scroll and the noble life I had lived carried me along to each destination and the challenge that waited there for me. Each time I would board the boat triumphant and return to my throne to gather Isis within my arms as the boat once again slid forward. Each time I returned to the boat I felt more confident to triumph over the next of my confrontations and even started to anticipate my next achievement.

I knew that as each one was overcome then I was closer to paradise. I had twelve stops to make on my way, one for each hour of the night as I approached a new dawn that symbolised the beginning of my new life here in the afterworld. As the boat moved onwards I could start to make out shapes within the dark and saw there was much more within this world than I first thought.

I saw that we floated upon a great river and upon the banks figures twisted and convulsed as though caught in a grotesque dance they could not end. I leaned to the side, almost dropping Isis upon the floor, to see them clearer.

"Do not waste your eyes trying to see them Thutmose," Osiris said firmly, still looking ahead. "These are the ones who forgot their way and will not make it to paradise."

It was too late though and as my eyes became clearer it was as if this allowed them to see me and they then began to call out to me. Some begged for help, others pleaded with me to carry them upon my boat. These were probably some of my very own subjects, ones who could not afford full burials let alone a funeral scroll. I looked to Osiris but he knew what I was about to ask before I spoke and he turned to me furious. "They are no longer your responsibility Thutmose! This journey is yours and yours alone. Do you wish to remain here with these heretics? For if we stop the boat along these shores this is exactly what will happen." His voice was so loud within me that I felt my essence shake. I turned to face forward and stare into the void that was all I could see ahead. Eventually their images and cries faded and our next stop appeared before me.

This one was not a temple; it was a grand hall that stood with bright flags rippling upon their poles along its high roof. The light around it was a low gold colour as though the dawn was about to make herself known above us. I was so anxious to have this one finished off that I almost outpaced Osiris as he walked once more before me. It was all over quickly, as though this test was completed before I even entered and I felt like singing as I walked behind my guide to leave the hall.

As we stepped out of the doorway and back outside, all around us shone bright. There was not a sliver of black that remained and I looked out now to see what did indeed fill this space. The boat and the river it had sailed upon were gone. Ahead of me lay a field of wheat on the verge of turning gold and above us the most brilliant sky of the sharpest blue I had ever seen. In the distance I saw a palace and I knew it was mine. My final eternal home waiting for me with everything I needed and everyone I loved. I threw my scroll to the ground and ran.

The wheat pushed itself aside as I ploughed through it. I did not feel its whiskers brush against me nor did I feel its stems crack under my feet. All I knew was this palace ahead of me and it grew larger and larger with every step. I saw its patterns painted so bright come into focus and saw my cartouche upon the flags that lined an avenue that led to its doors. Then I saw her standing alone within the great doors like a frame around her. Her gown was spun gold and upon her chest the most beautiful ruby sat glowing like the sun itself. My Satiah was waiting for me and as I ran between the first of the flags she opened her arms for me.

The warmest sweetest embrace my soul had ever known welcomed me to paradise and we held each other as though it would never end. "Come and let the others greet you," she whispered, and the doors opened up behind us. Amenemhat and Nefertiry waited for me just as I always imagined and then I saw my father and mother with an endless stream of faces behind them. This may be my palace but it was theirs also. This was our eternal home to live as Gods and welcome those who were yet to come.

Each day was a grand occasion with the most lavish of feasts and entertainment. The days were spent relaxing with no fear of famine or attack. I had a new horse and I could ride as fast and as far as I could with no pain. At night I could eat and drink without fear of my waist expanding or my head hurting the next day.

Everything was pure bliss, but there was an ache from life that somehow still let itself be known. It was this ache that still kept us attached to the realm we had left and though none of us would speak of it we all felt it. It was this feeling that allowed us to still observe what we had left so that I watched my children continue after me.

I saw Amenhotep's great triumphs and knew when he was ready to join us. I stood at the doors of the palace as each one of my children arrived just as Satiah had done for me, knowing the exact moment they would be there. I even stood behind Matreya's mother as she greeted my second wife. We saw everything, and though it was with some detachment, I knew it was also because we missed all that we had left behind.

The ache did not lessen as we remained here and those we loved joined us. As we continued to watch we were just reminded more of what we were missing. All our lives we prepared for paradise and now that we were here we continuously thought of returning to that unpredictable existence of life. For some this was more powerful than others and suddenly someone would no longer be here anymore. Sometimes it was as though they swirled into a vapour before the rest of us as their final goodbye--for others they might simply vanish when you looked away. We never knew where they had gone to but we did know we would see them again.

One by one I saw my children leave like this, all ready to move on long before me. Satiah though remained by my side and we walked hand in hand constantly as though to anchor ourselves to each other. I remained for her as she did for me.

We watched together as my successors moved from triumphs to adversities. The empire shrunk but remained strong and then Arkhenaten, the family idiot, took to the throne and I watched as my dream prophecy became a reality. Somehow I was glad that most of my family had moved on so as not to witness this with me. Tutankhamun, the last male of our bloodline provided by those of Menkheperre's lineage, arrived at our doors, and I stood back amongst the crowd to welcome him, but as he walked in I felt no attachment to the young man.

I watched Egypt less and less but my observations were more out of habit than interest. I looked about me and there was no one here now aside from Satiah who made me feel that this was the paradise I had been promised. Satiah felt it also and one day she simply let go of my hand and began to drift away. "We will find each other again," I heard her voice within me, "I promise you."

Then I was truly alone.

The palace itself began to dissolve around me as though it was leaving me also, but it was my spirit letting go of this creation just as everyone else had done so. This was how they left--they simply created their next experience and now it was my turn to begin my next adventure.

I floated around my realm to see what else was available and saw how everyone else pictured paradise. There was everything from Greek festivals and Roman orgies through to people sleeping peacefully or men gathered along long tables gambling and drinking their way through eternity. Some were fascinating while some plain repulsed me. All of them were futile and barren, caught within a spiral of self-indulgence and apathy. Every one of them played with this place until they literally bored themselves to living again.

So many of them like me, wandered looking for our next taste of human life. This space was somewhat like the few months I spent as my funeral was organised. We were neither of the space we occupied, yet not sure of where it was that we were to go. We all eventually realised that this afterworld would not give us the answer and so, like all others before me had, I now turned my attentions back upon the world I had left.

As I let myself fall back towards this space I saw the energies of others floating by me. Some moved fast, while others hung in place as they watched below measuring their choice of where to go, and yet others who pulled back and returned to where we had left. They no longer held a human shape but appeared before me as wisps of colour turning and twisting as they moved. I suddenly realised that I too no longer held the shape I believed to be my body, and a surge of energy pulsed through me as I enjoyed this final shedding. I had no others around me to pull me back to my past, no images of paradise that I had to maintain, and now I had no physical image to identify with. I was completely free to begin again.

I floated around the earth plane observing all that there was to offer. I walked once more through Egypt without any emotion and I knew this place was no longer for me. I travelled up through the lands of Canaan and Persia and was tempted by their mysticism but knew these could wait. I floated over Turkey and smelt the coffee and sugars of their sweets but still there was not that pull of purpose that my being ached for.

I headed for Greece, the land whose people would dissolve the Egyptian empire--partly from curiosity to see what life they now all lived. I saw the men gathered in their plazas talking philosophy and the libraries full of books. I felt their love of the arts and the beauty they saw in nature. It was not hard to understand this last aspect of this people. Here lay a land lush with green and every turn of soil, even the crags of its mountains burst forth with life. There were none of the plains of desolate sand that had surrounded my time as Pharaoh. Here the plants touched every corner of their land only to end when they met the delicious blue-green of the sea.

The sun was bright but nurturing and people did not hide from it but built their homes to enjoy it as much as they could. They too had their Gods to care for them and the people celebrated them as Egypt did but with much more joy than we had ever known. Each delight I savoured as I walked here pulled me closer and closer to choosing this place to re-enter life.

I heard the murmurs of a place called Delphi. In fact I had heard of this place as those around me whispered it as we floated back to the Earth. My curiosity carried me there and encompassing the mountain I saw clouds of energy watching and observing. Some of these energies were far brighter and I knew they had not come from the afterworld as I or most of the other entities had. These were the archangels carrying messages for those that chose to hear them. I took my place amongst those like me and I watched as the angels communicated with the humans. It was amusing and inspiring all at once and part of me envied that they could bridge these worlds.

Atop one rock stood a young woman dressed in flowing robes and with her hair loose around her shoulders. Her face was beautiful, not only from the form that her human body had created, but as she closed her eyes and listened to the angels another beauty made itself known. Below her on the rocks a man knelt but looked up at the woman in awe, his hands gripped together as though begging for mercy, and I could feel his heart racing as he prepared to speak.

"What is it that you wish to know?" the woman asked, her eyes remaining closed, her expression serene.

"Most sacred oracle, speaker for the Gods, I wish to know of the child that my wife bears for me," he trembled as he spoke but the father within me felt and knew the joy and excitement of a new child. I rushed in closer to share this as much as I could.

I swept before all the others there and came in so close to the woman that she turned her head directly to where I was. Even though her eyes were closed I knew that she saw me and I was intrigued to see her smile. She kept her head turned and the man also looked to where her face seemed to be fixed.

"I see your son," she said smiling as though she wanted to say "I see you" to me. I hung in place now utterly curious as to what she would say next.

"A son!" the man beamed at the words.

"Yes, a son," she continued, and I felt as though she asked me to come closer so I did. Her head slowly moved as though she was examining every part of me and then she added, "He is a grand being, destined for amazing things." She smiled broadly now at me. "He is fit and strong with a mind to match--but it is his mind which will offer him grandeur in this life. Nurture this early and his name will be known by many."

"How should I nurture this?" the man's eyes were wide with awe, but now a fear set in of undoing this remarkable child who had not even been born yet.

"Egypt," was her answer.

"Egypt?" I cried out unison with the man.

"Yes, Egypt," she answered to us both. "The mathematicians of Alexandria will teach him much."

The smile that the woman had carried with her words now suddenly faded and I saw her body start to tremble. Two other women rushed forward to grab her arms just as her knees bent and she began to fall.

"The oracle has no more words for you today Sir," said one plainly as they carried her away.

The man stayed upon his knees for a moment and looked down in shock at what he had just heard. His mind raced over all that had been said, and then he remembered the one word that made him smile. "A *son*. I will have a son!" he repeated as he lifted himself to his feet and turned to leave.

At the bottom of the small mountain a young man lounged in a donkey carriage chewing on a twig, his legs hanging over the side of the seat. He saw the man making his way down the mountain sending small rocks ahead of him as he walked. The young man jumped up and stood as the man came towards him.

"Was it good news?" he called out to the man.

"The best news! I will have a son!" he exclaimed.

"Surely we must stop at a taverna to celebrate then?" offered the young man.

"Surely we must make haste to reach the shore lest I miss the last boat home," he said sharply as he lifted himself into the carriage. "One day you may understand that life is not about seizing every opportunity you can to drink! Now, get these animals moving."

Somehow I was tied to this man and I could not understand it. That woman had described me yet she had also described the child about to be born to this man. Perhaps she had confused the two, and my having stepped in so close had interfered with what she should have heard from the angels. Then again, perhaps she had said exactly what all three of us had chosen to be said. Either way, I decided to follow this man.

He bounced along in the carriage beside the young man and I saw his mind now race as they made their way. They arrived at a small dock and the man jumped from the carriage. He grabbed at a satchel and slung it over his shoulder. As he gathered another bag he spoke to the young man. "Tomorrow we rest, but the day after you will meet me here. I will come on the first boat and we will make our way to the open sea docks and sail to Alexandria."

The young man had groaned internally at the thought of meeting the boat that sailed at first light, but upon hearing of Alexandria, he groaned outwardly, "Ugh! Alexandria! We will be gone for a week."

"We shall be gone for two weeks!" said the man looking up. "We are long overdue a trip to Egypt for trade and I now have other business there to see to. If this does not please you feel free to seek another boss." He finished and tilted his head as though waiting for a reply.

"Fine, I shall meet you here," he groaned again.

The man smiled and went to climb aboard the boat that would carry him to the island he called home. His smile would not leave his face and the boat owner looked at him as they bounced over the waves. "I see you have had a good day of trade," he poked.

"The very best day has been given to me with even better to come," he teased in return, unwilling to tell his news lest the entire island know within a day. The oracles were supposedly omniscient but they were sometimes wrong. Despite his very heart knowing she was accurate, he would not embarrass himself with the possibility of sharing an incorrect message.

He jumped from the boat calling out his farewell and walked quickly to his home that was nearby the dock. He smelt the lamb before he was even in the door. It was the same aroma that greeted him whenever he was due home. A small comment made early in their marriage had led his wife to believe that slowly stewed lamb leg was his favourite dish and she excitedly had the maid prepare it every time he returned from a trip. Within the few months of their marriage it had indeed become his favourite as that smell meant the rigours of the road and dealing with merchants was over.

He entered the small courtyard that was the front of their home and called out to his wife. She appeared quickly as though she had run, and then stopped grabbing at a column to lean against while she held her rounded belly